WOODLANDS

WOODLANDS

OLIVER RACKHAM

Collins

This edition published in 2010 by Collins,
an imprint of HarperCollins

HarperCollins Publishers Ltd
77–85 Fulham Palace Road
London W6 8JB

Collins is a registered trademark of HarperCollins Publishers Ltd.

Originally published in 2006 as *Woodlands*, volume 100 in the New Naturalist series.

15 14 13 12 11 10
10 9 8 7 6 5 4 3 2 1

A catalogue record for this book is available from the British Library.

ISBN: 978–0–00–731514–7

Collins uses papers that are natural, renewable and recyclable products made
from wood grown in sustainable forests. The manufacturing processes conform
to the environmental regulations of the country of origin.

Designed by Myfanwy Vernon-Hunt
Typeset by seagulls.net
Proofread by Janet McCann
Printed and bound in Great Britain by Clays Ltd, St Ives plc

CONTENTS

In memory of Stuart Max Walters
1920–2005

For sixty years Max Walters was a pillar of the New Naturalist series. He was author with John Gilmour of *Wild Flowers*, no. 5 (1954), and with John Raven of *Mountain Flowers*, no. 33 (1955), and sole author of *Wild & Garden Plants*, no. 80 (1993). He served on the Editorial Board from 1981 until 2005.

He is the begetter of this book, first by being my teacher and lifelong friend, then by inspiring me to write earlier books beginning with *Hayley Wood* in 1975, and finally by persuading me over many years to write this one. He saw many of the draft chapters. One of the last things he did was to invite me to his home and put before me the cutting-edge articles on ant dispersal (p.254), published in obscure Swedish and German journals between 1896 and 1924; the sort of information that he loved to have at his fingertips. I am sad that he did not quite live to see it published.

He came from Yorkshire but lived most of his life in Cambridge. He was Keeper of Cambridge University Herbarium (1949–73), Director of the Botanic Garden (1973–83) and Fellow of St John's College and then (from 1964) of King's College. In retirement, Darwin-like, he kept and studied his own little botanic garden at Grantchester. One of his last projects was to re-establish the botanic garden at Sarajevo after the tragedy that ravaged his beloved Yugoslavia.

Max began as an experimental taxonomist. He became famous for the mighty works of reference that he organised and edited: the *Atlas of the British Flora* (with Franklyn Perring, 1962), *Flora Europaea* (1964–80) and *The European Garden Flora* (with James Cullen, 2000). *Flora Europaea* was perhaps his greatest achievement: nothing less than a complete Flora of a then battered and divided continent from the Azores to the Urals. Somehow he contrived to get the enthusiastic support of botanists in every country and province, and even to extract plant records from the prison-state of Albania.

He introduced me to the Mediterranean through field trips to southeast France, Slovenia and Croatia in the 1960s, when such excursions were more adventurous than they are now. (But was not every field trip with Max an adventure?) His interests, however, were not just continent-wide: he published three books concerned with Cambridgeshire botany and botanists, and in his later years he made Grantchester churchyard his field of study.

Max was a leading conservationist, especially in his work at the Botanic Garden. As a founder of Cambridgeshire & Isle of Ely Naturalists' Trust, he saw to the acquisition of Hayley Wood, the Trust's first big nature reserve, in 1962. Seven years later, he put his weight behind the campaign to prevent the destruction of the Bradfield Woods, Suffolk. Both events were turning points in woodland conservation; had they gone the other way, this book might not have been written.

As another of his old students has said, 'one of Max's greatest gifts was to inspire others to action, to reach heights of achievement they had not dared to contemplate'. He was a devout Christian; an embodiment of all that was good in old-fashioned socialism; a pacifist; he was upheld over 57 years by his wife Lorna. Like myself, he refused to recognise the distinction between amateur and professional: the *Atlas* contained tens of thousands of records by amateur members of the Botanical Society of the British Isles. In him 'the enquiring spirit of the old naturalists' lived on to inspire New Naturalist authors.

AUTHOR'S FOREWORD AND ACKNOWLEDGEMENTS

This is not a book about the Environment. It does not pretend that trees are merely part of the theatre of landscape in which human history is played out, or the passive recipients of whatever destiny humanity foists on them. This is a book about Ecology. It deals with trees as actors in the play, and with the multiple interactions between trees and the environment, trees and other trees, trees and other plants, trees and fungi, trees and animals, and trees and people. Unlike my previous books, it deals more in investigations than in results. For good or ill, I have no particular theory to promote.

I begin with chapters setting out the essential properties of trees, what woods are and how they work and why they are not all the same, before embarking on the thematic chapters that form the body of the book. Much of this has been said many times before, but it still needs saying. Knowledge, even of elementary matters, accumulates; it is now difficult to get ahead of the ever-increasing flow of publications and finish a book!

This is not a successor to *Trees, Woods and Man*, published by my great predecessor, H.L. Edlin, as New Naturalist volume 32, fifty years ago. He wrote as a then rather old-fashioned modern forester who still remembered something of the distinction between woodland and plantation. Timber prices were high, and forestry was the science of planting and growing trees rather than the art of selling them. Through the new technology of getting trees to grow on peatland, it then seemed possible to plant enough forestry to yield a substantial part of the country's entire timber consumption. Although Edlin appreciated natural woods and understood the importance of woodland history, for him the future of woodland lay with modern forestry, and he had little to say about woods that were unsuitable for it.

I am not a forester. I am a general practitioner of science, trained as a botanist – at first specialising in plant physiology, in how plants (especially woodland herbs) functioned. Cambridge had a tradition of plant ecology, including such illustrious names as Sir Arthur Tansley, Alexander Watt and Sir Harry Godwin, and my own teachers Clifford Evans, David Coombe, Peter Grubb, Max Walters, the mycologist Harry Hudson, and the tree pathologist John Rishbeth. David Coombe in particular directed me into historical ecology.

I write as a now rather old-fashioned botanist, concerned with woodland as an ecosystem with a life of its own, in which human agency is one among many environmental factors. In this book trees are themselves wildlife, rather than merely a habitat for wildlife.

Times have changed even since my own earlier books. Modern forestry is in decline, partly because the economic basis on which it was justified has collapsed. It will, no doubt, continue in a modest way, but it no longer dominates the woodland scene, and an ecologist need no longer be apologetic about having little to say on the ecology of plantations. Popular affection for woods and trees flourishes as never before, albeit sometimes embarrassingly ill informed. There has been a revival of the historic love of ancient trees, which were unfashionable in Edlin's time to the point that he regretted their existence.

I shall not be as comprehensive as Edlin. This is a book about woods rather than trees. I deal with trees in wood-pasture (as in Richmond Park) as well as woodland, but do not cover hedgerow, garden, or orchard trees.

I have always been concerned with the history of woodland – with the histories of individual woods, rather than the history of generalisations about woodland. This is not merely my own inclination: woodland by its very nature can be understood only in terms of historical processes. To describe it only at a moment in time, or in terms of a three-year PhD study, is like expecting to understand how a cornfield functions after one day's observations.

I was brought up on such classic New Naturalist books as *London's Natural History* by R.S.R. Fitter, *Mushrooms and Toadstools* by John Ramsbottom and *The Sea Shore* by C.M. Yonge. In that tradition I deal mainly in observations that do not call for specialised equipment and that any well-motivated observer can make. In this field amateurs can still do things that professionals, locked into their own ethos and culture (p.404), find difficult. I hope to inspire young readers to lay down the basis for long-term observations to be repeated in future decades. This book, I hope, may be useful to the growing number of people who have acquired woods and want to know what to do with them. (Woodland history has come to influence the estate agent's trade!)

New Naturalist books are traditionally about Britain and Ireland. Here, too, times have changed, and many readers are able to study woods and savannas in other countries. Although this book is still mainly about Britain, I have not hesitated to set it in a world context.

Woodland history is an international field of study. Much of what I say can be transferred to other countries. There are Forest History Societies in North America and Australia, and a *News of Forest History* published in Vienna. Not all these studies are ecological. Some are concerned with the mechanics of the first European exploitation of what were thought of as 'virgin forests' in other continents; others with forestry legislation, more prolific in other countries than in ours.

I draw attention to the work of Peter Szabó in Hungary. I would not have put Hungary high on the list of countries favourable for the study of historical ecology. It has had a succession of violent takeovers by outsiders – by the Magyar themselves, Mongols, Turks, Habsburgs and Soviets – each of which destroyed much of the archives and might have erased most of the evidence in the landscape itself. This ingenious and resourceful young scholar has found a remarkable amount of evidence still surviving, and has made the most of it in ways that are used in this book.

International comparisons are helpful in working out the effects of trees or people in the functioning of woods. The differences between England and Scotland are partly to do with Scotland having a different tree that behaves unlike any English native tree (Chapter 16). It is instructive to compare the interaction of broadly similar human cultures with much the same trees (England versus France) or with a broadly similar range of trees (Britain versus the British in North America), or an independent human culture with a broadly similar range of trees (England versus Japan), or a broadly similar human culture with an utterly different range of trees (Britain versus the British in Australia), or (as on another planet) an utterly different human culture with an utterly different range of trees (Australian Aborigines).

TABLE OF DATES

4,600 million	Origin of the earth
1,000 million	Green plants
500 million	Land plants
420 million	Vascular plants; clonal growth; mycorrhiza
340 million	Big trees (Archæopteris)
300 million	Trees that will burn
270 million	Four-footed herbivorous beasts
140 million	Broadleaved trees[1]
70 million	Present genera of trees
2.5 million	Hominids
2 million	Beginning of Pleistocene glacial cycles (glaciations and interglacials)
200,000	Present human species
10,000 BC	End of last glaciation; beginning of present (Holocene) interglacial; beginning of woodland history in Britain
6200–3800 BC	Atlantic Period; fully developed wildwood; Mesolithic people in Britain
3800–2000 BC	Neolithic in Britain; beginning of cultivation and woodmanship
2000–750 BC	Bronze Age in Britain
750 BC – 40 AD	Iron Age in Britain
40–400 AD	Roman England
400–1066 AD	Anglo-Saxon England
1066–1536 AD	Middle Ages (England)
c.1900 AD	Oak Change
1950–75 AD	'Locust Years'

Dates BC are derived from radiocarbon dates, calibrated to real calendar years, and will change slightly in future as the calibration is refined.

ACKNOWLEDGEMENTS

This book is based on information gathered here and there over nearly 50 years. I am indebted, first, to successive Masters and Fellows of Corpus Christi College, Cambridge, for their tolerance, encouragement, and the links they have given me to many fields of learning. Next, to hundreds of landowners who have welcomed me into their woods, and to scores of friends and helpers who have shown me their favourite places. I particularly thank:

Cambridge: Michael Astor, Paul Freeman, Nicholas Hammond, the late William Palmer, the late Franklyn Perring, Jon and Mark Powell, Chris Preston, Peter Sell, Ray Symonds, Edmund Tanner, Charles Turner, the late Max Walters, Harold Whitehouse, Richard Woolnough. *Cornwall*: Stephen Bott, Veronica Chesher, Oliver Padel. *The rest of England*: Margaret Atherden, Gary Battell, John Bloomfield, Len Cram, Richard Darrah, David Dymond, the late Ted Ellis, Andrew Fleming, Vikki Forbes, Peter Fordham, Mary and the late Eric Fox, Ann and the late James Hart, Hildegard Heygate, Anne Horsfall, John Hunter, Jack Kemball, Keith Kirby, Simon Leatherdale, Michael Martin, David Maylam, David Morfitt, George Peterken, Susan and the late Colin Ranson, Alan Rayner, Geoffrey Roberts, Dennis Seaward, Lawrence Sisitka, Margaret Slee, Nigel Spring, Alexander Wheaten. *Wales*: Paula Keen, Peter White. *Scotland*: HRH Prince Charles, Robin Callender, Professor James Dickson, the late Charles and Anne MacBurney, Professor Christopher Smout. *Ireland*: Professor Daniel Kelly, Professor Fergus Kelly, Alan Peatfield. *Northern Europe*: Professor Björn Berglund, Professor John Birks, Professor Richard Bradshaw. *Southern Europe*: Marco Armiero, Dick and the late Jean Grove, Jennifer Moody, Professor Diego Moreno, Philip Oswald, the late Madeleine Vuillermet, Professor Peter Warren. (I have touched on the work of the Sphakiá Archaeological Survey, directed by Jennifer Moody, Lucia Nixon and Simon Price.) *North America*: Bill Allen, Henry Art, Susan Bratton, Martin Canny, Wick Dossett, David Houston, Jennifer and Melissa Moody, Peter White, Hap Wotila, Vickie Ziegler. *Japan*: Professor Katsue Fukamachi, Professor Jun-ichi Ogura, Professor Toru Nakashizuka, Professor Hideo Tabata, Hiroshi Tanaka. Visits to Japan have been supported by the Japanese Academy of Sciences and the British Academy. *Australia*: Professor Bill Allaway, Katheryn Bennett, Daniel Lunney, Jenny Mills, Tim Nevard.

Much of the information is derived from research projects supported by the Natural Environment Research Council, the Nature Conservancy Council and Corpus Christi College, Cambridge.

CHAPTER 1

THE CONSTANT SPRING

What Trees and Woods Are and How They Behave

The commercial harvesting of timber, for use or sale, is often considered a prime cause of the disappearance of forests. But it need not be, and under proper management it never is. ... the mere cutting of timber need not seriously harm the woods. What does the damage is the prevention of regrowth thereafter ...

H.L. EDLIN, *TREES, WOODS AND MAN*, 1956

In an ideal world, trees would be like an inferior sort of animal or a very inferior sort of person. They would have their origin in the mysteries of sex, would grow up and become 'mature'; might die when smitten by disease or by the random violence of tempest or fire; would anyway die of 'old age' on reaching the equivalent of fourscore years; and would be replaced by new trees arising from seed.

Trees in this world would fit into the affairs of human society. They would grow close together in forests, each tree forming just one straight cylindrical trunk provided by a beneficent Providence for the north European timber trade: genetic modification might even induce them to grow square trunks.* They would die when cut down, and the land they grew on would turn into non-forest. Humanity would plant successor trees to create a new forest even better (by human standards) than the original.

This world sprang from the imagination of the scientists and savants of the Enlightenment in the eighteenth century. It captured the imagination of nineteenth-century governments, who sought to make their trees (and their people)

* Californian redwood often grows trunks that are squarish in section. Japanese cultivators grow square bamboos by confining the young stems in square tubes.

live in that world. Old-fashioned foresters and scientists, and many who write books on trees, still live in such a world. If you believe in a plurality of worlds, there may be, orbiting some far-off star, a world with green men and pink trees behaving thus. But in the real world of Earth, trees are wildlife just as deer or primroses are wildlife. Each species has its own agenda and its own interactions with human activities. If all trees were like the ideal, they would lose most of their significance, all their historic meaning, most of their beauty, and most of their value as a habitat.

SOME FACTS OF LIFE

Coppicing and pollarding

Older readers will have been taught that trees die when felled and woods disappear because people cut them down. The reality is more complex. Many trees, including most conifers, do indeed not survive felling, but most British trees either *coppice* – they sprout from the stump, like ash – or *sucker* from the roots, like most elms. Coppicing and suckering, familiar to any gardener, are the basis of nearly all historic management of woodland (Figs 2 & 171). The Bradfield Woods (Suffolk), a typical *coppice-wood* or *copse*, have been cut down at least 50 times and show no sign of disappearing: after each felling they constantly produce *spring*, coppice shoots or suckers (Figs 4,5 & 6).

Trees that are periodically cut tend to live longer (p.38). If an ash is felled at 12 years old it will sprout. If repeatedly felled every 12 years it will develop a permanent base, a *stool*, which will live indefinitely, getting a little bigger at each cycle.

An alternative is *pollarding*, cutting the tree 6 to 10 feet (2 to 3 metres) above ground to produce a crop of new shoots (Figs 3 & 7). Most trees that coppice will also pollard. The decision whether to pollard or coppice is the woodman's; the decision whether to sprout, sucker, or die is the tree's. Pollarding is harder work than coppicing and is normally done for some special reason, such as that it is impossible to exclude browsing animals that would otherwise eat the young shoots.* Pollards, too, have permanent bases that live longer than trees that are not cut.

---

* Some coppicing trees form a massive solid base called a *lignotuber*, from which new shoots arise every time the tree is felled or burnt. In Australia the seedlings of many eucalypts form a kind of fireproof wooden radish that persists throughout the life of the tree and can grow to 20 feet (6 metres) in diameter. Some American oaks and ashes form lignotubers that resist fire or drought. Californian redwood, that mysteriously huge tree that is even longer-lived through coppicing, forms lignotubers called *burls*, prized for their beautiful contorted grain. In Britain lignotubers are exceptional, though the massive bases of old coppiced ashes and the 'elephant's-foot' bases of some oaks would count as such.

A suckering tree tends to form an ever-expanding circular patch of genetically identical stems called a *clone* (Fig. 8). Clonal trees sprout when cut down, but do not form stools.

Timber and wood

The arisings from coppicing and pollarding are called *underwood*, which has been used for many purposes, but especially for fuel. In most English woods a scatter of bigger trees is left among the stools to grow to a size suitable for beams and planks (Fig. 4). These trees, usually oaks, are called *standard* or *timber* trees. Academic writers draw a distinction between the 'coppice-with-standards system', including timber trees, and 'simple coppice' without them; in practice, however, timber trees come and go, and these are not systematically different forms of management.

Timber is the trunks of big trees. *Wood* consists of coppice or pollard underwood plus the branches of timber trees: hence we talk of a *timber*-framed building, but a *wood* fire. There are similar words in most European languages: *bois d'œuvre* and *bois d'industrie, madera* and *leña,* etc. The distinction is weaker in Scotland than in England or Wales, and is not made in America.

Seed reproduction

Most trees can grow from seed, but not always easily. There is a long and perilous route from a seed to a tree producing more seed. The tree may seldom produce viable seed, like many elms and (until recent hot summers) lime. In oaks there may be a *mast year*: a huge crop of seed at long intervals. Most bamboos never flower until the last year of their lives, when all the world's bamboos of a particular species flower simultaneously, produce vast quantities of seed, and die.

Tree seeds may need to germinate at once, as with oaks and poplars, or be capable of dormancy: many tree seeds of middle weight (ash, hawthorn, lime) germinate in the second or third year after shedding. The seedling may be *light-demanding* like oak and ash or *shade-bearing* like beech and yew; not many British trees can grow up in the shade of trees of the same species. Seedling trees are bitten off by slugs, mice, deer, etc., or attacked by fungus diseases. Some, such as oak and ash, can survive being bitten off at least once, and produce a new shoot.

Seed reproduction enables trees to colonise new ground and create a new wood. Most trees have some *dispersal mechanism*: light, wind-borne fruits (birch), those transported by animals (jays carrying off acorns and dropping some on the way), those that pass through a bird's gut and germinate afterwards (hawthorn).

(Some eucalypts have walnut-sized seeds that seem to do nothing but drop off the tree.)

Trees such as birch are *pioneers*: they grow up more readily in the open than in a wood. Oak, which used to grow up easily within woods, mysteriously changed into a pioneer a century ago (p.59).

Gregariousness

Hornbeam is a *gregarious* tree. If a wood is 10 per cent hornbeam, that does not mean that every tenth stool is a hornbeam; more often the wood will consist of 10 acres (4 ha) of pure hornbeam and 90 acres (36 ha) of something else. Clonal trees, such as aspen, are of necessity gregarious, but hornbeam and lime are gregarious for some other, unknown, reason. Ash and maple occur more or less randomly scattered.

Crab-apple, however, is anti-gregarious: it is very unlikely that the next tree to a crab will be another crab. Many trees of tropical rainforest behave thus.

Trees and soil (see also Chapter 10)

Tree books usually claim that trees need soil to grow on, and that they protect the soil; if the trees are felled – it is said – rain washes away the soil and trees cannot return. This can hardly be true of Britain, which has been treeless for most of the last two million years except for interglacial intervals like the present.

In reality many trees grow perfectly well in rock fissures or on derelict buildings. Indeed, in landscapes which are a mosaic of soil and rock, trees often choose the rock, leaving the soil to grassland, heath etc.

Most trees in Britain will grow (though not necessarily well) on almost any soil, but with certain tendencies:
- Alder grows on *flushed* soils: spring-lines and places with moving water.
- Aspen favours *waterlogged* places with stagnant water.
- Oak and birch grow on the least fertile soils that support native trees.
- Oak is rarely on thin chalk or limestone soils (unless there is a surface layer of another material).
- Beech dislikes waterlogging.
- Elms are correlated with high fertility – but are the elms the result or the cause of the fertility?

Statistical analysis shows significant but weaker relationships. Maple tends to be on soils with a high clay content, and ash is more tolerant of waterlogging than maple, with hazel intermediate.

Storms

Twenty years ago people thought hurricanes occurred in other continents and killed trees. Learned writers treated 'storm mortality' as subtracting old trees from wildwood. Few remembered the 'Great Storm' of 26 November 1703 that sank the Fleet and destroyed the Eddystone lighthouse. Fewer remembered 15 January 1362, when (as Piers Plowman put it) 'pere-trees and plum-trees were poffed to þe erthe ... beches and brode okes were blowe to þe grounde'.

Reality intruded with the events of 16 October 1987 and with storms in 1990, 1999 (on the Continent) and 2002. The chief lessons learnt (or not learnt) were:

- Storm effects were greatest in the interior of woods and plantations; less on the edges (Fig. 9); least among freestanding trees. Crowding predisposes to both breakage and uprooting.
- Uprooting was commoner in planted than wild trees.
- Both uprooting and breakage were commonest among big, young, fast-growing trees. Ancient trees were least affected.
- 'Unsound', rotten and hollow trees were no more affected – sometimes less – than 'healthy' trees. Narrow forks predisposed to breakage. A tree that broke one limb often broke others, suggesting a genetic predisposition.
- There was no great difference among species, although certain exotics (Monterey pine, hybrid poplar) were more often uprooted.
- Root systems, where exposed, were unexpectedly shallow.
- Trees nearly always survived breakage, except sometimes at the base.
- Most uprooted trees survived, especially where a swathe or area of trees toppled rather than single trees here and there. Fallen trees, responding to the change in the direction of gravity, sprouted at least from the base, and sometimes all along the trunk (Fig. 19). If they died, this was usually due to the shade of neighbouring trees rather than drought. Thus lime (shade-tolerant) nearly always survived, whereas birch usually succumbed except in a swathe.

As in other countries, storms were an unmitigated benefit for wildlife. They broke up areas of monotonous shade and encouraged coppicing plants. They renewed the habitat of ground-nesting birds and (in France) of deer. They call in question the assumption that the 'normal' state of a tree is upright.[1]

While revising this book I was summoned to Slovakia to investigate the 'calamity' of 19 November 2004, when a local storm shattered or levelled many square miles of close-packed spruce forest in the Tatra Mountains (Fig. 10). Many of the characteristics of England in 1987 – not least the frantic overreaction of humanity – repeated themselves. Blowdowns probably form part of the normal ecology of spruce, but the overcrowding practices of Central European foresters encourage them.

Other countries and other trees

Table 1 summarises the properties of the commoner native British trees. The first task of anyone investigating an unfamiliar country is to make a similar table for trees there. This may not be simple, for these properties do not run along particular branches of the evolutionary tree. European beech coppices, but the almost identical beech of eastern North America, *Fagus grandifolia*, suckers (Fig. 11). North America, Europe and Japan each have one or a few species of elm that coppice and grow from seed, and other elms that sucker.

Travellers in other continents will encounter many of the properties in Table 1. Even Australia – which is, in effect, another planet – has trees that coppice, pollard and sucker, or are gregarious or not. In Mediterranean countries or North America the visitor encounters fire, and learns to distinguish between trees that are flammable and fire-adapted and those that are not. One can seldom look up the answers in a book. What happens after a tree is cut down or set on fire are questions to be answered by going out and looking.

Knowledge of properties changes with time, as the Great Storm showed. The effect of browsing animals on different trees, which has shaped the ecology of the Mediterranean since before human history, is coming to pervade Britain too, as deer get ever more widespread.

WILDWOOD

I use the term *wildwood* for vegetation before it was affected by settled human activities. In Britain, wildwood ceased to exist in the Neolithic period (or before) and has left no record or memory; it has to be investigated through pollen analysis. Even now it is unsettled what wildwood looked like (Chapter 4).

Over the last two million years there have been cycles of ice ages (glaciations) and *interglacial* periods with climates somewhat like the present. The current interglacial, called the Holocene, the last 12,000 years, differs from the others in the presence of *Homo sapiens*, who alters ecosystems in ways not given to his predecessors, Neanderthal or Boxgrove Man. Ecosystems can be affected at a distance by people exterminating animals and manipulating fire. It is debatable whether 'virgin forest' or 'primæval forest', unaffected by mankind, exists anywhere in the world, or whether it is one of those phantoms, like 'primitive man', that haunt the scholarly imagination. (For 'old-growth' forest see p.90f.)

TREE-LAND IN CULTURAL LANDSCAPES

In Britain there are three sharply defined traditions of growing wild trees:

1. *Woodland,* with trees so close together that their canopies meet. Trees are managed by coppicing or allowed to grow on into timber.
2. *Wood-pasture,** where the trees are widely spaced and grassland, heather, etc. grow between them (Fig. 12). There are grazing animals (cattle, sheep, deer), and the trees are mostly a secondary land use.
3. *Non-woodland* trees in hedges and farmland and around buildings.

Besides wild trees, there are *plantations,* orchards, gardens, etc., which differ from woodland in that the trees are not wild: someone has put them there (Fig. 13).

Managed woods, wood-pastures and non-woodland trees go back to prehistory; they are already there in the earliest records of landscape, around 800 AD. Plantations, with rare and unimportant exceptions, began around 1600 AD. They became the staple of modern *forestry,* in contrast to *woodmanship,* which is the art and science of growing trees in woodland and wood-pasture.

Woodland and wood-pasture are aspects of the world's great division of treelands into *forest* with a small *f* (in the sense of trees, trees and trees, with shade-bearing plants beneath them) and *savanna* (grassland with scattered trees).

WOODLAND

Woodland normally occurs as islands in farmland, seldom more than 300 acres (120ha) in extent, with sharp edges. In England every wood has its own name as if it were a village. Whether this results from fragmentation of what was once a continuum of woodland, or whether insularity is a necessary part of the story of how woods came into being, is discussed on p.437.

Woodland structure
In woodland, the trees, as well as other plants, are usually wildlife. They have grown naturally; they will usually have been cut down (often many times) and have grown again by coppicing. (For exceptions see p.264ff.)

On the trees are *epiphytes* such as mosses and lichens and polypody fern, best developed in damp western regions. Flowering-plant epiphytes (not rooted in the ground) are few in Britain except on pollards. Under the trees there may or

---

* I shall avoid the term 'pasture-woodland' because it suggests that wood-pastures are a derivative of woodland, which most are not: they can equally be thought of as tree'd grassland.

may not be layers of understorey trees and *shrubs* such as dogwood. (Both of these are better represented in Japan than in Britain.)

Britain has five species of *woody climbers* – honeysuckle, ivy, clematis, dogrose and woody nightshade. Other continents have many more (America calls them 'vines').

Ground vegetation is composed of herbaceous plants, undershrubs such as brambles, and ground-living bryophytes (mosses and liverworts). What distinguishes woodland from wood-pasture is that the ground vegetation consists of plants that evade shade or are adapted to it in one of the following ways:

1. Some species can live in permanently weak light, such as dog's-mercury and enchanter's nightshade.
2. Some evade shade by growing before the leaves come on the trees, like primrose and anemone. They get roughly tenfold more light than those that leaf in summer, and the light is more effective in photosynthesis than light that has already passed through tree leaves.
3. Some (*seed-bank plants*) evade shade by appearing every time the wood is felled, passing the years between fellings usually as buried seed, such as foxglove.
4. Some evade shade by moving around the wood by well-dispersed seed, seeking spots that have recently been felled, like marsh thistle.
5. Some need no light, deriving their substance from parasitising trees – either directly, like toothwort, or via mycorrhizal fungi, like bird's-nest orchid.

Underground are the mostly unseen mycorrhizal, litter-decomposing and rootparasitic fungi (p.35f, 369f).

For some of these assemblages of plants the trees provide an environment by casting shade or sucking moisture out of the ground, but for others there is a more intimate relationship (p.277).

Sometimes a set of woodland creatures appears to do much the same job, sharing what to the human observer looks like the same ecological niche. These constitute what American ecologists, especially ornithologists, call a *guild*. Warblers and nightingales that nest together in dense underwood form a guild. So do primrose, bluebell, anemone and violets on the ground of the wood; it seems a matter of chance which occupies any particular square inch. Ash, maple and hazel in a mixed coppice form a guild; so do the five woody climbers; so do the various mycorrhizal fungi that are attached to oak.

Coppicing and woodland grassland
Woodland is not wildwood. For centuries people have used and managed natural

woods, and ecosystems have organised themselves in response. Woods have been repeatedly felled and browsing animals excluded. Their present ecosystems are easily damaged by too much shade or by letting in sheep or deer, which they are not used to. Many ecologists call these woods 'semi-natural'; I shall avoid this term because it assumes the existence of a superior category of 'wholly natural' woodland, in which humanity is not an ecological factor. It is doubtful whether any actual examples of this category exist (p.91f).

Coppicing plants respond to felling by more vigorous growth or increased flowering. Violets (shade-adaptation category 1), primrose and bluebell (category 2) are visible all the time, but when the wood is felled they are suddenly exposed to nearly full sunlight; they take the opportunity of extra photosynthesis, the proceeds of which are put into extra flowering in the second or third year after felling. Buried-seed plants (category 3) appear from a seed bank laid down the last time the wood was felled. A few, such as dog's-mercury, appear to be set back by coppicing.

Coppicing plants vary unpredictably even from wood to wood, and are often different from one country to another. The Baltic island of Øland has ash–hazel woods like those in England, but the plants responsive to coppicing include cowslip and a dandelion, which never do this here (Fig. 14). Most countries with coppicing traditions, such as Greece and Japan, have coppicing plants.

Coppicing affects recruitment of trees. By providing temporary open spaces it encourages light-demanding tree seedlings such as birch, and allows others such as ash to progress from a seedling towards a tree. At the same time it prolongs the life of existing stools and gives less opportunity for such turnover. I know of no seed-bank trees in Britain, though North America has one (pin cherry, *Prunus pensylvanica*).

Open spaces in woods may arise regularly through coppicing, or irregularly and infrequently through death of trees, windblow or (in other countries) fire. There are also permanent open areas, kept in being either artificially or by browsing animals: these are *woodland grassland*, whose plants differ both from the coppicing assemblage and from grassland away from woods.

Ancient woodland

Thousands of apparently ordinary woods can be traced back to the Middle Ages. There are four ways to do this:

1. Documents, including surveys, maps and place-names.
2. Archaeology, including the boundary earthworks called *woodbanks*.

3. Woodland structure, including giant and ancient coppice stools.

4. Vegetation, including the occurrence of specific *ancient-woodland plants*.

In the 1980s the Nature Conservancy, predecessor of English Nature, produced an Inventory of Ancient Woodland (Provisional), mapping – county by county – the woods that appeared to be ancient, and whether they were still intact or had been grubbed out or replanted since the 1920s. They drew the line between ancient and recent woodland at *c*.1600. Similar surveys have been done in Wales and Scotland,[2] and are proceeding in Ireland.

Most ancient woods have been intensively used; their present state of comparative disuse is not historical. In principle, they could have begun from surviving fragments of wildwood that were demarcated, conserved and periodically felled. Doubtless many of them were, but others show evidence of having been open land in the distant past.

Woods in other countries

In Scotland (and to a lesser extent Wales and Ireland), measuring woods and defining ancient woodland is not straightforward. Woods, especially in the Highlands, lack nice sharp edges; they move around, so that a wood as a whole may have had a continuous existence but only some of its area may always have been woodland. Woods shade off into wood-pasture and moorland; it is a matter of opinion at what point the trees are big enough or close enough together to constitute woodland. The criterion that a wood should have woodland ground vegetation is problematic in a land with a history of grazing animals in woods and a weak distinction between woodland and wood-pasture.

Uncertainties occur in many other countries (Fig. 15). If, as according to official statistics, 31.57 per cent of the area of Ruritania was 'forest' in 1931 but only 15.67 per cent in 1991, how much of the difference is because forests have really declined or because the definition of what counts as forest has become more restrictive?

Recent woodland

In most of Britain, land lacks trees because people prevent trees from growing. If they stop ploughing land, mowing grass, keeping cattle and sheep, or maintaining factories or mines, trees invade by their dispersal mechanisms. The easiest way to create a new wood is to do nothing. I remember when railway banks were kept mown to prevent fires (p.46), and were beautiful with grassland flowers; since mowing was abandoned they have turned into oakwood. Slippery leaves on the track exhaust trains' sandboxes and give rise to special slow-running 'leaf-fall timetables' every autumn.

Acquiring trees is the first and easiest stage in creating a wood. The trees will be pioneer species, often hawthorn, oak, ash or birch, depending on which are available in the nearest existing wood or hedge. Hornbeam may come in the next generation of trees, but lime, an ancient-woodland plant, seldom comes at all. Herbaceous plants are less easy to establish. New woods often have little ground vegetation, except remains of the grassland or moorland that was there before, or farmland weeds like nettles (Chapter 12).

Many woods date from the 1930s or earlier periods of agricultural depression. The term *secondary woodland* includes all woods – including some ancient woodland – that show signs of once having been open land.

Secondary woodland is worldwide. Alongside the well-publicised destruction of forests, large areas of farmland turned into forest in the twentieth century. Mechanisation of agriculture put farmers out of business whose difficult land or lack of capital prevented them from mechanising; their land 'tumbled down to woodland'. This can be seen on a huge scale in most countries of southern Europe, in North America, and even in densely populated Japan (Fig. 16).

WOOD-PASTURE OR SAVANNA

Wood-pasture (Table 2) combines trees and livestock, either domestic or wild beasts such as deer, antelopes, American wood buffalo or kangaroos. There is a tension between these: the shade of the trees is bad for the pasture, and the livestock eat the regrowth of the trees. In woodland most of the edible matter is far above ground, where only sloths, monkeys, koala bears and tree-kangaroos can climb for it. Shade-bearing herbaceous plants make meagre sustenance, and many, such as lords-and-ladies, are distasteful or poisonous.

Cattle and deer love tree leaves and prefer them to grass, but soon eat all the foliage within reach, creating a *browse-line*; they eat the edible herbs, then the brambles, and then starve unless they can get out of the wood and find substantial grasses. If Nature had intended cattle and deer to be woodland beasts, evolution would have given them long necks; but the giraffe is an odd side-branch of ungulate evolution.

Most wood-pastures consist of trees scattered among grassland or heath, with a history of grazing by cattle, sheep or deer. These are so characteristic of modern English deer-parks that similar-looking ecosystems in other countries are called 'parkland'. They also occur in places like the New Forest and Epping Forest; rarely in East Anglia and Wales trees are scattered in farmers' fields. Usually the trees are wildlife: they got started either at times when grazing was in decline, or in the protection of thorny thickets that held off the animals.

Backward in time and outward in space, examples of tree'd grasslands multiply. A thousand years ago they cannot have occupied much less than one-tenth of the whole of England. They cover about one-sixth of Portugal and one-eighth of Spain (p.116). They are widespread in the Balkans, Greece and Turkey, formerly as far north as Sweden,[3] and even in Japan. In lower latitudes they merge into the savannas of Asia, North America, Africa and supremely Australia (Fig. 17).

Wood-pasture lacks shade-adapted plants. Savanna is grassland (or heather, etc.) with trees, and is similar to grassland or heather without trees (but see p.124).

Wood-pasture now attracts attention because of revived interest in 'veteran' trees. Other than coppice stools (p.202), trees seldom grow old in woodland: if woodmen do not cut them down, competition from neighbouring trees forbids them to live through a long period of decline. Ancient upstanding trees are a strong indication that a site is *not* an ancient wood.

Wood-pastures result where various factors – drought, grazing animals, fire – create conditions for trees to grow, but not forests. In historic England the predominant factor has been people keeping plenty of livestock. In Africa it may be drought. However, recent researches show the importance of human activities even in tropical savannas:[4] the distribution of tree'd grasslands would be very different if people had never existed.

Branches of wood-pasture

There are three forms of wood-pasture:

1. *Wood-pasture commons*, the original form in England. A common is a piece of land on which a particular group of people, not the landowner, has rights to keep livestock and sometimes to cut wood (rarely timber). Some commons were wooded (e.g. Burnham Beeches, Buckinghamshire), others not.
2. *Parks*. In the eleventh century, landowners began to add deer to the repertoire of domestic animals and to keep them in semi-captivity in *parks*, most of which were private wood-pasture surrounded by a *pale*, a deer-proof fence.
3. *Forests*, places on which the king (or some other very great magnate, not necessarily the landowner) had the right to keep deer, to kill and eat them, and to set up a special legal system ostensibly to protect the deer. Forests were introduced by William the Conqueror after 1086. They usually involved tracts of common

land in which the king's deer were added to – and did not displace – commoners' and landowners' normal activities. The difference between a park and a Forest is that a Forest is not fenced, the deer staying there by force of habit. *Forest* (with a capital F) must not be confused with *forest* in the woodland or plantation sense. A medieval Forest was a place of deer, not of trees. About half the English Forests were wooded, in the limited sense of having more woodland per square mile than the surrounding landscape. Only a small part of the woodland and wood-pasture of England was actively involved in Forests (p.119).

In the *uncompartmented* type of wood-pasture, livestock had access to the entire site every year, and the trees were normally pollards. *Compartmented* woodpastures were demarcated into coppices, one of which would be felled each year and then fenced to keep out the beasts until the wood had grown up sufficiently not to need protection. Many wooded Forests, such as Hatfield and Blackmoor (Chapter 20), were compartmented, many parks, and a few wooded commons.

Terms

I use *wood* and *woodland* in the original English meaning of the words. A *wood* is an island of woodland – what an American calls a *wood-lot*. *Woodland* has been used in distant countries to mean other things, such as savanna. In Australia *woodland* means savanna (at least the denser forms of it); tropical forest is called *bush*.

NON-WOODLAND TREES

Freestanding trees grow in hedges and fields and around settlements. Some are planted: there is a much stronger tradition of planting trees in hedges than in woods. Others have grown up out of bushes and underwood forming the hedge itself.

Hedges in Britain go back beyond the beginning of records, with archaeological evidence from the Iron Age and beyond.[5] They are not merely linear woods: they tend to be less shady, less stable and more fertile. A test of whether a plant is an ancient-woodland indicator (Chapter 12) is that it shall not grow in ancient hedges. A few hedges are *ghosts* of woodland, the edges of woods that have been destroyed: they retain woodland plants but do not acquire new ones.

Non-woodland trees have historically been an appreciable part of the total tree cover, especially in areas that also had woodland. Many hedges were regularly coppiced for fuel. However, even such a woodless place as medieval Bassingbourn (Cambridgeshire) had non-woodland trees: the parish derived a small income from the 'loppe' of 'Asshewel Strete tree', 'the asshes in the Marketsted', and other pollards growing on public land.[6]

PLANTATIONS

In plantations the trees have been put there, as an alternative to sugar beet or ryegrass; they have no relation to the natural vegetation. Usually they were transplanted from a nursery. They are meant to be cut down for timber when quite young (40 years for most conifers, 100 years for oak) and not to grow again: the stumps should die and the land be put to some other use.

Modern forestry, as concerned with planted trees, has two branches. The *commercial* branch mass-produces trees in even-aged plantations and fells them all at once; it was what the Forestry Commission did for most of the twentieth century. The *estate* branch operates in more complex and varied ways, felling small groups or single trees and even using *natural regeneration* by self-sown seedlings.

Plantation trees do not pretend to be wildlife. The ground vegetation, if any, is a remnant of what was on the site before. However, plantations if neglected begin to take on the character of woodland as the planted trees die and unwanted wild trees come in. They may begin to acquire a woodland flora as plants invade from nearby woodland. This depends on how near the plantation is to existing woodland, and whether the soil is too fertile (Chapter 12).

Some plantations are on the site of natural woods that have been *replanted* (or 'restocked') by killing the wild trees and planting trees instead. They retain something of the previous ground vegetation, and often also of the previous trees that resisted the killing. Such survivals result from neglect rather than intention: estate as well as commercial forestry drains out the distinctive features of ancient woods, leaving nothing (other than woodbanks) older than one generation of timber trees. 'Unreplanting' or 'deconiferisation' is now an important branch of woodland conservation (p.378f).

The plantation tradition is earlier and stronger in Scotland than in England. Scots travellers introduced exotica, several of which, such as Douglas fir and Sitka spruce, became fashionable foresters' trees. Scotland played the leading part in introducing modern forestry – based on the German model via British India – to Britain. The Forestry Commission was largely a Scottish invention.

EVOLUTION

Animals and plants, in theory, have become adapted to their environment by evolution and natural selection. Evolution acts through sexual reproduction, which for plants takes the form of seed. Animals, most of which are short-lived, keep up with changing environments through genetic change in successive generations. The textbook example used to be melanistic moths, which had changed their camouflage patterns in response to acid rain exterminating the lichens on tree trunks.

Most creatures evolve, but some evolve more than others. If an oak takes 50 years to produce its first acorns, evolution acts 200-fold more slowly than on mice. Longevity and vegetative reproduction delay its operation still further. A clonal oak can produce acorns a thousand years after it germinated. Many trees seem to have dispensed with sex as a means of reproduction: I have never seen a seedling English elm or black poplar, and in many years of exploring Greece I have only two or three times seen a seedling prickly oak, one of the commonest Greek plants.

With very long-lived plants, evolutionary adaptation is somewhat a relic of distant prehistory. It came to terms with the slow environmental changes of the Tertiary geological period, but has not caught up with the violent climatic fluctuations of the last two million years, still less with disruption by humanity in the last 7,000 years (but see p.436f). These events have thrust trees into environments to which they are not yet adapted; they may retain adaptations to environmental factors no longer operating, such as European elephants.

NATIVE, NATURALISED AND EXOTIC SPECIES

Native plants and animals are species which reached this country by natural means, usually while Britain was still joined to Europe before some 7,000 years ago: for example ash and badger. *Alien* species were brought by people, deliberately or accidentally, and behave in one of two ways:
1. *Naturalised* species, which once here propagate themselves without further human intervention. Central European sycamore and Asian fallow deer have become part of the wildlife of Britain.
2. *Exotics*, the majority, do not spread beyond where people have put them: South American guinea pig and Albanian horsechestnut are not wildlife here. (Horsechestnut can grow from seed, but seldom gets beyond the seedling stage.) This does not depend on the lapse of time: sweet-chestnut and walnut were both introduced by the Romans, but one has naturalised and the other not.

Naturalised species are divided into *archaeophytes*, historic (but not native) members of the British flora like sweet-chestnut, and *neophytes*, modern introductions like Norway maple; by convention the dividing line is set at 1500 AD.[7] *Casuals* are plants like borage that do not persist without reintroduction.

In principle (and in this book) these are matters of fact, to be resolved by scientific and historical investigation. Either maple was brought to Ireland on a ship, or it got there by natural means. At present sycamore counts as a neophyte, but if someone finds good evidence of its presence in the Middle Ages it will become an archaeophyte. But of late years the issue has become contaminated by value judgements and political correctness. The question of whether sycamore is native has become muddled with whether conservationists should approve of sycamore. The addition of species to the British flora has become confused with people's attitudes to human 'aliens' in the Customs & Immigration sense of the word.

Plants need not be native or alien everywhere. Scots pine was native in the early Holocene throughout the British Isles. It died out by Roman times from England and Wales, and probably rather later in Ireland. It was reintroduced in or about the seventeenth century and became naturalised, spreading on to heathland, but not into native woodland unless put there. Pine is thus native in parts of Scotland and naturalised (a neophyte) in the rest of Britain.

A recently prominent matter is introductions of 'native' species from foreign sources. Some writers refer to native species as 'true natives', the implication being that there are also false natives. Indeed there are (Chapter 13). Much of the introduction of 'Scots pine' was from Continental sources and is visibly different from the native pine of Scotland.

OAKS AND ELMS

There are two native oaks in Britain (Table 3): most other countries have more. To most readers the common oak will be *Quercus robur*, 'pedunculate oak'; *Q. petræa*, 'sessile oak', is the oak of oakwoods and of the north and west. They are very different ecologically, although they often overlap and hybridise.[8] Until 200 years ago only botanists recognised the differences: they thus have no common names, the English names being translations of earlier botanical Latin names.

Many alien oaks have been planted, of which Turkey oak* and the evergreen holm-oak have become naturalised. Besides the different species, it is possible to

---

* The European tree (*Quercus cerris*), not the American turkey-oak (*Q. lævis*).

distinguish wild from planted-type oaks (Table 17) and indigenous oak timber from Baltic oak (p.242).

There are arguably more kinds of elm in England than of all other native trees together. Wych-elm (*Ulmus glabra*) is a 'normal' species; it is not clonal, grows from seed, and coppices. It is the common elm of the north and west and Ireland, getting rarer towards the south and east. Clonal elms generate a host of 'microspecies', rather as brambles and dandelions do.[9] These fall into three main groups:

1. The English elm group (called *U. procera*): widespread but not very variable, the common elms of middle and mid-south England; seldom in woodland except at the corners, very susceptible to the current form of Dutch Elm Disease and now rarely seen except as suckers.
2. The East Anglian group (called *U. minor*): the common elms of eastern England and parts of the southeast; exceedingly variable; often in woodland; sometimes resistant to Elm Disease.
3. The Cornish group (called *U. sarniensis*): the common elms of Cornwall and southwest Devon.

There are many intermediates and possible hybrids. It has been claimed that some, if not all, the non-*procera* elms are ancient introductions from Europe, but so far this lacks confirmation.[10] Elms of the *minor* group occur throughout southern Europe and as far away as Crete. I have never seen any recognisable *procera* outside the British Isles. *Sarniensis* (as its name implies) occurs in the Channel Islands (Fig. 172).

SEVEN QUESTIONS TO ASK ON VISITING AN UNFAMILIAR COUNTRY

1. Which trees die when felled and which sprout?
2. Which trees are clonal?
3. Is pollarding a practice? Which trees respond to it?
4. Which trees are eaten by cattle? or sheep? or goats? or deer? Which recover from browsing?
5. Do trees on cliffs or islands differ from those of the rest of the landscape?
6. Which trees will burn? Which survive fire? Which germinate after a fire?
7. Which trees invade abandoned land?

CHAPTER 2

SOME LESS FAMILIAR PROPERTIES OF TREES

Roots, Partnerships, Longevity, Tree Rings, Sap-Sucking, Fire

... From 1940 to 1945 I was concerned with fire-fighting arrangements over many thousands of acres of forest in the South of England ... these were subject to unusual risks from large-scale military training and aircraft, and ... German incendiary bombs ... any kind of vegetation that could be set alight, was set alight, and had of course to be tackled by fire-fighters. Broadleaved woodland of any kind simply refused to burn at any time, although fires in coniferous plantations, and among heather and gorse, were serious and frequent.

H.L. EDLIN *TREES, WOODS AND MAN*, 1956

ROOTS

Who understands tree roots? In countries like Greece that are fond of the bulldozer, roots are exposed to view in road-cuts; but until 1987 few English people understood what a tree's root system looked like; some thought roots went nearly as far below ground as stems above it.

As the great storms of 1987 and 1990 showed, most trees in England are shallow rooted (Fig. 18).[1] It may be argued that deep-rooted trees were never uprooted, but anyone digging holes in a wood seldom meets roots more than 3 feet (1 metre) down. A giant beech can have a root-plate only a few inches deep, much less than the diameter of the trunk. A chestnut stool on clay or loess, 8 feet (2.5 metres) in diameter, has all its visible roots in 9 inches (23 centimetres) or so. Trees do not necessarily have deeper roots than herbaceous plants: I have excavated barley roots down to at least 8 feet (2.5 metres).

Is it true that trees in Britain have taproots? An oak, on germination, produces a vigorous vertical root that nails the acorn to the ground. Maybe people thought this went on developing for many years, but oaks uprooted in storms show that this is not so: the taproot goes down a foot or two (30 or 60 centimetres) and is then superseded. David Maylam tells me of oaks forcibly uprooted that proved to have taproots, but it is not clear in what circumstances these are developed. In Greece deciduous oaks generally have shallow roots like English oaks, but evergreen oaks are deep rooted, especially if rooting into rock fissures.

Roots and windblow

A tree's roots have three functions: to hold the tree up; to supply it with water; and to supply it with minerals. (Trees usually delegate the last to mycorrhizal fungi.) In England, generally, the holding-up function is the critical one. In the great storms many millions of trees were uprooted. To most people's surprise they stayed alive; many of them lived through the great droughts of 1989 and 1990, and some flourished better than many trees that had stayed upright (Fig. 19). The same happened after other hurricanes and in other countries. James Dickson points out that woods around Glasgow are full of living oaks and larches overturned in the great storm of 1968. Most trees lived (and are still alive if not shaded) if one-quarter or one-sixth of their root system remained in the ground.

The inference, that trees have four to six times as much root as is needed to supply them with water in an ordinary summer, explains some anomalies. Urban trees often have their roots severed by builders' or cable-layers' trenches: this can hardly be good for the tree, but it rarely suffers obvious above-ground effects. Ploughing around a farmland tree must play havoc with its shallow roots, yet the consequences are less severe than would be expected.

Trees should thus be able to grow so close together that they fail to stand up before they suffer unduly from root competition. They do: in the 1987 storm, trees in plantations were more often uprooted than in natural woods, in natural woods more often than freestanding trees, and in the interior of a wood or plantation more often than on the edges, *including the windward edge* (see Fig. 9). Evidently isolated trees can develop a bigger root system, which holds a greater weight of soil to counterbalance the wind pressure, than their sisters whose roots are restricted by neighbouring trees. A marginal tree develops half an unrestricted root system. Trees in plantations are even more crowded than in woods, partly because foresters earn their living by growing stems, not roots, and accept windblow as a normal risk of business, but also because they plant trees close together and often forget to thin them. Crowding turned out to be the most significant factor in uprooting – and also in wind-breakage, but that is another story.[2]

In other climates the balance between root functions is different. In the Mediterranean, summers are fiercely dry, and most trees have not adapted to drought by losing their leaves as they do in the seasonally dry tropics. Instead they have deep roots and grow widely spaced (p.201). In a high wind, most trees break before they uproot.

MYCORRHIZAS

There are thousands of species of specialised woodland fungi. Many conspicuous toadstools go with particular trees. The familiar fly agaric (is it still familiar?) is always near either pine or birch: its *mycelium* – the permanent, usually unseen vegetative network of microscopic hyphæ – is a partner with the roots of these particular trees.

Most land plants are dual organisms. Attached to their roots is a fungus, whose hyphæ are thinner and more richly branched than the root itself; they invade more soil than is directly accessible to the roots. The host plant supplies the fungus with the carbon needed to make its hyphæ. The fungus does much of the job which schoolchildren used to be taught was done by the root hairs. It supplies the plant with nitrogen, phosphorus and other nutrients, and sometimes water too; it can even defend its host against competition from nonmycorrhizal neighbours. Neither functions well without the other; seedlings use their seed reserves to make contact with the fungus, and die if they fail to find a partner.

Lichens, too, are dual organisms – a combination of a fungus and a green or blue-green alga. (So is the human body, as anyone knows who has taken an antibiotic that kills off, temporarily, the gut bacteria.) Mosses and certain families of herbaceous plants lack mycorrhizas, but most liverworts have them.[3]

Mycorrhizas have been known for more than a century, but their full significance has only recently been elucidated by such scientists as Professor D.J. Read.[4] Most plants have *endotrophic* or *vesicular-arbuscular* mycorrhizas. The fungus forms micro-trees inside the cells of the root, and sends out hyphæ that branch far into the soil. These simple fungi, which lack visible fruit-bodies, form a special phylum (Glomeromycetes). It is usually said that the fungal species are few and not particular as to their hosts, but this may be due to incomplete knowledge. Their hyphæ secrete glomalin into the soil, a protein that, like humus from worm casts, stabilises and aerates the soil. This plant – fungus symbiosis goes back to the remote geological origins of land plants.[5]

The second kind of mycorrhiza is *ectotrophic*: the fungus forms a sheath investing the root, from which strands of fungal tissue invade the surrounding soil. Host plants include trees such as pines, oaks, beeches, birches and hazels. The fungi include many common toadstool agarics and other basidiomycetes.* They tend to choose particular host trees: a whole genus (or subgenus), *Alnicola*, favours alder. They are particularly efficient on acid soils, where they recycle nitrogen and phosphorus out of fallen leaves. Even minerals in the pollen that birches, pines and oaks so copiously shed are not wasted but sent back into the tree by the root-fungi.[6]

The world's best-studied mycorrhizal is probably *matsutake* ('pine fungus'), *Tricholoma matsutake*, the fabulous edible toadstool which is part of any Japanese autumnal feast. (Slivers of it have passed down the author's – alas unappreciative! – throat.) It grows on the roots of Japanese red pine (*Pinus densiflora*). Starting from a particular tree, it forms a slowly expanding *shiro* (a clonal mat of mycelium), which is poorly competitive against other fungi and microorganisms, and sensitive to the amount and composition of leaf litter. Fruiting is influenced by the age of the pines and the abundance of the evergreen oaks and hollies that form the understorey: there is a complex underground interaction between this and other mycorrhizals and litter-decomposers. *Matsutake* has been getting rarer, partly because the pineries have been destroyed by a nematode (p.339), but also because declining management has altered the balance between pines and shrubs. Since one toadstool can easily sell at the equivalent of £20 (retail in 2004), *matsutake* is more lucrative than timber.**

Fungi, originating from trees, can transfer substance to other plants. This explains woodland plants that have no chlorophyll, such as bird's-nest orchid and yellow bird's-nest. Long regarded as saprophytes (feeders on rotten wood or leaves), they are really parasites on the 'wood-wide web' of ectomycorrhiza. Like the toadstools', their substance was originally made by the trees. A mysterious speciality of Groton Wood (Suffolk) is *Epipactis purpurata*, a big orchid growing and flowering in the densest shade of lime where there are few or no other herbs. I never see it not flowering, and it never comes up twice in the same place; presumably it lives for many years without coming above ground. Some plants

---

* Two other types of mycorrhiza are associated with Ericaceæ and terrestrial orchids.
** I am grateful to Professor Hideo Tabata and colleagues for an initiation into pityomycology.

are pink instead of green, with little or no chlorophyll. I have long suspected that it is really a parasite on mycorrhiza.

Mycorrhizal fungi form a fourth component in the ecosystem, along with trees and shrubs, herbaceous plants, and bryophytes. They are a factor in the behaviour of woodland in relation to waterlogging. Anyone trying to start a new wood has to consider them, especially if the site is fertiliser-sodden farmland (p.261): cultivation and fertilising are disastrous for many mycorrhizas.

A comparison of mycorrhizal fungi

This is a record of my own long-term observations and those of visitors, including distinguished mycologists, at four sites in eastern England: two boulder-clay woods 2 miles (3 kilometres) apart but of different character, an ancient mixed coppice on a wide range of soils, and a series of plantations in a 200-year-old Breckland park (Table 4). (The development of fungal communities and guilds in Brandon Park is discussed on p.369f.)

Most of the classic sites for mycorrhizal fungi are on acid soils. Boulder-clay woods have a reputation for being poor in species. This is partly due to their fungi fruiting less often on calcareous soils; the difference is reduced by recording over many years. Mycorrhizal fungi are often associated with particular trees: Spooner & Roberts (2005) give many such associations. In a mixed wood it can be difficult to decide which tree goes with which fungus, especially as many mycorrhizal fungi are clonal: starting from one tree, they spread out into the root-space of different trees. In Table 5 I list the associations that I have been able to identify, which are summarised in Table 6. They confirm some of the traditional associations, but not all.

In Brandon Park, although the greatest number of mycorrhizals go with pine, beech and birch have disproportionately many in relation to the abundance of the trees. Birch and pine have many species in common; these are both pioneering and relatively arctic trees, but did not much occur together in the early Holocene of Britain (p.71). Ectotrophic mycorrhizas get about by spores; plantations of exotic trees tend to make do with the local ectomycorrhiza and later to acquire their own species. Thus the conifer plantations, in 200 years, have acquired five species of the conifer-specialist genus *Suillus*, including two specialists from the far-away homeland of larch.

In Bradfield Woods, with no conifers or beech, the predominant hosts are birch and hazel; alder has unexpectedly few specialists. There are surprisingly many species in common between Brandon and Bradfield: beech associates in

Brandon (e.g. *Laccaria amethystina*) and even pine associates (e.g. *L. laccata*) occur with other trees in Bradfield.

In Hayley Wood, oak and hazel appear to be the predominant mycorrhizal hosts. In Buff Wood they are outdone by the small area of hornbeam, which has several specific mycorrhizals: some of these occur on beech in Brandon Park, even though hornbeam is more closely related to birch than beech.

Ash, maple, lime, hawthorn and blackthorn have few known associates. These have mainly vesicular-arbuscular mycorrhizas without visible fruit-bodies.

LONGEVITY AND DECAY

How long do trees live?
An anthropomorphic myth is that trees have a defined life span and die of 'old age'. This may be true of some short-lived species. Most of the flowering cherries that were fashionable street trees of the 1930s are now dead; birch and aspen seldom reach a century. However, in a civilised country, trees are normally felled before they get far into middle age and become too big to be easily handled. The public rarely sees an old tree of a long-lived species.

Oaks are not immortal: they die at random from unknown causes. At Polstead Park in Suffolk a gigantic, spreading oak at the corner of the park, 17 feet (5.2 metres) in girth, suddenly died in 1991 (Fig. 20). Like all freestanding oaks with a big spread of branches it was young for its size, dating from c.1736. A row of pollard oaks round the edges of the park, nearly twice its age and very stag-headed, hardly altered at all. Life expectancy has little to do with age: if one must be anthropomorphic, the battlefield is a better analogy than the almshouse.

Why are trees not immortal? Every year trees have to lay down a new annual ring all over their trunk, branches, twigs and roots. Most trees reach their maximum leafage in late youth. Thereafter, taking good years with bad, the material available for making new wood is roughly constant, but it must be spread over an inexorably increasing area. Obviously this cannot go on for ever.

Trees can retrench and reduce the area to be covered: they shed redundant twigs and branches. Pollarding and coppicing are a major retrenchment, which resets the ageing process and prolongs the tree's life. Most of the oldest oaks are pollards. Ash usually falls to pieces and disappears at around 200, unless growing in an adverse environment, but coppicing can extend this to at least 800. Some trees are self-coppicing or self-pollarding (p.64f). Lime, unusually, is able to miss one or more annual rings.

A *veteran* tree is one old enough to have gone through cycles of dieback and regrowth (Fig. 21). How old it is depends on the species: an 80-year-old aspen is a veteran aspen, whereas a 200-year-old oak is in early middle age.

Life expectancy depends more on size than age. Other things being equal, adversity, which slows a tree's growth, will prolong its age. Very old trees occur on infertile soils or at high altitudes. The world's longest-lived trees are the short, fantastic, gnarled bristle-cone pines at the limit of trees in the mountains of California. Among the oldest trees in Europe are the short, fantastic, gnarled cypresses at the limit of trees in the mountains of Crete (Fig. 22).[7]

Competition limits longevity by interfering with retrenchment. A tree that goes through a phase of dieback will not recover if a neighbour expands to fill the space. Although in other countries ancient trees can occur in woods, like the redwoods of California, in Britain they are normally freestanding (p.125).

Decay and compartmentation
Trees (God knows why) have evolved in favour of longevity. Decay is not a disease, but is part of that evolution and part of normal development. Any tree needs a mechanism to get rid of superfluous boughs formed when it was young. It must compensate for minor damage and survive injury by windblow (or fire, with fire-promoting trees).

Trees have no immune system and no wound-repair system. Vertebrate animals respond to injury by warring against the bacteria that invade wounds, and by regenerating damaged tissue. Trees react with a damage-limitation mechanism, walling off and bypassing both decayed and diseased tissue.

When a branch dies or is broken or cut, the tree lays down barriers in the surrounding wood which wall off a *compartment*, the size and shape of which are determined by the injury. Wood-rotting fungi (sometimes specific to particular living trees) invade the exposed surface and form a pocket of rot, which spreads up to the predetermined compartment boundary.

In Europe, research has been dominated by the interests of timber producers, who harvest trees before they are old enough to have incurred much injury. For them, decay is a nuisance like disease. Understanding of damage limitation comes from America, with its stronger tradition of arboriculture (caring for individual trees).

The barriers consist of pre-existing wood altered so as to block the spread of fungi. In broadleaved trees the water-conducting vessels are plugged with structures called *tyloses*: in conifers the microscopic *bordered pits*, acting as valves between the water-conducting cells, close. The wood becomes impregnated with tannins and other fungus-opposing chemicals. There are four types of barrier. The first three resist the spread of a fungus along the length of a stem or branch (important in blocking the spread of vascular diseases like Dutch Elm Disease), from one annual ring to another, or around the circumference of a stem. Type 4 is called forth by a major injury, and separates wood laid down before the injury from that produced after. This is the most effective type of barrier, often forming a bark-like lining to the interior of a hollow tree.[8]

Fungi themselves contribute to compartmentation. Some wood-rotters form a barrier of hard fungal tissue called a *zone-plate* on meeting the tree's barrier. If they meet wood occupied by another individual fungus, each makes a zone-plate, with a narrow 'demilitarised zone' between (Fig. 23). Zone-plates in beech or hornbeam, formed by the fungus *Ustulina deusta,* appear in sections of the tree as single or double sinuous black lines. 'Spalted beech' (full of zone-plates) is treated as decorative by some furniture makers.

Most trees reach their maximum height and spread quite early in life: they pass through a period of being vulnerable to breakage by wind, but go on indefinitely getting thicker. When a big tree goes hollow it is getting rid of internal wood no longer needed to hold it up. Minerals in the decaying wood may be recycled into the tree's roots. Although in Britain decay is a mainly fungal process, in lower latitudes termites help. In the Cape York Peninsula of tropical Australia most trees, even a few inches in diameter, are hollow (and are used by Aborigines for the musical horn called a *didgeridoo*).

American, European and Australian trees – broadleaves, conifers and eucalypts – have this mechanism. In the great storm of 1987, most of the trees that broke were big, young and perfectly sound. Many a rotten or hollow tree remained upstanding surrounded by younger trees that were broken or uprooted.

Trees exhibit *compensatory growth*, laying down extra wood where needed at weak points (see Fig. 26). The base of a big tree tends to be a weak point, where butt-rotting fungi can spread up from root injuries, and where the tree is unlikely to survive breakage unless it is a lime. (I have known a big oak break at the base, the wood having been turned by a white-rot fungus into a substance still identifiable as oak, but with the consistency of Camembert cheese.) Buttress roots may compensate for butt-rot: many a great oak is held up for centuries by its root buttresses, the centre of the base having disappeared.

Most decay fungi are symbiotic rather than pathogenic, but some can be either. Silver-leaf fungus, *Stereum purpureum,* is a weak wood-rotter, especially on birch, but on fruit trees it can enter through pruning wounds and secrete chemicals that poison the tree. All the almond trees around where I lived in Norwich died of it during ten years or so. After World War I the Government, thinking it could vanquish the fungi, made silver-leaf illegal. Forestalling silver-leaf is probably why arboriculturalists used to cover pruning wounds with tarry preparations 'to prevent decay'. In reality it is impossible to prevent decay, but there is something to be said for encouraging decay by symbiotic rather than pathogenic fungi. *

How effectively compartments confine pathogens depends on the fungus and the tree. The bracket-fungus *Inonotus hispidus*, a heartwood-rotter of ash, gets through compartment walls by growing in winter when the tree's reactions are slow. Thus a heart-rotted ash can withstand one winter storm but break in a less severe storm the following winter. *Ustulina deusta* is well contained by beech, but can penetrate the compartment barriers of lime.[9]

A pollard tree renews its Type 4 barriers each time it is cut. Inside a hollow tree there may be the shells of one or more previous barriers, superseded by the present lining of the hollow; they weather out as the surrounding, less rot-resistant wood decays. Roots can spread downwards into the rotten wood and debris that fill the cavity, extracting minerals. (Compartment barriers, formed when the tree was alive, occasionally weather out from decayed timbers in ancient buildings.)

Veteran trees as a habitat
Much of the value of trees as a habitat for other creatures attaches not to all trees, but to those few that are old enough to have hollow interiors. Beneficiaries include:
- hole-nesting birds;
- bats, using cavities and cracks of different sizes for roosting, hibernation and breeding;
- beetles, flies and other insects of rotten wood, especially of red-rotted oak, willow or hawthorn altered by *Fistulina hepatica*;[10]
- insects associated as symbionts or predators with bracket-fungi;
- invertebrates living on damp debris accumulated inside pollards;
- flies that breed in wet rot-holes, or on 'slime tracks' of exudate (especially those produced by bacterial wetwood),[11] dribbling down the outside of a tree;

---

* In America, wounds on live oaks are painted to deter insects that carry oak wilt.

- insects under old dry bark;
- spiders associated with these, and insects that feed on the spiders' leavings;
- specific lichens on old dry bark under overhangs;
- bryophytes and other lichens on rain-tracks or weathered-out compartment boundaries.[12]

A single 400-year-old oak, especially a pollard with its labyrinthine compartment boundaries, can generate a whole ecosystem of such creatures, for which ten thousand 200-year-old oaks are no use at all.

TREE RINGS AND DENDROCHRONOLOGY

Most native trees produce annual rings, whose structure is diagnostic of the species (p.242ff). The age and growth rate of a tree are given by counting the rings on a stump or in a core taken with a hollow borer. (Many trees, especially in the tropics, have no annual rings; one should be cautious with trees like lime that can miss rings, or with foreign trees that produce extra 'false rings'.)

Oak, by far the commonest timber in historic buildings, has well-defined rings that vary in width from year to year. The variation depends partly on weather; good and bad years are repeated in most trees within the same geographical region. Posterity will recognise the late twentieth century by the sequence of a bad year (1975), a worse year (1976), then 12 unremarkable years, then two bad years (1989–90), three unremarkable years, a bad year, an average year (1995), an average year, a rather bad year (1997), and so on. By comparing the early years of a living tree with the later years of a timber from a historic building, and by comparing its earlier years with the later years of an older timber or a log buried in a bog, these patterns have been extended back, even to the Bronze Age.

This procedure has grown into a considerable science. It is used to date historic buildings: the journal *Vernacular Architecture* publishes results of such work. The determined amateur can try it: it helps to have a travelling microscope to measure the rings to within 0.1 millimetre. There are computer programs to remove the effects of long-term trends, as the tree grows older or as neighbours compete with it, leaving the year-to-year variations that are useful in dating.

Tree rings have other uses. Because weather varies from region to region, the provenance of a timber can sometimes be determined: if the sequence matches a *master curve* from Poland rather than England, this is evidence that the sample is of Baltic oak (p.232). By removing year-to-year variation, leaving the long-term trends, it has been possible in America to use growth rates as a measure of climate change.

To get a result one normally measures at least 100 rings, preferably from each of several contemporary trees or timbers. Tree rings are affected by other factors besides weather, such as defoliating caterpillars (p.335).* In view of the statistical 'noise' introduced by unknown factors, it is surprising that the method has been so successful and so seldom at odds with dating by other means.

SAPSUCKING

A now familiar sight is a small tree trunk with horizontal rows of holes round the circumference, sometimes repeated from top to bottom. Americans recognise these as the work of sapsuckers (*Sphyrapicus*), a genus of woodpecker-like birds that peck holes in trees and then come back and lick up the exuding sap. Sapsuckers, however, are absent from Europe.

The trees most often affected are lime, elm and oak, typically stems about 4 inches (10 centimetres) in diameter with nearly smooth bark (Fig. 24). The holes are soon overgrown by new annual rings, but the scars persist for many years in the bark and permanently as little irregularities in the wood (to be treated as decorative by future veneer-cutters?).

This minor damage seems to be done by the great spotted woodpecker; other woodpeckers may be involved on the Continent. It is curious that such a conspicuous activity was not noticed in bird or forestry books down the centuries. I began to see it around 1970, but there are scattered records (more numerous in Central Europe) back to the 1930s. Have woodpeckers only recently taken to sapsucking?

FIRE

As Edlin noted (p.33), there is little hope of studying fire and trees in England. Readers visiting the Mediterranean, North America or the Scottish Highlands may encounter it, and in Australia certainly will.

---

* I am told that at conferences in this field high words, and occasionally blows, used to be exchanged between the supporters of weather and of caterpillars.

When fires happen depends on weather and on sources of ignition; but whether vegetation will burn at all depends on the plants. Trees are combustible by adaptation, not misfortune. Pines and eucalypts make flammable resins and oils, and it is their business to burn from time to time and destroy their less fire-adapted competitors. More subtle adaptations can promote fire. Fallen leaves may lie as a loose, airy litter; shed twigs may lie for many years without rotting; the trees may cast a light shade that allows flammable shrubs to grow underneath. Fires are reproducible: it is unusual for vegetation to burn that has never burnt before. Combustibility apparently evolved with some of the earliest trees in the Devonian; so presumably did adaptations to take advantage of it. Charcoal from Carboniferous forest fires is a major constituent of coal. Since the late Tertiary, fire has come to be a factor second only to climate in determining the world's ecosystems.[13]

Lightning often strikes a dead tree and sets fire to loose bark or dry debris in its hollow interior. Even now, in a tidied-up landscape, most fires in the Rocky Mountains are attributed to lightning. Climate can encourage fire, but does not cause fires unless the vegetation is fire-promoting.

Fires vary in intensity, duration and effects. A fire in ground vegetation or leaf litter is usually relatively cool. Its effects tend to be long term, killing seedlings and young trees of fire-sensitive species like beeches and maples. A crown fire, which happens with fire-promoting trees, is much grander: flames climb into the treetops and leap from tree to tree.

Certain plant families – pines, eucalypts, heathers, grasses and palms (Fig. 25) – are *fire-adapted*. Fires seldom happen without them. Some species are easily killed, but their seeds are stimulated to germinate by heat, and the tree starts producing new seeds when young: Aleppo pine in the Mediterranean can regenerate if fires are only 15 years apart. Others are killed to the ground, but sprout from the base as in coppicing, for example strawberry-tree. Others have thick bark or heat-resistant cambium, and a full-grown tree is little affected: the supreme example is cork oak. Some pines have cones that will not release their seeds unless heated. Many Australian plants have seeds that will not germinate unless exposed to smoke or water that has passed over charred wood: visitors to Perth Botanical Gardens are sold packets of seed and bottles of smoke-water to persuade them to germinate.

In Europe the pines of the north and the Mediterranean vegetation of the south are fire-adapted; not so the deciduous forests of the middle. Similar-looking ecosystems in North America are more fiery, with extensive pines and tall Ericaceæ and Rosaceæ, big flammable shrubs that accumulate fuel. America, however, also has anti-fire ecosystems. Sugar-maple, a strongly dominant tree whose shade-resistant seedlings are killed by even a weak fire, has dead leaves that compact into a dense, incombustible, ground-hugging mat. In turn the monocotyledonous spring flowers have upright, sharp-pointed leaves that pierce this papier-mâché-like layer. Fire may be linked to gregariousness (p.18): adaptations both to fire and to lack of fire work only if there is a considerable area of vegetation with the same characteristics.

Australia is the Planet of Fire. Except in the small area of rainforest, fire is as necessary to Australian native vegetation as rain to Britain. All the thousand species of *Eucalyptus* that dominate Australian vegetation appear to be fire-adapted. One cannot live long in Sydney without witnessing the awesome spectacle of a eucalyptus crown fire, or the nonchalant way in which the trees carry on growing afterwards. These eucalypts, although they may not have obviously thick or fireproof bark, survive and grow new twigs to replace the burnt ones. Some shed their outer bark to fuel a second fire a year later, mopping up any competitors that the first fire missed. Other species are killed to the ground but sprout, usually from a lignotuberous stool (p.16) that gets bigger at each fire cycle. Western Australia has many bizarre sights: none more so than an old marri (*Eucalyptus calophylla*) converted by repeated fires into the likeness of a pollard, a pillar of charcoal sprouting leaves. Possibly the grandest fire anywhere on the planet in human history occurred in 1939 in some of the world's grandest trees (*E. regnans* and *E. delegatensis*) between Melbourne and Canberra. These 300-foot (90-metre) eucalypts – themselves arising after a fire centuries ago – were killed, but their tiny seeds germinated to form a new generation, by now over half the height of their parents. All these notoriously do not regenerate without fire; apparently they need fire to set back antagonistic fungi in the soil.[14]

Fires can occur in ordinarily fireproof vegetation if a disturbance causes fuel to be drier or more compacted than usual. Debris left after logging is famously prone to ignition. In Borneo, fires occurred in tropical rainforest after drought killed some of the trees and a second drought dried them; this is probably a recurrent though rare event, and most living trees more than 28 inches (70 centimetres) in diameter survived the fire.[15]

The visible effects vary. Charred stumps and logs retain a coating of charcoal for several decades, and when it weathers away it leaves a smooth surface with a distinctive texture. On Mount Athos, the sacred mountain in north Greece, it was easy in 2001 to recognise traces of the great fire of 1991, but there were fainter traces of two previous fires beyond the present monks' memory.[16] Citizens of Sydney learn to recognise the stages whereby trees regain leafage burnt in a crown fire, as new growth sprouts from the bigger, living boughs and twigs.

A symptom of fire is a charred cavity at the base of a tree, usually on the uphill side, which is enlarged by successive fires. In Tasmania most of the big savanna eucalypts have conical bases (depicted by early English artists) resulting from compensatory growth around cavities eaten out by grassland fires in the nine-teenth century (Fig. 26).

Fire, like coppicing, stimulates a profusion of herbaceous plants, many of them from buried seed laid down after the last fire. This can be seen after fires in English gorse or Mediterranean maquis. Often the part of a forest richest in plant life is the part that has recently been burnt.

Forest fires favour deer, which can increase tenfold after a big fire. Human burning practices are the oldest detectable form of land management, and still almost the most widespread. The object is not to get rid of forest. It may be to make better pasture for wild or tame animals, or to create areas of improved pasture on which to find the beasts when needed, or to help in catching beasts by persuading them to leap over cliffs. There is abundant ethnographic evidence, especially from North America.[17]

Europeans (unlike Native Americans and Australian Aborigines) fear fire, and when they colonise fiery regions try to suppress it. A by-product of the fire-fighting industry is that small, controllable fires are replaced by vast, uncon-trollable conflagrations stoked by many years' accumulated fuel. However, if fires are delayed beyond the usual interval, the site may be invaded by fire-sensitive trees that alter the chemistry and structure of the vegetation so that it never burns again.[18] The sugar-maples of the southeastern United States have been suppressing shortleaved pines and the beautiful, fire-dependent ecosystems that go with them; the rainforests of eastern Australia have been expanding into the adjacent eucalypts.

Fire in Britain and Ireland

I remember when 'forest fires' were much feared in Britain, and in retrospect can see why. In the Forestry Commission's youth, young conifer plantations, packed with bracken and dry grass, were an admirable fuel; when he-men smoked and trains shovelled burning coals on to the track there was no lack of ignition. A ploughed strip was maintained where railways adjoined plantations. Even thunderstorms set plantations on fire, and the rain often did not extinguish them.[19] These conditions have passed away.

English *native* woods burn like wet asbestos. Even in the great summers of 1975 and 1976, when extreme drought coincided with a fashion for burning stubble fields, I never heard of a grown-up native wood catching fire – nor in the summers of 1995 and 2003. It happens that Nature has given England very few fire-promoting plants – heather, gorse, dead bracken, dry reed-beds, dry grasses – none of which is a tree. Fires happen in certain types of non-woodland vegetation, but run out of fuel and go out on reaching a wood (Fig. 27).

Although English *woods* appear to be immune from fire, *trees* may be involved in a fire in surrounding bracken or heather. Bracken in shade makes too little substance to sustain a fire, but a wood can burn a few years after it has been felled and the bracken thereby stimulated. In the exceptional summer of 1975–6 I encountered four instances of bracken or bramble burning in a sparse or recently felled wood: I doubt whether they did permanent damage. In 1326–7 there was a sale of £1. 2s. 9¼d.-worth of burnt underwood in a wooded part of the Forest of Dean, resulting from 'an unfortunate fire from a certain charcoal pit setting light to the bracken'; the wood was expected to grow again.[20]

In sparse oakwoods with plenty of bracken it is worth looking for charred cavities on the uphill side of tree bases. Professor Paul Mellars tells me the strange story of Treeton Wood near Sheffield, which he remembers as having bluebells and bracken, but which by 2000 was reduced to stumps as a result of a fire. This may be a repeated event; another of the three ancient woods in Treeton was named 'Burnt Wood' before 1860. All three, according to the Ordnance Survey, had conifers planted in them, which may have predisposed to fire.

Lack of fire as a significant factor in English woodland is not a legacy of past management resulting in an unnaturally tidy wood lacking fallen branches. It is due to the anti-fire adaptations of native trees. Most have a leaf litter that compacts into a soggy mass. Fallen branches quickly rot: combustible deadwood never accumulates to provide fuel. This leaves only trunks, especially oak, that are too big to burn on their own.

Burning is a method of rejuvenating (but not creating) heathland. In wood-pasture, grasses, heather and bracken provide fuel, and trees are involved only incidentally. Ancient trees are easily killed by fire, especially if hollow, which is a significant conservation problem: many of the ancient oaks of Ashtead Common (Surrey) have perished in a succession of fires. (Fires do not solve the problem of conserving heathland; birches spring up on the burnt surface and exert their anti-fire properties, shading out the heather to produce an undistinguished secondary wood.)

So much for England. In Scotland the native pine, like all the world's pines, is fire-adapted (Chapter 16). The 'natural' frequency of fires in the pinewoods of Scandinavia is said to be about every 80 years. Although fires in Scotland were probably less frequent, they are known from most Caledonian pinewoods, in some of which (as in Glen Tanar) areas of even-aged pine result from historic fires. Young pines are killed by burning the heather around them (as well as by too much grazing); occupational burning of moorland is probably one factor holding back the pinewoods from spreading.

In Ireland there is the strawberry-tree, now almost confined to the Killarney area, but which from place-names and other evidence was more wide-spread in historic times. This small, light-demanding tree is an outlier from the Mediterranean, where it is often dominant in maquis. It is flammable and fire-adapted: it makes Corsica such a fiery island. In Killarney it grows on cliffs and at the edges where oakwoods meet bogs, which have a history of burning. Its decline cannot be, as often said, due to people cutting it down, for it sprouts vigorously after felling as well as burning. Does lack of fire play a part?

Conclusion

Too many vegetation historians appeal airily to 'forest fires' without giving actual examples (localities, species and dates) of fire occurring in the kind of forest being considered. It is no good citing analogies from American Indian practices: North America is a different continent, has different trees, and is more flammable than this part of Europe can ever be. Grass fires in savanna are not evidence that forests will burn. One still encounters the nonsense that prehistoric people 'cleared the forest by fire' to create fields: nonsense because even in the most favourable circumstances fires may kill trees but do not destroy them, and there remains the immense task of getting rid of the dead trees and roots.

Charcoal occurs in prehistoric peat deposits: conscientious pollen analysts record the varying amounts. The fragments are often too small to identify, being charcoal dust blown in from a distance. In countries with flammable trees these may have come from forest fires. In England the presence of char-coal (unless it came from a very local fire on the peat surface itself) probably means that what burnt was not forest but heath or savanna, with grass, heather or bracken. Pollen deposits, moreover, are usually from wetlands, which can be more combustible than the rest of the landscape; in reed-beds, especially, the standing dead stalks are often burnt in spring by people for reasons of land management.* The relation between charcoal and a part-savanna wildwood, on Vera's model (p.79), needs to be explored.

---

* I am grateful to Professor Paul Mellars for discussing this point concerning the Mesolithic site at Star Carr, Yorkshire.

CHAPTER 3

OUTLINE OF
WOODLAND HISTORY

From rising ground England must have seemed one great forest before the fifteenth century, an almost unbroken sea of tree-tops with a thin blue spiral of smoke rising here and there at long intervals. Even after twenty generations of hacking at the waste, the frontiers of cultivation were rarely far away from the homesteads.

W.G. HOSKINS, *THE MAKING OF THE ENGLISH LANDSCAPE*, 1955

[He meant the fifteenth century AD, but the fifteenth century BC would now be considered a more accurate date for such a picture. Hoskins's own researches began this re-dating of the European landscape]

WILDWOOD

In countries that escaped the direct effect of glaciations, trees and woodland history have continued for millions of years, although even tropical rainforests had their ups and downs. In Britain woodland history is measured only in thousands of years. Ice ages covered most of Britain in glaciers, whose muddy debris constitutes the boulder-clay that forms the soils of many woods.

Woodland history began some 12,000 years ago, when the climate became possible for tree growth. Trees and woodland plants returned by wind- and bird-borne seed from their southern refugia to form a series of wildwood plant communities. There followed a long epoch of relative stability, the *Atlantic Period* (6200–3800 BC), with a climate not very different from that of the mid-twentieth century.

There are two theories of Holocene wildwood. Until recently it was thought that England was covered with trees – some said with giant trees, so close-set that there was barely room to squeeze between them – from coast to coast and far into the mountains. A proverbial squirrel could have leapt from Land's End to Ullapool without setting paw to ground. This traditional theory I shall call the *Tansley model*, after Sir Arthur Tansley in *The British Islands and their Vegetation* in 1939. Alternatively there was a patchy and changing landscape, with substantial tracts of grassland as well as woods, maintained by browsing multitudes of deer and wild oxen: the squirrel could have leapt, at most, from Loughton to Epping. This I shall call the *Vera model*, after Francis Vera in *Grazing Ecology and Forest History* in 2000.

How far Palæolithic and Mesolithic people affected wildwood is discussed in Chapter 4. Land management by burning had profound effects in other continents, but would have had less scope in Britain and Ireland, where not much of the aboriginal vegetation would have been flammable.

Mesolithic culture is best known from the site of Star Carr, Yorkshire, dated to the ninth millennium BC. Its people, as well as burning the local reed-beds, were carpenters, building platforms and boats.[1] They may have begun woodland management, at least to the extent of generating supplies of trees small enough to be useful – the guiding principle of most woodmanship until the invention of power tools (p.220).

Woodland and settled civilisation

There can be no doubting the impact of Neolithic people. Around 3800 BC they initiated a settled culture, with crops, domestic animals, buildings, private property, temples, tombs, a relatively dense population, and the work ethos – what constitutes civilisation as modern people understand it. Most of these things originated in the early Holocene in southwest Asia. Whether brought by immigrants or taken up by the existing population, they constituted a foreign culture, introduced from a very different environment. Virtually all European crops are plants of open, well-drained land and will not tolerate even slight shade or waterlogging. Domestic animals, in agricultural numbers, require grassland. On the Tansley model, people wanting to indulge in these would first have had to create open land. They would also have begun converting the remaining wildwood to managed woodland, generating a permanent succession of small trees.

In the Neolithic, human activity superseded climatic change as the leading influence on vegetation changes. That is not to say that climate became unimportant: and there was still unfinished business from the vicissitudes of the early Holocene.

Destruction of wildwood

Neolithic farmers began reducing Britain to that imitation of a Turkish steppe in which wheat and barley are at home. (Later their equivalents in Japan, deriving their staple crop, rice, from the wet tropics, had the task of converting mountainous Japan into the likeness of a Vietnamese fen.) Sometimes, as on Dartmoor, farmland was not sustainable and later became moorland. Destruction of wildwood continued through the Bronze and Iron Ages. England probably passed through the stage of being half woodland at some time in the Bronze Age (second millennium BC).

In Scotland too, wildwood was converted into open land from Neolithic times onwards. To the Romans the Highlands were a mainly open landscape. However, in Scotland (and Ireland) much of the wildwood went directly to moorland, and natural processes played a greater part than in England. In the peculiar climate of northwest Scotland, with high rainfall and cold summers, woodland was not sustainable indefinitely: progressive accumulation of blanket peat pushed the trees eastward.

Prehistoric woodmanship

Evidence for woodmanship becomes compelling in the Neolithic. Waterlogged excavations, in which wood is preserved, show the diversity and sophistication of prehistoric wooden artefacts. The trackways of the Somerset Levels – walkways giving passage across the soft peat from one fen island to another – were made of rods generated by a form of coppicing more elaborate than in historic times (p.220). At this stage woodland was so abundant that conservation was probably not the motive: rather, woods were managed to yield material for specific crafts.

The development of woodmanship has yet to be systematically studied. Besides the trackways (which continued in various styles into the Anglo-Saxon period), the making of wattle 'huts', which could be large and substantial but short-lived buildings, implies the regular production of rods and poles in coppice-woods. To make bronze and then iron implies the maintenance of regular fuel supplies.

Timber structures, too, ranged from trackways to immense post-built 'woodhenges'. Each of the innumerable post-holes that are the commonplaces of excavation contained a tree trunk. The late Bronze Age produced the biggest timber structure known from any ancient or modern period in these islands, the giant crannog or artificial island at Flag Fen near Peterborough (1350–950 BC), and the Brigg Logboat, the biggest known artefact made from a single tree (p.241).

The Roman period

Although the meagre written sources say little that is useful about landscape, it was in the Roman period (40–410 AD) that England, at least, became recognisable in something like its medieval form. It had cities, towns, villages and farmsteads. It already had much of the present road network – not only the recognisable straight 'Roman roads'. Settlement and agriculture had spread everywhere, even into inhospitable terrain such as the Fens. England (and probably Ireland somewhat later) had taken on its characteristics of dense population and relatively little woodland.

The reduced area of woodland – not much greater, and possibly less, than in medieval times – would have been conserved and managed. There was a wood- and timber-based economy operating on a similar scale to the Middle Ages'. Timber-framed buildings existed on a similar scale, and in a not very different style, from those of the Middle Ages. New or expanded consumers included towns and cities and many industries, all of which called for organised wood supplies, if not timber as well. Among major trees, chestnut was introduced, at this stage probably for its nuts rather than as a woodland tree.

A legacy of the Roman or Iron Age is the great division between *Planned Countryside* and *Ancient Countryside* (Table 7, Fig. 1). The distinctions now visible in the landscape arose at various times from Anglo-Saxon to Victorian, but they derive from a dichotomy in Roman Britain. Cities like CAMVLODVNVM (Colchester) or AQVÆ SVLIS (Bath) should be thought of as set in abundantly wooded terrain, like present Rouen; cities like RATÆ (Leicester) should be thought of as set in farmland extending to the horizon with little woodland, like Chartres today.

THE ANGLO-SAXON PERIOD

The transition between Roman Britain and Anglo-Saxon England is a great enigma in British archaeology. One culture disappeared, and after a dark age of 200 years a seemingly very different one emerged, with a much lower population, a different language, different heathen gods, a different Christianity, different institutions, different buildings – yet retaining much of the old infrastructure, especially in the countryside. Written sources emerge as evidence for the landscape. They appear as perambulations defining the boundaries of landed estates, or less definitely as place-names, many of which appear to be two-word descriptions like Marshwood. Neither source reveals much about a transition from a different landscape in the past.

The Dark Ages were the biggest recession of human affairs in the history of England, more likely from plague than from battle and murder. But people still tilled fields and maintained pastures and roads, although the pastures may have been bushy and some of the Roman roads were preserved piecemeal as farm tracks. Woodland probably increased, but not on the overwhelming scale of eastern North America or the south of France in the twentieth century.

The Anglo-Saxons were not primitive or small-scale people. If their timber buildings do not survive, this was not through lack of sophistication, but because they were based on posts set in the ground, which soon rotted. In the Suffolk and Essex estuaries they built gigantic fish-traps, among the largest timber structures ever known in Britain.[2]

The curtain rises in the eighth century on a landscape not very different from the present. Instead of vast, vaguely defined tracts of wildwood there were wood-lots having names (of similar form and antiquity to the names of hamlets and villages) and definite extents and boundaries. The area of woodland was probably 20–25 per cent of England, about the same as France today. Woods and wood-pastures were permanent: some exist to this day. They yielded regular supplies of timber and underwood. There were hedges and non-woodland trees. All these things leave little archaeological record; their emergence at this time results from the history of record-keeping and does not imply the origin of the things themselves.[3]

Woodland was unevenly distributed. Areas later to be Ancient Countryside already had much more woodland, heath and hedges. In areas with not much woodland the next stage towards Planned Countryside was beginning with an agricultural revolution: the landscape was being reorganised into *open-fields*, divided into a multitude of half-acre strips belonging to the various cultivators. This sort of collectivisation went with development of communal cultivation and gathering of houses into villages.

Viking incursions had little apparent effect on the fabric of the countryside; they are not correlated with the difference between the two landscapes. Many woods acquired Norse names, like Wayland Wood in Norfolk, which still exists (p.73).

THE MIDDLE AGES

Domesday Book, the great survey of England in 1086, is the earliest semi-quantitative record of woodland. The area (including wood-pasture) adds up to about 15 per cent of the land, more in Ancient and less in Planned Countryside (Table 11).

After Domesday came 260 years of expanding population and pressure on land. Cultivation expanded into heathland, moor and fens. Woodland shrank to something like 7 per cent of England. In areas with more woodland there was more destruction, leading to a less uneven distribution; however, the two biggest concentrations, in the Weald and Chilterns, remained very wooded until now. Outside woodland, open-field farming spread into nearly one-half of England, and similar practices emerged in parts of Wales, Scotland and Ireland.

Wood-pasture developed into its three branches of wooded commons, parks and Forests, the latter two being formalised for keeping deer as semi-domestic animals. The Normans introduced the rabbit, pheasant and fallow deer, each of which was to leave its mark on the landscape.

The twelfth century marks the beginning of houses and barns, built of timber and underwood, that endure to this day above ground. From the thirteenth century onwards, detailed surveys, modelled on the Ely Coucher Book (p.140), make it possible to follow the histories of individual woods, woodland management and its produce. As woodland declined, the remaining woodland gained in value and was more intensively managed. Many wood-pastures were enclosed with woodbanks and turned into coppices, often subdivided by internal banks. Timber began to be imported in bulk from abroad.

Recession returned with the Black Death in 1349. About one-third of the people perished; repeated visitations of plague held down the population until the seventeenth century, relieving the pressure on land. Any wood remaining in 1350 had a good chance of surviving the next 500 years. Some woods got bigger, and new woods arose on abandoned farmland, but on a modest scale.

Woods continued to be managed and used. Timber-framed buildings from the later Middle Ages and sixteenth century survive in increasingly larger numbers. Fuel-using industries, such as making bricks, iron and glass (but not bathing), expanded to regain roughly their importance in the Roman period.

THE POST-MEDIEVAL PERIOD

The sixteenth century brought no radical change. The dissolution of the monasteries in the 1530s, despite its huge effect on land tenure, seems to have had no decisive physical effect on woodland. Woods stolen and retained by the Crown were often neglected and damaged by cattle browsing, but usually remained on the map. Woods were still cut, but coppice cycles appear to have lengthened and timber trees grew bigger.

Deer-parks enjoyed a new lease of life, stimulated by Henry VIII's mania for hunting in parks. This habit went on into the seventeenth century, preserving or creating some of the most evocative savanna landscapes in England. In the eighteenth century it was joined by a rising fashion for designer landscapes around country mansions, many of which incorporated ancient woods and ancient trees.[4]

Woods could be grubbed out at times of high farming, especially the periods 1550–1600, 1625–50 and 1700–50. Smaller areas of new woodland arose at various times. Around 1600 we hear of tentative attempts at modern forestry.

Woodland economics changed: first with the introduction of chimneys, rising standards of domestic heating, and colder winters, especially in the 1590s (the second phase of the Little Ice Age). Fuel-using industries expanded, but also used wood fuel more efficiently. In the mid-sixteenth century the price of underwood rose in real terms by about 75 per cent; prices of timber trees rose by 50 per cent in the sixteenth and seventeenth centuries. The increasing use of coal then held the price of wood from rising further. Rising relative sea levels would have increased the demand for wood and timber in maintaining sea defences.

In the eighteenth century there was renewed destruction, especially in counties like Norfolk where agricultural improvement made it possible to cultivate the poor soils on which woodland remained.

From the late seventeenth century shipbuilding became significant in the economy of many woods. There was an exponential rise in both naval and commercial shipping, offsetting the decline in demand from timber-framed building. The effects on woodland, however, were at least equalled by an exponentially rising demand for oak bark from the leather-tanning trade.

Outside woodland, strip-cultivation landscapes were again reorganised. The beginnings of enclosure go back to the fifteenth century, but what remained by 1720 was then redistributed, parish by parish, by a series of Enclosure Acts going on well into the nineteenth century. Land was subdivided by straight hawthorn hedges, laid out hastily on a drawing board and transferred to the terrain, creating the distinctive appearance of Planned Countryside today. A side effect was the destruction of many wood-pasture commons and Forests, victims of Enlightenment philosophy that thought communal land uses were immoral.

Scotland, Ireland, Wales

Scotland has no Domesday Book; the earliest direct evidence of the extent of woodland is the maps made by the indefatigable traveller, Timothy Pont, in the 1590s. In c.1750, after the Jacobite revolt, General Roy was commissioned to make a military survey of mainland Scotland, lest King Charles III should rear his ugly head again. Estimates of 'natural woodland' area, county by county, were compiled by Sir John Sinclair in 1814 and 1845. There are also estate and county maps, and the Ordnance Survey large-scale maps (sometimes in great detail) from 1871 onwards.

As Professor Christopher Smout, Historiographer Royal for Scotland, points out, cartographers and their informants had different ideas about whether a scatter of trees or a patch of hazels constituted a wood. His researches indicate that Scotland had relatively more woodland than England before 1700, but less of it survived until 1900. Most of what did not survive went to moorland. Many woods in the Highlands supplied ironworks, tanneries and other industries; these woods either still survive or disappeared only after the industries had died.

Ireland presents somewhat similar problems: although some woods had definite names, boundaries and areas, there were also patches in fields and on islands in bogs whose extent was difficult to define. The Civil Survey, a kind of Domesday Book made in the 1650s, records much less woodland in Ireland than there would have been in England, but for some of the more wooded counties the record is lost. Paradoxically, Irish woodland as known in the nineteenth century is not only even less extensive than in the seventeenth, but is in different places (p.110).

Medieval Wales probably had more woodland than England, and a rather lower survival rate. A very large tract survived in the South Wales coalfield, used as fuel for ironworks, and later probably produced pit-props and mining timber for the coal mines. Most of it disappeared, mysteriously, in the late nineteenth and early twentieth centuries.

NINETEENTH AND TWENTIETH CENTURIES

Shipbuilding and leather-tanning went on rising until c.1860, when both markets rapidly collapsed. Meanwhile the railways (which for a time were big consumers of oak timber) undercut the rural fuel market by bringing coal to remote places. In places the growth of coal mines postponed decline for half a century, as pit-props provided a market for small timber and large underwood. These effects, in sum, were to reduce the value of woodland relative to other land, and to reduce the value of wood relative to timber.

The 1860s and 1870s were a time of destruction of woodland at a rate not seen for 650 years, to be followed immediately by an agricultural depression in which new woodland was formed. Plantation forestry began to overtake ancient woodland in area.

Next came the *Oak Change*. Hitherto oaks had grown more or less readily from seed within existing woods. With few exceptions, this ceased in the twentieth century. Oak now grows freely from the acorn almost anywhere – heathland, farmland, railway land – *except* within existing woods. It is disconcerting that a common tree should violate the Principle of Uniformity – that its present behaviour should furnish an interpretation of the past – and there has been much conjecture as to the cause.[5] The most plausible reason is the introduction from America of oak mildew (*Microsphæra alphitoides*), a fungus disease first noticed in 1908 that rapidly spread to every deciduous oak in Europe (p.335f). It has little effect on oaks growing in the open – but it may be death to an oakling in a wood struggling against shade. In effect, it seems to make oak a more light-demanding tree.[6]

In 1914 many woods would still have been recognisable to a medieval surveyor. Details would have changed: a piece subtracted from the outline here or added there; longer coppice rotations; often a high density of timber trees intended for a now vanished market. Woods attached to great estates changed in a particular way, with conifers planted among the old stools, or 'gamekeepers' plants' like snowberry or box. Coppicing had already declined in much of the north and west.

The period of relative inaction ended in World War I, when timber felling suddenly accelerated to meet the demands of the war economy and of war itself (p.356). After the war, forestry became an affair of state with the founding of the Forestry Commission in 1919. The Commission initiated a huge programme of new planting on non-woodland sites. More felling occurred between the wars, when one-third of England was put up for sale. Extraordinary felling was repeated during World War II. These fellings had a huge political impact, overshadowing woodland policies and management long after a new generation of trees had grown. Their effects were exaggerated: the majority of natural woods either escaped altogether or were left with a reduced but substantial complement of timber trees. As yet, plantation forestry had had little effect on natural woodland. Woodland increased as land went out of cultivation in the Great Depression of the 1930s.

Coppicing declined between the wars; it was sometimes briefly revived in the great winter of 1947 or when coal miners went on strike. It hung on in southeast England and East Anglia. Otherwise most woods became 'derelict' in Forestry

Commission terms. In biological terms they were recovering from the great timber-fellings.

Deer had been relatively rare at least since Anglo-Saxon times; they had been confined to parks and Forests, and woodland ecosystems elsewhere had developed without them. In the twentieth century there began a remarkable increase, of both native and introduced deer, with profound consequences (p.424f).

The 'years that the locust hath eaten'[7] – 1950–75

After World War II the idea got about that Britain was an overpopulated land: every acre ought to look as if it was doing something useful – even acres that the country had managed without in the dark and hungry years of war. From 1950 onwards, woodland was destroyed at a rate probably never seen before.

The chief agent of destruction was modern forestry: woods were felled and poisoned, and plantations made on the site. Usually the plantations were of conifers; foresters were obsessed with fast growth and had forgotten what woodland was for. Other woods were grubbed out and made into farmland. Development for housing, industry and roads came well behind these, though it attracted more attention.

The modern conservation movement had begun in England with the Epping Forest affair of 1878 (p.325f). It could not stem the destruction of woodland, indeed the planting ethos infiltrated conservationists themselves; but naturalists' trusts began acquiring woods as nature reserves, to prevent them from being destroyed and to reverse the decline in coppicing and revive the ecosystems that it generates.

The years of recovery

In 1975 it seemed that apart from nature reserves no native woodland would survive until the end of the century. This has not happened. The destroyers made little further headway, and by 1990 were in full retreat. The economics of forestry changed: even plantations on non-woodland sites were hardly worthwhile. A new generation of foresters had arisen, with better things to do with their lives than growing millions of identical trees. In agriculture, the need for more land was undercut by higher-yielding crops: food shortage had given way to overproduction.

Plantations on former woodland sites proved difficult to maintain. Native trees recovered from the poison and began to overtop the planted trees. Matters were helped by a series of great droughts. The hurricanes of 1987 and 1990 plucked out millions of planted trees.

Public interest in trees and woodland suddenly revived: a measure of this is the extraordinary success of the Woodland Trust. Much of the country's woodland is now in the hands of this and other conservation bodies. The Forestry Commission is now in the forefront of woodland conservation, especially in the 'deconiferisation' of replanted ancient woods.

At the time of writing virtually all the natural woods that existed in 1975 are still there, plus a goodly number of those then thought lost to replanting. Not everything is well: although 'conservation coppicing' still flourishes, commercial coppicing has continued to decline – partly because of the counterproductive efforts of conservationists in promoting the recycling of paper, partly because of the increase in deer. This apart, the prospects for woodland are better than they have been for a hundred years. Whether this will continue is discussed in Chapter 22.

CHAPTER 4

POLLEN ANALYSIS AND WILDWOOD

The dust might have come from anyone's coat ... pollen grains, including those of the sow-thistle, mallow, poppy and valerian.
AUSTIN FREEMAN, *THE GREEN CHECK JACKET*, C.1925

THE AGE OF EVOLUTION

The world is supposed to be about 4,600 million years old, and has been lived in for about four-fifths of that time, but mainly in the sea. About 500 million years ago land plants appeared, and in the late Devonian, 360 million years ago, there is the first evidence for trees – but trees more like those with which the imagination of C. S. Lewis peopled Venus than the trees of Earth today.[1]

Palæozoic trees had some familiar properties: clonal growth; annual rings; ability to burn, and adaptation to fire; ability to grow either in a forest or scattered among low vegetation; adoption of fungi to help out the functions of roots; and ability to go hollow when old. Then, as now, not all trees had these qualities. The continents were grouped together, with England roughly where Borneo is now.

Modern-looking trees – the first conifers – appear in the late Carboniferous, some 310 million years ago. Somewhat later came four-footed beasts, especially dinosaurs, which engendered adaptations to resist or recover from browsing.

Flowering plants, including broadleaved trees, emerged in the Cretaceous (150–65 million years ago). By this time the continents had moved some way towards their present latitudes. The Atlantic opened up, first in the middle, leaving North America and Eurasia joined through Greenland (well south of its present position), so that plants could move from America to Japan. Australia, isolated from other land masses, turned into what is virtually a different planet.

During the Tertiary (65 – 10 million years ago), many present genera, perhaps even species, of trees appeared. Broadleaved forests of oaks, beeches, laurels etc. dominated much of the world. They were predominantly evergreen, indicating a tropical or subtropical wet climate. Such 'laurisylvan' forests, which once flourished around London, are now reduced to the warmer parts of Japan, China and the southeast United States.

All this vast time, the environment was very stable. Climate very slowly changed; the earth's crust rose and fell; continents wandered at less than 2 feet (a half-metre) a century. Animals, rival trees and pathogens became able to devour, shade or kill particular species. But even long-lived trees could apparently adapt by evolutionary change to these slow events. Local disasters came by super-volcano or tsunami, and very rare worldwide catastrophes by the crash of asteroid. These one-off events had a less severe impact on plants than on animals; their effects would probably be indirect, through killing off the browsing animals.

Why do trees coppice?

A legacy of this period is the ability of trees to sprout after felling. Coppiceability can hardly have evolved in the relatively few generations of trees since people invented axes. Nor is it a universal property of trees. Nor is it related to the history of human contact; it is as common among the trees of North America (Fig. 28) and Japan as among their relatives in Europe; in Australia it is common among eucalypts and near-universal among rainforest trees. Although sometimes a fire adaptation, it is no less prevalent among incombustible trees.

To what influence is coppiceability an adaptation? Catastrophes like ice storms, avalanches and blowdowns (p.19ff) come to mind, but are surely too local to account for so widespread a phenomenon. Presumably it is some factor that no longer operates: was it super-elephants, of which more anon?

Some trees self-coppice. Hazel, if not cut or browsed, sends up new shoots from the base that ultimately replace the old ones. When old, *Tilia americana*, American lime or basswood, rots at the base and falls down, having sent up a ring of sprouts to form its successors (Fig. 30). So do two Japanese limes, and so, presumably, did *T. cordata* in Europe. Self-coppicing occurs in a Japanese beech, an American ash, American chestnut, Japanese and American magnolias, and in one of the world's rarest and most recently discovered trees in an Australian rainforest.[2] It is one of the mysterious ways in which trees – long-lived as they already are – further extend their life spans. In effect, they step off the ladder of evolution: ability to hold on to territory supersedes the ability to adapt to environmental changes.

A heroic example is the Californian redwoods, a very ancient tree genus and one of the few conifers that coppice. The huge blackened stump of an 800-year-old tree, felled by loggers a century ago, is surrounded by a ring of its sprouts now 150 feet (50 metres) high, which in turn forms part of a ring of rings. Some of these trees germinated at least half the Holocene ago.[3] Is this behaviour a relic of adaptation to browsing by dinosaurs? But what could even the mightiest dinosaur do to these giant trees?

THE AGE OF CLIMATIC CHANGE

Two million years ago, stability vanished: changes went into top gear with the coming of the ice ages. There were about 50 cycles of increasing intensity, during the last half-dozen of which plant life was wiped out at high latitudes; the last but one was probably the most severe so far. Trees moved south, and some of them returned northward when warmer temperatures returned. Glaciations have occupied at least three-quarters of the time; interglacials like the present are relatively brief. Even the Amazon rainforest seems at times to have been reduced to large patches.

In Europe the ice ages were more severe than in America or the Far East, partly because the barriers of the Mediterranean and Sahara left cold-sensitive plants with nowhere to go. Little of the laurisylvan flora survives compared to Carolina or Japan: only one species of holly, one of laurel, four evergreen oaks, no magnolia. In the Mediterranean glacial periods were dry as well as cold.

Evolution was no longer the dominating force in the functioning of trees. That is not to say that it no longer functions. Annual creatures (most animals are, in effect, annual) can keep up with not-too-drastic climatic changes. Perennial plants and trees migrate or sit out the change or go extinct. Trees of remote islands cannot migrate. In Crete three of the four high-altitude trees – cypress, Cretan pine, prickly oak – occur at all levels from the tree-limit at 5,600–6,000 feet (1,700–1,800 metres) down to the coast: they can endure a huge range of temperature. On the mainland prickly oak seldom occurs above 2,000 feet (600 metres). Ability to withstand cold has evidently been forced on insular prickly oak by the glaciations.

Perennial plants and long-lived animals, on the whole, found themselves not so much in environments to which they were adapted, but in those into which accidents of history had thrust them. This may explain why some alien species, like grey squirrel from North America, or Japanese knotweed, or gorse in New Zealand, fare better in environments to which they are manifestly not adapted than in their homelands.

In Britain, the last-but-one ice age covered most of the island in ice. Glaciers scraped up soft rocks from the bed of the North Sea and deposited them as moraines of mud, such as can still be observed around Norwegian glaciers. This formed the boulder-clay that underlies many English woodland soils. The last ice age, though covering less of the country in ice, converted Britain to tundra and probably left not a single tree alive.

THE AGE OF HUMANITY

Half a million years and two interglacials ago, a kind of superman, *Homo heidelbergensis,* lived at Boxgrove (Sussex), spearing super-horses and avoiding super-elephants. As far as is known, hominids used their stone tools for cutting up super-rhinoceroses, but not for cutting down trees.[4]

During the present interglacial, the *Holocene,* changes have gone into over-drive. The present human species enters the stage. By tradition, Upper Palæo-lithic and Mesolithic people were too few, and too limited in their technology, to have much more influence on the landscape than the beasts on which they preyed, or than Boxgrove Man. They prowled, it was supposed, through bound-less forest − trees and trees and trees, with patches of fen and reed-bed − from coast to coast and almost up to the tops of the mountains.

But mankind, even in small numbers, has powers not given to 'the beasts that perish': the power to exterminate large animals, to influence sites at a distance, such as by altering the fire frequency, and to introduce plants and animals from region to region.

Pleistocene elephants were not the puny monsters that we rode at the zoo, but dinosaur-sized creatures like the West Runton elephant, from the last-but-one interglacial, displayed at Norwich Castle. All continents had giant mammals in previous interglacials: super-elephants, super-rhinoceroses, super-sloths in South America, even an elephantine marsupial in Australia. They survived many glacial cycles, but died out around the last glaciation, when the super-fierce *Homo sapiens* expanded. If Upper Palæolithic people exterminated them – and what else could it have been? – the removal of these living bulldozers would have been the most profound effect so far of humanity on the world's vegetation. The Holocene may be the first period since the Permian without super-herbivores – but trees may not yet have adapted to living without them.

There have been forest fires almost as long as there have been forests (p.44). People could hardly have set fire to non-fire-adapted vegetation, such as a limewood or elmwood, but in America, Africa and especially Australia, people have influenced whole continents by altering the frequency of fire in combustible vegetation.

Islands

Islands are special. Those near the coast, such as Britain and Japan, get linked up during glaciations when ice on land takes water out of the sea and causes sea level to fall. They tend to have similar plants and animals to the Continent, but with some species missing. Britain never had bison, and some common European plants, such as the yellow thistle *Cirsium oleraceum,* reach Calais but no further. Some trees, like sycamore and spruce, are supposed not to have crossed the Channel after the last glaciation, but since they are not native in coastal France this cannot be the only factor involved. Others did not reach Ireland.

More distant islands, as in the Mediterranean, lack many Continental species and develop endemic floras peculiar to themselves. Endemic plants, such as those of Crete, have to withstand variations of climate: there is nowhere for them to go during glaciations. On very rare occasions mammals get stranded, to generate bizarre endemic faunas such as the tiny elephants, super-mice and mountaineering mini-hippopotamuses that once roamed Crete. A consistent feature is that they lack adequate carnivores. When people arrive, the surrealist mammals disappear, but the trees and plants – adapted over two million years to over-grazing – withstand cattle, sheep and goats.[5]

Oceanic islands, like St Helena, have almost entirely endemic plants and land birds, with no mammals except bats. When people and livestock (pigs, rats, goats) arrive, the consequences are disastrous. The entire ecosystem, with no resistance to browsing, collapses; the trees are relegated to cliffs, and universal tropical weeds inherit the land.

POLLEN ANALYSIS

The prime evidence for wildwood and prehistoric woodland comes from pollen. Many trees and other plants produce vast numbers of pollen grains, the shells of which are made of sporopollenin, one of the most indestructible of organic materials. They last millions of years in permanently wet or permanently dry places. To some extent they are identifiable. Any student can recognise pine, oak or lime pollen; to some extent the groups of pine species produce different pollens; hazel, embarrassingly, is easily confused with bog-myrtle; experts can separate the two native species of lime pollen; but so far only one group of experts has claimed to distinguish the two native oaks.[6]

Palynology, the study of pollen grains, goes back to the 1880s. It can be used to check whether 'thyme' honey really comes from thyme, or where a murderer or victim has been, or the provenance of a historic artefact like the Holy Shroud of Turin, or when sufferers from hay fever need to take their medicine. In the archaeology of vegetation it has grown since the 1930s into a science, practised all over the world.

One looks for a lake or peat bog with a stratified deposit: year after year a new layer of mud or peat is added and includes that year's fallout of pollen. (Sometimes acid soils and archaeological deposits preserve pollen.) A core is extracted with a hollow borer, cut up centimetre by centimetre, taken to the laboratory, and processed to get rid of material other than pollen. A specialist identifies the pollen grains and counts the number of each type from each sample. The result is expressed as a pollen diagram, in which the amount of each type of pollen is plotted against the depth in the profile (Fig. 173). Other samples are sent to a radiocarbon dating laboratory to get a sequence of approximate dates.

Pollen analysis is not straightforward. Pines, oaks and other wind-pollinated trees produce vast quantities of pollen; a yellow film forms on a water surface near pine trees in flower. Lime and blackthorn are mainly insect-pollinated and waste far less pollen, which travels much less far. So a sample containing 20 per cent lime pollen and 80 per cent oak pollen probably means a limewood with a few oak-trees. Poplar pollen has the reputation of being poorly preserved; chestnut is easily overlooked. Herbaceous plants, especially if insect-pollinated, produce less pollen still; the palynologist will be very lucky to meet primrose or bluebell pollen. Grasses are copious pollen producers, but mostly cannot be identified as to species.

Pollen analysis requires a fairly well-equipped laboratory, a good microscope, and a reference set of pollen grains from known species. Preparing the samples uses hydrofluoric acid to dissolve unwanted materials. A century and a half ago hydrofluoric acid was almost a household chemical; artistic young ladies would etch patterns on glass with it; it is now frowned upon because it dissolves most materials except sporopollenin, including the human body in a manner that I shall not describe.

Few readers will be tempted to do their own palynology, which is a pity because there are plenty of deposits worth looking at, especially in woodland ponds and small wetlands. Many have been destroyed by the fashion for de-silting ponds and moats. In theory the pollen should always be sampled and recorded before doing this, lest a unique document be destroyed unread. Pond-clearers are usually in a hurry; palynologists are few and busy and have their own research interests to pursue, and may not welcome samples randomly thrust upon them by others.

What pollen analysis does not reveal

Palynology records the sequence in which trees returned to Britain after the last glaciation and how wildwood developed. Suitably adjusted, pollen counts give some idea of the composition of wildwood, although this may be biased by trees such as alder that grow round wet places. Especially in drier countries, pollen deposits represent the wettest spots in the landscape and may not be typical.

In Britain, many pollen deposits come from wet hollows that are typically fringed by alder. Extensive deposits, such as from big lakes, tend to catch pollen from a wider area than small woodland ponds. However, dry country, such as chalkland, is difficult to recognise in the pollen record; here snail shells may be a proxy for indicating where woodland was and how long it lasted.[7]

How much pollen is needed to establish a tree's presence? Pollen analysts discount odd grains of wind-pollinated species, which could have been blown from a distance. Pine pollen is regularly blown from America to Greenland and from Norway to Shetland. Substantial amounts of pine pollen are needed to prove the presence of the tree, especially if the other contributors to a sample shed little pollen.[8]

Palynology may not reveal the structure of wildwood or what it looked like. The prickly oak of the Mediterranean, *Quercus coccifera*, produces the same pollen whether it is a great oak-tree or a shrub 2 feet (60 centimetres) high. However, hazel (as anyone can see who walks round a wood in February) is a prolific producer of pollen *provided its leaves are not shaded*. Hazel pollen is vastly common in samples of British wildwood, often exceeding all other trees put together. This used to be interpreted as a hazel understorey in 'mixed oak forest', which cannot be right, for understorey hazel produces no pollen and is masked. Nor can it mean hazels with a few catkins under a small gap in the canopy. Hazel dominating a pollen sample must mean areas of hazel *forming the canopy*.

Evidence for the stature of trees exists if the trees themselves are preserved in peat. As modern farming in the Fens dissipates the peat (and helps along global warming), there come to light 'bog oaks', occasionally of gigantic size.[9] These encouraged scholars to think of wildwood as composed of forest giants, but they grew in a very favourable environment and died a strange death. They were the last generation of trees to grow on the mineral soil before peat began to form. They were killed by water backing up from rising relative sea level, rotted at the roots, crashed down into the developing peat, and were entombed (p.76f).

Pollen analysts have assumed that trees mean forest, and express the degree to which a landscape was forested by the ratio of tree to non-tree pollen (AP/NAP). This is only a rough measure: it depends on whether the tree pollen is lime or pine, and whether the investigator counts hazel as a tree. Pollen records become difficult to interpret in later periods: woodland becomes fragmented, hedges and non-woodland trees appear, and the landscape gives the impression of increasing complexity.

Coppicing greatly alters the ability of a wood to produce pollen. Oak tends to be over-represented because it is a timber tree and produces pollen all the time. Hazel and birch are over-represented because they resume pollen production two or three years after felling. Lime, which usually takes at least ten years to produce pollen, is under-represented; if the felling cycle is shorter than ten years it may be missed altogether.

Palynological criteria are wanted to differentiate between the following:
- forest;
- savanna, that is grassland with trees;
- coppice-wood;
- hedges and non-woodland trees; and
- (in Mediterranean countries) maquis, that is trees like prickly oak reduced to the stature of shrubs by browsing, burning, or drought.

DEVELOPMENT OF WILDWOOD

About 12,000 years ago, after the last glaciation, trees returned to Britain. The first were birch and then pine, relatively arctic and easily dispersed (Fig. 29). Often a birch-dominated phase was followed by a pine-dominated. Less according to expectation, hazel came from the northwest and spread into England from Scotland; there was a combination of hazel and pine that has no close parallel today. Hazel then became exceedingly abundant, often dominant, over most of Britain and Ireland.

Oak, alder and lime followed, replacing pine and birch. Then came elm and then ash, displacing some of the hazel (or at least preventing it from producing pollen). Holly, beech, and probably maple and hornbeam were the last trees to arrive before a rise in relative sea level cut Britain off from the Continent, about 7,000 years ago.

The return was not always a slow creeping of each species from Kent northwards. Some trees appeared in small quantities – just enough pollen to prove they were here – hundreds or thousands of years before they became abundant. They had to replace existing trees, not merely to occupy vacant ground; they may have had to wait for mycorrhizal fungi to catch up with them.

Changes in climate played their part. There was a setback of re-glaciation in the early Holocene, known as the Allerød Interstadial. The ninth millennium BC saw the rise of lime, which must mean – considering the non-invasive behaviour of lime today – that summers were then hotter even than those of the last 30 years. (Lime probably benefits from unusual heat waves rather than from average summer temperature: today it extends further north in Scandinavia and higher in the Alps than oak.)

Despite some claims to the contrary, beech is native to England and Wales. Its wood and charcoal are known from the Bronze Age. Pre-Neolithic records are of pollen only: was there enough pollen to establish the presence of the tree? As Sir Harry Godwin, greatest of English pollen analysts, showed, beech pollen travels less well than that of some other trees. Even where beech was known to have been present from fossil wood, there was often little pollen in nearby deposits. This, he said, 'makes it difficult to dismiss as due to distant transport by wind the sites ... where beech pollen is present though sparsely'. On this basis beech got into Somerset and Dorset in about 7000 BC, about when Britain became an island. A thousand years later it was locally abundant at Wareham, but not until much later did beech, along with maple and hornbeam, become a main woodland tree.[10]

Ireland lacked lime. If beech got there – there is one find of its fruits – it did not persist. Maple is supposed to be an introduction in Ireland, but on no very good grounds: its pollen and wood have been found in prehistoric contexts.[11]

The fully developed wildwood

American ecologists, following F.E. Clements, and Europeans after them, believed that any sort of vegetation, if left long enough, would progress into a stable ecosystem, the *climax*, determined by climate. Climax theory gave respectability to the tradition of stable, immensely ancient 'primæval forests'; it was influential for much of the twentieth century, and still influences conservationists.

If ever there was a long enough period of stability in the Holocene for trees and plants to compete and achieve equilibrium in something like a climax forest, it would have been the 2,400 years of the Atlantic Period, ending in 3800 BC. (Whether it was really forest is discussed later; whether it was really 'virgin forest', unaffected by humanity, is considered in the next chapter.)

The Atlantic Period began with a sudden rise of alder, which had previously been present throughout Britain and Ireland, and now became one of the dominant trees. This is somewhat of a mystery: it has been attributed to the climate getting wetter and causing ground to become sodden, but alder is a tree of flushed, not waterlogged, ground (p.18), and is not very dependent on high rainfall. Moreover, if this were the explanation, the change should have been most marked in drier regions, which it is not.

Oak and lime, and later ash, rose to displace most of the pine, some of the birch, and to displace or mask some of the hazel. Around 4000 BC there were five broad regions of wildwood (Fig. 31):

1. *Lime Province*, comprising most of Lowland England. At most sites lime is present in the pollen record, and often turns out to be the commonest tree if adjustment is made for its poor pollen production.
2. *Oak – Hazel Province*, comprising regions of mainly Palæozoic geology and mountain landscapes.
3. *Hazel – Elm Province*, comprising most of Ireland and southwest Wales.
4. *Pine Province*, in the central and east Scottish Highlands.
5. *Birch Province*, in the northern Scottish Highlands, thinning out northwards into tundra.[12]

Each Province included several types and variants of wildwood, some of them related to present woodland types (p.86). There were (and still are) outliers of lime in the southern parts of the Oak–Hazel Province. Outliers of pine persisted in special places in all four other Provinces.

Pine declined to extinction except in its stronghold of the Highlands of Scotland. In England and Wales there is no good evidence for it beyond the Roman period; it is last heard of as a fossil in the Fens. In Ireland it lingered late enough to have written records. Birch also declined outside the Birch Province. In the Oak–Hazel Province it persisted in quite large quantities; even in the Lime Province it never quite died out.

LOCAL VARIATION IN WILDWOOD

The south Norfolk meres

In East Anglia there are many depressions, ranging in size from a few acres up to 100 acres (40 ha) or more. They are thought to be karst features, produced by local solution of the underlying chalk, although most are blanketed with Pleistocene deposits of boulder-clay, sand and loess. They include the famous fluctuating meres of the Breckland, which dry out periodically and do not preserve pollen. Others are permanent lakes, whose mud contains pollen, often from late-glacial times to the present.

Thirteen cores have been analysed from eight different meres,* located around the edges of the dry Breckland (Fig. 175). The soils and geology are most complex, with a patchwork of sand, chalk, loess and boulder-clay in different proportions. The region has been farmed since at least the Iron Age. Diss Mere is in the town of Diss, surrounded by a tract of ordered fields, probably Iron Age in date. There is one ancient wood in the region of the meres, Wayland Wood,** which has existed at least since Anglo-Saxon times; it is an ash maple–hazel wood with oak timber trees, a patch of hornbeam, and (unusually) many stools of bird-cherry (*Prunus padus*). To the south are Fakenham Wood (hazel) and Burgate Wood (partly hornbeam and partly ash–hazel), both with standard oaks. Further to the east the woods are predominantly of hornbeam; to the northeast is Hockering Wood, a great limewood. There are two small patches of lime (*Tilia cordata*) within the mere region.

---

* The smallest, the Oxborough site, is a hollow only 15 feet (5 metres) across and is apparently a pingo (p.169).

** The Babes-in-the-Wood wood; it belongs to Norfolk Wildlife Trust.

Godwin's two cores from Hockham Mere were the basis of the classic story of how wildwood developed in England (Table 8). Birch and willows appeared first. Then came the rise of pine, soon overtaken by hazel. Elm came next, followed by oak and by the decline of birch. Alder and lime came together as pine declined. The arrival of ash produced the fully developed wildwood, the end of which is marked by the sudden decline of elm at the beginning of the Neolithic.

What do the 13 cores reveal for the period between the rise of ash and the Elm Decline? This was the late Mesolithic, about 5000 to 3800 BC, when people should have been hunter-gatherers, not having much direct influence on vegetation. I have measured pollen counts off the published pollen diagrams.[13] To calculate the contributions of different trees to the canopy I have multiplied elm pollen by two and ash and lime by eight, which (very roughly) allows for them producing less pollen than birch, pine or oak. Hazel is taken to be a good pollen producer as a canopy tree, but to be sterile if shaded.* I have omitted alder and willow as being wetland trees, forming a separate plant community fringing the meres.

Throughout the period, each of the sites had five main dry-land trees: lime, hazel, oak, ash and elm. Pine pollen was scarce, and probably blew in from pinewoods in the Fens. Birch was locally present in small quantity. There were insignificant amounts of beech and yew, and only odd grains of hornbeam and maple.

At the beginning of the period most cores are dominated by hazel. The proportion of hazel generally fell, replaced by increasing amounts of lime and then ash. Following Richard Bradshaw, I would interpret this as the working of natural succession. Hazel and pine got in first; hazel then took over, possibly by suppressing the fires which pine needs to maintain itself. Hazel would be stable, being long-lived and densely shading, but later-comers slowly got in and replaced it. Some of the hazel was suppressed and presumably killed by lime. Later, ash began to take over: if modern ecology is a guide, the result would be an ash–hazel wood in which the hazels stayed alive but stopped producing pollen. Oak also increased in places.

This takes us to just before the fateful decline of elm. At most sites, as everywhere this side of the Alps, something caused two-thirds or more of the elm to disappear from the canopy in a few years around 3800 BC. What that Something was is considered in the next chapter.

---

* Some investigators did not distinguish hazel from bog-myrtle pollen. Although small quantities of bog-myrtle are known to have been present, I have taken all 'coryloid' to be hazel.

What took the place of elm? Overwhelmingly hazel: in all but one of the sequences hazel returned to being the commonest tree just after the Elm Decline. The inference is that elms had invaded part of the hazel-wood and converted it to elmwood with an understorey of hazel that ceased producing pollen. On the death of the elms the hazels produced pollen again. Experience in Madingley Wood shows that hazels can survive with little alteration for well over 50 years under elm, but produce no pollen;[14] my observation in Hayley Wood shows that when elms die the released hazels flourish and resume producing pollen. *

The pollen evidence now reveals, instead of the 'mixed oak forest', at least five types of wildwood within the Lime Province of south Norfolk:

1. Limewood. Lime in its present behaviour is very gregarious: patches of pure lime alternate with patches of other trees (p.18). It is unlikely that hazel could persist under the dense shade of lime.
2. Hazel-wood. Considerable areas of hazel remained in an unsuppressed state, still producing pollen, before the Elm Decline.
3. Elm–hazel-wood.
4. Ashwood, either as pure ash or (more likely) with suppressed hazel underneath.
5. Alder-wood, forming fringes round the lakes.

This is the minimum number of wildwood types consistent with the evidence. Birch could have been mingled with other trees – it is now one of the few that can (for a while) keep up with the height growth of lime – but more likely occurred as patches on its own. There is no means of telling whether oak was scattered among other trees (a forerunner of its historic position as standard trees among underwood) or formed patches of woodland on its own.

The five to seven woodland types were represented in very different proportions in no systematic way. Hockham core 1 was predominantly hazel-wood throughout. In the same mere, core 2 shows hazel temporarily overtaken by lime just before the Elm Decline. In neither core was any ash recognised at all. In Hockham 3, oak, lime and ash outnumbered hazel throughout, while in Hockham 4 hazel outnumbered lime, oak and ash. In the little depression at Oxborough, lime was dominant at first and mysteriously died out.

The wildwood of southwest Norfolk thus comprised a patchwork of tree communities, probably related in part to soil differences, from which the various

---

*   Is the excessive dominance of hazel after the Elm Decline due to insufficient allowance having been made for its high pollen production?

lake catchments received more or less random samples of pollen. The mosaic was on a small enough scale for more than one type to contribute to the catchment of any one mere. In general terms it resembles the patchwork of tree communities still extant (p.274). Limewood, hazel-wood, ash(−hazel)-wood, alder-wood and birchwood are familiar in ancient woods in south Norfolk today; elm−hazel-wood and oakwood are extant elsewhere in East Anglia.

There is little pollen evidence for woodland containing maple (insect polli-nated) and hornbeam. Is this because those trees became major components only after the wildwood period? Or is it a sampling effect − the meres sampled differ-ent parts of the landscape from surviving ancient woods? On present evidence we cannot be sure, although these pollen cores fail to document any subsequent rise in hornbeam or maple.

Regional differences

Other parts of eastern England tend to be more strongly dominated by lime, notably in the Norfolk Broads and the Epping Forest area, but have little or no ash. A core from Mar Dyke, south Essex, however, has oak, hazel, elm, lime and ash in much the same proportions as some of the Norfolk cores.[15] Cores from the Fens show a strong dominance of lime, and also considerable quantities of pine. The buried 'bog oaks' in the Fens, however, are indeed mostly oak, with pine, yew and even birch (preserved as bark), but bog trees of lime and hazel are not reported. This must be an effect of taphonomy: the more rot-resistant trees were engulfed by the peat and preserved, but limes and hazels rotted before they could be entombed.

Pollen from wildwood lime is found in Lowland peat, usually in abundance, almost exactly as far north (to the Lake District and County Durham) as lime still exists, but within Lowland England it bears no relation to whether or not lime is still extant.

The Oak − Hazel Province

The most extensive researches are those of Dr Judith Turner and colleagues at 52 sites in County Durham and the northern Pennines, covering the Boreal Period of about 8700 − 6200 BC. The principal trees (other than wetland alder and sallow) were hazel, birch, pine, oak and elm, this being outside the range of lime.[16]

There was local variation much as in East Anglia. Allowing for differences in pollen production, hazel was usually the commonest tree, sometimes very strongly dominant. Pockets of pine and birch occurred here and there. Elm was very prevalent, especially in the wildwood that then covered the highest fells of the Pennines.

This is an earlier and transitional period, preceding the fully developed wildwood of the Atlantic Period. The decline of birch and pine, and to a lesser extent of hazel, had not yet occurred. However, two peculiarities of the high dales, especially Swaledale, can be traced back to wildwood times: abundance of elm (in historic times often the commonest tree) and scarcity of oak (now absent from Swaledale except the lowest few miles).

WHAT DID WILDWOOD LOOK LIKE?

In a region absolutely covered with trees, human life could not long be sustained ... The depths of the forest seldom furnish either bulb or fruit suited to the nourishment of man; and the fowls and beasts on which he feeds are scarcely seen except upon the margin of the wood, for here only grow the shrubs and grasses, and here only are found the seeds and insects, which form the sustenance of the non-carnivorous birds and quadrupeds.
GEORGE PERKINS MARSH, NORTH AMERICAN ECOLOGIST, 1864

Wildwood as forest
Hitherto, for simplicity, I have treated wildwood as forest; but the story now becomes controversial. Scientists and foresters traditionally assert that the 'natural' place for trees is close together in dense forests. The Enlightenment ideal (p.148) seemed to be confirmed by climax theory. (Would palynology have developed differently if it had come before, rather than after, the development of modern forestry?) The discoveries of palynology were taken to reconfirm that 'mature' wildwood consisted of trees, trees, trees and trees, from coast to coast and from the Fens to Cross Fell. This was the 'Tansley' theory, in which only details still called for explanation: How big were the trees? How long did they live? How did they renew themselves? In what combinations did they grow: was there a monotonous 'mixed oak forest', or were there patches of different trees and mixtures of trees? How did Mesolithic people manage to squeeze between the great trunks and earn a living?

In the 1980s, I became dissatisfied. Pollen deposits have a continuous record of plants that do not flower in shade. Some of these are now plants of meadow or pasture; others are associated either with coppicing (wild strawberry, ragged robin) or with *permanent* open areas (betony *Stachys officinalis*, devil's-bit scabious). Their pollen was not abundant, but since such insect-pollinated plants waste little pollen even a few grains must be taken seriously. Wildwood therefore contained persistent open areas, the predecessors of the present woodland grassland of rides and glades.[17] These plants have a somewhat greater pollen record in previous interglacials.

Wildwood as savanna

A fable: Once upon a time there was a grassy plain interspersed with groves of trees. Deer, bison, wild horses and wild oxen grazed on it. They devoured most of the young trees that were forever springing up in the plain, but occasionally a few hawthorns or blackthorns would escape and form thickets. One such thicket gradually expanded into the fringe of coarse grass that surrounded it. Passing rooks and jays dropped acorns and hazelnuts; these germinated and grew up, protected by the thorns, to establish a grove of oak and hazel.

Folk in those days prowled around the edges of such groves, snaring the deer and eating the horses and carrying bags of hazelnuts to their camp on the edge of a nearby fen. Occasionally they speared a great bull – bigger than a rhinoceros and faster than a racehorse – and celebrated their valour with a feast, drinking out of its horns.[18]

Our grove slowly spread into the surrounding grassland as new thorns and then oaks sprang up in its edge; it grew into a roughly circular wood half a mile across. In the interior there were no new oaks or hazels, which need light, but there came a new generation of shade-tolerant limes and beeches. For the purpose of this story, trees have finite life spans, and after a few hundred years the grove would have broken up: as the trees in its interior died, a new area of grassland would have arisen to complete the cycle.

All this happened several times over 5,000 years, but there came a time when the cycle was not to be completed, because new technology intervened. People had acquired cattle and sheep and tame horses, which pastured in the grassland and stopped the grove from expanding. These people exterminated the terrible wild oxen and the deer; they dug up part of the plain and grew corn.

Their successors went on doing this until all the plain and some of the groves had been grubbed out and made into farmland. Our grove, however, survived. They cut it down from time to time; they made a bank, ditch and hedge round it to protect the regrowth, and it became a permanent island among farmland. They called the plain Cambridgeshire, and the grove they called Hayley Wood. A thousand years ago it passed into the hands of the Abbots of Ely, and in 1962 to the Cambridgeshire Wildlife Trust. It still keeps the roughly circular shape of its expansive origin. It is still full of oaks, but deprived of horses and oxen it has no younger generation of oak. (And the students of my college still celebrate their examination valour by drinking out of a super-bull's horn.[19])

The Vera model: My story illustrates (or parodies) the alternative model of wild-wood expounded by the Dutchman, Francis Vera, in his book *Grazing Ecology and Forest History.* His thesis is that wildwood was not all trees, but contained large areas of grassland, maintained by the grazing of wild beasts. It was not a stable climax, but was in a state of gradual flux. Wooded areas ('groves') would extend at their edges, invading the grassland, and decay at their centres, giving rise to open areas which would turn into new grassland. This went on, so he claims, from the end of the last ice age until the spread of farming and forestry put an end to the dynamics – although some of the groves survived into medieval and even modern times as woods with a characteristic compact, rounded shape.

For want of a better term, I shall call this the 'savanna' model of wildwood. Most savannas in the world today consist of single trees in grassland, which is not (in the main) what Vera had in mind, although one can imagine that some of the 'groves' might never have got further than a patch of thorns with one or two oak-trees. A closer modern parallel might be the mott savannas of Texas (Fig. 32), with clonal patches of oaks and elms in grassland, some of them two or three acres (0.8–1.2 ha) in extent, having woodland shrubs and woody climbers as well as trees. A model of a Vera-type landscape (although the dynamics are different) is the New Forest or Hatfield Forest, with areas of trees, some of them many acres in extent, in a matrix of grassland or heath (Fig. 33).

Vera claims that browsing animals affected the composition of woodland. In particular, 'without horse and ox oak will not survive': oak and hazel, trees from the middle of the successional sequence, do not now grow from seed within exist-ing woods, and need browsing animals to create fresh habitat.

Vera's thesis explains how there came to be large numbers of big game, and provides a role for them in maintaining the structure of the landscape. A savanna-like structure (rather than continuous forest) gives more scope for ancient trees. It allowed the first farmers to find pasture for domestic animals and open areas to grow crops without having to dig up trees.

Most large herbivores, like deer and wild oxen, find it difficult to make a living in continuous forest. They eat off the low tree leaves and brambles, creating a browse-line. There is not enough edible biomass within reach to sustain a reason-able density of beasts, especially of herd animals.

Deer today may live in woods, but earn a livelihood by feeding on fields outside (p.424). Elk (like moose, their North American brethren) are best at home among low trees or perhaps reed-beds. Red deer are mixed feeders, at home in moorland, but needing trees for shelter. Roe are the most wood-adapted of deer, but even they are not reliant on woodland. (It should be possible to tell whether fossil animals fed on woody or grassy vegetation by examining the microscopic wear of their teeth.[20]) Wild swine, feeding underground, can live in some types of dense forest, although in Spain they extend far into steppe.[21]

All this applies to large herbivores that no longer have natural predators. Île Royale is a big island in Lake Superior; it has never been much inhabited by people and is now a National Park. Originally it was densely forested and had few, if any, large ungulates. After logging and mining it developed clonal thickets of aspen and became suitable for moose, which swam across around 1910. They multiplied into thousands, helped by a great fire in 1936 that renewed their habitat, and by the 1940s were eating themselves out of a home: 'another of those big game ranges, degraded by overpopulation, where the animals hang on at the limit of numbers permitted by their food supply, to be decimated periodically by hard winters.' While the National Park authorities were searching their hearts about the propriety of introducing wolves, the problem solved itself. When the lake froze more extensively than usual, a wolf pack trotted across from Canada and began eating the moose. The interaction between moose, wolves, trees and weather will take many years to elucidate fully. Predation affects not only numbers of herbivores but also their behaviour: they avoid places where they cannot see who is coming to eat them.[22]

Mankind is often thought of as a savanna animal. Forest is an inhospitable environment because most of the action takes place in inaccessible tree canopies. Many authors point out that forests provide things like nuts, toadstools, 'roots' etc., but it is hard work living on them: many are seasonal, and some (especially berries) are not produced in shade. Anyone who tries to live off the tubers of an English wood is in for an unpleasant surprise on encountering lords-and-ladies. Forest peoples, like desert peoples, are specialised and few in numbers.

Discriminating between Vera and Tansley models:[23] An objection is that Vera's theory is too general (Table 9). His book is mainly about the Netherlands and Germany, but he draws on other countries, especially England, because of the abundance of historical records. Instead of going through all the evidence country by country, he combines evidence from half Europe: fieldwork from Germany can be used to interpret records from England.

The herbivores diminished westward. In Britain, reindeer, Irish elk, bison and wild horse did not survive into the Holocene. There were elk (down to the Mesolithic); aurochs (down to the Bronze Age), although historical records of aurochs associate it with fens; red and roe deer; wild swine; and beaver. In Ireland, Irish elk barely survived into the Holocene, and only wild pig was abundant: red deer, if present at all in pre-Neolithic Ireland, were rare, perhaps because there was too much forest. There should, therefore, have been a gradient from a Vera-type landscape in eastern Europe to a Tansley-type in Ireland.

The trees were different. Ireland lacked beech and lime, the principal trees of the last stage of the Vera cycle. In Britain, although beech has a historic association with wood-pasture, it was largely in the southeast. Lime in Britain avoids places with a browsing history; it is reluctant to spread to newly available ground, and seems to require a less dynamic landscape than Vera proposes.

It is hard to believe that after 70 years of intensive study of pollen deposits there should be any difficulty in discriminating between forest and savanna, but when I wrote this, few pollen analysts had responded to Vera. F.J.G. Mitchell applied three tests:

1. On Vera's model, oak and hazel should have been rare in Irish wildwood, because pre-Neolithic Ireland had only one abundant big herbivore, wild pig. But hazel and oak pollen are both abundant: 'there was no significant difference in the relative proportions of *Quercus* and *Corylus* in the primeval forests of Ireland and Europe'.

2. Mitchell examines contemporary pollen fallout in various parts of Europe, and shows that in 'closed canopy forests' trees account for 60–90 percent of total pollen, in 'open sites' less than 40 per cent, and in semi-tree'd landscapes 30–60 per cent. Pre-Neolithic samples typically have at least 70 per cent tree pollen, in both Ireland and Europe.

3. There should be fluctuations especially in non-tree pollen over the grassland–grove cycle. These would be detectable in small basins that record local pollen. In Ireland and Europe Mitchell has looked for such fluctuations, thousand years by thousand years, and not found them.[24]

Oak and hazel seem not to be maintained by browsing. Both got on very well in pre-Neolithic Ireland. In England there is not much correlation between browsing and oak regeneration. Oak certainly perpetuated itself without browsing in woods such as Hayley down to the time of the Oak Change, *c.*1900, as tens of thousands of oak timbers in buildings bear witness (Chapter II); recent browsing by deer has not brought it back. It might perpetuate itself today had oak mildew not been introduced from America (p.335). Non-reproduction of hazel is likewise partly due to the introduced grey squirrel. How much turnover of hazel there had previously been is unrecorded; my impression is that hazel stools are very long-lived and do not need much seed establishment.

Vera's model could operate without the oak and hazel story, but central to his thesis are hawthorn and blackthorn. These were present and were a favourite firewood; their charcoal is found in Mesolithic archaeological sites. They are insect pollinated; their pollens are not very distinctive and are probably often overlooked.[25] But they produce considerable quantities of pollen, especially when growing at the boundary between woodland and grassland, and had they been abundant this ought to have been recognised. In pre-Neolithic deposits their pollens are far rarer than lime.

Another difficulty concerns grasses, the predominant 'non-tree pollen' in most samples. Why is there so little grass pollen in pre-Neolithic wildwood? Vera's answer is that grasses were there, but the herbivores ate their flowering tops. But this calls for such intensive grazing that the thorns could not spread and the dynamics would come to a halt, as happens now in Hatfield Forest.

Tree-to-non-tree pollen ratio is a blunt instrument. Both sides of the ratio add up prolific and sparse pollen producers indiscriminately. If there were only oak, hazel and grasses − good producers − this might not matter too much, but if the trees were lime and maple the ratio would necessarily be low, and if the non-trees included plenty of pretty flowers and not much grass (like an alpine meadow) even scattered or distant trees would appear to be dominant.

Fire might be another way for open areas to form. However, pine, the only fire-promoting tree, was local by the mid-Holocene; it plays no significant part in Vera's scheme, much of which deals with such very incombustible trees as lime, beech and elm. Grassland might just burn, but the amount of grazing that prevented the grasses from flowering would prevent dead grass from accumulating as fuel. Wildwood tree trunks buried in peat, even pine, are seldom scarred by fire; however, heather charcoal has often been identified, showing that moorland fires go back to Mesolithic times.[26] If fire did occur its consequences should appear in the form of peaks of heather pollen or bracken spores. A study of charcoal in the Norfolk meres found no more evidence of fire than could be accounted for by Mesolithic campfires.[27]

A specifically savanna plant that has a pollen record is mistletoe. Palynologists regard it as an indicator of warmth, but it also indicates a habitat. In my experience the British subspecies is exclusively on orchard and freestanding trees, hardly ever in a wood. It is most familiar on domesticated apple, lime and poplar; its commonest wild host is hawthorn. In Hatfield Forest, its chief stronghold on wild trees, it occurs on old hawthorns and old maples, but only in the plains (p.122) and not in the woods. Its pollen would thus indicate freestanding trees, old trees, and especially old hawthorns. It is abundant in the last-but-one interglacial; in the Holocene it is uncommon before the Neolithic. (Many Australian mistletoes, too, grow on savanna eucalypts.)

Grassland plants that might show up in a Vera-type ecosystem are buttercups. These, though insect pollinated, are relatively prolific pollen producers, and are so distasteful that they flower even under severe grazing. Buttercup achenes and pollen are particularly numerous in the last interglacial, and occur in the pre-Neolithic Holocene, although they much increase in the Neolithic and after.[28]

Diss Mere (Fig. 175) is one of the best pollen deposits published in Europe. The pre-Neolithic portion indicates tree-land divided between oak, lime, ash and hazel. Among Vera-type indicators, there is a small amount of mistletoe, which disappears after the Neolithic, and the odd grain of hawthorn. There are a few plants that do not flower in shade, such as heather, sorrel (woodland grassland), *Angelica*-type and cow-wheat (now a coppicing plant), together with appreciable amounts of bracken, but no buttercup. Such plants greatly increase with the expansion of farmland in the Bronze Age and after. There can be little doubt that the landscape round the mere was predominantly woodland, with only small permanent open areas.[29]

Fossil evidence also comes from remains of insects. Although these are called 'old-forest insects', their modern ecology associates them with ancient *trees*, which are more likely in a savanna context. Many of them require flowers as well as trees, and some call for sunny situations.[30]

Outside palynology, some aspects of Vera's timescale are unpersuasive. Several thousand years elapsed between wildwood times and the earliest historic records – especially in England, which has been densely populated since the Iron Age. Vera could be right in claiming that in Germany and Poland, as late as the Middle Ages, cultural landscapes were still being carved out of primæval wildwood, although such assumptions tend to be based merely on lack of archaeological survey of earlier human activity. In England, however, all the unwritten centuries of late prehistory and the Roman period, with retreats and advances of woodland, lay between the times of elk and aurochs and the earliest written records. By Anglo-Saxon times every inch of England had an owner.

Other countries: Mediterranean islands had unbalanced faunas with elephants, hippopotamuses and deer – often in dwarf forms – but no effective carnivore until Man appeared, usually well into the Holocene. Here, if anywhere, the aboriginal landscape should have been savanna, especially as the dry climate would hinder regrowth of trees after browsing.

Of islands having a pollen record, Corsica apparently had forest and maquis in the early Holocene much as it has now, with some differences in the species. Native herbivores seem to have been scarce, the forest being too dense for them, or already extinct. On Mljet in Dalmatia, the indications also imply forest, including such palatable trees as elm, so herbivores too played little part.

In Crete, which is drier, the indications are definitely against forest. The pollen record includes non-shade-bearing plants such as asphodel, as well as trees. The diverse landscapes of Crete already existed; trees took the form of savanna or maquis rather than forest. The arrival of people is not very clearly marked. This is surprising, since on present knowledge the earliest evidence of human presence is around 7000 BC and the beasts had died out much earlier. The climate alone may have been dry enough to create savanna, independent of browsing animals.[31]

Provisional inferences
Pollen evidence is against the Vera model, especially in Britain and Ireland. However, it cannot be simply dismissed, for there are ragged robins and devil's-bits to be explained, as well as a place to be found for the beasts and the Mesolithic people who lived on them.

On Vera's model it is easier to find room for ancient trees and their specific invertebrate animals and lichens. Ancient trees fare better in savanna where they escape the competition of younger neighbours and can more easily resist windblow (p.18).

Vera's model needs to be developed in relation to the palatability, longevity and gregariousness of different trees. What part did elm clones play? Did they slowly expand as fixed objects in an otherwise dynamic landscape? Or were the suckers sought out by aurochsen and ruthlessly devoured?

The Vera model of wildwood would have been much more favourable to Mesolithic hunter-gatherers than the Tansley model. Whether people already at this stage were manipulating vegetation in favour of edible animals is still uncertain. Mesolithic people took advantage of the abundance of hazel: they were hazel-nut-eaters rather as north Italians used to live on chestnuts (p.338).

How can Vera's and Tansley's models be reconciled with the continued existence of woodland herbs, many of which do not survive grazing? Was there some form of compartmentation analogous to that in medieval parks and Forests? It is difficult to imagine a physical barrier, but were the depths of the groves no-go areas for deer and wild cattle, either because there was not much to eat or because of danger from carnivores?

Further work is needed on specific aspects of the pollen record chosen to differentiate between forest and savanna. Fossil insects too might help. It is too much to hope for a differential pollen record of primrose (forest) versus cowslip (savanna), but pollen data should be searched for other plants that do not flower in shade, preferably unpalatable species like buttercup. Published pollen diagrams do not always contain the information. A full pollen record is an unwieldy piece of paper, and authors too often leave out what they consider to be unimportant or irrelevant pollen types. Many diagnostic species leave little pollen and so are particularly liable to be omitted.

Could a few wildwood groves still be there in the shape of medieval woods with near-circular outlines? Hayley Wood is not a good candidate, for the faint earthworks that underlie some of it (Fig. 193) point to prehistoric activity. Nor are the coppices in Hatfield Forest. However, there are many others, especially in Lincolnshire, that would be worth searching.

Comparison with previous interglacials
Whatever may be said for the Holocene, Vera's model works better for previous interglacials. Non-shade-bearing herbs are then more strongly represented, as are blackthorn, hawthorn, mistletoe and buttercup. Oak, however, was not notably more prevalent than in the Holocene.

The landscape of Boxgrove Man, two glacial cycles ago, apparently included wide expanses of grassland. The trees were much the same, but the big game was bigger and more savanna-like: super-elephants, rhinoceroses, hippopotamuses, lions, hyænas, bison and super-deer.[32]

The Holocene stands out for the abundance of hazel throughout Britain and Ireland. Hazel as a dominant tree had been approached only late in the last interglacial. Spruce and fir (*Abies*) had been native in previous interglacials, but in this interglacial they never returned. This was probably not just an accident of rising sea level. Neither is native across the English Channel today; they probably had Atlantic ecotypes that were wiped out by the vagaries of glaciation.* Other unusual features of this interglacial are the abundance of alder and lime and the persistence of birch.

Is there a link between the peculiarities of this interglacial – lack of elephants and rhinoceroses, abundant hazel, sparse evidence of non-shade-bearing herbs – and the presence of that new and terrible monster *Homo sapiens*?

WILDWOOD VERSUS ANCIENT WOODLAND NOW

It is a theme of this book that ancient woodland is not the same as wildwood. Conservationists do no service to woodland if they try to remake it in the image of what they imagine wildwood was like, whether on the Vera or the Tansley model. Woodland comes of processes of development and management, discussed in the next chapter. Nevertheless, there is some continuity from wildwood. How far are the differences in tree composition due to actual changes on the ground and how far to pollen sites and surviving woods representing different samples of the prehistoric landscape?

The Lime, Oak – Hazel, Pine and Birch Provinces still mark major differences in woodland distribution; only the Hazel – Elm Province is barely recognisable, largely because little ancient woodland survives.

In the Lime Province, lime still occupies its whole range in wildwood times, but in vastly less quantity. The decline, however, is curiously uneven: there are regions, such as around Sudbury (Suffolk), where lime is still the commonest tree in ancient woodland, and others, such as northeast Suffolk, where it is entirely absent. Elm suffered the Elm Decline in the early Neolithic and never fully recovered; doubtless farmers grubbed it out first because it grew on the most fertile soils. Hazel is still abundant in the Lime Province. There is now much more ash and birch, but this is partly a twentieth-century increase. Oak shows an apparent increase, partly because of long-standing and increasing encouragement from woodmen, and partly because it would have grown on the less fertile soils.

In the Oak – Hazel Province, hazel is now much rarer as a woodland tree (though common in hedges). Probably it grew on fertile soils and has been grubbed out, leaving oak on less rewarding soils.

---

* The word *spruce* is short for 'spruce fir', meaning fir of Pruce, that is Prussia. 'Norway spruce' is a curious misnomer.

The prehistoric scarcity of hawthorn is an argument against the Vera model. Maple (also insect pollinated) and hornbeam (wind pollinated) are also rare. Were they indeed less common than now? Or do no pollen sites sample maple- or hornbeam-dominated parts of the ancient landscape? If there has been a real increase, it is difficult to explain in terms of processes now operating. Hawthorn is encouraged by hedge planting and intermittent grazing, but what human activity can have encouraged hornbeam and maple?

Beech also has a poor pollen record in Britain. There was apparently a real increase in the 2,000 years before the tree-planting period, probably at the expense of lime, but even the good historical records of beech fail to explain why.

CHAPTER 5

WILDWOOD INTO WOODLAND

THE WOODS

Item there is there one little park which contains in itself nine acres, with a laund, by the aforesaid perch. Which would be worth every year with the laund 4 shillings if there were no beasts. [Now the wood called Park Wood, 14.3 acres (56.8 ha). The laund would have been an open area (p.118), of which no trace survives.]

Item there is there one grove which is called tykele which contains in itself five acres by the aforesaid perch. [Now the wood called Titley Hill, 4.7 acres (1.9 ha).]

And a certain other grove which is called prestele which contains in itself thirty acres by the aforesaid perch. [Now Priestley Wood, 38.4 acres (15.5 ha).]

And another grove which is called Wetheresheg which contains in itself seven acres and a half by the aforesaid perch. And these three are worth every year sixteen shillings. [Now Swingens Wood, 14.2 acres (5.7 ha).]

Item there is there one great wood which is called boynhey which contains in itself ninescore acres by estimate. And it is worth per annum four pounds and ten shillings. [Now Bonny Wood, 126 acres (51 ha).]

THE WOODS OF BARKING, SUFFOLK, IN THE *ELY COUCHER BOOK*, 1251.

[The length of the perch is given as 16.5 feet (5 metres), the same as the modern perch; the acres thus need no adjustment. Priestley and part of Bonny Wood are nature reserves of Suffolk Wildlife Trust.]

DID WILDWOOD REALLY EXIST?

Conservationists for more than a hundred years were obsessed with preserving the world's 'primæval' or 'virgin' forests. Until lately they meant forests unaffected by human activity ('untrammelled by man'), or only by the sort of hunting, gathering and maybe rubber-tapping that seemed not to have much effect on the ecology.

Interest revived in the 1990s. Wildwood enthusiasts scolded conservationists for being concerned for coppices, wood-pastures and other 'artificial' kinds of vegetation. It was argued that even in Britain conservationists ought to turn all their energies to 'restoring' primæval vegetation, somehow unpicking the effects of thousands of years of management (p.430).

Ten years later, the old certainty, that wildwood meant forest, was challenged. If restorers of wildwood are to get anywhere they have to establish what it is they are trying to restore. The numbers, habits, tastes and effects of wild beasts are the most important unanswered question in prehistoric ecology.

The very concept of wildwood has shrunk in the face of archaeological and historical discoveries. Nineteenth-century explorers rediscovered the monuments of mighty civilisations in the jungles of Yucatán and Cambodia, grown up over the farmland that had supported these cultures. James Fairhead and Melissa Leach have demonstrated that much of the forest of West Africa was once savanna, maintained by a settled population (p.90). Even in the remotest reaches of the Amazon, clever people discovered how to make a living from the sodden, luxuriant, infertile vegetation: the present tranquil solitudes are not primæval but depopulated.[1]

It can no longer be assumed that absence of evidence of 'significant' human presence means evidence of absence; that forests not containing temples and pyramids have always been forest. Faint earthworks, termite mounds, and traces of human cultures that did not build in stone are easily missed if one does not know what to look for. Archaeologists avoid forests because dense vegetation and leaf litter hide scatters of flints or potsherds. Anyone who restricts the term 'natural woodland' to woods with no human influence risks creating an empty category.

Old-growth forests and their European equivalents

Old-growth forest is an American term for tracts that have escaped obvious logging or modern forestry practices within the life span of the existing trees (see Fig. 11). Some form the nuclei of National Parks; others come up from time to time for preservation or destruction, and are a political issue at which even Presidents shudder a little. These are wild and wonderful places, often containing very specific animals. It is easy to imagine them to be 'virgin forest' as it might have been had humanity never existed. But most were used by Native Americans and have been modified by the loss of their practices, as well as by the European habit of suppressing or postponing fires. George Peterken published a map of officially designated 'virgin forests' in Europe. Nearly half the sites were in the rather small country of Czechoslovakia (Table 10). Although this is partly due to a pioneering interest there in 'virgin forest' and its protection, it must mean that Czechs and Slovaks use a wider definition of 'virgin forest' than Poles, Germans or Hungarians. (Would Staverton Thicks in Suffolk or Ballochbuie Pinewood in Scotland count as 'virgin forests' in Czechoslovakia?)

According to Peterken, these tend to be designated according to whether they meet ecologists', and especially foresters', preconceptions of what a virgin forest should look like: 'if they have large trees, much dead wood, a patchwork of structure, and a full range of dynamic states, the supposed state of [wholly] natural woodland'.[2] There has seldom been any serious attempt to verify that they were left unused by the surrounding human populations.

Peterken shows, and on my more limited experience I agree, that where a historical record exists it often demonstrates a history of wood-pasture. I once visited a *gammelskog* ('ancient wood') of huge, ancient spruces in Sweden; the local Mayor took me aside and pointed out some yet older pines of spreading shape which indicated that the spruces had infilled between what had once been scattered trees; Richard Bradshaw cited a pollen diagram showing that the site had once been a heath.

Sites left unmanaged for a century or more (of which England is beginning to acquire a goodly store as the years pass) are of the greatest ecological interest and should be protected. But they are not relics of pre-Neolithic wildwood, and do not return to such with time. They are altered both by irreversible events in the more distant past and by events outside their borders. The very name of one in France, *La Tillaie* in the Forêt de Fontainebleau, proclaims that it was once a limewood, which could indeed have been a relict of Mesolithic times, but since then it has turned into an oakwood and then into a beechwood. A common sequence of events is a reduction of grazing as prehistoric people ate up the native herbivores; then a period of less tree cover and heavier browsing by domestic livestock in historic times; then a time of abnormally little browsing, after common-rights were suppressed; and lately resumed browsing as deer multiply.

Even such a seemingly feeble activity as fur-trapping can have an effect. In Ontario a major influence on forests is the food preferences of porcupines, which eat the bark off beeches and the leaves off hemlocks. If you ask why this happens in some areas but not others, you are told that it depends on the abundance of fishers, a kind of super-weasel, the only mammal that can digest a whole porcupine and live. The fisher has valuable fur on his back and in places has been kept down by trappers.[3]

Conclusion

The idea of wildwood, isolated from human activities, has so shrunk that one begins to ask whether it has existed at all since the last ice age, except on remote islands. The last extensive areas of wildwood could have been Madagascar and New Zealand, into which Polynesians burst about 1,500 and 800 years ago. On which lonely island did some storm-driven canoe or eighteenth-century ship bring the world's very last wildwood to an end?

THE NEOLITHIC

Neolithic culture in Britain is defined archaeologically by new styles of stone tools and the appearance of pottery. From pollen, cultivated cereals are distinguishable from other grasses. Another new feature is weeds, many of which came along with crops from southern Europe; plantains, however, were native. Small clearings can sometimes be identified, but a very distinctive feature of the beginning of the Neolithic is the Elm Decline. All over west and north Europe elm, and only elm, pollen suddenly and permanently declined.

A paradox of the forest model of wildwood is how and why Neolithic people should have abandoned hunting and gathering for the meagre yields of early cereals grown in competition with native vegetation. To do this at all they had to create fields and pastures. Why did they bring foreign crops and animals into an all-forest landscape that needed so much work before it became suitable for the new way of life? How did they find time and energy to dig up trees without metal crowbars and mattocks? What did they live on while doing it? On the Vera model the difficulty largely disappears: they would merely have to dig up grassland – leaving the wooded areas until farming was well established – and fence their cultivated plots to keep out tame and wild livestock.

In the seventeenth century Kentish clothiers and Buckinghamshire tailors abandoned good jobs to turn peasant in lonely, hostile, rattlesnake-haunted, poison-ivy-infested America. Somehow they found time and skill to make and fence fields as well as till them, but even the abundant records hardly explain what drove them or how they managed it. The problem is more severe for Neolithic farmers, unless they used land already cleared by wild animals – much as American colonists began on the savannas and farmland of their deceased Native American predecessors.[4]

The phrase 'clearing forest by fire' is a phantom that haunts discussions at this point. Here I dismiss it on the grounds that it cannot be done (p.47). To get an English wood to burn the trees have to be cut down, carried to a fire site, cut up, and densely stacked before a fire in one log will spread into the next. In the Norfolk mere deposits charcoal is even scarcer in the early Neolithic than at other times.[5]

Some of the remaining wildwood was converted to managed woodland, yielding trees small enough to be useful, whether for wood, leaves or timber. Evidence for coppicing is archaeological (p.220f); at this stage it is unlikely to be extensive enough to be discerned in the pollen record.

The Elm Decline

Elm – a moderate pollen producer – had amounted to about one-eighth of the trees of wildwood, but much more in some areas than others.[6] At the beginning of the Neolithic it suddenly collapsed by more than half. This seems to have been simultaneous, rather than tracking the spread of Neolithic culture over Europe.

What was the cause? Deterioration of climate is inadequate to explain so universal a change. Had the climate become less favourable for elm, it would not have affected elm everywhere and elm only: it would have wiped out elm in climatically marginal areas, but not in the middle of its range. It should have affected elms in America too, but did not. The same applies to deterioration of soils.

An alternative, proposed in 1941 by Iversen in Denmark, is that people were feeding livestock on leaves, especially elm leaves, instead of grass, as they still do in parts of Europe. Elm would have been the favourite tree, and pollarding for leaves would have reduced its pollen output. The objection is that the small population of the time could not suddenly have taken to holding down the pollen production of such vast numbers of elms, even if they had nothing else to do. Nor was there a decline in alternative trees, such as ash, in regions where elm was scarce. The Elm Decline affected only elm, regardless of how common or rare it was.

The obvious explanation is Elm Disease, the effect of *Ceratocystis* fungi (p.336f). The Elm Disease epidemic of 1965 onwards was preceded in England by several others; there is no reason in principle why there should not have been one in 3800 BC. What other cause could have been so sudden, so specific to elms, so universal in Europe and yet absent from America (where Elm Disease was unknown until introduced in the 1920s)? At least one of the bark-beetle vectors is known to have been present.

The matter seems to be clinched by the pollen diagram from Diss Mere, where the sediment contains annual layers (varves) that allow the Elm Decline to be followed year by year. Here elms comprised about 10 per cent of the wildwood; they produced varying amounts of pollen in good and bad years; this ended in one very good year, after which all the years were bad. Ninety-four per cent of elm pollen production ceased in at most three to four years: exactly like a bad attack of Elm Disease.[7]

Elm was substituted by an increase of hazel, as in the 1970s when hazels were released from the shade of elms. Although pollens of different elms are almost indistinguishable, Keith Bennett was able to separate two types at Hockham and Stow Bedon Meres (Fig. 175), of which the type attributed to wych-elm predominates before the Elm Decline and that attributed to East Anglian elm after the Decline; this too would be in line with modern Elm Disease outbreaks, which affect some elms more than others. At Stow Bedon Mere there was little elm, and the Elm Decline was very subdued: this too parallels modern Elm Disease, where some patches of elm, especially in the depths of woodland, escape.

A symbiosis between Elm Disease and Neolithic people remains to be investigated. The behaviour of modern disease suggests that it would have been promoted by people felling trees and creating woodland edges, isolated trees and pollards. At the same time the gods, through Elm Disease, would have rewarded Neolithic people with fertile pastureland ready made.[8]

LATER PREHISTORY

During the immense length of the Neolithic period, human settlement spread throughout the country. It was denser in some areas such as the Breckland, but seems to have been confined to river valleys in the claylands. Much of it was more than just clusters of huts in forest clearings. Most pollen diagrams show a great expansion of non-tree pollens. Monuments such as henges and long barrows involved precise alignments and called for a distant unobstructed horizon. Wide areas of what was later to be chalk downland and heath were already open country.

It used to be thought that 'primitive' people confined their activities to soils that were easily cleared and cultivated with their supposedly inefficient tools, especially the chalklands where Neolithic and Bronze Age monuments are so conspicuous. Forty years of archaeological survey and discovery have now shown how very pervasive prehistoric activity was in Britain, extending far into difficult terrain. The plateau of Dartmoor, now a place of punishment far above the altitudinal limit of modern settlement, is covered with Bronze Age houses and field systems. Most of the big wooded areas of medieval England contain traces of Iron Age and even earlier activity, for example the Neolithic chamber-tombs in Wychwood Forest. Prehistoric people could live where their successors, even in the medieval period of great pressure on land, did not.

Later prehistory gives the impression of a progressive advance of farmland, heath and moorland. Bronze and especially iron tools presumably made it possible to cut down trees faster than they could grow back up. Iron tools made it possible to till stony soils without having to get a new plough every day. Metal working created new requirements for fuel, stimulating the expansion of coppice-woods for conveniently small sizes of wood.

Lime declined more than other trees, but not everywhere simultaneously. At Diss Mere it disappeared in the mid- to late Bronze Age; in Epping Forest it went in the middle Anglo-Saxon period, although the site remained wooded. In some parts of the country lime is still undiminished in ancient woodland today (p.86). This whimsical decline (of a tree that is difficult to kill) is a mystery. It is all very well to say that prehistoric people harvested its leaves for fodder and its bark for fibre, or dug it up because it grew on the best soils, or that livestock ate lime in preference to beech, but if so, why did they attack it so unevenly?[9]

Woodless areas of the Bronze Age are marked by clusters of round barrows, placed where they could be seen from a distance, even if they were later to be in ancient woodland, as in the Forest of Dean or Wentwood Forest (Monmouthshire). Another indication of woodless areas is organised field systems. Field systems on the Dartmoor pattern – with bundles of parallel but sinuous axes in one direction subdivided by cross-walls at irregular intervals – are known in many parts of England and Ireland; some are in use to this day, including near Diss. They vary in date, where known, from Neolithic to Romano-British.[10] Whatever the motive behind this kind of geometry, they indicate large areas of non-woodland. So do the vast field grids in Japan of the early centuries AD, such as the one within which the ancient capital city of Nara was later to be placed.

As woodland decreased and the landscape got more complex, the number of plant species increased: at Diss Mere only some 20 pollen types per sample are identifiable from wildwood times, increasing to 45 in the Roman period and 60 in the Middle Ages.

Global warming?

One begins to hear the claim that global warming (p.422) has its roots far back in prehistory. Past concentrations of atmospheric carbon dioxide are known from fossil air trapped in polar ice cores. William F. Ruddiman notes that in the three previous glacial cycles CO_2 rose during glaciations to about one and a half times its previous level, and then gradually fell during interglacials. In the Holocene the peak occurred early, at about 11,000 BC, but the fall, instead of continuing until the era of burning fossil fuel, ended about 6500 BC (early Neolithic in Asia) and was replaced by a steady rise. He attributes this to the spread of agriculture, to people grubbing out forests and indulging in practices, such as rice cultivation, that released carbon to the atmosphere that would otherwise have been locked up in vegetation and soils. He even ascribes subsequent falterings in the rise to plagues killing off humanity and allowing forests to recover.[11] In my view this is exaggerated: how could cultivation on what can hardly have been more than 6 per cent of the world's land area (only 2 per cent of the whole globe) have been the cause of a 15 per cent anomaly in atmospheric CO_2? However, other human activities, such as altering the frequency and extent of fire, could have contributed. If Australian Aborigines, by land management through burning, maintained savanna and prevented the return of rainforest over much of the continent, and if similar activities occurred in Africa and the Americas, the total area affected could have exceeded the area of cultivation.*

Roman Britain

The Roman Empire did not suddenly import a colonial culture unrelated to what had gone before, like the English in America; rather, it took over and added to indigenous activities, like the British in India. Expansion was especially in domestic heating and fuel-using industries: hypocausts, baths, bricks, tiles, glass and iron. Ancient Athens grew its food and fuel locally, and imported timber; Rome

---

* There are other loose ends in the calculation, such as conversion of carbon into limestone in the sea or into peat in bogs, and the expansion of the Sahara desert (which seems to be independent of human action).

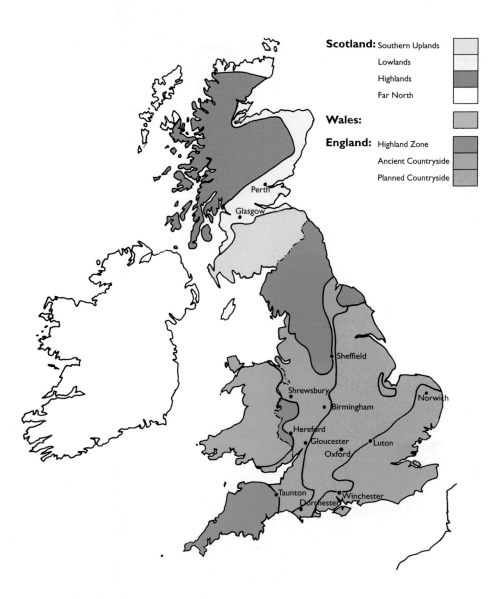

Fig 1. Regions of Britain and Ireland.

Fig 2. Consequence of felling a young beech tree. In this species the young shoots are organised within a callus at the junction of bark and woods. In others (ash, lime, etc.) the sprouts arise from pre-existing dormant buds under the bark. *Chalkney Wood, Essex, April 2003.* See p.16.

Fig 3. Hornbeam pollarded for the first time. Pollards in England are usually in wood-pasture or non-woodland situations, seldom in the interior of woods, unless the wood is more recent than the pollard. *Hatfield Forest, Essex, September 1980.*

Fig 4. Coppicing in progress. The underwood trees have just been felled, leaving a scatter of standard trees to grow on to timber size. *Bradfield Woods, Suffolk, January 1980.* See p.17.

Fig 5. Sallow and other underwood stools after three months' regrowth. *Bradfield Woods, Suffolk, August 1986*. See p.16.

Fig 6. Elm and other underwood stools towards the end of the coppice cycle. *Bradfield Woods, Suffolk, May 1978*.

Fig 7. Old pollard horsechestnut (*Æsculus turbinata*). *Norikura, Japan, October 1998.*

Fig 8. Clonal tree (p.17): European white poplar, which grows in a circular patch with a common root-system. *Kempton, Tasmania, July 2001.*

Fig 9. Pine plantation after the Great Storm. Youngish, crowded plantations were very susceptible. Trees on the edge – even though it was the windward edge – remain upstanding. *Rendlesham Forest, Suffolk, March 1988.* See p.19.

Fig 10. A crowded semi-natural spruce wood after the Great Storm of November 2004 (p.19). *Tatra Mountains, Slovakia, June 2005.*

Fig 11. Old-growth wood of beech and sugar-maple. American beech (*Fagus grandifolia*) is clonal: the fallen beech is surrounded by its own suckers. *Warren Woods, Michigan, May 1981.* See p.90

Fig 12. Wood-pasture; note cattle eating tree leaves. *Hatfield Forest, Essex, May 2005.* See p.21.

Fig 13. Plantation of Monterey pine (*Pinus radiata*). *Tasmania, July 2001.* See p.363.

Fig 14. Cowslip and dandelion as coppicing plants (see p.23). *Øland, Sweden, June 1995.*

Fig 15. Cypresses and pines invading pasture. Does this yet count as forest for statistical purposes? *Samariá Gorge, Crete, July 1987.* See p.24.

Fig 16. About to become a wood: pines and other trees invading grassland. *Kirigamine, Japan, November 1998.* See p.25.

Fig 17. A classic tropical savanna. Grassland (now mostly of introduced grasses, p.421) with scattered eucalypts and rock-like mounds made by wood-eating termites. *Laura, north Queensland, July 2001.*

Fig 18. Root-plates of beeches (p.33), *Box Hill, Surrey. March 1988.*

Fig 19. Chestnut flourishing 15 years after it was overturned. *Denstead Wood, Blean, Kent, February 2004.* See p.19.

Fig 20. A gigantic, not particularly old, oak that suddenly died from an unknown cause (p.38). *Polstead Park, Suffolk, September 1995.*

Fig 21. Some of the thousands of ancient pollard oaks in Staverton Park, Suffolk. See p.432.

Fig 22. Ancient cypress at the tree-limit. *Mount Kastro, White Mountains, Crete, July 1991.* See p.39.

Fig 23. Double zone-plate (zigzag pair of lines) between two *Ustulina* infections in a living old hornbeam. *Hatfield Forest, Essex, August 2005.* See p.40.

Fig 24. 'Sapsucker' holes in lime (p.43). *Chalkney Wood, Essex, April 1995.*

Fig 25. Burning palm-grove (*Sabal palmetto*). The palms are not much hurt, and will be back to normal in a week or two. They keep out oaks and other less fire-adapted trees. *Cape Canaveral, Florida, September 1993.* See p.44.

Fig 26. *Eucalyptus obliqua* with the conical, hollow, blackened base that is so evocative of Tasmanian savannas. Their present, Europeanised environment will no longer support a fire, and without fire they will have no successors. *North Bruny Island, July 2001.* See p.40.

Fig 27. Burnt bracken glade (p.47). Bracken is a clonal, strongly dominant plant that can overwhelm young trees and maintain permanent openings. Dry bracken in spring affords almost the only possibility of fire in English woodland. On reaching the trees the fire runs out of fuel and goes out. *Bradfield Woods, Suffolk, April 1970.*

Fig 28. Coppiceability in American trees (p.64): stools of *Quercus texana*, probably generated by prairie fires before European settlement. *Valley Mills, Texas, January 2002.*

Fig 29. Did early Holocene wildwood look like this? *Muskeg in Algonquin National Park, Ontario.* See p.71.

Fig 30. Self-coppicing in *Tilia americana* (p.64): a ring of stems surrounds the fallen original tree. *Near Duluth, Minnesota, December 1984.*

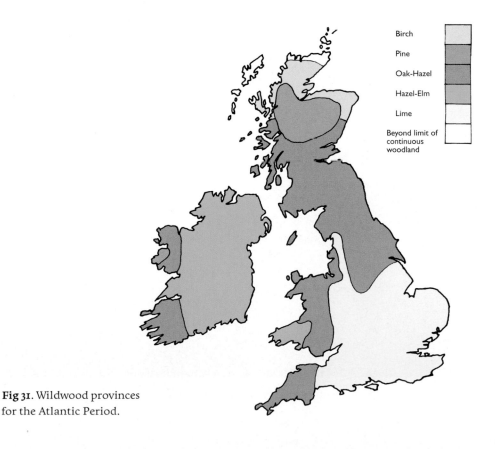

Birch

Pine

Oak-Hazel

Hazel-Elm

Lime

Beyond limit of continuous woodland

Fig 31. Wildwood provinces for the Atlantic Period.

Fig 32. Mott savanna (p.131), with clonal patches of oaks and elms scattered in prairie. *Valley Mills, Texas, February 2003.*

Fig 33. Did Vera's wildwood look like this? *Hatfield Forest, Essex, February 1981.* See p.79.

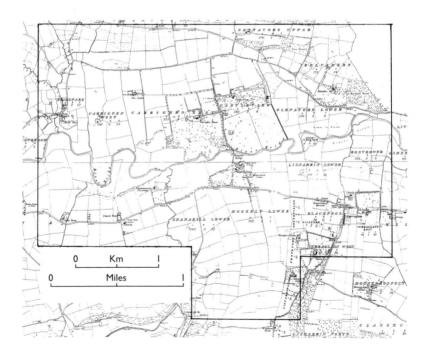

Fig 34. Woodland in Ireland, 1598 and 1903. (The Ordnance Survey of 1844 is almost the same as 1903, except that a number of very small fields were amalgamated in the interval.) Between 1598 and 1844 the landscape changed almost out of recognition. R = rath. *Mogeely, Co. Cork: the Raleigh map and the Ordnance Survey*. See p.109.

Fig 35. A fallow deer doing its duty, as imagined in the 1630s. Detail from *The Triumphs of Pan*, by Nicolas Poussin, © National Gallery. See p.118.

Fig 36. Approximation to a medieval park pale (p.118). *Moccas Park, Herefordshire, August 1974* (photo G.H. Rackham).

Fig 37. Pollard hornbeam, originally freestanding, now surrounded by infill trees. *Hatfield Forest, Essex, August 2005.* See p.125.

Fig 38. Savanna of junipers, each with a circle of different, greener grass under it (p.124). *Davis Mountains, Texas, August 2003.*

Fig 39. Ancient oaks, each pollarded at several points, every four years or so, for leaves on which to feed sheep (p.125). Annual rings show that this practice goes back at least to the fifteenth century. *Near Grevená, north Greece, May 1988.*

Fig 40. Australian infilling (p.126). Savanna eucalypts, blackened at the base by grass fires, are surrounded by younger trees from advancing rainforest, probably because of fire suppression. *Kuranda, Queensland.*

Fig 41. Oak surrounded and overtopped by giant hollies. *Staverton Thicks, May 2003.* See p.128.

Fig 42. Prairies and motts near the scene of a Wild West gunfight (p.204). *Menard, Texas, January 1996.*

Fig 43. The oak that thinks it's a holly (p.127). *Staverton Park, April 2003.*

Fig 44. The wood anciently known as Skotítas (p.135). *Káryai (Arachova), Peloponnese, July 1985.*

Fig 45. A wood mentioned in an Anglo-Saxon charter: the bank that marks the boundary through what was then *Wulluht graf. Ufton Wood, Warwickshire. March 1990.* See p.99.

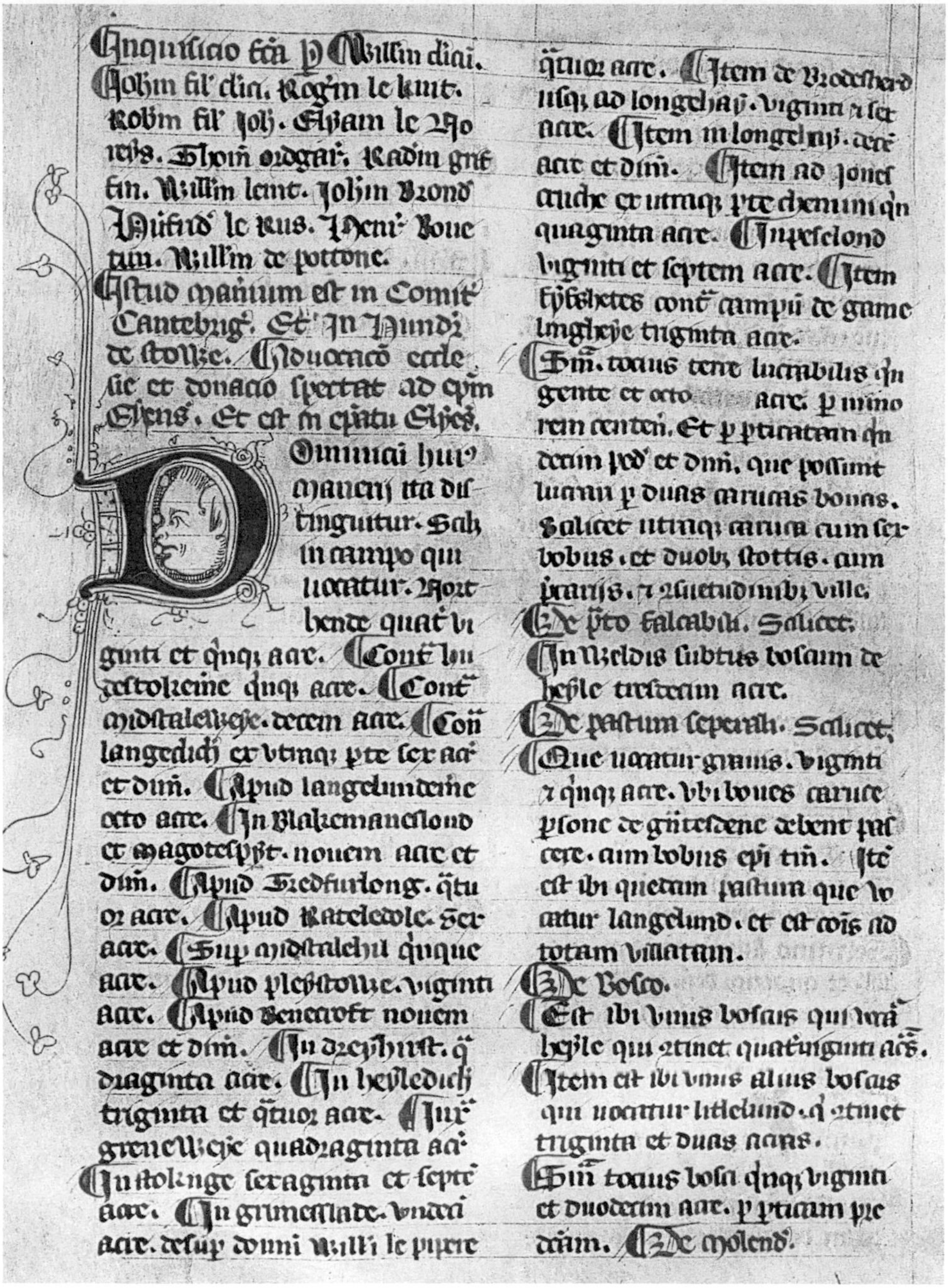

Fig 46. Part of the Ely Coucher Book entry relating to Little Gransden (p.139). Hayley and Litlelund woods are mentioned under the rubric *De Bosco* 'concerning the wood', bottom right. By permission of Gonville & Caius College, Cambridge, (ms 485/489).

Fig 47. Rising relative sea level in the Norfolk Broads brings fen woods within reach of high spring tides. *Surlingham Wood, October 1999*. See p.159.

Fig 48. 'Normal' woodbank with external ditch, exposed by coppicing. Note pollard tree. *Bradfield Woods, Suffolk, March 1997*. See p.160.

Fig 49. Bank round wood that was once a park, with internal ditch. *Monks' Park, Bradfield Woods, Suffolk, March 1997*.

Fig 50. Woodbank dated to 1297–8. *Hindolveston Wood, Norfolk, September 1994.* See p.161.

Fig 51. Nineteenth-century woodbank made when a wood was truncated (p.161). *North Elmham Great Wood, Norfolk, August 1969.*

Fig 52. A monks' woodbank, separating their wood from that of a secular landowner (left). *Chicksands Wood, Bedfordshire, March 1997.* See p.161.

Fig 53. Woodbank and wood-wall in France (p.164). *Le Bec-Hellouin, Normandy, July 1976.*

Fig 54. Tip-up mounds in America (p.164). *Alleghany Forest, Pennsylvania, April 1999.*

Fig 55. An unexplained woodland pond, with no corresponding bank. This pond contains a pollen deposit. *Chalkney Wood, Essex, April 2004.* See p.169.

Fig 56. Stump of oak felled 81 years ago (p.166). *Hatfield Forest, August 2005.*

Fig 57. A holloway (p.174): it divides the wood, with a woodbank on each side. *West Creech Great Wood, Dorset, June 2000.*

Fig 58. Flooded ridge-and-furrow. The ridges are seventeenth-, the woodland twentieth-century. *The Triangle, Hayley Wood, February 2001.* See p.198.

Fig 59. A Low-country limewood in the sixteenth century. Spot the oak, aspen, broom, elm, ivy, the pollard by the gate, male fern, shrubby honeysuckle *Lonicera xylosteum*, and the fungus *Oudemansiella radicata*. Where is the castle? © British Library, Add. ms 18855 f.108v. See p.187.

Fig 60. The other side of the page ('June'). Landscape and 'bushy-topped' trees are much less convincing in summer (p.187). © British Library, Add. ms 18855 f.108r.

Fig 61. *The Hunt of Maximilian*, tapestry, *c*.1500. An odd but possible landscape (p.188). © Musée du Louvre, Paris.

Fig 62. '*Cornard Wood*', by Thomas Gainsborough, *c.*1750. A Dutch wood pretending to be English? © National Gallery. See p.188.

Fig 63. *Salisbury Cathedral*, by John Constable, 1823. What are East Anglian elms doing here? © Victoria & Albert Museum, R.254. See p.189.

Fig 64. Hayley Wood in a very wet winter (p.198). *February 2001.*

Fig 65. Flush with alder and ramsons. *Chalkney Wood, Essex, May 1978.* See p.198.

Fig 66. Mediterranean savanna. The big tree (*Quercus macrolepis*) has roots still visible at the marker (arrow) and thus extending out for at least twice the radius of the branches (p.201). *Lésbos, Greece, September 2004.*

Fig 67. Ancient oaks clustered around a rock outcrop (p.202). (They are high-cut 'giraffe pollards'; they belonged to Queen Jane, and 'legend' has it that when she was beheaded in 1553 her oaks were beheaded in sympathy.) *Bradgate Park, Leicestershire, March 1995.*

Fig 68. Ancient stools: lime; note that the surrounding young trees are ash. *Groton Wood, Suffolk, March 2002.* See p.202.

Fig 69. Hornbeam; the diameter of the stool is about 1 ½ times the man's height. Hornbeam often does not form stools as well defined as here. *Blean Wood, The Blean, Kent, February 2000.*

imported much of its food, and grew most of its timber and wood within Italy.[12] Roman Britain, as far as we know, did all these things within its own resources. The magnitude of some industries implies very extensive coppicing.

What was to be England, in Roman times, could hardly have been as much as 20 per cent woodland (as wooded as France today); some would say less than 10 per cent. Most of that woodland was managed. As yet there is no means of locating the woods or relating them to the structure of wildwood. Probably there was much more woodland in what is now Ancient Countryside than in future Planned Countryside (p.102). It is possible that some medieval woods already existed, but there is no way to identify them.

Industrialisation

There have been wood-using industries since Neolithic times: some Somerset Levels trackways could have been built by trained carpenters. In the Middle Ages hurdles were usually made by specialists: there was a firm of hurdlemakers in the Hindolveston woods (Norfolk). Charcoal would have been made almost anywhere for local blacksmiths. As well as these dispersed, small-scale industries, there were heavy industries consuming enough wood to influence square miles of woodland.

The Romans had several such industries. Around Battle (Sussex) the iron industry appears to have produced 550 tons of iron a year in the period AD 120–240. If it took 12 tons of charcoal to make a ton of bar iron and 7 tons of wood to make a ton of charcoal, this would require 46,000 tons of wood a year, consuming the annual growth on about 23,000 acres (9,300 ha) of woodland. This calculation includes six out of the 36 Roman ironworking sites known in the Weald. The area of the Weald is 860,000 acres (348,000 ha). I guessed that in 1086 about 70 per cent of it was woodland, and at a further guess it was much the same in Roman times, giving 600,000 acres (242,800 ha) of woodland. The consumption figure may be an overestimate, for more recent experiments in making iron by Roman methods indicate a wood:iron ratio of 50:1 to 40:1.[13] Wealden woods would have been amply able to support the known Roman iron-smelting; and even with further charcoal needed to process the iron there would have been land left over to feed the labour force and the horses and oxen.

There were smaller iron industries in the Forest of Dean and elsewhere. Another calculation for the whole of Roman Britain is based on a population of 3.6 million using 3.3 lb (1.5 kg) of iron per head, that is 5,400 tons per year. At a ratio of charcoal to finished iron of 20:1 and a wood:charcoal ratio of 7:1, this gives 800,000 tons of wood per year, roughly equal to the annual growth on 400,000 acres (161,880 ha) of woodland. I suspect this is an underestimate (especially as regards population). The total area of England and Wales is 37 million acres (15 million ha), of which somewhat under 2 per cent would have been devoted to growing fuel for the iron industry, plus further land needed to support about 150,000 workmen and their families.[14] Although the total woodland area was probably much more than 2 per cent, it had to support several other industries as well as domestic uses. Roman woods are unlikely to have been over- or under-used.

ANGLO-SAXON WOODLAND

I was taught, following the traditional view, that the Romans 'made little impression upon the natural scene'. When their civilisation collapsed, most of the farmland was abandoned and reverted to woodland, from which the Anglo-Saxons slowly and laboriously carved out an independent cultural landscape. The 'colonisation of medieval England' continued even into the fifteenth century. If that were true, digging up trees should have been one of the best-known activities with which medieval men occupied their time. Familiarity with medieval documents showed that this was not so: there were records of *assarts*, farmland won from roughland, but most were of only an acre or two and some were from heathland or wood-pasture rather than woodland. The study of Domesday Book backdated the question to an earlier period: nine-tenths of the task had been accomplished before 1086.

Did Anglo-Saxons, then, spend two or three hours every day getting rid of trees? The entire corpus of Old English writing makes no direct mention of woodland being destroyed. No charter refers to land newly won from woodland; no boundary includes 'the site of the wood that Æthelstan grubbed up'. The earliest records describe a cultural landscape already fully developed, with no suggestion that it was rapidly changing. That is not to say that woodland was never grubbed, but the inference is inescapable that Anglo-Saxons took over a previous landscape as a going concern.

This is supported by the pollen record and archaeology. Woodland certainly increased locally after the Roman period, for example on the site of Stansted Airport (p.180). But there is no sign of a general or overwhelming increase. The excellent record for Diss Mere shows a small increase of hazel and birch. At Quidenham Mere, only 7 miles (11 kilometres) away, but lying outside the organised field system around Diss, the main clearance phase seems to have been as late as the end of the Roman period.* An increase could occur well into the Anglo-Saxon period, as in Oxfordshire.[15]

Names of settlements give some indication of where early woodland was. I ignore 'wood' (as in Brentwood) because it has a very wide range of date and gives no indication of the amount of woodland. Useful names are those of settlements in -leah ('wood' or 'clearing', as in Rayleigh or Leigh-on-Sea), -hyrst (similar, as in Crowhurst), the Norse equivalent – þveit (as in Bassenthwaite), and -feld ('open place in sight of woodland', as in Bradfield). These are prevalent in areas where there was later much woodland, as in the Weald and south Lake District; they are rare in most of the future Planned Countryside. Kent – then as now – combined much woodland and a dense population, and is particularly rich in woodland place-names.[16]

The Anglo-Saxons, being fewer and far less industrialised than the Romans, would have used the woods less intensively, but did not allow them to spread far. Roman roads are an indication of the continuity of infrastructure, for they could not survive in disuse. Main roads, maybe, were kept open by the much reduced populations of the cities at either end. More significant are the Roman roads that survive in part: they ceased to be through routes, but there was still a local population that kept them up, year after year, as lanes between farms and hamlets.

Anglo-Saxon and early Welsh perambulations (p.136) are the earliest documents to describe the landscape and to locate woodland. Already in the eighth century there were no vast and vaguely defined tracts of wildwood; there were wood-lots with owners and names of their own. Their boundaries were often marked by a linear feature called a wyrtwala 'root-bank' or wyrtruma. Something like one wood in four is still there, for example Ufton Wood (Warwickshire) (Fig. 45).

The division between the future Ancient and Planned Countryside is well marked in Anglo-Saxon charters, usually in features not directly related to woodland: hedges, open-field features, species of non-woodland trees. Woodland itself is more commonly mentioned in Ancient Countryside and often absent in future Planned Countryside, as in the Wiltshire chalklands and south-east Warwickshire.

The division between wooded and less wooded parts of England was established

---

* Neither mere has sediments suitable for radiocarbon dating, but the Roman period can be identified with certainty because it comes just before the first appearance of pollen of Cannabis, a specifically Anglo-Saxon crop.

in or before the Roman period. In the more wooded parts the Anglo-Saxons took over Roman clearings and called them leys and hursts; later they may have made clearings of their own, but did not radically alter the distribution. In less wooded parts they probably conserved such woodland as there was. It was in those less wooded parts, with little room for expansion, that the Anglo-Saxons reorganised the cultural landscape by setting up open-field strips and by aggregating the earlier hamlets into villages.

What the Anglo-Saxons did with woodland is less well documented. The distinction between woodland and wood-pasture already existed. Some places possessed woodland at a distance, especially in the Weald where such detached wood-lots appear to have been mainly used for feeding pigs. As woodland specialists, they had at least ten words for different kinds of woodland (p.138). Charters mention various kinds of coppice products, charcoal, and woodland designated for fuel for salt-boiling. Woods were valuable property and could be the subject of lawsuits.[17]

DOMESDAY BOOK

William the Conqueror's great survey of 1086 is a vast and mysterious record of land use throughout England, except the four northern counties and parts of the Welsh border. England then was not a very wooded land, even by twentieth-century standards. Only half the 12,580 recorded settlements possessed woods. Woodland was a common, but by no means essential, asset of an eleventh-century estate.[18]

For more than half the country Domesday gives the sizes of woods, and thus roughly their areas (p.140). For Eastern England woods are assessed in terms of the number of pigs they were supposed to feed, an unsatisfactory statistic that can be turned into areas only very approximately. For the southeast there is a still more nebulous assessment in swine-rents. Very seldom does Domesday name woods or say how many woods a place had.

The total area amounted to 15 per cent of the country. England thus had about twice as much tree cover (woodland, plantation, wood-pasture and non-woodland trees) as it has now. It was rather less wooded in Domesday Book than France is now. I first did the calculation 25 years ago;[19] it has not been seriously challenged, though I suspect the figure of 15 per cent is a little too high.

Woodland was very unevenly distributed, as it is in France today (Fig. 176). The biggest concentration was in the Weald and the second biggest in the Chiltern plateau. Near Wolverhampton there was a tract of woodland some 15 miles (25 kilometres) across, though it had settlements within it. Larger areas of the east Midlands, Breckland, Fens, and east Yorkshire had no woodland at all. Elsewhere islands of woodland were scattered among farmland. Wood-lots ranged in size from 38 square miles (the future Cannock Chase, Staffordshire) to many of less than an acre.

The three distributions of woodland – from place-names, charters and Domesday – record its distribution early in the Anglo-Saxon period, later in the period, and just after its end. On the whole they are consistent, and point to the Anglo-Saxon as a period of general stability. They all independently make the distinction that later developed into Ancient versus Planned Countryside. Documents fail to mention people digging up trees because they did not often do it.

In 1086 the future Ancient Countryside had well over twice as much woodland in relation to its area as Planned Countryside. The two tracts differ. The southeastern tract, containing both the Weald and Chilterns, was one-quarter woodland; the northwestern tract only one-sixth. Much of the difference is due to the moorland in the northwestern tract. If moorland is excluded, Ancient Countryside had three times as much woodland in 1086 as Planned.

For Lincolnshire, Nottinghamshire and Derbyshire, Domesday separates coppice-woods from wood-pasture. Coppices tend to be smaller, and add up to 2 per cent of the total area of each county. This suggests that people encoppiced as much woodland as they needed and let the rest go to wood-pasture. Most of the 'woodland' area would thus have been wood-pasture, except in densely populated or sparsely wooded counties such as Cambridgeshire and west Suffolk.

Domesday says little about the composition of woods, though it occasionally mentions spinneys and carrs (woods of thorn or alder), and rarely oakwoods or willow-woods. It refers to industrial woods, such as those supplying the saltworks at Droitwich (Worcestershire) and Northamptonshire ironworks. It never mentions individual trees.

Domesday Book compared with modern figures
The earliest reliable county figures are for 1895 (Table 11). Most counties had more woodland in 1086 than 1895: Worcestershire had nine times as much. Leicestershire and Herefordshire, however, had not much more, and Devon apparently had less woodland in 1086. Generally regions with much woodland in 1086 lost more of it than regions that had little. Exceptions were the Weald and Chiltern plateau, which remain well wooded even now, although the woods are now less

continuous. All England in 1086 had three times as much woodland as in 1895. The distinction between Ancient and Planned Countryside was still very marked in 1895, although the former had lost more woodland than the latter. The 1895 statistics, however, include plantations, by then not much less in area than natural woodland.

Comparing the 1086 figures with the area recorded as Ancient Woodland in the late twentieth century, between one-fifth and one-sixth of the Domesday woodland apparently survived until the 1930s, but only one-tenth was still intact (not grubbed or replanted) by 1990. (Most of the change was in the Locust Years 1950–75, p.60.) The distinction between Ancient and Planned Countryside is still visible; losses since 1950 have been greatest in Planned Countryside.

The survival rate is somewhat exaggerated, because figures for Ancient Woodland include woods originating between 1086 and c.1600; this, however, is offset by the inclusion as Intact of some woods that were successfully replanted before 1930. Losses since 1930 are overestimated, because much of the loss was to replanting, some of which is reversible (p.378ff).

AFTER DOMESDAY

After Domesday Book comes an active but poorly documented period, sparsely illuminated by charters and land-grants in monastic archives. When systematic documentation reappears in the mid-thirteenth century, much of the change to the modern distribution had already happened. Something like half the woodland of 1086 had turned into farmland or heath.

Under the rising population after 1086, farmland expanded to its sustainable limits and beyond. New land was won not only from the less-used woodland, but also from heath, mountain and the Fens (helped by low relative sea level). Most of the woodland on what is now Stansted Airport was assarted by the monks of Colchester Abbey and their neighbours (p.179). (For examples in Dorset see p.390.) Grazing animals might turn wood-pasture into heath by preventing the trees from replacing themselves, as in Thorpe Wood, whose owner, the Bishop of Norwich, could not prevent it from turning into Mousehold Heath in the twelfth century.[20] The few woods in southeast Warwickshire were more often conserved than the extensive woodland in northwest Warwickshire.[21]

Pressure on land also advanced the conservation and encoppicement of the remaining woodland. Woodland in formerly well-wooded areas became more intensively used and acquired scarcity value.

The change from wood-pasture or mere pannage to coppices sometimes came later in northern England.[22] Growing industries of iron-smelting and ironworking maintained concentrations of coppice-woods. The growth of London as a market for fuel and timber came too late to save the great woods of Middlesex, but it did maintain an outer ring of woods in the northern Weald, Kent, Chiltern plateau and Essex. (Most of the woods of north and middle Surrey, however, are recent.) Paris, likewise, developed a system of supply and transport from distant woodland.[23]

Norwich Cathedral Priory owned two woods at Hindolveston, north Norfolk. In 1272 the monks contrived to sell £214-worth of timber at once, a vast quantity. They needed the money because they had been sacked and burnt by the revolting townspeople (the fire-reddened stonework is still visible inside the Cathedral). In subsequent years they converted the woods to produce income from underwood rather than capital gains from timber. This involved especially attending to boundaries and security, and building woodbanks (p.159ff). This was a considerable capital expense, roughly one-quarter of the cost of a great barn.

LATER STABILITY AND CHANGE

By 1250 woods in England were fully developed. They had names, ownerships, boundaries and regular management, which were to remain for the next 700 years (Figs 177 & 179). Not that woodland was static: some woods were extended or curtailed, with new boundary earthworks recording the changes. Woods were grubbed out; new woods were formed as farmland or heath was abandoned. Even the many woods that did not change in extent had coppice cycles lengthened, rides cut through them, species added or subtracted, wild oaks replaced with planted oaks, and doubtless changed in other ways of which there is no record. Even if the underwood was more or less regularly cut, timber trees might be allowed to accumulate and then be suddenly felled to meet some disaster or to supply a big building project. However, all these are changes of detail, rather than affecting the continuity of the wood. Two big groups of woods illustrate some of the vicissitudes.

The Bury Abbey woods[24]
The great Abbey of Bury St Edmunds was endowed by Anglo-Saxon kings with about 221 estates: about half of West Suffolk, extensive tracts of northeast Suffolk and southeast Norfolk, and a few outliers. Of these estates 100 are known to have

had woodland, recorded by Domesday Book in terms of swine. Of the others, 23 were in the woodless Breckland, and many others were very small. Where there was woodland in 1086, in 34 places it is not heard of again, and in two more it is not heard of after 1200 (Fig. 178).

The distribution of places that lost woodland is not random. In Norfolk and east Suffolk half the estates that had woodland in 1086 lost it by the later Middle Ages. The bigger woods disappeared: Mendham, with the biggest swine-entry of the Bury estates in Suffolk, is not heard of again. Chippenhall, the second biggest, is not heard of after the twelfth century; its ghost may, however, still be there as Chippenhall Green, now a splendid old grassland. In west Suffolk, however, only 11 out of 51 Domesday wooded places lost their woodland. A pattern emerges: the nearer a wood was to the Abbey the more likely it was to survive.

Maybe the monks had a deliberate policy of conserving the nearer woods and letting their tenants grub or graze away the more distant ones. The Abbey itself was a large user of wood and timber. Coppice-woods were becoming more valuable than arable land, and there were markets for timber and underwood in Bury and other west Suffolk towns, in the nearby woodless Breckland, and in the expanding economy of the woodless Fens. A hint of this is in a dozen places in west Suffolk where woodland is known to have existed, but is either not recorded in Domesday or gets a disproportionately small swine-entry. It is hardly credible that these woods came into existence between 1086 and 1250, especially as the Bradfield Woods, for example, contain no archaeological evidence of this. Probably they had already been encoppiced and were not used for swine; and since the form used by the Suffolk enumerators had no box for coppice-woods they were left out.

At the Dissolution in 1538 the Abbey owned about 150 separate woods. Some 17 woods (or the equivalent in fractions of woods) were destroyed between 1538 and 1700; about 30 in the eighteenth century; about 23 in the nineteenth (Fig. 180). Very little was lost between 1900 and 1950. Between 1950 and 1975 nearly one-third of the remaining woods (by number) were grubbed or replanted. About 38 appear to survive today either intact or coniferised, with fragments of a dozen others. Compared to other Abbey possessions, the woods have survived relatively well, but big woods have fared worse, especially in the twentieth century. In 1538 the Abbey had 13 woods of more than 100 acres; by 1950 six were still reasonably intact; today the only intact survivor is Felshamhall Wood (Bradfield Woods), nearly the smallest of the 13.

The Bishop of Ely's woods[25]

The endowment of St Etheldreda's Abbey at Ely was on a similar scale to Bury, with about 225 estates, comprising most of the Isle of Ely, much of the Breckland and Norfolk Fens, and outliers extending into Hertfordshire and Essex. Only 52 of these estates had woodland in 1086. When the Pope founded Ely diocese in 1109, the endowment was split between the Bishop and the Abbey. The Bishop got 58 estates, but these included most of the bigger ones and those with woodland.

The Ely Coucher Book of 1251 (p.140) records existing woods, and former woodland as assarts and as fields called *Stocking* (a place of 'stocks' or tree-stumps). On the estates round Somersham (Huntingdonshire), where the Bishop had a Forest (p.120), about 900 acres (364 ha) of woodland remained in 1251; stockings and assarts add up to 389 acres (157 ha) of arable land, whereas the Bishop's arable land not remembered as former woodland came to 530 acres (214 ha). The general impression is that wooded estates lost about one-third of their woodland between c.1000 and 1251, whereas woodless estates (with rare exceptions) had no memory of former woodland. The pattern of survival is concentrated on Cambridge, not Ely.

After 1251 the rate of destruction slowed. The survey ordered by the king in 1356, when the Bishop was wanted for murder (p.141), generally records much the same woodland as in 1251.

Of 49 woods in the Ely Coucher Book, about 17 still survive as a whole or in substantial part, plus fragments, especially boundaries, of others. Big woods and especially common-woods disappeared: only two of the survivors, Hayley Wood and Bonny Wood (Barking, Suffolk), are bigger than 100 acres (40 ha). Six Coucher Book woods are nature reserves or belong to the Woodland Trust.

Industries

This pattern of slow attrition of woodland, but only minor changes in the woods that survived, is probably typical of areas with relatively little woodland and only 'domestic' uses of woods. Heavy industries bring booms and busts into the picture: the rise and collapse of an industry both have to be considered.

In the Middle Ages some industries operated at a similar scale to those of Roman Britain. Baths and hypocausts were forgotten; bricks and glass were being rediscovered; but the population was on a similar scale, and presumably dropped pots and wore away ploughshares at a similar rate. Ironworking was mainly in three of the biggest concentrations of woodland: the Weald, Forest of Dean and southern Lake District.

It used to be claimed that industries caused 'deforestation' – converting forest to non-forest. This rests on three misapprehensions: that fuel-using industries burnt timber; that they made no provision for future fuel supplies; and that trees once felled never grew again. Timber (p.17) can, at a pinch, be used as a fuel or made into charcoal, but it would not chark all the way through unless laboriously chopped into billets. (The wages of charcoal-burners often came to more than the cost of trees or of felling them.) Here, as ever, the shoots from a stump were more useful than the original tree. Then as now, an industry was an investment in buildings, furnaces, equipment, manpower, horses etc., not to be jeopardised by letting the fuel supply run out. Industries tended to settle in large areas of woodland because charcoal is fragile and more difficult to transport than other raw materials.

The chemical reaction of converting iron ore to iron

$$2Fe_2O_3 + 3C = 4Fe + 3CO_2$$

calls for only one-sixth of a ton of carbon to make a ton of iron; the rest of the charcoal is spent in creating the high temperature needed, and can be saved by more economical furnace design. By 1550 England was said to produce about 5,000 tons of iron a year, much as in Roman times, but the wood: iron ratio was reduced to 30:1. This would be roughly equivalent to the annual wood yield from 75,000 acres (300 square kilometres) of woodland (on the basis that no timber was being grown). By 1700 production increased to 24,000 tons a year, but improved blast furnaces used wood at about 18:1, so the woodland needed was 220,000 acres (900 square kilometres), about one-seventh of all the woodland in England.[26]

Industrial and domestic uses clashed, since industrialists, with many bigger bills to pay than that for trees, could buy up woods at prices that domestic users could not afford. By the fifteenth century, most of the woods around Sheffield were producing charcoal, much of it for making blades and nails. Even into the nineteenth century charcoal was used for making the best steel.[27]

London depended on a great ring of woods outside its agricultural and market-gardening belt. On the south side, approaching the Weald, the conflict with the expanding iron industry became an affair of state, in which a statute of 1580 tried to prevent ironworks from using charcoal made within 22 miles (35 kilometres) of outer London.

Another clash was with the Cornish tin industry. Tin was more economical of fuel than iron, and less particular about which fuel, although charcoal was preferred. A ton of tin called for roughly ten tons of wood, and at its peak, c.1700, the Cornish tin industry would have been using about 15,000 tons of wood a year or its equivalent. Although this should have been within the capacity of the 30,000 acres (12,000 ha) of wood in Cornwall, these woods were already fully used, and as the industry moved westward from Dartmoor to Land's End it bought up the meagre local woods. Around the Helford River:

... their few parcels [of woodland] *yet preserved are principally employed to coaling, for blowing of tin. This lack* [of domestic fuel] *they supply either by stone coal fetched out of Wales, or by dried turfs.*
R. CAREW, *THE SURVEY OF CORNWALL*, 1602

The port of Gweek, in the midst of the Helford River woods, was importing charcoal.[28]

Industrialists expanded into Wales, Scotland and even Ireland, not because they had destroyed the woods of England, but because they were expanding production. In Wales a sixteenth-century bard denounced the felling of the great wood Coed Glyn Cynon in the area later to be Merthyr Tydfil and Aberdare, where an iron industry was expanding.[29]

SCOTLAND

The owners and occupiers of land are often averse to give correct statistics on a matter which might afterwards affect their interests.
A.E. SMITH ON THE BOARD OF TRADE, 1874 (CITED BY T.C. SMOUT *et al.*, 2004)

Scotland is another country, and even the nature of woodland is not the same as in England. Woods less consistently have sharp edges. Pinewoods and birchwoods have a history of moving about within the same general area, but even the oakwoods were often not sharply demarcated from moorland.

In the post-medieval period, coppicing seems not to have been universal, developing chiefly through the influence of industries. Banks and walls around woods were apparently made from the seventeenth to the nineteenth century where there had previously been no fixed boundary.

At the same time, many woods were used as pasture and shelter for livestock (p.296). This must mean that the trees were not continuous but widely spaced enough to allow a worthwhile growth of grasses and other edible plants between them: they would thus have counted as wood-pasture rather than woodland.

This emerges from the researches of Professor Smout and his colleagues for the period after 1590.[30] Whether it is also true of the Middle Ages is less clear. As in England, many medieval Scots consumed timber and underwood, and (especially in the Lowlands) would have had cause to conserve the sources. However, Scotland had more alternatives, especially coal and peat. Even timber did not have to come from trees; it could be imported from Scandinavia, or dug up as fossil 'bog fir' from peat, or picked up on Hebridean beaches having drifted from an unknown western continent.

Industrialisation spread to Scotland. Greedy or impoverished lairds began leasing woods to optimistic English and Irish capitalists for various industries. Ironworks were among the most successful, beginning at remote Loch Maree in 1611. One of the latest and longest lived, the huge Lorn Furnace at Bonawe in Argyll, opened in 1752 and drew its supplies from oakwoods within a 50-mile (80-kilometre) radius, mostly by sea (which made transporting charcoal easier).

Decline was not, as many writers have assumed, due to English or Irish tree-fellers. On the contrary, the woods that were exploited are, for the most part, those that are still there: the disappearances were among those woods not known to have been exploited. In the post-medieval period conservation practices, such as keeping livestock out of woods after felling, were practised only sporadically unless there was a prospect that the wood might have more than a local commercial value.

In 1750, according to Smout, woodland occupied nearly 10 per cent of Scotland, falling to 3 per cent by 1900 (excluding plantations). I suspect that the former figure stretches to the limit everything that could come within the elastic Scottish definition of woodland, including scattered trees and bitten-down bushes. On this basis, the survival rate of Scottish woodland was less than in England, but more than in Ireland.

I agree with Smout in attributing the disappearance of Scottish woodland to these causes:

- Continuing natural succession from woodland to peatland in the Holocene.
- Increased grazing pressure in the nineteenth century: the substitution of multitudes of sheep for modest numbers of cattle and goats.
- Human depopulation, reducing the motive to conserve.
- Short-cycle burning on grouse moors, restricting the scope of birch and pine to move around.
- Encroachment by modern forestry, turning woods into plantations.
- Twentieth-century proliferation of deer.

None of these processes was uniform. It would be worth studying what happened to woodland in glens that escaped Highland Clearances, or on estates that promoted grouse versus deer.

IRELAND

The Old Irish texts, according to Professor F.S. Kelly, nowhere suggest that there were large areas of unused woodland in medieval Ireland. The impression is of a wood-based economy, using many smallish woods. The few medieval surveys and cartularies do not suggest much woodland.

The Irish Civil Survey of 1654 gives areas of thousands of woods, located by townland (subdivision of a parish) but seldom named. The published volumes of the Survey cover just over half of Ireland, in which the woodland adds up to 2.7 per cent of the land area (Table 12). In an earlier version of this calculation I added in seven more counties with no published volumes, but for which Eileen McCracken, Irish woodland historian, cited woodland areas from Survey manuscripts. All these counties had 1 per cent of woodland or less, making the recorded total for Ireland 2.1 per cent of the land area.[31]

I now think that McCracken's figures are much too low (even though she maintained that Ireland had much more woodland than this). Her counties include Offaly and Leix, for which a famous map of 1562, although small-scale and vague, shows them to have been well wooded;[32] and Kerry, which now has the biggest concentration of ancient woodland in Ireland. For nearly one-third of Ireland the Civil Survey seems not to survive at all; this includes what were probably the well-wooded counties of Wicklow and Fermanagh.

I conclude that the Civil Survey information is somewhat biased towards poorly wooded counties by the survival of the data. Allowing for this, the true total in the 1650s is likely to have been somewhat higher, perhaps 3.5 per cent. Ireland would still have been less wooded than England at the time.

What happened to the Irish woods? By c.1845, when the Ordnance Survey mapped every wood in Ireland, the woodland area was down to 1.5 per cent (albeit probably with a restrictive definition of woodland: see the Eagle's Rock story, p.297). However, most of these woods were in different places. It is remarkably difficult to identify the same wood in the Civil Survey and the Ordnance Survey, less than 200 years apart. (Would it be easier if the Wicklow and Kerry data had survived?)

Sir Walter Raleigh, who had lifted some lands with the sword from the great Desmond Estate, commissioned a map of Mogeely, on the Cork–Waterford border, in 1598: an exceptional map, drawn to English standards of cartography, with the boundaries of every wood (Fig. 34). It was an agricultural countryside, with no visible bogs or mountain, big enclosed and named fields, and the remains of a big deer-park. About one-fifth of the land shown is woodland. Unknown to the cartographer, it was a land of ancient agriculture: there are several raths (Iron Age farmsteads) in the area mapped.

By 1844 there was a remarkable transformation. Nearly all the woods had vanished; so had most of the infrastructure. It had become a landscape of small fields and a few small woods (with un-Irish names like Belvidere Wood). There is little correspondence in the location, and none in the boundaries, of woods between 1598 and 1844. Only the main road and the village of Curraglass remained to identify the spot, together with the river Bride (which had lost its islands) and the church (in ruins).

One should not make too much of one map, although it is said to be the only surviving map of its type. If it is representative, then Irish woods were victims of a huge reorganisation of landscape, probably in the eighteenth century, without parallel either in England at the time or in Ireland since. In Ancient Countryside in England the infrastructure, including the woods, changed little from 1598 to 1844 (see Fig. 177); even if woods were grubbed out they usually left ghost outlines (p.27) in the hedges. In Planned Countryside the woods usually survived even if the infrastructure did not (see Fig. 179).

On the 1598 map the woods are not defined wood-lots, but patches of wood within fields, rambling inconsequentially from field to field. (None appears to contain a rath.) Was this a landscape of decline, with no longer enough people to hold back the trees? If the Irish woods of the 1650s were in part relatively recent, the result of a century of sword, pestilence and famine, they might have been destroyed without much comment when prosperity returned. Not being demarcated from fields, they would have disappeared without even a ghost remaining.

EIGHTEENTH- AND NINETEENTH-CENTURY INFLUENCES

Alternative energy

In 1550 the woods were fully used: industries like Wealden iron and glass, and cities like London and Canterbury, had come to terms with their local woodland. Where did energy and timber come from to supply the huge later expansion of population and industry?

Coal had been used since Roman times. By the Middle Ages most surface coalfields were being worked, and coal was preferred for certain trades. When Edward I was building great castles in North Wales in the 1290s he first needed limekilns: although there was plenty of local wood he shipped coal from distant mines.

Coal was cheaper in labour costs. A miner was reckoned to raise about 250 tons of coal a year, about a ton per working day. A woodcutter would find it difficult to produce a ton of made-up wood a day from the tree to the roadside: this would be equivalent in heat produced to at most half a ton of coal, in practice less because of the water content of wood. The difference in labour cost paid for long-distance transport. Coal was cheap even at a distance.

In 1550 the population of London was about 90,000. Most of their domestic and industrial fuel came from the ring of woodland 20–40 miles (30–60 kilometres) out. They were using about one-fifth of a ton of coal per head per year, shipped 300 miles (500 kilometres) from northeast England. Fifty years later, the population had roughly doubled, and so had the fuel consumption. The woods were producing roughly the same, but coal consumption had risen to about three-quarters of a ton per head per year.

England has an area of 30 million acres (12 million ha). In 1700 about 1.8 million acres (730,000 ha) were woodland. If those woods yielded 2 tons of dry biomass per acre per year, half of which was used for fuel and half for timber and other purposes, this would make 1.8 million tons of dry wood fuel per year, equivalent to 0.9 million tons of coal per year. The actual coal production was at least 1.2 million tons per year. The calorific value of the coal consumed in England had overtaken that of wood in the mid- to late seventeenth century – 200 years before the United States reached that point. By 1815 England was digging 22.6 million tons of coal a year, more (it is said) than all the rest of the world, equivalent to nearly 50 million tons of wood, the annual production of woodland as big as the whole of Great Britain.[33]

As E.J.T. Collins points out, industrial use of wood fuel in Britain declined uniquely early. Charcoal iron production in England peaked at about 25,000 tons a year in the 1750s, but in the United States rose to 680,000 tons in 1890, and in the one state of Michigan to 300,000 tons in 1907. This is to do with England having more expensive labour, worse ores, and competition from coal.[34]

De-industrialisation

The thesis that woods were destroyed by heavy industries cannot be sustained. On the contrary, wherever there remained a big concentration of woodland, there is an industrial or urban use to account for its preservation. It was the 'unexploited' woods that disappeared from the map.

Industries, however, are liable to sudden death through technological change or foreign competition, leaving their woods unemployed. In Cornwall the woods, when the tinners had finished with them, reverted to domestic use, leaving charcoal-hearths (p.166ff) as witnesses to their industrial phase.

Disused industrial woods could pass to other industries. Northern and western coppiced oakwoods were taken over by an expansion in leather-tanning, which used bark and could be combined with other industries using the wood. Others produced pit-props for holding up the roofs of coal mines. The Chiltern woods, as the London market for billets and charcoal declined, were gradually taken over by a mechanised furniture industry (p.284). So thoroughly were they converted from coppice and pollarded wood-pasture to timber production that by the nineteenth century this was regarded as the normal state of a beechwood. The rise of shipbuilding (p.57) would have found a use for the oaks no longer wanted through the decline of timber-framed building.

Specialised underwood trades expanded, especially in southern England, to take advantage of increasing markets for mass-produced hop-poles, barrel-hoops, and other industrial, agricultural and domestic artefacts; this was probably related to the replacement of mixed underwood by chestnut (p.287). Indeed, Collins has termed this 'the golden age of English woodlands'.

The decline of industries left woodland open to destruction. Coed Glyn Cynon (p.107) was still very much alive in the 1810s, when again there were complaints that its valleys had been 'stripped of their grown timber'. After the iron industry had died, it seems to have produced pit-props and then passed to modern forestry, which lasted for only one generation of planted trees. On the Ordnance Survey of c.1870 the South Welsh valleys were still one of the biggest wooded areas in the British Isles; by 1950 the woods had faded away, mostly into moorland. In Kent and Sussex, although there is still plenty of woodland left, much was grubbed out in the nineteenth century, the golden age of hop growing. Elsewhere, woods were saved by agricultural recession and fell into disuse or were used as pheasant shoots, until the great onslaught of the 1950s (p.60).

CONCLUSIONS

Woodland is not wildwood. What wildwood was like in the pre-Neolithic (Peterken's 'past-natural' state) is open to interpretation. What it would be like by now had human activity remained at a Mesolithic level (the 'present-natural' state) is open to conjecture. What present woodland would develop into in future if human activity were to be withdrawn (the 'future-natural' state) is open to hypothesis.

Turning wildwood into woodland involved at least the following processes:

- Fragmenting continuous forest (on the Tansley model) or stopping the dynamics of groves (on the Vera model).
- Instituting coppicing and the production of small timber trees.
- Giving woods boundaries, ownerships and names.
- Withdrawing browsing.
- Selecting guilds of plants that take advantage of cyclical changes in shade.

These are not recent events; woods have had an appreciable fraction of the Holocene in which to come to terms with them. Some aspects, such as the removal of upstanding old trees and large deadwood (apart from boundary pollards) have presumably reduced the fauna and flora of the wildwood, though wood-pasture gives an alternative means of survival. However, woodmanship is an ecological factor in its own right, just as mowing is the defining factor in meadows.

Coppicing has produced several guilds of plants that respond to it (p.211ff). Where did these come from? What were they doing before people invented axes? Neither Vera's nor Tansley's theory of wildwood seems to provide for large temporary openings every 7 to 30 years.

Fire, where it is possible, stimulates the germination of buried-seed plants, but woods with coppicing floras tend not to be combustible, least of all in England. Alternative natural processes are avalanches, windblow, beaver activity and ice-storms; although some of these can stimulate buried-seed plants like coppicing,[35] they are too sporadic in time or too limited in space to be a prototype of coppicing. Are trees and woodland plants still conditioned to some factor from previous interglacials that no longer operates?

CHAPTER 6

OF WOOD-PASTURE AND SAVANNA

While [the wood] *is Inclosed the Commoners & Sharers can have no benefit by the feeding therein Except it be by reaping the Grass & carrying it away in Baggs wch would be a great hindrance to them in neglect of Business of greater Weight. ... Except it be a poor Body that hath nothing else to do ... and he perhaps may lye in a Copice reaping grass a whole day together.*
ABELL HURLEY, REPORTING ON HATFIELD FOREST, 1612[1]
[In this compartmental Forest, each coppice was fenced for nine years every time it was cut, which the holders of common-rights regarded as a grievance. Note the grassy vegetation, typical of grazed woods (p.215f).]

Wood-pasture is a neglected biome. The eighteenth-century Age of Reason decreed that trees belong in forests and grassland on farms; tree'd grassland was ignored by foresters as not being forest, by agronomists as not being grassland, and by ecologists as an artificial ecosystem beneath their notice. But it is of immense historical and ecological importance. On the Vera model (p.79), pre-Neolithic wildwood had more in common with savanna than with modern forestry. Are people's love of parkland, and their edginess about entering woodland, relics of the human species' origin in African savannas? Most 'common-or-garden' birds – robin, blackbird, rook, starling – are more at home in savanna (or edges of woods) than forest; countless butterflies,[2] hoverflies and bees require some combination of trees and non-tree vegetation.

Wood-pasture exists in many European countries, although compartmentation seems to be an English refinement. In Spain the various types of *monte* (conifer forest, coppice-wood, maquis etc.) contrast with what academic writers call *dehesa,* grassland bright with spring flowers, interspersed with millions of pollard evergreen oaks, grazed by merino sheep, fierce with brave bulls, and grunting with the viper-fed pigs that turn into fine hams. The Romans distinguished between *silua* (woodland) and *saltus* (savanna).[3] In the Old Testament, Absalom, riding hastily off a battlefield, came to a sticky end when his head caught in the boughs of a low oak (or was it a terebinth?), 'and the mule that was under him went away'[4] – as once nearly befell the author in the Wild West.

In other continents tree'd grassland or savanna forms a wide transition zone between forest and prairie or steppe. European explorers of North America found mainly forest in the east, mainly prairie west of the Mississippi, and between them such formations as the Oak Openings of Michigan and the Post-Oak Savanna of Texas. Africa is a land of tropical forests and savannas. In Australia, various densities of savanna cover half the entire continent, between the rather limited extent of forest and the central desert.

Ecologists, obsessed with 'wholly natural' vegetation uncontaminated by human influence, have tried to distinguish the savannas of other continents from the wood-pastures of Europe. The former were supposed to be 'natural': some influence, especially drought or fire, allows trees but not forests to grow, in contrast to the tree'd grasslands of Europe, maintained by domestic live-stock. However, this is partly a false distinction, and it is impossible to draw a line between them. Savannas in North America were largely maintained by Native Americans' land management, which involved periodic burning. In Australia the ecology of an entire continent has been altered, ever since the last ice age, by Aboriginal land management involving particular burning regimes. Tree'd grasslands are the result of various limiting factors – drought, fire, cold (as at high altitudes), natural or artificial grazing. The savannas of other continents are part of a continuum that passes gradually into the uncom-partmented wood-pastures of Europe. The relation of savanna to drought is discussed later (p.201).

WOOD-PASTURES IN BRITAIN AND IRELAND

In England, wood-pastures and woodland presumably go back far beyond writ-ten record, either to the Vera model of wildwood or to the Neolithic beginnings of livestock keeping.

Wooded commons

The earliest allusions to common woods or wooded commons are in Anglo-Saxon charters; there is nothing to suggest that they were then new. By 1086 they seem to have been the predominant type of 'woodland'.

Like commons in general, wood-pastures had a characteristic straggling shape, with concave outlines, different from the more compact shape of woods (p.159). Houses – the dwellings of some of the commoners – fronted on the common and backed on to their private land.

Commons in theory belonged to the lord of the manor. They were regulated by manorial courts, staffed by the body of commoners, which made and enforced regulations for their use. Thus they did not incur the 'Tragedy of the Commons': the theory that communal land uses are not sustainable because each of the participants will exceed his rights to the detriment of the commoners in general.*

Wooded commons were only part of commons in general. They could lose their trees and still remain commons; as when Thorpe Wood, Norwich turned into Mousehold Heath (p.102). Conversely, a woodless common could gain trees in a period of slack grazing. Like other commons they could be privatised – by agreement among the parties or by Act of Parliament – and turned into ordinary farmland. Or the lord of the manor and the commoners could agree to divide the common between them (p.158).

Wood-pasture commons having ancient trees include Burnham Beeches (Buckinghamshire), Ashtead Common (Surrey) (Fig. 181) and The Mens (West Sussex). Hampshire is noted for wooded commons. Many, such as Southampton Common, have become wooded comparatively recently, but others have ancient pollards, such as Gosport Common. A curious one is Binswood, still grazed and having the characteristic shape of a common with funnel-like entrance horns (p.159), but enclosed within the outline of a somewhat larger medieval park.[5]

Parks

Wood-pasture gained a new impetus from the husbandry of deer as semi-domestic animals. The practice was known to the ancient Romans,[6] but there is no telling whether they had parks in Britain.

---

* A doctrine that has had more influence than it deserves; it was invented by Garret Hardin, an American with no experience of how commons actually worked. See Grove & Rackham (2002) p. 88.

The prototype deer-park may have been Ongar Great Park in southwest Essex, mentioned in an Anglo-Saxon will of 1045. This huge park, 3 miles by 2 (5 × 3 kilometres), was presumably for native red deer; it remained substantially intact until the 1950s (Fig. 182). Surviving fragments include a massive boundary bank, with ditches on both sides. (However, R. Liddiard proposes that other parks existed in late Anglo-Saxon times, developing out of corrals for catching wild deer.[7])

The Normans favoured deer husbandry, and c.1100 introduced fallow deer, an oriental beast that was easier than native deer to keep on a limited area of land. Parks multiplied from 35 in Domesday Book to well over 3,000 around 1300.[8] Most were not 'hunting parks' but deer-farms producing venison for the table as well as providing pasture for cattle and sheep. (I have very few medieval records of hunting in parks, and most are of foxhunts.) At least 40, however, were country-house parks, forerunners of the designer parks of the eighteenth century.[9] A deer-farm park, and the feasts it engendered (Fig. 35), was a status symbol somewhat higher than a manor house; a country-house park would symbolise the greater nobility.

The medievals assumed the fallow deer to be a woodland animal, and nearly always provided it with woodland or wood-pasture. Parks were typically shaped as a rectangle with rounded corners, a compact shape for economy in fencing. Deer, stronger than pigs and more agile than goats, had to be confined by a special cleft-oak fence called a *pale* (Fig. 36) or a wall; this characterises a park and distinguishes it from a Forest, where the deer stay from force of habit.

Many parks – but few wooded commons – were compartmented, divided into woods that were fenced after each felling to keep out the deer (and other livestock) until the underwood had grown up out of their reach. There would also be one or more *launds*, open areas accessible to the deer at all times, in which any trees would be pollarded. Launds would have waterholes and a park lodge where the parkers did their business.

In the later Middle Ages parks were revived, this time for ceremonial hunts (in addition to their deer-farm and ornamental functions).[10] The sixteenth century introduced a new kind of hunt in a confined space: according to Christopher Taylor's researches, it was the forerunner of the modern dog-track, with spectators betting on greyhounds that sprinted along a fixed course after a live deer (sometimes reuseable) instead of an electric hare.[11]

The third age of parks was the eighteenth century, when country-house park design became an art form in the hands of Lancelot 'Capability' Brown, Humphry Repton and their contemporaries. There was a fourth, little-known age of parks in the nineteenth century, when country-house and municipal parks were involved with exotic trees and with the estate branch of modern forestry (p.346).

Parks preserve features from previous landscapes: especially ancient trees, but also moats, ridge-and-furrow, and sometimes the earthwork remains of whole medieval villages. These were often consciously preserved. A park that contains medieval oaks may look like a medieval park, but is not necessarily one.[12]

Some examples of parks
- Medieval, compartmental: Monks' Park (Bradfield St Clare, west Suffolk); Sutton Coldfield Park (Warwickshire).
- Medieval, non-compartmental: Staverton Park (east Suffolk, private); Blenheim Park, Oxfordshire.
- Tudor and Stuart: Kentwell Hall (Long Melford, Suffolk); Grimsthorpe (southwest Lincolnshire). Moccas (Herefordshire, private) is a famous and mysterious park, in which extensive research, and even the publication of a book, has failed to elucidate its origin.[13]
- Eighteenth century, incorporating earlier non-park features: Ickworth (Suffolk); Felbrigg (Norfolk).

Forests
The idea of Forests originated in the ethos of Merovingian France, where ownerless land belonged to the king, who was entitled to the wild beasts living therein. In contrast, an Anglo-Saxon king – the first among equals – might honour huntsmen and hunt deer, but only as any other landowner would.

William the Conqueror introduced Forests to England, but in a modified form, since everywhere in England already had an owner. He asserted the right to keep deer, and to set up Forest courts and a Forest officialdom. William was no first among equals: the kingdom and all that was in it was his, and he asserted his supremacy by keeping his deer on other people's land and by setting up officials to protect the deer's interests. In Domesday Book there were some 25 Forests, including the New Forest, Dean and Sherwood. William's successors multiplied Forests, especially after the introduction of fallow deer, until King John went too far and was arraigned by his nobles for (among other things) declaring too many new Forests.

Forests were not linked to woodland as were parks. Most were large commons. There were wooded Forests (like Epping Forest), moorland Forests (like Dartmoor) and heathland Forests (like most of Sherwood). Forests were sited near royal palaces or estates; on some the king owned the land and on others it belonged to someone else. The king could dispose of the land but keep the Forestal rights, as with Hatfield Forest in 1238.

Beasts of the Forest were overwhelmingly fallow deer, but also red deer (especially in moorland), and rarely roe deer. Wild swine were included in the two Forests where they survived, Dean and Pickering (Yorkshire). In the Forest attached to the royal manor of Somerton, which was entirely farmland, the hare was a Forest beast, and when one was found dead, 12 jurymen would sit on the body and hold an inquest, as if it were a deer or a man.

The legal limits of a Forest were established by a perambulation, going from point to point as in an Anglo-Saxon charter (p.136). This defined where people could be prosecuted for snaring deer or otherwise breaching Forest Law. It was *not* the extent of the *physical Forest*, the tract of wood-pasture, moorland, heath etc. where the deer lived. Usually the *legal Forest* was several times the extent of the physical Forest. Confusion between legal and physical Forests, combined with confusion between Forests and woodland, is partly responsible for the belief that medieval England was very wooded. The legal bounds could be extended or reduced by a stroke of the pen without any noticeable effect on the ground.

Forests were established in a poorly documented age. No record survives of setting one up (unless the early perambulation of Blackmoor Forest (p.389) was part of the original proclamation). It would have involved proclaiming the boundaries (much as with a modern National Park), appointing officials, and often introducing some deer (especially if these were fallow).

Forests were not 'set apart for the king's hunting'. His deer were added to the pre-existing activities. Cultivation, pasturage and woodcutting went on much as outside Forests. Assarting (p.98) was illegal under Forest Law, but was usually condoned for a modest fine.

The parties in a Forest were:
- the king, as owner of the Forestal rights (the right to keep deer, to kill and eat them, to make appointments to offices in the Forest bureaucracy, and to pocket the fines);
- the landowners, some of whom owned also the trees;
- those with common-rights; and
- the Forest officials, who soon became hereditary.

A Forest, the royal status symbol, was aspired to by those demonstrating that they were nearly as good as the king. Already by 1086 the Earl of Chester had declared a few Forests. In England most Forests were always royal; the others belonged to high nobility, down to the level of the greatest bishops (Durham, Winchester, Ely). It is unlikely that all private Forests (often, but inconsistently, called *chases*) had the trappings of courts and officers, as Cranborne Chase (Wiltshire and Dorset) did.[14]

In Scotland, whose kings were weaker, Forests were more numerous than in England; only a minority were royal, and the link with woodland was even more tenuous. The system went on much longer than in England – in the Highlands well into the nineteenth century.[15] In South Wales every petty marcher lord, seeking to be as good as the English king, declared the local mountain to be a Forest: there were more Forests than in all England, but hardly any were royal. North Wales, however, which remained independent until after the Forest system in England had passed its peak, had very few: Welsh princes were known to be as good as the English king and had no need of the trappings of Saxon royalty.

What did the king get from 90 Forests? Venison: entertainment was an essential part of the prestige by which he reigned, and he needed to produce hundreds of noble beasts and birds at Christmas and other feasts. He gave deer to favoured subjects, as carcasses, permissions to hunt, or live to start parks. Where he owned the trees, he used timber and underwood to build castles and palaces, for equipment when fighting in France, as gifts to friends and relations or to religious orders, or to sell to pay his debts. Some Forests (especially Dean) were the source of especially large trees, sent hundreds of miles for cathedral roofs and other special uses. Twelfth-century kings got a large income from Forest fines; later this seems to have been reduced, perhaps because much of the proceeds disappeared in the bureaucracy. An important function of the Forests was as an honours system. Chaucer, for meritorious services as diplomat and Customs officer (and, maybe, as poet laureate), was awarded the honorific sinecure of under-Forester of the Forest of North Petherton, Somerset.

Wooded Forests (that is, Forests containing more woodland or wood-pasture than the surrounding landscape) comprised about half of English Forests. They were shaped like commons, with horns and boundary-houses (Fig. 183); they operated much like any other wood-pasture common. The king's deer were usually a minor addition to the pre-existing land uses. In a Forest with many landownerships, like Epping, the Forest courts might take on the regulation of common-rights. Felling timber and wood, though breaches of Forest Law, were seldom prosecuted unless excessive or unusual.

About half the wooded Forests were compartmental (Fig. 184). In Hatfield Forest there were 17 coppices, which in theory were felled on an 18-year cycle;

for six years after felling all the livestock were fenced out, and for three years after that only deer were let in. The remaining one-third of the Forest was *plains*, grassland with pollard trees, in other Forests called *lawns*. Similar arrangements operated in Wychwood (Oxfordshire), Cranborne Chase, Rockingham Forest (Northants), Writtle Forest (Essex) and Blackmoor Forest (see Chapter 20). Non-compartmental wooded Forests included the New Forest (for most of its history), Epping and Hainault Forests (Essex), Savernake (Wiltshire), and the Forest of Dean.

After their thirteenth-century heyday, Forests gradually fade from the record. As Graham Jones points out, few were formally dissolved, and some were very much alive in the sixteenth century.[16] Possibly private Forests, though less well recorded, lasted longer than royal: Cranborne Chase was formally (and disastrously) abolished in 1828. Even if the legal status fell into abeyance, the physical fabric often survived.

Wooded Forests where the Crown still owned the land fell on evil days in the nineteenth century. Some, such as Alice-Holt (Hampshire), Salcey (Northants) and Dean, were converted into plantations that never fulfilled their purpose. Others were privatised: the destruction of Hainault Forest in the 1850s was a landmark in the histories of the bulldozer and of the modern conservation movement (p.325).

Forests existed in different forms in other countries. In Hungary they played a very large part in the medieval landscape.[17]

The Forest of Galtres and the Archbishop of York's woods: For medieval kings, York was the northern capital of England, where they liked to keep Christmas. Like Norwich (but unlike London or Canterbury) it was under-provided with woodland; it was chronically short of wood, but well placed to import timber.

The Vale of York (Fig. 183b) was ill-drained and infertile. To the modern visitor it seems a flat, low-lying, dull region of ordinary farmland; its few ancient woods were ferociously replanted in the Locust Years; only place-names like Sutton-on-the-Forest hint at a more distinguished history. That history, however, has been ably investigated by the Woodland History Group of the Yorkshire Philosophical Society. For much of what follows I am indebted to the account by Jane Kaner.[18]

The later Norman kings surrounded York with a ring of Forests: Galtres to the north, Ouse & Derwent to the east, Ainsty to the southwest. The chief recorded product of the latter two was money from fines for infringing Forest Law. Ainsty, where the king owned little or no land, was perhaps the first Forest to be abolished: in 1190 its inhabitants paid Richard I the rather small lump sum of £31 to buy themselves out. Ouse & Derwent was likewise ransomed by Fountains Abbey and others in 1234.*

This left Galtres as the most significant wooded Forest in northern England. Its topography is rather shadowy, for it was never properly mapped. The legal Forest stretched 12 miles (20 kilometres) north-northwest from York city. Unlike Sherwood, one cannot find an uninhabited gap in which to place the physical Forest. The area is dotted with ancient settlements, between which the physical Forest probably reticulated itself like a Norfolk or Dorset common.

Galtres was a huge source of deer for the king's feasts: the biggest producer of fallow deer in England and the second biggest of red and roe. It was not very wooded, even in Domesday Book. Surviving records indicate more heath and fen than woodland. However, it had timber trees and pollards: the part which the king owned was a source of great (though perhaps not outsize) timber trees, which supplied royal building works in York down to the mid-fourteenth century, after which there seem to have been no more. Despite the large numbers of deer, there seems to have been no attempt to compartmentalise the Forest.

Islanded within the Forest were monastic and private coppices and parks. The Abbot of St Mary's, York, sweetened King John with 40 marks and a palfrey to be allowed to make the Abbey's wood into a park – which was compartmentalised and seems to survive, badly damaged, as Overton Wood. St Leonard's Hospital in York also made its private wood in Beningbrough into a park, whence timber was rafted down the Ouse to York in 1409; part of the park bank survives.

Galtres survived into the reign of James I, at which time there were still pollard oaks. In the 1610s and 1620s the Forest was abolished, privatised and very thoroughly destroyed. The Woodland History Group found one mighty pollard oak big enough be a survivor of the Forest.

York Minster, with its huge width, called for many exceptionally long, as well as ordinary, oaks. As far as is known, the Minster got timber from private woods, including Stillington in the legal Forest, none of which survives. The king was not in the habit of granting timber to York Minster from Galtres Forest, nor from Sherwood as he did to Lincoln Minster.

---

* The king still kept some deer for ready use at Langwith Hay, 4 miles (6.5 kilometres) from York. This, rather than Langthwaite in Swaledale, appears to have been the 'Forest of Langwast' from which he placed a last-minute order for roe deer for his famous Christmas dinner in 1251 (Rackham (1986a) p. 119).

The biggest wood near York, then as now, was Bishop's Wood. It was apparently, in all but name, a small Forest belonging to the Archbishop and containing his deer; it was compartmented, with several named woods or 'haggs', and 'outwoods' corresponding to plains in other Forests. In the fifteenth century the Archbishop provided oak timber from here for the Minster, including boards for the nave ceiling, which were sawn on the spot instead of coming as usual from the Baltic (p.232). By the eighteenth century the wood was a huge but conventional coppice, providing thousands of tons of timber as well as underwood. There have been several phases of planting – conifer symbols appear as early as the Ordnance Survey of 1845 – 8 – but enough yet remains to identify it as an ash – hazel wood.

Medieval timber buildings in York ought to be a rich source of information on the ecology of growing trees (Chapter 11). York Minster, alas, has attracted several fires and the wrath of restorers, so that little ancient timber remains, except the thirteenth-century Baltic pine doors of the chapterhouse. The countryside, though not prolific in such buildings, has the early Norman door at Stillingfleet – made of crooked, fast-grown 'local' oak, presumably before the Baltic trade – and the ancient doors of Cawood Palace. I remember, at Selby, the last timber bridge to take a main road over a tidal river.

OPERATION OF WOOD-PASTURE

Ground vegetation

The essential difference between woodland (or forest with a small f) and wood-pasture (or savanna) is the ground vegetation. In woodland the ground vegetation consists of plants that tolerate or evade shade (Table 2). Wood-pasture has grassland or some other plant community that calls for unshaded conditions.

Ground vegetation under savanna trees may not be quite the same as that between them. In southern Portugal and Spain, as T. Marañon has shown, there are two types of grassland, one beneath the evergreen oaks, the other between them.[19] In the arid Davis Mountains, west Texas, I find that every tree of juniper has a circle of the grass *Stipa tenuissima* exactly beneath it, in contrast to the mixture of grasses constituting the general prairie (Fig. 38). A similar difference should be looked for in the few English wood-pastures that still retain their ground vegetation. Is it due to:

- the shade of the tree canopy?
- a dry zone created by the tree roots taking moisture out of the ground?

- a damp zone created by the tree canopy combing moisture out of fog or low cloud – adding to the rainfall under the tree at the expense of that between the trees?
- a fertile zone created by minerals brought up by the tree roots and shed in fallen leaves?
- cattle lying in the shade of the tree and adding their dung to the fertility? or
- the tree canopy protecting the ground against slight frosts?

Pollards and veteran trees

Wood-pasture trees tend to live longer than upstanding trees in woods. This is partly because the lack of neighbouring trees allows them space to go through phases of retrenchment and regrowth. Also, as timber trees, oaks would be difficult to replace, so landowners would allow them to grow to unusual sizes, worth more per cubic foot than ordinary oaks. However, most trees in uncompartmented wood-pasture were pollarded, going on to become veteran trees (p.42).

In other countries' wood-pastures the trees, as well as the grassland, often feed the livestock. Leaf-fodder is a tradition of Norway, the Alps and Balkans, and through Turkey on into Central Asia and the Himalayas.[20] There are many styles of pollarding or sometimes *shredding* – cropping the side branches leaving a tuft at the top. Leaves are often dried like hay and stored to feed animals in the winter (Fig. 39). This was less important in Britain, where animals could feed out of doors in winter. However, there is evidence for it from the Somerset Levels (p.220). Pollard hawthorns in Hatfield and Savernake Forests may have provided iron rations for the deer to gnaw in hard winters.

Not all wood-pastures have ancient trees: most Spanish and Portuguese savannas (with a notable exception near Trujillo) have trees no more than 130 years old, the result of an expansion in the recent past.[21] Greece and especially Crete, however, are (with England and southeast Sweden) the great stronghold of ancient trees in Europe.

Infilling

In the last 150 years, besides widespread destruction of the world's forests and savannas, those that remain have changed. Many forests have got denser and savannas have turned into forest. The student should be alert to discrepancies between old trees and their surroundings: to the process of *infilling*, where big spreading old trees, which grew up with room to expand, have tall young trees crowded between them (Fig. 37).

Infill trees may be of the same or different species. In Savernake Forest (Wilt-shire) the great spreading oaks of the seventeenth century (and a few medieval pollards), which grew up scattered on heathland, now stand in woodland with twentieth-century oaks crowded between them. In Epping Forest, young hollies infill between the pollard oaks, hornbeams and beeches (p.326).

I have seen infilling in many European countries, in Turkey, North America and Australia (Fig. 40), have heard of it in Africa, and would expect it in South America. In Japan sacred groves around temples and shrines are not untouched wildwood. Many consist of great evergreen trees of *kusonoki* (*Cinnamomum camphora,* camphorwood), *tabu* (*Machilus thunbergi,* a laurel-like tree), or a dozen other species – sometimes pollarded – with younger trees such as the giant conifer *sugi* (*Cryptomeria japonica*) crowded between them. A century ago manage-ment evidently changed. Pollarding was abandoned, and a new generation of trees was either planted by the faithful or allowed to grow up, creating the dark and numinous shades which so impress the pilgrim today.

In West Africa much of what was thought of as 'virgin forest' is really a legacy of the slave trade. Previously it had been a cultural savanna. In the eighteenth century slavers murdered or carried off the people; their pastures and fields turned into forest, in which huge savanna trees and the remains of villages and termite mounds are still embedded.[22]

Hollins, holly-hags, bursts and hats

Holly and ivy are the only British evergreens that are both edible and (in moder-ate quantity) non-poisonous to livestock. (Pine is rather unpalatable; yew is palatable but poisonous.) Holly was iron rations for sheep in snowy winters. It has an Atlantic distribution, easily set back by drought, dying at the top as hedgerow hollies in Norfolk often do. Nevertheless, it is now on the increase.[23]

Holly grows easily from seed. Although browsed by most herbivorous mammals, it is not killed; repeated browsing turns it into a spiny topiary-like bush, recalling the bitten-down prickly oak bushes on many a Greek hillside. If browsing stops for a few years it is well placed to grow into a tree. It thus prospers under intermittent browsing, especially in the twentieth century. It acts as an infill in wood-pasture; notably in Epping Forest, where prohibition of pollard-ing and decline of browsing after 1878 resulted in holly bushes growing into great trees. I suspect that the story of Sutton Coldfield has an element of browsing, turning coppices into wood-pasture, followed by lack of browsing allowing holly to take over.

Mayhew, chronicler of the Dickensian lower classes in London, mentions the trade of 'Christmasing', stealing holly by moonlight for sale.[24] A happily forgotten use of holly bark was to make bird-lime, instant glue for sticking small edible birds to twigs: Waterton, the eccentric Yorkshire naturalist, complained in the 1850s that his hollies were being damaged by bark-gatherers.[25]

Hollins – wood-pastures of holly-trees – are a feature of mountain regions. Near Sheffield in 1442 there was a sale of holly in winter. Later, in 1725, the Earl of Oxford found, also in the Sheffield area:

...the greatest number of wild stunted holly trees that I ever saw together.... This tract of ground they grow upon is called the Burley Hollins ... their branches lopped off every winter for the support of the sheep which browse upon them, and at the same time are sheltered by the stunted part that is left standing.[26]

This was evidently a tract of pollard hollies, like the famous hollins still extant on the Stiperstones in Shropshire. Hollins should be looked for in other moorland countries; I have seen great pollard hollies above the Killarney woods in southwest Ireland.

Holly occurred in woodland also, and sometimes formed the underwood of coppices called 'holly-hags'. These extended into lowland England, but were sufficiently unusual to be named after the tree. In the Middle Ages holly is occasionally heard of as timber. In 1196 there was a *hulnetum*, one of the rare Latin wood-names in *-etum*, meaning a wood composed of a particular kind of tree, in Bentley (Suffolk).[27] This later became Hulney Wood, which is still there, but suffered very drastic replanting followed by very drastic windblow in 1987; I cannot say what happened to the holly.

Sutton Coldfield Park (Warwickshire) is a big medieval park with embanked woods called *hursts*. One of these, Holly Hurst, is a solid mass of holly with birches and standard oaks. Less of the holly is in the form of coppice stools than one would expect. However, the other hursts are also thickets of holly; Upper and Lower Nut Hurst, despite their names, are holly-woods in which I have found no hazel.

The enigmas of Staverton Park: Staverton Park (Suffolk) is an oak savanna, divided into two areas (Fig. 185). In the more open part holly trees have arisen, not in gaps between oaks as they would in a rational world, but under the oaks' canopy (Fig. 43). The denser part, 'The Thicks', looks like a later stage of the same process: hollies grow in rings round the bases of living or dead oaks or the mouldering remains of oaks that have almost disappeared. Students, when asked to speculate, produce the following interpretations:

- Birds sat on the oaks eating holly berries and excreting the seeds (which, like tomato seeds in Man, survive passing through the gut).
- The presence of the oak in some way alters the sandy soil and makes it more favourable to holly.
- The hollies came first; they lived for centuries as prickly, bitten-down shrubs that protected the oaks arising among them and, long afterwards, grew up into trees during a lull in browsing. *

There is a similar association between oak and holly in the New Forest. Hollies, according to Colin Tubbs, colonise heathland, where they survive burning in the fire-dominated landscape. Patches of holly are invaded by rowan and yew, and give rise, Vera-style, to a central group of oaks. These 'hats' or 'holms', although ultimately impermanent, last for centuries and give rise to place-names.[28] I have seen a similar association, between a different oak and a different holly, on Cumberland Island (Georgia).

The grandest of all holly infills is Staverton Thicks. The mighty hollies, up to 70 feet (20 metres) high, are said to be the biggest in the kingdom, accompanied by some of the biggest birches and biggest rowans. They have overtopped and killed many of the pollard oaks (Fig. 41). The great storm of 1990 uprooted some of the giant hollies, but they go on growing as if nothing had happened. Any gaps are filled with prickly, deer-bitten masses of young holly. What set off this change from what would previously have been a conventional pollarded wood-pasture? How can an Atlantic, drought-sensitive tree reach its greatest development in the driest part of Britain on blown sand, the least moisture-retaining of soils?

Holly is not new at Staverton: thirteenth-century estate accounts record nil entries for sales of holly. When I first knew the Thicks, in 1969, the oaks killed by holly shade were already in all states of decomposition, from those still retaining bark to those mouldered away to meagre traces. Since a dead oak takes at least a century to disappear completely, they must have died at various times from the mid-nineteenth century onwards. For the hollies to grow up and out-compete the oaks would take nearly another hundred years. The hollies, therefore, would have begun to get away in the mid- to late eighteenth century. ** There was evidently a temporary relaxation of grazing, which could have given rise to the last generation of pollard oaks in the rest of Staverton.

---

* John White proposes another explanation in the form of 'bundle-planting' (p.204); but apart from the lack of evidence of any planting in Staverton, the oaks and hollies are usually too far apart to have originated in one hole.

** Holly produces indistinct and unhelpful annual rings.

The Staverton hollies are perhaps the oldest example of holly infilling. The reason for their grandeur is probably geological. The Thicks, although on a sandy plateau, has wet seeps that persist in most summers. Under the sand is a thin bed of Chillesford Clay, absent (or patchy) in the rest of Staverton, which evidently holds up a perched water table that feeds the hollies.

Forests and deer

Popular and even learned writers reiterate the belief that Forests were 'hunting preserves', 'reserved for the king's hunting', which has become a literary *topos*, a factoid not requiring illustration. In reality normal agriculture, pasturage and woodmanship went on in Forests, royal and private, much as they did in the outside world. Deer were added to these pursuits. How large a part did hunting play in the life of the average king, and in which Forests?

The most convincing account of an English king hunting is from before there were Forests, in the reign of King Edmund the Magnificent (939 – 46). The king rode out from Cheddar Palace in the Mendips in pursuit of red deer. He singled out a hart and went after it through a 'wood' (*silua*); it cannot have been much of a wood, for he rode through it at speed, without looking where he was going; the hart plunged into Cheddar Gorge and was 'ground into little pieces', and the hounds ditto; the king was enabled to pull up his horse on the last tussock (*in ultimo … cespite*) by the miraculous intervention of St Dunstan, whom he then promoted to be Archbishop of Canterbury. This was a real adventure, written down shortly afterwards, and repeated by similar accidents in 1240 and to the Wells Harriers in 1895.[29]

The early Norman kings hunted. William the Conqueror introduced the Forest system, as his obituary in the *Anglo-Saxon Chronicle* records to his discredit. William II met his death in the New Forest in a hunting accident (or was it an accident?); so did his nephew, who got spiked in the throat by a branch, as could happen to anyone, and his brother, who rode into a cloud of poison gas.[30]

Tudor and Stuart kings and queens hunted in person. Henry VIII, halfway through his reign, became 'passionately fond of the chase', and developed a mania for parks, to which the English landscape is permanently indebted. Elizabeth liked to be thought of as 'a weak and feeble woman' who could not keep up with her father's manly activities, but in practice seems to have outdone him as the greatest sporting sovereign before George V. Charles I and Queen Anne were mighty hunters, and even Oliver Cromwell took a passing interest.[31]

It is easy for historians to project Tudor royal hunts back into the Middle Ages and to transfer them from parks to Forests. For the four centuries after 1100 there is no lack of writing about European kings hunting. In Spain, Alfonso XI (1312–50) wrote a *Book of Hunting*, dealing with the strategy and tactics of the chase, veterinary medicine and field surgery, and hundreds of localities from Santander to Algeciras. Alfonso's hunts were real adventures: disdaining pitiful deer, he stuck mighty sows and lanced raging bears.[32] French kings hunted in person, and at least one was a martyr to the chase. (For the Hunt of the Emperor Maximilian (1493–1519) see p.188.)

All this, however, is Continental. English nobles liked to translate books on hunting, and there is some English material on the management of parks. There are 'legends', such as the story of Henry III sparing the White Hart of Blackmoor Forest in Dorset and punishing Thomas de la Lynde who slew it (p.392). Henry's relatives, Richard and Edmund of Cornwall, were keen sportsmen and volunteered to catch deer for the royal table. This apart, historians of hunting and biographers of kings are short of particulars of hunts giving names, dates and places. There is little to justify modern scholars' obsession with hunting as the *raison d'être* of English Forests. In contemporary records, deer appear far more often at feasts than in hunts. The ordinary medieval king apparently had little time or inclination for Forest hunting; his dinner was caught for him by professional hunters. Hunting was a courtly science, its etiquette to be learnt from books, not field trips. A royal hunt was full of symbolic meaning, like a coronation, and almost as rare. It has been claimed that Henry VIII was the first to develop the knack of delegating his workload to administrators, giving himself leisure for a life of 'aristocratic ease ... hunting and obesity'.[33]

What kept down the numbers of deer? Writers insist that in Forests the king's deer were protected by 'savage laws and cruel penalties'. They have in mind the *Anglo-Saxon Chronicle*'s statement that King William '... set up great protection for deer, and legislated to that intent, that whosoever should slay hart or hind should be blinded ...' (1087 AD). The Conqueror, it seems, objected to the death penalty. But were such Byzantine punishments ever inflicted? I have challenged the academic world for examples of the confiscation of eyes (or even testicles) for Forest offences – names? places? dates? – but no reply has come.

To keep the numbers of deer constant one normally needs to kill about one-quarter of the stock each year. According to his correspondence, Henry III in an average year ordered some 600 fallow deer, of which 530 came from Forests; this includes those which he ate himself, or gave live or dead to his friends. He consumed 160 red and 45 roe deer a year. These are absurdly small numbers. The fallow, even if we double the figure to allow generously for unrecorded orders, would be in equilibrium with at most 5,000 fallow deer in all the royal Forests in England. From Hatfield Forest he took a dozen deer a year, about one-fifth of those that now need to be killed there to keep the numbers constant.

There are now thought to be at least 100,000 fallow, 100,000 red and 200,000 roe deer free-ranging in England; motorists kill tens of thousands annually.[34] If the twentieth century could not hold down the numbers of deer using cars and guns, how could the thirteenth with nets and arrows? And yet in the Middle Ages there were complaints of not enough deer: in 1257, gifts were suspended in some twenty Forests for that reason.[35] During the Middle Ages red and fallow deer remained constant or declined; roe became almost extinct. Something does not add up.

Records of poaching offences in Forest courts are remarkable in three ways:
1. the long interval between the date of the offence and its clearing up, often 20 years, so that many defendants had died or left the area;
2. the lenient penalties, deterrent fines or imprisonment being seldom inflicted unless there was a commercial poaching gang; and
3. the high status of most of the defendants: nobility, gentry or higher clergy.

The courts, it seems, were concerned mainly with raising revenue from fines; probably most of the money had been collected long before at lower courts whose archives do not survive.

What could have kept down the numbers of deer, other than a great deal of unprosecuted and unrecorded poaching? The king oppressed the nobility – that was his job – but had no interest in antagonising the middle and lower classes. There was normally no point in prosecuting the ordinary individual snaring a deer for the pot.

The motts of the Wild West

I have written about savannas based on single trees scattered among pasturage. In Texas, however, several savanna trees are clonal, growing from suckers, especially inland live-oak (*Quercus fusiformis*) and cedar-elm (*Ulmus crassifolia*). The prairies are thus dotted with patches of these trees, called *motts* (Fig. 32). Usually all the stems in each mott share a clonal peculiarity of habit or branching, but occasionally one can detect two clones in a mott, or even a mixed oak–elm mott.

Motts tend to be based on patches of thin soil or rocky ground amid the clayey prairie. Each mott is a wood, with a shrub layer (elbow-bush *Forestiera angustifolia*), woody climbers (cat-brier *Smilax rotundifolia* and the local species of grape) and herbaceous plants. In the nineteenth century the landscape was privatised and divided up by fences, which run in straight lines through prairie and mott alike; many of these, over the years, have turned into mixed hedges.

Although superficially motts look like Vera's wildwood groves in action, this is a cultural landscape. It is now grazed by declining herds of cattle, sheep and goats and increasing hordes of deer and feral hogs. Without enough grazing the prairie rapidly infills, especially with the local juniper, *Juniperus ashei,* formerly confined to canyons, but now forming dense 'cedar-brakes' between and around the motts.

In pre-settlement times this was fire-dominated: travellers such as the Santa Fé Expedition of 1841 often mention fires. Fires in the flammable grassland would limit the spread of the fire-sensitive juniper. They would less often have spread into the motts, but a fierce fire would have killed the trees to the ground, leaving the suckers to sprout. Burning continued for some time after privatisation: hidden in the hedges are the pioneers' long-lasting juniper fence stakes, charred by prairie fires.

Mexican land perambulations of the 1830s, written in a pidgin of Spanish and English, show that the infrastructure already existed. Woodland, savanna and prairie were located generally where they still are; even the tree species are often the same, although few of the individual trees are still alive.

How old are the motts? The stems on each mott are usually about 80 years old, probably arising after the last fierce fire or after settlers had felled the motts for fuel. A few much bigger live-oaks have stories associated with them, for example those, now 2–3 feet (60–90 centimetres) in diameter, supposed to have been already there when the city of Waco was started c.1842 and thus now about 200 years old. The motts, however, must be much older than the stems.

On 2 November 1831 there was a desperate gunfight between a war-party of Tehuacana and Waco and their foes, a gang of adventurers including James Bowie (toting his Bowie knife) looking for silver. The scene was:

... a cluster of live oak trees, some thirty or forty in number, and about the size of a man's body. To the north of them there was a thicket of live oak bushes about ten feet high, forty yards in length and twenty in breadth ... The surrounding country was an open prairie, interspersed with a few trees, rocks and broken land.
J.W. WILBARGER, *INDIAN DEPREDATIONS IN TEXAS,* AUSTIN 1889

I have been there and find it still a land of prairies and motts with even-aged stems.

The savanna infrastructure has passed through at least four human cultures. The barbed-wire fences and hedges are a legacy of settlement and of a short-lived attempt to cultivate the prairie. This was preceded by the cowboy culture of the Chisholm Trail, which itself lasted only about 30 years. Before these, in the eighteenth century, were the Plains Indians, horsemen ranging over hundreds of miles, and hybrid cultures like the Waco who, though nomadic, had permanent bases and grew crops. But these too had predecessors, before the coming of Europeans and horses, known to archaeologists as the Woodland Culture; there can be little doubt that the motts and prairies originated under their influence.

STATE OF THE WORLD'S WOOD-PASTURES

In Britain, the wood and pasture components seldom both survive. Many wood-pastures have infilled into woodland, losing the pasture altogether. Parks tend to belong to people who can afford to 'improve' the grassland, keeping the ancient trees, but reducing the ground vegetation to ryegrass. Even in Hatfield Forest the National Trust was persuaded into a brief but disastrous phase of improvement in the 1950s; 50 years on, the old grassland has still only partly recovered.

In other countries the original pasture has been replaced by invasive exotics. In Californian savannas one is depressed to find the indigenous evergreen oaks remaining, but the grassland replaced by familiar European annuals such as *Bromus* species, clovers, and southern European plants such as *Kohlrauschia prolifera* and *Parentucellia viscosa*, with hardly a native herb in sight. This is a new plant community: the species come from different habitats and do not form such grasslands in the Mediterranean. The traffic has been one way; Spanish *dehesas*, in a similar climate, are not overrun with Californian plants.

In Australian savannas, likewise, kangaroos and emus now feed on European herbs or, further north, universal tropical grasses that have displaced much of the native ground vegetation. This in turn affects the fire regime, for the invaders often burn hotter than the original grasses (p.421).

Pollarding was an aspect of European culture that was rarely transferred to North America, and only sporadically to Australia, but it exists in Tasmania. The great savanna eucalypts there, now in farmland, are relics of an Aboriginal cultural landscape. Many are pollarded: was it black or white people who did this, and why did they undertake the immense labour of pollarding these iron-hard trees? The present Tasmanians, whose magnificent landscapes are among the island's few remaining assets, are distressed to find these trees gradually dying. No human ingenuity, it seems, can persuade new eucalypts to arise in farmland, either because the soils are altered or because of lack of fire.

CHAPTER 7

ARCHIVES OF WOODLAND AND HOW TO STUDY THEM

On the way from the Hermai the entire place is full of [deciduous] oaks. The name of the place, Skotítas [the Dark], did not come from the density of the trees, but from Zeus surnamed Skotítas, and there is a sanctuary of Zeus Skotítas on the left of the road if you turn aside approximately ten stadia. Going back from here, going on a little and turning left again, there is an image of Herakles and a trophy ... The third turning off the direct road, to the right, leads to Káryai and the sanctuary of Artemis ... and the Nymphs.
PAUSANIAS, *DESCRIPTION OF GREECE* (C.150 AD), III.10.6

Reader, go to the remote byways of Mount Párnon in the Peloponnese, above the village whose modern Greek name is Káryai, previously known by the Slavonic name Arachova – both meaning 'nuts'. The sanctuary of Artemis and the Nymphs is now a chapel, with wonderful plane-trees, among the biggest in Europe, beside a spring.[1] As far as I know, this is the earliest account of a named wood in Europe. Skotítas Wood was 'rediscovered' by the explorer Jochmus and a local priest in 1834. It is now probably bigger than in Pausanias's time. The dominant tree, as in other ancient woods in the Peloponnese, is the deciduous oak *Quercus frainetto*. It is a rather open coppice (Fig. 44), with some ancient stools, and a rich flora of shrubs and herbs in glades and newly felled areas. Some of the oaks have been shredded.

Skotítas, as far as I know, is the only surviving wood in Europe to have its own god. Pausanias, unusually among ancient writers, was writing to tell posterity where things were in the landscape. Far more often we have to make do with incidental mentions in records written for some other purpose. This chapter explains what archives can and cannot achieve.

CHARTERS AND PERAMBULATIONS

The earliest writings in Britain to describe specific pieces of landscape are *peram-bulations*, descriptions of boundaries appended to conveyances of landed estates. For example, the bounds of Long Itchington, bearing date 1001, run:

>...*from Ycenan* [the Warwickshire river Itchen] *to the cress well; to the alder-stub; to a high oak in the middle of Wulluht grove; to a withy-bed; to a barrow; to a little barrow* ...²

A thousand years later the alder-stubs and the barrows have gone, and so has the high oak, but its site is on a massive bank that now divides what was Wulluht Grove into Ufton Wood and Long Itchington Wood. (The orientation of the bank shows that it was made by the lord of Itchington.)*

About 840 perambulations are attached to charters bearing dates from about 600 to 1080 AD. For many the authenticity of the title deed is questionable, which in effect means that the date is uncertain.³ They are usually written in Old English, sometimes Latin.

Perambulations exist in later centuries, especially for defining the legal boundaries of Forests. Many other countries have them: for medieval Hungary they are a large part of all the documentation.⁴ In Europe a few are earlier: in Crete (where they are set in stone) they begin in Ancient Greek times. In the United States, survey perambulations and their 'witness trees' – a few of which survive – are an important source for the landscape just before settlement.

Anglo-Saxon perambulations are numerous enough to provide material for statistical analysis, though this is not straightforward because the distribution is very uneven: there are dozens for Berkshire, but none for Norfolk.⁵ They are the earliest evidence for names, locations and boundaries of woods, and for the distinction between woodland and wood-pasture.

Many perambulations can still be followed on the ground (p.387f). Something like one-quarter of the woods are still there. Charters also mention hedges and hedgerow trees and freestanding trees in downland. The trees most often mentioned, in descending order, were thorn, oak, apple (or crab), willow (including sallow and withy), ash and elder. Oak, lime and birch are among the trees associated with well-wooded areas later to be Ancient Countryside (Table 7); thorn, blackthorn, apple and elder are mentioned especially in areas without woodland, later to be Planned Countryside.

---

* I am indebted to Dr David Morfitt for showing me the spot. For a discussion of woods in Warwick-shire charters and later documents see Wager (1998).

PLACE-NAMES

Place-names, including names of woods, are derived from Old English, Old Norse or (rarely) Norman-French or Old Welsh. They offer a second window into the age of the charters. They once meant something, but over the years they have diverged in spelling and pronunciation from the everyday language: their meaning has been forgotten and sometimes misinterpreted.

To interpret place-names one needs to look at the spelling in early documents. The county volumes of the English Place-Name Society (not yet complete) give early spellings and offer interpretations.

Anglo-Saxon names of villages and hamlets sometimes indicate substantial amounts of local woodland. Those ending in *-ley*, *-hurst*, *-field*, and Old Norse *-thwaite* give an insight into the general distribution of woodland (p.99).

Place-names are only vaguely datable, and their study is not an exact science. The earliest document containing a name is only the latest possible date for either the name or the feature itself. One should beware of over-interpreting names. A *Brentwood* 'burnt wood' could arise at any time from the sixth to the fifteenth century; it should not be interpreted as 'wood destroyed by fire', for there is no knowing whether the fire was a bracken fire (p.47) or merely charcoal-burning.

Names of woods
A peculiarity of England is that almost any old wood, however small, has a name, which is often the name of the wood itself and not of some nearby farm or village. The further one goes back in history the more such names emerge. Hayley Wood is still called by the name that it had in the Ely Coucher Book; but in 1251 Hardwick Wood, now called after the parish, had its own name, Bradelegh; Hockering Wood in Norfolk was called Swinnow. Gamlingay Wood (see Fig. 179) was called Short Wood, and the two parts into which it was subdivided before 1601 were called Mertonage Wood and Avenells Wood. Eversden Wood was divided among three parishes, and the part in Great Eversden was subdivided into Granditch Wood, Stockings Wood and Snapdean Wood. Some wood-names are forever lost. Epping Forest used to be Waltham Forest, both being names of nearby towns: presumably it had a name of its own before it became a Forest in c.1100, of which no memory survives.

Names of recent woods are often distinctive. 'Plantation' is normally just that, although the name may stick long after the planted trees have died out.

'Hundred Acre Wood' is probably recent: an ancient wood of that size would have had a more distinctive name. 'Spinney' means a wood of thorns – Latin *spinetum* – and remembers an abandoned field in the process of turning into a wood. 'Fir Wood' implies a pine plantation, but can be confused with 'Furze Wood' referring to gorse. 'Conifer Wood' usually alludes to a *conyfare* or organised rabbit warren.

Wood-names sometimes allude to uses or management. 'Coppice' or its spelling variant 'Copse' or its dialect equivalent 'Spring' often mean coppice compartments (p.27) in a park or wooded Forest. There was a wood called Colyers Tayles in Castle Camps (Cambridgeshire) in 1411:[6] *collier* being a charcoal-man, and *tailz* a coppice (Modern French *taillis*).

Besides *wudu*, 'wood', the Anglo-Saxons had words for what were presumably different kinds of wood-lot: *bearu, fyrhðe, græfe, graf, hangra, holt, hyrst, sceaga, strod, wald*.[7] Although most of these still survive in the names of ancient woods – Frith, Grove, Holt, Shaw – their meanings are doubtful, except for *hangra*, 'Hanger', a wood on a slope. 'Shaw' is now used of a narrow wood, but Old English *scaga* seems not to denote any particular shape. The common wood-name ending '-hay', usually reduced to '-y' (e.g. Easty and Northy Woods in Cavendish, Suffolk), apparently means 'enclosed wood'. There were many unenclosed common-woods, whose names might include *gemæn*, 'common', as in Man Wood or The Mens (Sussex). 'Grove' (*graf*) usually means a small wood, but the word is once used for a type of woodland produce; and the present area of the wood *Wulluht graf* (p.136) is 194 acres (78 ha), which even by the standards of the eleventh century was not small. *Hris* (now Rice or Royce) meant 'underwood'. The Norse word for grove, *lúndr*, survives as 'Lound', 'Lownde' or the ending '-land'.

Tree names usually indicate the presence of the tree, but not how much there was of it. One knows how many oaks to expect in 'Oaken Grove' and perhaps in 'Notoaks Wood' but not in mere 'Oak Wood'. Does 'Birch Wood' mean a wood composed of birch or a wood distinguished by having one conspicuous birch tree? A wood composed of birches would be 'Birchen Wood' or 'Birchet' (like *Biolet* in French or *Birchat* in German); Birch Wood in Dedham (Suffolk) appears as *Birchetum* in medieval Latin.

Many woods are named after owners or tenants, but were not kept up to date. Alsa Wood (Stansted Mountfitchet, Essex) is the medieval *Asishey* and Anglo-Saxon 'Ælfsige's hay'. One of the Hindolveston woods, Norfolk, was still called 'Robin's Wood' in the eighteenth century, after John Robynes, an unfree tenant of Norwich Cathedral Priory, who had leased it five centuries before.

Wood- and tree-names are liable to misinterpretation. The parish of Lindsey (Suffolk) is corrupted from *Lelesey* and cannot be named after the lime (*linde*) trees in the local woods – although Groton Wood in the next parish may have given rise to the surname *de Lyndewode*. The wood next to Hayley Wood was called Littlehound Wood when it was grubbed in the seventeenth century, and gave rise to the later place-name Houndwood Field. The Ely Coucher Book of 1251 (Fig. 46) spells it *Litlelund*; it has nothing to do with hounds, but is the little *lúndr*. The 1251 scene was not new, but remembered Viking times. If there was a little *lúndr* there must (must there not?) have been also a great *lúndr*, which can hardly have been other than Hayley Wood itself.

Woods called 'Long Wood' are long, but a 'Round Wood' can be angular and a 'Short Wood' is not necessarily short.

Wood-names in Wales are disappointing, usually being no more than the name of an adjacent farm. Cornwall has a few wood-names in the extinct Cornish language: the great Merthen Wood on the Helford River was thought of as three woods, Coesenys ('Island Wood'), Coose-Carmynowe and Cosabnack. In Ireland a few ancient names of big woods are known, but even if the wood survives it seldom has a Gaelic name today. Gaelic wood-names are sadly lacking in the Highlands of Scotland.

In France only woods of more than 100 hectares or so have names, which are often those of some nearby village or town. Very big woods (more than 400–1,000 hectares) are called *forêts*, but there is no apparent difference between *bois* and *forêt* except size. This seems to be a nineteenth-century corruption: in the eighteenth century there were fewer *forêts*, and even a huge wood (or group of contiguous woods) could be a *bois*. Bois de la Reyne, 'Queen's Wood' (near Toul) of Cassini's map (*c*.1755), about 50 square kilometres (12,000 acres) in extent – as big as the Forest of Dean – had become Forêt de la Reine by 1834. (It had been through a period when queens and Forests were both politically incorrect.)

SURVEYS

Domesday Book

A stage in investigating an ancient wood is to see whether it is 'mentioned in Domesday Book'. Numerous modern editions make it possible to trace the record, if any, of almost any settlements in England. If, as often, there was more than one manor in a parish, or two parishes with the same name, the names of the landowners will help in working out which was which.

Domesday rarely names woods, and never records trees. In counties where it gives the dimensions of woods – x leagues long by y furlongs wide, at 8 furlongs to the mile and 1½ miles (2.4 kilometres) to the league – these sometimes make sense when compared to the present size of the wood. Where an estate had more than one wood, Domesday somehow combined them into one pair of dimensions. The woodland belonging to a place was sometimes located at a distance.[8]

The Ely Coucher Book

My own interest in woodland history was inspired by Hugo de Northwold, Bishop of Ely 1229–54. Forty years ago I was involved with Hayley Wood, recently acquired by the then Cambridgeshire & Isle of Ely Naturalists' Trust. Through Reaney's *Place-names of Cambridgeshire* I found a reference to the *Ely Coucher Book*, compiled by the Bishop's orders in 1251. Having been taught medieval Latin at school by a friendly master, Samuel Bate, I ordered the manuscript in Cambridge University Library and found what is now a well-known description of the wood:

'Est ibi vnus boscus qui vocatr heyle, qui continet quat'uiginti acras'
There is there one wood which is called heyle, which contains fourscore acres.

This was a startling discovery for a young don who had been taught (as one was taught 40 years ago) that the countryside had always been changing and that the present woods, hedges, etc. were the product of farming practices no older than the eighteenth century.

It took some years of research to document *boscus de heyle* through the intervening centuries and to show that it was indeed the present Hayley Wood. The next step was to show that it was not a unique survival. To commemorate the three-quarters of a millennium of the *Coucher Book* I published an analysis of what had happened to each of the 49 woods in it (p.122ff).[9]

Hugo de Northwold was apparently a pioneer. Since Domesday Book there had been sporadic surveys of institutional estates, but the *Coucher Book* seems to be the first to descend to the detail of giving the names, areas, boundaries and uses of woods (Fig. 46) – besides fields, meadows, fens, heaths, and naming thousands of people who held lands from the Bishop, with their feudal duties, such as carting his underwood or gathering his nuts. This wonderful volume (called a *coucher* book because it lies down, being too big to stand on a shelf) is still unpublished.[10]

Later surveys

The Hundred Rolls of 1279 were a greater and more detailed Domesday Book, setting out to list the assets of all estates in England, including the area of woodland (though not usually the name) belonging to each manor. Alas, the rats in the Tower ate most of it (or was it ever finished?); but the Cambridgeshire part survives and was a link in demonstrating that the survival of Hayley Wood was not especially unusual. The surviving parts were transcribed and published in 1818.

Estates found their way temporarily into the hands of the king: those of a bishopric, during vacancies of the see; those of private lords, whenever the owner committed high treason or died without an heir; those of dependencies of French monasteries, when England was at war with France. The Crown would hold an *inquisition* into the property, making *extents* of the manors, including their woods and parks. The king's agents would administer the estates; they would file accounts, occasionally (as with Staverton Park) for useful runs of years. Thus in 1356 Thomas de Lisle, Bishop of Ely, was on the run for the murder* of William de Holme, and Edward III's valuation of his estates makes a useful comparison with that of a hundred years before: for 'Heylewode' it gives the coppice cycle (seven years), which the *Coucher Book* omits.[11]

Lands belonging to monasteries were seized by Henry VIII in the 1530s. Most of them he sold off and frittered away the proceeds on obscure French wars. A department of state was set up, the Court of Augmentations, for receiving the king's stolen property. Anyone making an offer for monkish land had to get a valuation, which is filed in the Public Record Office, for example:

Growton woode conteyneth 37 acres
howe wood conteyneth 4 acres
S[um]ma of acres 41
Wherof 10 acres of 3 yeres growth, 10 acres of 7 yeres growith, 15 acres of 10 yeres growthe and 6 acres resydue of 14 yeres grouth, all whych woods be dyuysed [leased] ... *except great trees growing in the same by the late abbott and convent* [of Bury St Edmunds Abbey] *to Wyllyam Gooche* [in 1533] ...   £5
And in the seyd woodes be growinge 200 sapling okes of 30 and 40 yeres growthe whereof 80 reseruyd for tymber for the ffermor [lessee] *to repayre the howses ... and 120 resydewe*

---

* This was, it seems, a genuine murder: the gangster-Bishop's hand did not strike the blow, but did arrange the contract.

valluid at 4d. the tree wch is in the bolle 40s.

PARTICULARS FOR GRANT OF GROTON, SUFFOLK, TO ADAM WINTHROP, 1543

[He was the ancestor of the Winthrops of Massachusetts and Connecticut. Half the wood is incorporated in the present Groton Wood.][12]

Among documents containing incidental references to woods are *cartularies*, registers of land transactions kept by monasteries and other institutions. The transactions themselves seldom involve woodland, but woods appear among the abuttals that define other pieces of land. These may identify the location of the wood with respect to fixtures such as manor houses, roads or churchyards.

Many cartularies have been published. It is worth searching the index for incidental mentions of woodland. However, mentions tend to be scarce, and only those fluent in reading medieval manuscripts should try searching unindexed cartularies.

ESTATE ACCOUNTS

Although any large estate, from Roman times onwards, presumably had some sort of book-keeping, estate accounts survive from the thirteenth century onwards. An account roll typically covers one financial year (New Year's Day often being Michaelmas, 30 September). It lists income and expenditure, grouped under heads such as 'Carts' or 'Buildings', to arrive at a net profit. On the back of the parchment roll, worn by many grubby fingers, is a list of stock, live and dead, from swans to tree trunks. There may be a heading covering the wood, with sales of faggots and the cost of making and carting them, and sales of timber. Other references, including to non-woodland trees, can be scattered through the roll, for instance purchases of hurdles or underwood for making them, or trees felled or bought for repairs or new buildings.

Account rolls can give a detailed picture of woodland management and the place of woodland in the economy. They record functions that involved money. Trees felled in the wood for repairs to the lord's barn may appear under the cost of felling, or from sales of the resulting branches or bark. Sometimes there is a separate little account of the 'servile works' owed by tenants by way of rent – someone might work off *x* works by acting as woodward.

In the late Middle Ages, unfortunately, estates were often 'farmed', leased as a whole to a tenant whose records rarely survive. Estate accounts flourished again in the eighteenth century. The account books prepared by agents of the Ashburnhams, woodland owners in Sussex and Suffolk, record, year by year, income from so many acres of underwood which produced so many hundred hurdles (at six score to the 'hundred'), 'pease sticks', 'hurdle brush', 'short wood', 'cow bins' etc., etc. – a mass of minute detail whose exact meaning was then familiar to everyone and is now forgotten.

Scottish native pinewoods are documented in estate records from the seventeenth century onwards. Some records are preserved because of lawsuits, especially over lands confiscated from earls who committed high treason in the Jacobite Rebellions. We learn of the traditional local uses of pine, birch and other trees, of commercial logging, and of the arrival of sawmill technology in the seventeenth century. They are the basis of Steven & Carlisle's study in the 1950s (p.302) – a work ahead of its time, not least because it went through the evidence wood by wood instead of working downwards from generalities – and Smout's more recent work.

MAPS

Medieval maps

As far as I know the earliest surviving map to show a British wood is the famous Boarstall Map of c.1445. Boarstall in Buckinghamshire was a curious place, embedded in the wooded Forest of Bernwood. The map shows a very small village with its church, moated manor house and wayside cross, surrounded by open-field arable and also hedged fields. The periphery is almost all woods and wood-pastures, some of then named ('Ffrith', 'Costowod', 'Pannsale' etc.) and subdivided by hedges. A fallow buck and doe are drawn – to show that this is a Forest – and there are pollards and coppice stools of two unidentifiable kinds of tree. In the foreground is an anachronistic scene showing an early Forester [!] presenting the gory head of a wild swine to King Edward the Confessor, and in return getting a coat of arms [!] and a grant of land.

The purpose of the map was not topographical accuracy; much ink has flowed in a vain effort to reconcile it with what is known from other sources.[13] It seems to represent a compartmental wooded Forest, with areas of grassland and pollard trees and other areas, hedged off, with coppice stools.

It might be thought that the medievals could not produce detailed maps of woods, but for two mysterious surveys, of Sibton (Suffolk) in 1325 and Leaden Roding (Essex) in 1439, each of which gives the areas of woods to within a quarter of a square perch, that is to within one part in 10,000 for a 15-acre (6 ha) wood.[14] Such precision would be hard to attain even now (supposing the boundary of the wood could be precisely defined). However, at Leaden Roding three of the woods still survive, and have areas within 1 to 4 per cent of those cited in 1439: as close an agreement as could be expected, given that woodbanks have a finite width. People who could measure the area of an irregular wood with such accuracy would necessarily have been able to construct a detailed map. (Measuring woodland is more difficult than for other land because the trees get in the way.)

Elizabethan and later maps

The craft of mapmaking ought to have been stimulated by the dissolution of the monasteries and privatisation of their lands. Thousands of new owners of monkish land and woodland would have wanted to know what they had acquired. However, it was 40 years later, in the 1570s, that detailed maps began to appear, showing all fields, hedges, woods, roads and buildings.

Early maps are usually of landed estates, at a scale of around 1:5,000, showing the shapes of fields and woods. They were often made when an estate had changed hands. Historians may philosophise eloquently about maps as expressions of 'power', but mere information was often needed: complexities of land tenure required research before a purchaser knew exactly what he had bought.

Mapmaking did not evolve out of crude beginnings, and accuracy does not go with late date. Elizabethan maps range from the sketchy to the extremely accurate. The best surveyors, such as Thomas Langdon who mapped Gamlingay (Cambridgeshire) in 1601, and John Norden who mapped the complex Stanhope estates, including Staverton Park, in 1602, bear comparison with any cartography since.

Maps were made down the centuries, with changing fashions in style but (as regards woodland) no great changes in content. The existence of a map, its quality and survival are matters of chance. Maps show the outlines of woods, sometimes indicating the nature of the boundary. Individual trees are not shown, apart from a very few acting as boundary marks, or occasional mentions of service and other rare trees. An early convention appears to indicate timber trees scattered among underwood, and in wood-pasture cartographers sometimes indicate where the trees were dense or sparse. Many cartographers indicate trees in hedges, but usually at an even spacing, which must be conventional.

Areas of woods are often shown (in acres (often, but not always, the modern acre of 0.405 hectare), roods at four to the acre, and square perches at 40 to the rood). Very rarely we are told of how many years' growth the underwood was.

Maps of counties and larger areas
Small-scale county maps of the sixteenth and seventeenth centuries, such as the Norden series, show conventionalised parks, but are of little use for woods. Patches of trees fill inelegant blank spaces rather than indicating reality. Only Rutland and Middlesex, tiny counties, are mapped at a scale big enough to show individual woods. Woods near roads may be shown on road maps, beginning in 1675.[15]

Knowledge of the Scottish Highlands has been transformed since Steven & Carlisle's time by the rediscovery of the sketch maps made by Timothy Pont, indefatigable explorer of the wild Highlands between 1585 and 1596. These maps, recording every shieling, burn and wood, were never published. Later they were worked on by the learned Robert Gordon of Straloch, and sent to the Dutch cartographer John Blaeu, who published some in a heavily revised form in his great *Atlas* in 1654, and lost others. Blaeu's version is simplified from Pont's original, and woodland is usually exaggerated; whence (in part) the belief that as recently as the seventeenth century the Highlands were much more wooded than they are now.[16] The next maps to show individual woods in Scotland were General Roy's Military Survey, made in 1747–55 after the Jacobite Rebellion.[17]

Mapmakers later published county maps, at scales of 1 inch to the mile (1:63,360) or larger, showing the sizes and rough shapes of woods. These include Rocque of the London area in the 1750s, Chapman of Nottinghamshire in 1774, Hodskinson & Donald of Cumberland in 1774, Chapman & André of Essex in 1783, and Faden of Norfolk in 1795. Woods, however, are often shown inaccurately (as compared to contemporary large-scale maps). Any wood that was not visible from a public road, or had recently been felled, might be omitted. County maps are often better for Forests, wooded commons or parks than for woodland; some have a special symbol for differentiating wood-pasture (see Fig. 183a).

Enclosure and tithe maps
Each Enclosure Act (p.57) required hiring a surveyor to make a large-scale map showing the proposed state after reorganisation. Such maps, dating between

c.1720 and c.1850, exist for nearly half the parishes of England. Although woodland was seldom directly involved, many enclosure maps cover the entire parish and thus show woods: the earliest map to portray Hayley Wood is the enclosure map of 1816 which shows the wood, already surrounded by 'Ancient Inclosures'. Wood-pastures, especially wooded Forests, often had separate enclosure proceedings and maps (which usually led to destruction of the site, p.325).[18]

Between 1838 and 1845 there was a campaign of mapmaking on account of the Tithe Commutation Act. Tithes, originally every tenth sheaf, lamb or faggot, paid to the provider of the parish priest – or, by then, often to some third party whose ancestors had purchased the entitlement – were to be replaced by a 'rent-charge', a money tax on almost every field, pasture, meadow and wood in England and Wales, which therefore had to be measured. If there was not already an enclosure-award map a new map was made, together with a schedule or list of lands.[19]

The student will probably find either an enclosure or a tithe map covering any wood. The acreage, owner and occupier will usually be given, but the land use seldom goes beyond differentiating 'wood' from 'plantation'. Usually these maps are reliable, but they do not always prove the non-existence of a wood. Small areas of woodland among moorland, if they do not have definite boundaries, may be overlooked; some tithe maps, particularly in Dorset, are rather perfunctory and may leave woods out.

The Ordnance Survey

The national survey, at 1 inch to the mile, began in 1795, and worked northwards, reaching the north of England by the 1860s. Scotland was covered from 1847 to 1878. At first the OS was similar to county maps; some of the same people worked on both. The early sheets, of the southern one-third of England, suffer from the same weaknesses. Often there survive 'surveyors' drawings' (not field notes but an intermediate stage in publishing the map); these may give details of woods that disappeared from the published version, but they can also contain fictitious details such as field boundaries that bear no relation to the real fields as known from larger-scale maps.

After 1830, fieldwork was done more conscientiously and in greater detail; as far as I know woods from this point on are reliably shown. Some of the previous surveys were left unpublished; for a few sheets there were two published versions, before and after 1830. The metal plates from which the maps were printed remained in use (though sometimes copied electrolytically) for most of the century, railways and other new details being added in later impressions.

The large-scale OS, at 6 inches to the mile (1:10,560), began in Ireland in the 1830s. This was followed by the tithe-award maps; then the surveyors were employed on a 6-inch and 25-inch (1:2,500) survey of Britain, beginning in Scotland and northern England where the 1-inch coverage was still unfinished. The 6- and 25-inch scales show almost the same information, except that the 25-inch adds acreages of fields and woods.

The 25-inch OS of the mid- to late nineteenth century is the most detailed and accurate map of Britain ever made, especially regarding trees and woods. Wood-names and acreages are given. Perhaps the most detailed of all the sheets are those covering Hatfield Forest in 1874, distinguishing woods (with rides), scrub, grassland, small ditches, hundreds of wood-pasture trees (each one, as far as one can verify from air photographs, measured in by men dragging a chain), and even woodbanks. This is exceptional, but in general the first edition 25-inch tried to show every non-woodland tree in Britain, and as far as it can be checked got them right.

The OS convention for 'normal' woodland depicts standard trees among underwood, but there are many other signs, which vary with date and are not fully explained. They include bracken, rough grassland, bushes without trees and trees without underwood. Conifer symbols must indicate planting, except in parts of the country where native yew or pine are possible. Even if the conifers have now disappeared, their former presence can explain other trees planted along with them, such as plantation-type oaks (Fig. 203), or trees such as birch that are successors to the defunct conifers.

Later editions of the OS decline in content and accuracy: the first details to go were individual trees. Nevertheless, they are the chief documentary source for woodland in the twentieth century. The primary material is the 6-inch or 25-inch surveys, from which other scales are derived. A 1-inch map published in the 1950s can thus show woodland as it was in the 1920s. A wood may be shown as 'rough grassland', the result of a 1920s felling, and yet long ago have reverted to being a normal wood with surviving ancient stools. The date of survey, not of publication, should always be quoted.

LEGAL DOCUMENTS

Statutes and regulations

In most countries governments, in their vanity, have tried to regulate the behaviour of trees with masses of statutes. At international conferences on forest history about two-thirds of the papers are on the history of forest legislation and one-third on the history of forests.

Although this began in the Middle Ages, legislation vastly expanded after 1750, the time of Enlightenment, when writers on modern forestry sought to bend the ear of government and invest their theories with the majesty of law. Typically they sought to replace the earlier, often communal, links between people and trees with something reflecting the Age of Reason (whether it was good or bad reasoning would emerge later). Woods were to be separated from pasture and farming, and to be managed henceforth on 'scientific' principles of modern forestry (Chapter 18).[20]

Britain was a disappointingly un-Enlightened country with no tradition of top-down regulation until the Forestry Act of 1919. Charles Mynors has written a wonderful book, *The Law of Trees, Forests and Hedgerows*. Exhaustive and very readable, it goes back in some detail to the nineteenth century, but before 1919 deals almost exclusively in case law.

One can almost count the relevant English statutes on one's ears. The two that concern us are medieval Forest Law and the Statute of Woods of 1543. Forest Law, though mainly concerned with deer, in theory forbade people to cut down their own trees within the legal bounds of a Forest. The Statute of Woods required woods to have a minimum of 12 timber trees per acre, to be fenced after felling to prevent them from turning into wood-pasture, and not to be grubbed out.

It is an anachronism to read early statutes as if they were intended to stop people from doing things; their purpose was often to raise revenue from fines. They are of value only in conjunction with records of prosecutions: what cases were brought? were the fines deterrent? People did cut down trees and woods within the legal bounds of Forests, and used or sold the timber and underwood. 'Offences' were prosecuted only if there was an aggravating circumstance, such as the perpetrator being the Prioress of Felsted (representative of a French religious house), or there being a large commercial interest, or the penurious and greedy Charles I being on the throne. Prosecutions under the Statute of Woods seem to have been very rare, although it could be cited in the terms of leases even 200 years on.

Court rolls

The legal documents relevant to the woodland historian are not the top-down ones. The minutes of local manorial courts record things people were not supposed to do, how often they did them, and how much they were fined. Non-woodland trees appeared before the courts more often than woodland: disputes over who owned a hedge, trees allowed to grow out and obstruct the highway, turning timber trees (which belonged to the landowner) into pollards (whose regrowth belonged to the tenant), and so on. Manorial courts could and did amend the rules from time to time.

Read with patience, court rolls can yield a vivid picture of how a wood or wood-pasture actually functioned. Species of tree are often named. One must note whether a type of 'offence' was a regular and repeated occurrence. Court proceedings seem often to have been used to collect a reasonable grazing or woodcutting rent under the guise of a fine.

Forest proceedings

Administrative records of English Forests, especially wooded royal Forests, attracted much attention a hundred years ago. Selections can be read in many published works, such as J. Charles Cox's book *The Royal Forests of England* in 1905, and chapters by Cox and others on 'Forestry' in the earlier volumes of the *Victoria County History*. Many a wood was saved from oblivion because it happened to lie within a legal Forest and its owner committed a prosecutable breach of Forest Law.

For Epping Forest there are numerous fragments of the proceedings of lower Forest courts, which in this particular Forest handled the sort of business that manorial courts would have done were it not a Forest – people cutting wood who were not entitled to it, grazing illegal goats, removing wood under woodcutting rights on an 'unreasonable great Cart' instead of the prescribed sledge, etc.[21]

However, most of these are selections, made on an unknown basis, rather than a systematic analysis of all the Forest files in the Public Record Office. An exception is the compendium, compiled c.1400, of the archives of Sherwood Forest and edited by Helen Boulton, with its extensive records of timber, deer and Forest offences.[22]

EARLY BOTANICAL RECORDS

The earliest botanical record of a plant in a definite place is of nearly the rarest British plant, *Sorbus domestica,* the Whitty pear or 'true service', which has ash-like leaves and fruits like tiny apples. The author of the seventh-century *Historia Brittonum,* 'Nennius', records 'apples ... found on an ashtree' on cliffs near the mouth of the Wye.[23] This wondrous tree was not noted again until found far away in Wyre Forest (Worcestershire) a thousand years later. After three centuries of further oblivion it has lately been found again on various cliffs, including the Wye, where it doubtless lurked unseen all the time.

Systematic records begin in a small way in the sixteenth century. In the seventeenth century Thomas Johnson recorded the plants in Ken Wood next to Hampstead Heath, and John Ray in Madingley and Kingston Woods near Cambridge. These can be compared with later records for those woods and with what is there now. They establish the important fact that woods lose species with time: thus in Madingley Wood, out of 31 species recorded in *c.*1660, 14 are no longer there. Extinctions are not at random, but are especially of non-shade-bearing plants of woodland grassland and coppiced areas, such as saw-wort and the grass *Calamagrostis canescens.*[24]

Other historic records lurk in herbaria. Besides being biased towards rare plants, herbaria are organised by species rather than locality: it is easier to find out localities where *Serratula* used to occur than to find out what plants there were in Hayley Wood in the nineteenth century. Computer catalogues may help to solve this problem.

HOW TO FIND WRITTEN RECORDS

Each English and Welsh county has one or more record offices, run by the county council and open to the public. Their map collections are a good place to begin. They should have sets of nineteenth-century Ordnance Surveys, and maybe copies of the survey drawings. They will have most of the Enclosure-Act and Tithe maps for the county, and many earlier estate maps. They usually have a map index, parish by parish, as well as indexes to other types of document.

Eighteenth- and nineteenth-century county histories often reveal whether a wood, or the estate of which it formed part, belonged to the Crown, or a private family, or a monastery, or a diocese, or a Cambridge or Oxford college. This indicates the type of archive in which its earlier history is likely to be found. The *Victoria County History* – still incomplete – contains detailed accounts parish by parish, often identifying the archive and giving a reference to each document. English Place-Name Society volumes give references to documents mentioning particular woods.

The Public Record Office (National Archive) at Kew contains the records of Crown (and Duchy of Lancaster and Duchy of Cornwall) estates. For the Middle Ages many items have been published as abstracts in the hundreds of volumes of the king's business correspondence known as the Rolls Series, including (among others) the Close and Liberate Rolls. These are to be found in big libraries; the volumes have excellent indexes of places. For many purposes it is unnecessary to see the original documents. The PRO has many other types of record, including early maps and surveys. Consulting the catalogues used to be a research task in itself, but many of them are now on computer files. The British Library contains some important manuscript maps, such as Roy's Military Survey. Pont's maps are in the National Library of Scotland.

Records of monastic estates were scattered to the four winds at the Dissolution. By now they may have got into almost any archive: a useful source is Davis's *Medieval Cartularies*.[25] Most monastic estates make an appearance in the PRO, either in the Crown records (if Henry VIII retained them) or in those of the Court of Augmentations (if he frittered them away).

Diocesan archives have sometimes been transferred to public repositories: thus those of Ely diocese are in Cambridge University Library, but Canterbury has an excellent record office in the Cathedral. Every Cambridge (and Oxford?) college, and the university, has its own archive, containing records of each estate they have ever owned, some inherited from before the college was founded.

Private estates sometimes still have their own archives; they vary from those with muniment rooms staffed by professional archivists to those that are so secretive as to cast doubt on their confidence in the title to their lands.* Deposited private archives form the bulk of the collections of county record offices (not always in their own county). Private estates appear sporadically in the Public Record Office, for example the administrators' accounts of high traitors or vacant bishoprics. Entries in the *Calendar of Inquisitions Post-Mortem* (Rolls

---

* Another reason for being refused access to an archive is that the documents are lying in sacks on the floor.

Series) may mention an extent, but to find out its contents one has to consult the original document.

Useful pieces of information often turn up in unexpected contexts: woods may be named in the context of highwaymen, murders, heretics, accounts of unrelated estates, inquests after accidents, and woodsale advertisements in newspapers.

Archivists are responsible for producing documents, but not normally for reading or translating them, though they give friendly help with the occasional difficult word. Some record offices offer a research service for a fee.

INTERPRETING DOCUMENTS

Much ecological history is written by either:

- historians who fail to understand the ecology, who write (for example) about people 'destroying' forests by cutting down trees, not realising that cutting down an ash-tree is a different action from cutting down a pine;

or:

- ecologists who fail to understand the history, who assert that 'ancient authors say ...' without stating which ancient authors, what exactly they say, what exactly the Greek or Latin words mean, and what are the grounds for believing them.

The subject is plagued by factoids or canards: statements that look like facts, are treated with the respect due to facts, and have all the properties of facts except that they are not true. I do not mean conflicts of evidence or differences of scholarly opinion, such as the Vera controversy, but beliefs that persist even though they are easily disproved. Examples include:

1. The landscape has always been changing (instead of periods of stability alternating with more or less widely spaced phases of change).
2. Forests were 'cleared' by setting fire to them.
3. Hedges are no older than the eighteenth century.
4. The roofs of Westminster Hall and King's College Chapel, Cambridge are of chestnut, not oak.
5. Erosion is necessarily the 'fault' of people destroying forests (rather than of ploughing land, or being part of the normal order of nature, the process that gives sedimentary geologists a job).

Not all factoids are relics of past ignorance: in 2001 it became accepted (despite public denial by the Director of the Animal Health Laboratory) that casual passers-by can transmit foot-and-mouth disease from animal to animal.

The ecologist needs to assess what weight to put on each item. Oak is often mentioned in documents: it was a common and expensive tree; it was easily recognised; it had many specific uses; it belonged to landowners, who kept records, rather than tenants who did not. Hornbeam is rarely mentioned: it was difficult to identify; there was little reason to recognise it, because it did nothing that other trees would not do; it sank into the general anonymity of underwood. Hence any mention of hornbeam is worth many mentions of oak.

Some pitfalls and sources of false information
1. *Misunderstanding landscape history.* The history of the countryside is not the same as the history of country *people* nor of what people have *said* about the countryside. There are other actors in the theatre besides Man. Landscape history is the history of human default as much as of human action.
2. *Tradition of plagiarism*: writers have copied one another. If John Evelyn said something in the seventeenth century, that was good enough to be repeated in the twentieth, without checking whether Evelyn was rightly informed or drew the right conclusions.
3. *Expecting the history of the landscape to be simple.* If some chestnut-woods can be shown to be planted in the eighteenth or nineteenth century, that does not make all of them post-1700 or all artificially planted.
4. *Using only documentary evidence*, which shortens perspectives and precludes knowing what was happening at times when people were not writing. In Britain most of the really big steps in making the landscape had already happened before the earliest documents. Even in the best-documented sites, such as Gamlingay Wood or Hatfield Forest, the fieldworker discovers things that are not in the written record.
5. *Using documents of a generalised nature.* The history of woodland is the sum of the histories of hundreds of individual woods. The history of people's attitudes to woodland, however interesting, is not the same thing: it can hardly be understood without first knowing what it was they were attitudinising about.
6. *Obsession with the history of forest laws.* Writers accept legal documents at face value and interpret them in terms of modern legal practices.
7. *Not knowing what to make of tradition.* Almost any popular book on trees has masses of 'legends', often treated as evidence. These are colourful stories, which it seems a shame to ignore. The question is not so much 'are legends

reliable?', but 'is a particular story a legend or not, and where did it come from?' For centuries, in a cosmopolitan country like England, country folk have been reading books and acquiring facts and factoids from other countries or from works of fiction.

8. *Using generalised 'human activity' as a let-out.* Biologists and historical geographers too often invoke human activity as an explanation of any pattern or phenomenon that they think is anomalous, as if this dispensed them from further investigation. But details are needed. If tree-planting is to explain an apparently anomalous tree distribution, one has to demonstrate that the pattern of planting activity fits that distribution.

9. *Translation.* Translators tend to know little of woodland history and fail to get the technical terms right. They can use 'clearing a wood' without saying whether they translate *amputare boscum,* felling a wood (expecting it to grow again), or *evellere boscum,* digging up a wood (to make a field). 'Brushwood' properly means birch twigs or other material for making brushes, but translators sometimes use it for the Latin *subboscus,* underwood in general. The student should make every effort to test the translation, if not to go back to the original record.

How to write pseudo-history
- Do no fieldwork.
- Confine yourself to written documents.
- Use contemporary documents of a generalised nature.
- Use forest laws as direct evidence of what was or was not done.
- Rely on other people's translations.
- Pay attention to contemporary writers who had much to say for themselves.
- Assume that everything presented as 'legend' or 'oral history' is what it claims to be.

How to write pseudo-ecology
- Confuse trees and other plants and animals with 'The Environment'; do not investigate their behaviour.
- Assume that all trees behave alike.
- Confuse the history of the countryside with the history of country folk or of what people have said about the countryside.
- Copy what previous authors have said.

- Expect the history of the landscape to be simple.
- Take official statistics at face value, without reading the small print of how they were arrived at or what exactly they mean.
- Never admit you don't know something.

CHAPTER 8

ARCHAEOLOGY AND LAND-FORMS OF WOODLAND AND WOOD-PASTURE

One of the features of an ancient forested soil surface, one that had or has been continued thru several generations of trees, is the presence of mounds and depressions ('pillows and cradles') resulting from blown-over and uprooted trees. This pillow-and-cradle topography – widespread in northeastern [United States] never-ploughed lands, and elsewhere in the world – is destroyed in the process of ploughing, a land-use which leaves a smooth surface and clean-cut plough-line in the soil horizons ... These ploughland features will then persist even for two hundred years after abandonment, or until new pillows and cradles start forming when trees are again wind-blown.

F.E. EGLER & W.A. NIERING, 1976 [REFERRING TO CONNECTICUT][1]

Archaeologists tend to avoid woods: either because they are assumed to be relicts of wildwood that have never known human activity, or because tree roots are assumed to have destroyed the underground stratigraphy, or because dense vegetation interferes with archaeological survey. In reality, English and Welsh woods contain as much archaeology as anywhere else, if not more. Potsherds rarely lie on the surfaces, but badgers sometimes excavate them, and they should be looked for in the tip-up mounds of uprooted trees.

Some features belong to the functioning of woods themselves; others (e.g. coal mines) may have been in a wood but not related to it; others may survive from something on the site before it became a wood. Woods can contain remains of almost any terrestrial human activity, including some seldom preserved outside woodland. The investigator should not pass over the inexplicable: people often send me drawings and photographs of strange earthworks in woods, which I am seldom able to identify.

Natural features are not always distinguishable in the field from artificial earthworks. Landslip terraces (natural) are easily confused with lynchets (artificial); with ponds it is often impossible to be sure which is which.

This chapter deals with the non-living part of woodland archaeology; but ancient trees, especially coppice stools and pollards, are as much part of the archaeology as barrows and charcoal-hearths. Anyone surveying a wood should record both. Archaeology can manifest itself indirectly in such things as nettle-beds growing on accumulations of phosphate (p.200).

Faint earthworks may not be visible all the time. They may be revealed when a wet spring temporarily floods the surface, or enhanced by vegetation sensitive to slight differences of drainage. Faint banks or ridge-and-furrow can appear as lines of dog's-mercury, bluebell or primrose (p.175ff).

SITES OF WOODS

Woodland often occupies particular positions in the landscape, usually not places that are good for growing trees, but places bad for anything else: steep slopes, rock outcrops, flat ill-drained clayland, or old landslips.

Large areas of sandy or stony terrain tend to be heath or moorland, some-times with woods round their edges. In England most big heaths date from the Mesolithic to Bronze Ages, but there are later examples of woodland turning into heath: for example most of Thorpe Wood near Norwich turned into Mousehold Heath around the twelfth century AD. The heaths of Wollin on the Polish coast arose out of woodland a little earlier, supposedly as a result of too much harvest-ing of trees.[2]

Often a medieval coppice-wood adjoins a common pasture or wood-pasture, with a stout bank between. Cheddar Wood adjoins Linwood Common in the Mendip Hills: Wall Wood and Monk Wood adjoin Woodside Green near Hatfield Forest, Essex. Probably the whole was originally wood-pasture, and the lord and tenants did a deal: the lord got exclusive control of the more wooded part in exchange for relinquishing his rights to the trees on the rest.

Ancient woodland strongly avoids ground liable to flooding: that was the most valuable land as meadow. In other countries, woods occur on the flood-plains of rivers such as the Rhine, Danube and Mississippi. A fragment still remains of the last flood-plain wood in Ireland (the Geeragh in Macroom, County Cork). Only in the twentieth century, as meadow lost its importance, have woods arisen on wetland; for example, the birchwood now covering Holme Fen nature reserve near Peterborough, or most of the alder and sallow carrs of the Norfolk Broads. Rising local relative sea level is bringing the latter within reach of high tides: it is an uncanny experience to stand in Surlingham Wood and watch the spring tide creeping around the tree trunks (Fig. 47).

SHAPES OF WOODS

Shapes of woods can be constrained by the environment, for example a long narrow wood following a steep escarpment, or the 'gallery' woods bordering streams that are common in Cornwall and in many other countries. Otherwise, the shape of a wood tells a tale. Does it have the shape of a field that has turned into a wood? Or is it the shape of an ancient wood? Or of a park? Or a common?

Typical shapes of ancient woods (Fig. 187) are sinuous, as in Hayley Wood, or zigzag, as in Kingston Wood nearby. The irregular curves date from a period before people saw any virtue in straight lines; they may represent a boundary that had to find its way between the trees of a wood-pasture. Zigzags may represent successive stages in grubbing out a bigger wood. Woods seldom have roads within them: where a road appears to cross a wood, either the wood or the road is modern, or the road really separates two woods, with a woodbank on either side.

Wood-pasture commons (including wooded Forests), in contrast, have straggling outlines, funnelling out by *horns* into the verges of the roads that cross the common. The houses of commoners, scattered round the edge, often define the outline. There can be enclaves of private land, including private woodland, within the common. Wooded commons are no different in this respect from unwooded commons. Norfolk and Dorset, before the Age of Reason caught up with them, were permeated by a spider's-web of ramifying commons, some wooded, some not.

Parks often have a very distinctive shape, a rectangle or pentagon with rounded corners. The special feature of a park was an expensive deer-proof fence or boundary wall, hence the need to shorten the boundary.

EARTHWORKS BELONGING TO WOODS

Woodbanks

In much of England ancient woods are surrounded by banks and ditches, following all the bends and zigzags of their outlines. Normally the bank is on the inside and the ditch on the outside (Fig. 48); exceptions raise the suspicion that the site was once a park (Fig. 49).

The earliest woodbanks that I know are faint ones bordering the holloway of the 'Roman Road' – really an Iron Age road – through Chalkney Wood, Essex. Most big woodbanks seem to be of Anglo-Saxon or early medieval date.

At Hindolveston (Norfolk) the monks of Norwich Cathedral, having converted their two big woods from timber to underwood production, hired contractors to make 3½ miles (5.5 kilometres) of new woodbank round the woods (p.103). Their account-rolls record the following:[3]

Branches of trees and underwood sold on the bank [in 1297–8]
Westwood: Richard Gilbertson   2s.

    John Hunny   4s.

    Henry Leper   3s. 6d. ....

[30 purchasers in all, total £10. 12s. 1d.]

Adam Draper For making 4 hundred [i.e. 480] perches of

    Woodbank [*ffoss' Bosc*] at 2d. a perch   £4

    To the same for repairing banks, by the day   10s. 3d.

[5 contractors in all; total length 1186½ perches, i.e. 3.7 miles, 6.0km]

In pulling thorns ... by the day   4s. 10½d.

    [elsewhere it says 'pulling thorns to plant']

Total expenses   £10. 9s. 10¼d.

And so receipts exceed expenses by   2s. 2¾d.

The Wood [1299–1300]

To mending gates of the wood, 8 days as required   2s. 8½d.

To 1 staple for the gates   1d.

To 5 locks bought for the said gates   8d.

Item, in mending the banks of the woods in places, with planting

    little plants and thorns, for 33 days   5s. 4½d.

Paid to the woodward [for 52 weeks], he gets 7d. a week [a full-time

    job at the minimum wage rate]   36s. 6d.

They built bridges at the entrances, supplied gates with 'feterloks', and planted a hedge, all at a cost of £10. 10s. [roughly £7,000 in the money of 2006]. The date, 1297–8, is rather late for a major woodbank. One of the woods still exists, surrounded by a massive bank and ditch at least 30 feet (9 metres) in total width

(Fig. 50). Accounts of woodland in the Blean, east Kent, record the making of what appear to be new woodbanks in the 1230s, 1250s and 1290s.[4]

Woodbanks were made whenever a new wood-edge was created by subtracting from, or adding to, a wood. By the eighteenth century wood edges were often in straight lines. Banks became steadily less substantial, until in the nineteenth century they were no more than a hedge of the same period, with a feeble bank and a single row of planted hawthorns (Fig. 51). The latest woodbank known to me was constructed through Gravelpit Coppice, Hatfield Forest (Essex), when it was reduced in size in 1857.

Internal woodbanks were made when a wood was subdivided between owners. In Gamlingay, when the biggest manor was divided in the twelfth century, two-thirds and one-third, so was the wood (see Fig. 179). The predecessors of Merton College and of the Avenells insinuated a ditch between the trees; each began at the perimeter bank, keeping the bank on his own side of the ditch, and met in the middle where the bank switches sides. The ditch is still there, 400 years after Merton bought out the Avenells and no longer needed it. In Hockley Woods, south Essex, such a process continued when successive farms were split off the big estates, each taking and embanking an acre or two of wood. Subdivision typically went on until the late Middle Ages, after which the woods were gradually re-amalgamated into one ownership.

Presumably banks originally had a triangular section, which would slowly wear down to a rounded profile; leases of woods often required the lessee to clear out the ditch. Later banks tend to be more triangular and less worn down, though I hesitate to date an earthwork by its state of preservation. Banks are often asymmetrical, steeper on the outside.

Where a wood is on a slope, a *lynchet* tends to obliterate the ditch. If there is a field below the wood, the soil creeps away down the slope, leaving the woodbank at the top of a little cliff; if a field is above the wood soil creeps down to fill up the ditch and pile against the bank (Fig. 188).

Very big woodbanks were made by ecclesiastical landowners. In Chicksands Wood (Bedfordshire) a huge bank stands on the monks' side of the ditch that separates their part of the wood from the secular Pedley Wood (Fig. 52). In the woods around Canterbury one can detect the different styles of woodbank profile favoured by the Archbishop, Christchurch Cathedral, St Augustine's Abbey and other, mostly spiritual, wood owners.

Not every ancient wood was embanked. Richard Gulliver comments on the scarcity of woodbanks in the Vale of York.[5] Forest regulations sometimes stipulated that woods shall have a 'low bank and hedge' so as not to discommode the deer. This rarely seems to have been observed. The banks of the woods in Hatfield Forest are not much less substantial than those of non-Forest woods. However, the nearby wood called Canfield Hart and some of its neighbours, although unquestionably medieval, are surrounded only by a ditch with no bank: although a bank helps to stabilise a wood's outline it is not essential. Wychwood Forest (Oxfordshire) was a large wooded Forest compartmentalised into Copses (woodland) and Lights (grassland) (Fig. 189) . In what is left of the Forest the Lights follow dry valleys and the Copses occupy the limestone ridges; although they have been stable for centuries the divisions are not marked by any earthwork. (Soils over the limestone are thin, making this an example of the 'trees on rock, grassland on soil' principle.)

In stone-wall country, such as west Cornwall, there may be a boundary wall as well as, or instead of, a woodbank. The wall may act as a facing to the outer slope of the bank. On the top boundary of Cheddar Wood, Somerset, dividing the wood from Linwood Common (Fig. 190), the bank evidently came first and was then revetted with a wall, which was left unfinished. Around Sheffield, Melvyn Jones distinguishes three types of woodbank profile and three types of bank-plus-wall, as well as walls only.[6]

Woodbanks and wood-walls may not coincide with the present edge of a wood. Most of the woods of the Mendips (Somerset) extend beyond their banks: the woods increased in the twentieth century as the adjacent commons fell out of use. At the top of Cheddar Wood a fringe of woodland outside the woodbank was already there on the Ordnance Survey map of 1883; this fringe is of hazel and therefore antedates the coming of the grey squirrel (p.278).

The investigator should make a map at a scale of 1:2,500 of all the woodbanks and other earthworks, recording their width, on which side is the bank, any notable features of the profile, and any significant trees.

Trees on woodbanks: On many woodbanks are pollard trees of various species, typically halfway down the outer face of the bank. These are usually the only ancient upstanding trees in an ancient wood.

On slippery clays, woodbanks, even worn down by centuries of rain, are not negligible obstacles to getting into a wood. They were reinforced by a hedge at the level of the pollards. Remains of the hedge may have grown out into mighty and grotesque shapes. An ancient ash stool, its horizontal boughs plashed ('laid') in the line of the hedge, is a surreal object, as are the towering gnarled beeches that surround some woods in southeast Wales.

In southeast England, coppice compartments (*cants*) in woods are defined by low pollards called *cant-marks*, often not on a bank. These established the boundaries whenever a cant of a wood came up for sale at a coppice auction.

Woodbanks in other countries: Woodbanks were an investment expressing the value of woodland and the importance of woodland conservation, especially round small woods where the bank can, on occasion, take up one-sixth of the entire area of the wood.

In Wales, the bigger and more compact woods are often embanked, but mosaics of woods on rock outcrops and fields on pockets of soil are not demarcated. Many woods do not fill the space inside the wood-wall, as though they have shrunk at their up-slope edges.

In Scotland, the story is more complex. Pinewoods and birchwoods are not confined; indeed the biology of the trees requires that they have room to move around (Chapter 16). Professor Smout demonstrates the 'dyking' of woods, especially oakwoods, in the seventeenth century and later.[7] Whether this happened in the Middle Ages is uncertain; some Lowland woods, such as Garscadden Wood near Glasgow, have ancient banks around and within them.

In Ireland, some ancient woods were embanked, although with rare exceptions (such as St John's Wood, p.298) so little remains of their perimeters that woodbanks seldom survive. Often, as at interfaces between wood and bog in Killarney or between wood and limestone pavement on the Burren, I can find no boundary feature.

In Belgium, boundary banks, sometimes very thickly set with pollard trees, are a feature of big ancient woods such as the Forêt de Marchiennes. From the early sixteenth century there survive a series of drawings of a massive bank defining a monastic property boundary (p.188): it had gates and stiles, and sizeable coppice stools and a plashed hedge grew on it.[8]

Woodbanks are common in northern France. Around the (part-wooded) Forêt de Fontainebleau, south of Paris, I found a bank and ditch with reverse orientation (ditch on the inside), having sarsen-stone pillars to mark the boundary. A stronger bank, with normal orientation, marks the boundary of the (wooded) Forêt de Chantilly northeast of Paris. In both places the wood now sometimes extends beyond the bank. The monks of the great Abbey of Bec (Le Bec-Hellouin, Normandy) took the boundaries of their local wood seriously. Its perimeter, 5 miles (8 kilometres) long, is surrounded by a massive, sinuous bank with a mortared stone wall on it; lesser banks subdivide the interior (Fig. 53).

In America, woodland was usually too plentiful and labour too scarce for making woodbanks. I have found banks between wood-lots and fields on Cumberland Island off the Georgia coast, but that was a land of slavery where jobs might need to be found to keep slaves busy at slack times of year. In Japan, weak banks, with pollard trees on them, sometimes demarcate lanes between private coppices, or the boundary between the sacred grove of an ancient Shinto shrine and a private pinewood. Where a wood adjoins a rice-field the farmer has the right to maintain a ribbon of grassland to prevent the trees from shading the crop. These buffer zones, *imbatsuchi,* are old grassland, part of the elaborate interrelation of semi-natural habitats that forms the *satoyama* landscape of old-fashioned Japan.[9]

Woodbanks as habitat: Woodbanks create a special environment and add to the diversity of a wood. In wet woods such as Hayley badgers make setts in the bank. Woodbank soils tend to be less acidic, better drained and often more clayey than the rest of the wood, and may have distinct vegetation: in an ashwood with bluebell the bank may be a strip of maple-wood with dog's-mercury.

Tip-up mounds
Why is the general surface of English woods (away from earthworks and geological features) usually almost smooth? Successive storms ought to have uprooted trees, which – decades later – would have died and rotted away, leaving a pit where the roots were torn up and a mound beside it representing the root-plate.

Tip-up mounds are common in northeastern North America, and indicate which areas are primary forest that has usually been felled but never cultivated, and which are secondary on ex-farmland. In New England historical ecologists, by studying the rate at which mounds degrade and the superposition of successive mounds, have identified traces of hurricanes of 1944, 1938, 1821, 1815, 1635, and c.1450.[10] The Alleghany National Forest, Pennsylvania, is full of 'pillows and cradles' except in parts that have been cultivated (Fig. 54); these result from tornadoes, and when I was there in 1999 a tornado had just generated a new crop.

Tip-up mounds are rare in Britain. They have been reported by archaeologists from sites now outside woodland: at Sutton Hoo (Suffolk) pits and mounds were found with Neolithic pots carefully deposited in the pits.[11] On Rodborough

Common near Stroud (Gloucestershire), Dr Michael Martin tells me of pits, now in grassland, but with wood-anemone (an ancient-woodland plant, Chapter 12) growing round them, possibly due to the storms of 1602 or 1703. The blowdown of 2004 in the Tatra Mountains of Slovakia (p.19) was not a unique event; there are plenty of tip-up mounds from previous storms.

Most ancient woods have had centuries of coppicing, with little opportunity for trees to grow big enough to get uprooted. Even so, there ought to be traces of mounds dating from before coppicing began. They should be visible in woods such as Hayley, on clay soils that preserve earthworks well, and in seasons when waterlogging brings out details only an inch or so high, but I have never found them.

Tip-up mounds are generated now, especially when great beeches uproot; in Hayley Wood the storms of 1987 and 2002 produced some from ashes and maples. In the Middle Ages there were regular arrangements for disposal of *cablish*, windfallen wood, not only after exceptional storms like that of 1362. However, trees often fall or perish without generating mounds. An elm that dies standing and falls to pieces gradually will not leave a hole, nor will a lime that rots and breaks at the base. An oak that dies of *Phytophthora* or honey-fungus stands until the roots rot, and falls leaving only a small hole.

In overcrowded plantations and neglected woods there are now far more trees of the size and age to uproot than in past centuries. But why are there not faint pits and mounds from prehistory? Did trees then not fall in ways that created them?* Were there not enough big youngish trees to uproot? Or not enough great storms? Or is there some process that effaces mounds?

In the redwood forests of California I can find no trace of ancient pit-and-mound, although today these colossal trees quite often topple over leaving prodigious root holes.

Stumps

Another surprisingly rare feature is oak stumps in the last stages of decay. Many woods are full of stumps of oaks felled during or between the World Wars; these are eroded at the surface and the older ones are detached from the ground, but they are still very recognisable: a dead oak stump evidently takes more than a

---

* A hint that points in this direction is the clonal distribution of lime. If limes habitually blew down, they ought to have taken root along the fallen trunk, giving rise to a linear clonal patch. I have been unable to find such patches.

century to disappear (Fig. 56). (Most other species last less long.) Why are there not very degraded remains of stumps from earlier fellings? Fewer oaks than usual were felled between 1860 and 1914, but some were, and they should have left recognisable stumps. Is this due to a change in the method of felling?

'Grub-felling' by cutting through the roots is recorded for certain Norfolk woods in the nineteenth century. It would have the advantage of yielding a foot or two more of the valuable butt end of the tree. It ought, however, to leave a recognisable pit. Documents and place-names from Anglo-Saxon times onwards prove that stumps and stocks of trees were familiar objects. I have often seen medieval timbers with the marks of an axe on the butt end (showing that they were felled in the conventional way), but never with the stumps of roots.

The investigator should get into the habit of noting stumps, whether they are oak, their size, and (with experience) how recent they are.

Charcoal-hearths
Walter [de Fynchyngfelde] *had four charcoal hearths in the said cover, to the destruction of the forest and the detriment and escape of the king's beasts.*
HATFIELD FOREST, CLOSE ROLLS, 1336 (EDITOR'S TRANSLATION)

Charcoal is made by setting fire to wood and cutting off the air supply. Once started the process is self-sustaining: the chemistry of the wood is broken down, the volatile constituents evaporating as gases and fumes. What remains is a fraction of the weight of the wood with a larger fraction of its heat of combustion. The structure of the wood is unaffected, and microscopic details can still be identified in charcoal thousands of years old from archaeological sites.

Charcoal is a lightweight fuel, cheaply transported, though fragile and difficult to carry more than 15 miles (25 kilometres) unless by barge. A pound of charcoal produces more heat than a pound of wood, though less than the 2½ pounds or more of dry wood needed to make the pound of charcoal. It was favoured as an urban fuel, where the cost of transport mattered more than the cost of trees. Charcoal can be made to burn at a higher temperature than wood, or any other fuel before the invention of coke (which is coal converted to charcoal). It was used (and still is to a smaller extent) in high-temperature industries like iron working. It was produced in bulk in the Chilterns and other woods that supplied London, or that supplied iron-furnaces (p.105) as in the Weald, southern Lake District, Forest of Dean, South Wales and Argyll. It was also made wherever there were woods, to supply blacksmiths and other local users: charcoal was a convenient way to use up branchwood and oddments.

Often the species does not greatly matter, though hard charcoals such as oak are more transportable than fragile species such as pine. For gunpowder the charcoal was normally alder, whose structure produces the intimate mixture of carbon and potassium nitrate needed to achieve a predictable explosion. Alder coppices established round the Royal Gunpowder Factory at Waltham Abbey are still there.

The Italians, who took charcoal seriously, worked out the weight of charcoal produced by a given weight of wood: 16 per cent with pine, 18 per cent ash, 19 per cent beech, 20 per cent oak, 24 per cent maple, and 25 per cent larch (apparently based on the fresh weight of wood).[12] In practice wastage usually reduces the yield to 12–15 per cent.

Underwood of no more than 12 years' growth or branchwood was normally preferred. Charcoal was at first made by burning wood in a pit, hence the 'coalpits' in medieval documents in places where there was no mineral coal.

The classic method, recorded by Theophrastus in the fourth century BC,[13] was to build a stack of logs, cover it with earth and straw, ignite it from within by a secret method, and watch it day and night for a week as it smouldered into charcoal. In the New Forest this method flourished in the nineteenth century, but mysteriously collapsed after 1880, apart from a brief revival to make charcoal for gas masks in World War II.[14] Charcoal was later a by-product of pyroligneous acid factories (p.293), and is now made in steel kilns.

Details are poorly documented: writers and artists were more interested in the charcoal-burners' cabins than in what they did. A charcoal-stack requires a circle of level ground 20–40 feet (6–12 metres) across, often misleadingly called a 'pit' or 'pitstead'. On flat ground, as in Hatfield Forest, there is little hope of finding the site, but on a slope it appears as a circular platform scooped into the hillside. Charcoal-hearths were used time and again as the woods were felled and grew up. They are often in groups, served by one track, as men watching a stack burn could use their time building another stack and dismantling a third. Under the leaf-mould there is a layer of charcoal fragments, from which the species and size of wood can be identified.

Charcoal-hearths can be found in most sloping woods of north and west England, and in Wales, Scotland and Ireland. In the Derbyshire Peak six patterns of charcoal-hearth have been distinguished, two of them on level ground. Sometimes there are so many that scraping up earth to cover them would have significantly affected soil and vegetation.[15] Around Coniston Water are woods that supplied the ironworking activities of Furness Abbey and its successors from the twelfth to the eighteenth centuries. The woods contain pitsteads at about one per 2 acres (0.8 ha).[16] The woods around the Helford River, Cornwall, contain charcoal-hearths that probably served the tin industry, operating in that area in the seventeenth century (p.107).

Charcoal-hearths can occur on moorland that used to be woodland. Above the oakwoods north of Abergavenny (Monmouthshire) are brackeny slopes with faint depressions, which turn out to be scooped platforms containing oak charcoal. Charcoal-hearths on moorland, without charred wood, may be for peat charcoal; on the Lizard, Cornwall, these are rectangular.[17]

Charcoal was a big industry in Italy (which never had a coal age), leaving innumerable hearths in the Apennines.[18] I have found charcoal-hearths in surprisingly remote places on Athos, the Holy Mountain of the Ægean: the monks, who made a living from their vast mountain woods, evidently shipped charcoal to urban markets in Thessalonica and Constantinople. There are charcoal-hearths in the gorges of Crete, sometimes where there is no longer woodland.

Whitecoal: This mysterious fuel consisted of wood (of bigger sizes than usual for charcoal) dried in a kiln. It was especially used in lead smelting from about 1550 to after 1750, when a process was invented using coal. Lead smelting used typically one ton of wood (fresh weight) per ton of lead. Whitecoal was added to charcoal to give the right temperature: charcoal alone would burn too hot and volatilise the lead.

For unknown reasons whitecoal was made in the woods, rather than being dried immediately before use. Structures known from their shape as Q-pits occur in woods in lead-working areas, especially north Derbyshire. They are circular, with an entrance gap ('mouth') and a trench ('tongue') extending downslope from it. How they were used is unclear; some have evidence of a secondary use for charking mineral coal into coke.[19]

Limekilns

A limekiln was a rough stone tower with an arched entrance, built on a slope. Chalk or limestone and fuel were fed in at the top, and lime extracted through the arch. The heat of combustion decomposed the limestone (calcium carbonate) to quicklime (calcium oxide), used to make mortar or as a fertiliser.

The high temperature melts or calcines the inside of the kiln, depending on the kind of stone.

Limekilns were often built near a source of limestone or fuel or both, although even in woodland they might burn coal (p.396). Cathedral builders, needing hundreds of tons of lime, often got a friendly king to give them dead trees for a *rogus,* a kiln attached to the cathedral (where stone-working debris would provide the limestone). In Crete one often finds remains of a limekiln next to an isolated masonry chapel or fort.

WOODLAND PONDS, DELLS AND HOLLOWS

One might expect fewer ponds to the acre in ancient woodland than elsewhere, since most of the activities that create ponds took place outside woodland. This may not be so. The biggest concentrations of ponds in England are in Cheshire, south Lancashire, south Norfolk and north Suffolk; in East Anglia there are even more ponds per square mile in ancient woods than in the rest of the landscape.[20] Wolves Wood (Hadleigh, Suffolk) has more than three depressions per acre of woodland. Are these there by chance? Most show no characteristic artificial features nor any plausible explanation for their presence (Fig. 55). Were natural ponds among the obstacles to cultivation that caused a site to be left as woodland?

Ponds, pits and dells (dry depressions) have many different origins. In New England or Ohio innumerable 'ponds' represent natural hollows in the landscape as retreating glaciers left it, and this may partly be so in Old England also. They can result from other natural processes and from many kinds of human activity.

Some clusters of ponds are *pingos,* the melted-out remains of great lenses of ice formed in glacial times where water welled up from under frozen subsoil; they appear as ponds with banks round them, often in recent woodland, but so far not reported from ancient woods.[21] *Swallow-holes* occur where limestone or hard chalk is dissolved by acid waters or reacts with adjacent acid rocks, especially in Hertfordshire and Dorset. They are often conical, with streams mysteriously disappearing into the underworld.

Artificial ponds may or may not be related to happenings in the wood. 'Hammer Ponds' in the Weald are dams made to supply water wheels that worked mechanical hammers for processing iron, located in or near woods to be near the fuel supply. The five dams still holding water in Sutton Coldfield Park were made about 1420; they drove, among other industries, fulling mills, a sword mill and a button mill.[22]

In most coalfields mining goes back to the Middle Ages or before, and has left remains inside and outside woods. *Bell-pits* are shafts sunk to a shallow coal seam; the miner would undercut the bottom of the shaft as far as he dared and then dig another shaft. They appear as swarms of pits with rings of spoil around them. *Drifts* or *adits* are tunnels dug into a seam from its outcrop on a hillside. These too are often in groups, with remains of an access road in front.

Landslips

When a slope is too steep to stand up it gives way. It usually tilts as well as sliding. The breakaway part comes to rest as a terrace, often crescent-shaped and sloping back into the hillside to form a dell. Landslips are commonest where clay underlies other strata and springs lubricate the slip-plane. They occur especially on the coast, where marine erosion takes away the fallen material that would otherwise buttress the slope against further slumps, and in railway and motorway cuttings.

Inland landslips are commoner in woodland than in the rest of the countryside. The trees probably had little influence: tree roots are too shallow to reach the slip planes, although trees could have a minuscule effect by promoting the infiltration of rainwater to activate the slip. Landslips favour the formation or survival of woodland by preventing cultivation.

Good localities for woodland landslips are the Isle of Wight, the Ironbridge Gorge (Shropshire) and west Dorset. In Dorset, with its complex strata of clays, weak sandstones and chalk, they can occur on slopes as little as 5°, making a visit to even the smallest wood an adventure. They appear as steep banks with hollows behind them of bottomless black ooze, sallow-wood full of golden saxifrage, marsh violet, wood horsetail and unusual sedges; they can be lairs of wild sows, liberated in the 1990s. Many landslips are probably of Pleistocene age. More recent ones can be vaguely dated by relation to archaeological features and the growth of trees.

Britain is a stable country where landslips seldom still occur inland; but in the Alps, the Mediterranean and Japan the mountains are still being upheaved and are still shedding loads of sediment. Landslips are a well-known ecological factor in tropical forests, where the exposed rock may only slowly be recolonised.[23]

WOODS AND ROADS

Now you would never know
There was once a way through the woods.
RUDYARD KIPLING, *REWARDS AND FAIRIES*, 1910

By far the greater part of modern roads go back at least to the Saxon age, and many thou-
sands of miles of them, the ridgeways, have had a continuous existence going back into times
long before history began.
G.B. GRUNDY, 1933

Many parts of England once had a denser network of roads than today, and woodland is a likely place to look for extinct roads.

A difference between woods and wood-pastures is that wood-pastures have roads *through* them, but woods have roads *between* them (Figs 187, 208). An example from east Kent is the *radfalls*, a number of wide, muddy lanes between massive banks that straggle between the Blean Woods. Some of these are through routes, but one seems to be an access lane ending in North Bishopsden Wood, surrounded by woodbanks that suggest it was the last wood in that part of the Blean to remain as common after all the surrounding woods had been embanked.[24]

Trenches

Commanded … that the highroads from merchant towns to other merchant towns be
widened, wherever there are woods or hedges or earthworks, where a man may lurk to do
evil near the road, by two hundred feet on one side and by two hundred feet on the other
side; but that this statute extend not to oaks nor to great trees, if they be clear underneath.
And if by default of the Lord, who may not want to level earthwork, underwood, or bushes as
provided above, and robberies be done, the Lord is responsible. And if there be murder, let
the Lord be fined at the King's will. And if the Lord is unable to level the underwood, let the
country [folk] help him to do it. And the King wishes that in his demesne lands, and woods
within Forests, the roads be widened as is said above. And if by chance a park be near the
highroad, it is convenient that the Lord of the park adapt his park so that it have a space of
two hundred feet next to the highroad … or he make a wall, earthwork, or hedge such that
malefactors may not pass or return to do evil.
STATUTES OF THE REALM 1 97 (1285)

Woods were feared as dangerous places; travellers expected to be mugged when passing them. Two travellers were murdered in the Prior of Barnwell's wood at Bourn, alongside the road from Huntingdon to Royston, and the Abbey chronicler claimed that the above statute – the earliest legislation concerning woods – was a response. The new woodbanks made on that occasion, by owners of woods in Bourn and across the road in Longstowe, are visible to this day.[25]

Not all owners of roadside woods hastened to cut *trenches,* as these clearings were called, because the statute told them to: that is not how medieval legislation worked. Trenches, to give travellers a sense of security against highwaymen, had long been made where roads passed woods, and I know of no new ones after 1285. Whether they did deter highwaymen is unknown: then as now, the *sense* of security was what mattered.

Some trenches still survive as long narrow fields between woods and roads – sometimes surprisingly minor roads. Others have long since grown over again, but traces can be found as woodbanks set back from the road. A trench, if correctly identified, proves that both the wood and the road existed in the thirteenth century, but its absence does not prove the contrary. Some landowners, such as the De Bohun family in Essex, took their chance of a holdup occurring: their Dunmow High Wood adjoins a Roman road with no trace of a trench.

Watling Street, now the A2, was the great road for pilgrims to Canterbury and travellers to France. The pilgrims in Chaucer's *Canterbury Tales,* having escaped the perils of Shooter's Hill, Oxleas Wood and Bexley Heath, would have passed through the great ring of woods surrounding Canterbury, in sight of their destination. This large and armed party, telling merry tales, would have given no thought to highwaymen; but others might have been glad of the trench through the woods (Fig. 191). It varies in width from 280 to 420 feet (85 to 130 metres), not the 400-plus feet (120 metres) provided by the statute. It is bounded by sinuous woodbanks, evidently fitted in among the trees. At least four owners were involved; Fishpond Wood, which had a private owner, is less strongly embanked than the others, which were ecclesiastical.

Another trench borders the present A121 road through Epping Forest (see Fig. 183). Being in an uncompartmented Forest, it has no woodbanks; it is now overgrown, but can still be detected as the ancient pollards stop abruptly at a line about 180 feet (55 metres) from the road on either side.

Edward I, when invading Wales, conscripted hundreds of woodcutters to fell trenches along the roads to protect his communications.[26] Whether they grew up again as soon as Edward's back was turned, is not recorded.

In France concerns about highwaymen lasted much longer. The Cassini maps, c.1755, show hundreds of *tranchées* where main roads traversed woods, and many still survive. Trenches are typically 200–230 metres (about 650 feet) in total width, often used as arable fields (e.g. 'Les Cinq Tranchées' in the Forêt de Haye outside Nancy). Some are sinuous and could be medieval, as along the main, supposedly Roman, road through the Forêt de Sommedieue from Verdun to Metz. Others border the straight main roads attributed to Louis XIV.

Roman roads

Disused Roman roads quite often run through woods, appearing as low, flat-topped earthworks, for example in Grovely Forest west of Salisbury. The main Roman road to Dorchester through Cowpound Wood, Athelhampton, has massive earthworks to overcome a steep gradient. Most disused Roman roads lack trenches and woodbanks; they probably fell out of use before these came into general use.

Occasionally an unknown Roman road comes to light in a wood, as with the faintly raised, flat-topped earthwork across the Bradfield Woods, west Suffolk, overlain by the spoil-banks of the later excavation called the Fishpond. Conversely, a search of ancient woods can disprove the existence of a Roman road. At Barking (Suffolk) the known Roman road from Long Melford, if prolonged in a straight line for COMBRETOVIUM (the predecessor of Ipswich), has left no trace in Priestley or Swingens Woods, documented to the thirteenth century (see Fig. 186). It must have turned aside to join a preceding road (still in use) to reach its destination by a less direct route, avoiding a steep descent.

Holloways

Lanes sunk below the land surface are erosional features: centuries of hooves, wheels and feet have ground away the soft surface, and heavy rain has washed away the debris. They are especially common in Monmouthshire, Dorset, west Suffolk and the Weald. They are undatable: many are already cited as *holan weg* in Anglo-Saxon charters. Holloways tend to turn into linear woods as trees grow on the steep or rocky sides: they may acquire woodland plants such as bluebell, primrose, and even moschatel. Further erosion undermines the trees and leaves their roots dramatically overhanging the road.

Many lanes through, or rather between, woods are holloways (Fig. 57). A narrow lane, which can hardly have taken carts, descends through Merthen Wood, Cornwall, to a quay on the Helford River.

A holloway that enters a wood-pasture common by one of its horns, or by a ford across a stream, may split into several tracks, either to reach different destinations across the common, or because travellers would divert round difficult parts of the track. In disuse these can create puzzling bundles of gullies.

Tracks within woods

The common pattern of straight woodland rides, often with ditches on the uphill side or both sides, is usually of eighteenth-century or later date. However, the rides that divide Norsey Wood, Billericay, into six divisions appear on a map of 1593.[27] In French Forests, such as Fontainebleau, grids of straight rides radiating from a point known as a *patte d'oie* ('goosefoot') are said to have enabled eminent hunters to ride around on horseback or in carriages. English examples are in Hatfield Forest (eighteenth century), Savernake Forest, and Oakley and Hailey Woods (Cirencester), all associated with important estates. Rides *within* woods must not be confused with highways *between* woods (with a woodbank on either side) or the tongues of plain that sometimes separate woods in a compartmental wood-pasture (see Fig. 184).

Constructed tracks on slopes often lead to mines or clusters of charcoal-hearths. In Cheddar Wood in the Mendips hollow tracks leading straight up the very steep slope are said to have been for sliding down wood or timber.

EARTHWORKS THAT HAPPEN TO BE IN WOODS

Barrows

Barrows – burial mounds ranging from Neolithic to Anglo-Saxon in date – were normally built in grassland or heath, often carefully sited to be visible from a distance. Some, however, are now in ancient woodland. Within Wychwood Forest are several long and round barrows and chamber tombs (see Fig. 189). Wychwood was one of the big wooded areas in medieval England, but much of it was evidently non-woodland from the Neolithic to the Bronze Age.

Field systems

Most ancient woods show no traces of cultivation, but there are many exceptions. Strip lynchets are narrow fields (like terraces but lacking stone walls) that follow the contours on steep slopes, usually on chalk or limestone. Sometimes they extend into ancient woods, as in Westridge Wood, Wotton-under-Edge.

Madingley Wood, Cambridge, is the scene of 350 years of botanical studies. Some of its earthworks relate to the medieval boundary of the wood, some to the grubbing of four small fields from the wood in the seventeenth century and their subsequent re-incorporation into the wood. Underlying all these is a grid of massive banks and ditches, which seem to define a system of small squarish 'Celtic Fields' (Fig. 192). This was confirmed when a pipe-trench in 1994 revealed a large Iron Age to Roman settlement just outside the wood. What then was probably a clearing in the boulder-clay woods had, by the Middle Ages, turned into an island of woodland surrounded by fields.[28]

What may be a planned field system extends under the Blean woods north of Canterbury. Deep ditches define a grid of rectangles, 550 × 210 yards (500 × 190 metres), aligned along the Roman road through Blean village.[29]

In the last 30 years coaxial field systems, believed to be of various prehistoric dates, have been reported in many different places, including Dartmoor and south Norfolk (p.95).[30] Parallel but not straight main axes, often roughly north and south, are connected by cross-hedges at irregular intervals.

A test for any such planned field-system is to see what happens when it meets an ancient wood. The clay uplands of west Cambridgeshire, once thought to have changed from wildwood to farmland as late as Anglo-Saxon times, are underlain by about 30 parallel but sinuous north–south axes, visible in the landscape as roads, furlong and parish boundaries. Susan Oosthuizen draws attention to these and shows that they are older than the Roman roads that intersect them.[31] Her interpretation is extended and confirmed by including the low bank and ditch that bisect Hayley Wood, which conforms to this system and is extended outside the wood by further parish boundaries (Fig. 193). This in turn is underlain by fainter, apparently older, banks and ditches within the wood, visible as strips of bluebell in an otherwise meadowsweet-dominated area. Even Hayley Wood has not the simple history that we envisaged on p.78.

Ridge-and-furrow

This is the physical expression of open-field strip-cultivation, widespread in midland and northern England from late Anglo-Saxon times until the eighteenth or nineteenth century (p.55). It consists of ridges, usually curved or with a double 'reversed-S' curve, typically around 33 feet (10 metres) in wavelength and one furlong (220 yards, 200 metres) in length. Ridge-and-furrow was also formed in later centuries and outside the 'classic' area; late ridges tend to be straight and narrow (Figs 192, 58). Several different profiles have been recognised.[32] Anyone interpreting ridge-and-furrow in a wood should remember the need for a *head-land*, a strip of land at the end of the ridges on which to turn the plough.

Many ancient woods in the east Midlands contain areas of ridge-and-furrow, which have therefore not been woodland all the time. Some ridged areas are outside the woodbank and are an enlargement of the original wood. In Buff Wood (East Hatley, Cambridgeshire) four areas of ridge-and-furrow appear to have been added to the wood in the late Middle Ages: they contain ancient coppice stools, and a map of 1750 knows no difference between the additions and the original wood. Out of 18 ancient woods in the west Cambridgeshire group, 11 have expanded over ridge-and-furrow; in five instances these represent medieval, and in six post-medieval, additions to the wood. In two woods (Madingley and the Triangle at Hayley Wood) the ridge-and-furrow itself is of post-medieval date.

Less often, ridge-and-furrow occurs inside the woodbank: sometimes it is faint, and apparently represents an experiment in cultivation that got no further. In Monks' Wood near Huntingdon about one-sixth of this very large wood is ridged.[33] Among ancient wood-pastures, some of the ancient oaks of Moccas Park (Herefordshire) and Dalkeith Park near Edinburgh stand on ridge-and-furrow that must antedate them.

Ridge-and-furrow witnesses to the well-documented increase of woodland in the nineteenth century, but also to an earlier increase in about 1350 to 1500, after the Black Death had reduced the population of England by about one-third. In both periods woodland increased at a time of agricultural depression.*

An example – Swithland Wood: The Charnwood area is an outlier of Highland England in the midst of Leicestershire, of hard rock, crags and thin soils, and ancient mixed hedges. In Domesday Book this was the most wooded part of a poorly wooded county.

Swithland Wood has been investigated over many years by Stephen Woodward. At first sight it is an obvious secondary wood, with no distinctive boundary earthworks, and most of it overlying ridge-and-furrow. It has a number of ponds

* For the Ruddiman hypothesis, this happened on a world scale so vast as to produce a remission in the rise of atmospheric carbon dioxide and in global warming: see p.96.

and dells and strong internal banks and ditches. The parts lacking ridge-and-furrow include rocky outcrops containing recent quarries. The name Swithland Wood is anomalous, for the wood is in Newtown Linford parish, not Swithland, which adjoins it to the east.[34]

The wood has a rich woodland flora including species characteristic of ancient woodland, such as native lime, and a number of great stools of lime, ash and oak.

The ridge-and-furrow forms an irregular pattern around the internal banks, dells and outcrops (Fig. 194). It seems to have been fitted into pre-existing hedged fields. The names of these fields may have been remembered in a record that Mr Woodward found of the wood in 1677, when it was called Great Lynns, Little Lynns and Donham Lynns. This name probably refers to *linde* or lime-tree; 'Great Lynds' was already a wood and was coppiced in 1512.

One expects ancient secondary woodland in Leicestershire. The total woodland area diminished only 20 per cent between 1086 and 1895, so most woodland grubbed out in the twelfth and thirteenth centuries was replaced later. The men of Linford probably hewed some fields out of a wood on the edge of their territory. They left strips of woodland to act as hedges, and groves on thin soils and around dells and other uncultivable patches. Later, imitating their open-field neighbours in east Leicestershire, they created ridge-and-furrow on the new fields. After the Black Death these poor fields were the first to be abandoned and to tumble down to woodland, which they have been for at least 550 years.

The oak coppice, as expected (p.285), is on the thin, acid soils of the rocky patches. Big coppice stools, as expected, are near the hedge lines. Most of the lime today is on or near hedge lines and other places where the tree would best have survived. Lime away from these places represents occasional colonisation by seed in favourable years. Another factor favouring lime is that some of the trees on this site are of the variant that has weeping branches that hang down and take root.

Terraces
Terraces are the Mediterranean equivalent of ridge-and-furrow. They run horizontally across slopes like strip-lynchets, but are built with stone walls. They are notoriously difficult to date, but some are datable from ancient trees standing on them.

In the twentieth century woodland increased in most southern European countries. Terraces in woods are familiar to Mediterranean travellers; often they are revealed after a fire.[35]

Moats

Moats are dry or wet ditches round houses, castles, orchards, churches, wind-mills or haystacks. House moats, typically of a fraction of an acre in extent, were dug in their thousands round farmsteads between 1150 and 1330, with a revival at a higher social level in Elizabethan times. Moats may have deterred burglars and highwaymen; they served for drainage, sewage disposal and fishing; but they are now thought of mainly as a status symbol – the middle-class symbol of a man whose house is his castle, but who does not run to a park. Moats are commonest in Suffolk, Cambridgeshire, Essex, Worcestershire and Warwickshire; there are many in Ireland.

Many deserted moats appear as groves among fields. Often they are elmwoods, now full of dead elms and live elm suckers, with ivy, nettle, cow-parsley and other plants of woodland with accumulations of phosphate (p.200). They rarely have rich floras, though some have been woodland for centuries.

Moats also occur in bigger woods: sometimes by chance, but also there is a definite association with woodland. The west Cambridgeshire woods have 11 moats in or adjoining them. Kingston Wood and its outliers surround a moat that still contains a medieval house; this remarkable arrangement has changed little since before 1720, though the woodbanks indicate changes before then. East Hatley is a shrunken medieval village with 12 moats – an apparently unique concentration – lining the village street. Two of the moats are now in Buff Wood; one of these overlies earlier ridge-and-furrow; nine elm clones are associated with them. In Overhall Grove a big, apparently unfinished moat, with medieval pottery, forms the core of a wood largely on ridge-and-furrow; it is surrounded by massive multiple banks and ditches that may be prehistoric. This is one of the biggest surviving elmwoods in England (p.282).

East Anglia has some notable woodland moats: Gawdy Hall Wood (Norfolk), divided by an internal bank into two parts, each containing a moat; Hedenham Wood (Norfolk) and Burgate Wood (Suffolk), each with a huge 'Hall Yard' moat; Hockering Wood, with a moat in the middle of a big lime-wood. Some people evidently liked to live in the shelter of a wood. Woods may also contain ditched enclosures like miniature moats, for example in Hayley Wood, or Bonny Wood (Barking, Suffolk). Did woodwards' cottages aspire to moat status?

Hillforts

Hillforts are embanked enclosures of the Iron Age. Some big ones, like South Cadbury in Somerset, enclosed permanent towns; others are interpreted as refuges for times of trouble.

Many hillforts, like Maiden Castle or Hod Hill in Dorset, are in grassland. Others, like Wandlebury near Cambridge, had trees planted in the eighteenth or nineteenth century. But many others are in ancient woodland or wood-pasture. Were the woods there when the hillforts were in use? If not, how much of the present woodland did the forts and their surroundings occupy? Two in Epping Forest, Ambresbury Banks and Loughton Camp, remind us of (they could even have inspired) Julius Cæsar's statement that the Britons forted up in 'impassable woods'.[36] Neither has any visible field system attached.

The great hillfort of Welshbury, outside the Forest of Dean, with its triple fortifications, is in an ancient limewood. The limes, last coppiced in the 1930s, form huge stools and clonal patches, recognisable by differences in time of leaf-fall (p.203). The two biggest lime clones, one 40 × 39 feet (about 12 × 12 metres), both sit on (or emerge from under) the ramparts. Their size raises the question of their relation to the fort. Were they already there before it was built? A recent survey (which does not discuss the limes) reveals the further complication that the fort sits partly on an earlier field system.[37]

It might be thought that trees would shelter attackers and impede defence. But Dr David Morfitt drew my attention to the custom, in Continental fortifications, to plant the earthworks with trees that, when the time came, could be felled to form a defensive *abattis* (p.181) that attackers would have to struggle through under fire.

Conclusions

Not all ancient English woods (or all tropical rainforests) have been woodland throughout the Holocene. Most of the big and some smaller wooded areas of medieval England contain evidence of Roman or earlier settlement and cultivation. However, it can seldom be shown that the whole of a medieval wood was non-woodland at an earlier period.

By the Iron Age, population had grown until it was no longer possible to cultivate the easier soils and leave the rest. People were tilling land later thought to be uncultivable. Was this was because of extreme pressure of population or because standards of what was cultivable were different then? Or was it a mistake, like modern attempts to cultivate deserts in America and Uzbekistan?

The second-largest wooded area in eleventh-century Essex lay east of Bishop's Stortford. Although Domesday Book records woods here only roughly, in terms of swine (p.100), woodland must have predominated over several square miles. Most of it was grubbed out in the twelfth century, remained as farmland, and long afterwards became the site of Stansted Airport. The southern part remained as the woods of Hatfield Forest. In the 1990s investigations in advance of extending the airport found numerous settlements from Bronze Age to Roman in date. How much woodland survived through this earlier period of habitation is not known, but settlement had predominated over woodland for some of this time. Hatfield Forest has two known Iron Age sites, one with a small field system, and several other mysterious features which are unlikely to be natural.

An example pointing in the other direction comes from the coaxial fields of southeast Essex, an ordered landscape with a large hole in the middle containing the ancient woods of Hockley, Rayleigh and Hadleigh. Evidently there was a central block of infertile land that was left as woodland or heath. The woods have complex woodbanks that do not conform to the field system; in some there appear to have been two or three successive cycles of subdividing and embanking the woods.[38]

How many of the settlements and field systems recovered from under destroyed medieval woods could have been detected when the woods were intact? Are there unsuspected non-woodland features under surviving woods? These questions might have been settled in the 1950s and 1960s by surveying woods before and after they were grubbed out, to see whether they overlay archaeological features invisible in the intact wood. Alas, surveying practice developed too late, and woods were destroyed unrecorded. The compartment boundaries in Monks' Park (p.119) are visible both as soil marks in the destroyed wood and as banks and ditches in the remaining wood; but the soil marks also reveal faint, unrelated structures, probably Roman or earlier, which are confined to the part of the wood that was grubbed before recording began. Woods are now rarely destroyed, and opportunities no longer arise.

WOODLAND AND WAR

Battles in woods ... are usually long and murderous.
LA GRANDE ENCYCLOPÉDIE, C.1882

Military remains tend to be less tidied-away and better preserved in woodland than elsewhere. They include practice trenches of World War I, sometimes dug into a pre-existing earthwork, with their characteristic zigzag or crenellated plan, changing direction every few yards. Along the old Lavenham railway (Suffolk) the medieval woodbank of Lineage Wood was pressed into service in World War II as part of a defence line supposed to keep invading tanks away from Cambridge.

Eastern England had more than a hundred military airfields in World Wars I and II. Their barracks, hospitals, ammunition stores, etc. were hidden in woods from enemy reconnaissance. After the war these structures rotted away (latrines being the last to go), but there are still remains. Stansted Airport began in 1942–3 as a bomber base; in Table Coppice, Hatfield Forest, are rows of iron stumps, the remains of hutments; the hard roads built to service them are still in daily use. Earl's Colne airfield (Essex) resulted in bunkers in Markshall Woods, now adapted as bat shelters; in Chalkney Wood the huts are marked only as patches of nettles and other phosphate-demanding plants.

Woods have been used as strategic and tactical obstacles. The battle of Agincourt in 1415 is said to have been fought in a confined space between the woods of Agincourt and Tramecourt, but Azincourt has had no wood for at least 250 years, and the topography is now uncertain. Elizabethan accounts of warfare in Ireland make much of the difficulty of getting through woods. Having struggled through Irish woods on scree slopes, I am thankful not to have been wearing armour and under fire.

What of the effects of war on woodland? The military have at least temporarily destroyed woods, as along roads in Wales (p.172). Unusual quantities of timber have been consumed for military purposes or to sustain war efforts. And not only timber: Henry III when he went to war would order large quantities of hurdles, and down the centuries underwood was used to make gabions and revetments to trenches. But this should not be exaggerated. The period 1914–45 was unusually stable for ancient woods in England (apart from destruction by airfields), even though the amount of timber in many woods diminished (p.358).

In the nineteenth century European tacticians developed a system for turning woods into improvised forts, by creating an *abattis* of felled trees with defensive positions round the edge.[39] This was tried in the Franco-Prussian War and World War I. It would leave archaeological traces, especially of the trenches and parapets recommended 60–100 feet (20–30 metres) inside the wood edges.

Generations have wondered at the devastated woods photographed in World

War I, with the top shot off every tree. But woods quickly recover, as they do after hurricanes (p.19). Some shot-up woods and trenched and cratered ground were seized upon by the French and Belgian forest services for a spree of replanting in the 1930s. The effects of the War on the topography vary. Around Verdun, where a million men were slain in very wooded country, the woods are still much the same as on the Cassini map of c.1755, but both natural woodland and plantations have increased (the Forêt de Verdun) where the blood poured thickest. The woods that I have seen had returned to the appearance of a normal coppice-wood by the 1970s. The notorious Thiepval Wood on the Somme has recovered as a natural wood, but is still full of bodies, unexploded munitions, trenches and craters.[40] In Flanders many small woods disappeared, but probably long after the war.

Wars can favour woodland by restraining unfavourable activities, especially pasturage. Parts of the Pindus Mountains were depopulated in World War II and the civil war that followed. When the people returned they found their lands seized by the Greek Forest Service on the plea that trees were now growing on them. Land rendered inaccessible by uncharted minefields has had the effect of protecting forests and allowing new ones to arise.

WOODLAND AND ARCHAEOLOGICAL CONSERVATION

Some archaeologists object to trees. Trees are supposed to promote erosion as raindrops coalesce on them and splatter the ground; this can be a useful corrective to the doctrine, common in other countries, that trees (and only trees) protect against erosion. Tree roots disrupt buried features. Tree-felling brings machinery that wrecks earthworks. When trees blow down their root plates tear up surface and buried features. For such reasons archaeologists in the 1960s destroyed the ancient wood on Llanmelin hillfort not far from Welshbury, losing any prospect of ever understanding the relation between the trees and the hillfort.

If trees take over grassland sites the ecology as well as the archaeology is damaged, which should be opposed by both kinds of conservationist. Cambridge-shire Wildlife Trust has spent many years on the laborious task of reversing the invasion of the great earthworks of Devil's Ditch and Fleam Dyke.

With ancient woodland the trees may well be part of the archaeology, like elms at Buff Wood and Overhall Grove. At Welshbury the ramparts are in excellent condition despite centuries of coppiced limewood; the state of the underground features is unknown, but any damage by roots will have been completed long ago. The conservation of the archaeology depends on suitably managing the trees. If lime is allowed to grow up to tall trees, this will indeed result in windblow at the next big storm. As has been shown at Overhall Grove, timber can be removed without damaging the earthworks by attention to detail, such as not using machines in wet weather and filling ditches temporarily with logs.

The Forestry Commission has recently surveyed its woods in the east Midlands for archaeological features, entering the results on constraint maps that identify areas out of bounds to certain types of operation. This should set an example, ending the tradition among archaeological and biological conservationists of not talking to each other, even when they war against the same foes.

CHAPTER 9

PICTURES AND PHOTOGRAPHS

PICTURES AND PHOTOGRAPHS

How strange that among all this painting of delicate detail there is not a true one of English spring!
JOHN RUSKIN ON THE PRE-RAPHAELITES, C.1860

Here I am concerned with the humble practicalities of what paintings, drawings and photographs (rarely sculpture) have to say about trees, woods and the landscape themselves. Constable's paintings show that trees and other vegetation have dramatically increased in almost every one of his scenes on the Suffolk–Essex border in the 200 years since his time. The scattered pines in Cézanne's pictures of southern France have, over a century, turned into vast, fire-promoting extents of pinewood.

Art has another significance. Much of what is written on landscape history is really the history of what literate people wrote about landscape and what people are supposed to have thought about landscape. Paintings reveal another aspect of the relation between people's attitudes to landscape and the actual landscape that they were attitudinising about. Writers on trees and woods have waxed eloquent on how pictures reflect the artist's supposed ideology or prejudice: Gainsborough has been rebuked for not being a socialist before his time. However, this kind of writing is seldom based on anything that the artist actually said, and often reveals more about the writer than the artist or the landscape.

Landscape pictures may be topographical, of a known place; or generic (*A Wooded Landscape*); or forming the background to a portrait, battle, martyrdom etc. There are landscapes designed as works of art; maps as works of art; portraits of trees; and botanical illustration as a branch of art.

The earliest European landscape paintings are frescoes, some 3,500 years old, excavated on the Ægean island of Santoríni. They appear to depict the cavernous red, yellow and black cliffs unique to that sea-volcano. One shows *Phœnix theophrasti,* the Cretan palm, now one of the world's rarest trees. However, many of the plants are stylised to the point at which, for example, commentators argue whether sea-daffodil (*Pancratium*) or papyrus is meant.[1]

In 336 BC the warrior-king Philip of Macedon was buried in the great barrow of Vérgina. On the façade of his tomb is a wall painting, still just recognisable, which shows the king and his courtiers in the field, pig-sticking and spearing other fierce beasts.[2] A luckless lion fights a losing battle against the combined assaults of Philip and Alexander the Great. Probably the king wished to be remembered by an actual deed of valour: there were still wild lions in north Greece. As in many pictures, the interesting part is the background: a grassy savanna with rock outcrops and scattered trees, apparently beeches, either in clumps or as massive individuals. There are still savannas with coppice-like clumps of massive beeches in remote parts of Macedonia today. Most of the trees are shown as dead. Savanna-like landscapes and dead trees were to be an artistic tradition for over 2,000 years.

Artists add or omit trees for reasons of taste (or to save time?), especially if they are working up studio pictures from field sketches. If, in the studio versions of *The Hay Wain,* Constable left out one bay of the ancient house now called Willy Lott's Cottage, he could easily have omitted a tree or two. But this hardly accounts for his views, like *The White Horse,* that now cannot be painted at all because trees have grown up and hidden them. Nor is it likely with pictures painted specifically to depict recognisable places, as in Humphry Repton's Red Books.

Topographical views

Pictures of cities or country mansions begin around 1500, for example Hoefnagel's views of Norwich and of Nonsuch Palace (Surrey) in *c.*1580. They are useful for hedgerow and park trees, less so for woods. Probably they are more accurate than 'artistic' pictures, being commissioned for people who could check the details.

Oblique aerial views were invented probably in Venice in the late fifteenth century, and continued until just before it became possible to draw real aerial pictures from balloons. They can be works of surprising accuracy, intermediate between pictures and maps. Examples are the 'map' of north Dorset c.1570 (p.394) and Kip's view of Grimsthorpe Park c.1710, which shows the layout of that most important of designed parks (p.119) already complete by then.

Can artists draw trees?
One of the greatest European landscape artists, Simon Bening or Benninck (c.1483–c.1565), worked mainly in what is now Belgium. John Hunter drew my attention to 'November' in a series of the *Labours of the Months* (Fig. 59). Bening shows two spearmen going out and slaying a wild swine and blowing a horn and letting the dogs eat it – as one did in November on the Continent. But the landscape is the point of the picture: a hilly land of dispersed settlement, hedges and small fields and scattered farmsteads. It could be Essex or Herefordshire (but not Cambridgeshire). In the foreground a coppice-wood shows three stages of felling and regrowth. There are recognisable oaks, aspens and elms; the coppice stools are small-leaved lime, with its floppy habit and heart-shaped leaves. Lime at one year's growth still retains its leaves, but grown-up lime has already lost them (as indeed it does). Bening puts in coppicing plants, such as broom and brambles. All this – on a leaf of parchment smaller than this page – is not just a 'A Wooded Landscape', but an individual wood with a personality still recognisable now. One day someone may identify the spot.

Bening is exceptional. Go into a gallery, take a landscape painting at random, and ask 'What is that tree?' Surprisingly seldom can you give a definite answer. Representing trees is perhaps the most difficult task in art, and few artists succeed. No picture (or photograph) of a big tree can be naturalistic: life is too short to depict the complex reality. Any tree picture is a caricature. The art of caricature is to identify the distinctive features (the 'jizz' of a tree, as bird-watchers would say) and discard the non-distinctive ones. Most artists keep the non-distinctive features and get no further than the traditional Army classification into Fir-trees, Poplars and Bushy-topped trees.

Pictures of trees in leaf are more problematic than of leafless trees, and even Bening seldom made them recognisable (Fig. 60). Out of 41 book illustrations by him that show trees, I can recognise the trees in 16 out of 25 that depict leafless or dead trees, but in only one or two out of 16 that depict fully leafy trees.[3]

A Belgian contemporary (or maybe Bening himself?) sketched a summer wood-land interior. Although his purpose was to record a woodbank, he shows coppice stools and timber trees, and nearly (but not quite) makes them identifiable to species.[4] Another rare exception is the Louvre tapestry of the *Hunt of Maximilian,* c.1500 (Fig. 61). A luckless wild pig, as big as a horse, fights a losing battle against the mounted hero and his courtiers; his rear is assaulted by a rabble of poodles, rottweilers and a greyhound in armour. The December landscape is unmistake-ably an opening in a coppiced alder-wood with tufts of holly, clonal patches of aspen, and a beech-tree on a knoll. It looks like a park that has been made by partly grubbing out a coppice-wood. I have never met this plant community, but would recognise it.

Maybe artists could portray trees if they wished, but thought it unimportant. One hardly expects El Greco or Turner or Picasso to get the trees right: that was not their job. For many others trees are mere fillers of unoccupied spaces. But an artist may take immense pains with the details, yet still fail to draw a convincing tree, especially in a studio painting. Even pictures specially commissioned for identifying trees do not always capture their jizz: for many years a tree-recog-nition poster hung in conservationists' offices without anyone noticing that the trees on it were not recognisable.

I once tried to locate Gainsborough's picture, today called *Cornard Wood,* in the actual woods around eighteenth-century Great Cornard (Suffolk) (Fig. 62). Taking the recognisable church in the picture as a point of reference, I could not reconcile Gainsborough's woodland with any of the woods known in contemporary maps. The trees, though beautifully detailed, are barely identifiable. The scene lacks infrastructure: coppice stools, banks and ditches bordering the lane, etc. Is it a work of imagination bearing the sort of relation to real landscapes that Piranesi's *Carceri d'Invenzione* did to real Italian jails? No: Susan Foister has shown that it is derived in detail from a landscape by Ruisdael.[5] A picture that has appeared on the cover of a book about English woodland is thus of a foreign wood. Ruisdael himself (who often depicted recognisable trees, even in leaf) was part of a long tradition among Dutch and Flemish Old Masters: whether it was true to the landscapes of their countries I cannot say. But Gainsborough was no mere plagiarist: he made the scene bland and generic by leaving out the dead tops and eroded roots that gave personal-ity to Ruisdael's oaks. These were not to be long out of fashion: in Leicester Museum is a view of the Blean near Canterbury, by Thomas Sidney Cooper in 1832, which has two great oaks with the shattered tops and dead branch-ends so characteristic of oaks on the Blean.

John Constable sketched trees convincingly in the field. He loved elms, and on a good day could master the features that distinguish the many kinds of elm. In his studio pictures, however, trees lose much of their distinctiveness – except for Lombardy poplar, then just entering the English landscape with its very distinctive shape. A remarkable exception is his painting of Salisbury Cathedral for the Bishop (Fig. 63). The spire is framed between two magnificent leafy elms – but they are East Anglian elms, not English elm, the common species around Salisbury. Were they a real outlier of East Anglian elm? Or did Constable import them from an East Anglian sketchbook? His original sketch of 1811 shows some of the other trees in the picture, but not these.

Painters of the Barbizon School, in mid-nineteenth-century France, lived outside the Forêt de Fontainebleau, then (before the foresters got at it) a majestic and distinctive landscape, with its extraordinary sandstone rocks and multitude of ancient trees. They rarely appreciated it. Most of their paintings are unresponsive to the majesty and distinction, giving the impression that Barbizon could have been anywhere. Narcisse Diaz, indeed, went to the trouble of reworking *Cornard Wood* or a Flemish predecessor.

In Britain, the Glasgow Scots and the Pre-Raphaelites were contemporary schools to Barbizon. Horatio McCulloch appreciated the ancient and majestic trees of Cadzow Park, and spent many an hour portraying them.[6] The mid-nineteenth-century Pre-Raphaelites lavished their skill on plants and trees, influenced by the popular craft of botanical illustration. John Everett Millais and Ford Madox Brown got every leaf and petal right, and every lenticel on oak marble-galls (then a new curiosity). John Samuel Raven could depict a sainfoin field with 19 species of weed. The Tate Gallery exhibition in 2004 brought together about 140 of their works.[7] Trees are recognisable if drawn from close enough to show individual leaves. More distant trees are seldom identifiable, except for Lombardy poplars and Scots pines, a few beeches, and some elms (but the artists turned a blind eye to the Elm Disease then raging!). Great spreading hedgerow oaks never appear. Only one picture, John Brett's *The Hedger*, is of a convincing wood, with stools of oak and ash (but the cataloguer called them 'birch'!) and in the foreground a woodbank with a man plashing a hedge on it. Pre-Raphaelites painted in the field, usually in summer, and encountered the extra difficulty of depicting leafy trees.

Portraits of trees

This art form, widespread in Europe from the sixteenth century, was especially developed in England. Strutt published a book in 1822, *Sylva Britannica*, portraying 48 famous trees and groups.[8] Those still extant include the Tortworth Chestnut, which had already been a famous tree for more than a century (p.287) and has not greatly changed since Strutt's time. In Savernake Forest (Wiltshire) I identified what he portrayed as the King Oak shortly before it collapsed in 1990. There was apparently another King Oak nearby that collapsed in the nineteenth century and of which no trace now remains; thus are the identities of even famous trees sometimes confused.[9] Strutt's, like most veteran trees (p.125), are freestanding or in wood-pasture, not in woodland. Many are pollards. He measured many of them: the giant trees of 200 years ago were not very different in size from giant trees today. Chance once led me to lecture in the rooms of the Royal Agricultural Society in London, beneath a portrait of King George V as Patron. The king was shown under some of his ancient oaks, symbols of majesty, in Windsor Great Park. I happened to illustrate my lecture with those same oaks, this time as relics of Windsor Forest and home of its special insects.

Artistic preferences

Artists choose some features of landscape and shun others. They love dead trees (because dead trees are easier to draw?). Dead elms in paintings are part of the evidence for early Dutch Elm Disease. They love badlands, landscapes of erosion gullies that are common in Italy but adopted by French artists such as Fragonard and even by Flemings, who would have seen badlands only on their travels. Many love pollards, which occur from the medieval *Très Riches Heures du Duc de Berry* through Dürer, Rembrandt, even Gainsborough (though rarely), and on to Arthur Rackham and later.

Artists mysteriously avoid certain features known to have been common, such as open-field strip-cultivation. In Italy they shun cultivation terraces (p.177), preferring to depict sloping hedged fields. (Was there a textbook which said 'Never paint terraces'?) Except for a few Belgians and Pre-Raphaelites, they avert their eyes from coppice stools and trees with more than one stem. Before Dürer they seldom show recognisable mountains: Europe was slow to appreciate the spiritual qualities of mountains. They rarely get timber-framed buildings right, even though timber-framing was itself an art form.

Landscape imitating art

People remake the real world in the image of art. Park landscapes of the eighteenth century (p.118f) are supposed to imitate the works of Claude Lorrain and Poussin. Landscape designers cited these Old Masters, whose pictures they might have seen on their patrons' walls, but the reality is more complex. Parks were rarely set up on a *tabula rasa* without pre-existing features. The designers 'Capability' Brown, Humphry Repton and their colleagues worked round and incorporated existing woods, hedges and ancient trees. Repton's famous Red Books included 'before and after' pictures for his clients' benefit.

Baroque artists such as Poussin (1594–1665) established the belief in the 'ruined landscape' of Southern Europe. They depicted the nymphs and heroes of ancient Greece disporting in noble forests and crystal fountains; the scenery was typical of the lush badlands of middle Italy, which they knew. Travellers who, a century later, reached the real, dry, 'barren' Greece concluded that the landscape had gone to the bad since Classical times by human mismanagement. They could not know that ancient Italy was rather like Poussin's Italy, but very unlike ancient Greece and ancient Spain. This deep-seated misunderstanding contributed to the modern belief in desertification. (The Spanish Forestry Commission has striven, so far with little success, to remake Spain in the image of Italy.)[10]

Artistic cultures independent of Europe have different priorities and values. The Chinese and Japanese have for centuries understood the personalities of trees. Not for them the bland, straight-grown, bushy-topped: their space-fillers are golden clouds, not trees. They love dead boughs and eroded roots. A few flicks of a tiny brush define the jizz of a pine and its difference from other species of pine. European artists in Australia set about learning the individualities of a thousand species of eucalyptus, and used them to define the different landscapes of the new continent. (Some of them were clanking around Australia for forgery, unfettered by European artistic tradition.) Euro-Australian tree art is still very much alive, for example, in the works of John Duncan Firth.

PHOTOGRAPHS

Photography began as an art form, concerned with people, buildings and gardens. Most of the many volumes compiled on the lines of *Barsetshire in Early Photographs* are disappointing for woodland. However, the tradition of portraits of great trees continued: Menzies' book on Windsor Great Park in

1864 has photographic prints of ancient trees pasted into the text that can be compared with the same trees now.[11]

Many professional photographers, like artists, do not appreciate what makes a tree distinctive, and have an unerring nose for the commonplace. A standard composition is of a big, young tree against the sky, telling nothing. I once contributed to an article on Grimsthorpe Park, that amazing landscape of picturesque trees which, surely, even the least appreciative cameraman could hardly miss. The professional photographer that we sent − alas, without detailed instructions − ignored the wonderful ancient trees and sought out some horsechestnuts that could have been anywhere. (An exception is Thomas Pakenham, whose *Meetings with Remarkable Trees* and *Remarkable Trees of the World* are a superb continuation of the tradition of tree portraits.)

Woodland photography can be difficult. As with paintings, it is impossible to record all the complexity of a big tree. Branches against the sky tend to disappear. Matters are worse in summer, when the light is weak and green, and especially on a sunny day when sunflecks create awkward contrasts. (Will electronic photography make it possible to correct for these hazards?)

Woodland crafts were illustrated in Edlin's *Woodland Crafts of Britain,* with its wealth of pictures taken in the 1930s or earlier. Woods themselves began to be illustrated in the 1920s: the photographs published in the *Journal of Ecology* and in Tansley's books reveal what English woods looked like before deer attacked them, or the boundary between chalk grassland and beech- or yew-wood before the woods began to spread in the 1950s.

Better than any early woodland photography in Britain is the magnificent record of Californian redwood forests by A.W. Ericson and others.[12] The task of reducing the world's grandest trees to roof-shingles and railway sleepers was a world-celebrated triumph of technology. In recording it, these photographs explain the initiation of what are now the world's grandest coppice-woods (p.65).

As well as recording woods and trees that have disappeared, photographs document stability and change within existing woods and trees. They show that dead branches in oaks can persist for well over 50 years and are not necessarily the result of recent pollution. For this purpose it is important to relocate the original viewpoint. Fixed-point photography is dealt with in Chapter 21.

Fig 70. Ash stool, medieval in age, newly cut. The pigmentation of all the shoots is the same, showing that it is probably one and not two stools. *Bradfield Woods, Suffolk, June 1981.* See p.203.

Fig 71. Exceptional ash stool, half with dark-pigmented shoots and half with green shoots, which is therefore two stools fused. *Bradfield Woods, May 2004.*

Fig 72. How a lime, overturned in a storm, might give rise to a linear clone (but seldom does) (p.203). *Groton Wood, Suffolk, March 2002.*

Fig 73. Ancient coppice stools in other countries (p.204): Chestnut on *Mount Athos, Greece. May 2003.*

Fig 74. Ancient coppice stools in other countries: *Prunus yamazakura* in Japan. *Kiga, Tango Peninsula, October 2004.*

Fig 75. The oldest coppice stool of all? *Silk Wood, Westonbirt, February 1980.* See p.204.

Fig 76. A wood that escaped the Oak Change (p.205) and is still in its medieval state with a multitude of young oaks. *Bradfield Woods, Suffolk, October 1996.*

Fig 77. Polypody and other epiphytes on oak: this requires a combination of crooked trees, damp climate and lack of acid rain. *Winding Stoy, Hilfield, Dorset, March 2005.* See p.386.

Fig 78. Herbaceous communities in Hayley Wood, Cambridgeshire (see page 210): Oxlip (after coppicing and in the absence of deer). *April 1987 (photograph by D.E. Coombe).*

Fig 79. Herbaceous communities in Hayley Wood, Cambridgeshire: Bluebell avoiding waterlogged areas. *April 2001*.

Fig 80. Dog's-mercury (and little else). *May 1966*.

Fig 81. Primrose one year after coppicing (p.211): a spring-leafing persistent perennial. *Buff Wood, West Cambridgeshire, May 1969.*

Fig 82. Oxlip and water-avens behaving like coppicing plants after a blowdown. *Tatra Mountains, Slovakia, June 2005. See p.213.*

Fig 83. Wood-spurge one year after coppicing: a buried-seed plant (and also an ancient-woodland plant, Chapter 12). Ramsons, however, also in this picture, is set back by coppicing. *Bradfield Woods, May 1987. See p.252.*

Fig 84. Yews on cliff. *Swaledale, Yorkshire, February 1994.* See p.217.

Fig 85. Young ashes, fourteen years and one coppice cycle after deer were excluded. *Hayley Wood, February 1994.* See p.426.

Fig 86. Horsechestnut in its native environment as a cliff endemic (p.217). *Zagori, Epirus, Greece, September 2005.*

Fig 87. The author cleaving oak into radial planks with a froe (p.222). Photo © R. Darrah.

Fig 88. A Norman church door, its planks sawn from fast-grown, crooked, uncleavable oak (p.223). *Stillingfleet, Yorkshire, October 1981.*

Fig 89. Two-band faggot. *Bradfield Woods, March 1984.* See p.278.

Fig 90. Hall-house of c.1400 (p.229). *Flatford, East Bergholt, Suffolk, April 2005.*

Fig 91. Interior of hall. Each rafter represents a small oak-tree. The internal wall is partly elm (p.230) . *Flatford, East Bergholt, Suffolk, April 2003.*

Fig 92. Wattle-and-daub exposed (p.234). This very tall panel has five horizontal staves instead of the usual three; the wattle rods are lime. *Lavenham, Suffolk, May 1988.*

Fig 93. Wheat Barn, Cressing Temple, Essex. *December 1988*. See p.231.

Fig 94. An American log 'cabin'. Although small, it is a stylish and expensive cabin, built of great logs thinned down. *Great Smoky Mountains, Tennessee, May 1981*. See p.235.

Fig 95. Seventh-century pagoda (p.236).
Horyu-ji, Nara, Japan, November 2004.

Fig 96. Japanese monumental carpentry not
meant to be seen (p.237). *Senjokaku Temple,
Miyajima, January 2001.*

Fig 97. Monumental symbolic gate of *c.*1200 (p.236). Note the sacred deer (Fig 168).
Todai-ji, Nara, Japan, October 1998.

Fig 98. Japanese workaday carpentry: interior of a thatched roof. The bigger timbers are whole small pines; the smaller components are giant bamboo. Rope lashings are preferred to pegged joints. *Arakowa, Lake Biwa, December 2003.* See p.237.

Fig 99. Shipbuilding as a cottage industry (p.238). *Near Bozburun, southwest Turkey, July 1996.*

Fig 100. *Tilia cordata*, a tree – here as a 'ghost hedge', the remaining woodbank of a wood grubbed out in the eighteenth century (p.250). *Shelley, Suffolk, May 1987*.

Fig 101. Herb paris *Paris quadrifolia*, a clonal plant unresponsive to coppicing (p.250). *Buff Wood, Cambridgeshire, May 1985*.

Fig 102. *Lobaria pulmonaria*, one of the few big lichens associated with ancient trees (p.255). *Asi Gonia, Crete, April 1988*.

Fig 103. *Helleborus viridis*, apparently very long-lived (p.250). This scene has hardly changed in 50 years. *Buff Wood, Cambridgeshire*.

Fig 104. Alder-woods in a landslip swamp; even in this perilous place the alder has been coppiced. *Kingcombe, Dorset, June 2000.* See p.289.

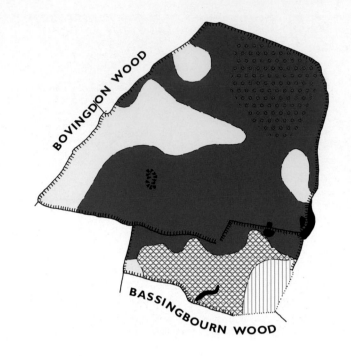

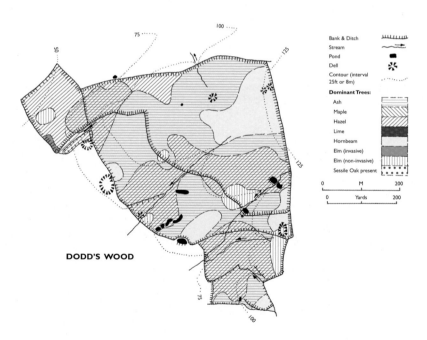

Fig 105 and Fig 106. Variation within woods in Bovingdon (Essex) and Benhall. See p.275.

Fig 107. Ashwood on acid soil, with bluebell and bracken. *Coombe Wood, Langdon Hills, Essex, May 1977.* See p.276.

Fig 108. Pure hazel-wood, showing hazel as a canopy tree (p.276). *Hatfield Forest, Essex, February 1981.*

Fig 109. Great stool of maple (p.276). *Lawford, Essex, August 1994.*

Fig 110. Hazel-wood with bluebell. *Cranborne, Dorset, May 2004.* See p.276.

Fig 111. Limewood (p.279). *Shrawley Wood, Worcestershire, May 1985.*

Fig 112. Pure hornbeam-wood composed of old stools of hornbeam (p.280), invaded by birch at the last coppicing. *Wormley, Hertfordshire, June 1975.*

Fig 113. Beech timberwood (p.284). *Penn Wood, Buckinghamshire, June 1974.*

Fig 114. A rare eastern oak coppice (p.286). The pines give it an air of Scotland, but are almost certainly introduced. *Swanton Novers Great Wood, Norfolk, March 1970.*

Fig 115. Former wood-pasture (p.284). *Frithsden Beeches, Hertfordshire, June 1974.*

Fig 116. Ancient beech coppice stools (p.284). *Denstead Wood, Blean, Kent, February 2004.*

Coppiced oakwoods that have escaped oak replacement: **Figs 117–120** (p.292f).
Fig 117. Cornwall: one of the few places where ancient woodland meets the sea. Not grazed.
Bonallack Wood, Constantine, July 1986.

Fig 118. South Wales: severely grazed, with giant stool. *Coed Fforest-uchaf, Cwm Cynon, Glamorgan, April 1982.*

Fig 119. Derbyshire, on scree. *Yarncliff Wood, Hathersage, June 2003.*

Fig 120. Near the northern limit. *Torvaine, Inverness, February 1985.*

Fig 121. Irish oak coppice (p.294). *Kilteel Wood, Co. Kildare, February 1994.*

Fig 122. Irish oak timberwood (p.294). *Portlaw Wood, Co. Waterford, September 1985.*

Fig 123. Devon hazel-wood. *Okehampton Park, November 2005.* See p.297.

Fig 124. Ash stool in Atlantic hazel-wood. *Eagle's Rock, Burren, Co. Clare, September 2004.*

Fig 125. Glen Tanar pinewoods in c.1595, on Pont's map. Printed at the same scale and orientation as Fig 126. © National Library of Scotland. See p.306.

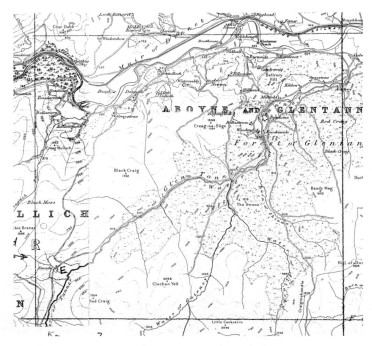

Fig 126. Glen Tanar pinewoods, from the Ordnance Survey of 1871. The woods are of much the same extent as in Pont's time or today. E = Etnach (Pont's 'Attanich').

Caledonian pinewoods: **Figs 127–130**(p.314).
Fig 127. Patchwork of even-aged stands.
Glen Tanar, Aberdeenshire, October 1993.

Fig 128. Queen Victoria's pines. *Ballochbuie,
Aberdeenshire, April 2000.*

Fig 129. Old pioneer tree on rock outcrop, surrounded and hemmed in by its children.
Glen Tanar, October 1993.

Fig 130. Pines precariously surviving among blanket peat. *Achanalt, Ross & Cromarty, September 1977.*

Fig 131. Stag-head, a normal condition in old (and not so old) non-woodland oaks (p.323). *Near Abergavenny, Monmouthshire, June 1999.*

Fig 132. Active group-killing of beech (p.326). Note the horsepath. *Verderers' Ride, October 1990.*

Fig 133. Bog that provided the pollen core, surrounded by dense, dark, outgrown beech pollards, with not a single lime tree. *Lodge Road, September 1997.* See p.326.

Fig 134. Old killing group, invaded by birch (p.326). *Hangboy Slade, September 1997.*

Fig 135. Dutch Elm Disease (p.336) on *Ulmus americana*. *Williamstown, Massachusetts, May 1981.*

Fig 136. Chestnut-blight canker (p.338), due to a virus-infected fungus that has not much harmed the tree. *Liguria, Italy, September 1984.*
Fig 137. Oak mildew (p.335). *Blackmoor Forest, Dorset, September 2002.*

Fig 138. Oak wilt in Texas inland live-oak (p.339). *Valley Mills, Texas, August 1983.*

Fig 139. Red pine subtracted from the forest by a nematode worm (p.339). *Near Hiroshima, Japan, January 2001.*

Phytophthora effects: **Figs 140–143.**
Fig 140. Bloody flux on birch. *Arger-Fen Wood, Bures, Suffolk, April 2005.* See p.339f.

Fig 141. Killing circle in jarrah forest. *Near Byford, West Australia, December 1996.*

Fig 142. Alder disease. *Hereford, October 1995.*

Fig 143. Group killing of horsechestnuts. *Hatfield Forest, Essex, September 2003.*

Fig 144. Oak plantation, probably of the 1830s, on site of former wood. The trees are uniform in age and appearance. When they come to be felled there will be nothing to maintain the character of the wood. *Salcey Forest, Northamptonshire, April 1984.* See p.354.

Fig 145. Monument to an unhappy age. *Frithsden Great Copse, Hertfordshire, June 1976.* See p.359.

Twentieth-century plantations on ancient-woodland sites. **Figs 146–149.**
Fig 146. Successful replanting, probably for the second time. No trace remains of the wood except for buried seeds. The Douglas fir has grown well, but is neglected as regards thinning. *Wentwood Forest, Monmouthshire, August 2005.* See p.373f.

Fig 147. Successful Corsican pine plantation: the planted trees have survived and produced saleable but poor timber; little ground vegetation, but some previous trees survive. *Chalkney Wood, Essex, April 1996.*

Fig 148. Marginally successful plantation: planted trees (or some of them) have stayed alive, but will never produce timber. *Horwood Forest (Wetmoor Woods), Gloucestershire, November 1998.*

Fig 149. Failed plantation on a limewood: hardly a trace remains of planted trees. *Shrawley Wood, Worcestershire, May 1985.*

Fig 150. Early deconiferisation (p.378). *Layer Marney, Essex, July 1998.*

Fig 151. Needle's-eye tree, characteristic of small-leaved lime that has recovered from assault with a poisoned jimjam (p.380). *Chalkney Wood. Essex, March 2002.*

Hemispherical photographs

The fish-eye lens, invented by Robin Hill the biochemist,[13] takes a picture of approximately an entire hemisphere projected on to a flat surface. Originally intended for studying clouds, it was applied by Clifford Evans, David Coombe and Margaret Anderson to the measurement of shade.[14]

Shade is measured by taking a photograph of the canopy and overlaying it with one of three grids, dealing with the three sources of light: direct sunlight, light diffused from blue sky, and light reflected from clouds. The first grid gives the sun's position at different times of day and of year, from which one can record how much of its track is obscured by leaves or branches. The second and third grids divide the hemisphere into sections each giving the same amount of light from a standard blue or overcast sky, on which one counts how many sections are clear or obscured. Two photographs, one with the trees in leaf, the other leafless, measure shade with a precision that could otherwise be got only by round-the-clock light measurements lasting a whole year. This method avoids the great uncertainties that arise from using photoelectric cells, which respond very unevenly to light of different spectral compositions, or coming from different directions in different weather and at different times of day.

Hemispherical photographs are a simple way of recording changes in woodland canopies, for example round a coppice cycle or following disuse of coppicing (Figs 195, 196). The camera needs to be returned to a fixed point year after year, preferably to a permanent cradle fixed in the ground.[15]

Fish-eye lenses have been made for various models of camera. It is convenient to mount the camera, facing upwards, on a board with arrows at the ends that can be levelled and oriented north and south. These arrows will appear on the photograph and will indicate where the horizon lies as well as the orientation.[16]

Aerial photographs[17]

Photographers could have taken to the air almost as soon as photography was invented, but they seldom went up in balloons, and air photography became a source for woodland only in the 1920s.

In late summer 1940, during the Battle of Britain, the German Luftwaffe flew what amounted to a great survey of England, mainly the east and southeast, but sometimes extending even into Wales. The excellent original prints (and those of many other countries) are now in the Cartographic Division, United States Archives in Washington.[18] They complement the Royal Air Force's wartime photography of Germany, Austria, Italy and other countries in Europe and beyond, now in the Department of Geography, University of Keele.

Wartime aerial photography is the best record of woods just before the Locust Years (Fig. 197). The German photographs (a triumph of both valour and technology) record the last phases of coppicing in many woods. The replanting movement, however, had barely started. The usurpation of woods by military airfields (p.181) mostly came after 1940 and was not recorded by the Luftwaffe, but sometimes was by the RAF.

Air photographs are an excellent record of the structure of woods. An early example, taken in 1930 in the beechwoods of the Oxfordshire Chilterns, shows the effects of selective logging, drought and fungal attack, as well as distinguishing woods from plantations and picking up abandoned pasture invaded by trees.[19]

Black-and-white photographs seldom identify tree species, apart from the circular patches produced by elms and other clonal trees. Colour photographs, which begin about 1960, are better (especially in autumn); infrared false colour are better still. Earthworks are normally visible only in felled areas. Crop-marks and soil-marks, natural or artificial, such as the 'stripes and polygons' produced by freezing and thawing in glacial times, or those due to Iron Age field-systems and Roman villas, can normally be identified only in grubbed-out woodland, but can sometimes be observed extending into a wood from adjacent fields.

Distinguishing woods from plantations should be easy because most plantations are in rows. In practice it is less simple. As a plantation gets older or is neglected, its canopy flattens and the tree rows become indistinct. Worse, photographs of natural woods, with their uneven canopies, give the illusion of rows that are not there. Especially on slightly oblique photographs taken in sunshine, the parallel shadows and the apparent tilt of the taller trees seem to line up into rows. Having looked in vain on the ground for such rows as seen in aerial photographs of ancient woods, and having seen apparent rows in an air photograph of New Guinea rainforest (and when overlooking a wood from a mountain), I distrust such evidence without confirmation.

Thermal infrared images, which indicate the surface temperature of objects, measure the microclimate in woods, an important influence on both trees and woodland plants and animals. They reveal, for instance, the warmer temperatures of recently coppiced areas, or the difference in temperature between the two sides of a woodbank.[20] (A hand-held apparatus is used on the ground to detect deer.)

Air photographs and satellite images are used to measure ecological change and deforestation. This is more difficult than it looks. 'Deforestation' itself is hard to define in many tropical countries, where forests do not have sharp edges, farmland can be full of trees, and changes are more complex than acres of forest turning into acres of non-forest. What is to be done statistically with forests that have been depleted or burnt but still remain forest?

CHAPTER 10

WOODLAND IN THE FIELD

Evidence of Present Soils, Trees and Vegetation

Contrary to what we used to think, the 'memory' of the forest is not of just one, two or three centuries, but of at least 2000 years.

E. DAMBRINE AND J.-L. DUPOUEY, FRANCE, 2003

WOODLAND SOILS

Woodland can grow on almost any soil or rock except deep acid peat (though 'bog firs' and other fossil trees show that it occurred even there in the past). Woodland soils, however, are not a random selection of all soils. Woods tend to be preserved or formed in particular places, and their soils develop differently from elsewhere.

Woods in Britain and Ireland, to a large degree, are survivors of periods of land hunger in the thirteenth and nineteenth centuries. They are normally not on land that is good for growing trees, but on land that (by the standards of those times) is bad for cultivation through steepness, infertility or poor drainage. Secondary woods have arisen on abandoned settlements or ex-industrial land, heaths and commons, and lately even meadows.

Characteristics of woodland soils[1]

Soil texture: Readers may have been taught that soils are formed by the weathering of underlying rocks. That is so to some extent, but especially in lowland areas soils often derive from separate superficial deposits that may be too thin to appear on a geological map. Thus woods mapped as chalk may have intensely acid soils formed from surface loess, dust that has travelled in the atmosphere.

Because woods escape ploughing, they are likely to preserve thin deposits: this is one way in which woodland soils differ from farmland.

Soils contain four main size-classes of material: *clay* (smaller than 0.001 millimetre), *silt* (0.002–0.1 millimetre), *sand* (0.1–2.0 millimetres) and *gravel* (bigger than 2.0 millimetres), besides coarser cobbles and boulders. These may come from the solid geology, from glacial deposits like boulder-clay, or from blown sand. Silt often comes from *loess*, wind-blown dust. This mostly results from dust storms around the end of the last glaciation, although it is still being deposited in areas downwind of deserts, like Japan, Texas or New South Wales; Sahara dust rains down every year on Crete, and as I write a cloud of it has even strayed to Britain.

Wet places: A very important factor is whether water accumulates in wet seasons, usually in spring. *Waterlogging* occurs where there is not enough slope to carry rainwater away, so that stagnant water fills air spaces and deprives the soil of oxygen. It thus encourages plants, such as aspen or oxlip, that tolerate these consequences. It does not have to be continuous or even annual. In Hayley Wood – on a flat hilltop in a low-rainfall part of the country – there has been significant waterlogging in 14 out of the last 42 years, culminating in the supremely wet spring of 2001 (Figs 58, 64).

Flushes are where the surface is irrigated with moving water, especially from springs. Moving water picks up oxygen where it passes cracks or root-holes, and has different effects from stagnant water. Flushes with alder, sometimes bordered with ash, occur in sloping woods in many parts of the country (Fig. 65); on nearly level ground they are associated with the remarkable 'plateau alder-woods' of the Bradfield Woods (Suffolk) and in north Norfolk.

Acidity: Soils can be acid or calcareous. Their acidity is measured on a scale of pH, which varies from 3.0 (the most acid soils) to around 8.0 (the most calcareous).

Soils develop with time. Rainwater percolates through the soil and *leaches* out soluble minerals, at a rate depending on the composition of the soil and its humus content. It may also wash out clay particles, a process known as *lessivage*.

Woodland soils tend to be acidic, even if they overlie chalk, chalky boulder-clay or limestone; they get more acid towards the top. Part of the acidity may originally have been there in layers of loess or sand, and part has developed over time. Carbon dioxide, which is acid, is drawn out of the atmosphere and synthesised into leaves, which when they fall and rot release organic acids, fizzing away any calcium carbonate that they meet. So a soil profile under bracken, with pH of 3.1 in the bracken litter, may rise to pH 5.6 in the sandy mineral soil and 7.8 in the underlying boulder-clay.

Surface acidification tends to be counteracted (if the soil is not too acid or too waterlogged) by earthworms and moles, and by tree-fall mounds if any (p.164f), which mix the layers. In well-drained parts of Hayley Wood, pH rises from 6.1 at the surface to 7.1 in the boulder-clay.

In ancient woodland, surface acidification may have accumulated over thousands of Holocene winters of rotting leaves. On earthworks such as woodbanks it is observable in miniature. The bank itself usually has an inverted profile, with the calcareous subsoil, dug out of the bottom of the ditch, on the top of the bank. The bank is therefore less acidic than the rest of the wood, but has a surface-acid layer a few inches deep, produced by hundreds of winters of rotting leaves.

Leaf litter and humus: When leaves, twigs, bud-scales etc. fall, one of two things may happen. Earthworms may come out of their burrows at night and drag down leaves to eat below ground: the worms and their gut bacteria disperse the breakdown products among the soil in the form of wormcasts. As Charles Darwin, the great earthworm ecologist, showed, worms are choosy: they take soft tasty leaves like elm first and leave the tough, nasty-tasting oak leaves till last.[2]

Alternatively, leaves pile up on the surface and are broken down gradually by mites and fungi; they form a stratified humus layer of many years' leaves in successive states of disintegration. Fungal hyphæ and mites' excrements give leafmould its distinctive smell.

Leafmould soils are known by the general Danish designation of *mor*; earthworm soils are called *mull*. The distinction depends partly on worm activity and partly on the trees. Acid soils are hostile to mull-forming types of earthworm, and the trees that grow on them tend to have unpalatable dead leaves. The transition from mor to mull is typically around pH 4.0, although I have found mor under beech in soils as weakly acid as pH 4.6, and mull under maple at pH 3.5 (on a rare occasion when maple grew on acid soil). Mull is also encouraged by coppicing.

More detailed studies subdivide mull and mor into many different categories. In America, where some forests have great thicknesses of 'duff' and leafmould, the matter is complicated by uncertainty as to which earthworms are native and which are European introductions.

Other countries have other ways of disposing of leaf litter. A loose, airy litter structure, as with pines, encourages ground fires. In Australia, many eucalypts produce a litter so unpalatable that fire is the only way of recycling it. In North

America, however, sugar-maple leaves pack down into a cardboard-like layer that appears to be a means of suppressing fires (p.45).

Fertility – woods versus farmland: Woodland soils are not a simple extension of the soils of the surrounding farmland. They would not have remained as woodland if they had been attractive for agriculture. Early farmers depended on the natural fertility of the soil, since they could not buy fertility in a sack: infertile soils remained as woodland or became heath. In infertile parts of Scandinavia, or in Japan where there was little animal manure, people would gather leaf litter and bushes from the woods to fertilise their fields, but in Britain they have seldom been reduced to such desperate expedients.

Woodland soils have developed independently of farmland. They are not ploughed or limed. They tend to retain their stratification and their top layers, such as thin layers of loess. Ploughing (rather than deforestation) promotes sheet erosion: soils on sloping arable fields creep downhill away from the bottom edges of woods and pile up against the top edges of woods lower on the slope (see Fig. 188).

Ancient woods have escaped the centuries of manuring, followed by two centuries of imported or artificial fertiliser, that farmland has had. They would lose phosphate as successive crops of wood were removed. The phosphate never came back, but ended in gardens, dunghills and churchyards, to nourish plants such as stinging-nettles. Occasional accumulations of phosphate may result from phosphate-bearing rocks, or historic or prehistoric settlements where people have lived and gardened and died, or maybe from a big roost of starlings.

In high-rainfall areas woods may be especially infertile, because nutrients have been washed out by 10,000 years of rain. This is partly why woods have turned into moorland as the Holocene has progressed (p.316). It happens to some extent all over the world. Some tropical forest soils, developed over millions of years, are extremely infertile. Many a settler in the tropics has been lured to ruin by the misbelief that the 'luxuriance of nature' implies fertile soil.

A growing conservation problem is contamination of woods and other nutrient-poor places by fertiliser dust or fertilised soil blowing off the fields, so that common, vigorous phosphate-dependent plants overrun the historic woodland vegetation. To anyone wanting to imitate an ancient wood a chief obstacle is that an ex-farmland site is too fertile (p.260). In very low-nutrient environments such as Atlantic oakwoods, nitrogen deposition may affect bryophytes and lichens on trees.[3]

Moisture: Drought can cause dieback of trees (p.323) and even in Britain can affect woodland. Places waterlogged in spring may be droughted in summer: water-logging prevents the plants from putting down deep enough roots to withstand drought. Drought in dry summers is apparently what stops oxlips in Hayley Wood from being immortal, rendering them liable to extermination by deer (p.423).

In other countries drought has more obvious effects on wild vegetation. In the Mediterranean, summer is the dry season, to which many plants are ill adapted because their evolutionary ancestry obliges them to grow in summer. Trees are often lacking, or reduced to the stature of bushes (maquis). Alternatively, trees may be widely spaced to form savanna (p.26): widely spaced above ground, but filling the whole below-ground space with their roots, so that they capture rain falling between the tree crowns as well as on them (Fig. 66).

It used to be claimed that the Mediterranean was originally covered in dense forests, and that the present savannas, maquis and garrigues are forest that has been 'degraded' by thousands of years of people cultivating, cutting wood, keeping livestock and burning vegetation to create pasture. Important though these have been, there can be little doubt that the limiting factor has been moisture, ever since the climate reached approximately its present state some 5,000 years ago. Moisture depends on rainfall, on whether the soil or bedrock can retain rainfall, and on whether the roots can penetrate the rock to get at the water. Moisture-retaining schist rocks may be more vegetated than limestone in the same climate; karstic limestone (with holes and fissures) may be more vegetated than solid limestone. Trees tend to grow on screes, or along a geological fault, or on the ruin of a Roman farmstead, or over an ancient tomb – features that promote root penetration.[4]

Mediterranean savannas are chiefly in the region of roughly 16 to 24 inches (400 to 600 millimetres) annual rainfall: less rainfall and there is steppe, more rainfall and there is forest. In Texas, where savannas are, again, partly cultural, and where rain falls all the year, they occur in the 16 to 40 inch (400 to 1,000 millimetre) belt. Although much of England falls within these limits, the less hot summers make moisture go further, so that climatic savanna is hardly a possibil-ity – with the possible exception of Staverton Park, an extreme combination of low rainfall and poor moisture retention (p.128).

Trees on rock, grassland on soil

In hard-rock landscapes, trees or woodland tend to be on rock: areas where there is soil are grassland or heath. An English example is Bradgate Park, a Midland outlier of the Highland Zone in which the ancient trees are mostly on rock out-crops (Fig. 67). In South Wales small, irregular woods followed (and occasionally still follow) very closely the rocky patches in the landscape.

In Estremadura (Spain) the *dehesa* wood-pastures (p.116) are on shallow soils over granite: areas where clay has accumulated tend to be treeless farmland. In middle Texas (p.79) woods tend to be in canyons and on limestone outcrops; where clay overlies the limestone, trees are lacking. Although large extents of clay were cultivated by settlers, land-grant surveys show that when they arrived in the nineteenth century the claylands were prairie, the limestone soils were savanna, and the canyons were wooded. In west Texas, savanna on the Davis Mountains ends abruptly at the base of the volcanic rocks and gives way to the stoneless plains of the Chihuahua Desert. I could multiply examples from Crete, Japan and other countries.

This phenomenon − trees on bare rock, grassland on soil − has escaped the attention of ecological writers, who were taught that trees cannot grow without soil. It is more than the mere effect of people cultivating the areas with soil. Rock fissures may have some attraction for tree roots, such as access to deep stores of moisture in a semi-arid environment. Or (in flammable countries like middle Texas) rocky areas may interrupt the spread of prairie fires. It is a reminder that in tree'd grassland the trees are not always the dominant partner.

WOODLAND STRUCTURE

Underwood stools
In most natural woods the trees have been coppiced: lack of coppice stools raises a suspicion that the wood is either recent or much altered by modern forestry.

Cut down a maple-tree, and it will sprout and form a small stool; cut it again after ten years, and it will sprout again and form a bigger stool; after 300 years it will be some 3 feet (1 metre) in diameter. In New England, where coppicing was introduced by English settlers, wood-lots contain stools of *Acer rubrum* of up to that size. In Old England, stools of *A. campestre* can be much bigger, resulting from cycles of felling and regrowth over a much longer period.

Such *giant stools* (Figs 68, 69) are living archaeology, independent evidence of the age and management history of a wood. Their ages can be estimated by look-ing for the biggest stools of a given species in a wood of known date of origin. In the Baltic islands of Åland, Carl Hæggström found hazel stools more than 6 feet (1.8 metres) in diameter, the oldest of which he estimated − from the date when the land they stand on emerged from the sea – to be 990 years old.[5] Hazel in nineteenth-century plantations is up to about 2 feet (60 centimetres) in diameter.

Alternatively, annual rings can be counted and measured in a section of the above-ground base of a stool. Giant stools are hollow, and usually have only a shell of wood from which to estimate the rate at which they have expanded. The last few coppicings can be dated by looking for cycles of narrow and wide annual rings. This source of information was all too common in the 1960s and 1970s, when ancient stools were destroyed every day, but is now less easily come by.

As a very rough guide, a coppiced ash stool 4 feet (1.2 metres) in diameter would be 400 years old, and one 8 feet (2.4 metres) across would be 800 years old. On wet or infertile sites stools are likely to expand more slowly than this.

Lime, oak and hazel stools probably grow about as fast as ash; maple a little faster. Sycamore stools must grow faster, for they can be 10 feet (3 metres) in diameter, although the tree has been in Britain for only 450 years. (It was fashionable in the seventeenth century, and many sycamores planted then, or their children, must still be alive.) Chestnut is also a fast grower: in Felbrigg Great Wood (Norfolk), where it was first planted in the 1670s (p.350), some stools are 7 feet (2 metres) across. The biggest chestnut stools that I know are up to 16 feet (5 metres) across in Holbrook Park (southeast Suffolk) and Stour Wood (northeast Essex).

Very large coppice stools grow out into rings, raising the question: Is this one individual, or an amalgamation of two or more? This can be decided if all the stems on a stool are one clone, sharing some individual peculiarity of bark, branching habit, time of leaf-opening or leaf-fall, etc. In ash the first-year shoots after coppicing contain a red pigment that distinguishes them as individuals by the intensity and colour of the pigment and its distribution – whether it is diffused or concentrated around lenticels. Usually all the stems of a big stool share the peculiarity and differ from neighbouring stools (Figs 70, 71) : they are thus parts of the same individual. Occasionally a big stool shows two peculiarities divided by a line through the middle: it thus consists of two individuals close together.

Lime shows similar peculiarities, but as with ash some of them are visible for only a short time in the year or in the coppice cycle. Lime, unlike ash, might reproduce vegetatively in two ways. Some limes are self-layering: weak stems bend over to the ground and take root at the tip, which should generate circular clonal patches. Alternatively, limes can blow down in storms and take root along the trunk, creating linear stands of genetically identical stems (Fig. 72). Both are probably uncommon: in my experience identity extends to no more than three adjacent stools.*

This inference is confirmed by David Morfitt's detailed observations in Piles Coppice (see below). He searched for neighbouring stools sharing some peculiarity of habit, pigmentation, time of leafing or leaf-fall, etc. The results were largely negative. Many stools are distinct from all their neighbours; possible clonal patches seldom extended to more than four stools in a row up to 120 feet (35 metres) apart. Some of these, inevitably, will be false matches, for it is easy to prove that two individuals are genetically different, but (even with DNA analysis) less easy to prove that they are identical. Vegetative reproduction has been less important for these limes than propagation by seed. If, as is likely, the limes were coppiced from the Middle Ages until the twentieth century they have had little opportunity to blow down.

Giant stools occur in most other countries with a long coppicing tradition, such as France, Norway, Sweden, Italy, Hungary[6] and Greece; also in Japan, though less commonly than here (Figs 73, 74). In many countries one must beware of coppicing as a response to fire, or of self-coppicing, as in Japanese or American limes and magnolias (p.64). The live-oak motts of inland Texas (Fig. 42) are, in effect, super-stools.

The biggest coppice stool that I know of is the now famous lime (*Tilia cordata*) in Westonbirt Arboretum, Gloucestershire, some 50 feet (15 metres) in diameter; it is a relic of the medieval Silk Wood (Fig. 75). It all has the same time of leafing, and I am told has the same DNA. Nearly as large is a lime ring in Gosling's Corner,** a surviving fragment of the great Langton Wood near Wragby, Lincolnshire. Such stools have a claim to be the oldest trees in Britain and the last surviving trees of the wildwood: they could well have originated by self-coppicing.

Timber trees

Oaks: Oak has been symbiotic with people. For over a thousand years, it was the commonest and most expensive timber tree. Woodmen, finding a young oak, did not cut it with the underwood, but let it grow to a timber tree. Although oak will

---

* The method could also be used to test the 'bundle-planting' theory invoked by Ted Green to explain multi-stemmed trees in eighteenth- and nineteenth-century parks. Planters, it seems, would sometimes dig a hole and shove a number of nursery transplants into it, of which several might survive and fuse to give the illusion of a single tree. If this were so, then the stems should *not* be identical. So far, I have failed to find the expected differences, and have to infer that multiple stems result from coppicing or the equivalent, such as a beast eating the top out of a single tree when it was small. (*Tree News* spring/summer 1995; replies, autumn 1995.)

** Lincolnshire Wildlife Trust.

grow in almost any environment in Britain except on thin chalk soils, this gave it a competitive advantage. In the eighteenth century rising prices of oak bark and oak timber encouraged landowners to increase the proportion of oak. Even after the bottom dropped out of both markets in the 1860s, many owners still encouraged oak.

Then came the Oak Change, around 1900: both species of oak largely stopped replacing themselves within existing woods (p.335f). With a few exceptions such as the Bradfield Woods (Fig. 76), most woods are now in an unhistorical state as regards their standard oaks. Instead of a mixture of ages, with young trees predominating, there are now only oaks of 100 years old or more.

Standard trees in woods that have escaped replanting now tend to be in one of three states:

1. Most of the oaks were felled between 1914 and 1945 and have not been replaced (except for sporadic regrowth from stumps). The stumps remain and give a rough indication of the date of felling (p.165f). About one-third of ancient woods are in such a state, mainly the bigger ones (p.205)

2. The oaks are still a wild population, but few or none are younger than a century. The *smaller* oaks now are roughly as big as the *biggest* oaks would have been in the Middle Ages. Stumps indicate whether there has been any felling since 1900. The oldest oaks are seldom much over 200, although there are exceptions (Ken Wood in Hampstead, London, has some from the 1680s).

3. The oaks are not a wild population, but result from replacement of wild-type oaks with nursery-grown trees of what were regarded at the time as 'good' genetic stock, as was the practice between about 1820 and 1920. These oaks have a degree of uniformity that distinguishes them from wild oaks (for details see Chapter 13). This has happened in a large minority of woods (often only part of a wood), probably more in the Highland Zone (Chapter 15).

In a rational world, timber trees would not be scattered throughout a wood, but would all be together in one part. This arrangement should result in better timber and better underwood, but was not often practised. The oakwoods of west Cornwall (and I am told south Devon) are divided into a timber part, located in a sheltered ravine, and a wood-producing part occupying the more windy slopes. In some of the woods on the Blean (east Kent) timber oaks are concentrated into particular parts of the wood, delimited by rides, the rest of the wood often being chestnut coppice.

Other species: The beechwoods of the Chilterns, consisting entirely of timber trees, appear to be a nineteenth-century development from coppice and wood-pasture (p.283f), but have still some connection with natural woodland in that most of the beeches are wild-type.

Other timber trees for which there was a market were elm and ash. Most of the elm came from non-woodland sources, but surviving elmwoods have standard trees as well as outgrown underwood. Ashes as timber trees are rarely more than 150 years old. Those that are older, as in Hayley Wood, go hollow and begin to take on the character of ancient trees.

Other native species were historically regarded as underwood, and rarely allowed to reach timber size before the twentieth century. Miller Christy, nearly a century ago, remarked of hornbeam: 'a mature wild-grown example in its natural condition is very seldom seen', but such are now not uncommon. The same is true of maple, lime, cherry, crab and even service. Woodmen have allowed these to grow up, as a curiosity or in the hope that a market for their timber might arise. Latterly it has become the custom, when coppicing in nature reserves, to promote these other species instead of the missing young oaks.

Ancient trees

Ancient woods are *not* the place to look for ancient trees, apart from coppice stools. Indeed the presence of ancient trees, unless they are boundary pollards, indicates that the wood is not ancient, but has grown up around freestanding trees (infilled savanna, p.125f). However, some standard trees in woods are on the way to becoming the old oaks and ashes of the future: they are acquiring conservation importance because they are difficult to replace.

Epiphytes and woody climbers

No visitor to the Australian tropics can forget the massive 'fern-gardens' high in the crowns of rainforest trees, or the climbing rattan palms that hang down from far above, armed with razor-wire prickles whose least touch draws blood. Most of the action in such forests, and the diversity of species, happens out of sight high in the trees. As memorable are the gnarled wisterias of Japanese sacred groves, their empty coils enveloping the ghosts of the trees that once they climbed, or the mysterious little ferns that proliferate on the soft bark of the giant *kusonoki* tree. In the southeastern United States mighty vines loop from tree to tree and even, enigmatically, across roads.

Britain has few of these. We have five woody climbers: ivy, adhering by aerial roots; honeysuckle, twining; clematis, using its leaf-stalks as tendrils; woody nightshade, scrambling informally; and dog-rose, hooking itself up, rattan-wise, on prickly flagellar shoots. Epiphytic vascular plants – rooted on the tree rather than climbing up it from the ground – are mainly in western oakwoods, especially the polypody fern on big horizontal boughs (Fig. 77), or wood-sorrel in rot-holes.

Pollards have many more epiphytes, even, on occasion, including other trees. A few big pollard willows, like a few big coppice stools, are genetically more than one tree. A second willow may start from seed in the crown of the first tree, root through the central cavity into the ground, and mingle its tissues with those of the host tree.

An investigation of woodland structure: Piles Coppice

Rural Warwickshire is traditionally divided into two halves. To the northwest is Arden, an Ancient Countryside of hamlets, ancient hedges, lanes, holloways and the ghosts of former heathland, often mistaken for Shakespeare's Forest of Arden.* To the southeast is Feldon, a Planned Countryside of villages, Enclosure-Act roads, hawthorn hedges and straight lines. In Anglo-Saxon times Arden had a huge extent of woodland, much of which had already gone by the thirteenth century; the monumental work of Sarah Wager describes – as far as documents reveal – what happened to each of the woods.[7]

On Arden's eastern fringes, extensive ancient woodland lingered until the twentieth century's vogue for grubbing and replanting; much of the replanting was unsuccessful and the ancient woodland has reasserted itself. This area has been studied by David Morfitt. Around Coventry, Domesday Book records a big concentration of woodland, which probably already contrasted with Dunsmore Heath to the east – an example of the ancient association between woodland and heath.

On the very edge of Arden is Piles Coppice in Binley (52 acres/21 ha), where Dr Morfitt's studies were concentrated (Fig. 198).[8] It is now crammed between a railway, a motorway, electricity pylons, a housing estate and a conifer plantation on the site of an ancient wood; but like many urbanised woods it is in surprisingly good condition. It has belonged to the Woodland Trust since 1987.

Piles Coppice sits on a ridge between two shallow valleys; it has sandy-silty soils probably containing loess, and quite strongly acidic (pH 3.5–4.6). It is

---

* The 'Forest of Arden' in *As You Like It* has more to do with the Ardennes in Belgium. The myth that Warwickshire Arden was a Forest was apparently invented by Michael Drayton, Shakespeare's senior contemporary.

largely surrounded by a woodbank with ditch on the outside, except on the southeast where the earthwork is poorly preserved and faces the other way, showing that it belonged to the adjacent territory of Brandon. It has an impressive spring flora.

The characteristic trees are lime and sessile oak. Small-leaved lime is dominant on the sloping parts of the wood, as stately coppice stools long outgrown to nearly 100 feet (30 metres) high; they are mixed in the usual way with standard oak-trees. Dr Morfitt found that the stools are of various diameters and ages, the largest some 11 feet (3½ metres) in diameter and evidently many centuries old. The commonest size, around 5 feet (1½ metres), indicates that there has been some more recent replacement of lime. In each part of the wood that he examined, giant and big stools occur together.

Lime is infrequent in the surviving Arden woods, but there is an area of lime-wood in the interior of the next ancient wood but one, Birchley Wood; this too has big stools in an embanked wood that is well documented back to c.1150. (The name, anciently *Burtleia*, has nothing to do with birch.)

The oaks in Piles Coppice comprise *Quercus robur, Q. petræa* and intermediates which are usually regarded as hybrids.[9] This was confirmed by Dr Morfitt using leaf measurements for the two species. There are both timber trees, interspersed among lime and hazel coppice, and coppice stools. Timber oaks, mainly in the lime area, were of both species with many intermediates. Coppice stools were overwhelmingly sessile oak, varying in size from those only once cut to ancient stools 8 feet (2½ metres) across.

Binley, anciently *Bilney*, is fairly well documented. A map of 1746 shows 'Piles Coppice' almost exactly as it is now, but before this there is a gap of nearly five centuries, bridged by a complex and confusing series of charters. Dr Morfitt identifies Piles with a private wood 4 × 2 'furlongs', which Domesday Book traced back to before 1066; the area and shape (½ × ¼ mile, 0.8 × 0.4 kilometres) are about right. At some time after 1150 it was bestowed on the Cistercian monks of Combe Abbey, who had it for the rest of the Middle Ages.

A wood called Coppice or Copse is likely to have been so-named to contrast with a nearby non-coppice wood, probably a wood-pasture. Near Piles Coppice was Binley Common Wood, now mostly swallowed up in the new town of Binley Woods. (Housing developments tend to be named after what they destroy.[10]) On the south, the anomalous woodbank was part of the compact curved outline of Brandon Old Park. In 1279 what appears to be this wood is recorded as '42 acres of land'[11] of which 2 acres are included in the park of Brandon by payment of 2 shillings and a buck per annum.' This would have been a common transaction: a rich man planning a park would pay large money for projecting bits of his neighbour's land, in order to square off the outline of the park and make it economical to fence.

GROUND VEGETATION

Herbaceous plants, like coppice stools, are a defining feature of a wood. The *National Vegetation Classification* is, to a large extent, a classification of woodland ground vegetation as it was in the 1980s.

Much is known about the range of environments in which specific plants grow, or (at least as important) in which their competitors do not grow.[12] Environmental factors vary in several independent dimensions: soil texture; soil acidity; waterlogging; flushing; degree of shade; time elapsed since last felling. Trees also act as an environmental factor for the herbaceous plants, though the correlation is not particularly close (Chapter 14).

Herbaceous plants (and tree seedlings and ground-living bryophytes) may form *guilds*, assemblages of species correlated with a particular environment of soil, shade or state of coppicing. Alternatively, one species may become so strongly dominant as to squeeze out all others. Dog's-mercury is very competitive, being clonal and not needing to establish from seed, and also because it produces a dense canopy of nearly evergreen leaves. Where the environment is ideal for it, it flourishes and squeezes out all other species, even tree seedlings. In less-than-ideal circumstances it coexists with other species as one of a guild. Plants like primrose and orchids, or non-gregarious trees like crab, always appear within guilds.

Why do guilds exist? Why does one best-adapted species – dog's-mercury, bramble, bracken – not always out-compete the others and take over the site? (Believers in the 'Tragedy of the Commons' assert that this is what happens in human affairs.) Are guilds chance groupings of plants that happen to grow in the same environment, or are they plant 'communities' in a real sense, with mechanisms of integration between species? These questions have been debated for 70 years.[13]

Relation to soil factors

Herbaceous plants are related to particular soil types more closely than most trees. A classic example of such relations is in the west Cambridgeshire woods,

where there is (or was) a series of plant communities associated with waterlogging (Figs 78, 79, 80) :
- big sedges (*Carex acutiformis* and *C. riparia*) – in the wettest places;
- oxlip and meadowsweet;
- bluebell and oxlip (with the richest guild of other species);
- bluebell as sole dominant;
- bluebell coexisting with dog's-mercury; and
- dog's-mercury alone or with occasional bluebell – in the driest places, on slopes of more than 2 degrees.

These zones were studied in the 1940s by B.A. Abeywickrama, and after him by successive students of Alex Watt, David Coombe and Donald Pigott – combining field, garden and laboratory experiments. It was first established that competition was involved: oxlip and bluebell would grow well in mercury territory provided the mercury was suppressed. Next it was shown that waterlogging determined the competition; this was done by raising or lowering plots of vegetation, which adjusted themselves to the new drainage status. Waterlogging might be expected to act via poor aeration, lack of oxygen in the soil or accumulation of carbon dioxide, but turned out in practice to work through converting iron compounds from the ferric to the ferrous state. Ferric iron is harmless, but ferrous is toxic to plants, whose sensitivity closely corresponds to their position in the waterlogging scale. Oxlip is very tolerant and mercury very sensitive: oxlip grows in the worst-drained places, not because it prefers bad drainage, but because it cannot compete with mercury.[14]

In runs of dry winters, mercury, which is clonal, advances into hollows, and dies back when these are flooded. To a lesser degree waterlogging affects soil acidity: soils are more acid in areas liable to waterlogging.

Flushing attracts a different guild of plants, including ramsons *Allium ursinum*, golden saxifrage, *Equisetum telmateja* and *Carex strigosa*.

Soil acidity is another determinant of ground vegetation. All the plant communities mentioned above are relatively calcareous, though bluebell can extend on to very acid soils. Woodland plant communities on strongly acidic sites involve bracken, some brambles, the grasses *Molinia cærulea* and *Deschampsia flexuosa*, or *Sphagnum*. The *National Vegetation Classification* assigns most ancient woods to variants of just two groups, W8 (calcareous or less acid) and W10 (strongly acid), the line being drawn around pH 4.8.

Places with accumulations of phosphate, natural or archaeological (p.200), tend to have a distinctive suite of plants, especially nettles, but also goosegrass, ground-ivy and the grass *Poa trivialis.*

Light and shade

The degree of shade under different trees varies rather little in winter, but much more in summer, when most of the light has to pass through leaves. Ash (for example) casts a light shade, whereas lime is heavily shading. Another factor is the time when the tree canopy comes into leaf: early-leafing trees can deprive the ground vegetation of three weeks' extra light at the brightest time of year.[15]

Some woodland plants avoid shade (p.22); others tolerate it, responding to lack of light by producing thinner, more spread-out leaves that capture photons more efficiently. Many, such as meadowsweet or *Deschampsia cespitosa,* die out under dense shade (e.g. hornbeam); they persist in moderate shade, but flower only under light shade (e.g. ash). A few, especially parasitic orchids and some bryophytes, appear to prefer the densest shade. Shade maintains some guilds by keeping out aggressive, light-demanding species, especially grasses.

Woodland grassland plants, which need to see the sun through permanent gaps in the tree canopy, include valerian, devil's-bit scabious and some sedges.

Coppicing plants[16]

Woods were not always dark and gloomy as they often are now. When they were regularly felled a profusion of plants responded each time. These would build up reserves in the first year after felling, flower in the second (less often the third) year, and gradually decline as the underwood grew up and re-established the shade.

Felling a wood (but leaving a scatter of timber trees) typically increases light in summer by at least 20-fold; increases light in spring (before the trees come into leaf) three- or four-fold; and in many woods extends the period of spring light by about three weeks, because the remaining shade comes from standard trees that come into leaf later than the underwood.

Coppicing plants form a number of guilds (Table 13):

1. *Spring-leafing persistent perennials.* These dozen or so species include some that are common and important: bluebell, primrose (Fig. 81), anemone, lesser celandine, early purple orchid. They are there all the time, but rejuvenate themselves every time the wood is felled. They respond strongly to coppicing, even though they do most of their leafing in spring when the effect of removing the shade is less than in summer. The shade phase is necessary to them because it keeps down stronger-growing competitors that require continuous light.

2. *Summer-leafing persistent perennials.* This larger group includes violets,

meadowsweet, water-avens and several grasses such as *Deschampsia cespitosa* and *Melica uniflora*.

3. *Buried-seed plants*. This large group (at least 100 species) are plants invisible between coppicings. They emerge from a seed bank laid down the previous time the wood was felled, spring to life, flower in the second year, renew the seed bank, and return to dormancy. Foxglove in woods on acid soil can appear in millions where not one was visible in shade. This mysterious capacity is widespread: one-third of the entire flora of the wood may be invisible if there has been no recent felling. Many rushes, speedwells, St John's-worts, brambles, wood-spurges (Fig. 83), ragged robin and even heather behave in this way.

Buried-seed plants discriminate between individual woods. The 'signature plant' of Hayley Wood is ragged robin, of the Bradfield Woods wood-spurge *Euphorbia amygdaloides*, of Hempstead Wood (northwest Essex) wood forget-me not *Myosotis sylvatica*, of Chalkney Wood red campion and wild raspberry, of Groton Wood trailing St John's-wort *Hypericum humifusum*. Although these are plants with definite ecological ranges, it is difficult to account for this local abundance in terms of environmental factors. The development of a distinctive set of coppicing plants for each separate wood may be one of the processes in the change from wildwood to individual woods.

I leave as an exercise for the reader this question: how do buried seeds know that the wood has been felled and it is time to germinate? Being buried, they can hardly see the extra light. It could be some microclimatic effect, such as higher temperature in a coppiced area; but if so, why does not the whole seed bank germinate in vain every time there is a season a few degrees warmer than average? Or are a few per cent of the seeds programmed to germinate every year – but only if there is extra light do they grow into plants? (Without extra light they succumb to something – let us call it slugs – before they get big enough to be noticed.)

4. *Mobile species*. These, especially willowherbs and thistles, have an efficient dispersal mechanism and move around the wood, chasing newly felled areas.

5. *Tree seedlings*. Trees such as ash and birch, and formerly oak and hazel, rely on coppicing to progress from the seedling to a young tree.

6. *Aquatics*. Aquatic plants, such as brooklime speedwell and water violet, occur in woodland ponds, but are visible only after felling. Water violet probably spends the interval as vegetative buds buried in the mud.

7. *Casuals*. Many plants, such as hemlock, mullein, borage or the occasional

stray cereal, do not persist in woods, but come haphazardly into felled areas from outside.

8. *Unresponsive*. A dozen species appear to be unaffected or even set back by coppicing. These include ramsons, adder's-tongue fern and herb paris. Dog's-mercury is damaged by coppicing, which may benefit other plants by breaking (for a time) its competitive monopoly in woods that favour it.

Much recent 'conservation' coppicing is akin to silvicultural thinning, leaving (by historical standards) too many trees standing and providing more continuous shade. Where there are deer this weakens the regrowth; where there are not it favours brambles over more specialised coppicing plants. Thinning versus coppicing, when compared experimentally in a French hornbeam–oakwood, produced strikingly different results. Thinning produced a 'spectacular spread' of brambles, and also grasses and sedges. Other guilds of coppicing plants were fully developed only after coppicing. Although thinning was presented as a 'close-to-nature' practice, it did not replicate the way that woods actually work.[17]

The appearing of coppicing plants is one of the changes that transformed wildwood into managed woodland. Where did they come from? They are not pioneer plants of open ground, nor are they the same as plants of permanent open areas (woodland grassland plants), nor (apart from casuals) are they universal weeds. They are by no means related to the sort of woodland that can be burnt (p.44f). In wildwood, natural treefall, from storm or avalanche, seems too rare an event at any one place to give rise to them. However, part of the Tatra Mountains, Slovakia, where blowdowns repeatedly occur (p.19f), has something closely resembling the coppice-plant guilds of England, including oxlip, water-avens, raspberry, hemp-nettle and other species (Fig. 82). Whether evolution was involved is discussed in the final chapter.

BROWSING

The biggest immediate threat to woodland is browsing animals: deer, sheep or feral goats (Chapter 22). Large herbivores subtract much of the woodland ground vegetation, replacing it with browsing-adapted plants, especially grasses. They render coppicing impracticable. They convert a woodland ecosystem into trees plus grass, with no long-term future for the trees. This has been shown by numerous exclosure experiments. Hayley Wood was established in 1962 especially to protect oxlip; oxlip has declined ever since except where protected from fallow deer. Since seven-eighths of the wood was deer-fenced in 2001–2 there has been a notable recovery except in the one-eighth left unfenced.[18]

What difference did it make if a wood was in a Forest?
There is one set of woods that has been exposed to *intermittent* browsing for centuries, namely compartmental wood-pastures, especially Forests such as Hatfield or Wychwood Forest.

These had a specific grazing regime, typically ungrazed in the first half of each coppice cycle (p.121f) and grazed in the latter half. Recent observations on grazing in woods are mainly concerned with deer or sheep, but in historic wood-pastures there were usually all the domestic animals, and often deer too. If the system worked as it was supposed to do, trees would be protected from browsing in the vulnerable first few years after felling. At the same time herbaceous plants would be freed from browsing as well as shade. Shade-bearing herbs, if palatable, would be exposed to attack in the second half of the cycle; buried-seed plants and mobile plants would be exempt, being no longer visible.

Historical surveys rarely identify underwood, but an exception is the 1564–5 surveys of Rockingham Forest, analysed by G.F. Peterken, which report thorn (hawthorn or blackthorn) in nearly every one of 106 coppices and maple in the great majority; ash was notably rare.

Pasturage in Rockingham continued well into the nineteenth century. J.A. Best has compared trees and ground vegetation in the formerly grazed Rockingham coppices with woods that have no history of intermittent grazing. I shall put this study beside my own records of the 12 surviving coppices in Hatfield Forest, compared with the two purlieu woods close to the Forest and with 12 similar woods outside the Forest and within 10 miles (6 kilometres) of it (Table 14). All sets of woods are on predominantly calcareous substrates, although the soils may be acidic.[19]

The Hatfield Forest woods have a history of periodic browsing by deer, cattle and sheep; the purlieu woods, in theory, were accessible to deer only; the other woods should not have a browsing history. In recent decades the separation has to some extent broken down as deer have increased outside the Forest: the records date mainly from 20–25 years ago when this was less of a problem.

Trees favoured by periodic browsing: Maple and hawthorn have long been more abundant in Forest woods. This was found by Best in Rockingham and appears strongly in the Hatfield records. In Hatfield, however, most of the hawthorn is a recent invasion: in the 1920s the wood-fences were allowed to decay and let in cattle, which devoured the underwood, creating gaps which hawthorn later filled.

Blackthorn has been favoured by intermittent browsing in both Rockingham and Hatfield. (It is significant in Rockingham as the food-plant of the rare black hairstreak butterfly.) As with the previous species, this is a matter of abundance rather than presence or absence. The purlieu woods follow the non-Forest woods. Unlike Best, I do not find crab-apple to be commoner with browsing.

Aspen is known in Hayley Wood to be distasteful to deer and to be encouraged by coppicing plus deer.[20] In Hatfield Forest it is a clonal and rather uncommon tree, and is limited by requiring waterlogged ground, standing out in wet places where deer have eliminated everything else.

Oak as underwood is a special and anomalous feature of some of the Hatfield coppices: it is not on the very acid, infertile soils where it occurs elsewhere in Lowland England. I have argued that this relates to a breakdown of the separation of coppices and plains, perhaps in the seventeenth century, which allowed cattle to get into the young underwood. Oak, being then prolific and somewhat resistant to browsing, filled the resulting gaps, creating the unusual situation that there were so many oaks that it became worthwhile to treat some of them as underwood rather than timber.[21]

Elm is palatable to all livestock; continuous exposure to deer is the main reason for woodland elm failing to recover from recent Elm Disease. It is surprising to find elm systematically more abundant in Hatfield Forest than in non-Forest woods. However, browsing *in the latter part of each coppice cycle* might well do it no harm. After each felling, suckers would arise from the roots and in six years would be big enough not to be much harmed when the animals were let in.

Trees disfavoured by periodic browsing: Ash is the only tree which Best or I found to be disfavoured compared to other trees. It is very palatable; but deer normally do not kill ash saplings, but reduce them to gnarled stubs, which wait until reduced shade and reduced browsing let them get away. In Hayley Wood a period of coppicing and severe browsing in the 1960s killed many of the stools. Part of the area was fenced in 1980, and within 14 years was crowded with pole-sized ashes with gnarled bases, filling the gaps.[22] This might be taken to indicate that intermittent browsing favours ash (Fig. 85). This, however, is contrary to Best's experience in Rockingham and mine in Hatfield Forest. Were the seven-year fencing phases too short to sustain ash? Or were cattle involved, which destroyed ash more effectively than deer?

Herbaceous plants favoured by periodic browsing: Best remarks on the 'grassy' appearance of Rockingham coppices subjected to grazing, especially due to *Deschampsia cespitosa*. This grass is more abundant in Hatfield Forest than in purlieu or non-Forest woods, often dominant in coppiced areas; its history in Forest coppices appears to go back to the seventeenth century (p.115). *Brachypodium sylvaticum* adds to the grassy appearance. Although European grasses are adapted to grazing, woodland grasses are either tough and relatively unpalatable, like *Deschampsia*, or feeble and not worth eating, like *Brachypodium*.

Best notes barren strawberry, burdock, ground-ivy, wood-sorrel and sanicle as 'apparently more frequent in grazed coppices'. Barren strawberry and ground-ivy are among the rather peculiar set of coppicing plants in Hatfield Forest; burdock, however, is a generalised mobile coppicing plant and is not more common in the Forest. The most distinctive (though no longer common) coppicing plant of Hatfield Forest, almost unknown in the non-Forest woods, is hound's-tongue, a very distasteful plant which nothing will eat. Wood-sorrel, a shade-bearing plant, is more common in grazed coppices in both Rockingham and Hatfield. With sanicle there is no appreciable difference at Hatfield.

Stinging-nettle is eaten by cattle (though without relish) but not by deer. As a phosphate plant, it might be favoured by cattle feeding outside the wood and lying up and depositing dung in shade. At Hatfield the net effect is a modest increase in the Forest compared to non-Forest woods.

The big sedge *Carex pendula* has increased in many woods, sometimes to the point where it suppresses other plants. Although elsewhere it is favoured by large numbers of deer (which dislike it), it is not more prevalent in Hatfield Forest.

Herbaceous plants and undershrubs disfavoured by periodic browsing: Plants sensitive to continuous browsing include bramble, primrose and oxlip. Brambles are among the favourite foods of deer, although not often eliminated by them, especially as they have a seed bank. Bitten-off bramble leaflets are a sign of deer browsing that one looks for in an unfamiliar wood. Brambles are distinctly less abundant in Hatfield Forest. Oxlip, a shade-bearing perennial with no seed bank, barely survives at all in Hatfield Forest, though it was formerly abundant in some of the comparison woods. With primrose the difference is less obvious. Hatfield, however, lies on the edge of a geographical boundary between primrose and oxlip regions; some of the comparison woods lie well within the oxlip region and would not be expected to have primrose.

Best gives bluebell and dog's-mercury as adversely affected by browsing. At Hatfield, this seems to be corroborated for bluebell – almost absent from the

Forest but common outside – but dog's-mercury is indifferent. In Hayley Wood bluebell is not much eaten by deer (unless starving) and mercury hardly at all, but severe deer pressure probably diminishes these plants, perhaps through trampling and soil compaction.[23]

Other plants 'apparently absent or less frequent in grazed coppices' in Rockingham include anemone, herb paris, pignut and wood speedwell *Veronica montana*. This can be confirmed in Hatfield only for anemone, which is strikingly absent from the Forest. Its susceptibility to browsing is somewhat surprising: although shade-bearing, and exposed to animals in the latter part of the coppice cycle, it is very unpalatable. The same is true of herb paris, which is rare and declining in Hayley Wood, perhaps because of predation by deer (which I cannot confirm).

A regular cycle of periodic browsing lets woods survive for centuries, but in a modified form. Browsing for half the time probably has a less drastic effect than browsing all the time at half the intensity. Trees and buried-seed plants are protected in the first half of the cycle, when they are at their most vulnerable. Shade-bearing plants – those that are still visible, and struggling against shade – are at their most vulnerable in the second half: not only palatable species like oxlip, but even the distasteful anemone, bluebell and dog's-mercury, tend to die out in the long run.

Cliffs
Cliffs, out of the reach of browsing animals, are the habitat of many of the world's rare and endemic plants. The familiar horsechestnut was originally a cliff endemic of Albania and Epirus (Fig. 86).

Palatable trees may grow on cliffs. In Swaledale and many other limestone areas yews and ancient wych-elms occur in cliff refugia (Fig. 84). Limes and rare whitebeams are a feature of the towering cliffs of the Avon Gorge, Bristol. The same happens in foreign countries, supremely in Crete, an island with a history of thousands of years of browsing by domestic livestock preceded by hundreds of thousands of years of browsing by wild beasts, but with a profusion of inland cliffs. A visitor to a foreign country, investigating the browsing history, should first see whether trees on cliffs differ from those in the rest of the landscape.

Even modest crags, which goats and even sheep ought to climb, serve as refugia for palatable trees (e.g. lime in Wales). As fruit-growers and tree-planters know, grasses are powerful competitors against young trees. Do rocks, by reducing grass competition, encourage young trees to grow faster and get away sooner from the attentions of sheep and goats?

CHAPTER 11

USES OF WOOD AND TIMBER

*Reconstructing the Woods from Buildings,
Hurdles and Ships*

I have also consulted the available museums, only to find that many devote far more space to the war-gear of Polynesian tribes or the internal structures of obscure marine worms, than they can spare for the native arts and peasant crafts of our own people.

H.L. EDLIN, *WOODLAND CRAFTS OF BRITAIN*, 1949

Any writer on trees feels obliged to relate the peculiar uses to which each species is supposed to have been put. Herbert Edlin, besides *Trees, Woods and Man*, wrote *Woodland Crafts of Britain*, an invaluable record of 'woodland' crafts as they survived into the 1940s. As a student of craftsmen at work, he was rivalled only by Helen Fitzrandolph and Doriel Hay, Oxford dons of the 1920s. However, it lacks time-depth: this is one of those books that give the impression that 'traditional' practices are all of the same remote antiquity. It also lacks sources for most of the information. Another useful study, based on written records and limited to the period since 1750, is by E.J.T. Collins.[1]

Since Edlin's time, although the crafts themselves have further declined, much more material has come from archaeological excavations and the study of antique furniture and standing buildings. (Built-in furniture, made by local carpenters, is especially instructive.[2]) Woodworkers such as Richard Darrah have been studying the crafts to the point of being able to replicate ancient artefacts. Museums have responded to Edlin's stricture, though objects are still displayed without saying what they are made of. The time has come for an authoritative book on ancient and early-modern woodworking: its materials, methods and products. This chapter is concerned, not with makers and manufacture, but with what timber and wooden artefacts reveal about trees, woodland and woodland management.

EARLY WOODMANSHIP

Woodland management goes back at least as long as agriculture. Whether it goes back further is uncertain: the Mesolithic excavation at Star Carr produced evidence for carpentry and reedbed management by burning, but so far not for woodmanship. There is, however, a scrap of archaeological evidence in the form of buried multi-stemmed alder stools.[3]

The obvious motive is producing trees of manageable size. It is not too difficult to fell a tree, and experimenters have claimed that stone tools compare favourably even with chainsaws, but what happens next? Reducing a great tree to pieces that can be carried away and used is no light task, especially if one has not invented saws. Most human cultures use the smallest tree that will do the job, leaving the converting and extracting of huge forest trees until machines have been invented.

It is a surprise to go to Cartagena, Colombia – one of the best preserved of old Spanish towns – and find so much seventeenth-century timber surviving within 8 degrees of the equator. Much of this is not rainforest giants but small trees, one log per timber. Even slaves hated to waste effort cutting up big trees.

Other motives for woodmanship might have been producing a continuous supply of rods, poles and firewood, and producing leaves for feeding livestock. Conservation is unlikely to have been a motive until later: at first woodland was very abundant, though much of it would have consisted of trees too big to be useful.

Somerset trackways

Early woodmanship is known from 'trackways' preserved in peat, especially in the Somerset Levels. From Neolithic to Anglo-Saxon times people lived on fen islands and made walkways across the soft peat between, which have been engulfed and preserved by the growth of the peat. They are made of underwood, branchwood and cleft oak planks used in many different ways. Some materials probably grew on the peat and some were brought from the upland.

The famous Sweet Track, of early Neolithic date (about 3900 BC), is made of large poles and small timber. It has the greatest variety of species and the most elaborate carpentry. Some of the ash, oak and hazel poles apparently came from coppice-woods.[4]

Walkways of woven wattle hurdles are known from the middle Neolithic to the Iron Age. The earliest, Walton Heath and Rowland's Tracks, are made of rods of hazel and a few ash. Like a modern wattle hurdle, they have straight *sails* (stout rods) interwoven with long flexible *ethers* to form a panel about 4 feet 3 inches by 8 feet (1.3 × 2.4 metres). The rods were rent from the stool by a blow with a stone axe. They are all used in the round (there being no metal tools needed to split them). Hence they are very uniform in size, but not in age. It was not the practice, as now, to fell a whole stool at once and split the thicker rods; instead, rods were drawn from each stool one by one as they reached the right thickness. Many rods had their tops cut off two to four years before being felled. Topping and felling were done in summer (the last annual ring is incomplete), which suggests that the main product of the wood was leaves.[5]

CONVERTING TIMBER AND WOOD

Timber (or wood) may be used either as the round log, or *scappled* into a square or rectangular section, or split or sawn into two or four or smaller divisions. Figure 199 shows various types of subdivision of the log and the shapes into which they *warp* as the timber dries out and shrinks.

Scappling
Many cultures use poles and small timbers in the round, lashed together with fibres. Carpenters' joints and nailed joins, however, are best worked on flat surfaces.

In scappling a log, the excess may be hewn away with an adze or a special tool called a *broad-axe*. Or an ordinary axe can be used by the 'notch-and-chop' method, common in medieval England and modern Australia. Every 2 or 3 feet (60–90 centimetres) a notch is cut down to the required level; the hewer then turns the axe round and splits away the unwanted timber, leaving the bottoms of the notches still just visible. Saws were used only if enough timber was removed to yield a useful offcut.

The flat faces may extend to the corners of the beam; but usually in England the corners are left rounded (*waney*), often with the bark left on. Waney edges indicate whether the beam is from a whole log, and the diameter of the original log. They are the stuff of tree-ring dating (p.42): the outermost annual ring on a waney edge gives the year that the tree was felled.

A medieval carpenter would normally fell the trees and work them while still green, saving the labour and wear on tools of working seasoned oak. As a log dries out it shrinks: very little along its length, more in the radial direction, and still more in the circumferential. With some trees the difference may be taken up by the timber stretching circumferentially: some eucalypts are notoriously unpredictable to work because they have internal stresses lying in wait for the unwary carpenter. Oak usually cracks along the line of least resistance. An oak beam made from a whole log typically displays four cracks called *shakes*, from the pith to the middle of each face (Fig. 199); these wax and wane along the length of the beam as the pith wanders towards one face or another. If the tree is allowed to dry out before working the cracks will be distributed at random around the circumference.[6]

Cleaving

Before the invention of saws, people might split a log lengthways. This is the earliest known form of carpentry, going back to the Mesolithic hunter-gatherers of early postglacial Yorkshire.[7] It calls for co-operation from the tree, especially for big trees in which it is difficult to influence the direction of the cleft as it progresses.

Woodmen make thatching-broaches or hurdle-ethers by cleaving rods of hazel or sallow, less often ash, using a metal edge tool called a *froe*; the workpiece is gripped in a frame called a *brake*. If the split runs off course it can be corrected by bending the thicker side.

The Pacific Coast Indians of North America, superb carpenters and architects, are said to have had a method of splitting huge planks off standing Douglas fir and other conifers. The Japanese, down to the seventeenth century, would split big trunks of *hinoki* (*Chamæcyparis obtusa*) and *sugi* (*Cryptomeria japonica*) into standard-sized pieces, small enough to carry, which were the usual stuff of the timber trade for middle- and upper-class buildings.[8] Both technologies demand conifers with a very regular wood structure in which a split, once begun, proceeds along a predetermined plane, even if it is not along the radius of the tree.

Cleaving most pines, oaks or other of the world's crooked, knotty trees is difficult, especially for people who have to make do with wooden wedges. It is an unrewarding task to propagate a split (Fig. 87) along the length of a long log if the grain is spiral or there are knots in the way. Nevertheless cleavable oaks were not uncommon in Anglo-Saxon England, to judge by their use in carpentry.[9]

In the Middle Ages there were enough cleavable oaks for the regular manufacture of cleft objects such as park pales, barrel-staves, clapboards (where not imported), laths, tile-battens and the thousands of shingles used instead of tiles on castle roofs and church spires. Edlin describes the Lake District craft of making *spelk* baskets from thin laths cleft from oak timber, a small-scale use in which the craftsman could be choosy about which logs to use.

Sawing

The Bronze Age invention of saws gradually spread from furniture making to coarser carpentry and finally to tree-felling: saws were once made that would get through a giant Californian sequoia. Saws can save labour and wastage and will go through knots and crooked grain (Fig. 88); but they are expensive and need regular doctoring; landowners disapproved of them because they made less noise than axes when trees walked off at night.

The Ancient Egyptians sawed lengthwise by lashing the timber to a post,[10] but European practice uses a two-man saw. The accounts of any medieval building project include payments to sawyers at so much a square foot. At first one end of the log was propped up on a trestle, but in the fourteenth century the sawpit was invented, in which the log lies over a pit like a churchyard grave; the top sawyer stands on the log and the bottom sawyer in the pit. Each method produced characteristic changes in the direction of the saw-scratches as the saw reached the support and the log had to be moved along. When the sawyers got near the end they often split the last foot or so.

Mechanical saws, driven by water wheels, were invented probably in France in c.1200; they spread to much of Europe and then Scotland and America, but in England sawyers did not tolerate them until the eighteenth century.[11] An early sawmill produces a pattern of parallel scratches, getting closer together on encountering a knot with its greater resistance.

The chainsaw, originally a surgical instrument,[12] came into use for felling in the 1950s. It produces distinctive semicircular patterns on the sawn face.

CHOICE OF TREE SPECIES

Writers often claim that particular trees are necessary for specific uses, and even exist because of such uses: as if someone wanting to make chairs might plant beech trees, and come back and make the chairs when the trees had grown. There may occasionally be something in this 'orchard' ethos: the Royal Gunpowder Factory at Waltham Abbey had alder plantations (which still survive) because the wood structure of alder charcoal results in the particular intimate mixture of carbon, sulphur and potassium nitrate that gives gunpowder its bang. More often industries adapt themselves to the available trees or migrate to where suitable trees grow. To some extent trees are interchangeable: different cultures use the same tree for different purposes and different trees for the same purpose.

Fitzrandolph & Hay and Edlin describe uses of specific trees in the 1920s and 1940s. Significant properties include strength at right angles to the grain (in which oak is weak and elm strong); splittability (chestnut best, followed by oak); and 'woolliness', resistance to abrasion (poplar best).

Furniture

Furniture timbers depend more on fashion and custom than practicality. Almost any species has been used, even alder. Upper-class furniture of tropical hardwoods had its imitators in pine or beech, coloured with dragon's blood – or, when the dragon-trees of the Canary Islands were not supplying it, with *kino*, the exudation from damaged eucalypts that is said to have been Australia's first export to Europe.

Modern 'Windsor' chairs are factory-made of beech; those of the eighteenth century were made in local workshops of whatever was available, such as ash for the bow and sallow or birch for the legs; but the seat was always elm, whose high transverse tensile strength allowed it to be less than an inch thick. Beech, although otherwise an inferior timber, works well with woodworking machinery; it took over gradually as the craft became industrialised around High Wycombe (p.284). The last component to be made in beech was the seat, sometimes with disastrous results. America, however, has its own tradition of Windsor chairs and other furniture, in which the kind of timber does not matter: seats are made thicker to compensate for a weak material, and since American chairs are painted nobody notices the timber.

There are occasional medieval references to beech furniture, but it remained local until the nineteenth century. Much vernacular furniture, especially big table tops and built-in settles, is elm.

Wheels

George Sturt's *The Wheelwright's Shop*, published in 1923, is a classic account, by a practitioner, of one woodworking craft in its highly developed nineteenth-century form, which included making vehicles as well as wheels.

The spoked wheel was invented in the Iron Age and probably reached its highest development then. Two refinements, the shrunk-fitted iron tyre and the one-piece bent rim, were later lost: the tyre was reinvented in the eighteenth century, but even Sturt never recovered the bent rim. Wheelwrighting has two branches, dished wheels and flat wheels; in Britain the flat wheel is known chiefly in spinning wheels, but in Asia and Sardinia it is used for load-bearing wheels.

Sturt never made the nave, spokes, felloes and axle of a wheel of anything other than elm, oak, ash and beech. Other cultures use other timbers, although elm is generally used for the nave where obtainable: its high tensile strength in all directions is useful for a structure that has mortices cut in it all round. But I have heard of an Iron Age wheel with an ash nave; the Japanese use the elm-relative *keyaki*. Wheelwrights in Australia soon learnt to adapt their craft to different species of eucalyptus instead of European timbers; they made flat wheels on a heroic scale, such as 12-foot (3½-metre) wheels on the wains, drawn by herds of oxen, that moved logs of the giant, heavy *karri* eucalyptus in south-west Australia.

Turnery

Wooden cups, known as *mazers*, were made in their millions in Anglo-Saxon and medieval England. Coppergate in York is not the street of policemen, but of cuppers or cupmakers: its excavators found great quantities of spoilt cups and cup-cores of the tenth century. Cups were normally made by splitting a short log, about two and a half times the diameter of the mazer, into four billets, which were then made into cups on a lathe. Maple was specifically used for cups, but other species such as ash would serve. About 80 mazers survive above ground; almost all are 'fine' mazers with a ripple or bird's-eye grain, banded with silver-gilt.[13]

Mazers were probably the commonest product of the turner's art, which ran also to tool handles, chair-legs, balusters, reels and much else.

Bark

For most of history the bark of oak was a by-product for tanning leather; no other native tree has nearly as much tannin. It must be removed in May when the cambium is beginning the new annual ring. Medieval accounts include sales of bark when oaks were felled, but it was not very important: until the seventeenth century bark was commonly left on if the timber was felled at the wrong time of year to strip it.

In later centuries bark increased in value faster than timber. By the early nineteenth century mountainous stacks of bark came from every wood and hedge in the country, so valuable that thousands of acres of western oakwoods were managed solely as coppice; timber was foregone for a greater yield of bark. Those who think of the Navy as the great consumer of oak-trees for ships should contemplate the Army's consumption of oak-trees for boots and saddles. After

1860 the value of bark sharply declined as other sources of tannin came into use, such as valonia, the giant acorn-cups of *Quercus macrolepis* from the Ægean. Bark-gathering lingered late enough to be described as a curiosity by Thomas Hardy (p.396) and photographed by Edlin.

FAGGOTS AND FUEL

1 hundred wood faggots 6s. . . . ½ hundred furze faggots 3s. 4d.
BILL FOR BURNING ARCHBISHOP CRANMER, 1553[14]

At most times fuel has been the chief product of woodland, in terms of tons per acre per year. Logs, faggots and charcoal would come from underwood (the residue after the more exacting trades had taken their pick) and the branches of timber trees. Timber itself would be more valuable for other purposes, and would incur the extra expense of chopping it into burnable sizes.

Faggots were bundles of rods, compressed in some sort of vice and tied with bands of twisted hazel (Fig. 89). (In Japan they are still made and are tied up with wisteria.) They came in various sizes, defined by market regulations, from the little *ostrey* faggot (a firelighter) through *kids* and *bavins* to the *two-band* faggot. In 1461–2 Canterbury Cathedral sold from Short Wood (the long wood in the Blean now called Church Wood) *courtfagot*, *kechynfagot*, *balfagot* and *salefagot*, besides logs in the form of *belet*, *talwode*, *ostwode* and *orwe*, rods, bark and charcoal.[15]

Faggots were used in brewing, baking (until the 1970s), brickmaking and land-drains (faggots laid in a trench). Sea defences included (and still include) long faggots placed to trap silt in salt-marsh creeks, or interwoven between upright stakes; these were significant products from woods near low-lying coasts. Late-medieval Calais was an English outpost: keeping out the sea and the French (it was doubtful which would get Calais first) called for large quantities of timber and underwood, most of which was brought from England.[16]

Logs came in various sizes of *billets*, *shides* and *talwood*. A consumer-protection statute (1542) laid down the permitted sizes, normally 4 feet (1.2 metres) long and of various girths from 20 to 44 inches (50 to 110 centimetres) which were supposed to have identifying marks cut in them. At Cambridge we find 40,000 billets, valued at £36, confiscated for being under size. In 1523 a licence was issued to export four million 'byllet' from England to France.[17]

How much notice was taken of the species of firewood? Almost any tree will do. Elm, despite common belief, is excellent fuel if well dried, but in my experience ash does not live up to its reputation. Woodmen need marketing skills when it comes to disposing of alder or sallow.

For charcoal the species matters more. Some processes, like smelting, call for specific sizes of charcoal; some trees, like pine, produce a soft charcoal that easily abrades into unusable dust. Oak makes a good hard charcoal. The Japanese use charcoal as a domestic and cooking fuel, and are particular about its quality: it has to be made of oak (even the species of oak matters) and must not be excessively charked. Good Japanese charcoal is almost as hard as the original wood. It is made in a semi-permanent kiln near a water source, used for damping down the fire. Charcoal sites are often to be seen in mountain woods.

TIMBER AND WOOD IN BUILDINGS

The choice of whether to build in timber or some other material is not merely utilitarian. The distribution of timber-walled buildings in Britain is not related to the distribution either of woodland or of stone. The Weald (with superabundant timber) has a strong timber-framing tradition, but so have Essex (with average supplies) and Cheshire (with little). In the Middle Ages, timber and stone were both often brought from a distance. To generalise, where there is not much timber building it will be urban, as in Devon, Dorset, Gloucestershire (east of the Severn) or Scotland. Medieval Norwich had mud houses, none of which appears to survive; these were superseded by timber-framing, especially in that characteristically urban form with a timber façade (often of very thin timbers) on a brick or stone rear structure.

Timber was an architectural medium, not merely structural; it could be a status symbol. Wattle-and-daub was designed to expose the timbers at least inside, and in middle- or high-status buildings on the outside as well. Timbers often have traces of original paint.

Species of timber

Oak, though it was expensive, is the commonest timber in standing buildings. This is partly a matter of survival: less durable timbers, and buildings containing them, will have disappeared more often. Until recently, other species were thought to be a mark of late date and were under-recorded. Elm occurs from the thirteenth century onwards, often in regions without much woodland, although sometimes in well-wooded areas such as northwest Kent. Ash and even aspen and black poplar survive from the Middle Ages, and are not usually in the last stages of decay: if kept dry they are quite capable of lasting 700 years. Pine occurs espe-cially in Scotland and Cambridgeshire; it was always imported in England and usually in Scotland. Beech is curiously absent as a structural timber, although it functions perfectly well in France.

In underwater carpentry oak is not so obviously prevalent − either because the species was thought to matter less, or because waterlogging preserves non-oak species.

Timber-framing

Timber-framing in the medieval manner goes back at least to the Roman period. In Roman London, above-ground timbers are sometimes preserved through reuse in waterfront structures. The carpentry and the wattle-and-daub infill were similar in concept to medieval structures, although details differ and joints were rarely pegged. The timbers came from whole oak logs scappled from trees 25 to 65 years old. If the small amount of material is representative, the regular produc-tion of conveniently small oaks was as much a feature of Roman woodmanship as of medieval.[18]

Medieval timber-framing involved large numbers of small oaks. Normally each timber represents one log, scappled leaving waney corners. Bigger components come from bigger trees. Any house represents 150−300 such trees, a minority of which were bigger and used for such things as tie-beams and principal posts. Components such as floorboards and curved braces were sawn several from a log.[19]

Medieval sawyers could (if they had to) saw a great tree lengthwise into ordinary-sized timbers. At Gloucester in the thirteenth century, Henry III gave the Dominican Friars 82 huge oaks from the Forests of Dean and Gillingham (Dorset). The roof rafters, which still exist, were sawn four or six out of a tree.[20] Some similar reason probably explains why Great Livermere, in the woodless Breckland, has a church with a fourteenth-century roof (now hidden) sawn with great skill from big, crooked oaks. However, outsize trees − and their transport − were normally too costly to waste in this way.

There was a change to using bigger trees and sawing them into smaller compo-nents; in eastern England this can be dated to the late sixteenth century. Prob-ably the growth of oaks had been gaining on felling. Another possible factor is the falling cost of sawing, as better saws were invented and sawyers' wages fell.

An analysis of a small two-and-a-half-storey house in the Weald of Sussex, dated to the 1560s, reveals at most 39 trees, all between 1 and 2 feet (30 and 60 centimetres) in diameter (and thus big trees by medieval standards), sawn into

280 components. Very few of the trees were more than 14 feet (4½ metres) in useful length; they are interpreted as hedgerow oaks.[21]

There are regional differences. In northern England ordinary timbers appear to be more often sawn out of big trees than in the middle and south. In the western half of England, for unknown reasons, *cruck* construction prevails. Every 10 to 15 feet (3 to 5 metres) a house is spanned by two great curved timbers running from the base of the walls (stone or timber-framed) to the apex of the roof. Often they are black poplar (which grows into that shape); sometimes they are the two halves of one tree. These support a frame made of lesser timbers.

In the Middle Ages, and down to the Oak Change of *c.*1900 (p.335), oaks grew readily from seed in existing woods: any long run of woodland accounts records the felling of hundreds of small oaks, and replacement could not have been difficult (see Fig. 76). The woods being coppiced, browsing animals could not have favoured the regeneration of oaks, contrary to Francis Vera's theory of wildwood (p.79f).

An example: Valley Farm, Flatford, East Bergholt

This is a hall-house in Suffolk, nearly typical of thousands that still exist and perhaps typical of hundreds of thousands that once existed. (It belongs to the National Trust, but is not generally open to the public.)

The house is in three parts (Fig. 90). The middle was a great hall open to the roof, heated by a fire smouldering in the middle of the floor. Both ends of the house are two-storeyed. The 'service' end has two rooms downstairs, the *buttery* and *pantry*, supposedly for storing drink and food, with a *solar* (a bedroom) upstairs. At the other end is a *parlour* (the sort of 'best room' that would later be used for weddings and funerals) with a second solar.

This is a middle-class house: the owner is thought to have been a modest farmer who was also a fuller, one of the small processing businesses that clustered around the towns of the cloth industry. In size it is in the middle of the range; there are many hall-houses both larger and smaller in East Bergholt. The few decorative details suggest a date of around 1400. (The timbers, as often, contain too few annual rings for a dendrochronological date.)

Alterations to the house were almost as standardised as the original plan. In the late fifteenth century a chimney was inserted in the hall, a brick tower projecting through a hole in the roof. A little later the hall was divided into two storeys by inserting a floor of massive timbers, in the makeshift manner of inserted floors.

The original fabric is identifiable by the soot-blackened timbers, the soot dating from the first hundred years before the chimney was added. Besides the hall, one of the service rooms is sooted inside, and so is the service solar; a fire was somehow contrived on the floor of an upstairs room.

Not all the timber is oak. Elm is used for some of the big timbers; ash appears in the service end. Generally these less durable timbers are used in places well away from the weather, although one wall top-plate is ash (and has rotted in one place and been fished by bolting on another timber with an early type of bolt). The original service-end stairs are still in use, with treads partly of elm, enclosed in a cage of black poplar boards.

In houses of this period one can often work out how many trees were used. A house of this size would normally contain 200–250 oaks, most of them about 9 inches (23 centimetres) in diameter, with a few bigger, and about 20 feet (6 metres) long. It would represent one year's growth of timber trees on something like 150 acres (61 ha) of woodland; or (to put it another way) the timber component of a 50-acre (20 ha) wood could produce one house of this size about every three years for ever.[22] In Valley Farm trees of even smaller size form the rafters of the roof (Fig. 91). They are sooted on worked faces, but where the corners are waney the soot deposit is patchy, showing that the bark was left on and slowly curled up and fell off. (A few rafters still have soot-covered bark attached.)

Much of the timber here, however, did not come straight from the tree. Many components are short, crooked, knotty bits of oak, oddments left over from some more important job. Others contain empty mortices, sooted inside, showing that they are reused. This was not just a matter of salvaging pieces from whatever building was on the site before: East Bergholt evidently had a recycling business, re-scappling second-hand timbers to new dimensions.

The use of oddments, recycled timber and non-oak looks like a concession to economy: the householder was building a little beyond his means. Economies are mainly in inconspicuous places, except for some elm timbers at the (socially) high end of the hall. These, however, are painted red (beneath the soot), so would not have looked different.

Lower-class houses are scaled-down hall-houses, sometimes lacking the parlour. In towns (like Hadleigh, Suffolk) they may be built in terraces.[23] The trees used were often small, little more than coppice poles. They often include timbers other than oak, for example being all elm (even where oak was available). However, a little oak is usually present: perhaps its distinctive smell enhanced the status of even the humblest house.

Great barns

Among the biggest and oldest timber structures built from ordinary trees are aisled barns (often miscalled 'tithe barns'). They are the barns of big, usually monastic or collegiate, farms. They may have stone or brick outer walls and huge timber roofs covered with tiles or tilestones; in east and southeast England they are wholly timber-framed. They were not just workaday sheds, but were built by architects (whose names are occasionally known) and were meant to be impressive.

The Knights Templars, soldier-monks, built two giant barns at Cressing Temple in Essex, the Barley Barn in c.1210 and the Wheat Barn in c.1270 (Fig. 93). Each is built round 12 great posts in two rows. As originally built they contained some 480 oaks per barn, mostly less than 10 inches (25 centimetres) in diameter. In the Barley Barn the trees are less completely scappled, leaving waney corners, giving an impression of rugged, massive solidity – a Durham Cathedral among barns. In the Wheat Barn slightly smaller trees were used and more was removed in scappling, giving a more elegant appearance – a Wells Cathedral among barns. The Knights had about 110 acres (44 ha) of woodland, which might have yielded one barn's worth of oaks every five years.[24]

The rafters of the Barley Barn (originally about 300) were about 21 feet (6½ metres) long and made the best of a tree trunk that was not much longer. The crooked shape and pattern of branch-scars shows that there was only moderate competition from surrounding underwood. The Wheat Barn rafters were from rather smaller trees, drawn up straight by greater competition, such as might arise if oaks grew in a well-grown lime coppice. Much of the roof of the Barley Barn was replaced later in the Middle Ages, using oaks grown with more competition still.

The problem in both barns was getting 12 trees big enough for the posts. The trees, probably hedgerow oaks, were not especially big by modern standards – in the Barley Barn some 2 feet (60 centimetres) in diameter, in the Wheat Barn a little smaller – but in each barn the four best oaks were used for the conspicuous central posts, and the worst, waney and even rotten, oaks were put in dark corners. The wood likely to have supplied the other timbers was grubbed in the eighteenth century. A fragment of a contiguous wood survives (Lanham's Wood, Rivenhall) – a lime and hornbeam wood, now containing several oaks big enough for barn posts.

Around Canterbury, despite thousands of acres of woodland in the Blean, post-sized oaks were even scarcer. The barn of St Augustine's Abbey at Littlebourne had originally 22 posts, 'curved like snakes', as Alexander Wheaten put it. Faversham Abbey's two barns have 29 surviving posts, three of them forked at the top of the tree.[25]

Timber quality and Baltic oak

Nearly all medieval structures, from barns to cottages, were built of what would now be very poor-quality oaks. Good-quality timber was normally imported in the form of 'Baltic oak' boards. (Those who think that the future of woodland is in growing 'quality' oak should reflect that this has not been done here before.)

Accurately cut boards from huge, slow-grown, straight-grained oaks came in bulk from what is now Germany, Poland and Lithuania. The trade began (as far as is known) around 1170 and ended c.1610. 'Wainscot' boards were not too expensive to use for ordinary purposes.

Baltic oak is stable, soft and easy to carve, and light in weight (p.242f). It was never used in floorboards, probably because it abrades easily. It is encountered in church doors, carved tracery and some linenfold panelling.[26] In church screens the frame timbers are of English oak; the painted panels and carved tracery are usually of Baltic oak, though in Welsh screens I have seen even the most intricate carving done in fast-grown, hard 'local' oak.

Outsize trees

Cathedral roofs and royal palaces called for oaks bigger than barn posts. Lincoln Cathedral, planned in the twelfth century, called for tiebeams 46 feet (14 metres) long. Any oak much more than 2 feet (60 centimetres) in diameter or 30 feet (9 metres) in useable length would have been an outsize tree. These were very expensive per cubic foot and were hauled long distances, for instance from Northumberland to Walsingham in Norfolk. Such trees were probably at their scarcest in the fourteenth century, when great building projects such as the Lantern of Ely Cathedral or Westminster Hall were in progress.

The ordinary manor possessed one such timber, the post on which the windmill revolved. Such posts did not normally grow in the local woods, but had to be fetched from a special source. At Hatfield Broadoak (Essex) in 1328 the blacksmith's perquisite was the second-best oak in the Forest every year, which was worth 13s. 4d., about ten times the value of an ordinarily big oak-tree.[27]

By the sixteenth century, oaks had got bigger, and trees of this size were not so exceptional. One was inserted into the medieval Old Court of my Cambridge college to carry the weight of an upstairs chimney. In 1503 two carpenters competed for the contract to replace a great beam in the church roof at Bassingbourn

(Cambridgeshire). The timber cost £2 3s. 8d., a huge sum for a single tree, even including workmanship; it was fetched 16 miles (26 kilometres) at a cost of 9s. 5d.; it came from Datchworth (Hertfordshire) and was probably a non-woodland tree.[28] The greatest such project was the replacement of the giant roof of Old St Paul's Cathedral, London, after a fire in 1561. This called for 25 tiebeams 50 feet (15 metres) long and 16 inches (40 centimetres) square, and 2,440 rafters of 40 feet (12 metres) by 12 inches (30 centimetres). These were found, and the roofs prefabricated, at Welbeck Abbey (Nottinghamshire) and Guisborough (Yorkshire).[29]

Outsize timbers are sometimes elm. The keel of a ship – the biggest component in the hull, and one of the most important – would be a huge elm-tree. Two examples, 337 years apart, are the *Mary Rose* (1512) and the *Jhelum* (see below); each has a keel about 90 feet (27 metres) long, scarfed out of three great overlapping elms.

Wattle-and-daub

All-wattle structures: An entire one-storey building can be made of wood – of stout rods set in the ground, interwoven with flexible rods (ethers) to form a wall. The Iron Age roundhouses, replicated at Butser Hill, Hampshire, were 30 feet (10 metres) in diameter, with a conical thatched roof. Whole towns could be made of wattle, as in Viking Dublin and medieval Aberdeen which imply coppice-woods on a huge scale. 'Caber houses', sometimes stiffened with a few cruck frames, survived late enough to be photographed in the more wooded parts of the Scottish Highlands.[30] I have found wattle-built outhouses, and the occasional dwelling, in the remote province of Grevená in the Pindus Mountains, Greece. Most early hurdlework involves whole rods. Often the sails (p.221) are double.

Hurdlework was used as formwork to support concrete and rubble vaults or door and window openings while the mortar set. Usually the formwork was removed when no longer needed, or rotted away, leaving an impression on the underside of the vault. In medieval Ireland anyone building a vault had first to construct a wattle 'vault' on which to set it up. There are examples in Anglo-Saxon churches in England.

Hurdlework was used to form minor waterfronts, as excavated in Reading and many other places. Major quays, built to withstand the battering of ships rather than boats, were made of timber, new or reused. Hurdlework fences are depicted in many medieval pictures of gardens, but never survive; nor do the wattlework bodies of carts known from medieval drawings.

In timber framing: The commonest infill between timbers is wattle-and-daub (Fig. 92). Alternative materials include stone, interwoven oak laths (in Welsh Border barns and high-status work elsewhere), mud (in Normandy), special bricks (in medieval York and Norwich), half-baked brick (in New England), or air trapped between layers of lath and plaster.

Usually oak staves are fixed horizontally into small mortices cut in the upright timbers; stout underwood rods (whole or split) are set upright, passing in front of the top and bottom staves and behind the middle one, and tied on with string. The whole was then covered with daub, made of clayey subsoil with chopped straw added to prevent it from cracking; it was usually given a plaster finish. This is the commonest method for the tall narrow panels customary in medieval East Anglia, Essex and the east Midlands. In somewhat higher-status work cleft oak laths can replace the rods.

There are regional variations. Square wattle panels, favoured in west and south England, commonly have three vertical staves. Roman London had wide upright panels, each with about six horizontal staves, interwoven with thin vertical rods. Of medieval London, because of the Great Fire, little survives above ground: reused timbers from waterlogged excavations indicate horizontal staves, set in continuous grooves in the uprights, interwoven with vertical rods.

Wattlework, like some other aspects of woodmanship, was not much used in colonial America, but was introduced later into Australia. The name 'wattle', meaning species of *Acacia*, is said to derive from their use for this purpose for a few years in pioneering times.

Significance of wattle: For hurdlework, using interwoven rods, hazel or sallow (or osiers, as in basketry) are preferred because of their flexibility. Otherwise, the species did not much matter. For wattle-and-daub infill (excluding oak laths) in Eastern England I have found sallow to be the commonest, followed by hazel, ash and aspen, with small percentages of elm, maple, oak, lime, birch and willow.[31]

Wattlework on any but the smallest scale implies coppice-woods or coppiced hedges. Authors who wrote about 'building huts from branches of trees' could not have tried it themselves. Without regular cutting the supply of suitable-sized straight rods soon gets exhausted. Although wattle infill can last as long as the timbers, wattlework set in the ground would need renewing every ten years or so, calling for a continuous supply.

Wattle in standing buildings or excavated structures is probably a smaller sample than timber of the produce of the local woods and hedges. It is unlikely to be a random sample: the wattler would probably have taken first pick of the underwood, before less specialised users whose work never survives; the bulk of underwood would have gone for fuel. I usually find seven or eight annual rings in underwood rods, this being the length of the coppice rotation.

Why were sallow and aspen so abundantly used? Since they are among the least durable species, there was probably originally even more of them than survives. Aspen occurs as timber as well as underwood: being a weak competitor, it would be encouraged by short-rotation coppicing. Growth rate may have been decisive. The wattler, building a child- and burglar-proof partition, would choose the stoutest rods irrespective of species. Sallow and aspen, the fastest growers, would be more likely to reach the required size within a seven-year cycle.

Log building

There is another way to build in timber: by laying horizontal logs one on top of the other, notched where they overlap at the corners. It occurs in the Alps, Scandinavia and eastern Europe, transgressing national and tribal boundaries. It is unknown in Britain, but quickly got into European North America – it is uncertain how – which developed its own traditions (Fig. 94).[32]

The timbers are normally smallish conifers, whose straightness helps in this type of construction. The bottom log may be oak to resist rot. In the mountains of Norway I have seen a hut ingeniously built of curved rowan logs (there being no other tree) with the curve of each log matched to its fellows. America more often uses oak for the whole edifice.

Log building is sophisticated and lends itself to elaborate architecture, even churches with onion domes. I call the components 'logs', which in some workaday structures they are, but usually they are half logs, or scappled to a square section, or worked to an accurate cylinder or a more complex shape. There are different traditions in the jointing of corners, in door and window openings and gables, and in the method of fixing each log to the one above and below.[33] In American high-class log cabins the 'logs' are often fractions of a log, widely set with mud or moss *chinking* between, and have axe-marks giving a decorative texture.

THE JAPANESE PARALLEL

It is instructive to compare Europe with how an independent civilisation used its trees. In Japan, monumental buildings – the equivalent of cathedrals – are all built of timber, for the Japanese never invented mortared stone construction.

The world's oldest reasonably complete timber structure above ground is the Five-Storey Pagoda of the Horyu Temple in the countryside near Nara, Japan.* This skyscraper tower (Fig. 95) is built from moderate-sized trees of the exceedingly rot-resistant, cypress-like *hinoki* (*Chamæcyparis obtusa*). It has been dated from tree rings to around 670 AD. Like all pagodas it is built round a central mast, a giant *hinoki* trunk nearly 3 feet** (90 centimetres) in diameter and apparently 80 feet (24 metres) high, which mysteriously is dated around 594.[34] This venerable structure, wherever the timbers are protected from rain, looks deceptively new; the round posts and great doors retain their faded red paint overlying the distinctive tool-marks produced by a small convex adze.

In the eighth century the Emperor Shomu built a capital at Nara on a scale of grandeur that only Nero, Louis XIV and Peter the Great could rival in Europe. His palace − nearly a mile (1½ kilometres) square − has been excavated. In its hundreds of buildings most of the timbers were *hinoki,* which was evidently not expensive and was used in workaday as well as monumental structures. Where could all this large *hinoki* have come from? What set its growth in motion, some 200 years before? As with oak in England, there is a discrepancy with its present ecology. Although much grown in plantations, as a wild tree *hinoki* is not common and tends to be a light-demanding pioneer of disturbed ground. Had it been encouraged by a period of renewed erosion in the mountains?

In Japanese monumental carpentry there are never waney edges where they will be seen. (Most tree-ring dates are therefore approximate, for the last rings are missing.) *Hinoki* trees used as columns do not follow the shape of the log, but are worked to exact (usually tapering) cylinders. Sometimes they are full of knots, indicating that the top length of a tree was being used. Such lower-quality timber may be put in less conspicuous places, although paint would originally have hidden the defects. The giant hall of the Todai Temple in Nara, as built c.1200, used about 80 *hinoki* posts each 4 feet (1.2 metres) in diameter and about 60 feet (18 metres) long, but this was (and remains) the biggest timber building that the world has seen. Its gatehouse, with similar posts, survives (Fig. 97).

From the fourteenth century onwards *keyaki* (*Zelkova serrata*) or *kusonoki* (*Cinnamomum camphora*) were used, either because *hinoki* was getting scarce or because red paint was becoming unfashionable and these trees have a beautiful

---

* The oldest functional timbers in the world are probably the olive-wood blocks that join the columns of the Parthenon in Athens (fourth century BC) and prevent them sliding apart in earthquakes.

** The Japanese foot (*shaku*) is nearly the same as the English foot.

grain. The present giant hall of the Todai, dating from 1709, has only 64 columns a little smaller than the originals; they are not single trees, but are built (like a medieval ship's mast) of pine beams fastened with huge nails and iron bands to a *keyaki* core. (Where did all that *keyaki* come from?) The Senjokaku Temple on the sacred island of Miyazaki near Hiroshima, built by Hideyoshi Toyotomi, was left unfinished at that potentate's death in 1596; unfinished it remains, revealing roof carpentry of huge, rough, crooked pine logs, not meant to be seen (Fig. 96).

Japanese vernacular houses

Rural houses, in contrast, are made of small timber, large coppice poles and bamboo, finished to similar standards to those of medieval England. Timbers are of small oaks, pines and the less durable *sugi* conifer (*Cryptomeria japonica*). Waney edges and crooked shapes are tolerated, indeed appreciated for their beauty. One enters the 'service' end of the house. The step where one leaves one's shoes, and the post in the middle of it, are often *keyaki* with its distinctive grain. In the floor of the soot-blackened main room is a square *irori* pit on which a charcoal fire smoulders, reminiscent of a medieval English hall. A ladder ascends to the soot-blackened loft and the underside of the thatch (Fig. 98).

Urban houses, which are rarely ancient, tend to be of sawn *sugi*. This would have been needed suddenly in huge quantities whenever there was a great fire, like the one that consumed two-thirds of Kyoto in 1864.

Japanese wattle-and-daub, which is still regularly made, is normally of split bamboo, though underwood is sometimes used.

Japanese log-built strongrooms

These (*azekura*) are rare, but a handful of them are among the oldest timber structures in the world. The Shoso-in, a three-storey log structure of the 750s, held the treasures and curiosities of the Todai Temple for over a thousand years. They are apparently derived from granaries built on stilts. The 'logs' are *hinoki* timbers cleft to a hexagonal section with three wide faces and three narrow. Of the four buildings that I have seen, three got at least six 'logs' split out of a single length of a huge tree; the fourth derived most of its timbers from small knotty trees.

SHIPBUILDING

Most of the oak used in the [Lowestoft] *yards was obtained within a radius of about fifteen to twenty miles … when buying standing trees Mr William Parker, the wood yard manager*

and draughtsman, would get on his cycle, go out into the country, visit the various sources
of timber for sale and decide what to buy ...
Ted Frost, old shipwright, 1985

Shipbuilding is the stuff of myth. It is supposed to have consumed more trees than anything else, devouring the ancient forests (or, alternatively, preserving ancient woods). In reality, one can read long in woodland history without meeting it: the records of Hayley Wood, the Bradfield Woods and Hatfield Forest never mention it.

Let us begin with practical works, such as Ted Frost's account of building steam drifters at Lowestoft in the 1910s. The shipyards produced about ten vessels a year, about 90 feet (27 metres) long and 20 feet (6 metres) wide, measuring about 45 tons. Even in meagrely wooded northeast Suffolk there was no difficulty in getting timber.[35]

Let us visit shipyards building vessels of similar construction in Turkey (Fig. 99), where I have calculated that one ship of similar size represents about 3 acres (1.2 ha) of pine savanna at 50 years' growth. The present industry around Bozburun turns out some 30 ships a year, that is, 1,500 ships in 50 years, and would be in equilibrium with the growth of pines on about 4,500 acres or 18 square kilometres of pine savanna, much less than the actual area of pineries available.[36] This is quite intensive shipbuilding by ancient standards, and the calculation (however rough) does not support scholars' obsession with shipbuilding as the great consumer of trees.

Timber did not have to be local: shipbuilders are the best placed of craftsmen to import their materials. As ancient Athens or early-modern Holland bear witness, a country can be a naval superpower without growing its own ship timber.

Shipbuilding was not a constant consumer of trees. Medieval cargo ships were mostly about the size of a Lowestoft or Bozburun ship. Between 1295 and 1348 the cost of timber and plank amounted to some 30 per cent of the cost of building a ship; in the fifteenth century this fell to 17 per cent. The fifteenth century began an escalation in both merchant and naval shipping that continued at an exponential rate until the mid-nineteenth. Cargo ships came to exceed 300 and then 1,000 tons. Specialised battleships were built, such as Henry V's mighty *Grace Dieu* of 1,500 tons, now buried in the mud of the River Hamble.[37] Ships went to other continents and shortened their lives in tropical waters being eaten by shipworms. They were built to carry great guns or to take cargoes of railway locomotives through a Cape Horn gale. The quantity of English-owned shipping increased from 50,000 tons in 1572 to a million in 1788, and continued to increase until the mid-nineteenth century.[38]

There were setbacks: the *Mary Rose* was less than half the size of the *Grace Dieu* a century before, and the largest ships on either side in the Armada (1588) were little bigger. However, by the late eighteenth century, although the biggest ships were much bigger, the Navy had more than a hundred battleships as big as the single *Grace Dieu* or bigger. Had there been the slightest difficulty in finding timber for the ships that defeated the Armada, it would have been utterly impossible to build the fleet that defeated Napoleon.

Medieval ships usually had one huge mast, built of many oak timbers around a pine core, held together with rope belts and great iron hoops. The tower-like mast of the *Grace Dieu* was at least 190 feet (60 metres) high. From the late fifteenth century ships acquired multiple masts and topmasts, and masts began to be made from single giant conifers.[39] The provision of masts was more critical than of hull timbers; they were brought from America in special ships.

Complaints about shortages of timber came from the Navy: commercial shipbuilders, although they built far more shipping, seldom had any difficulty. The Navy was short of money rather than short of trees: it needed large sizes and special shapes of timber, but without paying extra for them. And there is a strange discrepancy between the amount of timber going into naval dockyards and the amount coming out as warships. The hull of a regular 74-gun ship 'needed' at least 3,000 loads of timber at 50 cubic feet to the load. This would be a stack of solid timber bigger than the entire volume of the hull, leaving no room for officers, men, guns, powder, shot, salt beef, or room to swing a cat. A rough calculation, based on measured sections, shows that the actual timber content of the ship would be at most 500 loads. Maybe as much again was lost as sawdust and offcuts: what happened to the other 2,000 loads? It was not there to build the ships, but to pay the men. Until 1801 shipwrights kept the 'chips' as a lawful perquisite; some chips were very large; and Deptford still has well-built timber-framed houses made from them. When the Navy Board offered gold instead, the men went on strike.[40] (There was a similar discrepancy, and a similarly privileged labour force, among Portuguese naval shipbuilding in Brazil.[41])

While complaining of shortages, the Navy only very slowly took to using foreign timber, species other than oak, or iron components, or moving the dockyards to the Empire as the Spaniards and Portuguese did. John Ramsbottom, the mycologist, stressed how bad ship design and poor seasoning resulted in dry and wet rot, wasting timber in repairs. The limiting factor was probably not the growth of timber, but the seasoning: 'had the nation faced another 20 years of war the domestic timber supply would have performed far better than it had between 1793 and 1814.'[42]

Other countries had curious statutes regarding shipbuilding timber. In Spain there was 'an ancient law by which the king was proprietor of every tree which his officers judged fit for any purpose of naval construction'. In the territory of Venice anyone who let his trees reach shipbuilding size risked having his wood-land banned to the State by sound of trumpet; the trees and their successors were confiscated, and he might have to provide free labour to transport them. I cannot say whether this really discouraged the growth of big trees.[43]

Roughly half the timber shipping ever built in Britain was between 1800 and 1860. Only at this time did the price of oak timber (but even more of oak bark) rise enough to affect nearly every wood and hedge in Britain. This market, lasting only 60 years, began the dissociation between trees and local uses. Even so, lack of timber was not a constraint on shipbuilding. An example from the multitude of cargo ships is the *Jhelum*, 430 tons, built at Liverpool in 1849 and now stranded in the Falkland Islands. The hull timbers seem to be still all English oak, although much of the planking was foreign and there were many iron components.[44]

'Old ships' timbers' in timber-framed buildings are somewhat of a canard. Land and ship carpentry are not interchangeable: ship components were more easily cannibalised into other ships. There are a few authentic examples of ships' timbers and masts being used in late carpentry on land, especially in Norfolk and the Channel Islands, where shipwrecks would be a source. M. Sinclair tells me that the straight timbers out of barges were used in houses along the Severn. Bits of boats are commonly met with reused in waterfronts.

Dugouts

What can you do with a big tree other than make it into a dugout boat? Logboats were used in Europe from the Mesolithic into the nineteenth century, and are still in use in many tropical countries. I have travelled in a dugout boat, 3 feet 6 inches (107 centimetres) in the beam, hewn from a tree of somewhat greater diameter.

Logboats are usually flat-bottomed like a punt to be more stable. The sides may be heated to make them flexible, and then forced apart to give more capac-ity. Logboats can have a mast (with integral step), but one of their limitations is the difficulty of providing a keel. Logs, moreover, tend to crack, especially at the ends, making fissures that are difficult to caulk.

Dugout boats give a clue to the largest trees available. Those excavated in Britain range in date from late Neolithic to medieval. Nearly all have been identified as oak, which is not an obviously suitable tree: it is hard, heavy, liable to split, and liable to weak spots and holes where dead branches have rotted. In other countries more suitable trees have been used, such as lime; in early-modern Greece sea-going logboats were made of giant white poplar trees. Maybe oak logboats are better known (and logboats better known than other types of boat) because they are more often preserved and recovered.

The biggest single timber known from any period in Britain was the Brigg Logboat, made in the Bronze Age from an oak log 48 feet (15 metres) long and 5½ ft (1.7 metres) in diameter at the small end (without sapwood). (The Hasholme Logboat, Iron Age and slightly smaller, is on display in Hull Museum.) In Scotland, although some logboats were 4 feet (1.2 metres) in diameter, most were less than 2 feet (60 centimetres), and at 60 feet (20 metres) long or more were disproportionately slender.[45]

Dugouts also include coffins, early church chests and many other kinds of container.

QUESTIONS TO ASK OF TIMBERS IN BUILDINGS (AND ALSO EXCAVATIONS AND SHIPS)

- What species of timber?
- Were they felled specially, or reused?
- Are they whole logs? Half logs? Quarter logs or less? With practice this can be ascertained without seeing a cross section. A beam that is waney on two diagonally opposite corners must be a whole log.
- What were the longest and the thickest trees used?
- What was the basal diameter of the trees? Measure the scantling (the nominal width and depth) of the beam. If it represents a whole log calculate its diagonal. Then estimate, from the amount of wane, by how much the diameter of the tree exceeded, or fell short of, the diagonal of the timber (see Fig. 199).
- How old were the trees? For this you need a cross section or a core; remember to include the sapwood.
- Were they woodland or non-woodland trees? Non-woodland trees will usually be faster growing, more crooked, and branched lower down. With woodland oaks one can sometimes make out how fiercely the surrounding underwood competed with the timber trees by suppressing their branches.

- Were the timbers running out of length? – that is, getting thinner, crooked and branchy at the top where they were reaching high in the tree?
- Was the timber worked fresh, or was it seasoned (cf. Fig. 199)? Medieval house-carpenters normally cut down the tree and worked it before it could dry out.

TIMBER AND WOOD IDENTIFICATION

This requires a book to itself. Identification of samples of wood by cutting sections and examining the cellular structure under the microscope is well understood. Most of the commoner timbers can be identified in a clean transverse section seen with a ×20 lens.[46] But the student is often presented with radial or tangential sections, or with bark, or the surface under the bark, or charcoal, each of which has its own characteristics, usually subtle and difficult to put into words. Diagnosis often has to be attempted through a layer of dirt, soot, or paint, or the ancient lichens that grew on bark (themselves of interest as indicators of acid rain or lack of it).

There is no substitute for experience: for examining logs of known trees and building up a body of knowledge and of reference samples. Here are a few diagnostic characteristics most often met with in ancient timbers.

Oak

Oak in cross section is unmistakeable. It is ring-porous: each annual ring begins with two or three rows of big *vessels* visible to the naked eye, followed by a darker mass of late-wood with light-coloured streaks ('flames') running through it in a radial direction. Every few millimetres the annual rings are interrupted by a conspicuous, light-coloured *ray* that runs from the middle of the tree towards the outside.

The outermost inch or so of an oak-tree consists of *sapwood*, tissue that performed most of the tree's vital functions. It is much lighter in colour than heartwood and is more easily attacked by insects.

Oak is very prone to differential shrinkage. Most oak beams that contain the pith show at least two radial cracks. Contrary to common opinion, ancient oak does not go 'black with age' but with soot. Old oak is very variable in colour.

Baltic oak, although probably of the same species, is different from British oak. It usually occurs as planks cut in an almost exact radial plane, thus displaying the rays as a pattern ('figure') on the face, often treated as decoration. The annual rings are very narrow (typically less than 1.5 millimetres (more than 15 rings to the inch)) and the grain very straight and lacking knots. It is more stable than British oak and does not warp, and being slow grown is light in weight (Table 15).

Under the microscope oak is very distinctive. The late John Fletcher, dendro-chronologist, claimed to be able to distinguish pedunculate from sessile oak, but his work was based on a narrow range of planted trees and has not been confirmed. Since the two species often grow intermingled, anyone investigating must collect samples of timber, leaves and acorns *all from the same tree* so that there shall be no doubt of its identity.

Elm

Elm in cross section is ring-porous. The annual rings have within and parallel to them a series of banded structures (as if there were 'monthly rings'), which are diagnostic of elm and related trees (e.g. mulberry and Japanese *keyaki*). Rays are many and just visible to the short-sighted naked eye. Elm is tough, stretches as it dries, and does not form many shakes.

Different elms have variations on this structure. From a whole log, preferably with bark on, the big, fast-grown, straight trunks of English elm can be distinguished from the slow-grown, crooked, often bossy stems of East Anglian elms. Chair-seats – massive, fast-grown, with annual rings often ½ inch (10 millimetres) or more – are likely to be English elm.

The under-bark surface of elm may have bark-beetle galleries – big ones of *Scolytus scolytus* or small ones of *S. multistriatus*. These were formed within a year of the tree dying. The brood-gallery, from which the others branch off, was formed in a vertical direction, and is normally at right angles to the length of a horizontal timber. If it is parallel to the length of a timber, this raises the suspicion that the tree died upright – of Elm Disease?

There may be direct evidence of past Elm Disease. Vessels invaded by *Ceratocystis* are visible as dark streaks along the length of the log. Usually they occur in one annual ring, or several if there have been repeated attacks. Close inspection may reveal white structures, *tyloses*, formed by the tree inside individual vessels to block the advance of the fungus. An infected ring, followed by a sudden decrease in ring width and then gradual recovery, indicates that the tree was damaged and recovered.

Ash

Ash is ring-porous: the annual ring typically begins with two rows of big vessels, followed by smaller ones scattered in the late-wood; there are many narrow rays. It too can have bark-beetle galleries, not unlike those of elm, but made by a different beetle. It is generally pale or greyish in colour. When encountered as rods, the combination of branches in opposite pairs and smooth bark is distinctive.

Conifers

Pine is much the commonest conifer among ancient timbers. Distinction between conifers is a microscopic matter; however, all pines have resin-canals penetrating the wood structure. Any pre-1700 timber that exudes resin is likely to be pine.

'Scots pine' (often imported or fossil) has pronounced annual rings, but no other structures visible to the naked eye. Within each ring, the darker-coloured early wood begins suddenly and gradually fades into the late-wood.

Cypress, occasionally met with among ancient chests, is most easily recognised by its distinctive, non-resinous scent. It came from Crete, and the short, broad, oddly shaped planks speak of the ancient gnarled mountain cypresses.

Poplars

Black poplar is not uncommon among timber and planks and in the half-cylinder lids of medieval chests. The body of the chest is often pine, although I know a huge chest dug out of a massive, contorted poplar log. Its 'woolly' texture on worked faces and its tendency to woodworm hide the inconspicuous annual rings. A yellowish colour is diagnostic.

Aspen, met with both as timber and wood, is similar; microscopists will not commit themselves beyond a diagnosis of 'poplar'. However, the bark of aspen, with its diamond-shaped lenticels, is very distinctive. (The phloem under the bark is easily confused with lime, both being in the form of sheet-like layers of fibres.) Whole-log timbers of black poplar may show rugged bark and bosses on the trunk.

Beech

Beech is most often encountered in late furniture. Like most broadleaved trees it is diffuse-porous, with annual rings distinguishable only by colour. The rays are well visible in transverse section; in tangential section they appear as a myriad of little brown flecks, darker than the rest of the wood.

Chestnut

In England chestnut is a phantom timber: I have yet to find any supposed ancient 'chestnut' that is not oak,* though I am familiar with it in southern Europe. It should be looked for in regions where the tree has long been prevalent (p.288), especially among wattle rods. It is ring-porous, with tracts of visible vessels extending into the late-wood, and barely visible rays. It looks very like oak and is similar in colour range. I suspect the misidentifications are by people who see only the tangential section, in which the strong rays that are diagnostic of oak can be difficult to detect.

Hazel

Hazel appears only in the form of wood. The bark is the most recognisable part, dark brown and shiny, with raised rectangular lenticels at intervals.

Sallow

Sallow wood is one of the commonest constituents of wattle. If, as usual, it is *Salix caprea*, it is recognisable by short, raised ridges under the bark. Older stems develop diamond-shaped lenticels.

---

* At Wingham church in Kent the octagonal posts of the nave are supposed to be chestnut, but the only one that I could identify as such is a Victorian replacement.

CHAPTER 12

ANCIENT-WOODLAND PLANTS AND OTHER CREATURES

Our original old woods may, I believe, be readily identified, because every wood containing the wild hyacinth I take to be such. Outside the wood, bluebells rarely appear in the hedge-row, if so they proclaim a woodland that has disappeared ... You may meet a planted wood of hundreds of years old, but how much does it fail in charm compared with the primaeval wood, with its glory of bluebells.

SIR HUGH BEEVOR, NORFOLK WOODLAND HISTORIAN, 1924[1]

FLORAS OF OLD AND NEW WOODS AND PLANTATIONS

Eighty years ago a fashionable branch of ecology was *succession*, for example, how an abandoned field or pasture, given 20 years, turns into the semblance of a wood. Later this study was eclipsed by the less well-researched fashion for plant-ing trees, sometimes expressly in imitation of an ancient wood. In either way it is easy enough to acquire trees, and presumably their mycorrhizal fungi; but what about the other components of a wood?

A fox-covert study

In 1917 the Revd E.A. Woodruffe-Peacock wrote up 50 years of observations in Poolthorn Covert, a 32-acre (13 ha) grove near Brigg in Lincolnshire. It had been planted as a fox-covert in 1797, on grassland with no adjacent hedges, apparently 3½ miles (5½ kilometres) from the nearest ancient wood. Thirteen tree and shrub species were planted including oak, ash, privet and four exotics; ten survived in 1917. Woodruffe-Peacock found a total of 179 flowering plants and ferns, which would be a very respectable degree of 'diversity' for an ancient wood of that size (p.435) if diversity is taken to be merely the number of species. However, he regarded 38 species as survivors from the previous vegetation (mostly grassland plants such as clovers, plantains and *Luzula campestris*), and 41 as casuals, including agricultural weeds such as groundsel and *Euphorbia peplus*. It had acquired only a few specifically woodland plants: bluebell, primrose (which Woodruffe-Peacock thought was a survivor), common spotted orchid *Dactylorhiza fuchsii* and *Viola riviniana*. The most remarkable (as it now seems) was one plant of anemone, which arrived in 1892 and spread into a clone. The wood notably lacked such species as spindle, hazel, aspen, yellow archangel and dog's-mercury. Even after 120 years it had the air of grassland that had acquired trees.[2]

This is a cautionary tale. Poolthorn Covert had vanished by 1975; we shall never know what another 120 years might have brought. The existence of previous investigations, even if they seem not to be still ongoing, ought to be grounds for preserving a place as a Site of Special Scientific Interest.

Historical ecology as an experimental science

Norman Moore, veteran conservationist, planted a 1-acre grove at Swavesey (Cambridgeshire), and 20 years later wrote a book about the result. The site, a pasture field on mineral soil on the edge of the Fens, was bordered by an ancient hedge. The trees were chosen to be roughly those of ancient woodland.

He had no great difficulty in establishing 21 tree species. Trouble came with the ground vegetation. The grove was soon taken over by cow-parsley, goose-grass and ivy, plants of fertile soil (p.200). He introduced bluebell, anemone, dog's-mercury and primrose, but these had to be kept going by weeding the stronger-growing fertility plants; only daffodil could compete with them. In 20 years, as Dr Moore had expected, the site was taking on the character of the many much older plantations and secondary woods which he knew from his work as an ornithologist, and which even after 150 years are still utterly different from ancient woods.[3]

The Lincolnshire study

Attached recent woods (adjacent to older woods) must be distinguished from *isolated* recent woods (separated by fields, or joined only by hedges). George Peterken and Margaret Game in the 1970s listed the herbaceous plants of woods in middle Lincolnshire, comparing 79 ancient, 34 secondary attached and 170 secondary isolated woods. Some secondary woods were natural and some were plantations (not differentiated in the published results); they originated at various eighteenth-, nineteenth- and twentieth-century dates. Species lists (omitting trees, shrubs and woodland-grassland plants) were generally shorter for isolated secondary woods, and varied less with the size of the wood. Ancient woods had the longest lists; attached secondary woods were intermediate. They compiled a list of species having more or less affinity with ancient woodland; for example, *Carex pallescens* was found in 28 woodland localities, 27 being in ancient woods.[4]

In secondary woods the commonest plants were 'universal weeds'. Cleavers (*Galium aparine*) was almost universal, followed by bramble, nettle, avens, *Poa trivialis*, hogweed, cow-parsley and creeping buttercup. Of the 30 commonest plants only *Mœhringia trinervia* and the ferns *Dryopteris dilatata* and *D. filix-mas* had any particular association with woodland; others were strong-growing plants of fertile soils. Species in secondary woods increased for the first hundred years, but thereafter there was no increase; some of the early colonists (or survivors) died out as later colonisers, such as dog's-mercury, moved in.

Two Cambridgeshire examples

My own experience bears this out. Toft Plantation is a 4½-acre (1.8 ha) plantation, dating from *c.*1820, originally attached to Hardwick Wood, west of Cambridge, an *Ely Coucher Book* wood with a rich flora. It became isolated when the part next the old wood was grubbed out *c.*1950. It is mainly of wych-elm, which had enjoyed a brief fashion when the wood was planted. In 1975 the species list stood at 54, surprisingly rich for a small grove; it included woodland plants such as spindle, *Cratægus lævigata*, early purple orchid and primrose, which had migrated from the old wood before it was cut off. Like the old wood it was carpeted with bluebell and dog's-mercury. Even oxlip (and oxlip–primrose hybrid) was there. It still lacked hazel.

Attached to Hayley Wood is the Triangle, a field which 'tumbled down to woodland' in the 1920s. It bears the ridge-and-furrow of seventeenth-century cultivation, giving a variety of different habitats that (were it in ancient woodland) would provide niches for all except woodland-grassland plants. Originally dominated by oak and hawthorn, it is now being colonised by ash. Ground vegetation is comparatively sparse; competition cannot be much of an influence.

Since 1973 I have mapped various species in the new wood.[5] Oxlip – strongly associated with ancient woodland – spread out from the old wood at about 3 feet (1 metre) per year, the pioneer plants giving rise to clusters of their children. It had still not colonised all the new wood when it suffered a severe setback in the 1990s from dry summers combined with increasing deer activity. Dog's-mercury (less strongly associated with ancient woodland) spread from the old wood at a similar rate; the pioneer plants expanded into clonal patches. By 1987 it was present in about five-sixths of the Triangle, but has since not advanced further. Bluebell spread at a similar rate, both from the old wood and from an ancient hedge; it too advanced more slowly in the 1990s and has still not occupied all the Triangle. Sanicle and anemone are still confined to within 150 feet (50 metres) of the old wood.

The felling of a deer-fence corridor in Hayley Triangle in 1991 gave a rare opportunity to observe coppicing plants in a new wood. It produced a curious, attenuated selection of them. Most of the coppicing plants of the old wood did not appear. The commonest were bristly ox-tongue, a generalised farmland weed, and a further crop of ash seedlings. Also abundant were *Viola* species, enchanter's nightshade, wild strawberry, creeping cinquefoil and *Veronica serpyllifolia*. The last three could have come from buried seed shed when the site was still grassland.

Toft Plantation and Hayley Triangle are (or were) attached secondary woodland. Colonisation would be less favoured if species had to jump across farmland to get to the new wood. Only to a very limited extent do hedges, even ancient hedges, act as corridors for plants.

ANCIENT-WOODLAND INDICATORS

I have before me 18 regional lists of plants characteristic of ancient woodland, including Peterken & Game's and the list that I developed in the 1970s for evaluating woods in eastern England. They cover most of England except the far north. Southeast England and parts of the Midlands are covered only by the single South Region Survey of the Nature Conservancy Council.[6] Individual lists contain from 11 to 100 species. In all, 155 species (nearly one-tenth of the British native flora) have been regarded by at least one author as ancient-woodland indicators.

One plant, the grass *Melica uniflora* (Fig. 201), is unanimously declared to be an ancient-woodland indicator. Woodruff (*Galium odoratum*) is on all the lists except that for Cornwall.

There are four reasons for a plant being on some lists but not others:

1. It may be a weak or questionable indicator not accepted by all authorities. I am surprised to find hazel cited on lists for Worcestershire, Hertfordshire and the Sheffield area, although it may become an ancient-woodland indicator now that grey squirrels have destroyed its capacity for reproduction (p.278).

2. It may be absent from some regions. Oxlip, although one of the best-

established indicator species, occurs on only two lists; a western equivalent would be bastard balm *Melittis melissophyllum,* on three lists. Wood-spurge occurs on 12 out of the 13 lists on which it would be geographically possible.

3. It may be confined to ancient woodland in some regions but not others. Bluebell, as Beevor pointed out, is largely confined to ancient woodland in eastern England; in Belgium it is an even stronger indicator; in Cornwall, however, it grows in nearly every ancient hedge as well. In the Chilterns (for which I have no list) I have found woodruff in secondary woodland.

4. Some recorders may have left it out because they thought it was not a 'real' woodland plant. They may omit trees (on the grounds that they cannot distinguish planted trees) or woodland-grassland plants.

How to compile a list

Ancient-woodland plants vary from region to region: a list from one region should not be used uncritically elsewhere. One approach is to compare lists of species between woods known (on other grounds) to be ancient and woods that originated at some approximately known date.[7] Another is to map species advancing (or failing to advance) into a recent wood adjoining an ancient wood.

Some species have alternative habitats. Pignut is equally at home in woodland and grassland, and indicates continuity of either. Oxlip was formerly in old grassland as well as old woodland. Anemone (15 lists) can occur in churchyards, and in Scotland loses its association with woodland.

A short cut is to ask 'What species occur in ancient woodland but not in ancient hedges?' Especially in Ancient Countryside with many ancient hedges, hedgerow species can normally be excluded as ancient-woodland indicators. However, there is such a thing as a *ghost hedge*, the relict edge of a destroyed wood. The now famous lime hedge at Shelley, Suffolk is the edge of a wood grubbed in the eighteenth century; it contains lime, service, anemone and bluebell (see Fig. 100).[8] Some ancient-woodland species persist in hedges, but do not colonise them.

The number of species dependent on ancient woodland is likely to be underestimated, because it is difficult to be sure about rarities. If species X has only one locality, which is in ancient wood A, this could be by chance, unless this is the only wood in the region that is ancient. However, if species Y occurs only in woods A and B, which are the only ancient woods out of a total of 20 woods, one begins to infer a real connection.

Use of ancient-woodland indicator species

No plant is an infallible indicator of ancient woodland. Even anemone got into Poolthorn Covert, as a single clone. The test is whether a wood contains a suite of ancient-woodland plants, the number varying with the size of the wood. An ancient wood of 5 acres (2 ha), for example, might be expected to have about one-tenth of the regional list of indicator species, rising to between one-third and one-half of the list for a wood of 100 acres (40 ha).

How ancient-woodland indicators work

Plants of ancient woodland can play almost any part in the woodland ecosystem. In Table 16 are 80 species, including:
- 8 trees and shrubs;
- 28 clonal plants;
- 4 annuals;
- 5 parasites (either directly on plants or on mycorrhizal fungi);
- 6 woodland-grassland plants;
- 1 plant characteristic of medieval woodbanks (*Melica uniflora*, the best established of all the indicators);
- 43 species that respond positively to coppicing (see Fig. 83); 5 neutral; 5 with a negative response.

The number of ancient-woodland indicators in each of a group of woods tends to increase with the size of the wood to the same degree as the general flora (p.435). Indicators show no special tendency to occur in bigger woods; crab-apple and *Melica* are commoner in small woods.[9]

What are the characteristics of ancient-woodland indicators? Very few ancient-woodland plants require continuous shade; about two-thirds of the herbaceous species show a positive response to coppicing. Of the 43 that respond, 8 belong to the guild of spring-leafing perennials (e.g. anemone), 13 are summer-leafing perennials (e.g. woodruff) and 20 are buried-seed plants. There would probably be more in all these categories if my information were more complete. The link between spring-leafers and ancient woodland is particularly strong: most of the perennials that leaf (or flower) in spring after coppicing have some claim to be ancient-woodland plants. Not surprisingly, mobile coppicing plants and casuals are few. There are no woody climbers.

Annuals are greatly under-represented: only one-twentieth of ancient-woodland indicators are annual, compared with one-quarter of the whole British and Irish flora.

These inferences are based on the whole table. They are not much altered if ancient-woodland indicators are defined more rigorously, restricted to those that appear on at least ten lists.

Ellenberg indicator values:[10] These are a rough indication of the occurrence of species in relation to environmental factors. (The data are partly derived from Central Europe, where the plants, although of the same species, may not behave identically to those in Britain.)

In terms of light, on a scale of 2 to 9, ancient-woodland indicator species cluster around the semi-shade values of 4 and 5; those more rigorously defined are more shade-tolerant (value 4). Only ten are plants of dense shade. Despite their shade-avoidance behaviour, only nine species − all among the less strong indicators − reach the light value of 7; but three-quarters of the whole British flora are open-ground plants with values of 7 or above.

In terms of moisture (scale 1 to 12), ancient-woodland plants are overwhelmingly in the middle of the range: half of them have value 5 ('average dampness'), which is the commonest value among the whole flora. In woodland, moisture has the two independent aspects of flushing and waterlogging (p.198); ancient woods tend to alternate between wetness in winter and drought in summer.

In terms of soil acidity (scale 1 to 9), ancient-woodland plants follow the distribution of the general flora, with a peak at point 7 ('weakly acid to weakly basic'). This is surprising in view of the acidic tendency of woodland soils (p.198): is this acidity a recent phenomenon to which the flora has not yet adjusted?

In terms of fertility, ancient-woodland indicators also tend to follow the general flora. However, Ellenberg's data relate mainly to nitrogen, whereas in woodland phosphorus is probably the limiting factor. Ancient-woodland plants, indeed woodland plants in general, are poorly competitive against high-fertility species such as nettle and goosegrass.

Prehistoric evidence
Indicator species are indicators of ancient woodland, not of wildwood. Nevertheless, at least 13 species that are now ancient-woodland indicators have wildwood pollen records. To judge by their present behaviour, they included both forest and non-shade-bearing components of wildwood (p.77f); several coppicing plants are among them. Whether wildwood had indicator species is not known. I shall not offer an opinion on whether the guilds of ancient-woodland indicators also

constituted guilds in wildwood times, or whether they emerged as part of the process of turning wildwood into woodland.

Why are there ancient-woodland indicators?
Plants may be confined to ancient woodland because:
- they lack seed production;
- they lack seed dispersal (they cannot reach new woods);
- the environment of new woods is unsuitable for them; or
- the environment of new woods is more suitable for competing species.

Lack of seed production or dispersal or both: The many clonal plants among ancient-woodland indicators are, self-evidently, species that rarely reproduce by seed even when the habitat is favourable.[11] They may produce seed and it may germinate, but seedlings do not easily generate a new clone. Some are species of old grassland as well as old woodland.

Few ancient-woodland indicators have wind-dispersed seeds. Many have fleshy fruits which are meant to be dispersed by birds or mammals, but the wrong sort of birds eat them, or else fail to disperse the seeds: for example service and herb paris. Have these lost their vectors?

Plants may disperse effectively and still be unable to establish. Small-leaved lime (*Tilia cordata*) produces abundant fruits with a wind-dispersal adaptation. Whether they are fertile depends on a high summer temperature.[12] After recent hot summers the limes of some Essex and Suffolk woods have often produced seedlings, but I have never found a seedling outside a wood. Ancient hedges near limewoods, showered with lime fruits for centuries, contain only a very thin scatter of lime stools.

Ramsons is a curious case. In the Bradfield Woods (west Suffolk) it occurs in huge, dense circular patches, which are stable over many years. I cannot find any clonal connection between the bulbs; I suspect that it grows from seed with no dispersal mechanism, spreading at only a few inches a year as the seeds fall.

Ant dispersal: The world's plants, over millions of years, have co-evolved with ants in many ways to their mutual benefit. An example is seed dispersal. As Axel Lundström found 120 years ago, the seed of cow-wheat (*Melampyrum pratense*) is exactly like an 'ant's egg' (cocoon) in size, shape, colour, weight, smell, and in having an 'excrement capsule'; even ants cannot tell the difference, mistake them for stray cocoons, and carry them to the nest.[13] Many seeds have *elaiosomes*, oily appendages attracting ants, which carry off the seed, eat the elaiosome and discard the rest. Ants, however, will carry off most seeds of suitable size, even though they have no obvious attractant. Rarely do they grow the seed – as do the Agricultural Ants of Texas with grass seeds – but they are a most significant dispersal agent.

Rutger Sernander in the 1900s spent hundreds of hours watching seeds exposed to ants (hence much of the information about ants in Table 16). Primrose seeds, with attached elaiosomes, were taken by the ant *Lasius niger* within 20 minutes. Oxlip seeds, which lack elaiosomes, nevertheless disappeared in half an hour.[14] Oxlip, with no evident dispersal mechanism other than ants, spreads into attached recent woodland at about 3 feet 3 inches (1 metre) a year; primrose is less related to ancient woodland.

Ants do not crawl far; seeds carried by them are unlikely to traverse a field or even a hedge to get to another wood. A plant species might be immobilised altogether if its particular ant went extinct. (Does the presence or absence of wood-ants (*Formica rufa*), a large, lively, patchily distributed ant, determine which plants get into new woods?)

Cow-wheat is a well-defined indicator species among the guild of buried-seed coppicing plants. *Melica uniflora* has all but one of the florets in each spikelet adapted into an elaiosome; it is dispersed only by ants.

Unsuitable environment of recent woods: New woods and plantations are seldom coppiced. Often they are too shady for many ancient-woodland plants. Ex-farmland, with its soils altered to suit agricultural crops, may be directly hostile to some ancient-woodland plants. It may be hostile to the ants that disperse them – a point that some reader may wish to investigate. More significantly (on present evidence), it encourages strong-growing, phosphate-demanding farmland weeds that out-compete the woodland species. If a new wood lets in enough light to have ground vegetation, it will probably be overrun with nettles.

OTHER ORGANISMS

Lichens

Many lichens are cited as 'old-forest' indicators; there is a lichen-based *Index of Ecological Continuity*.[15] Most are small and identifiable only by lichenologists, but a few, such as *Lobaria* species, are conspicuous (Fig. 102). They are sensitive to acid rain and have disappeared from polluted parts of the country (p.320f).

Most such lichens live on old, big, well-lit trees and dislike the abrupt changes of microclimate that are typical of the woodland cycle. They are really indicators not of ancient *woodland*, but of ancient *trees*. It is argued that such lichens indicate places where there have been successive generations of old trees. However, in the clean damp air of the west, some *Lobarias* and other species occur on younger trees and in woodland – sometimes on only one tree per wood.[16] The supreme area for such lichens, probably in all Europe, is the New Forest, with multitudes of ancient wood-pasture trees in a moderately unpolluted atmosphere. These specialised lichens form their own plant communities, often on specific trees (e.g. the rough bark of pollard oaks) and in specific situations. Big, old trees are the hosts of a similar group of lichens in Sweden.[17]

Lichen indicators, maybe, represent the savanna or non-woodland aspect of wildwood (Table 9), whereas flowering plants represent the forest aspect.

Mistletoe

Mistletoe is a flowering plant usually seen on exotic trees – cultivated apple, hybrid lime, hybrid poplar – with a preference for old specimens. It is magnificently developed on the ancient planted limes of Kentwell Avenue (Long Melford, Suffolk) and Grimsthorpe Park (Lincolnshire). It very rarely occurs in woods, ancient or recent.

It has a natural habitat on ancient native trees, especially hawthorns. In Hatfield Forest, that great stronghold of mistletoe, it is abundant on non-woodland pollard hawthorns and maples. It behaves like the special lichens. (It is very rare on oak: does it ever occur on *ancient* oaks?)

Insects

Insects can exhibit either the ancient-woodland or the ancient-tree pattern of behaviour. The black hairstreak butterfly is confined to certain ancient woods in the east Midlands: why is not clear. It should be able to fly easily between woods – but does not; its food-plant, blackthorn, is common. The heath fritillary butterfly, in its southeastern population, is confined to the Blean in Kent, where coppicing maintains its food-plant, the ancient-woodland cow-wheat *Melampyrum pratense*.[18] (Its other population, in Devon and Cornwall, feeds on plantains and is not a woodland insect at all – but by convention mere ecological differences are not grounds for subdividing a species.)

---

* A poor translation of German *Urwaldrelikte*, 'wildwood relicts'.

More numerous are 'old-forest relics',* associated with ancient trees. Many species live in particular, sometimes very specific, parts of hollow trees, for example spiders' webs under loose bark, or wood rotted by a specific fungus. Some of the beetles have a fossil record, indicating that wildwood possessed ancient trees; these are now either extinct or linked to savanna-like wood-pastures such as Windsor, Sherwood, Epping or Hatfield Forests.[19]

OTHER COUNTRIES

Ancient-woodland plants have been described from France,[20] Sweden, Germany and other countries, and have equivalents in North America. Not all studies are strictly comparable: they differ in whether they use plant records in a wood as a whole or in samples of its area, and in their approach to attached versus isolated secondary woodland. However, they have detected a similar pattern in more or less different environments and floras.

Belgium

Martin Hermy, historian of woodland, and his colleagues compared species lists from 101 woods in Flanders that could be classed as either ancient or recent. Two later studies involved mapping the spread of different species into attached secondary woodland resulting from a land abandonment.[21] In all they found 71 species with statistically significant affinity for ancient woodland.

The Belgian lists agree on the whole with the British (although they lack the parasites). Of 21 species on nine or more of the British lists, 16 are also indicators in Flanders. Some of the discrepancies may result from the Belgian study being differently planned; thus a detached wood was counted as recent even if 10 per cent of its area was ancient woodland.

Ancient-woodland plants tended to be less light demanding and to grow on more acid soils. In the earlier study, environmental differences, especially too much phosphate and the resulting competition, appear as the chief factors keeping them out of recent woods. Later studies show that lack of dispersal is the limiting factor for anemone, lack of establishment for herb paris, and both for oxlip and archangel.

Some species are ancient-woodland indicators in Flanders, but not Britain. Excluding some weak indicators, they comprise:
- maple, dogwood (common in ancient hedges in England);
- lords-and-ladies (common in recent woodland in England, limited by dispersal

and recruitment in Belgium);

- ground-elder (alien in Britain, aggressive in gardens, but clonal and not spreading far from the point of introduction);
- *Brachypodium sylvaticum, Deschampsia cespitosa* (general woodland grasses in England, but in Belgium lacking dispersal);
- lesser periwinkle *Vinca minor* (supposedly alien in Britain), lungwort *Pulmonaria officinalis*;
- bilberry, heather, bracken, wood-sage, *Carex pilulifera,* heath bedstraw *Galium saxatile.* These are partly heath and moorland plants in Britain. Their restriction to woodland in Flanders is probably because of the extermination of heathland there. (In the same way the destruction of old grassland in England has resulted in many of its species becoming restricted to woodland grassland.)

Sweden

A study in south Sweden investigated 12 deciduous plantations, 30 to 75 years old, all attached to ancient woods. Lack of dispersal was found to be the main factor for ancient-woodland plants. Many species with the slowest migration rates are the 'usual suspects' in England: woodruff, anemone, *Veronica montana*, yellow archangel, *Oxalis, Melica uniflora, Maianthemum, Convallaria* and herb paris. Eleven of the 20 species most typical of ancient woodland are said to be dispersed by ants. Anemone migrates at a fraction of a foot a year: pioneer plants arise from ant-carried seed and are infilled by clonal spread.[22]

Poland

Studies began with an investigation of the clonal spread of anemone into an abandoned clearing around the town of Biaowiez'a in the middle of the famous forest.[23]

A study on ancient versus attached recent woodland investigated the relation between colonising and non-colonising plants in relation to dispersal, shade and fertility (here interpreted in terms of nitrogen rather than phosphorus). Species characteristic of ancient woods include anemone, *Maianthemum* and *Luzula pilosa*, as in Belgium and England, but also bilberry and bracken as in Belgium, but not England. Ant dispersal and clonal spread are very significant factors. Ivy, a plant of recent rather than ancient woods in England, is the reverse in Poland.[24]

North America

Eastern North America has old farm wood-lots, relics of pre-settlement forest, embedded in a huge extent of recent woodland on ex-farmland. Compared with Europe, the farmland was usually cultivated for much less time and accumulated less fertiliser. After a hundred years 'much forest remains unoccupied [by woodland plants] in the Piedmont landscape' and is likely to remain so for at least a further century. One begins to ask how slow-dispersing plants could have got there within the time available since the last glaciation.[25]

Studies reveal patterns of invasion or non-invasion comparable to those in Europe, although all the species are different. Both ancient and recent woods can be composed either of conifers or of broadleaved trees; the flora is more affected by the ancient versus recent contrast than by the difference between broadleaves and conifers. Isolated recent woods have acquired fewer woodland species than attached.

Several of the many shrubs are characteristic of old woodland: *Viburnum alnifolium, V. acerifolium, Acer pensylvanicum* and *Taxus canadensis*. Some *Trillium* species go with old wood-lots, like their English relative herb paris. A number of *Aster* species, although wind-dispersed, are also more abundant in old wood-lots.[26]

Ant dispersal (at 3 feet 6 inches (1.1 metres) per year or less) and clonal spread again make their appearance. Huckleberries (*Gaylussacia* species, Rosaceæ) are very reluctant to invade woodland on former arable land in New England. They are clonal, and although their seeds should be dispersed by animals that eat the berries, in practice they rarely establish from seed and invade ex-farmland only by vegetative spread from the boundary.[27]

Many plants are characteristic of recent woodland. The timorous explorer soon learns to recognise and avoid the poison-ivy that covers the field-walls that pervade the ex-farmland woods: a plant (*Toxicodendron* species, Anacardiaceæ) that behaves curiously like European ivy, though unrelated (and poisonous by touch).

Japan

A pine plantation on a coastal sand dune, some 12 miles (19 kilometres) long, is attached to a natural forest at one end. After 44 years a study recorded how far plants from the natural forest had penetrated along the dune, and by what mode of dispersal. Out of 495 species in the natural forest, only 75 had moved even 300 yards (100 metres) into the dune. None of the 37 species known to be carried by ants occurred in the plantation, and only one of the pteridophytes that propagate by spores. One-third of the 132 species carried in the guts of birds and mammals had colonised.[28]

CONCLUSIONS

Ancient woodland and its characteristic plants have parallels all over the north-temperate world. These have been found even in studies that are confined to attached recent woods, in which colonisation is relatively easy. Even in Tasmania, acacia-woods that spring up on abandoned farmland can be strikingly different from the native eucalyptus-woods, whether intact or felled and regrown. Ancient-woodland floras in three continents share such features as clonal spread, ant dispersal and lack of competitive ability.

Attached secondary woodland of the Middle Ages or earlier may become almost fully assimilated to the adjacent primary wood. Ridge-and-furrow areas in Buff Wood, Cambridgeshire, which probably became woodland 600 years ago, have a full complement of woodland plants, and but for the archaeology would hardly be distinguishable from the original wood. Madingley Wood, which overlies an Iron Age field system and presumably was then a clearing surrounded by woods that disappeared more than a millennium ago (p.175), is now a fully developed ancient wood. Detached secondary woods of medieval age, however, often still lack many ancient-woodland plants.

Environmental differences in secondary woods can persist for centuries. Overhall Grove, Cambridgeshire, which overlies a medieval manorial site and possibly a prehistoric predecessor, is still dominated by stinging-nettles and cow-parsley that thrive on the accumulated phosphate. The nettles that mark an Iron Age town extend into Stockton Wood, Wiltshire.

Within certain limits, ancient woodland has thus been re-created in the past, albeit on a timescale too long to plan for within the vicissitudes of human affairs. But this may not be repeated in the future. Woods like Poolthorn Covert or Toft Plantation were established when farmland was still 'organic'. Woodland plants colonising them had only to overcome the obstacle of dispersal (or, maybe, lack of mycorrhizal fungi). Only on former farmyards, gardens or churchyards would they have had the obstacle of over-fertility. (Later, for ten years, Poolthorn Covert was fertilised by a million and a half starlings using it as a roost.)

Future plantations, or new natural woods, will usually be successors to farmland or improved grassland, because other non-woodland sites are of more conservation value in themselves. The difference between woodland and farm-land soils has been increasing. For nearly 200 years, farmland has been soaked successively with ground-up cab-horses, Egyptian mummified cats, guano from Pacific islands, *poudrette* from cesspits, 'coprolites', sewage sludge and superphosphate. It is now too phosphate-sodden for most woodland plants to survive in competition with high-fertility weeds. In this as in other respects, tree-planting is no substitute for woodland conservation.

CHAPTER 13

WILD AND PLANTED TREES

Tree planting is not a gift to nature ... [it is] like trying to teach kids about dairy farming by letting them play with milk bottles.
P. EVANS, *TREE NEWS*, 1993

Planting distorts the ecological 'story' the [Australian] *bushland holds and considerably reduces the value of bushland for ecological research and education on the operation and resources of existing natural systems and their response to disturbance.*
L. MCLOUGHLIN, 2001[1]

People have planted trees in orchards and gardens probably since Neolithic times, and since Roman times have imported fruit trees from Europe. Planting *areas* of trees for timber or underwood was very rare before the seventeenth century. In the twentieth century, tree-planting took off on a far larger scale (Chapter 18). The Forestry Commission established, or encouraged others to establish, timber plantations, first on heath, moorland and poor agricultural land, and then in the third quarter of the century on the sites of existing woods. Then from 1973 ('Plant a Tree in '73') the conservation movement took up tree-planting on an increasing scale, mainly in non-woodland situations. Between them these people have probably planted more trees in Britain, outside gardens and orchards, than in the whole of history before 1900. Most of the Commission's trees were exotics such as Sitka spruce and Corsican pine. Most of the conservationists' were thought to be native.

Motives for planting have been varied and sometimes incompatible. Common to many of the motives are the assumptions (usually unspoken and untested) that existing or past trees were themselves planted, that planting is needed to replace them, and that the trees now being planted will reproduce the properties for which their predecessors were valued. Is this so?

The fashion for transplanting trees from somewhere else leads to damaged or altered trees. Digging up a tree leaves much of the roots and mycorrhiza behind; growing a tree in a container constricts the roots. (Does it ever recover a normal root system?) Trees moved to another climate or a new soil may lack the proper mycorrhizal fungi and may be exposed to a world of new and hostile micro-organisms. Transplanted trees often die, and if they survive may suffer more than wild trees from drought or windblow. More surprisingly, some exotic trees, such as sycamore in Britain or Monterey pine (*Pinus radiata*) in Cornwall or Tasmania, fare better in new environments to which they are not adapted than in their home environments to which they should be adapted.

RECOGNISING PLANTED TREES

The simplest characteristic is age: any tree or coppice stool more than 400 years old is unlikely to have been planted, unless it is a relic of a garden (cf. p.278).

Trees in rows normally indicate a modern plantation, unless there is some underlying cause such as ridge-and-furrow. Rows, however, are not always easy to distinguish (p.194). Exotic trees, by definition, are usually planted. Some introductions, like sweet-chestnut and sycamore, or Corsican pine and Sitka spruce, are naturalised and seed themselves. I cannot recall any trees introduced by accident, like wool-shoddy aliens and other herbaceous plants.

Sweet-chestnut is widely naturalised as well as planted on both woodland and ex-farmland sites (p.287) . Plantations on former woodland are best recognised by the absence of ancient stools and the presence of areas of stools of more or less the same size, especially if there are few other trees.

Planted native trees

What of planted native trees, especially oak (Table 17)? Some types of plant-ing may be ecologically insignificant: the proverbial retired admiral, dibbling acorns into the ground with his walking stick, would have given them a slightly greater chance of survival. However, sometimes the wild oaks in a wood have been destroyed and replaced by oaks from an 'improved' source (p.265).

Replacing oaks was stimulated by the abnormally high price of oak bark and timber from 1790 to 1860. It is well documented for wooded Forests where the

Crown owned the land, such as Dean and Salcey (Northamptonshire). Oak plantations were also made on non-woodland sites, especially later in the century when agriculture was in decline but it was still hoped that the price of trees would recover.

Plantations usually occupy well-defined, sharp-edged areas. In itself this does not indicate artificiality, for clonal and gregarious trees (p.17, 18) naturally occur in sharp-edged patches. However, a boundary that runs in a straight line or coincides with a ride or internal woodbank raises suspicions of planting.

Wild populations of oak, as in the Bradfield Woods and Hayley Wood, show all the variability expected of a wild plant (Fig.203). The trunk may be straight, crooked, or corkscrew; epicormic twigs, sprouting through the bark, may be absent, or grow in patches, or cover the whole trunk with a 'furry' growth; leaves may open early or late, and may fall in October or linger into January; shape and colour of leaves vary; leafage may be dense, sparse, or patchy; lammas shoots are sometimes scarlet. Some of these features are affected by environment, but many are constant throughout a tree (or on all the stems of a multi-stemmed tree) and are likely to be genetic.

Oak plantations within ancient woodland, as on ex-farmland, tend to be monotonous: all the trees are nearly straight, with the same density of twigs, all leafing and losing their leaves at the same time, and with a small, constant presence of epicormic twigs. They are all the same age and set at much the same, rather close, spacing – which may give the illusion of different ages if some trees, losing to competition, have lagged in growth behind their sisters. They are usually *Quercus robur* except in areas where *petræa* is much the commoner oak. There will usually be a remnant of the previous underwood struggling to survive. Plantation oaks themselves seldom show signs of regular coppicing, but occasionally a stand has been felled once since it was planted and has sprouted from the stumps.

Landowners would want to grow superior oaks, as they would superior cows, and would select acorns from what was then regarded as an oak of superior timber qualities, of which I have just given a portrait. (Bark qualities seem to have been less highly regarded.) Oak is wind pollinated and is probably an inbreeding tree, so that acorns from a selected tree, like the daughters of a champion bull, will replicate the parent's peculiarities. Whether they grew their oaklings themselves or bought them, the resulting oaks would be similar within a wood, but would vary somewhat from wood to wood and ownership to ownership.

Although woodland owners tried to exterminate the pre-existing oaks, they might spare the younger ones and miss a few others. Stands of replacement oak occupy either the whole wood or defined areas within it. There is usually the occasional 'oak that got away', often multi-stemmed, a dissident standing out by its irregularity from the uniformity of its neighbours.

Groton Wood, Suffolk, is an ancient wood. The northern third, dominated by lime, represents one-half of a wood belonging to Bury St Edmunds Abbey. The southern two-thirds is ancient secondary woodland probably of early seventeenth-century date; it is a coppice-wood of hazel with some ash and cherry. The oaks, however, are more numerous than usual, forming a closed stand to the detriment of the hazel and even of each other, and are suspiciously uniform in appearance, compared to wild oaks. When Suffolk Wildlife Trust acquired the wood in 1972 they thinned some of the oaks, whose annual rings all dated from c.1925. These oaks were undoubtedly planted into an existing wood, without much disturbing the underwood. Here and there an anomalous oak survives from the previous population. How the substitution was done, and the planted trees enabled to compete with the underwood, is not known. In the part dominated by lime, a much stronger competitor, it seems not to have been attempted.

This has happened in a large minority of ancient woods: an earlier example is Hardwick Wood near Cambridge. In the nineteenth century, when the price of oak-trees (bark and timber) was high relative to underwood, woodland owners evidently tried to replace the wild standard trees with a higher density of oaks that were of better quality, according to the criteria of the time. This occasionally continued long after the economics had collapsed, of which Groton Wood is an example. Replacement of oaks may be accompanied by other planted trees, although Groton Wood has no evidence of other planting.

Oak replacement is probably commoner in the Highland Zone (Chapter 15), where wild-type oakwoods were replaced by planted oakwoods. In eastern England, out of 288 ancient woods where I recorded the type of oak, I found at least some planted-type in 65 woods, a little under one-quarter. This may be an underestimate, because woods with planted-type oaks may have been more liable to felling in the twentieth century, and maybe also to subsequent replanting, which would destroy the evidence. Replacement probably went with particular estates: it is particularly frequent in Suffolk (36 out of 85 woods).

ALIENS AND FALSE NATIVES

The current state of the commercial sector is insufficient to enforce the necessary controls over provenance of material used for hedge renovation.
A.T. JONES AND COLLEAGUES, 2001

Objections to alien species

Introducers of plants and animals usually expect the new species to 'enrich', rather than replace, the flora and fauna of the host country. Often they are right, but in a disastrous minority of cases either the introduced species, or something inadvertently introduced with it, gets out of hand and displaces the native plants or animals. It is impossible to predict which these will be. Those who persevered in introducing the grey squirrel (p.420) had no idea that it would lead to the loss of the red squirrel and would jeopardise most of British forestry.

The best-known invasive aliens in Britain are animals: rabbit (which has been here for 850 years), brown rat, grey squirrel, mink and introduced deer. Well-known invaders among land plants are ground-elder, sycamore, rhododendron, cherry-laurel, Himalayan balsam, giant hogweed and Japanese knotweed. The ill-effects of these seven 'villains' tend to be overstated, except rhododendron, which in western oakwoods can exterminate all other plants and jeopardise the future of the oaks. It grows prolifically from tiny seeds; to remove it requires digging up every stool or repeatedly felling and poisoning the stumps.

False natives and lookalikes

New amenity woods, motorway plantations and hedges often claim to imitate native woodland and ancient hedges, but the imitation is superficial. Some features, such as big coppice stools, cannot be copied; but even the maples and hawthorns are often not quite the same as native maple and hawthorn.

With oaks this has gone on for centuries. The two native oaks differ in ecology (Table 3); although they hybridise there are many populations that are recognisably one or the other. They are very variable within each species − surprisingly for trees that probably originated from only a few individuals when they returned after the last ice age. When planting oak, people have rarely sought to preserve this variability by gathering a few acorns from each oak. They tend to gather all their acorns either from the first oak they come to or from what by their standards is a 'good' oak. When they learnt to distinguish the two species of oak in the late eighteenth century they preferred pedunculate: a fashion to be suddenly reversed in the twentieth century.

Down the centuries, tree-planters have been far more enthusiastic about oak than any other native tree. They have imported foreign species of oak, and with them foreign gall wasps and other parasites. They have gone to great lengths (for acorns do not travel well) to import foreign populations of pedunculate oak that they considered superior to the native tree. The present position is complex, but not entirely beyond understanding. Oaks on estates with a strong history of planting may have come from anywhere in non-Mediterranean Europe: often (as at Moccas, Herefordshire, p.441) different age-cohorts of oak differ systematically in appearance. Wild populations most often survive in woods with a weak estate history, in ancient wood-pastures, in woods that are mainly sessile oak, and among oaks more than 350 years old.

Importation moved up a gear when planting became fashionable in 1973. Work was delegated to agents and contractors, whose ethos of tendering, profit margins and timetables clashes with the properties of trees. Oak, especially, does not work to a timetable, and if England does not produce acorns this year, the contractor, needing to spend the grant by the end of this financial year, will go to a country that does. The matter was made worse for a time by a European Union regulation that seed for commercial sale had to come from trees designated for their forestry qualities, of which there were few in Britain. More than 90 per cent of the 'native' trees planted in the late twentieth century were from unspecified Continental countries, and many were selected for mid-twentieth-century ideals of timber quality, whether or not that was relevant.[2]

In the 1980s the Forestry Commission began to remedy the situation by introducing an identification system for seedlings of local provenance. 'Local' was widely drawn – seed for Kent could come from anywhere between Somerset and Yorkshire – but even so, it seems, the scheme was not watertight: contractors felt at liberty to get stock from Europe if they were running out of time. In 1998 a new system was introduced, but the geographical regions are still not small: Anglesey and Monmouthshire count as 'local' to Aberystwyth.[3] The new scheme, however, reminds propagators to seek seed trees that are themselves of local origin, rather than the product of earlier planting from elsewhere.

This applies also to pine. In England most plantations of 'Scotch fir', from the eighteenth century onwards, were of Continental origin; even in the Scottish Highlands there are plantations of Continental pine and of Caledonian pine alongside natural woods of Caledonian pine.

In the twentieth century this habit spread to other trees and shrubs. By 1987 about 80 per cent of commercial hawthorns were imported; they often grew less well and suffered more mildew than native hawthorn. Many hawthorns planted after 1970 come into leaf about two weeks earlier than native hawthorns. Even hawthorn sold as originating from the Forest of Dean behaved suspiciously like Hungarian material.[4]

As Peter Sell, the great taxonomist, points out, some of these variants are

European forms of British species, but some are identifiable as distinct species. Dogwood in the 'Standard Broadleaf Mixture' planted on road-cuts is often not the native *Cornus sanguinea*, but its lookalikes *C. australis* from the Black Sea or *C. koenigii* from Russia. 'Free trees' given out by a generous county council to farmers in the 1980s included what was labelled 'field maple' but turned out to be the Japanese *Acer miyabei*. One of the Woodland Trust's new 'woods' near Cambridge includes native alder, the Central European *Alnus incana,* and their hybrids. Native wayfaring-tree, *Viburnum lantana*, has an eastern and western English variety; what is often planted, in new hedges or in gaps in ancient hedges, can be either of these, or the Asian *V. rhytidiophyllum,* or its hybrid with the eastern variant of *lantana,* or Chinese *V. veitchii.* Mixed hedges, planted in imitation of an ancient hedge, can consist entirely of 'false natives'. One of the 50 Heritage Trees of Britain and Northern Ireland, designated in 2002 in the belief that it was *Sorbus leyana,* one of the world's rarest trees (confined to two cliffs in Breconshire), turns out to be merely Swedish whitebeam, *S. intermedia.*[5]

How this happened has not been fully investigated, but let us make a generous guess. The nursery trade, especially its gardening branch, had for a century dealt almost exclusively in exotics: bluebells had to be the Spanish species, as though there were something wrong with English bluebells, which was to cause trouble when the two hybridised. (I can remember when gardeners were taught to despise all native plants: even daisies on lawns were a blemish.) It is difficult to keep track of large numbers of species in cultivation; labels migrate and identities get confused; mistakes get perpetuated from year to year.

When planting native trees came into vogue, the trade was suddenly called upon to supply large numbers of unfamiliar species. A Continental variety or Asian lookalike could easily be substituted for the 'true native', accidentally or even intentionally, given that the importance of the difference would not have been fully appreciated. Surplus stock, turned into 'free trees' at the end of the season, might change its identity.

This problem is not confined to trees and shrubs. 'Wildflower' seed mixtures often fail to contain English wildflowers: as Nigel Spring points out, cowslips planted on motorway verges are bigger and earlier than real cowslips. In 1989 a careful attempt was made to reconstruct chalk grassland on the Gog Magog Hills near Cambridge by sowing seed from commercial sources. When the plants came up they included some of those intended, and also cornfield weeds remaining from the previous arable use of the site, but there were many surprises: agricultural forage crops; garden ornamentals; Continental relatives of the species intended; and aliens from the Mediterranean. This was not a cheap or stand-ard scheme, like landscaping a motorway. The organisers spared no trouble or expense in choosing seed suppliers 'with excellent credentials', and yet the result, however instructive, was far from what was intended.[6]

Do imported native trees and shrubs matter?
The extension of gardening methods into the landscape at large erodes the distinction between them. Gardens should be special places; they lose their value if the wider countryside turns into a second-rate garden. Nursery varieties of trees such as hawthorn come into leaf earlier than wild trees, which starves the ground vegetation of light (p.211).

Non-local stock often performs less well in its new environment. For many purposes the differences are merely quantitative and may not matter much. Adaptation to local climate may be insignificant because climates vary with time as well as place: an oak that germinated in the Little Ice Age may be 'adapted' to a climate that has now moved up the mountain.[7] However, two spectacular historic examples show what can go wrong.

The Forest of Dean was for centuries a source of 'super-oaks', transported all over England and Wales and even to the Tower of London, wherever exceptional timbers were wanted. Those who replanted the Forest in the early nineteenth century (p.353f), having learnt that there are two species of oak, were not content with the local *Quercus petræa*, but preferred the 'superior' *Q. robur*. This has not prospered, hardly reaching even average size. For centuries the favourite elm was English elm, *Ulmus procera*, a super-elm – easily propagated, an excellent shade tree with a long leafing season, fast-growing, producing timbers bigger than any oak – but it was to prove super-susceptible to a future disease epidemic in the 1970s, and to involve the other elms in its downfall.

Alternatively, non-local stock may perform super-well. Gardeners must needs grow yellow archangel, not in its ordinary and beautiful form, but as a cultivar with variegated leaves, which is invasive: in gardens it becomes a pest to rival ground-elder, and is beginning to take over native woodland. Ordinary reed (*Phragmites australis*) is a species native to both Eurasia and North America. There are three forms, identical to the eye but distinguishable genetically: types E and S in America and type M in Europe. For three centuries after the Pilgrim Fathers, reed E and reed S were well-behaved members of wetland ecosystems, like reed M in Europe. But about 1900 someone must needs bring in reed M, which not only replaces the native reeds but spreads far and wide to turn indigenous wetlands into reed-beds, calling for expensive and destructive action to try to control it.[8]

Commercial trees may not replicate all the values of their wild predecessors. Especially if selected for timber quality, they may not reproduce the variability on which the beauty of wild trees depends. Nor may they be much good as a habitat: for example, epiphytic ferns and the creatures that live in them call for crooked oaks with wide spreading branches (see Figs 77, 203).

Conservation of 'biodiversity' is usually thought of in terms of species: it might not matter much if Hungarian *Quercus robur* were to replace Welsh *Q. robur*. However, this is more a convention of how ecologists think than an expression of biological reality. It is hard to argue that species are worthy of conservation and lesser units – subspecies and varieties – are not: that the native pine of Scotland is 'only' a subspecies and not worth protecting. These categories are inventions of the human mind, not measured units of genetic difference, and taxonomists are forever changing their minds about which is which.

As Sell points out, the biological reality has only recently come to light and is not fully understood. Many trees widely distributed in the northern hemisphere exist as *clines*, varying gradually from western Europe to east Asia or even into America. Travellers to the Caucasus or Japan might describe the local variants as species distinct from those of western Europe, without realising that they were connected by intermediates. Conventional taxonomy is not good at handling clines: the authors of *Flora Europaea* repeatedly refused to name a geographical variant on the grounds that it is connected to the named 'typical' variant by intermediates. (If developers or polluters were to exterminate the intermediate forms, would this increase the world's biodiversity by creating a new species?)

Importing false natives arbitrarily mixes up variants from one point on the cline with those on another point. (Whether the variants are regarded as different species is a historical accident.) The consequences vary according to whether the introduction performs better or worse than the true native, whether it hybridises with it, and whether it has the same relation to associated plants, animals and fungi. (Rosebay willowherb comprises two distinct forms: the native *Epilobium angustifolium* on rocky streamsides in mountain areas, and a lookalike introduced probably from North America in the seventeenth century, which behaves quite differently and has altered many British ecosystems.[9]) In general such introductions advance the cause of homogenisation and dilute the world's biodiversity.

Potentially more significant still, importing millions of live plants, and therefore thousands of tons of foreign soil, defeats attempts at keeping out foreign plant diseases such as new strains of *Phytophthora* (p.428).

CHAPTER 14

SOME TYPES OF WOODLAND

Lowland Zone

WHY ARE WOODS NOT ALL THE SAME?

Facile adaptationist guesswork used to explain everything that we observe in nature scarcely serves to make ecology an effective medium for teaching the principles of science.
J.L. HARPER, 1982[1]

Every ancient wood is different from every other. This chapter deals with the Lowland Zone of England, excluding the Highlands of the southwest, north and Welsh border (see Fig. 1). It corresponds to the Lime Province of prehistory.

I remind the reader that most 'woods' are plantations, where the trees have been planted on former non-woodland, just as most grasslands consist of cornfields and sown agricultural leys. This chapter is concerned with natural woods, much as a grassland ecologist writes about old meadows and pastures and leaves wheatfields and football pitches to specialists.

The many kinds of natural woodland
Sir Arthur Tansley, in *The British Islands and their Vegetation* (1939), devoted 91 pages to oakwoods, 63 to beechwoods, 18 to ashwoods, 12 to alder-woods, 7 to pine-woods, 9 to birchwoods and 4½ pages to yew-woods. Hornbeam-woods, most ashwoods, hazel-woods and maple-woods were subsumed under oakwoods on the grounds that the biggest trees were oak; limewoods were overlooked.

Tansley was a pioneer in appreciating that even natural woods had all been altered by management, but did not fully explain what management had done and had not done. The role of oak in his time (and now) was a legacy from two historical factors: centuries of woodmen favouring oak by treating it as a timber tree, and the former ability of oak to grow from seed in existing woods. Before the Oak Change, oak was a natural constituent of many types of woodland, but it was the intervention of woodmen that made it the principal timber tree.

There is a fundamental difference between oak in oakwoods, where the coppice stools as well as the standard trees are oak, and oak in other kinds of woodland (see Table 18). Timber oaks, unless felled very young, seldom sprout and do not give rise to permanent stools. Before the Oak Change they were a relatively transient feature. The continuity of a wood, and its difference from other woods, reside in the long-lived underwood stools, the ground vegetation, and probably the fungi. I shall define woodland types mainly in terms of underwood. Ground vegetation deserves its own classification. Although some types tend to go with particular trees the relation is statistical, not absolute. Trees are one of the factors that create the environment of the herbs, along with waterlogging, soil acidity, coppicing, deer, etc. These may affect the trees in a different way, or on a different timescale, or not at all. There is also much more information about trees than anything else: in most woods the ground vegetation is unknown before 1970, and it is unlikely that the fungi will ever be adequately known.

There have been three recent classifications of woodland. In *Ancient Woodland* (1981) I recognised 31 woodland types, mainly from eastern England. George Peterken in 1981 divided the 'ancient, semi-natural woodland' of Great Britain into 58 'stand-types' and subdivisions, based on tree assemblages and subdivided by ground vegetation. In 1992 the *National Vegetation Classification* (NVC) recognised a different 58 'subcommunities' of woodland in Great Britain. This last was based mainly on ground vegetation, although it has often been used as if it were a general-purpose classification. Ancient woodland probably contains 34 of the subcommunities, the others being short-lived stages in succession. Combining the three systems, I find a total of 83 types of semi-natural woodland recognised up to 1992, leaving out rare types discovered and subdivisions recognised since then. Of these, 53 are wholly or mainly within the Lowland Zone.[2]

Tansley presented the distribution of different trees as mainly due to environment. Matters have not much progressed since his time, and there is a curious lack of information on why trees occur where they do. Species have natural limits correlated with climate, but many grow well when introduced well outside those limits. Although some trees prefer or avoid particular soil types, most species can be found on most of the soils on which native woodland occurs at all.

Although I write about 'ashwoods', 'limewoods', etc., most Lowland woods are not wholly composed of just one tree species or one mixture of species. Even a small wood commonly varies from one part to another (Fig. 105). The scale of the variation differs: in some Essex woods every acre is different from every other acre.

Are tree communities natural?

One hears it argued that silvicultural treatment, mainly planting, has been such an overwhelming influence that it is no longer possible to understand the distribution of trees in terms of natural processes. If part of a wood is dominated by lime, another part by hornbeam, and a third part by hazel, it depends on the whims of past woodmen in favouring those trees. This theory was rejected in 1910 in the first attempt to classify English natural woodland,[3] but it has been revived since, most recently by the authors of the NVC.

Planting is easily invoked by ecologists to explain any tree distribution that they find anomalous or embarrassing: it is a let-out, removing the distribution of trees from the field of ecology, where they feel obliged to offer an explanation, into that of anthropology, outside their province. However, planting is not beyond the reach of rational investigation, whether anthropological (how people decide whether and how to plant) or ecological (what happens to the trees once planted). It is an activity with definite limits in time and space, discussed in Chapter 18.

Here I am not concerned with plantations on former non-woodland, whose tree composition is usually dominated (but not entirely, and to a decreasing extent with time) by whatever trees were originally planted. The question is: how far has planting influenced the tree composition *within ancient woodland*?

Silvicultural treatment has favoured certain weakly competitive trees: aspen (by coppicing) and oak (for timber). It may have helped in the disappearance of pine, one of the few trees always killed by felling. Other examples are the development of pure beechwoods, the spread of chestnut (in part) and the partial replacement of wild by planted oaks. With these specific exceptions, I have never found evidence (nor does the NVC offer any) that differences in underwood composition result from differences in silvicultural treatment. On the contrary, these differences persist side by side in the same wood under the same treatment. The only relevant treatment was coppicing, together with maintaining variable numbers of timber oaks. It is not the case that (for example) Merton College favoured maple in one part of Gamlingay Wood, the Avenells favoured ash in their part of that wood, and the Bishops of Ely favoured hazel in Hayley Wood. That is not how woods vary: the Bishops' woods in Cambridgeshire and Suffolk resemble the woods of their neighbours in those counties, and do not follow a general pattern of Ely bishopric woods. Variations in canopy survive despite, not because of, centuries of coppicing.

This chapter is not an exhaustive treatment of all the kinds of woodland, and does not cover fine distinctions or rare types. For more detail I refer the reader to *Ancient Woodland* and to Peterken's *Woodland Conservation and Management*.

WOODS OF ASH, MAPLE AND HAZEL

These are the core of ancient woodland in much of Lowland England; they are a specially British kind of woodland, being less common elsewhere (though probably under-recorded). There are steep dry hazel–ashwoods on the middle slopes of downland dry valleys in Wiltshire and Dorset, where sharp flints chink under the boot and dog's-mercury wilts in the summer drought; soggy ashwoods, impenetrable with blackthorn, on Midland clays; sparse ashwoods on acid, fertile gravels on the Essex–Suffolk border, with sheets of bluebell and patches of bracken; hazel-woods, crowded with stools, producing high-quality underwood in Wiltshire; and maple-woods on boulder-clays in Cambridgeshire and Essex (Fig. 107). Between these extremes are countless intergradations that defy divisive classification.

These woods may have almost any proportions of the three trees. Usually there are timber oaks (or timber ashes on thin chalk soils). On waterlogged soils they have clonal patches of aspen. They can adjoin hornbeam-, lime- and alder-woods, usually by a sudden transition. All three trees form ancient stools.

In *Ancient Woodland* I had Pure Ashwoods, Mixed Ashwoods, Ash–Hazel, Mixed Hazel, Pure Hazel, Maple–Hazel and Maple-woods as subdivisions within a continuum, but this does not do justice to some of the extreme types. Peterken has ten stand-types. The NVC has five subcommunities, three of which are parts of W8, the 'dump' category for any site that does not key out to one of the others.

Almost any ground vegetation, except some very acidic kinds, can be found under different variants of ash–maple–hazel woods. The commonest associate is bluebell. Hazel-woods and hazel–ashwoods carpeted with bluebells are one of the specialities that make Britain what it is. Maple-woods tend to be carpeted with dog's-mercury.

Hazel forms an underground stool that lives for centuries (p.202f). I have known it persist almost unaltered for over 50 years in the shade of elm.[4] It is self-coppicing: the stems, after 50 years or more, are replaced by 'water-shoots' growing up from the stool. These are brittle and not much use for hazel crafts: to produce useable wood hazel needs to be regularly cut. Occasionally hazel has a trunk more than a foot (30 centimetres) in diameter, which may be the effect of sheep eating the secondary shoots.

Hazel-woods are a relict of the early Holocene. Hazel was one of the early trees to colonise Britain, and in the Boreal Period became dominant (p.71). Its longevity, dense shade and self-coppicing would enable it to hold on to existing ground. However, a tree of relatively small stature could hardly resist invasion by taller trees for ever. It has been partly squeezed out by oak, elm, lime and later ash; these may or may not have killed the hazels, but would have overtopped them and prevented them from producing pollen. The Elm Decline brought some respite (p.75).

Determinants of ash, maple and hazel

Ash and hazel will grow on most soils that are not too infertile. Maple is one of the few common trees with a definite soil preference, for well-drained, clayey soils with little sand. However, it occasionally grows even on acid sandy soils, perhaps where the subsoil is less extreme.

In clayey woods (boulder-clay or Oxford Clay) ash tends to grow on the most winter-wet sites, hazel in the middle of the range, and maple on the more sloping ground (although the slope may be as little as 2 degrees). In Hayley Wood, ash is mostly dominant on the central plateau and maple on the sloping fringes, with hazel in between and overlapping both. Ash correlates with oxlip and meadowsweet, hazel with bluebell, and maple with dog's-mercury. Although the relations are significant, they are statistical and not obvious: I knew the wood for 40 years before discovering them. On ridge-and-furrow, stools on ridges tend to be maple and in furrows to be ash.[5] Ash seedlings cannot easily get through well-grown dog's-mercury: in the long term ash needs waterlogging to keep out mercury.[6]

Where there is not much maple, it will usually be on woodbanks (marginal or internal); woodbanks have an inverted soil profile, less acidic on the top (p.199).

Twentieth-century changes

Ash did well in the twentieth century. It sprang up on abandoned land, such as chalk grassland (after hawthorn had begun the process of succession) or limestone scree and quarry debris. It also took over existing woods. Hayley Wood has ash stools of all ages, indicating a continuous history of ash. But many a wood has few or no ancient ash stools and a preponderance of maiden or once-cut ashes. C.E. Moss, pioneer of woodland ecology who described the Mendip ashwoods in 1907,[7] apparently did not realise that they had been hazel-woods and limewoods in which ash had only recently become dominant. The same holds for others of the 'ashwoods on limestone', which were all that Tansley recognised. Peterken's 'ash–wych-elm woods', of which he recognised three variants, tended to turn into ashwoods after wych-elm was set back by Elm Disease.

Ash may take over from many other trees. Its seedlings are relatively shade-resistant and can live many years in a dwarfed state. If deer are present the seedlings are repeatedly bitten but not easily killed, and if browsing ceases for a few years get away. *Intermittent* browsing, therefore, sometimes favours ash (p.215).

Hazel has fared badly. Grey squirrels have taken away its means of reproduction. Usually all the nuts have disappeared by August while they are still green and unviable, and a young hazel is a rarity. Hazel is thus a threatened species, although its longevity will see it through some centuries to come.

Uses of hazel

Hazel, to some degree, moulded the civilisations of Britain and Ireland. Mesolithic people ate the nuts on such a scale as to create the suspicion that people had found some way to favour hazel above other trees. (This could not have been done by burning, for hazel is a fire-suppressing tree; the notion that it is encouraged by fire appears to be derived from other species of hazel in America.)

Hazel, as the commonest wattlework tree, encouraged a wattle-based civilisation. Its rods can be bent through 360 degrees, or even tied in knots, provided they are twisted to separate the fibres (Fig. 89). Hazel wildwood would have been the easiest to convert into managed woodland, avoiding the problem of handling or disposing of inconveniently large trees.

Hazelnuts were eaten long after they ceased to be a staple diet.[8] In the Middle Ages nut orchards were planted with cultivar hazels, cobs and filberts, some derived from the southeast European *Corylus maxima*. Until the 1950s, as Peter Sell records, there survived on a Cambridgeshire moat a row of gigantic cultivar hazels, probably relicts of the orchard of Sir John Tiptoft, celebrated humanist and judicial murderer, dating from c.1465.[9]

Nut gathering could be one of the labour services owed by manorial tenants. Hazelnut oil could be used to make soap. Nutting was a lively social occasion, affording 'opportunity for all sorts of Debauchery', into the nineteenth century.[10]

In recent times hazel underwood has been difficult to manage economically. If of best quality it has commanded fancy prices – and still does, in that shrinking area where it is not attacked by deer. People would plant it as an understorey to oak plantations well into the nineteenth century. However, once the ethers and thatching wood have been selected, hazel of ordinary quality leaves a bulky residue of small, crooked stems, which are difficult to sell.

LIMEWOODS

Since the Neolithic, lime has declined, to the point that Tansley was able to miss limewoods altogether. But in some areas it is still the commonest tree in ancient woodland. In Shrawley Wood (Worcestershire), or Hockering Wood (Norfolk), or Great Monk Wood (Coggeshall, Essex) or the Forêt de Chantilly (northeast of Paris) it does not take much imagination to see oneself back in wildwood times. Under the majestic limes, towering over all other trees, one asks why all ancient woods are not still like this.

Lime is very gregarious. Within a wood it forms solid areas of lime (Fig. 111), or at least clusters of stools. Limewoods are clustered in some parts of the country: the Lincolnshire limewoods, those of south Suffolk and north Essex, the Mendips, Worcestershire, Warwickshire, the Lake District and others. Elsewhere there are ancient woods but no lime. (Unfortunately the first edition of the *Atlas of the British Flora* under-records native lime, while the second edition fails to distinguish wild from planted lime.) It is the only abundant tree to be an ancient-woodland indicator. With few exceptions it avoids woodpasture.

Lime is very robust. It is difficult to kill: felling it is useless, and the regrowth is relatively unattractive to deer. It survives uprooting; I have known a stool fall over a cliff and continue growing. It withstood determined attempts by the unreformed Forestry Commission to eliminate it (p.376). Its one weakness, difficulty in growing from seed, is partly outweighed by extreme longevity.

Many of the larger stands are pure limewood, often on strongly acid soils (especially loess) with mor humus and brambles, or bracken: some are magnificent bluebell woods. On less acid soils or where the acidic surface layer is thinner (as in Groton Wood, Suffolk, or Cheddar Wood, Mendips) lime coexists with ash, forming mull humus and having primrose or dog's-mercury. Most limewoods have had a succession of standard oaks, despite the strong competition from the lime. An unusual variant has sessile instead of pedunculate oak. Peterken recognises four variants. Limewoods, like other unusual tree communities, get short shrift from the NVC.

Lime, or *linde* or *bæst* or *pry*, is a well-documented tree, partly from the use of its phloem fibres (bast) as fibre: a second-class fibre in a country that grew *Cannabis*, but much used.[11] Its other specific use, for wood-carving, is well known on the Continent, but English examples appear to be rare before Grinling Gibbons in the late seventeenth century. (A single limewood should have kept Gibbons's workshop going in perpetuity!)

Documentation, together with place-names and ancient stools, shows that most lime regions go back for at least a thousand years. Areas where lime survived into Norman times and that still have ancient woodland still have lime. An exception is the loss of a fen-edge distribution indicated by the place-names *Bastwick* in Norfolk or *Linwood* in March (Isle of Ely). (The one surviving fen-island wood, Higney Wood in Woodwalton (Huntingdon), is a maple–blackthorn wood – perhaps unique – with no lime.) There is still an unexplained gap between the general lime decline of later prehistory (p.95) and the historic distribution. Why did lime go extinct in Hertfordshire and remain abundant in mid–north Essex?

HORNBEAM-WOODS

Hornbeam, like lime, is strongly gregarious without being clonal, strongly coppicing, densely shading, and usually dominant if it occurs at all (Fig. 112). It grows on a wide range of soils, predominantly on acidic clays. Unlike lime, it grows readily from seed, and is not related to ancient woodland, but gets into new woods as a late-successional tree.

Hornbeam is perhaps the common tree least specifically related to human affairs. It makes heavy and good firewood, but has no specific use and is easily confused with elm and beech. There was a brief vogue for planting it (why?) in the mid-nineteenth century, often outside its native range.

Hornbeam is the commonest woodland tree within 25 miles (40 kilometres) of London. It has a second area of distribution within 15 miles (25 kilometres) of Harleston on the Norfolk–Suffolk border, and a scatter of other clustered occurrences. This behaviour, too, is like that of lime. But not often do both trees occur in quantity in the same wood: in Chalkney Wood (Earl's Colne, Essex) lime is dominant on the loess-covered boulder-clay plateau, and hornbeam on the London Clay and gravelly slopes, with a broad area of overlap. Unlike lime, hornbeam is abundant in wood-pastures like Epping and Hatfield Forests.

Hornbeam-woods in Hertfordshire were investigated by E.J. Salisbury in the 1910s, who recognised two types: '*Quercus robur* – *Carpinus*' woods and '*Quercus sessiliflora* [now called *Q. petræa*] – *Carpinus*' woods. These occur in south Essex and Kent too. The former, which I later called Pure Hornbeam, are on acid, often loessy soils; they have a normal woodland structure with standard oaks (or their stumps) of the pedunculate species. They tend to be bluebell and bramble woods.

The latter, which I later called Oak – Hornbeam, are on very acid, infertile, often gravelly soils; they often have an unusually large number of standard trees, which tend to be sessile oak; the ground vegetation is often bracken. This type is often a transition to oakwood on still less fertile soils.

Two other types of hornbeam-wood occur on clayey, less acid soils, usually in small patches and outlying from the main hornbeam areas. Hornbeam – Ash is often on wet sites with wood-anemone and primrose, forming a transition to Mixed Ashwood. Hornbeam – Maple is on areas with better drainage, with dog's-mercury; it is transitional to Maple-wood.[12]

Peterken recognises four types of hornbeam-wood (two with sessile and two with pedunculate oak). The NVC confounds them with other types.

Historically, archaeologically and palynologically, hornbeam is under-recorded. Its main area around London is documented in the last 500 years, but the earlier history is little known. Fossil hornbeam begins as late as the Neolithic: since it is recognisable both from pollen and fruits this is unlikely to be due to vagaries of preservation and analysis, although there are few pollen deposits within present hornbeam areas. It is hard to resist the conclusion that hornbeam has displaced lime by some process that no longer operates. Lime is not losing ground to hornbeam in Chalkney Wood now.

ELMWOODS

Elm was not doomed by the Elm Decline. On a reduced scale it continues to the present: several woodland stands of elm have survived modern epidemics of Elm Disease. Elmwoods are of two main types:

- of suckering elms in the *Ulmus minor, stricta* and *procera* groups (East Anglian, Cornish and English Elms). Woods of English Elm, never extensive, have been hard hit by Elm Disease;
- of non-suckering but nevertheless gregarious elms: wych-elm (*Ulmus glabra*) and related forms.

Suckering elmwoods
These have clonal circles of elm often embedded in a wood of other species. Different clones vary in appearance, ecology and susceptibility to Elm Disease. Some started from ditches or other earthworks: in Overhall Grove, an ancient, mostly secondary wood near Cambridge, some of the clones may have begun, around 600 years ago, as farmyard trees around a deserted settlement. Many clones send

out suckers into the surrounding non-elm wood well in advance of the circular front, assisting the advance of the clone the next time the wood is felled.

A wood may have two distinct sizes of elms, corresponding to the elm timber trees and elm underwood when the wood was last coppiced. Ground vegetation often consists of nettles and other phosphate plants. Sometimes these are related to underlying deserted settlements, but elms may have a greater power than other trees of extracting phosphate from the subsoil.

Suckering elmwoods are common in north Essex, Suffolk, Cambridgeshire and the east Midlands, but I know outliers elsewhere, one (of East Anglian Elm) even in South Wales.

Non-suckering elmwoods

Non-suckering elms are, or were, a constituent of many ashwoods, especially on limestone soils: often a patchy constituent, although Bunny Old Wood (Nottinghamshire) is dominated by wych-elm. Peterken recognised at least seven variants of ash–wych-elm woodland. Some of them have a particularly rich mixture of herbaceous plants, the micro-topography allowing plants of acid, calcareous, flushed and well-drained sites to grow together.

Effects of Elm Disease[13]

In general woodland has been unfavourable to Elm Disease, and woodland elms have suffered less than non-woodland. Suckering elms vary in susceptibility. In Overhall Grove the disease appeared in 1973 and subtracted one elm clone after another until by 1990 about one-third of the elms remained. Since then there have been few further losses. The disease (or its bark-beetle vector) is well versed in elm taxonomy, responding to slight differences in the phenotype of the trees. Much the same has happened nearby in Madingley, Buff and Gamlingay Woods, where big elm clones survive.

What happens after an attack depends on the suckering capacity and shade tolerance of particular elms, and on deer. Some parts of Overhall Grove display a new generation of elm suckers; other elm clones have disappeared altogether, and the vigorous growth of phosphate plants has delayed colonisation by other trees. In Hayley Wood a very big elm clone was destroyed as fallow deer devoured the young shoots. Wych-elm and other stool-forming elms are often killed to the stool and sprout from its edges: one of the few big wych-elms in the Bradfield Woods has survived two severe attacks. Here too browsing animals can determine whether the tree lives. The state of elms is a measure of the health of a wood.

BEECHWOODS

Beech is gregarious; it tends to be dominant if it occurs at all, although this is partly an artefact of management. It occurs as native in a number of separate areas (Fig. 202): Epping Forest, the Chilterns and Chiltern plateau, Cotswolds, north Norfolk, Forest of Dean, southeast Wales, and sporadically in southern England. I have found rare ancient stools, big enough to date from before the planting era, even near Durham. Soils include acid gravels, acid clays, thin chalk soils, and limestone scree and cliffs; the sites have little in common, except that many have a history as common wood-pasture.

As an introduced tree beech prospers and grows from seed almost from end to end of the British Isles. Occasional beech pollards on boundaries, outside beech areas, possibly represent early planting as distinctive markers. There are various kinds of evidence for its native distribution:

- place-names: unfortunately 'beech' is confusable with 'beach', 'book' and 'buck';
- archaeological finds of wood, charcoal or cupules;
- historical records naming the tree;
- ancient living trees (pollards and coppice stools); and
- pollen analysis (although few pollen deposits are from surviving beech sites).

Watt and Tansley classified native beechwoods into three categories: 'heathy' (*Fagetum ericetosum*) on strongly acid soils; 'brambly' (*F. rubosum*) in the middle of the range; and 'calcicolous' (*F. calcicolum*) on thin chalk and limestone soils. These were further subdivided on the basis of their ground vegetation. Calcicolous beechwoods comprised those with sanicle (on thin soils), with dog's-mercury (on deeper soils), and the curious beechwoods with ramsons on limestone scree.[14] Peterken and the NVC each recognise six types within the Lowland Zone; those of the NVC approximate to Tansley's.

Beech and early modern forestry

Most beechwoods have a peculiar structure, with only standard trees – nearly all beech, sometimes with a scatter of oak, ash, or cherry. Underwood is often absent, but there may be a few hornbeam stools, sometimes along internal wood-banks. They are not plantations, although they may look like it: they have a history of management for timber by the 'selection system'. Single stems or small groups were felled, the stumps died and were replaced by seedlings. Beech, being shade-bearing, lends itself to this treatment; many beechwoods have thickets of saplings awaiting the next felling to get away.

This type of woodland (Figs 113, 115, 116)has been in existence just long enough to be thought traditional. It is, however, an early form of modern forestry, dating from the end of the eighteenth century. Previously the beechwoods had been less monotonous: mixed coppices with a predominance of beech, or wood-pastures with pollard beech. These earlier structures survive in Epping Forest with its great pollards (p.324ff), Felbrigg Beeches (Norfolk), Frithsden Beeches (Berkhamsted) and parts of the New Forest. Coppice beech can be seen around Bix and Nettlebed (Oxfordshire Chilterns), and Westridge Wood (Wotton-under-Edge, Cotswolds, with its remarkable ramsons carpet).

The conversion to beech timberwoods has Continental parallels, especially in France where beech is still the staple of modern forestry. For the Chilterns it has been investigated by Leslie Hepple and Alison Doggett. Beech had not been much of a timber tree. Evelyn in *Sylva* (1664) said beech was 'good only for *shade* and for *Fire*', though by the 1706 edition he wanted to ban its use in making cheap furniture. The timber-framed houses of the Chilterns are made of oak. The job of Chiltern beechwoods was to provide London with fuel, a market that largely disappeared in the late eighteenth century with the growing coal trade and the coming of canals. This vacuum was filled by the growth of the Wycombe furniture industry: 'not a traditional rural craft, but a response to new market opportunities'. Craftsmen did not wait for trees to grow to timber size: the components (except for elm chair seats) were quite small and were made in the woods from large underwood. Gradually the processes became mechanised in factories and came to use bigger trees. For a short time there was a symbiosis between the industry and the woods, but then the timber trade became globalised and the factories got much of their material from America. Beech has to be grown in competition with France, which grows it better (especially through not yet having grey squirrels). The state of the Chiltern beechwoods is a monument to the industrial use of a century ago.[15]

Prehistory and early history

Beech got to Britain (and Ireland?) in wildwood times (p.71f), but on present information it was scarce for the first 2,500 years. From the Neolithic onwards it locally increased and was often dominant, but not necessarily where it is now. Because this increase did not happen in previous interglacials, some have inferred that it was due to human activity, but the nature of that activity remains obscure.[16] Beech does not readily invade felled woodland like birch, or abandoned farmland like oak; it was not a favourite hedgerow or homestead tree like elm; until recently it was not a favourite timber. It is, however, a characteristic wood-pasture tree.

A regular succession in wood-pastures is from lime to oak to beech, and recently to holly. This is clear, first from the pollen record and then from written records, in Epping Forest; different stages can be demonstrated in the New Forest (where the original lime stage gave rise to place-names like *Lyndhurst*), the Forest of Dean (where the surrounding woods are full of lime), the Avon Gorge woods at Bristol, the Forêt de Fontainebleau (France) and Draved in Denmark. Somehow the rise of browsing discourages lime and its decline encourages holly.

Beech has disappeared as a native from much of its prehistoric range and is now only a planted tree. Most of the disappearances were before historic times, although in Writtle Forest (Essex) there were huge pollard beeches even in the fifteenth century.

OAKWOODS

Oak can occur in seven situations (Table 18). This chapter and the next are restricted to the third: long-established woods in which oak is naturally so abundant that woodmen have coppiced it. Oakwoods in this sense are the commonest woodland type in the Highland Zone, but in the Lowland Zone are uncommon and specialised. They have three characteristics:

1. Oak is usually sessile oak – *Quercus petræa*, the oak of oakwoods. (The existence of two oaks, known to some botanists since 1586, was apparently not recorded by woodmen until the 1790s.)
2. Oakwoods are on the most acidic and infertile soils, especially leached hilltops, in which few other trees will grow.
3. Oak in this context is gregarious: oak stools are not scattered among other species as timber oaks usually are.

Oakwoods usually contain big stools, the product of centuries of coppicing. Among the intermingled trees are birch, occasionally chestnut and beech. Ground vegetation is often limited to bracken or *Deschampsia flexuosa* (the woodland grass of very acid soils), sometimes with woodrush (*Luzula sylvatica*) or bluebell. The many coppicing plants come mainly from buried seed, such as foxglove, heather and cow-wheat.

Relation between oakwoods and woods of other species: the Grovely Ridge[17]

On the chalk ridge west of Salisbury are three big woods: Grovely Forest, Stockton Wood and Great Ridge. All three appear to have a history of compartmental wood-pasture. The chalk ridge is mantled with a plateau of Clay-with-Flints, the middle of which is capped with loess.

There are three well-defined woodland types. Chalk-derived soils have ashwood. Acid clay soils have maple – hazel, or in one place the famous Ebsbury Beeches. On the loess plateau there is an abrupt transition to coppiced oak, in this case *robur*. Oakwood soils (pH 3.5 – 4.5) produce mor humus.

The woodland is partly ancient secondary: it overlies Iron Age settlements and enclosures, and part of it is described as heath in an Anglo-Saxon perambulation. It is threaded lengthwise by the prehistoric Grim's Ditch. The oakwood is an ancient feature, as shown by the huge stools (up to 16 feet (5 metres) across). The Grovely survey of 1566 mentions 'divers crooked oaks to get firewood from' (*pro Fyerwood inde habendo*).

Lowland distribution of oakwood

Oakwood is rare in East Anglia, becoming more common westward. In the Bradfield Woods, Suffolk, with their complex soil and vegetation patterns, the largest of the acidic sand-lenses has a few oak stools (but not sessile oak). Norfolk has a few patches of typical oakwood – they look like outliers of Scotland – in Swanton Novers Great Wood (Fig. 114) and others on acid, gravelly soils. In the Blean (Kent) and on similar terrain in southeast Essex patches of oakwood occupy gravelly ridgetops, with chestnut, hornbeam and (in Blean) beech on lower, less infertile ground. Oakwood becomes more common approaching the Highland Zone. Piles Coppice (p.207f) is typical of Warwickshire woods, with a patch of predominantly *petræa* oakwood. In Dorset many woods of other species, with *robur* standards, suddenly switch to patches of brackeny oak coppice that is *petræa*.

The boundary of the Highland Zone, of the present region of dominant oakwood, and of the Oak – Hazel Province of wildwood times (p.72), corresponds, in the main, to the extent of Palæozoic geology. Rainfall, moreover, rises from about 20 inches (500 millimetres) a year in East Anglia to 40 inches (1,000 millimetres) at the edge of the Highland Zone. If this difference has existed throughout the Holocene, there will have been twice as much leaching in Dorset as in Norfolk. More soils in the west than in the east are thus impoverished to the point of supporting only oakwood.

CHESTNUT-WOODS

The boundary between plantation and woodland is blurred with sweet-chestnut. Chestnut is apparently a Roman introduction that has persisted and spread; before pollen analysis it was undecided whether it was native.

In the Middle Ages it was a rare woodland tree, valued chiefly for nuts. Chestnut produces abundant nuts, though not every year, and now grows from seed more readily than the other big-seeded trees. The nuts are, as Evelyn put it, 'a lusty, and masculine food for *Rustics*' ; in southern Europe there are special varieties bearing big nuts that are easier to skin. It is very long lived. The Tortworth Chestnut (Gloucestershire), possibly the survivor of an orchard, has been celebrated since the fourth edition of his *Sylva* as a famous ancient tree (p.190).

History of chestnut

Is chestnut native or not? This was the earliest question in historical ecology, argued in the *Philosophical Transactions* of the Royal Society in 1769–72. Daines Barrington, correspondent of Gilbert White, argued that chestnut was a comparatively recent introduction; Hasted, the Kentish antiquary, and his colleagues claimed that it was 'the indigenous growth of Britain, planted by the hand of nature'. Arguments now familiar were used: historical records, ancient stools and pollards, place-names, timbers in ancient buildings, ability of chestnut to grow from seed, presence or absence of planting rows. Not all the data were sound: the place-names are still dubious, and most of the timbers were misidentified. In logic, Hasted produced the better case; but as often happens in science the more respectable man won. Barrington's argument passed into tradition and Hasted's was forgotten.[18]

Where chestnut came from is uncertain; as a native it is apparently confined to parts of southern Europe and Turkey. Archaeologists have identified its wood or charcoal at many Roman sites from Essex to Dorset. Its pollen is unknown in prehistoric deposits, apart from odd grains dismissed as contamination with modern pollen. It is thus an archæophyte (p.30), introduced probably by the Romans, which has persisted and has become a component of native vegetation.

Chestnut-woods are abundant in southeast England and in coastal districts from Essex to Norfolk. Many are plantations on former non-woodland sites, but others occupy ancient woods. How did they get there, and what happened to the previous trees? Chestnut stools are typically 3 to 4 feet (0.9 to 1.2 metres) diameter, suggesting an eighteenth-century date (p.203), but bigger ones are not uncommon. Medieval records are mainly in two areas: the site called Chestnuts in the Forest of Dean, and south of Sittingbourne in Kent.

As underwood chestnut excels wherever rot-resistance or cleavage matter. In the Middle Ages, chestnut wood seems not to have been specially regarded: it should be looked for in the wattle-and-daub of timber-framed houses in southeast England. Evelyn commends chestnut as providing the best hop-poles. It became fashionable as underwood in the eighteenth and nineteenth centuries: evidently the high price that it fetched outweighed its greater durability and thus smaller volume of sales.

As timber the tree has never been much grown, for it has a reputation for developing shakes (p.222). This has not prevented it from being a favourite timber in much of the Mediterranean, where carpentry is simpler and makes fewer demands on the material.

Chestnut today

Chestnut-woods have long been thought of as a recent artefact, neglected by ecologists. They are nearly always on acid soils (the Tortworth Chestnut being an exception). In *Ancient Woodland* I recognised three types, associated with lime, hornbeam and sessile oak. The NVC relegates them all to a variant of acid oakwood.

Chestnut stools in ancient woodland could result from various processes: survivals of Roman chestnut orchards; deliberate destruction of hornbeam or oak coppice and replacement with chestnut; and the tendency of chestnut to spread naturally from planted stands (ancient or modern) and take over existing woods. So far, the evidence for replanting remains circumstantial.

Chestnut still flourishes in Chestnuts, just inside the Forest of Dean, where Flaxley Abbey had the tithe of chestnuts in the twelfth century. The site adjoins Welshbury, the limewood crowned with a hillfort (p.179), which has a few ancient chestnut stools. This area could well be derived from a Roman chestnut orchard. Most of the woods in the medieval localities near Sittingbourne have been grubbed out. Other possible derivatives of Roman introduction have stools 15 feet (4½ metres) or more in diameter, as in Holbrook Park (southeast Suffolk) and Stour Wood (northeast Essex). Chalkney Wood, one of the few woods for which there are records of its underwood composition 400 years ago,[19] then apparently had no chestnut, but it now has stools scattered among lime and hornbeam. Since the biggest stools are only some 4 feet (1.2 metres) across it is probably derived from trees planted around 1700 and generations of their children.

In Kent, there are monotonous stands of chestnut, often with little else except birch and the occasional oak, with uniform, middle-sized stools, yet within

Fig 152. Blackmoor Vale from below Dogbury (p.386). *September 2002*.

Scenes from the physical Forest of Blackmoor: **Figs 153–157.** See p.397. **Fig 153.** Failed plantation, which has damaged the wood without producing timber. *Prince's Wood, April 2004*.

Fig 154. Surviving hazel-wood with wild daffodils. *Prince's Wood, March 2005*.

Fig 155. Woodbank, with remains of its hedge, amid a successful plantation. *West-upon-Hurdley Coppice, March 2005.*

Fig 156. Intact alder-wood on a big landslip. *Lyons Wood, April 2004.*

Fig 157. Ancient farmland oak. *Hartley, March 2005.*

Fig 158. A fallow-deer exclosure. It was set up in 1968, when the density of oxlip plants was roughly the same inside and out. After 25 years, oxlip has almost disappeared outside, but remains abundant inside. This is the scene in the year after coppicing: the pollard ashes inside the fence have sprouted all up the trunk, those outside only above the deer browseline. *Hayley Wood, April 1993. See p.408.*

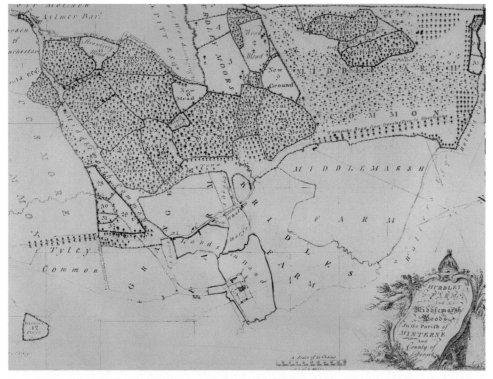

Fig 159. Isaac Taylor's map of the Cerne Abbey – later Winchester College – part of Blackmoor Forest, *c*.1770 (Dorset Record Offce). North to right. See p.395.

Fig 160. Scene in Buff Wood, Cambridgeshire, photographed by Peter Sell in April 1963. Prodigious flowering of oxlip, especially on the left.

Fig 161. The same, April 2005. The area to the left was coppiced in 1991. This photograph has been repeated 21 times in all, showing that oxlip greatly declined on the ride in the 1970s and 1980s (though it remains abundant in the adjacent wood); grasses (especially *Deschampsia cespitosa*) and *Rumex sanguineus* became dominant in the late 1980s; brambles flourished in the 1990s after coppicing; and ivy on trees has slowly increased. See p.409.

Fig 162. A Texas savanna. Note exposed limestone in foreground. *Valley Mills, August 1983.*

Fig 163. The same 20 years later. Note infilling by juniper: the viewpoint has had to be changed slightly. The dead tree on the left is still there, but now hidden. *August 2003.* See p.410.

Fig 164. What little was left of Hainault Forest (Essex) became a public place in 1906 (p.417). *May 1991.*

Fig 165. Californian savanna of native trees (the live-oak *Quercus agrifolia*) and exotic grasses. *Ukiah, April 2005.* See p.421.

Fig 166. A wood with the bottom eaten out by deer (p.424). Thirty years before, it had been the best oxlip wood in England. *Hempstead, Essex, April 2002*.

Fig 167. Effect of Japanese deer in Dorset (p.425). Note the lack of low cover, especially ivy. *West Creech Great Wood, June 2000*.

Fig 168. Effect of Japanese deer in Japan (p.425). *Mount Odaigahara, October 1998.*

Oaks of Moccas Park, Herefordshire, May 1998: **Fig 169–170.**
Fig 169. The Beetle Oak.

Fig 170. The Club Oak.

medieval woodbanks. Landowners apparently went to the trouble of grubbing or otherwise exterminating the original woodland – maybe oak or hornbeam – and substituting chestnut. This would have been a considerable industry: except in bracken glades, converting a wood to chestnut would require hardly less labour than converting it to arable land, yet neither of the books on Kentish woods[20] reveals how or when it was done. (See also Markshall, p.376f.)

ALDER-WOODS

Alder is one of the few trees with a narrow habitat requirement, for moving water. It is the familiar non-woodland tree on river banks, where its water-borne seeds germinate along flood-lines. It is not otherwise particular as to soil; in the Bradfield Woods (Suffolk) the pH under alder ranges from 3.3 to 7.3. Fen alder-woods are nearly always secondary, on abandoned meadow (p.158f). Alder forms coppice stools, which in the Bradfield Woods incorporate great mounds of woody debris.

Alder grows within ancient woodland along spring-lines and flushes. Typical situations are the *ghylls* of the Weald (ravines that penetrate a spring-line) and the landslips of west Dorset (Fig. 104).

There is a rarer kind of alder-wood, mixed with other trees, on plateaux irrigated, at least in winter, by seeps of water at contacts between boulder-clay and deposits of loess or sand. The classic site is the Bradfield Woods. Alder avoids waterlogged sites in which the water is stagnant: in woods such as Hayley these give rise to an aspen variant of mixed ashwood.

Alder-woods of all types tend to have ramsons and sometimes nettle as ground vegetation. They join on to many kinds of surrounding woodland, often with an intervening ash–hazel zone. Peterken has four variants, differing in acidity of the flush water, within ancient woodland. The NVC recognises only one in the Lowland Zone, alder–ashwood with nettle and yellow pimpernel (*Lysimachia nemorum*).

Alder is well represented in archives. In the Middle Ages it did many of the jobs for which conifers are now used. The Hindolveston (Norfolk) accounts in the thirteenth and fourteenth centuries mention woodland and non-woodland alder; the surviving wood still contains plateau alder.

Alder has root-nodule bacteria that fix nitrogen and fertilise the soil. This property has been utilised in a particular form of tree'd farmland in northern Italy.[21] As far as I know it has not been consciously used in Britain, although it probably makes a difference to small pasture-fields with alder in the hedges in Wales and southwest England.

CHAPTER 15

SOME TYPES OF WOODLAND

Highland Zone and Ireland

Despite the immense size of the charcoal store, there was at least as much land under oakwood in Argyll when [the ironworks] ceased operations in 1876 as when they commenced in 1753.

T.C. SMOUT, A.R. MACDONALD & F. WATSON ON THE LORN BLAST FURNACE

This chapter concerns southwest England, Wales and the Welsh Border, the Pennines and North York Moors, and southern Scotland (see Fig.1). This region corresponds roughly to that of Palæozoic rocks and closely to the Oak–Hazel Province in prehistory (see Fig. 31). Many woods adjoin moorland as well as farmland. I also include most surviving Irish woods; little survives of the prevalence of elm in wildwood times.

Woods are somewhat less uniquely different from each other than in the Lowland Zone. However, as the *National Vegetation Classification* showed, there is more variation if bryophytes and lichens are taken into account as well as flowering plants. The latter might display more diversity if they had not been browsed into extinction by sheep, as is shown by the oakwoods of Cornwall, which have escaped that fate.

The effects of tree-planting are widespread and sometimes difficult to detect. Anyone who travels through mid-Wales knows how seldom woods there lack conifers, even though no conifer (except yew) is indigenous.

HIGHLAND-ZONE OAKWOODS

Ancient oakwoods are by far the commonest type from Cornwall to Argyll and from Yorkshire to Killarney (Figs 117–120). They share some characteristics of their Lowland outliers: acid, leached soils with mor humus; prevalent *Quercus petræa* rather than *robur*; scarcity of other trees; and calcifuge ground vegetation, with bracken and *Deschampsia flexuosa*. Often they are on rocky slopes and screes.

Most of these woods have ancient coppice stools, though stool bases may be lower and less conspicuous than in Lowland oakwoods. Many, however, contain timber trees only – perhaps with a few stools in inaccessible places. Often this results from oak-replacement planting.

The woods around Sheffield have been investigated by Mel Jones (1998). Originally there were extensive wood-pastures, encoppiced in the later Middle Ages and used to supply the edge-tool and nail-making industries of Sheffield with charcoal. This use in turn declined in the nineteenth century, when most of the woods were replanted or at least oak-replaced.

An ancient oakwood: Mugdock Wood
Twelve miles (19 kilometres) northwest of Glasgow is a wood to which I was introduced by James Dickson, Scottish ecological historian. It is defined by banks and massive walls, though the wood now spreads well beyond its former limits. The geology is boulder-clay overlying basalt; the soils are strongly acid.

The wood is of oak and birch, with cherry, hazel and many others. Along a stream are ash and a few elms. The oaks are a mixture of the two species and hybrids; few are coppiced, but there are stools up to 8 feet (2½ metres) in diameter. Nearly all the alder and some ash consist of coppice stools. The wood is varied in structure; there are extensive bracken glades, now partly infilled with oak and birch. In shaded areas there are wood-sage and *Deschampsia flexuosa*; the generally grassy appearance may be due to roe deer.

A pollen diagram from a nearby moor shows birch as the dominant tree since Mesolithic times, with some hazel, alder and oak, but only traces of pine.[1] The area contains abundant prehistoric antiquities and is traversed by the Roman Antonine Wall. The place-name Mugdock is Welsh (Maesiddwg). The wood is documented back to the time of King Alexander III in the thirteenth century; it appears on Roy's military map of c.1755. In the eighteenth century it was regarded as an oak coppice.[2]

This wood (like others around Glasgow) seems to have been a permanent coppice with fixed boundaries, on the English model. Internally it has been unstable, with periods of neglect and recovery and of shifts between oak and birch. Other mountain woods are like this, for example, around Strata Florida in mid-Wales. An unexpected recent change is the increase in ash, growing from seed despite the deer. The next generation of trees is likely to make this an acid ashwood.

Oak replacement: Inchcailloch

The 'bonnie, bonnie banks o' Loch Lomond' are lined with steep, ancient oakwoods. These have a history as coppices supplying bark (p.225f), small timber for boat-building, and wood for that romantic enterprise, a pyroligneous acid factory (a kind of wood-burning gasworks).[3] (Does its ghost yet haunt chemistry textbooks, as it did in my schooldays?)*

Professor Dickson introduced me to some of the odd and mysterious islands, and asked my opinion on Inchcailloch, which had been declared a National Nature Reserve in 1962 for its oakwoods.

Inchcailloch (about 150 acres/60 ha), called 'Old Woman's Island' or 'Nuns' Island' after a convent founded in the eighth century, is said to have been a deer-park of King Robert the Bruce. It has a record as a coppice-wood from the seventeenth century down to 1845, involving sales to tanneries and ironworks. A fifteenth-century record, however, refers to timber. Although rocky, it also has a farming history and a church, and is supposed to have been 're-afforested with oak in the 1770s'.[4]

Oakwood now covers almost the whole island, including the ridge-and-furrow of former fields, but the oaks are not those of an ancient coppice. Nine oaks out of ten are timber trees, evenly and rather closely spaced, uniform and apparently a hybrid between the two native species; they lack the gnarled bases of oaks promoted from former coppice stools. They are evidently a plantation of *c.*1890. Some, uprooted in the hurricane of 1968, are still flourishing.

But this is not the whole story. Here and there, great oaks of markedly spreading habit had evidently been big, widely spaced trees before the planted oaks enveloped them. There are remains of a previous plantation of pines from the 1820s and 1840s. By careful search we found about 150 oak coppice stools, a few of them 6 feet (2 metres) in diameter, on cliffs and ridgetops or on the shore. There are also ash and alder stools in inland fens and on the less steep shores.

Inchcailloch has little of the infrastructure of an ancient oakwood. It has been replanted twice (three times if the 1770 story is to be believed). Before then it may have been less oak-dominated than it is now. The native trees were exterminated

---

* In Japan I met a man who made pyroligneous acid as an 'organic' pesticide.

and replaced, but not completely: some stools were overlooked in out-of-the-way places, and a few maiden oaks, perhaps standard trees in the coppice, were spared

Other examples

Around Sheffield there was so much replanting in the late nineteenth century that intact native oakwoods are now few. Yarncliff Wood, Hathersage, lies in a side-valley of the Derbyshire Derwent.[5] Most of it is even-aged sessile oak, with a few remaining pines, apparently dating from a replanting in *c.*1870: the Ordnance Survey map of 1876–80 records coniferous mixed with deciduous tree symbols (p.147). The planted oaks are all sessile and somewhat variable, suggesting a local provenance less strongly selected than usual. A few coppice stools survive, especially on unplantable rock outcrops; the oak stools indicate many previous centuries of felling and regrowth. A tract of hazel grows where a flush provides a patch of more fertile soil. Charcoal-hearths and a kiln witness to an industrial history. The plantation ends at a boundary wall, not including the whole of the original wood; outside it oak coppice stools continue, around a quarry where millstones were hewn from Millstone Grit, to the edge of the moor. This moorland edge is not demarcated; a fringe of birch marks a phase of expansion of woodland.

Yarner Wood, a great wood on the edge of Dartmoor, has a most complex history. Outside its ancient woodbank are plantations and natural woods on former fields. The interior is divided between coppice and timber areas. The timber oaks are all sessile, uniform in age and appearance and of good timber quality, probably planted *c.*1870. Coppice oaks, which include ancient stools, are variable; occasional relict stools lurk among the planted oaks.

Irish timberwoods

Oak coppices were probably not uncommon in Ireland before modern forestry (Fig. 121). Surviving examples include Kilteel Wood, Co. Kildare (embanked like an English wood) and fragments on steep slopes in Co. Waterford.

The *Civil Survey* of the 1650s often specifies 'Timberwoods', a category that would have been unfamiliar to English surveyors. These, presumably, yielded the high-quality timber implied by the Irish barrel-stave industry of the seventeenth century. Some Irish oakwoods today lack coppice stools and yet do not have the uniformity of planted oak. Portlaw Wood, Co. Waterford, probably a surviving part of the Great Wood of Kilconish, has remains of a variable stand of big timber trees, all *Quercus petræa* and having the variability of wild-type oaks (Fig. 122). Another, containing old oaks, is the old wood of Charleville (Co. Offaly), on an island in a bog. The origin, dynamics and functioning of such woods need investigating.

Oak replacement, widespread in Ireland, may account for the notion that Ireland had little history of coppicing. At Glen of the Downs (Co. Wicklow) a well-constructed earth road separates coppiced sessile oak, with stools up to 7 feet (2 metres) in diameter, from a uniform stand of maiden trees, also sessile, apparently of c.1840. In Tomies Wood, Killarney, most of the oaks are attributed to a planting of 1805 (my ring-counts make them a little later). Although widely spaced for a plantation, they are uniform in size and appearance, and appear not to be pure sessile oak as would be expected in southwest Ireland. Between them grow small pollard hollies. One rectangular compartment of the wood escaped planting and remains as regular oak coppice. Most of the oaks in Derrycunihy, another Killarney oakwood, appear to be of similar origin, although a few coppice stools survive. A pollen diagram from within the wood shows that it had a long history of roughly equal quantities of oak and birch. The replacement of birch by more oak is clearly shown in the uppermost layer of the deposit: 'at no time in the last 5,000 years has *Quercus* had such a dominance in Derrycunihy Wood'.[6]

Other trees in oakwoods

Many oakwoods now contain little but oak, sometimes with patches of hazel or alder. The commonest associated trees are birch and rowan, or holly in Cornwall and Ireland.

Many oakwoods were once more mingled with other trees. Where oak was wanted for bark, other species might be extirpated. In Scotland these were called 'barren timber' and might be felled at any time of year, whereas oak was sometimes restricted to early summer when the bark would peel.[7] How energetically or effectively extirpation was applied would have varied from place to place: it has had no lasting effect on Mugdock Wood. At least as important may have been browsing, which would favour oak as relatively unpalatable and more likely to recover from damage.

Ground vegetation

Highland-Zone oakwoods can develop specifically woodland vegetation, including buried-seed coppicing plants, like Lowland woods. This is best seen in woods among farmland, as in Cornwall or middle Monmouthshire. Many woods, especially if they adjoin moorland, have three other types of ground vegetation. The flora may be nothing but grasses or bracken, the wood being little more than grassland with trees. Or it may be reduced to heather, the wood being moorland with trees. Or there may be a rich bryophyte flora, as in many woods of the far west of Scotland and Ireland.

The *National Vegetation Classification* is at its best when dealing with oak–birch-woods, recognising nine subcommunities, distinguished mainly by their ground vegetation (including ferns), with some contribution from ground bryophytes.

Livestock have been let into woods, either deliberately or by not maintaining the boundary fences or walls. In Scotland this was a regular practice, to the extent that a landowner wanting to fence a wood after felling it was obliged to compensate tenants for the pasture lost. Woods were used especially, but not exclusively, by cattle and in winter; having woodland dispensed farmers from keeping beasts indoors and giving them hay and straw. Woodland was valued as shelter, but the pasture was worth having. What was that pasture?[8]

Some grasses, such as *Anthoxanthum odoratum,* tolerate shade but are tenuous and of little nutritional value. Other woodland plants are distasteful, or poisonous, or die down in winter, although brambles and dead leaves might serve as iron rations. Most bryophytes are not eaten. Holly might be pollarded for animals to browse, as in the famous hollins of the Stiperstones (Shropshire) and in the Pennines and possibly Killarney, although Smout has few examples from Scotland. However, when Sir John Sinclair referred to 'the fine strong grass with which the woods abounded'[9] this must mean that the woods were sparse enough to have real grassland between, not just under, the trees: they were not really woodland, but tree'd grassland. (According to Monteath's *Forester's Guide* (1814), an oakwood ought to have stools only 8 feet (2½ metres) apart, which would have precluded any pasturage; but this was a counsel of perfection, seldom achieved.)

This history doubtless explains why many Highland-Zone woods are poor in woodland flowering plants. Browsing would have subtracted most of the characteristic woodland plants, eaten when they emerged in the hungry season of late winter and early spring. It might have prevented a 'normal' woodland flora, with buried-seed plants and others adapted to coppicing, from ever arising.

HAZEL-WOODS AND HAZEL–ASHWOODS

Hazel-woods survive less often than oakwoods, probably because hazel grew on more fertile soils and was grubbed out to make farmland. Many an oakwood has patches of hazel within it, often on less infertile soils (marked, for example, by bluebell instead of bracken).

The extent of Highland-Zone hazel-woods, however, is probably under-recorded. More extensive hazel-woods can survive; I have seen one in lowland Aberdeenshire. The most remarkable are on the west coast and islands, woods in an extreme Atlantic climate (a temperate rainforest) with many special lichens, including at least one known from nowhere else in the world. They are supposed not to have been coppiced, although this seems hardly likely in an area with little woodland, and Smout gives a record of hazel 'cabers' for roofing.[10]

Hazel – ashwoods are frequent on limestone, as in South Wales. Peterken recognises three Highland types, and the NVC adds a fourth. A famous example is Rassall Ashwood on Loch Kishorn.

An Atlantic hazel-wood

The Burren, that famous limestone plateau in west Ireland, is an outlier of the dry, sunny, flowery *garrigues* of the Mediterranean; it may have been less distinctive in the past when it had more soil (since vanished into the underworld of karst caverns). It has long been noted for its hazel 'scrub'. The *Civil Survey* of the 1650s has many entries of 'rockie dwarf wood'.

At the base of Slieve Carran, beneath the towering east-facing cliff of Eagle's Rock, is a dense hazel-wood.* It is a nameless but sacred wood, for here (the Ordnance Survey avers) are the ruins of St Mac Duagh's Church, his Bed, the Grave of his Servant, and his Penitential Stations. A cluster of tiny fields could have been where the hermit grew his beans and cabbages, as holy men still do on Mount Athos.

Physically, too, it is an extreme of what woodland can do, a place not quite of this world. The wood is almost all hazel, with stools up to 6 feet (2 metres) in diameter. There are occasional ashes, all of them huge stools 5 to 8 feet (1½ to 2½ metres) across (Figs 123, 124). These establish that it is an ancient coppice-wood, last cut probably more than a century ago. Unusually, ash shows no sign of taking over the wood.

The ground is rounded limestone boulders, evidently a Pleistocene scree that has been so long without moving that the sharp edges have been dissolved away by karst action. Pleurocarpous mosses and liverworts form a thick ground layer and hide treacherous gaps between boulders; they form bulging masses on hazel stems, as in cloud-forests on tropical mountains. Everything not moss-covered is lichen-covered. Ferns and sparse flowering plants struggle through the bryophytes; one of the commonest is helleborine (*Epipactis helleborine*).

The wood is not specifically mentioned in the *Civil Survey*. The Ordnance Survey

* I am indebted to Dr Sasha van der Sleesen for introducing me to this wood. It is a breakneck place and should not be visited too much because of damage to bryophytes.

of 1840 and its successors down to 1913 show it only as scree. However, the ash and hazel stools leave no doubt that at least the upper part is ancient woodland. It was visited by the British Vegetation Committee in 1908; it was then 15 to 20 feet (4½ to 6 metres) high and contained much the same plants as it does now. Sir Arthur Tansley, who took a dim view of 'scrub', admitted that it could have 'a perfectly good woodland flora, though not numerous in species'.[11]

The wood has probably extended downhill in the twentieth century. Wind-stunted, goat-bitten hazels are scattered in the fissures of the adjacent karst plateau. The wood itself shows little sign of browsing except on hawthorn. In the past it may have had a functional wall separating it from the pasture.

An Irish mixed hazel-wood: St John's Wood

This is a huge wood (for Ireland) of 200 acres (81 ha) on flattish ground between a bog and Lough Ree. The free edges are bounded by a massive wall. The wood is a coppice, last felled c.1920; a small area was cut c.1990. It is remarkable for its rich flora; it has almost all the possible Irish trees and shrubs except *Arbutus*.

There are two distinct types of woodland. Most of it is dominated by hazel stools, with occasional ash, wych-elm, crab, bird-cherry and cherry, and a scatter of small timber oaks and oak stumps. Ash and hazel form big stools. Ash is on the increase. The oaks are mostly *robur*, rare as a native in Ireland. Soils are chiefly mull, possibly overlying karst limestone. The ground is covered in ivy, primrose and bryophytes (but not dog's-mercury, uncommon in Ireland). Here, too, the hazels are mantled in bryophytes. At the bog and lough edges the wood is fringed by spindle, blackthorn and other shrubs.

Here and there are patches of coppiced oakwood, mingled with holly, hazel, birch and occasionally *Sorbus hibernica* (the only tree endemic to Ireland). These have mor humus and are carpeted with *Luzula sylvatica*, the common ground vegetation of ungrazed oakwoods. The oak stools are up to 12 feet (3.6 metres) across.

As a varied mixed coppice, probably of monastic antecedents, this is the Irish equivalent to the Bradfield Woods. It is one of the very few surviving descendants of the Hazel – Elm Province of wildwood times, predominantly calcareous and even retaining a few wych-elm stools.

OTHER WOODLAND TYPES

Alder-wood

Alder occurs on flushed sites within Highland, as in Lowland, woods. It is especially common in South Wales, where *gwern*, 'alders', is one of the common-est tree place-names. Its unpalatability to sheep would favour it. Peterken has four types of Highland alder-wood, one characterised by bird-cherry.

Outliers of elm-, lime- and beechwoods
As outliers of oakwood occur in infertile parts of the Lowland Zone, so do outliers of Lowland woodland types in the more fertile parts of Highland woods.

Small patches of elm occur throughout Wales, Scotland and Highland England, often as groups of huge wych-elm stools within other types of woodland. Elm, very palatable, has probably lost ground to browsing; it tends to survive on cliffs or in woods among farmland. Peterken recognises three Highland-Zone variants of ash–wych-elm wood.

Swaledale (Yorkshire), with its extensive limestone, is one of the largest areas of the British Isles with no oak. In historic times elm was one of the commonest trees; it survives as great stools (along with yew, also susceptible to browsing) high on cliffs.

Patches of lime occur in Devon, South and mid-Wales and the Lake District, up to the limits that the tree reached in wildwood times. Often they are in ravines or on rocky ground, although the connection is weaker than with elm.

Ancient beechwoods extend into the Forest of Dean, Wye Gorge and south-east corner of Wales, on both limestone and acidic rocks and on wood-pasture and woodland sites. They reach high altitudes on Mount Blorenge between Aber-gavenny and Blaenavon. Blaenavon Beeches include a coppice-wood at 1,100 feet (335 metres), which nevertheless produces seedlings. The Punchbowl is a tract of surrealistic beech pollards at a similar elevation, affected by avalanches that roar down from the mountain above. This is one of the nearest approximations in Britain to a natural tree line, as with the tree-limit beeches in the outer French Alps and in the Balkans.

The Highland-Zone catena
In many places, in the mountains of Britain and in the glens of the south of Ireland, a wood occupies a steep valley-side of some relatively infertile rock. Typically the upper and middle slope is oakwood (or oak–holly), with hazel on the footslope, a narrow fringe of elm at the bottom, and alder lining the stream. I interpret this as sequence due to a *catena* of soil development: thousands of years of rain have washed out minerals from the upper and middle slope, to accumu-late at the base where the more demanding trees take advantage of them.

CHAPTER 16

CALEDONIAN PINEWOODS

Natural ecosystems have a great propensity for resilience and self-regeneration, but not when you wedge them in a corner with nowhere to go. Scottish native woodlands will happily seed and naturally regenerate given the opportunity, but do not readily do so beneath their own canopies, and historically have quietly pottered about the landscape as seedlings established beyond the limits of the existing tree cover.
ANDREW BERRY, 1997[1]

The Scottish Highlands and their woods are almost a different country from the rest of Scotland. The Scotch Fir or Caledonian Pine, queen of Scots trees, has three peculiarities:

1. it is killed by cutting it down;
2. it reproduces only by seed, and does so easily if the ground is somewhat disturbed; and
3. it is fire-adapted: it makes flammable resins and grows with fire-promoting plants such as heather. Fire is part of its ecology: a fire kills young pines, but some old trees survive, and a new generation arises from their seed. The fire cycle, however, needs to be not much shorter than a hundred years.

Even the familiar distinction between woodland and non-woodland hardly transfers to the Scottish Highlands. Pinewoods and birchwoods lack the fixed boundaries that are a defining feature of English or Lowland Scots woodland. They have no banks and ditches, and often one cannot say that one acre is woodland and another not. Woodland plants – those that grow in woodland but not moorland – are mainly mosses and liverworts rather than flowering plants.

Highland pinewoods are special because of the different behaviour of the trees. Highland birches, likewise, are shifty trees: they invade moorland (perhaps when browsing relaxes for a while) and live usually for one generation of birchwood before dying out. Birch, however, is not flammable and is less related to fire.

There are about a hundred Caledonian pinewoods scattered through the middle Highlands from northeast Argyll to the fringes of Sutherland: the big woods are along the Spey and Dee in the east. To the southwest is a region of oakwoods, to the north birchwoods, and hazel- and ashwoods to east and west.

The name Scots pine applies to the whole species *Pinus sylvestris*, which is unfortunate as most planted pines, even in Scotland, are introductions from Europe. Caledonian pine, *Pinus sylvestris* subspecies *scotica*, is endemic, peculiar to the Scottish Highlands. It is distinguished by its round-topped shape and short needles, and its thick bark at the base and thin red bark above (the correct combination for surviving a heather fire). (It has been claimed on genetic grounds that pines southeast of the Great Glen are less distinctive than those to the northwest.[2]) This is one of innumerable 'subspecies' of *P. sylvestris* forming clines (p.271) from Spain to Siberia. These in turn are part of the great subarctic belt of red pines extending round the globe, those in America and the Far East being regarded as different species. All are fire-adapted: for example, the Japanese and Korean *P. densiflora* has a history related to that of human burning.[3] They are highly gregarious: if Caledonian pine occurs at all, it is usually the dominant or only tree in a wood.

Caledonian pinewoods are among the best-studied native woodland of Britain, beginning with that pioneering work in historical ecology, *The Native Pinewoods of Scotland*, by H.M. Steven & A. Carlisle. The authors, excellent historians, made critical use of the materials available in 1957, including pollen analysis and early maps and written records. Their woodland history was written, as it should be, from the bottom up, being the sum of the separate histories of each native pinewood.

PINE IN PREHISTORY

Pines are very copious producers of pollen, which blows long distances and is the easiest of pollen grains to recognise. Soon after the last ice age, pine entered England and spread northwards, becoming the dominant tree over most of the landscape in succession to birch. With hazel it formed a plant community that is now difficult to visualise (p.71). It got into Ireland, and from Ireland into south-west Scotland, spreading northwards. It also, somehow, got into the northwest and spread southeastward.[4]

In England and south Scotland, pine was displaced by oak and other trees, leaving relicts (to die out much later) in the Lake District, the Fens and Ireland. In the middle and north Scottish Highlands a tract of subarctic vegetation was left, dominated by pine in the middle and by birch further north.

Why was this? Pine is not just a northern relict: even such a southern tree as beech fares well where introduced next to modern east Scottish pinewoods. Had fire, perhaps influenced by Mesolithic people, encouraged pine at the expense of its non-fire-adapted competitors? In wildwood times 'large Scots pine woods were a [peculiarly] Highland vegetation just as their remnants are now' (James Dickson). It is not yet known what part Caledonian pine played in this curiously complex story. Were the lost pines of England and Ireland of the Caledonian or Continental subspecies?

In the Boreal Period of dry climate, 8700–6200 BC, pine extended further north and to higher altitudes than it does now.[5] Since then the climate has got wetter and blanket peat has grown to cover much of the landscape, especially in the west. For a time, pines continued to grow on peat, as they still do in Sweden and Germany.

The present mosaic of pinewoods and birchwoods around Loch Maree has changed little for over 8,000 years. In the Dee basin, too, the Glen Tanar area has been dominated by pine since wildwood times. At higher altitudes birch predom-inated over pine, up to a tree-limit at about 2,300 feet (700 metres), a little above the present limit of pine.[6]

The Great Wood of Caledon
I was brought up on Fraser Darling's wonderful book, *Natural History in the High-lands and Islands,* published as New Naturalist no. 6 in 1947. Before me lies his evocation of the Great Wood of Caledon which – he claimed – had extended over the whole middle Scottish Highlands, joining up the present pinewoods. It was burnt down in the Viking wars, or burnt to deny cover to wolves, moss-ers and gallowglasses, and the remnants were felled by English businessmen in the eighteenth century, never to grow again. The destruction was progressive: a single felling or fire destroyed the forest forever. He wrote in sorrow and wrath of the continuing destruction of the (supposedly) meagre remnants of 'primeval' pine- and birchwood in the World Wars, and in apprehension at their future. The

woods, Darling thought, had been contracting for a thousand years until about one-twentieth remained. Had this continued that last remnant should be vanishing about now.

Darling did not invent the Great Wood of Caledon, but his great and well-earned authority gave further currency to the idea. To this day, guidebooks refer to the Highlands as an 'artificial' or devastated landscape, a sort of green desert which visitors appreciate but shouldn't. The restoration of the Caledonian Wood is dear to the heart of the Scottish Nationalists.

The Romans believed in a Wood of Caledon, *Caledonia silva*, which few of them had ever seen, in a vague and proverbial way, much as modern journalists think Cambridge is in the Fens.[7] Ptolemy, the second-century geographer who got no nearer Scotland than Egypt, had heard of a tribe called the Caledonii who lived east of a *Kaledónios drymos*, 'Caledonian Copse'. *Drymos* literally means 'place of deciduous oaks', but in Ancient Greek inscriptions it appears to mean 'coppice'.[8] Whatever Ptolemy meant, it does not easily construe into a vast pinewood. His map, copied and miscopied and recopied from his original manuscript, puts it vaguely in the middle Highlands. The belief was repeated many times by learned authors such as Hector Boece in the sixteenth century, but without fresh evidence.

Eighteenth- and nineteenth-century scholars thought they had confirmed a Caledonian Wood when abundant stumps and logs of trees were dug out of peat in the drainage operations then fashionable. (They ignored the Welsh claim that *Coit Celidon* – it would now be *Coed Celyddon* – where King Arthur fought was somewhere in the Southern Uplands.)

But knowledge accumulates. Steven & Carlisle showed that in general modern pinewoods were not the shrunken remains of much larger woods. They began to cast doubt on the reality of the Great Wood of Caledon, and the researches of James Dickson, Christopher Smout and D.J. Breeze have sent it to the dustbin of historical myths. Radiocarbon dating finds the bog-trees to be thousands, not hundreds, of years old. Their charred appearance is often misleading, the effect of blackening and cracking which waterlogged wood undergoes as it dries out. Pollen analysis shows that Scotland had lost most of its wildwood before the Romans came.[9]

Reports of woods being deliberately burnt are based on writings from centuries after the supposed event: Steven & Carlisle do not mention them. When historical records do appear, they refer to woods in definite places, mostly where there are still woods today. Records of logging by English and Scots entrepreneurs are nearly all from woods that still exist.

In historic times the Caledonian pinewoods have never been much more extensive than now. Romans, natives and English have cut down trees – how could they not have done? Woods have been burnt from time to time by lightning or accident or even deliberately. But boreal pinewoods are used to such disturbances, indeed probably need them to remain pinewoods; they recover, though not always in quite the same place. The theory of progressive destruction is no more plausible for Scotland than for anywhere else.

Why was there not a historic Great Caledonian Wood?
In Scotland, as in England, five-sixths of the original wildwood disappeared too early to be put on record. In England this is attributable to the inroads of early farmers creating fields, pastures and heaths. Scotland is different. The Highlands were much more densely peopled in the seventeenth century than now, and many a wood was nibbled away into fields and pastures at its lower edge. However, most Scottish pinewoods partly adjoin moorland: unless the blanket peat still hides vast Iron Age field systems like those of Dartmoor, wildwood usually went to moorland without an intervening phase as farmland.

Much of Scotland was always near the Arctic–Atlantic limit of tree growth. Woodland was a precarious and temporary phase of the early postglacial period, overwhelmed by the inexorable growth of blanket bogs as time passed, the climate grew wetter, and phosphate washed out of the soils.[10] The less favourable the environment for trees, especially in the northwest Highlands, the more readily farmers' livestock would prevent the trees from replacing themselves.

How far the great 'wilderness' of Scotland, the 'man-made desert' that Darling deplored, is indeed man-made or results from environment and the lapse of time, is debatable. In the northwest, environment was probably the dominant factor; trees now cling to rock outcrops and places where peat has not drowned them. In the drier, warmer, less peaty east and south, human activity predominated. Here pinewoods still grow by the square mile, despite centuries of browsing by cattle and goats.

The theory can be tested by asking how far cliffs differ from the rest of the landscape (p.217). To some extent they do in Scotland, but not always: many a low-altitude cliff is treeless.

HISTORY OF PINEWOODS

Middle Ages

Medieval Scotland was almost two countries. Almost all the action was in the south and east: Scots kings and nobles seldom ventured far into the Highlands. There are few records of pinewoods. Robin Callander tells me of the Bishop of Aberdeen's exploitation of the pinewoods of Birse on Deeside, where there are now very few pines. Castle Grant, on Speyside, has a fine late-medieval roof of presumably local pine. In the late Middle Ages the Bishops of Moray were in the habit of floating timber from Rothiemurchus down the Spey.[11] But in general the Scots, even in Aberdeen, got pine timber from Norway.[12]

Pinewoods were presumably used for local purposes, as in later centuries. Much patched and cobbled together, pines could roof great cruck-built halls.[13] Even with the then dense rural population, some of the eastern glens were well wooded. If living trees failed, fossil pine could be dug from peat as 'bog fir'.

The Scottish Normans instituted Forests on the English model. Most were outside the Highlands, but there were some inside the Highland border in Perthshire and Aberdeenshire. The association between Forests and woodland, weak in England, seems to have been non-existent in Scotland. (In post-medieval times Forests were designated all over the Highlands: credulous supporters of the Caledonian Wood point to their names on the map as evidence of former woodland!)

The age of exploitation

Pont's maps show that Caledonian pinewoods were somewhat, but not vastly, more extensive c.1590 than they are now. Glen Tanar illustrates this point (Figs 125, 126) . Then as now, it was the easternmost and second-largest pinewood, 30 miles (50 kilometres) west of Aberdeen. Pont depicts the Water of Tanar and its tributaries, and roughly indicates the extent of the woods. Although it is somewhat sketchy, and not all the tributaries are in the right order, the map establishes that woodland was of no more extent than it is now, and roughly in the same place, mainly on the east bank of the Tanar.[14] There have been local gains and losses, as there still are in progress today, but the agreement after 400 years of fires and logging is surprisingly good. Pont shows a number of settlements as well as woodland in Glen Tanar, including 'Attanich', evidently Etnach, which at 1,250 feet (380 metres) was one of the highest farms in Scotland to survive into the twentieth century.

Higher on the Dee there is only the published Gordon–Blaeu version (p.145). It shows 'Balamor' (Balmoral) with a settlement, a ribbon of woodland along the south side of Dee, and a patch of woodland on top of the prominent mountain 'Crag gewis', now Creag Giubhais. Many more agricultural settlements are shown than now survive, and only two small patches of trees. Given Blaeu's propensity to exaggerate woodland, one might infer that there was less woodland on the upper Dee in c.1590 than 200 years later, and much less than today.

An account in Latin, apparently by Gordon, describes the Dee pinewoods:

... woods with tall firs are not absent to look at; here raises itself a very high mountain, as if chopped off from the others, all clothed with woodland all round: the peaks, rocks, and the summit itself hold a pretty grove of immense evergreen firs; the slopes of the mountains and the fields nearest the river, the pleasant green of elms* and birches. Crag-Gewis [Creag Giubhais] is the mountain's name, crag meaning mountain, but gewis fir ...

Below Glen Muick on the same bank Pannanich wood [Pannanich hill southeast of Ballater] is seen, from which timber is often transported down to Aberdeen, but prepared suitably for transport and subdivided for country uses. For beams and whole tree trunks cannot be brought down, neither by the rough and rocky road, nor can they safely be trusted to the very fast river (even if there is enough water).[15]

Creag *Giubhais*, 'Pine Crag', is less piney now than the other crags above the Dee. Was it so-called because it once had the *only* conspicuous pines in the area?

The Ballochbuie dispute

How pinewoods functioned is recorded in a lawsuit of the 1750s. It all began with the Earls of Mar. The Mormaer of Mar had held a vast estate on the upper Dee since the days of Malcolm, slayer of Macbeth. His last descendant had instigated the 1715 Rebellion and lost not only his head; the estate, forfeit for proper treason, had been broken up.

Much of the land was bought in 1731 by the Earls' tenants, the Farquharsons of Invercauld. It included Ballochbuie, the second most valuable pinewood on the Dee. The western half was the Invercaulds' property; in the eastern half of Ballochbuie they owned the *land*, but the *trees* on it had been bought by the Earls of Fife. Invercauld's subtenant farmers, however, had a *servitude* on all trees on Invercauld's land: that is a right – like housebote and ploughbote in England – to take timber from those trees when they needed it to maintain their houses or equipment for 'bigging and labouring of the ground'.

---

* The original says *tiliarum*, 'limes', which is hardly possible: is elm meant?

The principles at issue were:

1mo, *How far* [Invercauld or his tenants] *has Right to plough or plant any ... of the Grounds which belong in Property to him, but lie adjacent to, or intermixed with, the reserved Fir Woods belonging to* [Fife]? *And, 2do, How far he is intitled to take Fir Timber from* [Fife's] *other Woods ... when he has Sufficiency of Birch, or other Timber, upon his own Lands, proper for the Purposes ...?*[16]

On the first point, it was agreed that Invercauld's people could graze cattle in the pinewoods under common-rights, but could not cultivate any land on which pines were growing or on which a future generation of pines might grow.

There was a flat terrace between the bottom of Easter Ballochbuie Wood and the river, partly wooded and partly open, where Invercauld owned the land and Fife owned the trees. Invercauld had encouraged a tenant of his, one Calder, to set up a smallholding on the unwooded ground. He claimed that his tenant's cultivation was not interfering with the Earl's trees, and was doing a public service by preserving the open ground:

If [the open lands] *were not cultivated, the adjacent Fir-woods would in time spread over them, and render this Country, what it originally was, namely a wild uncultivated Desert, the Habitation of wild Beasts only.*

The Earl of Fife did not agree:

... this Croft of Calder's, so far from answering to the pompous Description of it given by [Invercauld], *is a small Spot of Ground, of no larger extent than about three Acres, and that quite surrounded by* [the Earl's] *Fir-woods, except on the North-side, where it is bounded by the River. On the East, South, and West, it is surrounded by the large Wood of Ballochbuie, which consists of the finest, tallest, and most thriving Trees, belonging to* [the Earl], *and the large Trees were not, on any of these three Sides, at a greater distance than three Yards from Calder's House and Yard ... upon these three Acres of Ground there were above 12,000 young thriving Trees, from one to three Yards high, before they were destroyed by this Cottar ...*[17]

Fife furthermore complained that Invercauld's tenants had been helping themselves to Fife's trees growing on Invercauld's land, in preference to Invercauld's own trees; they had been using them improperly, taking pine where they should have been using birch, and selling the produce:

The Fir-woods of Braemar, even at that Time [1715], *were justly esteemed to be of very great Value, though they had been greatly deteriorated by the Wast and Abuses they had suffered. The largest and finest Trees, four or five Feet diameter, were frequently cut down by the Root ... when all that was wanted was Roof and Couples for their little Huts, though the*

Tops and Branches of such large Trees were more proper for these Purposes ...

Under Colour of this Servitude, they drove a Trade of carrying large Quantities of Timber out of these Woods to the neighbouring Markets, and every Tenant, who removed out of the Ground, demolished his House, and carried away the whole Timber, which required a fresh Supply for the Incoming Tenant.

... for the same Reason that the Birch is so fit for making Ploughs and other Instruments of Tillage, it is extremely unfit for making the Roofs of Houses, because, by its Crookedness ... it makes the Roofs uneven, and full of Hollows, and therefore not water-tight; besides, that it is of no Duration; and therefore Fir is generally used in this Country, both for the large and small Timbers, unless when either Laziness, or the Difficulty of obtaining it from [the Earl's] Factors, hinders the Tenants from getting it.[18]

These (probably inconclusive) legal proceedings record a number of ecological insights. Pinewoods were different from conventional woodland, did not coppice, and had shifting boundaries:

... as Fir-woods do not spring from the Root, but are propagated by the blowing of the Seed in the Grounds, immediately adjacent to the old Woods, or in the Openings, ... these highland Fir-woods are not fixed to a particular Spot, but gradually shift their Stances; and, it was plainly for this Reason, that, in the original Feu-charters, not only the Woods then growing, but to grow, were specially reserved; ... because, if the spreading of the Wood, and Growth of the young Timber, could be impune stopped in those Parts, where it naturally expands itself, its Existence would be of short Duration.

... the Woods in their present Situation, have undergone great Changes since the original Constitution of these Feus. There is scarce a Year wherein they do not make such Change greater or lesser, shifting backwards and forwards ...[19]

Opinions differed on whether cattle-browsing was sufficient to interfere with the propagation of the trees:

... it is very evident, that, if the Country had been always peopled, and stocked with Cattle, as it now is, those fine Fir-trees, which it has been the Work of Ages to rear, never would have risen.

If young Trees are cropt by the Cattle, thee is no help for it. It is an accident that there is no avoiding ... the Trees upon that Moor run very little Risk from the Cattle, as there is hardly any Pasture on the Moor adjacent to the Woods ...

Fire was much more feared:

The Danger of Fire to these Woods, is scarce to be conceived: The smallest Spark will set Fire to the Heath, which immediately communicates to the Trees, when the whole goes up in a Blaze; and if there is the least Breath of Wind, spreads with such Violence, that it is scarce extinguishable . . .

. . . since the Commencement of this Process, a Fire actually broke out, and destroyed part of the Wood in the Neighbourhood of this Calder's House, and, if it had not been that the whole Country rose, and Invercauld himself was very active in extinguishing those Flames, the Damage would have been fatal and irreparable.

Another action of the Farquharsons was to expel their tenants in Glenlui in 1726:

. . . that the due managdement of the Woods may meet with no obstruction, and that the Land may be ordered so as is proper for carrying on the Improvement and sale of the Timber.[20]

This was a very early Highland Clearance, and for an unusual reason, in order to grow trees; but was there also unfinished business from the 1715 Rebellion?

Commercial exploitation

The other great group of pinewoods is on the River Spey. Here too there was a dense local population and a large country trade, which according to Smout may have been so great that few trees were allowed to grow beyond a size that could be conveniently handled. The woods were roughly as extensive as they are now, but the trees were smaller. Here too, fire was feared: anyone (even a juvenile delinquent) burning heather near the woods might for a first offence be nailed to the gallows by an ear, rising to hanging for a fourth or subsequent conviction.

The River Spey is more navigable than the Dee. From the seventeenth century the Grants of Grant, Grants of Rothiemurchus and Dukes of Gordon tried to relieve their poverty or profligacy by rafting timber down it to reach coastal and southern markets. For two centuries they indulged in booms and busts on a grand scale. To obtain know-how they brought in businessmen from England and Edinburgh who, with (as Smout puts it) 'the eternal optimism of half-informed outsiders', took leases on the woods. These introduced state-of-the-art technology, sawmills in the American manner to produce 'deals', and blast furnaces; they called on their landlords to defend them from the 'violence and oppression' of other 'inland hielandmen'. An enterprise for boring out pine logs and selling them to London for water pipes failed to compete with English elm and ran out of logs of 10 inches (25 centimetres) diameter. The York Building Company of London had a go at using pine charcoal to smelt iron, only to find that it disintegrated into dust. A shipyard built hulls of pine at the mouth of the Spey; trunks were sent to the Navy mast-yard at Chatham, to be received there as 'sorry stuff'.

Like many small enterprises trying to break into an established trade, few of these made much money and most were short-lived. Apart from difficulties of transport, Caledonian pine was of worse quality than from overseas: fast-grown (a defect in pine), knotty and liable to blue-stain fungi.[21]

Logging overlapped with the beginning of tourism. The Honourable Mrs Sarah Murray rode into Rothiemurchus in 1790 and was delighted with the 'venerable extensive woods', which she contrasted with plantations elsewhere. For 80 years visitors were attracted by the 'sublime beauty of the woods', which, alas, they described only in vague and bland terms, allowing no comparison with what is there now. Somehow they failed to notice the logging and milling going on under their noses. Probably these were concentrated in particular areas at a time, and a few spots may have escaped: Sir Thomas Dick Lauder in 1834 reported 'gigantic skeleton trees', over 20 feet (6 metres) in girth, in a corner of Glenmore.[22]

In the nineteenth century Speyside industries were documented by Elizabeth Grant, daughter of a laird who was using the trees to pay off his debts in England. The coming of railways opened up markets for sleepers and pit-props. The stock of fellable trees sometimes got very low, but replacement seems to have been easy in those deerless times. Industrial felling petered out in the late nineteenth century, with brief resumptions in both World Wars.

Browsing

The 'traditional' livestock of the Highlands were not sheep and deer, but cattle and goats. Pines regenerated in the face of cattle browsing at Ballochbuie and of goats at Glen Tanar.[23] (I cannot say whether goats will eat Caledonian pine, but I find in Crete that *Pinus brutia* is one of the least palatable trees to them.) Deer have more effect: pine seems to be less palatable than Norway spruce (though tastier than Sitka), but is more easily killed if it does get browsed.

It is often said that large numbers of red deer did not appear until the twentieth century; in Rothiemurchus there were apparently none until they were introduced in 1843.[24] The Monarch of the Glen, when Landseer painted him, was no common beast. However, in some glens deer were always significant.[25] Deeside has long been their stronghold: did not the 1715 Rebellion grow out of a 'traditional' deer-battue organised by the Earl of Mar for his henchmen? Thomas Pennant, tourist, in 1769 noticed red and roe deer in the Ballochbuie area, but they do not appear in the lawsuit. In the late eighteenth century it was said:

From the great care and attention which has been paid to these animals for some years past, they are now so numerous and domesticated, that they are to be seen in numbers from the windows of the houses of Invercauld and Marr-Lodge. At the latter place ... 100 stags have been seen at once feeding on the lawn.[26]

By the 1880s – when cattle- and goat-browsing had probably disappeared – deer were numerous enough to be considered the cause of lack of regeneration, which was confirmed by exclosure experiments.

Ballochbuie and Queen Victoria
Pennant visited the upper Dee in 1769:

Brae-mar. [Rocks are] *exceedingly romantic, finely wooded with pine. The cliffs are very lofty ... with vast pines growing out of their fissures.*

...

Invercauld. *On the northern entrance, immense ragged and broken crags bound one side of the prospect; over whose grey sides and summits is scattered the melancholy green of the picturesque pine, which grows in the naked rock ...*

The hills that immediately bound [the plain of Invercauld] *are cloathed with trees, particularly with birch.*

... the mountains form there a vast theatre, the bosom of which is covered with extensive forests of pines: above, the trees grow scarcer and scarcer, and then seem only to sprinkle the surface: after which vegetation ceases ... the great cataract of Garval-bourn, which seems at a distance to divide the whole, foams amidst the dark forest ...

[Crossing the Dee on a stone bridge] *... entered on excellent roads into a magnificent forest of pines of many miles extent ... I measured several that were ten, eleven, and even twelve feet in circumference, and near sixty feet high ... These trees are of a great age, having, as is supposed, seen two centuries ... Mr. Farquharson informed me that by sawing and retailing them, he has got for eight hundred trees five-and-twenty shillings each: they are sawed in an adjacent sawmill, into plank ten feet long, eleven inches broad, and three thick, and sold for two shillings apiece.*[27]

People were then beginning to understand annual rings. James Farquharson had counted 214 rings in a pine 2½ ft (75 centimetres) in diameter.[28]

Compared with the present, the natural woods of the Upper Dee were not very different in extent 240 years ago, but there was not the great area of plantations now connecting them. There is a suggestion of rather more birch then than now, and a little less pine. Old pines on cliffs were as much a feature then as they are today.

In Pennant's account, Ballochbuie, though not named, is recognisable as the greatest of the Deeside pinewoods. It was probably less dense than now, especially where it thinned out at the top; the trees were not thick enough to conceal the Garbh Allt burn. Like many pinewoods, it consisted of apparently even-aged stands, each presumably resulting from the last fire or logging. The big trees were roughly as big as the big trees now. Ballochbuie was going through an episode of commercialisation. In selling 800 pines, the owner had made a moderate inroad into the stock of big trees. He got a low price by English standards, indicating difficult transport, despite the then good road.

Sir John Sinclair in the 1790s mentions attempts to industrialise other Dee pinewoods. At Braemar there were 'extensive natural fir woods' on the four principal estates; but the picture was already complicated by planting of 'Scotch fir' as well as larch. 'The forest of Glentanar' was described as being 6 × 10 English miles (10 × 16 kilometres), which must have been exaggerated. It brought in a regular income, although there was no sawmill, and it was difficult to export the timber, since the Dee was a hazardous river for rafting. It had been burnt twice: the fires consumed young woods, but merely singed the old woods.[29]

In September 1848 Queen Victoria toured Deeside, and was impressed especially by the 'beautiful wood' of '*Balloch Buie*', while Prince Albert went off to bag red and roe deer. They bought Balmoral when it came on the market, and later the Queen bought Ballochbuie Wood to keep it out of the hands of industrialists.[30]

The 6-inch maps of the upper Dee, surveyed in 1866 under the Queen's eye by Captain Pratt, R.E., are among the finest ever productions of the Ordnance Survey (cf Fig. 204). They appear to show not only woodland but every free-standing tree, and even individual bushes. They distinguish woods with fenced or embanked edges from those not demarcated from moorland. They differentiate conifers from broadleaved trees, but not woods from plantations. In places there is some indication of the density of trees.

Since the previous map by J. Robertson in 1822 woodland had apparently somewhat diminished. A notable change was the decline of human population. Most of the many moorland farms in 1822 were 'In Ruins' by 1866. Queen Victoria was never accused of perpetrating Highland Clearances, but she offered the population an easier way of life than growing barley on moorland, by creating jobs in Balmoral Castle and stimulating the growth of the Deeside towns.

In the Balmoral–Ballochbuie area the distribution of woodland was very little different in 1866 from today. The edges are shown as perhaps sharper than in reality; there were outlying tracts of bushes, and occasional scatters of pines, on the moorland beyond the woods. Elsewhere on the Dee there have been wartime fellings, regrowth after wartime fellings, new plantations, and a general increase of birch.

PINEWOODS AS THEY ARE NOW

Pinewoods today (Figs 127–130) result from the history of logging and fire over 200 years or more. As with other light-demanding trees, it is not in their nature to conform to the conservationists' model of a mixture of all ages. Young pines may colonise rocky, disturbed or eroded patches in moorland, roadsides and the edges of peat-hags. These pioneers grow into a widely spaced stand, and then – if there is no fire – are infilled by a second generation from the seed that the pioneers shower into the undisturbed heather. The result is a two-aged stand: tall straight crowded pines with big, branchy 'granny pines' scattered among them.

Pinewoods, given the chance, still 'shift their Stances'. At the limit of the Glentanar woods, on one side of the glen, young pines are colonising moorland; on the opposite slope, the woods are retreating, leaving a scatter of old and dead pines among moorland.[31]

Pines may have been less gregarious in the past. A number of eighteenth-century accounts mention 'firr' mixed with other trees;[32] whether these mixtures were stable can no longer be ascertained.

In prehistory pine sometimes grew on blanket peat, but it no longer does so. At Achanalt in the wilds of Ross & Cromarty, in 1977, a pinewood of a few acres was fighting a losing battle on a knoll of mineral soil, drowning in the rising tide of peat. The pines, then at least 120 years old, were confined to hummocks where bracken and heather still held out against encroaching *Sphagnum* and *Molinia*. The only young trees were where the windblow of their predecessors had exposed a patch of rock or moraine. They were further threatened by a Forestry Commission plantation of Sitka spruce. Smout cites examples, from eighteenth-century travellers' descriptions, of western pinewoods sinking into blanket bog 'without even being touched by human hand'.

Ballochbuie is exceptional. The huge old pines that Queen Victoria loved are widely spaced, but many of them are not of pioneer habit with big low branches; they seem to have grown up among neighbouring trees that were felled long ago, but have permanently altered the architecture of the survivors. Steven & Carlisle in 1959 said 'the trees in the greater part of the forest are in the 150 to 200 age class', with occasional trees or small groups under 100 years, and others up to about 300. This would imply that most arose between c.1750 and 1800, some as far back as 1650 and others as recently as 1850. (I am told that recent ring counts tend to make them somewhat older.) Pine seems to have regenerated well in the eighteenth century, when there were cattle browsing; it stopped regenerating roughly when deer became numerous. A partial felling around 1810, followed by little intervention since, might account for the open structure of the pine-wood. By 1848 it would have recovered sufficiently for Queen Victoria to think it a special place, while noting the ruins of a sawmill.

Pinewoods tend to have remnants of a moorland flora rather than a distinctive woodland flora. As with other Scottish Highland woods, one speculates that browsing by cattle, goats, sheep and deer, though failing to suppress the trees, prevented the emergence of distinctive vegetation such as exists in England. However, they have some woodland specialists: wood-anemone, *Luzula pilosa* and cow-wheat, as well as distinctive plants such as *Trientalis europæa*, *Moneses uniflora* and *Linnæa borealis*, and the orchids *Goodyera repens* and *Coralorrhiza trifida* – the last being a bizarre mycorrhizal parasite (p.36). They can be rich in bryophytes, and it is partly on that basis that the *National Vegetation Classification* divides them into four subcommunities.

CONCLUSIONS

Pinewoods have had their ups and downs, but have declined less than other Scottish woodland. Large-scale losses have been few: the present pinewoods have 'shifted their Stances' within the same general areas for at least 400 years. Peat-bound pine stumps in now pineless glens are mostly far older. There are a few place-names in Gaelic *giubhas*, 'pine', where pine is now either absent or only at lower altitudes, but some of these may refer to fossil pines.

Why are there pinewoods in some glens and not in others? It is not that they survive in remote and underpopulated places. As Smout comprehensively shows, it is not the pinewoods that have been frequently felled that have disappeared, but those (as in Glencoe, Glen Etive and Glen Orchy) with little or no record of exploitation:

The most dramatic examples of English external interest in Scottish pinewoods occurred not in areas where the pinewoods have since declined, but in areas where they still flourish.

The most extensive and flourishing tract, on Speyside, has a history of dense population and the most intensive history of exploitation. Does clear-felling act as a substitute for periodic fires?

Pine has retreated eastward: most of the losses have been in western Scotland, where pine has been less common since wildwood times. In the far north, pine has partly been replaced by birch in the Strathcarron woods. Like other trees, it survives better on rocky ground than on smooth slopes or soil. Increase of sheep-grazing in the nineteenth century undoubtedly restrained its capacity to expand outside existing woods. The wrong fire cycle may contribute: instead of the fires at long intervals to which pine is adapted, there is now either too frequent fire (on grouse moors) or no fire at all. However, Smout supports the view that much of the change was natural. Woodland is not sustainable for more than a few thousand years in the wet climate of western Scotland, in which minerals left by the last glaciation are leached out of the soil, and blanket peat inexorably spreads over hill and glen. The eastward retreat of pine is an 8,000-year process.

Native pinewoods, defying Fraser Darling's prediction, fare as well as they have done for a thousand years. Scotland has had more than its share of forestry scandals, and at least one of them – the plantation made, and later grubbed up, in Beinn Eighe National Nature Reserve – touched on pinewood.[33] But there have been few losses in the last 50 years. Even the smallest native pinewoods, as at Achanalt, have been listed by the Forestry Commission and carefully freed from surrounding plantations which would have overwhelmed them.

The Great Wood of Caledon still has a hold on the patriotic and political imagination of Scots, and there is a movement to 'restore' it. (Can one restore something that didn't exist?) But does Scotland really need yet more tree cover after all the plantations of the twentieth century? Is it Scotland's duty to turn into a second Norway?

The main obstacle to conservation, as in England, is deer – more deer than ever before, which are often reduced to eating young pine for want of anything better. Since before Fraser Darling there have been complaints of too many deer. Fences are not entirely effective, for deer get in (as when snowdrifts bury the fence) and multiply on the wrong side. Even so, they can work: experimental exclosures in Ballochbuie Wood are embarrassingly crowded with young trees, albeit birch and alder as well as pine. But Scotland has a fencing problem all its own. There are two big rare lumbering birds: blackcock, which is native, and capercaillie, once native, but now stemming from a nineteenth-century reintroduction. They flap about at night, blunder into fences and break their necks. The conservation of these birds is at odds with that of the pinewoods that are their habitat.

What are the prospects for controlling deer? Deer-stalking is a good source of income in a poverty-stricken region: people pay surprisingly large money to slay big game. But they expect to have plenty of not too difficult male targets with good heads, which does nothing to keep down the population. Deer migrate: they spend the summer in the mountains and go down to the valleys and the pinewoods in winter. People think it unethical to shoot their neighbours' deer: you don't kill 'my' deer even when they are on your land eating your trees.

CHAPTER 17

ENVIRONMENT, PATHOLOGY AND ECOLOGY

Damage, Disease, Defoliation

In spring we see the leaves sprout forth from the venerable trunks in all the luxuriance of vegetation, when of a sudden they are blasted as if by lightning, the bark falls from the stem, and long ere winter the finest tree perhaps in the park is only fit for fire-wood.
'DENDROPHILUS' ON THE ELMS IN ST JAMES'S PARK, LONDON, 1823[1]

Trees, being long lived, are parasitised by a huge variety of viruses, bacteria, fungi, mistletoes, nematode worms, mites, insects and other trees. Many of these are specific to a particular genus or species of host plant. Trees are damaged by frost, drought, waterlogging, pollution and browsing or gnawing mammals, or altered by genetic mutations. Almost any big tree can be called diseased – a fact well known to developers taking advantage of the loophole in tree preservation law which allowed 'diseased' trees to be dug up without too many questions asked.

In 1962, T. R. Peace's *Pathology of Trees and Shrubs with special reference to Britain* ran to nearly 800 pages, summarising hundreds of conditions. Cambridge University Botany School specialised in plant diseases for nearly a century, and two distinguished scientists, Dennis Garrett and John Rishbeth, taught the author.

Times have changed. The public has worried about tree diseases since the 1820s. Plant pathology became an affair of state with the Irish potato famine in 1845, since when there has been a succession of scares. But memories are short: the Elm Disease epidemic of the 1860s had been forgotten by the time of the next epidemic in the 1920s. Since the 1960s most research and teaching have turned to short-lived plants that are easier to understand. The public knows less, and fails to distinguish between short-term disturbances of little significance and less conspicuous but longer-term problems.

Most tree diseases are apparently trivial; most others affect the commercial value of the tree or its fruit without having much ecological significance. The rust fungus *Melampsora rostrupii* lives in spring on dog's-mercury and later moves to aspen, producing orange or yellow pustules on the leaves of both. It is unlikely to do more than slightly retard the growth of either host. Even weak pathogens, however, can have ecological effects if they attack seedlings. If as many as one in a hundred thousand ash-keys were to grow into a tree the world would be choked with ash-trees within a century; damping-off fungi are doubtless one reason why this does not happen.

Tree diseases can be difficult to investigate because several organisms are involved. The fungus or insect that did the original damage may be displaced by others: by the time the damage is noticeable the primary cause may have disappeared. Honey-fungus (*Armillaria* species) is a root parasite killing trees in gardens and forestry plantations; in an ancient wood, it is everywhere and likely to be found in any dead tree, regardless of what killed it.

ENVIRONMENT: ACID RAIN AND AIR POLLUTION

London has known acid rain for centuries. Royal Commissions on air pollution go back to 1285. By the 1620s 'the corroding quality of the Coale smoake, especially in moist weather' was blamed for dissolving Old St Paul's Cathedral.[2] Emission of sulphur dioxide from London probably reached a peak in the late nineteenth century.[3] In Norwich the facing stone of the Cathedral and Castle had partly disappeared by the eighteenth century. In Cambridge and Norwich, early photographs prove that much of the dissolution of medieval limestone stonework had already happened by the 1850s.

Nineteenth-century garden writers made much of the ability or otherwise of tree species to withstand urban conditions. The legendary success of the London plane was attributed to its periodic shedding of bark with accumulated dirt. R.S.R. Fitter's *London's Natural History,* published in 1945 as New Naturalist no. 3, has a chapter on 'The Influence of Smoke', but more in terms of soot than of acid rain.

The normal acidity of rain, which has dissolved carbon dioxide but nothing else, is pH 5.6. Rain may be more acid than this – that is, it may have a lower pH – because it has picked up acid dusts or gases, such as nitric acid made by lightning or by engines. It may be less acid because it has picked up alkaline dusts or gases, such as chalk or cement dust.

Lichens on trees are more sensitive to acid rain than the trees themselves. The presence or absence of particular lichens is one of the best ways of measuring the effective acidity of the rain in an area.[4] Big leafy lichens like *Lobaria pulmonaria* (see Fig. 102) are well-known indicators of clean air, as in west Dorset. Further east even the common *Parmelia caperata* has largely disappeared. The tolerant grey-green lichen *Lecanora conizæoides* is the last to go, leaving only the bright green alga *Pleurococcus*. In very polluted areas even this disappears, leaving bare, dark grey or black tree trunks, but still usually with no obvious effect on the tree. A classic illustration of evolution was furnished by the 'industrial melanism' of moths – an adaptation to concealment on bark purged of lichens. Pictures of trees painted when lichens were still abundant can now look odd for this reason.

In the 1970s the disastrous condition of trees in parts of Central Europe attracted publicity. On the border of Germany and Czechoslovakia, large areas of conifers died, giving rise to the term *Waldsterben*, 'forest dying'. The cause seemed to be gross air pollution from 'rust-bucket' heavy industries of the Stalinist kind. A possibly comparable place in Britain was the Cynon Valley in South Wales, where coal was made into 'smokeless' fuel – concentrating, it seems, all the smoke into one spot. Within a mile radius (1½ kilometres) oaks and sycamores were in poor condition and partly dead; birch, however, appeared to be stimulated.

Although actual death of forests was local, there was a reduction of 'vitality' among conifers, and to a lesser extent beeches and other broadleaves, over a much wider area of Central Europe. This vague term included vigour of growth and density of leafage. The cause was said to be some kind of atmospheric pollution, popularly thought to be acid rain.

Other causes are related to exhaust fumes from vehicles. Modern high-compression engines burn small amounts of atmospheric nitrogen, turning it into oxides of nitrogen, which in turn react with oxygen to generate poisonous ozone. Ozone formation is stimulated by sunlight: the stone-pines around sunny Florence were thought to be particularly affected,[5] although in Athens, with its uniquely hellish combination of sunshine and fumes, trees remain obstinately healthy. An alternative mechanism involves damaging trees' magnesium metabolism, especially important in Central Europe where magnesium can be in short supply.

Reports of reduced vitality spread to Britain, and some interpreted them as the beginnings of *Waldsterben;* as on the Continent, this was taken to be a new phenomenon, attributable to air or rain pollution. However, the Central European mechanisms would be less effective in Britain, cloudy and surrounded by stormy seas that blast magnesium-containing salt spray far inland.[6]

In the 1980s and 1990s the Forestry Commission and Greenpeace recorded symptoms on trees, principally conifers but including beech, all over Great Britain.[7] In some years at least two-fifths of the youngish beeches in this country fell short of the Central European standards for a healthy beech-tree. The shortfall varied from year to year in no very obvious pattern, nor was it related to the geography of any form of pollution. No evidence emerged that this state of affairs was really abnormal – that British beeches had measured up to those standards in the past.

Have woodland soils got more or less acid?

Tansley's book on British vegetation gives the impression that woodland soils more acid than pH 4.0 were rare in the 1930s. They are not rare now: in the 1970s I measured pH of between 3.0 and 4.0 in about one-fifth of the woodland soil samples that I examined from eastern England. This is a surprisingly large change to have occurred in only 40 years, given that at least twice as much acid deposition must have occurred in the century before Tansley. Has acid rain acidified woodland soils? Or were methods of measuring pH in Tansley's time less sensitive to low pH?

Since 1971, woodland soils in the rest of Britain have been getting less acid. The Bunce–Kirby comparison (p.408) reports a mean pH of 4.98 from 1,648 plots in 1971, and 5.31 from the same plots in 2001. The methods on the two occasions were comparable and the results appear to be real. The more acidic soils were more affected: some 12 per cent of soils had pH below 4.0 in 1971, but only 2 per cent in 2001.[8] Is this an effect of contamination by lime as an agricultural fertiliser (cf. p.419)? The data did not include any from East Anglia and Essex, where my 1970s measurements need repeating.

The return of lichens

From the seventeenth century onwards coal was the main urban and industrial fuel, and when railways came was the main transport fuel too. In the 1950s and 1960s, encouraged by the Clean Air Act, coal was partly replaced for heating by heavy oil, which was less smoky, but worse for sulphur dioxide. (Electricity, too, was dirty because of the coal and oil wastefully burnt to generate it.) From the 1970s onwards, oil was replaced by natural gas, which contains almost no sulphur.

After 1975, lichenologists noticed a dramatic change in acid-sensitive lichens in London. Pollution suddenly declined with the ending of heavy oil for heating, of coal-burning railways, and of Bankside and Battersea power stations. Species not seen for 200 years returned even to central London.[9] From 1974 to 1999 *The*

Lichenologist published annual bibliographies of articles on lichens and air pollution, documenting a similar recovery in cities all over the world.

STAG-HEAD: A NORMAL CONDITION?

When I first went to Australia my hosts took me into the bush and explained that Australia was a different planet, in which most trees were eucalypts, and fire and termites did the recycling job done by fungi and worms in Europe. Another unfamiliar feature, they said, was that Australia had droughts lasting years at a time: the leafage of eucalypts died back, economising moisture, and grew again when the rains returned.

But was this so unfamiliar? In the 1940s many hedgerow oaks in Norfolk had towering dead branches, which fascinated me. In the 1960s these 'dying' oaks were held up as an example of the ill effects of ploughing around them, toxic sprays, roadworks, 'old age' (but few were more than 200 years old) etc. In the 1990s they were still 'dying': similar trees were held up as an example of the polluting effects of Gatwick Airport. Those in Norfolk are mostly still there: over the years some of the dead boughs have rotted away, but others remain, and the trees have grown new leafage at a lower level.

Dead boughs on oaks last for about a century (Fig. 131). The bark rots and disappears, then the sapwood, leaving a sharp-edged core of heartwood. On oaks in Madingley Wood, photographed by D.E. Coombe in 1951, some boughs then already reduced to heartwood are still there now.[10] I suspect that the 'dying' oaks were survivors of the great droughts of 1911 and 1921, aggravated by a plague of defoliating caterpillars, by newly arrived oak mildew, and perhaps by frost and honey-fungus. Silviculturalists all over Europe debated whether oak had any future;[11] their French colleagues waxed eloquent on the *grande misère du chêne*. Oaks in Sussex were stag-headed long before Gatwick Airport was thought of.

Portraits of historic oaks, such as Queen Elizabeth's Oak at Huntingfield (Suffolk), show that they have passed through phases of dieback in the past: a 'high top bald with drie Antiquitie', as Shakespeare put it. In Sherwood Forest, successive waves of dieback, probably on the same trees, have been remarked on since the seventeenth century.

The 1921 drought was combined with other factors that have not recurred. Subsequent droughts have not produced oak dieback on the same scale. However, the 'oak decline', which attracted attention and concern in the 1990s, is likely to be related to a cluster of hot dry summers.

The drought of 1975–6, though it failed to reactivate oak dieback in Sherwood, was followed by a dramatic dieback of non-woodland ashes, especially in the east Midlands; by the 1980s there were whole landscapes of half-dead ash-trees. But ash does not remain stag-headed for long: by now the dead boughs have disappeared, and the trees have grown new crowns.

Stag-head illustrates a fundamental question in conservation: what is normal?

THE MYSTERY OF EPPING FOREST

In 1989 the Conservators of Epping Forest asked me to investigate why the great pollard beeches of the Forest were dying. The matter attracted much attention: 'Epping Forest in Danger'; 'up to half' the trees were said to be affected; I was told that a hapless councillor had been voted out of office for failing to keep them alive.

In Epping Forest there were several hundred manifestly unhealthy beeches and some dead ones. It was argued that the beeches of the Forest displayed an advanced state of *Waldsterben* symptoms; that this had the same significance and cause as in Central Europe; and that this was a recent and abnormal state of affairs.

Had the Continental parallel been correctly applied? Are the symptoms pathological at all, or are they part of the normal behaviour of beeches, which are not immortal? If pathological, are they specific to the *Waldsterben* syndrome, or can other adverse influences bring them about? Are they more severe in parts of the Forest particularly exposed to pollution? Have they increased recently?[12]

The story of Epping Forest[13]
Epping Forest, anciently Waltham Forest, is a huge, uncompartmented wood-pasture common (Fig. 183). It sits on a flat-topped ridge of Claygate and Bagshot Beds overlying London Clay. The trees are mainly hornbeam on lower ground, oak in between, and beech on the plateau. Beech is dominant over an area of about 3 miles by 1¼ (5 × 2 kilometres). Soils under beech are silty and seasonally wet, very unlike the well-drained sites on which beech typically occurs. They are acid: most pH measurements range from 3.7 to 4.2, typical for woodland soils in south Essex.

In prehistory Epping Forest was strongly dominated by lime, as shown by a pollen record from a bog in the present beech zone. The beech zone contains two Iron Age hillforts, connected with major settlements probably outside the present Forest. In Anglo-Saxon times the wood-pasture probably reached its medieval and early-modern form. Lime declined and then disappeared, replaced by oak and then beech.[14] Domesday Book shows the future Forest as the biggest concentration of woodland in Essex. By the fourteenth century it had reached almost exactly its present size.

Waltham was declared a Forest in the early twelfth century. The physical Forest lay between the king's palace at Havering and his royal abbey of Waltham. The land was owned by a score or more of private or institutional lords of manors, and used by several hundred commoners who had rights of pasturage and wood-cutting. To these other uses the king added perhaps 200 fallow deer and a few red deer. In the mid-thirteenth century he consumed, on average, about 20 fallow and four red deer annually from Waltham Forest.

Epping Forest produced wood, but not much timber. Since it was uncom-partmental and the commoners' animals could not be excluded, the trees were pollarded. Chapman & André's map of 1772–4 shows most of the Forest as wood-pasture, carefully differentiated from woodland (Fig. 183). There were a number of *plains*, areas of heather, grassland and bog, mainly on low or very ill-drained sites, grazed by deer and the commoners' cattle, sheep, pigs and illicit goats. It was crossed by one main road, the present A121, bordered by trenches (narrow clearings, p.171f) to give travellers a sense of security from highwaymen.

The Forest and its institutions changed little for seven centuries. In 1543 Henry VIII made a short-lived park on land whose ownership he had stolen from Waltham Abbey. He left behind a *standing,* an observation tower for ceremonial hunts, now miscalled Queen Elizabeth's Hunting Lodge. (The great oaks from which it is built probably came from elsewhere.)

Decline came in the nineteenth century from external causes. In 1830–4 the local turnpike trust split the Forest along its length by a new road, the present A104 (A11), which even then showed scant respect for the Forest's amenities. In 1851 the sister Forest of Hainault, where the Crown owned most of the land, was privatised and most of it grubbed out and made into poor-quality farmland. Epping Forest was saved by its fragmented ownership, but individual landowners began to encroach upon it. Its growing significance as a place of public recrea-tion led to the formation of the Commons, Open Spaces and Footpaths Preser-vation Society. The City of London Corporation, whose purchase of a property carrying grazing rights gave them a legal standing, were persuaded to intervene. The result was the Epping Forest Act of 1878, which abolished the rights of the Crown and the landowners and transferred the freehold to the City of London.

This was the first big victory in Europe of the modern conservation movement. However, it resulted in a transformation of the Forest and a series of problems that still continue. The early Conservators had little sense of history or ecology: the science of ecology itself had hardly begun. They were strongly prejudiced against pollards, and stopped the commoners from cutting them. The beeches grew up crowded and dense, suppressing other trees and ground vegetation – except holly, which has infilled wherever there is a space. The plains were not grazed enough, and the heather was overgrown with oak and birch. Although since 1980 the Conservators have recognised the losses resulting from these changes, they had gone too far to be easily reversed.

The problem: group killing
Beech is the only tree in the Forest commonly showing signs of damage. The original *Waldsterben* of Central Europe principally affects spruce and fir (*Abies*); damage to beech there is less conspicuous. There have never been any significant conifers in Epping Forest; those planted around its edges have not particularly suffered.

Dead or manifestly unhealthy beeches occur in groups (Fig. 132). A typical group centres on a cluster of dead trees or their remains; these grade through a zone of trees with more or less severe symptoms, to the 'normal' beeches of the surroundings. All the groups together amount to at most 5 per cent of the beech in the Forest. Hornbeams and oaks within a beech group are much less affected than beech; holly and birch flourish through lessening of shade. Group damage is not closely related to the age of the trees. It may be commoner in maiden beeches, dating from around the decline of pollarding, but affects pollards also.

Group damage is mainly in the northern, beech-dominated, half of the Forest. The sites tend to be just off the central plateau. They are usually on or near spring-lines, marked by patches of rushes or the wetland grass *Molinia cærulea*. They are associated not with vehicle roads, but with constructed horse-riding tracks.

Group damage goes back at least to the 1960s. On my first visit, in 1974, I noticed the Broadstrood group, which was evidently not recent. This group is no longer active, and the gap has been invaded by birch. Near High Beach there was a boggy area with 'dying' hornbeams and oaks as well as beeches; this too has not markedly got worse. The Hill Wood group is said to have begun in the late 1960s; some then attributed it to the effects of a World War II explosion. This group was aggravated by the 1975–6 drought, but later showed recovery. In the hot summer of 1989 some beeches on the edges of groups withered, but there was no general extension of the groups; indeed, there was a good deal of recovery, as marginal trees produced new shoots from lower in the crown.

Epping Forest was not much affected by the storms of 1987 and 1990. Trees bordering groups have sometimes been uprooted or broken by windblow. This is to be expected – the death of one tree exposes its neighbours – but is not an important factor in extending the groups. Beeches have often died after uprooting, which is unusual (p.19) and perhaps indicates pre-existing root trouble.

Of the five groups that began before 1970, three had stopped extending by 1989. At least eight others date from before 1980. Some of the big groups extended further by 1992. There was a general slow extension during the 1990s.

Recording symptoms

Symptoms of reduced 'vitality' on beech were published by D. Lonsdale,[15] following the practice of A. Roloff in Germany. They are:

- crown thinness – the amount of sky that can be seen through the canopy;
- branching pattern – in vigorous trees long-shoots predominate, whereas in less vigorous trees short-shoots take over;
- cluster-shoot formation – chains of short-shoots arising from other short-shoots;
- whether the leafage becomes thinner at the top of the tree;
- whether there are dead twigs or branches at the outside of the canopy;
- leaf rolling;
- fall of leaves while still green; and
- premature autumn colours.

Most of these 'symptoms' were present, but not always in the same tree. They were more marked in the damaged groups than in the general Forest. But their application is not straightforward. The list was intended mainly for use with younger trees; In trees of the ages usual in Epping some reduction of vitality may be normal. Epping Forest trees are wild, not mass-produced in a nursery, and some of the characteristics in which they normally vary overlap with those regarded as measures of vitality. Crown density varies from tree to tree because some trees have a strongly directional distribution of the foliage.

Areas particularly exposed to pollution

If vehicle fumes damage trees directly, damage should be more intense in places more exposed to fumes. In practice, none of the damaged groups directly borders a main road. The busy Epping New Road is bordered for miles by beeches, hornbeams and oaks no different in condition from those in the rest of the Forest.

Two places are specially exposed to fumes. Woodredon Hill is a busy, narrow main road climbing a steep hill. Trees come right up to the road. Beech is super-healthy, except for slight advancing of autumn colours. Careful search detected slight abnormalities on oak and hornbeam. In the south of the Forest the North Circular Road crosses a narrow part of the Forest in a cutting, and intersects the Epping New Road. There are slight but clear symptoms on beech, oak and hornbeam – which could as easily be due to the digging of the cutting as to traffic fumes.

Group killing can hardly be attributed to the direct effect of traffic pollution. Lack of association with roads is the more significant in that groups near roads are more likely to be discovered than those away from them. Several groups, however, adjoin horsepaths.

The rest of the Forest
Outside areas of group damage and of special exposure to pollution, most of the beech symptoms occur, but are never severe, and rarely more than two symptoms per tree. Chlorosis is probably the most frequent. In oaks, a common symptom in 1989 was patches of premature leaf-yellowing.

Although older, the beeches of the Forest at large in 1989 were no worse in terms of vitality, and probably better, than the average of those in Forestry Commission and other surveys of Britain in earlier years. There was no sign that the symptoms were getting worse or that the trees are suffering actual harm.

If general air pollution were the cause, trees on the western side of the Forest ridge should be more exposed and more affected than those on the east side. There was no sign that this was so.

Ecological history of the Forest
For most of its history the Forest was very different from today. Beech was less strongly dominant. The trees were much smaller, pollarded on a cycle of about 13 years. Although in places they were crowded, the Forest as a whole was less wooded and more savanna-like. The present Sunshine Plain – a narrow, boggy, open area – is almost the only survivor of the plains (mapped by the Ordnance Survey in 1881) that wandered irregularly across the beech zone. These were permanent: one is mentioned in a charter boundary of 1062.

After 1878 the Conservators suppressed pollarding and allowed grazing to decline. Trees, especially beech, were allowed to grow up very much bigger than before. The trees that overgrew the plains are, for the most part, oak and birch; beech is uncommon on former plains.

Pollarding often ended well before 1878. Views of the Forest, shortly before then, depict pollards of many more than the normal years' growth.[16] The pollard beeches of the Forest today have grown up for between 130 and 190 years; their bollings (permanent bases) vary from over 400 years old down to about 130. The oldest maiden (unpollarded) beeches date from about 1878.

The plains are not there by chance. Claygate and Bagshot Beds vary from clay to gravel, producing spring-lines and waterlogged patches. Here the growth of most trees is difficult and was easily prevented by the animals which grazed the Forest. Most damage groups are close to plains and on similar soils.

Beech is not abundant in the Forest because the environment favours it. The Forest is acidic and wet, and at best marginally suitable. Beech was favoured by the rise and fall of the wood-pasture ecosystem, which allowed it to predominate over competing species. It is passing through a phase of abundance that may not last for ever: in Writtle Forest it died out as a native.

The lichen story

Epping Forest is the classic locality for the decline of lichens in relation to pollution. J.M. Crombie, in a pioneering article, noticed that many of the lichens collected by Edward Forster in c.1790, which included even *Lobaria pulmonaria*, had disappeared when he first knew the Forest in the 1860s; one-quarter of them had disappeared by 1885. Further drastic losses were found by lichen surveys in the 1910s and c.1970.[17]

Sulphur dioxide output in London was increasing and shifting eastward to locations nearer the Forest, especially Liverpool Street Station, which opened in the 1840s. Houses – all burning coal – began to invest the south of the Forest in the 1870s, and by the 1930s had spread northwards. All but the more resistant lichen species were progressively lost.

Table 19 illustrates this progression. The lichens present in the Forest at each date have been classified on a 10-point scale of sensitivity to sulphur dioxide; from this it is possible to estimate the mean acidity of the atmosphere in winter, in terms of the sulphur dioxide concentration.

Although by 1970 acid rain in Epping Forest was severe, there are two worse degrees on the Hawksworth–Rose scale. As trees in Sheffield, the Welsh coalfield valleys and London show, beech can survive and even flourish in a greater intensity of sulphur pollution than Epping Forest had at its worst.

In the absence of fuller data, Paul Moxey kindly gave me some records by Professor Hawksworth in 1989. These, though incomplete, show a change for the better (as in many other places): the Forest had regained some lichens not seen for more than 70 years.

Measurement of acid rain

Paul Moxey measured the acidity of rain at High Beach, near the middle of Epping Forest, day by day from 1983 to 1989 (Table 20, by his kind permission).

Rain in Epping Forest is more often acidified (pH < 5.6) than not, but the pH varies according to which dust or gas the rain has picked up on a particular day. Acidity was lessening; very acid rain (pH < 3.6) happened only sporadically. De-acidified rain (pH > 5.6) was getting more frequent in the late 1980s. The change was too recent to have been responsible for bringing back the lichens: rain in Epping Forest would have been more acid still in the middle of the century.

Two comparisons

Hyde Park – very polluted: If pollution is bad for beeches in Epping Forest, it should have been impossible in the middle of London. Hyde Park and Kensington Gardens have a history of very severe acid rain, as shown by the erosion of Victorian statuary; they are surrounded and intersected by main roads. In 1989 there were almost no obvious lichens, even *Lecanora conizæoides* being confined to the relatively alkaline bark of ash trees.

In 1986 Dr Roloff declared: 'of the few beeches in central London (e.g. in Hyde Park), most are dying. Here a vitality loss because of ozone seems to be possible.' By 1989 there was a noticeable recovery: the nine beeches that I found, about 60–100 years old, displayed thinning of the crown, fastigiation, dieback and leaf-curling, but with one exception these symptoms were slight to moderate. The one tree faring worse was a copper beech next to a huge road junction. Hyde Park, though worse than Epping Forest, was thus not an impossible environment for beech.

Hyde Park has benefited from the decline of sulphur dioxide. In 1989, Professor Hawksworth found 12 species of lichens, though they had not yet grown big enough to attract attention.

Pindus Mountains – very unpolluted: In early September 1989 my duties on the Grevená Archaeological Survey took me to the Pindus Mountains around Perivólia and Vovoússa, northwest Greece: a remote and rustic place, not far from Albania; it is 110 miles (180 kilometres) southwest of Thessalonica, 180 miles (290 kilometres) northwest of Athens, and 220 miles (350 kilometres) east of Táranto. Here, if anywhere in Europe, should be a place to investigate the 'normal' condition of trees, unaffected by pollution.[18]

Beech is widely the dominant tree at altitudes of 4,330–6,000 feet (1,300–1,800 metres). The beeches are huge and magnificent. Many are well over

300 years old. Luxuriant lichens, including abundant *Lobaria pulmonaria,* confirm the lack of atmospheric pollution.

'Symptoms' were very frequent: chaining of short-shoots, dieback at tops, chlorosis, leaf-curling, early leaf fall. These are not confined to old trees. They vary with slope and aspect. In wet places, as at the edge of a small bog, the symptoms were very severe: some trees were withered and a few dead. Reduced 'vitality' is evidently chronic, not acute, and rarely kills the tree.

The Pindus beeches are in a 'worse' state than those of Epping Forest, but there is no suggestion that this is abnormal. They have been in a state of reduced vitality for centuries, as shown by narrow annual rings. Reduced vitality is one of the reasons for their long lives.

Inferences

Epping Forest reached its present state by a unique sequence of historical events. As the lichen history shows, acid rain is an integral part of the history of the Forest, like pollarding and the presence of beech itself. The trees were already exposed to acid rain when they began to grow up out of the pollarded state.

Beeches can withstand the recent degree of acid rain without overt damage to their health or even reduction of growth. They have survived greater acid rain in the past. They withstand – with survivable signs of distress – more severe pollution in Hyde Park.

Vehicle fumes, even where locally concentrated, have no visible effect on beech, and very little on hornbeam or oak. If the Forest were suffering a general decline, caused by a widely distributed form of atmospheric pollution such as ozone, symptoms of reduced vitality should be either randomly distributed, with local variation according to individual trees being more or less resistant, or else related to the intensity of pollution. In practice the random symptoms are very mild, and there is no reason to regard them as abnormal. The Pindus observations show that they can exist in the absence of pollution.

Group damage is better related to soils than to evident sources of pollution. It is related to springs and to horsepaths, both of which may interfere with the roots, and to the distribution of plains. I infer that group damage is a manifestation of an unfavourable set of soil factors, which when there was grazing prevented tree growth altogether, creating and maintaining the plains.

The symptoms, though severe, are not progressive. The tree may die, or live with the symptoms indefinitely, or recover. If pollution were the cause, affected trees would only get worse unless the cause diminished.

Interpretation

Lime, the aboriginally dominant tree of Epping Forest, disappeared a thousand years ago. Wood-pasture favoured beech, which became established even in moderately wet places. It could live there indefinitely provided that it was pollarded. Pollard trees, not allowed to form big tops, could withstand having their roots restricted by waterlogging.

After pollarding ceased, the trees grew up for a while, and maiden trees infilled between them. They had not room to form enough root to keep in balance with their enlarged tops. This would not matter in a normal year, but root-restricted trees would be at the mercy of the weather; they could be damaged in unusually wet and unusually dry years, of which there have been many since 1968.

Mounted visitors used to ride all over the Forest; horse trampling destroyed vegetation and soil, especially along wet tracks. By the 1960s this was causing trouble, which was met by constructing gravel paths. On wet ground, churning, excavation and compaction of the soil could all have damaged the shallow delicate roots of the beeches. Some, at least, of the group damage began at the time when this disturbance was at its worst.

It may be argued that pollution in some way interacts with soils – that beech could withstand waterlogging if it did not have to contend with pollution as well. This is a mere hypothesis; the soil theory covers the facts, and there is no reason to suspect any influence of pollution. Group damage occurs in similar wet places in the unpolluted Pindus. The puzzle is that beech should grow so widely on the unsuitable soils of Epping Forest, not that it should sometimes fail to prosper.

Time has passed and knowledge has increased, and there could be complicating factors. Beech is strongly ectotrophic-mycorrhizal: waterlogging, soil disturbance or compaction could damage the fungi rather than the tree directly. In the 2000s one suspects that a *Phytophthora* may be an intermediary – but in the absence of overt symptoms this would be difficult to prove.

Is group killing abnormal? Dead beeches are usually replaced by birch thickets, among which young beeches sometimes come up. To an American ecologist this would be a good example, the best in Britain, of *gap-phase regeneration*, one of the textbook methods by which forests replace themselves in the absence of human intervention. A big sugar-maple, for example, rots at the base and crashes down, forming a gap in which short-lived trees, especially other American maples, establish themselves and live for a few decades before being replaced by a new generation of sugar-maple. (American beech short-circuits the process by being clonal (Fig. 11): when a big beech crashes down the gap is immediately filled by its own suckers.) In the mountain forests of spruce and fir (*Picea rubens* and *Abies balsamea*) of New England, gaps are started by the assaults of spruce beetle, mistletoe and root diseases; they get bigger as honey-fungus, wind-uprooting and base-breakage take the trees on the edge of a gap. Here too, the abundance of gaps can depend on the long-term history of the stand as a whole.[19]

Group damage is part of the process whereby beech retreats from unsuitable soils. Had gaps had not been started by horse and horsepath damage, something else would have initiated them. In the long term beech will probably retreat on to well-drained sites, renewing itself there by gap-phase regeneration. The Forest will not revert to its original natural state dominated by lime.

PATHOLOGY: TREE DISEASES AND PESTS

Caterpillars

In May 1981 I was in a wood of many kinds of tree in Connecticut that a month before had been coming into leaf. Now it was almost leafless, and alive with the sound of myriads of tiny jaws. My host showed me the gypsy moth caterpillars (*Lymantria dispar*), then about 1½ inches (4 centimetres) long, and told me they would grow to 3 inches (8 centimetres) before pupating. I did not see how they could: they had begun on the black cherries and had already eaten almost everything except tulip-tree, which they would not touch.

Gypsy moth was in the last year of an 11-year population cycle that had repeated itself several times. In 1868–9 Monsieur E.L. Trouvelot, astronomer, had brought some caterpillars from Europe to teach them to be silkworms. He got no silk out of them, but lost a few of his livestock; he told the authorities, who were unconcerned. Twenty years later the caterpillars began marching across the United States at a rate of 13 miles (20 kilometres) a year. Attempts to control them by drenching the woods with poison, or by introducing more than 20 other insects, bacteria, or viruses to eat or parasitise them, have made little difference.[20]

Gypsy moth mainly troubles gardeners who squelch on caterpillars and whose prized and weakly trees die, and foresters whose tree growth is delayed. Its ecological effects are not dramatic, and are difficult to follow in a region where most woods are recent and changing through historical development à la Epping Forest. Most trees can withstand several defoliations: they grow new leaves and carry on as before, but with a shorter growing season and narrower annual ring for that year. A tree that is growing poorly, for instance because of competition, may decline further if defoliated and be gobbled up by honey-fungus.

In Britain, where gypsy moth was last seen in 1907, other caterpillars defoli-
ate oaks. In woods that are monocultures of oak, June can turn into December.
At least four species of tortrix-moth caterpillars are involved; defoliation results
from unusual abundance of common caterpillars, rather than the appearance of
rare caterpillars.

Staverton Park, which is effectively an oakwood, is perhaps the only place in
eastern England to be frequently attacked. I recorded attacks in the following
years:

1980   none (despite unusually severe attacks elsewhere)

1981   slight to moderate

1982   slight

1983   severe: 70% of oaks attacked to some degree, c.10% wholly leafless

1984   slight

1985   only one tree attacked

1986   severe on about six trees

1987   severe

1988–9 slight or none

1990   very slight

1991   slight

1992   severe but local

1993   very severe, except in The Thicks where oaks are mixed with hollies

1994   moderate but not in The Thicks

This pattern of attacks would probably be usual in north and west Britain, where
oakwoods are common; there are reports of such woods being defoliated one
year in three. Individual trees are affected haphazardly from year to year; they
tend to be clustered rather than scattered.

Freestanding oaks, and oaks in woodland of other trees, are much less prone
to attack. However, 1980 was a vintage year. In Hayley Wood many oaks were
leafless in June, and defoliation spread to ash, maple, hazel, elm, sallow, aspen
and sometimes birch. In Buff Wood nearby, these trees were affected, but not the
oaks. In northeast Norfolk attacks spread to hedgerow oaks.

What are the consequences? For ecology probably little, except that caterpil-
lar-eating birds have a feast. Oaks and elms are built to withstand defoliation. In
most years they expand their leaves rapidly in May (or latterly April) and then
stop growing for several weeks, producing lammas shoots in August (latterly
July) with a second flush of leaves. Oaks respond to caterpillar attack by advancing the lammas growth, which for some reason is never defoliated. The oaks of

Staverton remain conspicuously healthy despite repeated defoliation, which must be reckoned among the adverse factors that promote long life (p.39).

However, a tree that loses its leaves loses the substance that went into the leaves and would have been withdrawn had the leaves fallen naturally – plus the substance that the lost leaves would have made. Since excess substance goes into the year's annual ring, this should result in a narrow ring. Martin Bridge and I cored a number of oaks in Hayley Wood in 1981, and the results are shown in Table 21.

The annual ring for 1980 was reduced by about one-third (36 per cent) compared to that for the unremarkable years 1978 and 1979. The ring for 1976 (the drought year of the century) was reduced by 53 per cent. That is to say, an extreme caterpillar year had about two-thirds the effect of an extreme drought year. However, the caterpillars, as ever, attacked some oaks more than others, and the sample of 26 trees included two that declined by less than 10 per cent from 1979 and one that increased.

Caterpillar attacks annoy the forest economist, who hates trees to grow slowly. They annoy the dendrochronologist (p.43), who likes growth rates to depend on weather (that affects all the trees in a region alike) rather than insects that attack a tree here and a tree there.

Oak mildew

Everyone is familiar with the whitish bloom, like a thin coat of whitewash, on oak leaves in summer, especially on coppice and vigorously growing shoots (Fig. 137). This is the visible part of the fungus *Microsphæra alphitoides*, a mildew that spreads by wind-borne spores. Nineteenth-century mildew specialists knew it only as an American fungus. It suddenly overran Europe in 1908, much like two American mildews that had devastated European vines some decades earlier. It is now commoner on deciduous oaks in Crete and Britain than in America.

Oaks are not vines, and mildew at first sight seems to be trivial, at worst reducing the growth rate. But it may explain the Oak Change that happened at about the same time. In the Middle Ages and long after, oak had been a tree of established woodland, replacing itself in existing woods; millions of small trees were harvested to make timber-framed buildings (Chapter 11). In the twentieth century oak was a pioneer tree: it established itself easily on abandoned fields or along railways, but a young oak in an existing wood was a rarity. It is difficult to create a replica of a medieval building because of the lack of small oaks.

Maybe oak, especially *Quercus robur*, was always a light-demanding tree, encouraged in prehistory (as Vera would have it, p.79) by particular levels of browsing animals, and in historic times by coppicing. Where there are still abundant oaklings, either the wood is still coppiced (Bradfield Woods, Fig. 76) or the oaklings are concentrated along wide rides (woods on the Blean, Kent). But resuming coppicing has not brought back young oaks to Hayley, Chalkney and many other woods; nor has resumption of browsing by deer.

More plausibly, mildew, in effect, makes oak more sensitive to shade: an oakling may succumb to shade and competition if it has to contend with mildew as well. Mildew appeared when there had been abnormally little felling for half a century, and oaks were not regenerating well. If this interpretation is right, a seemingly trivial introduced disease has had a profound and irrevocable effect on the ecology of oak.

Epidemics

Dutch Elm Disease: Elms used to be the third commonest, and usually the largest, non-woodland tree in England. An epidemic of Dutch Elm Disease flared up in the 1960s and within 20 years had killed 90 per cent of the great elms in England.[21] A microscopic fungus, *Ceratocystis* (*Ophiostoma*) *novi-ulmi*, poisons the tree and blocks its water-conducting system (Fig. 135). It is carried from tree to tree by elm bark beetles, which breed under the bark of newly dead trees. It is controllable by immediately burning infected trees and to some extent by injecting a fungicide, but only East Sussex County Council and a few private landowners had the energy to do this.

Forty years on, the disease continues to smoulder. The most susceptible elm is English elm, the familiar elm of middle and south England, which no longer exists as a big tree except in East Sussex and among the urban elms of Scarborough and Edinburgh. Surviving big elms are of other species, especially some of the elms of East Anglia, the east Midlands and east Kent; they tend to be in woods rather than freestanding. However, elms have not been exterminated or even much diminished in their distribution. Most are clonal and continue to sprout from the roots. Wych-elm, the exception, grows from seed and within 15 years produces more seed; in regions like the Cotswolds it still flourishes as a small tree.

Ecological effects are less than might be expected. Gaps left by dead elms have been filled by elm suckers (deer permitting) or by other trees such as ash and maple. A few creatures that live on big elms have diminished, such as the white-letter hairstreak butterfly, the agaric bracket-fungus *Rhodotus palmatus*, and certain lichens. It is no longer so easy to demonstrate the wetwood condition produced by the bacterium *Erwinia nimipressuralis,* previously the commonest disease of elms, which produces the dark colour and sour smell of elm heartwood.

There was a previous *Ceratocystis* epidemic in the 1920s and 1930s, especially investigated in Holland (whence the name Dutch Elm Disease), and one in the 1830s and 1840s. Each epidemic attracted similar attention, with calls for infected trees to be felled and burnt, articles on the connection with bark beetles, an editorial in *The Times,* and attempts to make the government responsible. From time to time Elm Disease has flared up elsewhere in Europe, and lately has been gaining on growth of the elms: a big elm is now rather rare except in outlying corners such as Norway or Crete. The disease was unknown in America until it was introduced on imported logs in the 1920s, and has produced a widespread but patchy epidemic there. It seems to be unknown in Japan.

There can now be little doubt that Elm Disease is responsible for the well-known Elm Decline, which marks the early Neolithic period all over north and middle Europe. What else can have reduced elm pollen production – and only elm – by at least half, without affecting other trees, in at most four years at a site (p.94)?

Successive waves of Elm Disease have each killed some of the elms (a larger proportion each time round) and then mysteriously declined to an inconspicuous level. At least four organisms are involved: elms, the fungus, two or three species of bark-beetles, and viruses that parasitise the fungus. These are variable and some of them mutate, and from time to time a combination of circumstances generates a virulent form of the fungus that escapes from its limiting factors. A new factor is the tendency to ship logs and bark at random round the world in coals-to-Newcastle fashion. Thus was the disease brought to America, and it is widely held that the virulent strain of the 1960s arose in America and was brought back to Europe.

Chestnut blight:

Under a spreading chestnut tree
The village smithy stands
HENRY WADSWORTH LONGFELLOW (1839), REFERRING TO *CASTANEA DENTATA,* THE SWEET-CHESTNUT OF EASTERN NORTH AMERICA

As a student I was taught about *Endothia parasitica,* chestnut-blight fungus, which produces cankers on sweet-chestnut that spread and girdle and kill the branch or trunk. Its spores ride the wind, an insect vector not being essential. It is said to have come to America from Japan, where it occurs on *Castanea crenata* but is not a problem. (American horticulturalists, such as the great Luther Burbank, were not content with American chestnut, but must needs import quantities of Japanese material.) It spread unopposed through *C. dentata*, converting it from a great forest tree to a small understorey species. Chestnut does not easily rot, so the woods are still full of the mighty remains of multi-stemmed self-coppicing stools. It reached southern Europe to ravage *C. sativa* and the commerce in edible chestnuts, which in the Apennines had been a staple foodstuff.

Many years later, I was astonished when an Italian colleague told me that chestnut-blight was no longer troublesome. Chestnuts have been rescued by a virus that attacks and cripples the fungus. The disease still exists, but the cankers are limited and no longer kill the tree (Fig. 136). Chestnut is tenacious of life, and even a three-quarters-killed tree may fully recover. Once infected by a virus-infected fungus, a tree is permanently armoured against further *Endothia* attack.[22]

The northern Apennines are covered with chestnut-woods, stretching over hill and valley, except for beech on the higher mountains. They are often outgrown from chestnut orchards; there are remains of the *alberghi* that dried the nuts and the water mills that ground them into flour. A few groves are still productive; most are converted to coppices or neglected. Many of the great trees display high dead tops, relics of an *Endothia* attack defeated by the unseen ally. Woodcutters are familiar with *cancro del castagno*, which has left iron-hard lumps of canker, embedded deep in the trunk to take the teeth off an unwary chainsaw.

This is the story of chestnut-blight in the European heartland of chestnut, in Italy and southern France. The disease never reached outlying populations, such as the introduced chestnuts of England and Crete. On Athos, in north Greece, it arrived in the 1990s; the monks, who earn their living from chestnut coppice, have introduced the virus. With American chestnut the story has no happy ending. Although the virus got there, attempts to disperse it have been less successful, and the spreading chestnut-tree is now rarer than the village smithy.

Oak wilt: Forty years ago John Rishbeth lectured on a fungus that killed oaks in North America in the manner of Elm Disease. *Ceratocystis fagacearum* is mainly wind borne, and like Elm Disease persists for less than a year in logs. Since the 1920s oak wilt has been spreading out from a focus in Minnesota. It is assumed to be an introduction from an unknown country, but has still not been found outside America. It attacks two of the three groups of American oak species, red oaks and live-oaks, but white oaks were less affected. By 1983 it was killing the willow-oaks (*Quercus phellos*, a red oak) on the streets of Washington.

Oak wilt smoulders on. There is a second focus in middle Texas, where I have known it since 1983 (Fig. 138); it attacks the motts (clonal patches) of live-oak (*Q. fusiformis*) that dot the savanna (p.131). It usually kills an entire mott to the ground, but there may be regrowth if cattle allow it. (Elm motts are of *Ulmus crassifolia*, which seems to be unaffected by Elm Disease.) In 25 years it has killed about 15 per cent of the live-oaks, and seems to be slowing. It sometimes kills 'Spanish' oak (*Q. texana*), a red oak, but I have not seen it attack a white oak. It is carried partly by insects that are attracted to wounds on trees. It invades long-standing plant communities in the manner expected of an introduction.

For 40 years there have been rumours of oak wilt reaching Europe, and speculation on what would happen. It would probably not have the devastating effect of Elm Disease. There are no native red oaks in Europe; European deciduous oaks are white oaks and likely to be resistant. Whether the evergreen oaks of southern Europe, of the live-oak group, are susceptible is not known.

The dying pines of Japan: The mountains around Hiroshima look as if they have been hit by an atomic bomb: mile upon mile, millions of dead pines cover the slopes (Fig. 139). This is the latest stage in the spread of a microscopic, deadly nematode worm, said to have been introduced from America in the 1930s, which has gradually devoured the red pines of Japan.

Aka-matsu, red pine, *Pinus densiflora*, which resembles Scots pine, is a familiar and much-loved tree; its curved timbers are a feature of old-fashioned Japanese houses. It (and its edible *matsutake* fungus, p.36) was encouraged by a peculiar compost-gathering land-management practice that has no parallel in Europe. One of the profoundest changes between sixteenth-century pictures and the present landscape is the huge loss of red pine. Declining land management left the pines mainly on ridgetops that would have been their natural habitat, but the micro-worm has sought them out even there.

Pines have been replaced by evergreen oaks, hollies and others among the multitudinous evergreen trees of Japan. The parasite apparently does not matter in America, nor does it much affect other Japanese pines. What would happen if it reached Europe?

Bloody fluxes: Phytophthora is a large genus of microscopic fungi of the phycomycete kind (if indeed they are fungi), which thrive in temporarily wet conditions. Some 'damp-off' seedlings, or blight potato leaves and tubers. Those that attack full-grown trees are traditionally called *Ph. cinnamomi* or *cambivora*, terms that cover a group of species varying in host and in virulence. They spread by water-borne spores; they attack the cambium and may kill the tree. A diagnostic symptom is rusty-red, sticky exudations on the bark, looking like dried blood (Fig. 140).

The best-known European tree *Phytophthora* is ink disease of sweet-chestnut, which kills roots and sometimes the tree; it was a well-known problem before chestnut blight came. It favours wet seasons and waterlogged soils. It may be a native fungus, attacking what is usually an introduced tree.

In the 1960s John Rishbeth and I took an interest in an avenue of horsechestnuts belonging to our Cambridge college. Individual trees developed yellow, stunted leaves and died in two or three years. At first the cause seemed to be bacterial wetwood in the trunk spreading outwards and interfering with sap conduction. Later research found a *Phytophthora* damaging the cambium at the base of the trunk, which allowed wetwood to gain the upper hand and kill the tree. *Phytophthora*, in the manner of its kind, soon disappears, leaving other fungi to invade the dead tissue. The trees were planted c.1881, began to die at about 70 years of age, and by 2004, 26 out of 53 trees had died. They are not scattered at random: groups of dead trees alternate with stretches of healthy trees.

This set me looking for dried blood on wild trees. In the 1970s *Phytophthora*-like exudations were common on birch and sallow, and also found on beech, alder, willow, holly, cherry, aspen and oak. Some host trees were faring badly or dying from some other cause, but most recovered. The fungus probably entered through a small wound or twig scar, killed a patch of cambium, and then often died out, leaving a wound which was covered over by further growth of the tree. These limited attacks seem to have become less common since 1980.

As a student I learnt of the devastating effects of *Ph. cinnamomi* on the native vegetation of southwest Australia, especially on jarrah, one of the great timber eucalypts. Many years later I met Dr Frank Podger, whose articles I had read, and who explained how it had progressed by 1996. The scene is the mighty jarrah forests east of Perth, plant communities with hundreds of species, virtually every one peculiar to that small region, many of them lignotuberous (p.16n) and all highly fire-dependent. The climate is mediterraneoid, with hot, dry summers and warm, wet winters. Logging began in the nineteenth century: its effect might not have been too disastrous had it not happened that into this new planet, as it were, a common tropical root parasite descended in the 1920s.[23]

Phytophthora first takes out the banksias, small trees along whose roots it spreads to other species. Then it rots the blackboys (*Xanthorrhœa*) – an extraordinary plant, which flowers in profusion after each fire – and zaps the cycads.

Dryandra, a common genus of small trees, is not much affected, and only two of the six common eucalypts are susceptible. Ultimately it gets all the jarrah (*Eucalyptus marginata*), without hurting the other great eucalypt, marri (*E. calophylla*). The result is an impoverished native ecosystem, dominated by marri, from which jarrah and a random set of other species have been subtracted.

It was discovered, too late, that *Phytophthora* is spread by making gravel roads using gravel from infected pits. From these artificial sources it spreads at about 3 feet (1 metre) a year, faster in wet seasons. Its spread can be slowed, especially by keeping dirty vehicles out of uninfected areas. The cause is not lost: in an area about the size of Yorkshire nearly half is still unaffected.

In the 1990s another *Phytophthora* came to public attention in England through reports of sudden death of alders and oaks. Alder disease is a classic *Phytophthora*, attacking the cambium of the root and lower trunk, exuding dried blood, and more virulent near water. If the alders are felled the regrowth may escape. It was first noticed in the 1970s; it has killed probably about 10 per cent of the alders in some areas, such as Herefordshire and southeast England, and is beginning to attack East Anglia. It is widespread in Europe, and has attracted attention in Hungary where there are alder plantations. The causal species is reported to be a hybrid between two introduced *Phytophthoras*.[24]

At the same time dieback of oak was attracting renewed attention. On the Continent, there was some evidence for attack on oak roots by what was named *Ph. quercina*, which may be involved here too. *Phytophthora*-type exudations are scattered here and there in both dying and normal oaks.

Horsechestnut *Phytophthora* is now widespread.[25] A spectacular example is in Hatfield Forest, whose owners, the Houblons, whimsically introduced this tree in the 1850s. For a Balkan cliff endemic it fared surprisingly well on the Essex boulder-clay, and became the tallest tree in the Forest; but Nemesis has caught up with it. Year by year the horsechestnuts succumb, leaving mighty snags that are an excellent deadwood habitat (Fig. 143).

The scare of the year 2004 was the so-called *Phytophthora ramorum*, supposedly from Central Asia. On invading California and Oregon, it affected many trees, especially the local species of oak. At the time of writing it was reported in western England from rhododendrons and several other species of garden trees, but there was no sign that it would attack native oaks.

CONCLUSIONS

What is normal?

The first problem with environmental mishap and tree disease is defining normality. The public has been trained by 250 years of Enlightenment to expect trees to be upright and single-stemmed, not to have dead branches, not to be rotten, to come into leaf and to lose their leaves at the right time of year, and to die of old age. This may be what foresters and gardeners would like, but does not always agree with the agenda of trees as wildlife, nor with the concordat worked out between people and trees over the centuries.

High expectations can distort the views of scientists too. Reports of the declining health of beeches and other trees amounted to little more than that trees were failing to conform to standards of perfection set in Germany. One hardly expects the normal state of a human being to be perfect health: why should this be true of other creatures?

The Pindus beeches explode the implication that any tree that does not measure up to Central European standards of vitality must be a damaged tree. To achieve those standards, a beech needs to avoid being damaged and also to have the right climate and soil. Nature did not intend the Pindus, and maybe not England, to be the perfect environment for beech. In Central Europe, the tree is in the middle of its range, and perfect vitality may be its normal state when young. In England, beech is at the edge of its range, and perfect vitality may be unusual. In the Pindus, beech is at another edge of its range, and demonstrates that it can survive – indeed can be the dominant tree – despite poor vitality.

Much beech has been planted and suffers from the disadvantages of planted trees, especially trees introduced beyond their range or from foreign sources. People who plant beech often have no clear idea of where it will prosper. Exiled into a climate to which they are not adapted, dug up from a nursery bed, stuck into a hole in the wrong soil, exposed to hostile fungi and nematodes, separated from their mycorrhizal partners – it is surprising how often planted trees succeed at all, let alone conform to external standards of good condition.

Great storms are rare but normal events, to which trees are adapted. So are defoliations by native caterpillars. Stag-headed oaks are part of normal behaviour, a response to a rare but normal combination of events, except that a minor contributory factor may have been oak mildew.

Dutch Elm Disease is a borderline case. Epidemics may be part of the normal interaction between the fungus and its host: some might argue that the clonal habit of elms is an evolutionary response to the disease. Abnormality is shown by epidemics getting more frequent and more severe, and spreading round the globe. As with other conditions involving tree sprouting and reproduction, its effect is made worse by the increase of deer.

Ecology and evolution

Plants and animals often come to terms with parasites through evolution. Over successive generations, an annual plant species develops a reaction to infection, for example by secreting chemicals that attack the invading fungus. The fungus then develops a means of avoiding damage by the chemicals. This interaction works up to a point – if the life cycles of the host and parasite are not too dissimilar. In my plant physiology days I experimented with a variety of barley, bred for resistance to mildew, called Maris Concord, in the year when, alas, a Maris-Concord-resistant strain of mildew appeared. This problem has dogged plant breeders over the years.

The interaction works less well with long-lived or clonal hosts. In evolutionary terms, plant pathogens can run rings round trees. To develop genetic resistance to poplar-mercury rust, aspen has to start again from seed, which it does perhaps once in a hundred years, in which time the rust will have gone through 200 generations. A big elm clone may have had to cope with at least three epidemics of Elm Disease.

Disease resistance in trees has to be of a more structural and unspecialised kind. Sometimes it depends on symbiotic mycorrhizal or decay fungi. Dr Rishbeth invented a means of preventing the root fungus *Fomes annosus* from killing pine plantations. Usually it starts in a stump and spreads through the soil to attack living trees. New stumps can be deliberately infected with the harmless fungus *Peniophora gigantea*, which occupies the stump and denies it to *Fomes*.

Globalisation

Normal dynamics are circumvented by modern humanity's flair for mixing up the world's pathogens – human, animal and plant. Oak mildew shows how a seemingly insignificant introduction can profoundly upset the normal course of nature. The other oak conditions, dieback and wilt, seem not to be a problem for Britain, destructive though they are in other continents. Pine nematode, though it spreads relatively slowly, has changed the face of Japan. *Phytophthora* attack on the native vegetation of Western Australia has been called 'a biological disaster of global significance': it is comparable to the havoc wrought on small marsupials by introduced cats and foxes.

CHAPTER 18

MODERN FORESTRY

Its Rise and Fall

Some European countries have been slow in learning from Germany's mistakes ... A tragic example of this may be seen in Britain, where the countryside is being ruined by monoc-ultures. Large areas have been afforested with even-aged plantations of a single species, chosen because it was fast-growing or especially suitable for pit props ...
RICHARD ST BARBE BAKER, INTERNATIONAL TREE-PLANTER, 1948

Most forms of modern forestry rely on planting trees to create artificial vege-tation; this is what distinguishes forestry from woodmanship. Trees may be planted on moorland, heath or farmland, or into an existing wood, or the site of a destroyed wood; the intention is to create a crop, independent of the natural vegetation. Plantations are not permanent: the trees are intended to be cut down when 'mature', that is, saleable; the stumps should die, and something else will be grown on the site. Forestry, in effect, is the extension of arable farming to the growing of trees. (Selling trees has usually been someone else's business.)

Different countries have independent forestry traditions. Germany and Japan have probably the oldest, followed by France and Italy. England and Scotland began to develop their own practices, but in Victorian times were absorbed into a rigorous form of the German tradition. This was promulgated by the Forestry Commission from 1919 onwards, but never fully took over the practice of private landowners. Plantation forestry has won over many other countries, especially Tasmania, but has not taken over the whole world. (In New England I have been shown pine plantations as relics of an unsuccessful experiment.)

Modern forestry became linked to the eighteenth-century philosophical Enlightenment (p.148): the belief that all the world's problems can be solved by a combination of science (or what is presented as being science) and government. Land uses are to be categorised and simplified; common land and other multiple land uses are bad. Cultivable land should be used for conventional agriculture by private landowners. On other land, trees should be grown, but only for timber, not for wood, bark or other products. Timber production should ideally be organised by the state, both on its own lands and other landowners', on the model of either French or German forestry (depending on which state). Local knowledge should be ignored or marginalised.

These ideas captured the minds of governments, which tried to cajole or compel their subjects to follow them. (Politicians love to be told they can make even the trees grow or not grow, but do not remain in office long enough to find out.) The results depended on which style of forestry was adopted, how rigorously it was pursued, and against how much resistance. In Sweden or Italy modern forestry was taken up more thoroughly than in less Enlightened countries like England or Greece. England is remarkable in how late the government came to intervene. The German model of forestry was foisted on British India, whence it came back to this country. (What would have happened had it been the French tradition? Or the Indian?)

The application of science to forestry did not meet with complete success. Early science was reductionist, dealing with questions one aspect at a time, which is mismatched to such complex and long-lived organisms as trees. Seedlings do not behave the same as big trees, and Indian trees do not behave the same as German. Factors arise later that were not included at the start: foresters in southern Europe persistently leave fire out of their predictions. Globalisation meant that selling trees became as important as growing them. Nevertheless, Enlightenment ideas live on: in many countries research is being put into genetically modified trees that are to be propagated vegetatively, a recipe for future disaster given the importance of new plant diseases that cannot be provided against in advance.

Plantation forestry in Britain developed in two ways. The earlier form was estate forestry (p.28) growing trees for local use, especially on the estate itself, or to sell for furniture and other high-value uses. A motto often encountered is growing trees 'for pleasure and profit'; these coexisted uneasily, for most trees develop their profit aspects earlier in life than their pleasure aspects.

In the nineteenth century there diverged the practice of commercial forestry, foregoing the pleasure in the hope of profit, growing general-purpose timber as a commodity, often for low-grade uses such as pit-props – the great quantities of small timber or big underwood needed to shore up coal-mines – and paper pulp. For much of the twentieth century this was the more respectable and conspicuous branch.

Forestry books generally deal with successful plantations. An ecological book has to pay attention also to those that failed. There are degrees of success. The planted trees may stay alive; they may grow into usable timber; and (with luck) they may realise a profit on the money invested in growing them. This last depends on extraneous factors such as whether there is a market for the trees – and someone with the skill to find it – by the time they have grown. It is usually not known whether a plantation has made a profit, because by the time it is harvested the records needed for the calculation have been lost or destroyed.

HISTORY OF PLANTATION FORESTRY

Origins
The earliest account of a plantation of an area of trees is by Columella, the Roman agricultural writer of the first century BC, as an appendage to his account of vine-growing in Italy. To produce stakes for his vines he would plant a chestnut or oak coppice, citing an earlier author for the details. Chestnuts should be set half a foot* apart in rows 5 feet apart, and thinned to 2 feet apart; this would give some 4,000 stools per modern acre. The wood was to be cut at five years' growth, most of the stems being split into six small stakes. He was concerned only with chestnut as underwood: nuts were probably a staple diet in much of Italy, but would not have been produced at only five years' growth.

In the Middle Ages people often planted orchards, hedges and non-woodland trees. Planting an area of trees to create a new wood was a notable action to be recorded among the deeds of a great abbot – as rare and memorable as bringing a dead body back to life or recovering the abbey lands in trial by battle.

I know of seven English examples before 1500. The earliest and largest – but an uncertain one – is Soane (now Bullock) Wood, Colchester, which may have been enclosed and planted by the monks of St John's Abbey c.1242. The name (Latin *Boscus Seminatus,* 'sown wood') may imply a wood created by sowing acorns. The present wood is a large fragment of a much bigger wood, with no original boundary. In 1976 it was mainly chestnut (including giant coppice stools) and birch, with nothing definite to show it up as the oldest plantation known in England.

* The Roman foot was roughly the same as the English foot.

However, it lacked some of the characteristic plants of ancient woodland, such as lime and lily-of-the-valley, which grow in the other Colchester woods.[1]

A tiny plantation occurs in the *Ely Coucher Book* of 1251, recording a grove at Totteridge (Hertfordshire) of 4¼ acres (1.7 ha) 'including the land which was sown with acorns and [hazel-]nuts'. As John Harvey pointed out, two plantations were established by Abbot Godfrey of Peterborough in 1304 and 1310, who 'planted a wood where a wood had never been before' on the Fen edge, and others by Abbot John de Rutherwyk at the same time at Chertsey (Surrey).[2]

A few plantations on commons are known, for example on a sheepwalk at Gressenhall (Norfolk) in 1495.[3] At Dunstable (Bedfordshire) in 1247 the townsfolk agreed not to plant ash-trees except on their own land: if they planted them on the common, they might not sell them.[4] Was planting trees a device for appropriating public land?

In Scotland, Acts of Parliament, beginning in 1457, expressed the hope that landlords would encourage their tenants to 'plant wodds and treis make heggs and sowe brume [broom]'. The context is agricultural; hedges were not to be made 'of dry staiks na Rysh [underwood] or styks nor yit of na hewyn wode but allanly [only] of lyffand [living] wode the quhilk [which] may grow & plenyssh'.[5]

Sowing tree seed *in situ* was the usual practice down to the eighteenth century, when for uncertain reasons it was replaced by digging up transplants from a nursery. Sowing creates an undamaged root system and has much to be said for it.[6]

Evelyn and his predecessors
Eccentric abbots apart, plantations as a continuous tradition are foreshadowed by William Harrison in Holinshed's *Chronicles* in 1577. He thought woodland was diminishing, and proposed that 'Euerie man [that] enioieth fortie acres of land ... might plant one acre of wood, or sowe the same with oke mast, hasell, beech ...'

Modern forestry is often traced back to Arthur Standish, propagandist of the 1610s. Believing that the supply of timber and wood was diminishing (rather than the demand increasing), he made detailed proposals. Every farmer should plant hedges, and a quarter-acre plantation in the corner of each field. These would be growing so much firewood that 'within thirty yeares all Spring-woods [coppices] may be conuerted to Tillage and Pasture'.[7] Standish was not altogether mad. He was an agricultural writer who came apparently from the east Midlands, where hedges and woods were scarce. His sympathisers included the Winthrops, owners of Groton Wood (Suffolk), who went on to found the colonies of Connecticut and Massachusetts.

Besides being chattered about, a few plantations were actually created. Lord Burghley is said to have caused part of Cranbourne Walk, Windsor Forest, to be enclosed and sown with acorns in 1580. The site, if it can be correctly identified,[8] is now a wood-pasture, closely set with oaks that could be a plantation, but are unlikely to be more than 300 years old. In 1602 a 36-acre (14.5 ha) wood at Sudbourne (Suffolk) was described by Norden, the cartographer, as 'a newe Wood full of yong Settes'.

Government intervention began with the Commonwealth, which had inherited Crown lands, including those wooded Forests where the Crown owned the trees, from the headless Charles I. In the Forest of Dean the expanding Navy began to stake a claim to timber for shipbuilding – as well as being a large consumer of the iron produced by charcoal-burning blast furnaces. A few hundred acres of coppices and plains were enclosed by ditches, hedges or walls and sown with acorns and beech-mast between 1657 and 1660. Tens of thousands of oak and beech seedlings were transplanted out of other parts of the Forest. These attempts may have come to naught because they encroached on commoners' grazing rights. After 1660 the restored Crown made repeated efforts to establish enclosures and plantations. Although most of these failed, the Forest replenished its trees through a phase of natural regeneration that had begun in the 1640s; from this, presumably, came the large amount of timber that it supplied to the Navy in the mid- to late eighteenth century.[9]

More famous than Standish was John Evelyn, whose book *Sylva, or a Discourse of Forest-Trees*, published in 1664, went through editions and revisions for a century and a half. He was a learned man of many interests, a founder of the Royal Society, but his practical experience ran to gardening and arboriculture more than forestry. *Sylva* arose out of inquiries from the Commissioners of the Navy. Evelyn repeated what was now the traditional complaint:

Truly, the waste, *and* destruction *of our* Woods, *has been so universal, that I conceive nothing less than an universal* Plantation *of all the sorts of trees will supply, and well encounter the defect.*

This time blame could be heaped on the previous Parliamentary régime:

... our late prodigious Spoilers, *whose furious devastation of so many goodly* Woods *and* Forests *have left an Infamy on their* Names *and* Memories *not quickly to be forgotten! I mean our unhappy* Vsurpers, *and injurious* Sequestrators ...

Evelyn soon reveals himself as a landscape designer, more interested in walks and avenues than in areas of trees. English landscape architecture had existed since the twelfth century,[10] but he is the first surviving writer on it.

Evelyn's accounts of sowing, transplanting and pruning timber trees seem to derive from practical experience. He was well known among people able to put his ideas into effect, but as far as I know he cannot be linked with any surviving site. (It would be nice to think he designed Grimsthorpe Park (p.119), which is roughly contemporary with *Sylva*.) He visited Lord Arlington in the Suffolk Breckland, who got a licence for a gigantic park in 1671, of which the present Euston Park is a remnant. Relics of Evelyn's activity might be looked for there.

Evelyn's ideas were picked up in Scotland, where in 1683 John Reid published *The Scots Gard'ner*, which includes forestry as well as gardening. He apparently introduced the idea of timber trees 'for pleasure and profit', those mismatched motives that were to run through estate forestry to this day.

Eighteenth century

One of the first big plantations in England was in north Norfolk. Felbrigg Great Wood is not a medieval wood, but a series of plantations established by the Windham family from the 1670s onwards. Like most large plantations they are on very poor soil. Embedded in them are giant beech pollards remaining from a previous wood-pasture common. William Windham I began in 1676 by sowing 1,500 chestnuts in a nursery, to which he and his successors added many others, including such uncommercial trees as maple, birch and crab.[11] The chestnut stools (a fast-growing species) are now up to 7 feet (2 metres) across.

Early plantations copied natural woods, with underwood as well as timber trees, and were expected to be permanent – especially chestnut coppices. In the nineteenth century there was a brief vogue for hornbeam. In Dorset landowners put hazel in oak plantations almost up to the time that Thomas Hardy was recording the last flourish of the coppice crafts (p.396). However, timber plantations were meant to be felled after 50 to 150 years, and then either to revert to farmland or to be replanted. Even in parks, not many of the trees in boundary belts today are the same as were put there in 1750.

Oaks were still often grown from the acorn. At Stockton (Norfolk) in 1770 half a heath was planted, the other half sown with acorns among wheat; the sown oaks far outgrew the planted.[12] The practice gradually increased of planting timber trees only – which were coming to produce more income than underwood per acre per year – including conifers and other exotics. There was an increasing tendency to dig up seedlings grown in a nursery: conifer seed at first would have been too scarce to risk sowing in the field. The nursery trade, which had existed for garden plants since the Middle Ages, expanded from the 1720s onwards to supply both forestry plants and the huge demand for hawthorn to plant new hedges. Early nurseries might send plants hundreds of miles, but later local nurseries were set up, and estates took to growing plants themselves.

The Forest of Dean story was repeated 50 years later in the New Forest. This had always been less wooded than Dean, giving more scope for planting on heathland and grassland. An Act of Parliament in 1698 allowed the Crown, in spite of common-rights, to enclose and plant 6,000 acres (2,400 ha), and more when that had been completed. Had this been achieved, it would have been by far the biggest plantation that England had ever seen. It gave rise to the small wood-banks that surround some of the 'Inclosure' plantations in the Forest.[13]

The cause was promoted by what is now the Royal Society of Arts. In 1758, four years after its foundation, the Society awarded a gold medal to the Duke of Beaufort for sowing 23 acres (9 ha) of land with acorns; a silver medal to Mr P.C. Webb for 21 acres (8.5 ha), and another to Mr J. Burney for 5 acres (2 ha). Such awards continued until 1847, but they had not quite the influence on the development of the landscape that they have sometimes been credited with.[14] During 89 years, as its *Transactions* show, the Society offered about 2,000 medals and prizes for planting trees, but awarded only 178. Many medal-winning plantations were very small. Anyone sowing or planting 5 acres (2 ha) who applied for a gold medal would be almost certain to get it, unless the trees were the popular oak or 'Scotch fir'. Mr T. White of West Retford won 11 medals, six in one year. There was not much competition: people won more medals for things like 'true Rhubarb' or opium. (The Society was also interested in drugs, then a problem of under-supply.)

One of White's gold medals was for planting 10,400 'Lombardy or Po Poplars' − a tree lately introduced that was evidently thought to be a timber tree. The fashion in the 1780s was for trees from the late American colonies: awards were given for Red Virginia Cedar, Occidental Plane and Weymouth Pine, of which we now never hear.

What did the planting movement achieve by this stage? In England most plantations, as at Euston and Felbrigg, were estate forestry, part of the landscape parks of mansion houses; large plantations were seldom out in the general countryside. Park designers incorporated and adapted any woods already on the site. Some eighteenth-century parks such as Wimpole (Cambridgeshire) and Ickworth (Suffolk) were started in areas without much woodland though plenty of trees. Holkham (Norfolk) was a vast park − bigger than many Forests − begun in the mid-eighteenth century on an almost treeless site. Anyone starting a park in a woodless area would plant trees, but usually not large areas of planting: especially in flat terrain, groves and belts of trees would achieve the same appearance.

Norfolk had more than its share of landed estates and less than its share of ancient woodland, much of which was destroyed in the eighteenth century. However, on Faden's county map (c.1792) medieval woods still exceed plantations in area. Country-house parks had sprung up all over Norfolk, even where common-rights would have been an obstacle to acquiring the land. Few parks are shown as more than one-quarter woodland unless they incorporated an ancient wood. A boundary belt, typically about 150 yards (140 metres) wide, was a near-obligatory feature. Holkham, nearly complete by 1792, had such a belt, and a scatter of groves in the otherwise grassy interior. In the Breckland most of the big parks were already there in 1792 (or on Hodskinson's Suffolk map of c.1780); they generally had less woodland than they later acquired, and some were smaller – though West Tofts park, perhaps never finished, was intended to be even bigger than Holkham.

The Norfolk story may have been repeated in other parts of the country, such as Nottinghamshire, with many country mansions and not much woodland. Plantations had yet to become big business or to affect great areas of land. Until after 1800 most county maps were still dominated by medieval woods.

In Scotland, the plantation movement made more headway: with plenty of poor land and weak tenurial customs, landowners could more easily remove land from agriculture. It was dominated by a handful of very big lairds, notably the Dukes of Atholl and their rivals the Earls of Argyll. The ninth Earl, having consulted Evelyn about planting round Inveraray Castle, played politics and lost. In 1685 he found Atholl in temporary control of his castle, who – he said – dug up 34,000 trees and stole off with them to Blair Atholl.[15] For the first time they established big conifer plantations; the Dukes set a fashion for European larch. The Earls of Moray preferred native pines. Beech was introduced on a large scale, also sycamore, though mainly as a hedgerow and shelter-belt tree.

Wales, too, was the scene of more big plantations than England, beginning with Margam (Glamorgan). The most famous was at Hafod in a remote corner of Cardiganshire, where from 1782 onwards Thomas Johnes, friend of the landscape designer Uvedale Price, constructed an earthly paradise, a Gothic mansion house environ'd with contrived walks, his daughter's Pensile Garden, and 1,100 acres (400 ha) of larch and other exotics on the mountains.

In Ireland there may have been more pre-1800 plantations than in England. The Ordnance Survey of the 1830s records considerable woods, with English (not Gaelic) wood-names, in places without woodland in the Civil Survey 180 years before. Many were in or near demesne grounds, and were unlikely to have arisen by default. The maps do not suggest that they were new. Georgian Ireland enjoyed a little-understood period of prosperity, after the troubles of the seventeenth century and before the overpopulation of the nineteenth. The Royal Dublin Society offered more generous rewards than the Society of Arts; the jackpots were big enough to attract suspicions of fraud.[16]

Nineteenth century

This century saw a great increase in the plantation area (Table 22); the rise and divergence of 'commercial' forestry; and an increasing tendency to plant trees within existing woods.

Scotland continued in the lead. The *New Statistical Account* in 1845 gave the area of plantations in Scotland, which add up (adjusting for a few missing counties) to 573,000 acres (232,000 ha), or 3 per cent of the area of Scotland, against 0.93 per cent for 'natural woods'. This is beset by problems of definition, but the area of plantation had apparently overtaken that of woodland some decades before. (Professor Smout and colleagues put this point some decades later, on the basis that natural woodland had been underestimated by leaving out sparse or low woods.[17]) In nearly every county, plantations exceeded woods, Argyll being the only big exception. Later plantations began to extend into absurdly inhospitable places, as with Stirling Maxwell's efforts at afforesting the wilds of Rannoch Moor.[18]

The Scots set a fashion for Pacific conifers: Sitka spruce, Douglas fir and western hemlock. They began to publish textbooks, such as James Brown's *The Forester* (1847). Scotland was to have a disproportionate influence on English plantation forestry.

In England, during and after the Napoleonic Wars, the Crown tried yet again to convert those Forests where it owned the land to oak plantations, foreseeing the need for 74-gun ships-of-the-line and for boot leather and artillery-horse harness should there be a world war around 1940.

Admiral Nelson had visited (in spirit) the Forest of Dean in one of his rare spells of leisure, and had complained that it was not growing enough naval timber. An Act of Parliament in 1808 authorised the enclosure of about four-fifths of what the Crown owned. This task involved building 25 miles (40 kilometres) of stone walls and 70 miles (112 kilometres) of new woodbanks topped with furze, and digging hundreds of miles of drainage ditches. Most of the trees planted were oaks – still, in the main, by sowing acorns – and small numbers of pines and others. Existing trees, it seems, were felled but not grubbed or poisoned, and regrowth was cut back. Successive opponents, from mice to riotous commoners whose rights had been stolen, were overcome. No labour or expense was spared, and this time the planted trees grew. The ancient, complex wood-pasture structure was replaced with monotonous plantations; greens and commons were reduced to little more than roadside verges. Even the deer were officially banished, to protect not so much the trees as the morals of the inhabitants, lest they be tempted to the sin of deer-stealing. The undertaking was completed by 1855, just in time for the Navy to stop building oaken ships.[19] The wrong oaks were planted (p.270) and the result was barely successful even on its own terms. The entire Forest now contains less than 70 acres (28 ha) of ancient wood-pasture.

The New Forest was too big to treat thus. The area planted was about 19,000 acres (7,700 ha), less than one-third of the Crown land and about one-fifth of the whole Forest. The areas chosen usually adjoined and sometimes included existing tree'd areas: the big heaths were left alone. An attempt was made to get rid of the deer. The commoners more effectively defended their rights, especially in the latter part of the century when the Commons and Footpaths Preservation Society intervened to protect public amenity.

Smaller Crown-owned Forests were treated much as Dean. In Alice Holt and Bere (Hampshire), Whittlewood and Salcey (Northamptonshire) the natural vegetation and historic infrastructure – coppices, plains, most of the ancient trees – vanished under what would now be called 'blanket afforestation' of oak. The oaks of the 1820s grew, but never fulfilled their appointed destiny in World War II. These monotonous, even-aged stands of rather poor-quality oak became somewhat of an embarrassment.

Private landowners continued to develop country-house parks on the 'pleasure and profit' principle. Plantations arose away from parks and on a scale comparable to medieval woods. Bryant's map of Norfolk, c.1825, shows for the first time Emily's and Snake Woods and Bromehill Plantation on the Breckland, and several 'Fir Plantations' in northeast Norfolk, where the imitation of natural woods had been abandoned. Many small plantations were intended as coverts for foxhunting or pheasant-shooting, although existing woods were often used as such.

After 1860, agriculture became so depressed that plantations could compete with it for land. Landowners with money made by mining or trade began to think of trees as an investment. Although markets for oak bark and timber had declined, oaks were still planted, but were overtaken by conifers: spruce as well as the traditional 'fir' (pine) and larch. Successive Ordnance Survey editions record the infilling of many parks and extensions on to surrounding land. At Melton Constable in Norfolk the pre-1792 park was extended by plantations over the heaths outside, in which were embedded the ancient Swanton Novers Great and Little Woods.

Public authorities made plantations. Municipal reservoirs had a wide buffer zone of conifers around them, which kept away farmland effluent and the polluting public and were thought to improve the water. Examples are the Derbyshire Derwent, Haweswater (Lake District) and Lake Vyrnwy in mid-Wales.

According to Board of Agriculture Returns, the recorded area of woodland and plantation in England increased between 1872 and 1905 by 1.15 per cent of the land area (from 4.1 per cent to 5.3 per cent). Such figures should be taken with caution, and part of the change was due to natural woods growing up on heaths and other abandoned land; but it is an unexpectedly large increase in 33 years (although it fell far short of plantations in France). In Wales the recorded increase was 1.53 per cent, and in Scotland 0.69 per cent of the land. The scanty statistics for Ireland record no significant change: famine and emigration do not seem to have generated much new woodland.

Plantations on the site of existing woods
In a rational world, a site that already has trees on it would be the last place anyone would choose for a plantation: to the task of getting new trees to grow would be added the problem of preventing existing trees from competing with them. For most of history this commonsense attitude seems to have prevailed.

My earliest record of planting trees in an existing wood is at Cawston (Norfolk) in 1612, where the lessee of Southawe Wood:

shall yerely and everie yere of the 14 yeres putt a good number of Sallowes in the vacant emptie places of the ... two acres of underwood ... so that the sayd vacant and emptye places may be well planted and supplied with wood.[20]

Sallow may seem a surprising choice, but it was useful, especially for wattle-and-daub, and easy to establish. This, however, was merely filling gaps, not supplanting a natural wood. Gap-filling may have happened for centuries before, but not on a large enough scale to be recorded in writing.

Much later came what is now called 'restocking', in effect replacing a natural wood with a plantation. My earliest record is in Hatfield Forest, Essex, in 1759, when a 'fresh plantation' was made of Warren Coppice. By 1803 the wood was producing very little underwood, but timber trees being felled included beech and chestnut, which would not have grown there naturally. Half a century later it had disappeared: all but one of the other coppices, which were not replanted, are still there today.[21]

The Victorians often planted trees in existing woods without first destroying the wood: this is shown by scattered conifer symbols on first-edition 6-inch Ordnance Survey maps, or by scattered conifers still standing or rotting in the wood. How it was done – how they got the planted trees to survive the competition of the underwood – is unclear. Hardy's *The Woodlanders* records the attention given to planting and the harvesting of planted trees, a symptom of the decline of the woodmanship tradition in the Dorset of the 1880s when he was writing; this is confirmed by conifer symbols in woods on Ordnance maps.

In some areas replanting went far in the nineteenth century (p.264ff). Around Sheffield, where charcoal-burning had been abandoned, most of the woods had been converted to timber production, often as plantations, by 1914.[22] However, the main onslaught on existing woods occurred after 1950.

German influence

The British made forestry an affair of state in the Empire. The Government of India (including the present Pakistan and Burma), after the Indian Mutiny, had a department that tried to organise forestry throughout its own territories, and to set a European example to princes and maharajahs outside its jurisdiction. Perhaps because of Queen Victoria's German connections, the model imitated was German. Three distinguished German foresters were appointed to the Indian forest service from 1856 onwards: Sir Dietrich Brandis, Sir William Schlich and Berthold Ribbentrop. Their task was to impose German practice rather than learn from Indian, much as 'scientific' state foresters at home, with their strong emphasis on plantations, had marginalised Germany's own traditions of woodmanship and wood-pasture. How successful they were is hard to tell from this distance in time and space. Some of their activities, such as suppressing fires and squabbling over common-rights, had very different effects from those intended.

In 1878 the British foreclosed on Cyprus, collateral for a loan to the Sultan of Turkey, partly because they thought they knew better than the Cypriots how to manage the landscape of Cyprus. Here, after a period with P.G. Madon, a forester from the south of France, they appointed German-trained personnel from India.[23]

German forestry came to influence Britain itself via India and Cyprus. Brown's *The Forester* in 1847 had recorded mainly Scottish practice, without specific reference to Germany, although the 1882 edition has an appendix by Brandis on forestry in India. Its successor textbooks were German or heavily influenced by Germany. In 1889 Schlich began to publish his voluminous *Manual of Forestry*; in 1905 he became Professor in the new Forestry Department of Oxford University.

The twentieth century

State afforestation came before a Parliamentary committee in 1907, the motive being to find work for the unemployed.[24] Before this became more than an idea it was overtaken by the events of 1915.

The dependence of Britain on imported timber, going back to the thirteenth century, had become almost complete. Even pit-props were imported. One year into World War I, German submarines began to sink the ships fetching timber from distant lands. Although, in a rational world, the shortfall might have been made up from the vast forests of France, a shocked nation hastily began using up the trees that had accumulated in Britain since felling declined in the 1860s. This was more a matter of organisation than supply. It was later said that 450,000 acres (182,000 ha) of 'woodlands', about one-sixth of the woodland and planta-tion in Britain, had been felled in four years.

The Forestry Commission: The Government's Forestry Sub-Committee gave rise to the Forestry Commission, founded by statute in 1919. The first Chairman was a Highland chieftain, Lord Lovat, descendant of him who had lost his head in the cause of Bonnie Prince Charlie; for a long time the Commission had a Scots bias. The objective was to replace a 'strategic reserve' of general-purpose timber for use the next time there was a world war, to be grown on cheap land: heath, moor-land and poor-quality agricultural land.[25]

The Commission was primed by being presented with the 'Crown Woods' – New Forest, Forest of Dean and the like. Land acquisition was helped by low land values, but finance came and went at the whim of governments. (The Commission itself was nearly strangled at the age of three.) There was never a hope of developing a stable, independent agency like parts of the French forest organisation, which have gone on steadily growing trees down the centuries through thick and thin.

The Commission planted trees on its own land, and also made small grants to private landowners: £2 per acre was perhaps worth having in the Depression. Big early land acquisitions included the Ogmore and Margam areas of South Wales and in the Breckland and Sandlings of East Anglia.

In World War II the submarine story was repeated. About 500,000 acres (200,000 ha) of 'woodlands' were said to have been felled in six years, but not much on the Commission's lands, where the plantations were at most 25 years old. By an irony of history, the British in 1945 relieved conquered Germany of substantial quantities of timber by way of booty – but this was a drop in the ocean of German forests.

The Commission was not only concerned with planting trees. In the 1930s creating jobs had again become an objective: out-of-work miners were banished to remote new villages where, it was hoped, they would turn into forest workers and smallholders. For a time it organised the selling of trees, for instance through the Home-Grown Timber Marketing Association, established in 1934, although not much was left of the organisation when it was really needed 60 years later. The Alice Holt research station has published many scientific studies, some of them classics like *Utilization of Hazel Coppice* and T.R. Peace's *The Status and Development of Elm Disease in Britain*,[26] and still does excellent work, especially on tree pathology. Bedgebury Pinetum and Westonbirt Arboretum are, in effect, botanical gardens, and are likely to be the Commission's best-remembered legacy.

The Commission has organised censuses of woodlands, even censuses of trees, at intervals of about 20 years. These, though painstaking and detailed, lose much of their value through lack of consistency. Cambridgeshire in 1981 was taken to be a different area from Cambridgeshire in 1967, and Monmouthshire was counted with England in 1905 and Wales in 1948. Who knows how the surveyors of 1924 decided which woodland was 'uneconomic' and which was not? Or where boundaries were drawn in 1948 between the non-overlapping categories of 'felled', 'devastated' and 'scrub'? I understand that the original records, which might by now be more instructive than the published abstract, were thrown away.

It has often been claimed that the two World Wars destroyed vast areas of woodland, and the years between the wars destroyed even more. For woodland in the strict sense this is a myth, resulting from a confusion between felling the trees and destroying the wood. Even taking woodland and plantation together, it is not obvious from official statistics. For only a few, mainly agricultural, counties, do the figures for 1948 record a smaller area than those for 1905. In Suffolk many more acres were planted in the Breckland and Sandlings in the 1930s than were later lost to airfields or agriculture.

A search of part of my database shows, in eastern England, evidence of 'excessive' wartime or inter-war felling – pre-1950 stumps outnumbering surviving oaks – in only 90 out of 403 ancient woods, 22 per cent. This somewhat underestimates the extent of felling, for bigger woods were more often felled (17 out of 42 woods over 100 acres/40 ha); moreover woods in which the oaks had been felled were probably more likely to fall victims to grubbing or replanting between 1950 and 1975, which would often destroy the evidence. However, it disconfirms the popular belief in widespread destruction of woodland. On the whole, 1914–45 fellings did little more than make up for the lack of felling in the half-century before 1914.

My records for other counties are not very different. In many woods felling still left an unhistorically high density of oaks; in many others there is no evidence of twentieth-century felling at all. It is also common to find a wood with few oaks but no stumps remaining, showing that oaks had already failed to replace themselves well before World War I. Wartime and inter-war fellings were patchy and affected particular estates. In south Essex only one wood in ten was affected; in west Cambridgeshire there was at least some felling in most woods.

Planting was to increase still more after World War II. In the heyday of the 1970s it was running in Wales, Scotland and northern England at more than 0.15 per cent of the entire land area per year, some three times the nineteenth-century peak.

Triumph of the plantation ethos: Before World War II the Commission had seldom affected existing woodland. After the war, it purchased ancient woods, or acquired them on 999-year leases at a non-reviewable rent, or entered into dedication or approval agreements to subsidise private landowners to do the work. Woods came to be regarded as moorland. The existing trees would be ringbarked, poisoned, or both, and a plantation would be established, either of conifers or of a mixture of oak and a 'nurse crop' of conifers; the planted oak, in some cases, being later poisoned when a new boss took over. George Ryle describes the extraordinary efforts put into destroying the clay woods of the Midlands, even where it was obvious that the foresters would not win. This (had it all produced timber) would have been only a trifling part of the total area of plantations, but it had an impact on woodland ecology comparable only with the parallel fashion for grubbing out woods for a trifling increase in farmland.

Besides the Commission's own activities, it encouraged planting and restocking by private landowners: by exhortation, by grants, and by making replanting a condition of a felling licence. For a time – 1950 to 1975, 'the years that the locust hath eaten' – the plantation culture was pervasive. The Historiographer Royal for Scotland tells how the foresters were obsessed with non-native species and 'dismissive and destructive of the native woods'. Even the National Trust was persuaded to destroy historic woods in the cause of replanting (Fig. 145), and Cambridgeshire

Naturalists' Trust considered (briefly) a proposal to replant an arbitrarily chosen one-quarter of Hayley Wood. Scheduled Sites of Special Scientific Interest had no legal protection until 1981, by which time nearly all the damage had been done.

German-style forestry was the parting gift of the British to the Republic of Ireland. It was debated with rather more enthusiasm than in Britain, especially through the vivid writings of John Mackey.[27] In terms of area, the greatest achievements of the Forestry Division, as of the Commission in Britain and Northern Ireland, were after 1950. Much of the land planted was bog, either intact blanket bog or the remains of raised bogs destroyed by commercial peat digging. As an afterthought, most of the meagre remaining ancient woods were coniferised.

The rise and fall of forestry economics
When challenged, foresters would excuse their activities in terms of economics. In theory it should be possible to work out, with tables of discount and inflation, how much profit a plantation had made: to offset the cost of buying the land, planting, poisoning etc. against the income from sales of thinnings and of the final crop. The method was adapted from one devised in Germany to work out due compensation when someone's plantations were expropriated for public works. In practice, landowners rarely cared enough about profit to keep the archives from which to do the calculation. The great forest economist W.E. Hiley, who introduced the method to Britain, could not illustrate it from British examples, and used the Nilambur teak plantations in India, where meticulous records had been preserved since 1840.[28]

The new step was to apply the same arithmetic to *predict* whether a particular style of plantation would justify the amount spent on it. It was claimed that mass coniferisation and the restocking of existing woods were the only 'economically viable' form of forestry. This being a financial argument, it carried an authority independent of the quality of the data or the cogency of the logic. Modern foresters for a time promoted the idea that planting trees was not merely patriotic and conservationist but was an investment, an alternative to stocks and shares. Forestry companies flourished for a time. In Ireland in the 1930s forestry writers solemnly debated whether a farmer could expect more income from 10 acres of trees or 10 acres of sheep, and were disappointed when real farmers were not persuaded. Accountancy, however, was not enough: in Britain the forestry interest bent the ear of governments to help afforestation with tax exemptions, with a number of disastrous or comic consequences.[29]

Conservationists would sigh and say 'it's a pity that they have to do this, but ...', rather than picking holes in the calculation. Why the foresters chose this ramshackle apologia is a mystery. In practice, as Jonathan Spencer points out, the Commission was less concerned with economics than with finance – with staying afloat from one government to the next. Did they think accountancy was the way to persuade a stupid and hard-headed Treasury?

The first hole to pick is the discount rate used to link expenditure 40 years ago with income now. Because of the long time-interval the outcome may stand or fall on whether the rate is 3.1 per cent or 3.2 per cent per annum, yet the rate adopted was plucked out of the air, not derived from observation or measurement. This apart, the arithmetic would have worked only in a world where trees grew predictably and wages and prices were stable. Within 20 years the economics were falling apart, followed by the practicalities. The men doing the maintenance demanded more money, and then could not be found at all. Hot summers pinched the growth of spruces and other wet-climate trees and then killed them; storms plucked them out, and native trees recovered and out-competed them. If the trees grew, the markets disappeared. Hybrid poplars were planted all over river valleys when there was a good market for matches; by the time they had grown the matchmakers had decided they did not want them. Coal mines, the Commission's best customer, closed down. What was left was general-purpose timber, to be sold on a world market where prices were falling. There are many good reasons for growing trees, but as an investment they have been more like horses at Newmarket.

All these troubles were worse for plantations on woodland sites, which tend to be small, scattered, and troublesome to inspect. Heath and moorland plantations enjoy economies of scale and freedom from existing trees.

I am told that in Ireland plantations have fared better – but they are sustained by a perilously small number of pulp and chipboard factories. Other countries have similar stories. Japan has its own plantation tradition, which is as old as Europe's and has its 'estate' and 'commercial' variants. In 1998 I saw many abandoned sawmills and overstood plantations: it was explained that this was due to the rising cost of labour and falling price of timber. Japan, like Ireland and Britain, was going through a phase of plundering other countries' wildwood while neglecting its own forests. Abandonment, I am told, becomes irreversible as the skills of felling and hauling trees on steep slopes die out.

I was once scolded by a critic who told me that 'foresters ought to be growing trees for the industries of today': just what foresters can never do. This may be a justification for growing short-lived trees; yet even so, today's industries will have become yesterday's industries by the time the trees have grown. The landscape is full of trees grown for obsolete reasons, and probably always will be (cf. the 'Wycombe syndrome', p.284). Woods today are full of oaks that should have provided the ships and boots of World War II. Valleys are full of poplars that were to have ignited the cigarettes of the 1990s; many of these have grown into picturesque shapes after the 1987 and 1990 storms shattered or uprooted them.

The recent past and the future
Plantation forestry had six successive objectives in the twentieth century: creating jobs; creating a strategic reserve; saving imports; making money; and, now, providing public amenity and wildlife habitat. A lot of anthropology has unrolled within the life span of a short-lived tree.

When I first studied woodland those older and wiser than I were forever asserting that woodmanship was not 'economically viable' and the future was with even more plantations. They meant that woodmanship was labour-intensive and that the products did not sell themselves. These problems have now caught up with plantation forestry, especially the commercial branch. By the time the trees have grown, and the expense of establishing them has been forgotten, there is no telling whether a market for them will still exist. This, like the accountancy problem, may explain modern foresters' curious obsession with fast-growing trees: difficulties mount up the longer the trees remain standing. Timber nurtured over many years suddenly loses its value, as the market is captured by some distant country that has wildwood to liquidate or plantations coming into production or cheap labour. (The value of timber depends at least as much on costs of labour and transport as on the value of trees.) Fast-growing trees can hardly be left to grow on for a few more decades until the market recovers.

Planting passed its peak in the 1980s, and more of it is now of broadleaved trees. Although there will probably be some further increase, the immediate future for the commercial branch of forestry in Britain is poor. More and more of the world's production of general-purpose cellulose is coming from a less than proportionate area of plantations in continents with economies of scale impossible in Britain. This may not be sustainable, depending as it does on monocultures of alarmingly few species of exotic trees. But for the foreseeable future there is little prospect of a world shortage of timber, as the weak market for second-hand timber demonstrates.

Forestry, like much of agriculture, became a vested interest in search of a function. In 1980 a Select Committee of the House of Lords asked new and pertinent questions about its future.[30] The Forestry Commission reformed itself in the 1990s. A new ethos has grown up: previously it was, at best, a supporter of wild-life conservation *within* plantations; it now promotes conservation of woodland itself. This seems to be a permanent change. Partly it is a matter of survival: had the Commission continued to be at odds with conservation bodies and public opinion, as well as defying the economics, it would by now be dead. But a new generation of foresters has grown up with better things to do with their lives than grow millions of identical trees.

Estate forestry has found a new lease of life, presented as being a compromise between timber-growing, amenity and nature conservation.[31] Estate foresters are not bound to grow thousands of identical trees and fell them all at once: they are interested in natural regeneration, selection systems, continuous cover and the French forestry tradition. They are less obsessed with fast growth and early harvesting. They tend to grow 'quality' trees to sell for furniture and other special uses, rather than mass-produce ordinary trees to be ground into chips or pulp. They combine forestry with other land uses, and some have developed local trades that use the produce. (The Japanese equivalent of estate forestry, too, has fared relatively well.)

Estate forestry is a welcome change from the commercial branch that dominated the twentieth century. However, its claims can be exaggerated. Amenity and nature conservation will be dealt with in the last chapter. Like commercial forestry, it speculates on future value. It plans on the assumption that the wheel of fashion will be forever stuck in the year 2005; that definitions of 'quality' trees will not change in the future as they have in the past. High-quality timber is a new product in which Britain has not specialised before, and other countries may produce it better. Britain is not a good country for it, because of the ravages of grey squirrels, until very recently absent from the Continent.

With much of farming kept going only by subsidies, the question arises: Why should not plantations replace unwanted farmland instead of eating up moorland? This is the basis of the National Forests proposed, and in part begun, in the last ten years. They may not replace the ancient woods that farmers destroyed in the Locust Years, but they are very popular as a public amenity; they may produce a modest amount of timber. They could even be a minor insurance against the day when the natural enemies of trees like Monterey pine (*Pinus radiata*) catch up with Asian and Australian plantations (Fig. 13).[32]

CHAPTER 19

MODERN FORESTRY: ITS LEGACY

Plantations as Ecosystems

About 40 per cent of the vascular plant species in ancient woods have been unable to colonise new woodland even after 400 years, and there is no sign that they will do so eventually. While renewed attempts to plant more woodland on farmland are welcome because they create additional wildlife habitat, most of the characteristic and attractive plants of ancient woodland will not colonise without help.

G.F. PETERKEN

Plantations can have many different fates through design, accident or neglect. Weasenham Woods (west Norfolk), first appearing on Bryant's 1824 map, have been nurtured by generations of the Coke family in the estate tradition, and are now famous among dendrologists for their magnificent conifers. Some of the conifers have become naturalised and grow from seed.[1]

Hafod (p.352) passed to the commercial branch and became a Paradise Lost. The larches (or their successors) were felled in the 1940s in the ordinary course of business; the mansion was blown up as 'unsafe' in 1958; the Pensile Garden disappeared in Douglas fir plantations. By the 1990s only some beeches and the occasional cedar remained as stranded relics of the Johneses and Uvedale Price, plus one great pollard oak from a yet earlier period. The Hafod Trust was beginning the superhuman task of returning it to a Paradise Regained.

PLANTATIONS AND CONSERVATION

Objections to plantations are nearly two centuries old. Wordsworth the poet expressed a common sentiment:

Whole acres of artificial shrubbery and exotic trees among rocks and dashing torrents ... the whole contents of the nurseryman's catalogue jumbled together ... But this deformity, bad as it is, is not so obtrusive as the small patches and large tracts of larch-plantations that are overrunning the hill-sides.
A GUIDE THROUGH THE DISTRICT OF THE LAKES, 1835

Taste is fickle: why did the relatively inoffensive larch incur such eloquent disdain?

In the third quarter of the twentieth century the Forestry Commission was scolded for spoiling mountain landscapes by 'blanket afforestation', for obscuring the detail of rock and bog with monotonous spruce and larch (or, worse, 'pyjama-stripes' of alternate spruce and larch), and for making incongruous sharp edges at property boundaries. They responded by hiring Dame Sylvia Crowe, landscape architect, to advise them on a more naturalistic layout of plantations. Besides these usually minor concessions to appearance, they altered their design in practical ways, such as by not planting the banks of streams to reduce the harmful effects on fish.

Forty years on, was it wise to object so strongly to blanket afforestation? Ought plantations to be scattered over the country, rather than concentrated in a few areas? Blanket afforestation intrudes on fewer views than pepperpot afforestation; it affords economies of scale for the foresters; and it allows plantation ecosystems – whatever they might be – to develop on a large scale and with a wider range of habitats and of possible sources of animals and plants. (Do similar considerations apply to wind farms, now being objected to on similar grounds to plantations?)

In its early years the Commission was blamed for destroying antiquities. This has been rectified; constraint maps of plantations include antiquities among the features that limit operations.

Despite the huge increase in woods and plantations in the past 150 years, tree-planting is more popular than ever, as all conservation organisations know. Creating new woodland by letting 'scrub' take over abandoned land has been forgotten, although it happens daily before the eyes of millions of commuters on trains.

Motives (other than pleasure or profit) for plantations
In other countries, plantations have been made or forests preserved for environmental reasons. It has been widely believed that trees attract rainfall, prevent floods and prevent erosion. Thus Richard St Barbe Baker, founder of Men of the

Trees (now the International Tree Foundation), encouraged tree-planting all over the world, beginning in Africa.

The belief that trees increase rainfall had a scientific basis: John Woodward in the 1690s and Stephen Hales in the 1720s observed that trees transpire water vapour into the atmosphere, which returns in the form of rain. Well into he twentieth century savants claimed that deserts were created by people destroying trees. Baker in his early career was sceptical on this point, but later claimed to have demonstrated the increase of rainfall by measurement.[2] The effect is real, but probably so small as to be lost among the ordinary fluctuations of rainfall.

The beliefs that forests prevent floods and prevent erosion are still alive. In Japan, where there may be some truth in them, they apparently originated independently of European influence. Baker made deserts his mortal enemy; his Men of the Trees hoped to 'conquer' the Sahara.[3] (What happened to their trees? Did they conquer the Sahara? Have the vast tree-planting schemes in China held back the deserts?) These arguments are at their weakest in Britain, where it is difficult to argue that floods and erosion have much to do with lack of trees.

At the time of writing an oft-cited motive for tree-planting is to lock up carbon dioxide and thus reduce global warming. This, too, is a matter of scale: Britain is too small to make an appreciable difference (p.439).

PLANTATIONS ON NON-WOODLAND SITES

Are plantations really woodland?

At least nine factors may influence secondary woods:

1. age;
2. whether planted or natural;
3. tree species;
4. whether well managed or neglected;
5. previous land use: woodland, farmland, heath, moorland, or another plantation;
6. whether the site adjoins a pre-existing wood;
7. whether it includes pre-existing hedges or trees;
8. whether it is all tree-covered or contains open areas; and
9. deer and other browsing animals.

A full study would involve all these in different combinations. Published studies seldom deal with more than two factors at a time, or with plantations more than 50 years old.

Most plantations, especially small ones, pass through a period of neglect. Neglect is part of the essential anthropology of plantations, and should be provided for, not dismissed as an unfortunate lapse that will never happen again. Any plantation, especially a neglected one, is subject to natural succession as is a neglected field or heath and, if left long enough, will acquire some of the characteristics of a wood. The Sandlings pine plantations in Suffolk, when blown down in 1987, turned out to be full of young oaks. Even moorland plantations can be invaded by birch and rowan.

A highland example: Burrator

Burrator Reservoir, on the edge of Dartmoor, is surrounded by plantations created by Plymouth Corporation on moorland-edge farm grassland, mainly from 1925 to 1965. The plantations were very piecemeal, mostly of a variety of conifers. They fluctuated between management and neglect until much of them was harvested after the great storm of 1990.

The ground vegetation developed with the age and species of the canopy. Most conifers (even the deciduous larch) went through a thicket stage with no herbaceous plants; as they got older and let through more light they were colonised by grasses, bracken and heath bedstraw (*Galium saxatile*). What resulted was, in effect, a weak grassland with trees. Only a few woodland plants appeared: wood-sorrel, occasional bluebell, and foxglove (a buried-seed plant in felled areas).[4]

This supports my own impression that highland plantations preserve an impoverished fraction of the preceding flora, rather than developing much woodland vegetation of their own. (Oak plantations may preserve more of the preceding flora than conifers.) They can be colonised by wood-sorrel or *Luzula sylvatica*, less often by *Dryopteris* ferns or raspberry, and sometimes develop a bryophyte flora different from moorland; however, they resemble moorland-with-trees rather than woodland.

Plantations on heathland: fungi

Much of the Forestry Commission's activity in the 1930s was on heath or poor arable land, especially in the Breckland, east Suffolk and Dorset. They continued the heath plantations of past centuries.

At first sight heath plantations seem to lack a distinctive flora. Remnants of heathland survive precariously on rides, and if the canopy is not too dark a few moderately shade-tolerant plants such as the sedge *Carex arenaria* spread under the trees. Even old-established, coppiced plantations such as Emily's Wood in the Breckland have not much of a woodland flora.

There are a few exceptions. There was a sensation in the nineteenth century when *Goodyera repens*, a rare orchid of Caledonian pinewoods, turned up in pine plantations in north Norfolk. It still persists, and has also spread into pine plantations in Scotland: maybe it shares mycorrhiza with the pines. In the 1960s the big pinewood mosses *Rhytidiadelphus loreus* and *Ptilium crista-castrensis* turned up in 40-year-old pine plantations in Breckland. These remain a mystery: although spores could have come on the wind they are rarely produced. (Will the mosses survive the felling of the plantations?)

Fungi colonise more easily. John Rishbeth found in the 1950s that Breckland pine plantations on ex-farmland were menaced by honey-fungus (*Armillaria mellea* in the strict sense). It came either from spores germinating on stumps after thinning or by clonal spread from existing mycelia in the hedges.

Brandon Park in the Suffolk Breckland is a country-house park, founded *c.*1805 on treeless heath or strip-cultivation. Its nineteenth-century plantations were partly infilled by the Forestry Commission with Scots and Corsican pines *c.*1935. There are fine middle-aged beeches, Scots (not Caledonian) pines and larches. Flowering plants comprise considerable remnants of Breckland heath and grassland, but no characteristic woodland species.

I have recorded visible fungi there nearly every autumn since 1959. The list is still growing; at 469 species it is comparable in numbers with the ancient woodland of the Bradfield Woods (where, however, there has been less recording effort).

Over 200 years Brandon Park has acquired a respectable list of fungi, many of them specialised to particular trees (Table 23). (For details of the mycorrhizals see Table 5.) Grassland and heather fungi could have survived from the previous vegetation – although much of the grassland has probably undergone a period of fertilising. Beech, which could be native to Breckland but not here, is the predominant host of mycorrhizals and litter-decomposers, although it is not the commonest tree. Pines have acquired many ground fungi and predominate among the wood-rotters. Even larch and cedar, natives of distant lands, have acquired some specific fungi. Oak, however, has rather few as yet. The fungus flora is probably still incomplete: in its native Alps larch has a wide range of mycorrhizals comparable with pine.

There have been some changes. Fly agaric (*Amanita muscaria*), mycorrhizal with birch and pine, used to be common, but I have only once seen it since 1992. (The absence of fruit-bodies does not prove that it is not there.) *A. rubescens,* common in the 1960s, last turned up in 1995. *Collybia peronata* and *Helvella crispa,* on beech litter, have become commoner since 1975. Many litter fungi and mycorrhizals used to be abundant in pine plantations up to 60 years old, but where these have been invaded by the sedge *Carex arenaria* very few agarics are now visible. I am reminded of the Japanese work on *Tricholoma matsutake* and its relation to the vegetation in pinewoods (p.36).

Have Sitka spruce, Douglas fir and western hemlock brought any mycorrhizal fungi from the eastern Pacific? If so, would this be an ecological gain, or a mere stage in mixing up all the world's fungi? Should the conservation of such fungi, if needed, happen in Scotland or in Sitka?

As far as can be told, modern forestry has a bad effect on lichens. It destroys or weakens rock- or soil-growing lichens. By dealing in young trees, it favours quick colonisers that are already common.

Plantations and animals
Plantations are claimed to benefit birds and mammals. Much of what has been said is either vague and general or based on analogies with 'similar' natural forests in other countries. Many of the beneficiaries are species that are already common (in the case of deer, too common): for example rook and pheasant make use of plantations as well as all their other habitats.

It is plausibly claimed that the survival of the red squirrel depends on conifer plantations: the grey squirrel is a species of deciduous woods whereas the red is adapted to pinewoods.[5] If so, how did red squirrels flourish in the long centuries when there were no pinewoods south of Perth? Or did they? Could the native red squirrel be extinct, replaced by a Continental lookalike imported in the eighteenth century when numbers were low?

Many birds require trees, often a particular structure of trees, but have little preference for species. Plantations benefit these through an increase of trees in general. A few such birds have increased dramatically: the goshawk is well established in plantations in Wales, south Scotland and Breckland. Among conifer specialists, crossbill (*Loxia curvirostra*) is now widespread in big plantations all over Britain and Ireland. However, the Scots endemic species of crossbill (*L. scotica*) has not correspondingly increased: it appears to require *old pines,* which forestry does not provide.[6] Capercaillie, another conifer bird, is faring badly (p.316); blackcock is encouraged by young plantations, but then disappears.

Goldcrest and firecrest are less strongly associated with conifers than they once were. Poplar plantations on Lakenheath Fen, Suffolk (the only big plantations in the Fens) were colonised by the golden oriole, a fabled songster, a summer migrant spreading northwards into Europe. However, many woodland species require old, rotten or dead trees, which forestry provides only through neglect.

Forestry disfavours birds limited to open ground; but the bustard disappeared from heaths long before plantations encroached on them, and the stone-curlew depends more on Breckland cultivation than on heathland. Another heath bird, Dartford warbler, is deterred by any trees, whether forestry or wild.

Moorland birds

The Flows of Caithness and Sutherland are the nearest that Britain has to wilderness, a vast peaty tundra beyond the present natural limit of forest. They were the scene in the 1980s of a curious perversion of commercial forestry. As forestry terrain they are comically worse even than Rannoch Moor. Speculators brought out all the resources of technology to get trees to grow where nature did not mean them to, the trees being not veneer-quality oak or even Sitka spruce, but mere lodgepole pine, nearly useless and very liable to insect attack. The motive was not to grow cellulose, but to exploit a temporary tax loophole.

This affair attracted the wrath of the European Union because the Flows were the chief stronghold of greenshank in the Union (before Sweden joined!). There was plenty of theory on what moorland afforestation ought to do to birds, but little evidence. From what there was, C. Lavers & R. Haines-Young identified a dozen other species likely to be affected. Not all were equally at risk: some, such as golden eagle and buzzard, flourish elsewhere.[7]

Whether birds are displaced and what happens to them − whether they vanish or crowd in somewhere else − varies from species to species. Effects may not be limited to the mere subtraction of area: birds like dunlin avoid not only plantations themselves, but moorland in their vicinity.

Conclusions

Aquatic birds increased dramatically in England in the last hundred years, partly because of new gravel-pits and reservoirs. The increase in plantations has had less effect. It has reduced the habitat of some heath and moorland species, has brought back the goshawk, and has probably made some common species a little commoner. As with plants, neglect − deliberate or accidental − would improve the habitat. Blanket rather than pepperpot afforestation might have reduced the adverse effects and possibly increased the benefits.

For other animals there is less evidence. Conifer woods have a complex ecosystem of insects and spiders in the canopy, which conifer plantations to some extent reproduce. Broadleaved trees have similar creatures if there are shrubby lichens in which they can feed and hide. C.M.P. Ozanne and others have found strong edge effects in spruce and pine plantations. Thrips, for example, are largely confined to within 70 feet (20 metres) of the edge of a plantation, whereas some sensitive species avoid this zone.[8] Too little is yet known to put this observation into a wider context. Compared with tropical forests, these studies have been relatively neglected in Europe.

PLANTATIONS REPLACING EXISTING WOODLAND

Nineteenth-century plantings

The effects vary according to whether the planted trees lived, whether they were harvested, and what happened after the harvesting. At one extreme, after two cycles of replanting, a wood may be unrecognisable as an ancient wood, even the stumps having disappeared.

There are four possible fates for Victorian conifers. Some are still going strong, for example the ragged *Abies grandis* towering over an ancient wood close to a mansion, or yew as a specimen tree at a junction of rides. Some have died out or been felled and their stumps rotted away, but often a few survivors or mouldering logs remain: in Madingley Wood (Cambridge) a dwindling band of spruces remains from a planting of *c*.1870. Some have disappeared without trace, as in Gosling's Corner, a fragment of the ancient Langton Wood east of Lincoln, where scattered conifers shown on the 1886 Ordnance Survey have vanished and native woodland has closed up the gaps. Some have turned into birch (Fig. 206). The spread of birch in the twentieth century was helped by plantings in the previous century, which when they died made openings for the birch. In the Bradfield Woods (Suffolk) a patch of conifers is now a patch of birchwood with a few oaks; by 1973 a few stumps were still visible, but any specific larch or spruce mycorrhizal fungi were defunct.

Replacing wild with planted oaks

The most widespread legacy of nineteenth-century forestry is the substitution of foresters' for wild-type oaks. This was part of a process that increased during the twentieth century (Chapter 13). Replacement partly overlapped with the Oak Change (p.335), the loss of oak's ability to regenerate in woodland, for which foresters were not responsible. Did the loss of wild oaks (from a large minority of ancient woodland) matter?

Wild-type oaks are part of a wood's integrity, appearance and value as a habitat. It is part of the meaning of oak that oaks should not all be the same. It is irregularities that make oak such an excellent habitat for other wildlife. The accumulation of epiphytic ferns and bryophytes in western oakwoods, the nearest that Britain has to the massive 'fern gardens' high in the canopy of tropical forests, calls for trees with stout horizontal branches. Replacing wild-type oaks with uniform oaks of good timber quality (as a past century defined timber quality) was part of the homogenisation of woodland and the loss of local variation – within woods and from one wood to another – that conservationists would now resist.

Oak-replacement woods, however, include some nature reserves (p.293) and Sites of Special Scientific Interest. Scientists and the public persuaded the early Forestry Commission to retain much of the oak plantations of Dean and Alice Holt in the belief that these were the historic state of these Forests. Oak-for-oak replacement was not an ecological catastrophe, nor are wild-type oaks essential for a wood to be a nature reserve. But this is a factor that conservationists should routinely include in assessing the qualities of woods proposed as nature reserves, and in preparing management plans.

Twentieth-century replanting

Successful replantings: Borley Wood, south-east of Cambridge, is a big ancient wood (128 acres/52 ha). It is one of the drier boulder-clay woods, with patches of gravel. Two round barrows in the wood show that its prehistory was not simple. It had been mainly maple-wood, with ash and hazel and patches of elm, last coppiced in the 1920s. In *c*.1966 nearly the whole wood was felled and much of it grubbed out, leaving grasses and rosebay willowherb. The Forestry Commission then planted Corsican pine, Norway spruce and beech.

This had the makings of a successful replanting, favoured by a well-drained site, the use of Corsican pine, and the trouble taken to eliminate existing trees. By 1997 the growth of the planted trees had seen off most competition: of native trees, little remained except for a scatter of elm and maple and a few surviving ash stools. Dog's-mercury carpeted much of the ground; bracken and bluebell had probably somewhat increased. The flora was comparatively rich, but mostly on rides, and contained few distinctive species. Primrose persisted, but oxlip (never abundant) was not found. Distinctive species included deadly nightshade, a characteristic plant of woodland disturbance.

This is one of the few coniferisations with data on fungi. A fungus foray in 1999 found roughly equal numbers of residual species from the original wood and newcomers associated with the conifers. Residuals include a number of wood-rotters on elm, the tree of which there are most survivors. Mycorrhizal fungi were lacking, either of native trees or conifers; this in a season when *Russula, Lactarius, Laccaria* and *Boletus* were fruiting moderately well elsewhere. To judge by this one year's observations, Borley had lost the mycorrhizal agarics from the original wood without gaining those of the planted trees.

Nearby is Ditton Park Wood (185 acres/75 ha), a former ash–hazel-wood with some maple, a wet wood with extensive oxlip and meadowsweet as well as dog's-mercury and a small bracken area. Apart from the name it has little to show for its medieval history as a park. It was long reputed the wood with the richest flora in east Cambridgeshire, and in the 1950s was declared a Site of Special Scientific Interest. Notwithstanding, it was replanted in 1957–8; some original trees were left standing, to be poisoned later. Many different conifers were planted, besides oak and beech. The county Naturalists' Trust, in its report on SSSIs in 1965, made the best of a bad job: 'It is hoped that the retention of a wide diversity of habitats will enable future generations of botanists to grasp something of the whole range of habitats which occurred in the past.' This was not to be: the conifers grew only too well, and by 1976 I recorded fewer than half the plants known in the past – most of them on rides.

Much of the plantation was plucked out in the great storm of 1990, and the remainder, approaching commercial maturity, was drastically thinned, leaving planted oak and self-sown ash. Another threat to the flora emerged as *Carex pendula*, the aggressive sedge which suppresses most other plants and is encouraged by deer, took over thinned areas. In shade, dog's-mercury and meadowsweet persisted in an attenuated form, but under dense Norway spruce little survived. Oxlip was much reduced.

Simon Leatherdale discovered two lime stools, the only native lime on the Cambridgeshire–Suffolk border, overlooked by all previous botanists. Lime is very resistant to replanting, and this was probably all that there had been.

Stanstead Great Wood, near Long Melford, was one of the biggest ancient woods in Suffolk: a hazel–ashwood on acidic sands and gravels as well as boulder-clay. It was planted in 1960–4 with Corsican pine, Douglas fir and western red cedar. In 1967 it was sprayed Vietnam-style with 2, 4, 5-T from a helicopter:

apparently a unique event, for this notorious 'Agent Orange' poison was banned shortly after.[9] This either killed the underwood or, more likely, gave the planted trees (which were relatively resistant) a competitive edge. By 1981 some stools survived, but most of the native trees were self-sown birch and sallow. The flora, though quite rich (again including deadly nightshade), was largely confined to rides.

Donald Pigott investigated a wood at Leith Hill, Surrey, an apparently ancient wood partly of oak–holly with bracken and bramble on acid soils, and partly of less acidic hazel–ashwood with dog's-mercury and bluebell. Part of both types had been replanted by the National Trust [!] in 1957–8 with rows of sessile oak and Norway spruce or Douglas fir, the latter intended as a nurse crop. It was recorded in 1986, just before the great storm plucked out most of the conifers. Compared with intact parts of the wood, common woodland plants without long-lived seed, such as bluebell, anemone and bracken, disappeared from under the conifers, patches of oak acting as refuges. This Pigott interpreted as mainly an effect of the dark shade of spruce and fir, rather than of alteration to the soil. Only wood-sorrel benefited from replanting (as I have found elsewhere). After the storm, buried-seed plants, such as rushes, foxglove, woodrush and wood-sage emerged, as if after a coppicing.[10]

Partly successful replantings: Gamlingay Wood was recorded before planting (Chapter 21). Several methods of replanting were used, and parts were left unplanted. Many of the planted trees survived and produced a little timber. The effects, both on trees and on the ground vegetation, were complex and not altogether expected.

In the first 40–50 years, planting was good for birch (though birch was not planted) and bad for aspen. It was bad for oxlip (which additionally declined through increasing deer damage) and good for bluebell and dog's-mercury, as well as creating its own plant communities of relatively fertile and well-drained soil. It bore out the theory that replanting a wood damages its individuality and promotes commonplace plant communities at the expense of rare ones. However, the survival of so much of the original wood is due to this being, in forestry terms, an unsuccessful replanting.

Reydon-by-Southwold Wood (40 acres/16 ha) is one-half of an ancient wood in the northeast Suffolk hornbeam area. It was apparently a hornbeam–ashwood with patches of hazel. In 1960 a forestry company severely replanted it with conifers, especially the darkly shading Lawson cypress. Being a small and remote plantation it was neglected. Native trees reasserted themselves: some were surviving coppice stools, but predominantly they were self-sown ash and sallow. For a time the ground vegetation was very attenuated. In 1985 Suffolk Wildlife Trust bought the wood and began coppicing and removing conifers. This brought back much of the original flora, which had probably survived as buried seed.

Failed replantings: Shrawley Wood, Worcestershire, is probably the biggest lime-wood in England (340 acres/137 ha). Most of it is nearly solid lime (including one of the tallest native trees in the kingdom). It is such a remarkable place that before limewoods were well known it was supposed to be a plantation.[11] (The 'evidence' cited, that the lime stools are in rows, and that there is no lime in the surrounding country, was erroneous.) Some of the lime grows in huge rings (p.204). In the 1530s it had been a wood with common-rights of woodcutting, divided into ten named coppices.[12] Later, the lime poles were used for the curious metallurgical practice of *poling* copper: stirring the molten metal with green wood, which as it chars reacts with impurities.

Shrawley Wood fell into the hands of the Forestry Commission and was given the usual treatment. But Agent Orange here met its match. By 1985 Shrawley was back to being a magnificent limewood, and one had to look carefully for miserable remains of conifers.

The most evocative of limewoods is Lynwode Wood, Lincolnshire, by the lonely church and deserted village of Lynwode, named after the wood; John Lyndewode's funeral brass of 1421 bears his arms, 'a chevron between three lime-leaves proper'. This received the usual treatment from the unreformed Commission: George Peterken told me 'the air was acrid with herbicides'. But here too the lime-trees won. In 1993 they were alive and flourishing and beginning to overtop the drought-bitten Norway spruce. By 2005 most of the conifers had gone, revealing huge rings of multi-stemmed lime. They still bear the scars: each stem is hollowed into a kind of dugout canoe, the result of an assault on one side with a *jimjam,* a kind of poisoned axe.

Oak, beech and birch were easy to kill, followed by chestnut; hazel, maple, ash and hornbeam were intermediate; lime was apparently impossible. However, before poisons the order may have been different. In some of the Markshall Woods (Essex) the original limewood was replaced in Victorian times by chestnut, leaving strips of lime round the edges. The woods were later coniferised; they now have small dead stools of chestnut in the interior, lime round the edges, and occasional lime stools in the interior that survived both replantings. The nineteenth century had more success in getting rid of lime than the twentieth.

Conclusions

Effects of replanting vary from trivial to catastrophic. Whether the planted trees survive and whether they become dominant depends on the species previously existing, the species planted (Table 24), the site, and the degree of maintenance or neglect. To generalise from copious but unsystematic information, in eastern England the only planted trees likely to grow into timber on the site of an ancient wood were Corsican pine and oak. (Corsican pine, a Mediterranean mountain tree, resists both cold and drought.) In the West Country conifers from the eastern Pacific could be successful. Success was most likely on well-drained slopes or on the site of oakwoods; on flat clay sites or with limewoods the work swallowed up endless labour and was abandoned unfinished. The unreformed Commission put all the resources of science into destroying lime, and (as far as can now be told) had a success rate of zero.

Effects on ground vegetation depend on shade and leaf litter. At Gamlingay, poplars, inserted in rows among existing underwood, had little discernible effect. But *Thuja occidentalis*, almost as shady as a photographer's darkroom, eliminates all herbaceous plants. Spruces are nearly as bad. Corsican pine allows an attenuated set of herbs to survive. However, well-grown beech and oak plantations attenuate the ground vegetation by their long-lasting leaf litter. Beech can be almost as destructive as the more densely shading conifers. In Great Gransden Wood (Huntingdonshire) a dense oak plantation allowed oxlip and bluebell to survive, but eliminated most of the rest of the oxlip–bluebell guild.

A successful plantation is homogeneous and eliminates the patchiness that is an essential characteristic of ancient woodland. Even small areas of failure – surviving coppice stools or birch or ash invasion – break up the monotony and retain woodland plants. (Do they retain woodland animals? This would be an interesting study in island biogeography and the survival of small populations.)

Replanted ancient woods may retain woodland grassland on rides. An extreme example is Bernwood Forest (Oxfordshire), a sad remnant of what was once a compartmental Forest like Hatfield, but a famous butterfly site and a National Nature Reserve on the strength of its grasslands.

RESTORATION

And I [the LORD] *will restore to you the years that the locust hath eaten.*
JOEL 2: 25

As in ancient Israel, the Locust Years were not to last for ever. Many commercial forestry plantations have come up to saleable size. The trees will die on felling; the economics of replacing them are dubious. Why not try to regain wild vegetation?

Heathland is now internationally rare; the fragments of it in England are an appreciable part of all the heath in the world. Conservationists have long been interested in preserving the remaining heath, and now in recovering recently lost heath. Much heathland restoration starts from farmland or recent natural woodland, but some replaces plantations.

'Brandon Park Heath' (Suffolk Breckland) is on the site of about 150 acres (60 ha) of Corsican pine on blown sand. The pines were planted by the Forestry Commission c.1950; some blew down in 1987 and others were felled later. The area was fenced to allow sheep-grazing, to prevent it from turning into a natural wood as birch and pine seedlings colonise. By 2004 heather was reasserting itself, some from survivors on rides, some from buried seed dormant for 50 years. *Carex arenaria*, becoming dominant under the plantations, has declined, replaced by the grass *Deschampsia flexuosa*. Earth-lichen communities, a special feature of Breckland, have become prominent again.

Moorland is still so widespread that its restoration from plantation is not yet high on the agenda, with one notable exception: the Royal Society for the Protection of Birds has begun the huge task of getting rid of the ill-fated conifers from the Flow Country.

Unreplanting or deconiferisation
In the Locust Years, ecologists like myself wrote off about 40 per cent by area of ancient woodland as irretrievably lost to replanting: we accepted the foresters' claims to have killed off the trees, and shook our heads at the decline of plant life as the planted trees closed in. As time went on, we grew less pessimistic. Many woods were not so easily destroyed; the planted trees declined and native trees returned. Maintenance failed; rabbits devoured and squirrels crippled the beeches; the great summers of 1975–6, 1989–90 and 1995 took their toll of Pacific conifers and Norway spruce; even Corsican pine suffered from bark beetles.

In the 1980s the Commission, under a political cloud, sold many of its freehold woods. This was using the funds of one public body to pay the debts of another, for some of the woods were bought by county wildlife trusts with grants from the Department of the Environment.[13]

This opened opportunities for deconiferisation. Worcestershire Wildlife Trust bought Tiddesley Wood, a 230-acre (93 ha) wood near Pershore. This had been replanted with varying degrees of success. In places there was enough timber in the planted trees to be worth selling or growing on; in other places the conifers were alive but worthless, and in others there were only traces of the planting.

Chalkney Wood (Earl's Colne, Essex): This brings up to date a story that I have told elsewhere.[14] Chalkney (184 acres/74 ha) is one of the great limewoods of England, but includes areas of hornbeam, ash–hazel, and four steep little ravines with alder on flushed boggy slopes. It is one of the few woods to have records of its underwood composition going back 400 years. It had been the manorial wood of the Earls of Oxford, who liked to be thought of as swine: they imagined their family name, De Vere, to come from the Latin *verres*, a wild boar, which they bore as their crest and badge. In the later Middle Ages they made the wood into a park for wild swine.

In 1955 it was made a Site of Special Scientific Interest. (Why this one, out of about 30 limewoods in north Essex? Possibly because Sir Harry Godwin, the great ecologist, happened to know it; but one cannot disagree with the choice.) The Forestry Commission acquired two-thirds of it and applied the usual treatment. Limes and hornbeams were jimjammed; beech and a surprising variety of conifers were planted. Colin Ranson, the Nature Conservancy's man in Essex, and I watched with weary dismay as the wood seemed to decline into just another tree-farm.

The remaining one-third of the wood belonged to three sisters, two of whom continued to coppice the underwood. In 1973 it was acquired by Essex County Council as a public open space. They have continued coppicing, making this a classic wood for buried-seed plants.

The years rolled on. Chalkney, an outlying Commission property, fell into neglect. The planted trees, except Corsican pine, suffered setbacks and lost to the native trees; in some parts self-sown ash replaced the planted trees. The attitude of the Commission was changing: I found myself arguing on their behalf to retain the wood as an SSSI, on the grounds that they had failed to destroy its scientific interest. In 1989 their staff were planning the restoration of the wood. I argued that there was no great urgency to remove the conifers: most of the damage that they were likely to do had already been done.

Markets were found for the conifers, and as I write only a few Corsican pine remain. The wood changed, as if by magic, from a poorly grown plantation back to a magnificent limewood. Virtually all the limes have survived, many with jimjam scars as at Lynwode (Fig. 151). Surprisingly many surviving hornbeams and other trees have emerged. Buried-seed plants reappeared: the rare sedge *Carex strigosa* was, for a time, one of the most abundant. I sense a degree of friendly rivalry between the two owners in showing off Chalkney Wood to the public as an example of their styles of management.

Woodland restoration as Forestry Commission policy
Chalkney was a good place to start. The planted trees would have had to go while there was a market for them, and the native trees had put up a stout resistance. It was soon taken up all over eastern England, often with woods in a much more difficult state than Chalkney.

Unreplanting is not always straightforward. At Rowney Wood, near Saffron Walden, subtraction of conifers reveals a monotonous stand of oak, planted with them, but little surviving underwood. The ground has been taken over by *Carex pendula*. The wood is distressingly uniform, without the diversity that it must once have had.

Deconiferisation was put in hand in most of the Commission's ancient woods in the Midlands. Potton Wood in Bedfordshire (209 acres/84 ha) was where the replanting movement finally ran itself into the ground. Like Hayley, it is on a boulder-clay plateau that floods every wet spring. By the 1980s nearly half the area was abandoned as unplantable. Norway spruce grew for a time and then succumbed to droughts. After the great summer of 2003 there were more dead than alive; and as I write I hear that they have all gone (as have those in Ditton Park Wood). There is a population of oxlip that has increased – the only one in the county – despite fallow deer.[15]

I used to be told that successful plantations, even on Sites of Special Scientific Interest, ought not to be sacrificed to conservation interests. To this I would reply that a plantation, if successful, is likely to have been deleted as an SSSI. But even successful plantations rarely perpetuate themselves: the planted trees will be felled in the normal course of business, and the economics of planting another generation on an ancient woodland site are weak.

Estate forestry

This is the branch of modern forestry that appeals to the public. The Commission's most popular sites tend towards the estate tradition or inherit the estate forestry of previous owners. Should there be more of it? If so, should it take over ancient woodland or former farmland?

There are four main objectives: timber production (usually 'quality' timber); wildlife conservation; amenity; and gamekeeping. Estates combine these in various ways. Some set an example: they employ excellent ecologists, scrupulously distinguish between plantations and ancient woods, and invite the public to see what they are doing. Others are secretive and carry gamekeeping to excess.

The values of 'conserving wildlife in woodlands', mainly within the estate-forestry tradition, are set out by Esmond & Jeanette Harris (1991). Estate foresters can be vague about what they are conserving and why it needs to be conserved; it may mean little more than making a few common birds even commoner. Many of them fail to appreciate the conservation of ancient woods themselves: that some woods *are* wildlife and that each one is different. Ground vegetation and archaeological features survive, or not, by chance. As I have remarked elsewhere,[16] well-run estate forestry can very effectively drain out the meaning from an ancient wood, turning it into a grandiose tree-farm, with some trees of magnificent size, but leaving nothing older than one generation of planted trees.

Gamekeeping has its place: it promotes coppicing and woodland grassland, and produces excellent meat. Gamekeepers used to treat buzzards and polecats as deadly enemies, and a few still have brushes with the law over hen harriers. They created one peculiar ecosystem, gibbeted strings of sun-dried crows, stoats and grey squirrels and the special insects that inhabit them. Unfortunately there is a perversion of gamekeeping that breeds pheasants like battery chickens, in numbers such that even the shakiest marksman can hardly miss, and pays little attention to their eating quality. With this goes 'cutting back the undergrowth' by machinery, reducing a wood to a scatter of timber trees over tussocky, strongly competitive grasses and sedges, which is then particularly attractive to deer. This method of destroying a wood is legal as long as none of the trees cut is big enough to come within the scope of a felling licence.

If all estate forestry were up to the standards set by the best estates, I would not hesitate to recommend it as a model. My enthusiasm is tempered by the thought that of the few examples of degradation of ancient woodland by human agency I have seen in the twenty-first century, all but one have been within the estate tradition.

RESEARCH

Unless the original vegetation was recorded, it is virtually impossible to predict what had been lost.

C.D. PIGOTT, 1990

Plantations now cover about one-tenth of Great Britain, about one-third of the area of arable crops. This huge change to a new ecosystem in 120 years has attracted controversy, but remarkably little relevant research. Not that research on plantations is lacking, but it is mostly related to the planted trees and mostly to well-managed plantations. The examples that I have drawn on for this chapter could be multiplied, but would not amount to a systematic collection of data. Most plantations were not recorded before planting, so the consequences are not fully known.

Wildlife is not something homogeneous that can be discussed or provided for as a whole. Flowering plants respond differently from fungi, and one bird responds differently from another bird. The subject is far too complex to be resolved by a mere appeal to superficially similar forests in other parts of the world.

Do planted trees wage chemical warfare against their competitors? Pigott quotes a German study to show that the leaf litter of larch contains growth inhibitors, which may explain why little grows under larch although it is deciduous.[17]

A rudimentary scientific study would involve dividing a site, part to be planted and part not, studying each part before planting and after the plantation was fully developed, and comparing the effects of planting with those of not planting. Gamlingay Wood (p.405f) is probably the nearest there has been to such an investigation, involving several kinds of planting. Even it left much to be desired, especially in that two different people did the observations, and methods of recording had progressed in the interval. Would that I had had Adamson's original field notes from 1911 instead of having to make do with the selection of his observations that he published!

The constraints are anthropological (Chapter 22). Who, as a student, will record an area about to be planted and follow through its ecology over the next 60 years? But amateurs may succeed where professionals fail. Young readers are urged to begin recording sites or to continue records kept by parents and teachers. Nothing complex is needed; lists and photographs – with notes sufficient for the exact spots to be found again in the future – are far better than nothing.

Plantations are clearly not adequate substitutes for ancient woodland even if they consist of native trees. Farmers should give priority to conserving ancient woodland if they are lucky enough to own some, and developers should not pretend that plantations are adequate substitutes for ancient woodlands which they propose to destroy.

All this does not mean that plantations have no value for conservation. They are enormously better for wildlife than arable fields or grass leys.

N.W. MOORE, 2002

CHAPTER 20

ON INVESTIGATING A WOODED FOREST

Blackmoor

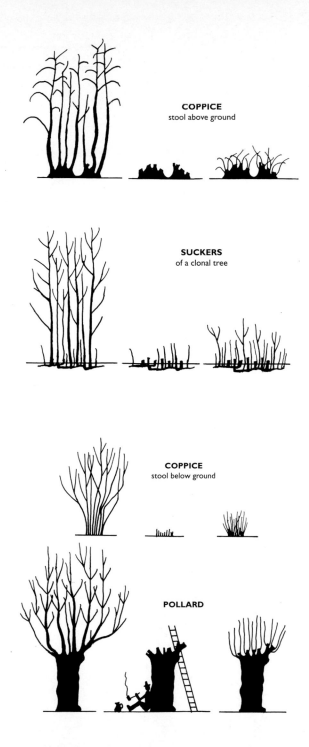

COPPICE
stool above ground

SUCKERS
of a clonal tree

COPPICE
stool below ground

POLLARD

Fig 171. Coppicing, pollarding, suckering. See p.16.

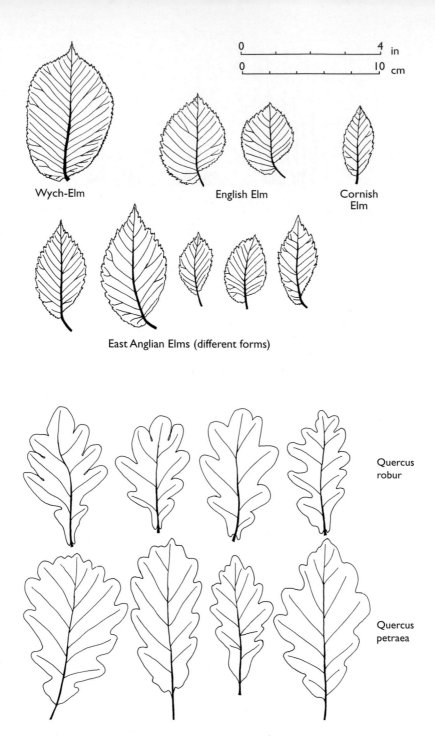

Fig 172. Leaves of British elms and oaks. See p.30.

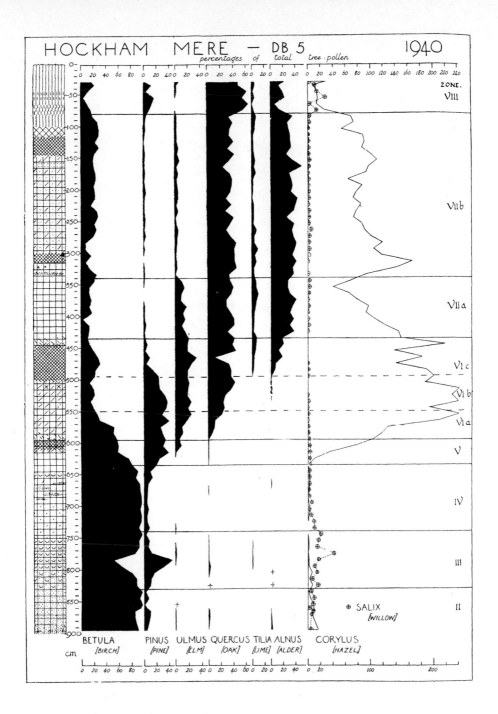

Fig 173. Godwin's first pollen diagram from Hockham Mere. The timescale runs from about 12,000 years ago (bottom) to the present (top). Pollen counts for each tree are expressed as percentages of all tree pollens (excluding hazel, which is shown separately on the right). Note the Elm Decline, which separates Zones VIIa and VIIb. The bar on the left encodes the nature of the sediments. Non-tree pollens were published as a separate diagram. More recent pollen diagrams are similar in principle, but more detailed; they include radiocarbon dates, which were not known about at this time. By permission of the British Ecological Society. See p.68f.

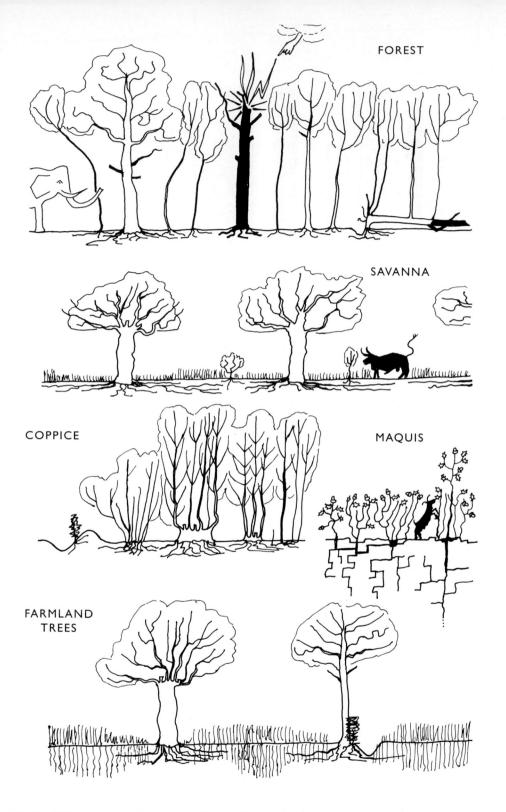

FOREST

SAVANNA

COPPICE

MAQUIS

FARMLAND
TREES

Fig 174. Different kinds of tree-land. What pollen would they produce? How could pollen-analytical criteria distinguish between them (p.68f)?

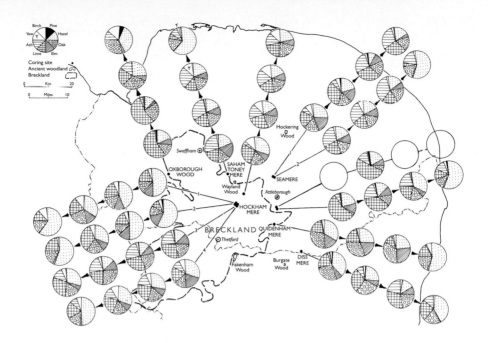

Fig 175. Pollen cores from the meres of south Norfolk. The outlined area is Breckland. For each site the four circles show the dry-land wildwood composition (1) early in the Atlantic Period, (2) average during the Atlantic Period, (3) just before the Elm Decline, (4) just after the Elm Decline. See p.73.

Fig 176. Area of woodland plus wood-pasture in 1086. Where Domesday Book (p.100) gives the dimensions (length x breadth) or areas of woods, these have been used to estimate the area of woodland in each 10-kilometre square. In 'swine' counties (eastern England) or 'swine-rent' counties (southeast) I have estimated the approximate area per county (for details see Rackham (2003) Chapter 9). Broken lines are the limits of Planned Countryside (middle third of England) versus Ancient Countryside (west and southeast).

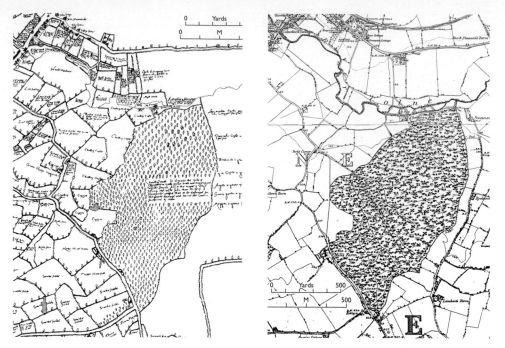

Fig 177. Woodland in Ancient Countryside, 1598 and 1876. Not only the wood (Chalkney Wood, often referred to in this book) but most of the infrastructure of landscape altered little over 300 years. The wood and the roads are still the same today, but many hedges were destroyed between 1950 and 1975. *Earl's Colne, Essex: the Harlackenden map and the Ordnance Survey.* See p.110.

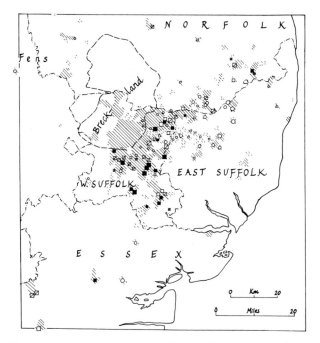

Fig 178. Woods of Bury St Edmunds Abbey, and what happened to them. Hatched: approximate extent of Abbey manors. Circles: woodland not heard of after 1200. Squares: woodland existing *c.*1500. White squares: nothing now remains. Hatched squares: fragments survive. Black squares: substantial Abbey woods still extant. Large and small symbols roughly indicate the size of the wood or woods; the woods themselves occupied a rather smaller area on the map than the symbols. See p.104.

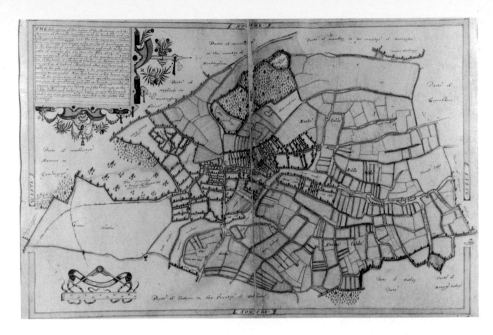

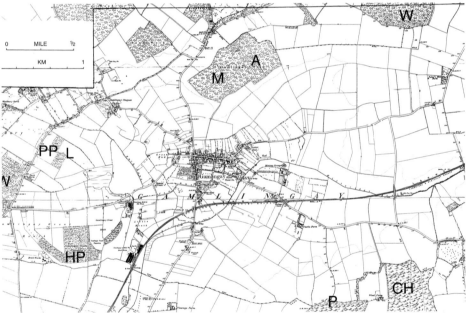

Fig 179. Woodland in Planned Countryside, 1601 and 1886. The landscape has been reorganised – not through continual changes, but because of a single far-reaching event, an Enclosure Act in 1848. The woods, however, remain as islands of stability, with certain exceptions. Avenells (A) and Mertonage (M) woods were amalgamated, without changing in shape, to form Gamlingay Wood. Broom Wood is now called White Wood (W). Potton Wood (P) is still there. Lambcott Wood (L) disappeared in the seventeenth century through the making of a deer-park; Park Plantations (PP – note the name) happened to be established later on nearly the same site. Waresley Wood (W) and Cockayne Hatley Wood (CH) are known from other sources to have existed in 1601. Waresley Wood later got bigger and extended on to the area covered by the map. Heath Plantation (HP) (note the name) is post-1848. *Gamlingay, Cambridgeshire: the Merton College map and the Ordnance Survey.* See p.110.

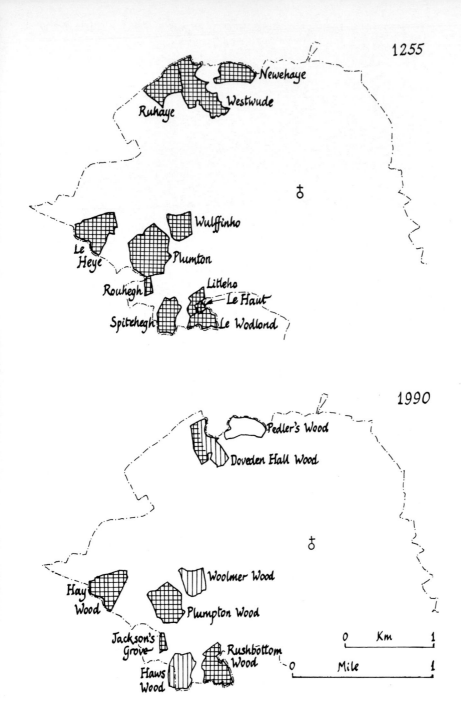

1255

Newehaye
Westwude
Ruhaye

Wulfinho
Le
Heye
Plumton
Rouhegh
Litleho
Le Haut
Spitehegh
Le Wodlond

1990

Pedler's Wood
Doveden Hall Wood

Woolmer Wood
Hay
Wood
Plumpton Wood
Jackson's
Grove
Rushbottom
Wood
Haws
Wood

0   Km   1

0   Mile   1

Fig 180. Survival of a group of Bury St Edmunds Abbey's woods (see p.104): Whepstead, Suffolk. On the 1990 map double-hatched woods are intact, single-hatched replanted, and blank woods grubbed.

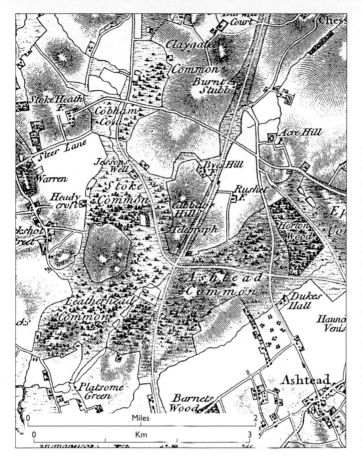

Fig 181. Wood-pasture commons in Surrey, ramifying from parish to parish, funnelling out into roads, and surrounding enclaves of private land. From the Ordnance Survey of 1816; note the distinction between woods (Horton Wood), wood-pasture, bushy common and treeless common. The area has since suffered from enclosure, development, forestry, golf and fire, but Ashtead Common still has some of its ancient trees. See p.117.

Fig 182. Site of Ongar Great Park, Essex, in 1873–4. The added broken line marks the original park perimeter, almost all of which survived as hedges or parish boundaries; note the shape. The woods within the park were probably compartmented. See p.118.

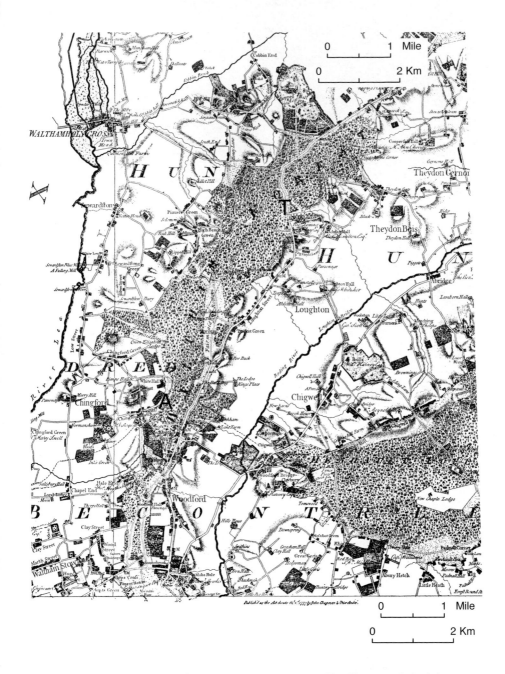

Fig 183 a. Part of Epping (anciently Waltham Forest), mapped by Chapman & André, 1772–4. What is shown is the physical Forest; the legal Forest covered nearly everything on this map and much more. This Forest was non-compartmental; note the distinctive savanna symbol for wood-pasture, contrasting with the darker symbol for woodland. A: here woodland adjoins, but is not part of, the physical Forest. T: anti-highwayman trench (p.171). See p.145.

Fig 183 b. The Vale of York.

Fig 184. Horwood Forest, now Wetmoor Woods, Gloucestershire: a compartmented Forest with 23 copses. Tongues of grassland (here called by the ancient name of *trenches*, cf. p.171) ramify between them and run out into the commons to the east. Note the houses adjoining the boundary.

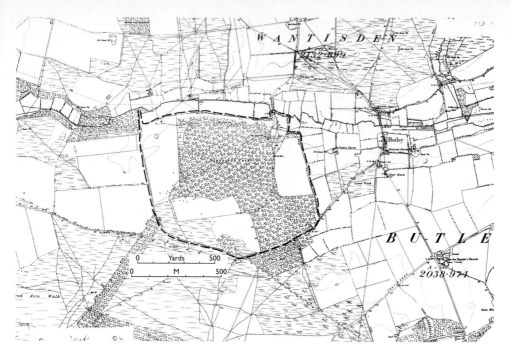

Fig 185. Staverton Park, Suffolk, in 1887 (p.127). The added broken line marks the original park boundary. It is not now very different except that the heaths inside the park are cultivated.

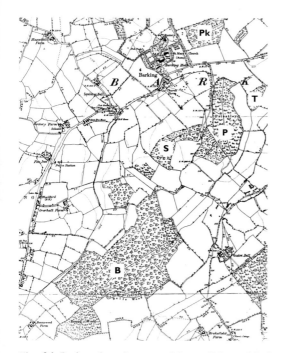

Fig 186. Reduced-scale copy of first edition of Ordnance Survey of Barking (Suffolk), originally 6 inches to the mile, surveyed 1884. Note the woods mentioned in the Ely Coucher Book (p.89): Park Wood (Pk), Priestley Wood (P), Swingens Wood (formerly Wethersheg, S), Titley Wood (T), and Bonny Wood (B). Several of the woods have been subdivided and are given separate numbers referring to the schedule. All are still there today. See p.173.

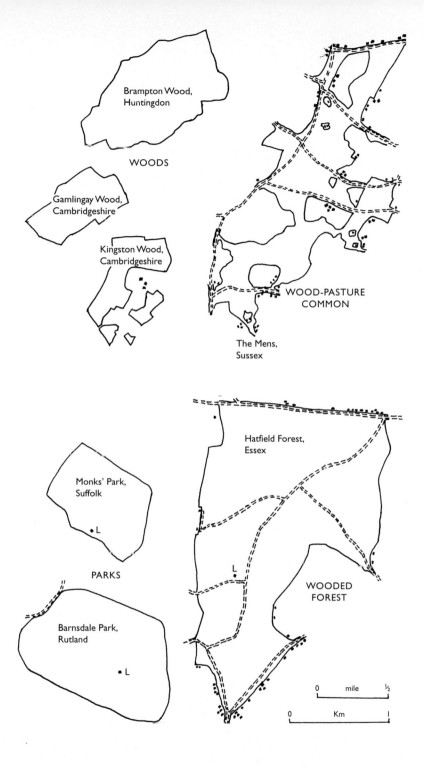

Fig 187. Shapes of woods, wood-pasture commons, parks and wooded Forests (p.159).

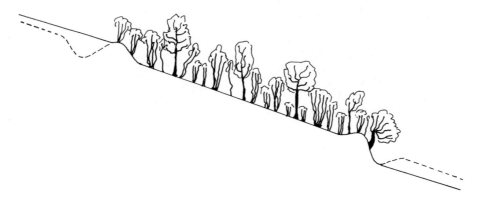

Fig 188. Lynchets and woodbanks on a slope. See p.200.

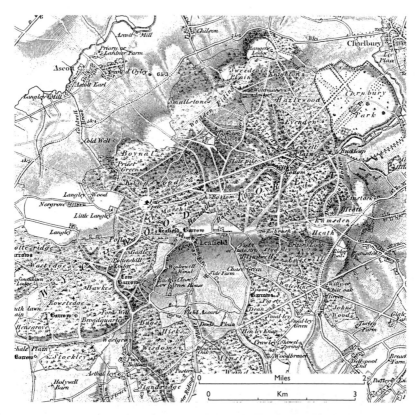

Fig 189. Wychwood Forest, Oxfordshire, in 1833 (p.174). The sinuous 'lights' follow dry valleys between the 'copses', some of which are named. Note the numerous prehistoric *Barrows*; village and fields of Leafield in the middle; the straight, radiating eighteenth-century rides (one of which follows the Roman road, Akeman Street); the lodges; and an ancient tree ('Fair Speir'). The Forest was privatised in 1857 and destroyed, except for the part north-east of Leafield.

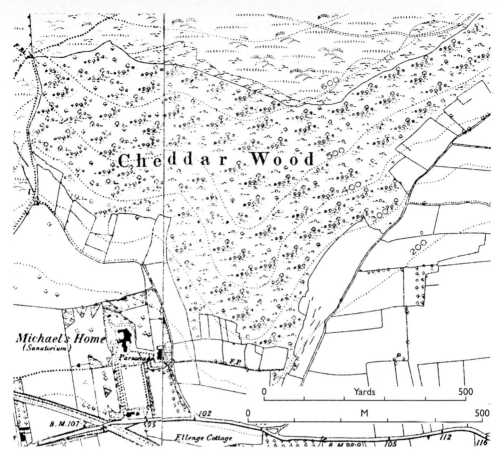

Fig 190. Cheddar Wood, Somerset, in 1883 (p.162). It climbs the steep south face of the Mendip Hills. The wood had already begun to invade the common to the north: it is much bigger now.

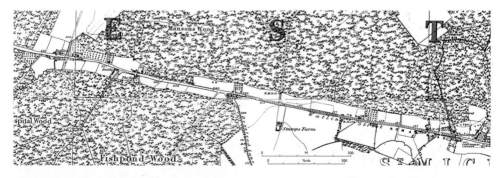

Fig 191. Trench where Watling Street, nearing Canterbury, passes through the Blean, Kent, as mapped in 1872–3. Part of it is still visible now. See p.172.

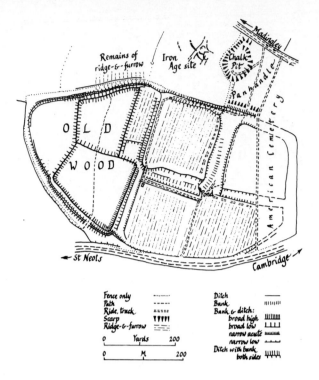

Fence only	....
Path	-----
Ride, track	=====
Scarp	ʏʏʏʏʏ
Ridge-&-furrow	===

Ditch	———
Bank	ɯɯ
Bank & ditch:	
broad high	ɯɯ
broad low	⊥⊥⊥
narrow acute	ɯɯ
narrow low	⊥⊥
Ditch with bank both sides	ɯɯ

0   Yards   200

0   M   200

Fig 192. Earthworks of Madingley Wood, Cambridge (p.175). Areas of straight ridge-and-furrow relate to seventeenth-century fields.

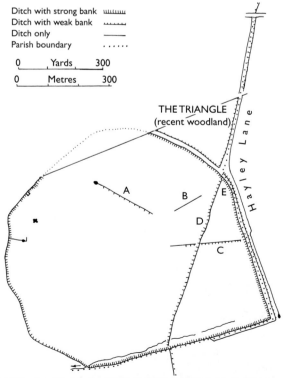

Ditch with strong bank	ɯɯ
Ditch with weak bank	----
Ditch only	———
Parish boundary	......

0   Yards   300

0   Metres   300

THE TRIANGLE
(recent woodland)

Fig 193. Earthworks of Hayley Wood, Cambridgeshire (p.85). A, B, C: faint prehistoric features. D: later prehistoric axis. E: Medieval woodbank.

N

0   100 m

| | = No earthwork
······ = Parish boundary in 1888
o = Boundary stones
||||||| = Bank (no ditch)
= Dry ditch
= Stream or wet ditch
= Ridge-and-furrow
= Disturbed areas (post 1900)
● = Pond or pit
= Marsh
= Outcrops & thin soil

Fig 194. Earthworks of Swithland Wood, Leicestershire, after S. Woodward. See p.176.

Fig 195. Hemispherical photograph, taken at ground level in the gap left by the fall of two great trees in a stand of outgrown beech pollards. Arrows locate true north and south and the position of the horizon. *Great Monk Wood, Epping Forest, 23 June 1975. See p.193.*

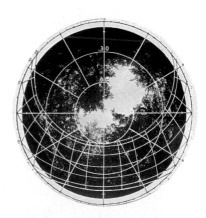

Fig 196. The same, with grid added. Curved lines show the position of the sun, hour by hour, at the summer and winter solstices and on the 21st of each month between (calculated by D.E. Coombe). This particular position gets no direct sunlight, except for small sunflecks, even in June.

Fig 197. Madingley Wood, Cambridge, photographed by an unknown German pilot. The four light-coloured areas had been small fields, hewn out of the wood probably in the seventeenth century, made into plantations in the late nineteenth. The shadows on the north edge of the wood are of towering elms. Compare Fig. 192. *About 3 p.m. on 31 August 1940.*

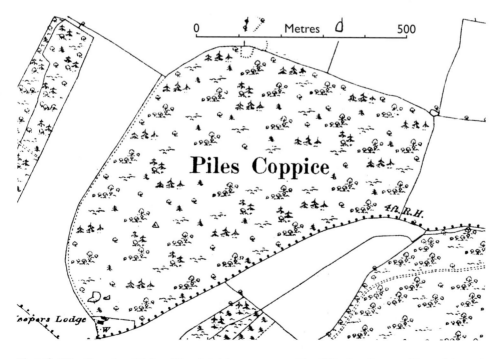

Fig 198. Piles Coppice, Binley, Warwickshire, as mapped in 1886 when it was still rural (p.207).

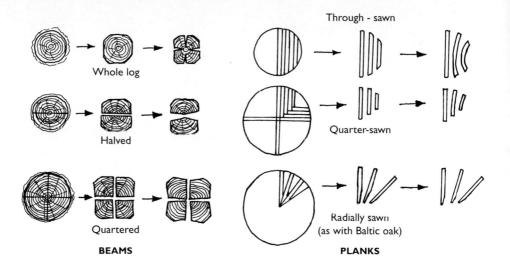

BEAMS

Whole log

Halved

Quartered

Through - sawn

Quarter-sawn

Radially sawn
(as with Baltic oak)

PLANKS

Fig 199. Ways of converting an oak log into beams and planks (p.221), and how they distort on subsequent shrinkage.

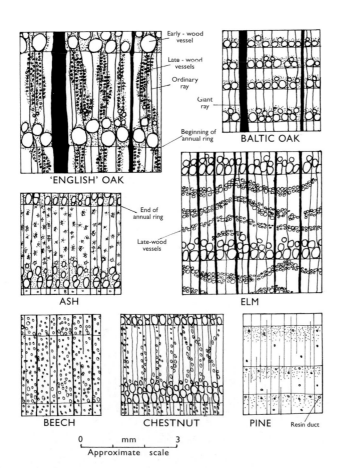

Early - wood vessel

Late - wood vessels

Ordinary ray

Giant ray

Beginning of annual ring

BALTIC OAK

'ENGLISH' OAK

End of annual ring

Late-wood vessels

ASH

ELM

BEECH

CHESTNUT

PINE   Resin duct

0   mm   3
Approximate   scale

Fig 200. Sketches showing characteristics of wood structure. See also p.242.

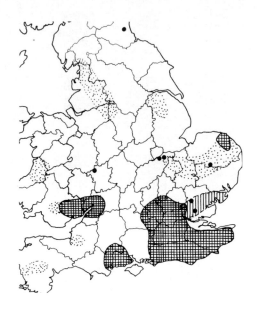

Fig 201. Plant characteristic of ancient woodland. *Melica uniflora*, the woodbank grass (p.250); the arrow marks the sterile floret which is an ant bait. By W. Fitch, the nineteenth-century botanical artist.

Fig 202. Distribution of native beech. Double-hatched: areas of survival. Black spots: outlying native localities. Single-hatched: extinct since Middle Ages, now only as an introduction. Dotted: prehistoric records only. See p.283.

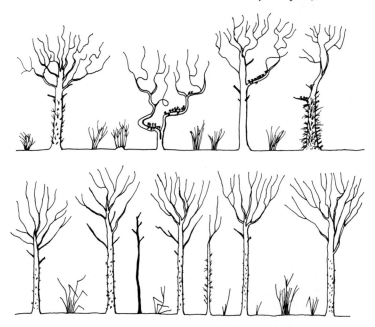

Fig 203. Wild-type oaks (above) and plantation-type oaks (below). See p.147.

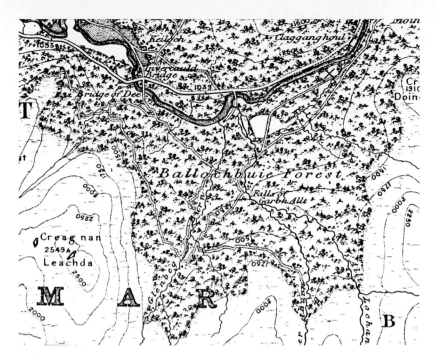

Fig 204. Ballochbuie Pinewood, from the Ordnance Survey of 1870, based on the larger-scale map of 1866 (see p.313). 'Forest' was a misnomer. X is the probable site of the clearing disputed in the 1750s.

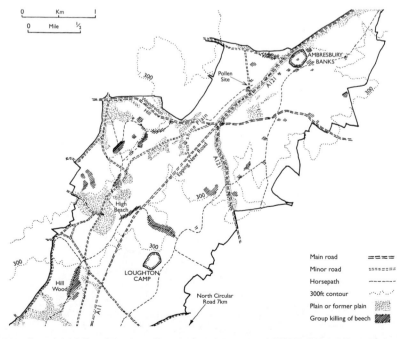

Fig 205. North and middle of Epping Forest, showing group killing of beech in relation to roads and paths, plains, and the 300-foot contour. Note the two hillforts.

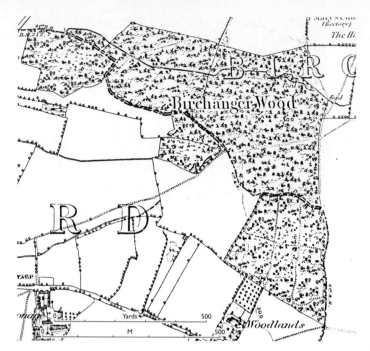

Fig 206. Birchanger Wood, Essex, on the Ordnance Survey of 1876. Conifers are shown in the large middle part of the wood. A century later they had vanished, leaving an unusually high density of birch among the old underwood of hornbeam and hazel (p.372).

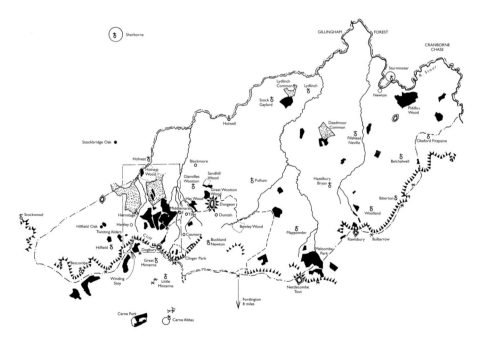

Fig 207. The legal Forest of Blackmoor, with bounds approximately drawn from the most extensive perambulation of c.1155. See p.387.

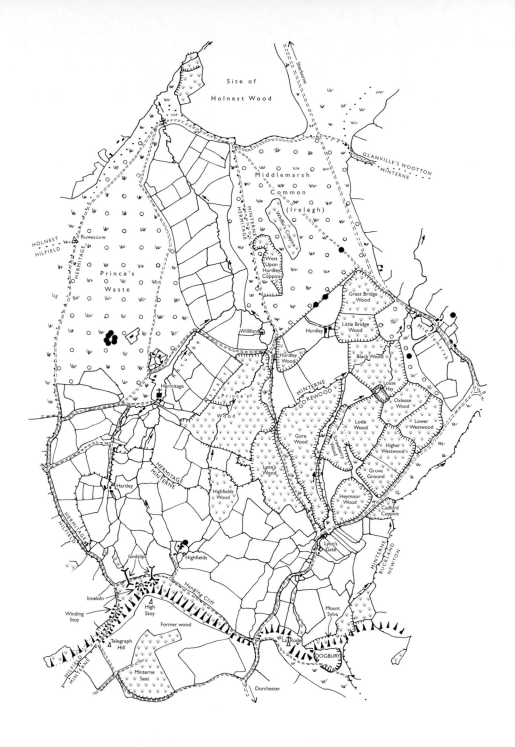

Fig 208. The physical Forest of Blackmoor, with earthworks and ancient trees visible on the ground. See p.390.

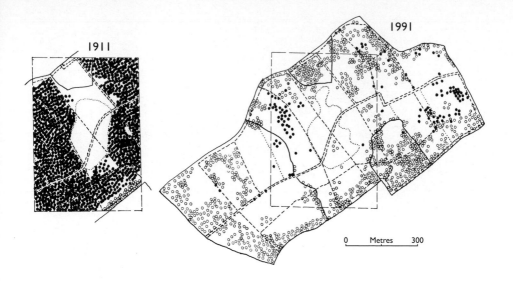

Fig 209. Distribution of meadowsweet (black dots) and dog's-mercury (white dots) in part of Gamlingay Wood in 1911 (middle of wood only, redrawn from Adamson's map) and 1991 (p.405).

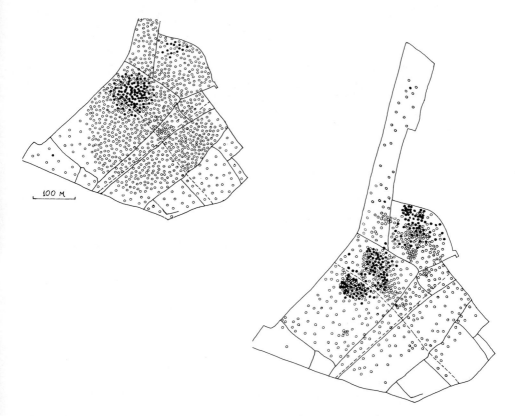

Fig 210. Primrose (white) and oxlip (black) in Buff Wood, Cambridgeshire, 1948 (redrawn after Abeywickrama) and 2002. The points give a general indication of the density, not individual plants. In this wood, with little deer activity, primrose has declined and oxlip increased. For intermediate maps see Rackham (2003) p. 394–5.

The traveller from the coast, who, after plodding northward for a score of miles over calcar-
eous downs and corn-lands, suddenly reaches the verge of one of these escarpments, is
surprised and delighted to behold, extended like a map beneath him, a country differing
absolutely from that which he has passed through. Behind him the hills are open, the sun
blazes down upon fields so large as to give an unenclosed character to the landscape, the
lanes are white, the hedges low and plashed, the atmosphere colourless. Here, in the valley,
the world seems to be constructed upon a smaller and more delicate scale; the fields are mere
paddocks, so reduced that from this height their hedgerows appear a network of dark green
threads overspreading the paler green of the grass ... Arable lands are few and limited; with
but slight exceptions the prospect is a broad rich mass of grass and trees, mantling minor
hills and dales within the major. Such is the Vale of Blackmoor.
Thomas Hardy, *Tess of the D'Urbervilles,* 1891

In 2000 I was invited to teach an advanced study course for the public at Kingcombe Field Centre, Dorset, exploring 'live' the historical ecology of a region,
doing 'real' research, making real discoveries, and asking questions to which the
answers were not known. It is time to record some results.

The Forest of Blackmore or Blackmoor lies between Sherborne and Cerne
Abbas in Dorset.*[1] It was an obscure and short-lived Forest, but it lived on in

---

* It was not an unknown region, and I particularly thank local historians Dennis Seaward and
Anne Horsfall for their help and contributions. Dorset Record Office were most co-operative. I
am indebted to the enthusiastic and energetic Nigel Spring, first Warden of Kingcombe, for
organising the course, and to successive participants.

memory. Its woods were never extensive and were badly damaged by modern forestry. But, as often happens, it turned out to have unanticipated distinctions. It is well represented in seventeenth- and eighteenth-century maps, including several by Isaac Taylor in the 1760s, who combined Rococo panache with meticulous accuracy. It is a singularly quiet and beautiful part of England, a place of prayer and meditation by the Friar Hermits of St Augustine in the Middle Ages and the Anglican Franciscan friars at Hilfield today.

THE SETTING

The dramatic view – best appreciated from below Dogbury hillfort – is still much as Hardy described it (Fig. 152). The eye roves from Alfred's Tower in Selwood Forest to the Mendips and Glastonbury Tor and the Somerset Levels. Beneath one's feet, across a confusion of old landslips, conifer plantations usurp the central woods of Blackmoor and Middlemarsh Common. In the cow-pastures of the Vale the ancient hedges are still there; most of the grasslands are no longer pale green, but have been 'improved' to the shiny emerald monotony of ryegrass or the tussocky blue of cocksfoot.

The southern rim of Blackmoor is the high, north-facing chalk scarp that ends the Cerne Abbas downs. On Telegraph Hill, a mile (1½ kilometres) west of Dogbury, anciently called High Stoy, a cell-phone mast replaces the shutter-telegraph of Napoleonic times. Below it a breakneck mule-track called Winding Stoy, worn to a deep holloway by a thousand and a half winters of rain and traffic, paved with loose and jagged flints, plunges headlong through tangled hazel-woods and towering ashwoods, fragrant with ramsons and toothwort, and under fern-garden oaks (see Fig. 77); it leaps down ledges of limestone-hard chalk, overlying weak greensand and slippery Gault Clay. Such is the gate of Blackmoor.

The combination of hard, weak and slippery rocks makes cliffs and landslips: 'Great Cliffs not able for menn to passe upe', as the Minterne map of 1616 says.[2] Near the foot of Winding Stoy, on 13 January 1583, a national event happened. As Camden put it (in stately Latin):

A field of three acres in Blackmore, with trees and hedges, was moved from its place and passed over another, leaving a mighty gap, and blocking the public road which leads to Cerne …from much moisture, with fountains abundantly welling up …[3]

There are now two grassed-over landslip mounds, one of them labelled on the Hermitage map of 1723 as 'The Ground which moved in the Year 1585' and 'The Hole from whence it moved'.[4] Whether there has been a mistake in the dates I cannot say. Landslips occur along the Blackmoor rim and in many other places in west Dorset, especially Kingcombe, and are still very active on the coast at Lyme Regis. Inland they often underlie, and evidently determine, ancient woods.

Blackmoor Vale itself (see Fig. 207) is on Oxford Clay, with gravelly islands on which most of the ancient farmland lies. The woods tend to be in wet places; the waters in half Dorset seem to converge on the central woods. Within 2 miles (3 kilometres) of the scarp, the land is covered with jagged, perforated, boot-eater flints of the kind that chink underfoot on the Winding Stoy. They must represent the residue of landslip after landslip as the chalk scarp has retreated southwards through the Pleistocene, the chalk itself having dissolved away with rainwater and acids from interglacial rotten leaves. This sort of flint is another reason why areas remain woodland: anyone trying to plough such soils soon has no plough left.

THE BLACKMOOR REGION BEFORE THE FOREST

'Dorset generally, and especially the chalk areas, is immensely rich in standing archaeological remains', as Christopher Taylor (2000) says: Neolithic and Bronze Age barrows on the hilltops, dykes, 'Celtic Fields' and strip-lynchets on steep slopes. On the rim of Blackmoor is a chain of hillforts: Rawlsbury Camp on Bulbarrow, Nettlecombe Tout, Dungeon on a mesa within Blackmoor, Dogbury, and maybe others. The Vale was evidently of some significance in the Iron Age. The Roman period is not much represented, but probably for lack of investigation rather than absence of activity.

Anglo-Saxon perambulations

Dorset has many pre-Norman charters. One charter, recording a gift by King Edmund the Magnificent to Ælfflæd, a nun, in 941, approaches what was to become the physical Forest of Blackmoor. She was a nun of substance, for the property was no less than the entire parish of Buckland Newton. The land is defined by its boundary:

First at Shordenberwe; along the way to a barrow; thence to a furze-row; thence southward to Langengrove; down by a ridge to a stream; along the stream to Doggenesford; thence up to Doggeneberwe; thence to Annesheal; thence to the old hinged gate ... [and much else] ... back to Scherdanbourh.[5]

This detailed perambulation, with 45 clauses in a length of about 15 miles (25 kilometres), includes a rushbed, five hedges, a wayside crucifix, an appletree, a willow, two thorns, four instances of *herepað* ('army path', *a road of middling importance),* * *and five ancient earthworks. Because of the complex detail it is not easy to follow now, but the sample cited above goes up the boggy stream that approaches Dogbury from the north. Dogbury* ** *is a small, prominent hillfort now hidden in trees. A mile (1½ kilometres) to the southeast, the ridgeway on which it stands passes a furze-row (not the one named in the charter) and bends at the feature* Annesheal *('Anna's Corner').*

Buckland Newton, a thousand years ago, was not very different from today. Its boundaries are described in terms of roads, hedges, trees and streams. Only one wood is mentioned, but there are four place-names ending in *-legh*, implying the existence (or former existence) of other woods close by (p.99).

In northwest Dorset as a whole, with 25 charters (including a few from just inside Somerset or Wiltshire) and 526 boundary points, woodland is slightly under-represented compared to England as a whole, but there are frequent references to *wyrtruma*, which may be the Old English for a woodbank. Hedges and hedgerows are abundant; there is about an average mention of trees, the commonest being thorn. There are few mentions of features associated with strip-cultivation. The character of the Vale of Blackmoor was already recognisable a thousand years ago; then, as in Hardy's time and now, it contrasted with the open chalklands to the south, where there are few mentions of hedges and many of open-field features.

Domesday Book

In 1086 Blackmoor was seen as somewhat of a hole in the map: many settlements within it are not mentioned, such as Hilfield, Leigh, Hermitage and Holnest. This does not mean that they did not exist, but that they were included in one or other of the great ecclesiastical manors adjacent: Middlemarsh belonged to Cerne Abbas and Hilfield to Milton Abbey. Even the central wooded area has Anglo-Saxon place-names – Holnest, Rocumbe, Hartley, Hilfield, Highfield – homesteads in the woods that seldom developed beyond hamlet status.

Domesday lists woods in Dorset by length and breadth, making it possible to estimate their approximate area. Dorset as a whole works out at 13 per cent woodland, a little below average for England, but over twice the area that there was in 1895. The record is unusually full, and shows pasture covering 28 per cent

---

* To see a *herepað* go to the west corner of Minterne-Seat Coppice. The Minterne-Hartley map of 1616 labels the present woodland ride 'haere path', a uniquely late instance of the word.

** Meaning unknown: the word 'dog' for a hound had apparently not yet entered the English language.

of the county, arable land nearly half, and meadow 1 per cent.[6]

The future Forest of Blackmoor was not an exceptionally wooded area. The Cerne Abbey, the principal woodland owner, had woodland one league long and eight furlongs wide: an area (1½ × ½ mile), not very different from the Minterne Woods and Middlemarsh Common today. A big wood in Buckland Newton was probably Bewley Wood, long ago grubbed out and its name corrupted into 'Beaulieu Farm'. Glanvilles Wootton had two woods of 5 × 4 and 5 × 2 furlongs, which could be the present Great Wootton Wood and Hay Wood. Not separately recorded are the woods of Hermitage: these, as we shall see, were a detached portion of the king's manor of Fordington, now a suburb of Dorchester. The Fordington entry is included with that of Gillingham, which had a huge wood later to be Gillingham Forest. To the north and east of Blackmoor were other big woods in Pulham (not heard of again), Sherborne (parts survive), and two in Sturminster Newton (one of which is now Piddles Wood).

BLACKMOOR AS A FOREST

The Forest of Blackmoor, like many others, was apparently first declared in the mid-twelfth century: a perambulation dated 1155 could belong to the original proclamation of the Forest. It was apparently named after Blakmore, a hamlet of Glanvilles Wootton near the heart of the legal Forest, whose most notable citizen was to be the seventeenth-century poet-highwayman John Clavel.[7] It is now reduced to a Tudor farm called Round Chimneys; the place-name survives as Blackmore Ford Bridge. There would have been many other black moors in the Forest, and a few still exist, such as Deadmoor Common in Fifehead Neville.

Dorset had six and a half Forests: Gillingham in the north, Powerstock (based on the present Powerstock Common), Bere Regis, Corfe (probably based on the heaths of the Arne Peninsula), Blackmoor and half Cranborne Chase. Each (except the last) had some pre-existing royal connection. At Blackmoor this was rather tenuous. Hartley and Hermitage were a small royal estate (a thousand acres/400 ha or so) forming a detached portion of Fordington, 10 miles (16 kilometres) away. This may have originated in the Anglo-Saxon practice of estates that had no local woodland acquiring detached portions in well-wooded areas at a distance.

The legal and the physical Forest
In all wooded Forests (p.120) it is essential to distinguish between the physical Forest (the contiguous tract of woodland and wood-pasture where the deer

normally lived) and the much larger surrounding extent of the legal Forest (where people could infringe Forest Law), most of which was ordinary farmland.

The legal Forest (Fig. 207) was some 13 miles by 6 (20 × 10 kilometres), covering some 20 parishes from Sturminster Newton in the east to Stockwood in the west. It bordered two other legal Forests, Gillingham Forest and Cranborne Chase.

The physical Forest (Fig. 208) was divided between Hermitage, Holnest and Middlemarsh, and Gore Wood, which is in no parish. It was compartmental: about two-thirds of the wooded area was divided into 20 coppices with woodbanks round them, which would be felled from time to time and enclosed for six to nine years, to keep out the king's deer and the commoners' livestock until the new shoots had grown out of reach. The remainder comprised Middlemarsh and Hermitage Commons, grassland with scattered pollard trees.

Blackmoor could barely be called a wooded Forest, even in the sense of having more woodland than the adjacent non-Forest. Some of its big woods were remote from the Hermitage nucleus. Scattered among the farmland were scores of private woods, often on patches of landslip, around which ramified common grasslands, moors and heaths. Some are mentioned in twelfth- and thirteenth-century perambulations,[8] but details are first given in c.1570 (see below).

The legal bounds waxed or waned as successive kings had more or less success in oppressing the local nobility. Changes in the legal Forest did not affect the physical Forest. Many perambulations survive, most of which mention Dogbury and the Winding Stoy holloway. They tell us little about the Forest as such, but reveal that the Vale in the thirteenth century was not very wooded: the few woods mentioned are mostly still there today. Sandhulle wood, lying between Pulham and Duntish in a perambulation of c.1230, is to be identified with Sandhill Coppice, still extant, whose earthworks show that it was part of a larger wood.[9]

Surviving records, copied into rolls of the Abbey of Glastonbury, show that some aspects of Forest Law were enforced in private woods throughout the legal bounds. The Abbot was fined in the 1320s for 'wasting' 100 acres (40 ha) in his own wood of *Puttelesworth* by [Sturminster] Newton 'and another part is ill-kept'. On other occasions he grubbed out 32 acres (13 ha) more of that wood, in the most distant corner of the legal Forest. Yet Piddles Wood, as it now is, is still very much alive – a big wood, part of it a nature reserve of Dorset Wildlife Trust. Between 1296 and 1323 the Abbot made his peace with the Forest authorities for grubbing out a total of 54 acres (22 ha) of wood and alders at *Beleyheg,* that is Bewley Wood (above). He grubbed or 'wasted' 47 acres (19 ha) of wood at *Corresmor,* now Cosmore, the north-facing combe beneath Dogbury which still has several small alder-woods in landslip hollows. His tenants did this too; for example one Rich-ard Molepuf (yes, he did exist, and had a brother Ralph) was wanted for 5 acres (2 ha) of assart in Brockhampton (unidentified). These are 'prosecutions' for *permanent* destruction of Forest vegetation; there is no suggestion of making the Abbot restore the woods he had grubbed out.[10]

Mere felling of wood or timber seem never to have been prosecuted. Only once does cutting trees appear among the surviving documents, when the Abbot was given a licence to fell six oaks in his wood of [Sturminster] Newton. It is not explained what made this seemingly trivial transaction unusual.[11]

Blackmoor, the King and the Earls of Cornwall

Kings hunted rarely, if ever, in Blackmoor. Dorset had royal palaces at Gilling-ham, Bere Regis and Corfe Castle, but each of these had a Forest of its own. Some-one in Purse Caundle held land by serjeanty of keeping the king's hounds that might be injured while he was hunting in Blackmoor;[12] but this may have been a jocular or sinecural tenure, like the man who held lands by service of counting the king's chessmen on Christmas Day.

Henry III gave Fordington, including Hermitage and Hartley, to his brother Richard, Earl of Cornwall, whose brother inherited it after him. These two seem indeed to have been mighty hunters, catching their dinners whenever they could get away from their high duties of state (such as being Emperor of Germany).[13] In 1236 the Earl cut down and sold some woods to pay for an outing to the Fifth Crusade.[14] Soon after, the Forest of Blackmoor became part of the permanent endowment of the Duchy of Cornwall. Then as now, the title of Earl (later Duke) of Cornwall, along with that of Prince of Wales, could be awarded to the sovereign's eldest son for his lifetime. When there was no Duke or Prince, the property reverted to the Crown. Hence the principal wood in Hermitage is called Prince's Wood, but during the reign of Elizabeth – who had no son – Hermitage was called 'The Queen's Waste'.

The hunting record of Blackmoor begins in 1215, when King John ordered Albert de Capell to take fallow deer, using two horses and 14 buckhounds. Between 1220 and 1272, Henry III ordered 350–400 deer from the Forest (Table 26). Unusually among Forests, they included all three species, fallow deer being by far the most numerous. Records of Forest courts show that people were fined for stealing harts (adult male red deer) as well as the usual fallow bucks.[15] This gives colour to the story, first recorded three centuries later:

king Henry 3. hunting here, and having run down several Deer, spar'd the life of a milk-

white hart, which afterwards T[homas] de la Linde, *a gentleman of this County, took and kill'd; but they were soon made sensible, how dangerous it is to provoke a Lyon. For the King, being highly incens'd at it, fin'd them severely, and the very Lands they held, do to this day pay into the King's Exchequer annually a ... fine, call'd White-hart-silver.*
CAMDEN, BRITANNIA, 1586 (TRANSLATED BY E. GIBSON, 1722)

In practice, Henry would have found it difficult to stage a royal hunt in this secluded place. He occasionally sent professional hunters to take deer for feasts, as in 1237:

May 4. [The king orders the head Forester] *to receive Roger de Stopham, whom the king is sending to him with his hounds to chase bucks in the forest of Blakemore ... and to cause the venison ... to be salted ...*

May 28. Order to send the venison to Westminster to arrive there by Whit Sunday [7 June].[16]

But a peculiarity of Blackmoor is that most of the deer were given away, either as carcases (or once as a pardon for poaching), or live to start parks. In 1244 the new Abbot of Cerne was given seven does to feast his installation. In 1241 three live bucks and five does went to the Knights Templars, who should have been fighting the infidel in Palestine. The excess of does given away live is roughly balanced by the excess of bucks presented dead.

Blackmoor was not a major producer of venison, and the numbers are absurdly small by modern standards. A mere 7 – 8 deer a year would be roughly in balance with a population of 30 animals, which must be well below the present number.

The king owned deer in the whole legal Forest, and consumed them throughout his reign. He owned trees only in Hartley and Hermitage, and last ordered them in 1239, after which the landowning rights passed to the Earl of Cornwall. He ordered timber on 13 occasions for repairing his buildings at Corfe Castle, Sherborne Castle, [Queen] Camel and Dorchester. He gave 209 oaks to various beneficiaries, such as the far-away Abbot of Bindon for his church. In all, these amounted to at least 500 oaks in 18 years, not a great quantity, and probably not especially big trees: sometimes they are specified as *cheverons*, 'rafter oaks', implying smallish size. They did not go to Salisbury Cathedral or Sherborne Abbey: Blackmoor was not a source of cathedral-size oaks as was Gillingham Forest.

Henry III gave 40 *robora* for firewood to the Abbess of Tarrant [Crawford]; the word *robur*, a big non-timber tree, probably means a dead pollard. The pollards still in Blackmoor are the remains of a tradition established by the thirteenth century. Three times he ordered an unspecified quantity of *busca*, apparently underwood used for fuel.

Hermits

No Forest was complete without a hermit, a holy man to pray for the welfare of the king and the souls of his predecessors, and minister to those few people who lived in the physical Forest. Even before the Forest, St Edwold had left the world as did many a Welsh and Cornish saint, dwelling at Stockwood, where a lonely and beautiful little church yet stands in a north-facing combe of the woods.

The holy men of Blackmoor belonged to the ancient order of Augustinian Hermits. By the thirteenth century they were settled in a place previously called Rocumbe, 'roe-deer valley'. They had a little monastery with a farm, under the patronage of the Earls of Cornwall. A hamlet grew up around, which manufactured pottery: a kiln of the late thirteenth century has been excavated.[17] Soon after, the parent order transmuted itself into the Augustinian Friars and became urban, leaving the hermits as an anomaly. They died out by the fifteenth century, and the settlement turned into a small but normal parish.

Does anything material remain of the hermitage? The lonely hamlet under the woods has a mysterious little church. It is said to have been rebuilt in 1800, and its fabric is at odds with earlier descriptions and with a sketch on the Hermitage map of 1723; however, the architecture is medieval rather than Georgian and reveals phases of alteration. Does some of it date from the time of the hermits?

What happened to the Forest?

Blackmoor, like many Forests, faded away without ever being formally abolished. It is last heard of on the death of Thomas le Brutt, hereditary keeper, in 1371.[18] Whether or not the institutional Forest still existed outside folk-memory, its physical infrastructure lasted with little change into the nineteenth century.

WOODS AND WOOD-PASTURES

Woods outside the physical (but within the legal) Forest

Not all these woods appear in the known records of Forest courts. Presumably every wood was cut down several times in a century, but this was rarely prosecuted; only woods that were partly grubbed out got into the court rolls.

Some of the small woods are on soggy, spring-ridden patches of landslipped ground with alder (see Fig. 104). Forest proceedings mention a wood called Sumptonalres. In 1397 Hilfield manor had a wood called Twysenalrs.[19] Twisting Alders Coppice still exists, but has not much alder; probably its name is a dialect form of 'Betwixt Alders'.

Coppicing is recorded in, for example, the court rolls of Wotton Glanville. The 1427 roll records income from areas of underwood in Hay Wood (still so called), le Iuere and New Wood.[20] (What can a 'new wood' have been in the fifteenth century?)

The breakneck wood beneath High Stoy aroused disputes between the Duchy of Cornwall and Cerne Abbey, involving the Duke of Clarence (he who for high treason was drowned in a butt of malmsey from Crete). The Abbot took fuel from 'the wood called Minters seate [now Mintern-seat Coppice on Telegraph Hill] alias Hanginge Clife' to burn lime. There are still remains of limekilns at the foot of the cliff.[21]

The aerial view

In c.1570 a cartographer imagined a view of the Vale of Blackmoor, looking south from a height of about 10,000 feet (3,000 metres) above Castle Cary. The town of Sherborne is laid out before the beholder, and all the landscape up to the jagged rim of High Stoy, which limits the view. The view − the inverse of Thomas Hardy's − is highly recognisable: most of the roads, villages and streams were much as they are now, although about half the nearer woods have since disappeared.[22]

There was, however, one great difference. Medieval and early-modern north Dorset, like Norfolk, was intersected with a ramifying spider's-web of commons; narrowing here and there into roads, broadening out where the ground was too wet or flinty to cultivate. Most were grassland, but some were tree'd. In the south of the Vale, farmland was often confined to islands of private land, sometimes shown in Hardy fashion intersected with massive hedges.

Commons, as elsewhere, became unfashionable in the eighteenth century, and most were enclosed and destroyed. Those few that remain, like Lydlinch and Deadmoor Commons, are nature reserves cherished for their fens and old grassland, though it is difficult to prevent them from turning into undistinguished woodland.

Coppices within the physical Forest

The coppices are set out in detail in maps of 1615, 1616, 1723 and c.1770.[23] Some of them adjoined each other; others were separated by lanes or strips of common. As in some bigger Forests (e.g. Cranborne Chase, Wychwood Forest) they were in different manors; Cerne Abbey and Winchester College, their successors, had the 14 coppices in Middlemarsh. Coppices varied in extent from 5 to 30 acres (2 to 12 ha); the bigger Prince's Wood and perhaps Gore Wood were outside the system.

The management regime is indicated in a report on Hermitage, Crown property seized by Parliamentary commissioners, 1650:

*... these Copses were formerly Inclosed and of good Improvement to the Lord and were
usually inclosed for 21 years or as there was Occasion for Raysing of the s[ai]d closes and
the young trees there growing and then layd open with the Rest till the Copses were Cutt
and then Inclos'd againe but for want of Inclosure for divers years past the Vesture thereof is
almost destroyed.*[24]

This sounds like a garbled version of a 21-year coppice cycle (the length of
the whole cycle, not the period of enclosure) in adjacent Middlemarsh. The maps
show that the only enclosed wood in Hermitage was Prince's Wood, which was
not subdivided – it would have been inconveniently small.

The coppices are enclosed, and mostly separated, by strong banks and ditches
(Figs 159 & 208). (In theory, woods within a Forest were supposed not to be
embanked, but like much of Forest Law this was disregarded – or did the banks
antedate the Forest?) The compartments were not laid out according to a plan,
and from the junctions of banks it is possible to work out how the system grew up.
For example, Grove Ground and Higher Westwood were originally one coppice,
to which Lower Westwood plus Oxlease Wood were added as one coppice; both
were later subdivided. Prince's Wood, in a different ownership, is only partly
embanked. Its bank is cut through by two small, elongated fields (originally four),
which are evidently a late intrusion with feeble banks. They are described as 'Assart
land' on the 1616 map, so the main period of embanking must be well before that
date. An internal bank within Prince's Wood may represent an attempt at its own
compartmentation. Most of Holnest Wood was grubbed out in the eighteenth
century to create a country-house park. The surviving fragment, which comprised
one or more coppices, has a massive bank on what is left of its original boundary.

Anyone interested in lime (*linde*) as a historic tree will ask where Thomas de la
Lynde, hero of the *faux pas* with the white hart, came from. The De la Lyndes were
local gentry from at least the twelfth to the sixteenth century; several generations were hereditary Foresters.[25] Two wood-names could allude to the tree:
Limeholte, as the 1615 map calls the Cliff wood, and Lyons Wood, among the Forest
coppices. 'Limeholte' may refer merely to lime-burning, but is named *Lyndenbolt*
in a document referring to events in 1277.[26] The latter, called *Lynis Wood* on the
1723 map, is the more likely, as the De la Lyndes were squires of Hartley. As far as
I know there is no *Tilia* anywhere in Blackmoor: but do there still lurk in Lyon's
Wood lime-trees that have defied poisoning and replanting?

Modern history and present state

With a bill-book in one hand, and a leather glove much too large for her on the other, she was making spars, such as are used by thatchers, with great rapidity. She wore a leather apron ... which was also much too large for her figure. On her left hand lay a bundle of the straight smooth hazel rods called spar-gads ... To produce them she took up each gad, looked critically along it from end to end, cut it to length, split it into four, and sharpened each of the quarters with dexterous blows ...

THOMAS HARDY, *THE WOODLANDERS*, 1887

Hardy set this scene in 'Little Hintock', a *nom de plume* for Hermitage, in the early to mid-nineteenth century. Making *broaches*, as this writer knows them, demands a quick eye and a strong wrist; they were used by the million for the temporary thatching of corn-ricks, and are now again in demand as people keep thatched roofs in better repair than they used to.

Woodmanship, however, was declining when Hardy wrote, though some of the specialised coppice crafts, such as making sheep-cribs, still flourished. Successive editions of *Kelly's Directory* list few woodland crafts in Blackmoor. At Middlemarsh a cooper worked from 1859 to 1890. At Lyon's Gate there was a brickmaker in 1855 and a firewood merchant from 1895 to 1915. Hurdle-making, as a speciality, had moved off to the Winterbornes and Bere Regis further east.

Woodmanship in Dorset had become dominated by the timber trade, and was infiltrated by tree-planting and other non-traditional activities. The first change was increasing the number of oaks. Trees and stumps still extant show that growing oak had often come to predominate over underwood. But not only oak timber: one of Hardy's characters 'did a large business in bark', which dates the story to the 1860s or earlier. Hardy mentions 'a curious sound, something like the quacking of ducks', as the barking-spade parted the bark from the oak.

Thirty years after Hardy, his commentator, Hermann Lea, noted:

The timber trade, of which we hear so much in the story, has declined, and with it has gone many of the smaller industries which were intimately connected with the larger business – hollow-turning, hurdle-making, splitting of thatching-spars, and the like.[27]

This change is illustrated by the coal lying among the ruins of the last limekiln at the base of High Stoy, still active until *c.*1901. Since 1857 coal had come by train even to this corner of Dorset, and lime-burners carted it 5 miles (8 kilometres) from the station rather than using the wood that grew on the spot.

In the mid-nineteenth century plantations had been established on the site of

Hermitage Common (Prince's Waste). They still imitated existing woods (p.350), with ash and hazel underwood, although timber oaks greatly predominate.

In most of the central woods the oaks were felled between the World Wars, leaving stumps still recognisable. *Kelly's Directory* records a timber merchant and sawmill, but no longer a wood merchant, at Middlemarsh from the 1930s. Nothing much then seems to have happened until the 1960s, when nearly all the coppices were destroyed and replaced by plantations. Different owners planted various species with varying degrees of success.

Not much native woodland now remains within the physical Forest (Figs 153–157). A fragment of the great Holnest Wood survives. In Prince's Wood the foresters spared (as foresters sometimes did) a narrow marginal fringe. On the edge of Lyon's Wood a curious salient of Great Minterne parish projects into Hermitage: this corresponds to a huge landslip, and on it is an intact fragment of ash- and alder-wood overlying a slump of bottomless black moor, decked with golden saxifrage. Part of Little Bridge Wood also escaped.

These fragments indicate what the coppices might have been like. They are usually ash–hazel-woods. Under regular coppicing, hazel would have prospered, except beneath the shade of the oaks. More recently, ash has increased, encouraged by felling the oaks at a time when there were no deer. Streams and landslip hollows are full of alder, which has resisted coniferisation better than ash. The ground vegetation is dominated by bluebell and ramsons.

Native woodland otherwise survives in Blackmoor in former non-woodland glades. The lane between Gore and Strawberry Woods is a curious and beautiful place. Isaac Taylor's map says 'W. Fox S. Fox and J. Gannot have each 2 Beast Leazes here', evidently a right to pasture cattle. Since 1900 the lane has turned into woodland of hazel and sallow, overhung with the boughs of its former hedgerow oaks, and carpeted with ramsons and moschatel. It adjoins the extra-parochial territory of Gore Wood, bounded on one side by the woodbank of that wood and on the other by those of the Middlemarsh woods, but being in a different ownership it escaped replanting. This winding lane collects water from many springs, but the watercourses, which would naturally follow valleys in the woods on both sides, have for some reason been diverted into the woodbank ditches.

At the heart of Blackmoor is another anomaly, Louse Hay, in c.1770 a two-acre (0.8 ha) field surrounded by woods. Its name suggests an Anglo-Saxon enterprise (Old English *blos* 'pigsty' + *gebæg* 'enclosure') which got no further than a single tiny field. In the twentieth century it turned into a tiny wood of ash and sallow, its delicate green carpet of moschatel in eerie contrast to the sombre, sterilised plantations that now hem it in. Why is so small an area, a mere piggery, defended by mighty banks and ditches?

In the plantations the original wood was thoroughly destroyed, though stools survived here and there. Most of the planted trees lived, but passed through periods of neglect. Some are now a tangle of wind-toppled larches; some grew into quite respectable Sitka spruce and Douglas fir, just in time for the market to decline. Ground vegetation under the dense evergreens is often reduced to a few attenuated bluebells. Banks and ditches, however, still snake through the coppices – with traces of their hedges – and tell of the compartmental Forest. When I was last there part of the woods was up for sale. Its likely future is to be devoured by unhistorical numbers of deer.

The commons

In the sixteenth century commons were roughly as extensive as the coppices. They seem to have been wood-pastures with pollard trees. Half the entire parish of Hermitage appears on the 1615 map as 'The Prince's Waste', meaning the common of which the Prince of Wales was nominal landowner. After the Prince had become Charles I and had forfeited his head, the committee for privatising his lands was petitioned by the commoners:

> ... their Auncestors haue for 60 yeares past & upward had right of Commonage for feed-inge their horses & Sheepe & other Cattle in & uppon the Commons of Hermitage & Hartley ... and Liberty to take Thorne ffurzen and Brambles ... for fuell.[28]

As in Hatfield Forest, the common-rights did not include woodcutting of the coppices or pollards.

Hermitage Common was the scene of frontier disputes with Holnest and Hilfield: all three manors have sixteenth-century perambulations. The bound-ary was marked by 'a great olde oke called the wynding oke' and another called Trimtree, and many stones, some being 'Ancient bound stones' and others set up to settle the quarrel, as well as 'ryme horn pitt ... in which pitt ... there hath been buried a boy which hanged himself in that pitt'. Although several of these survived late enough to be recorded by the Ordnance Survey, all the landmarks seem to have been removed since.[29] Hermitage Common was broken up probably in the eighteenth century and became ordinary farmland.

Middlemarsh Common, anciently Irelegh,[30] met a different fate. It had been an irregular-shaped area, funnelling out by horns at the corners into roads and the lanes between the coppices. Attempts were made to encoppice it. The c.1770 map shows two surviving coppices within the common, but woodbanks on the ground indicate that there had been others. Three sides of the common had been tidied into straight lines by encroachments and boundary settlements, and the fourth was about to be. The map shows the common as woodland, but mostly less dense than the coppice-woods, and intersected by informal paths; it suggests a halfway stage in 'tumbling down' to natural secondary woodland.

The Common remained mainly wooded through the nineteenth century. In the 1960s it was treated differently from the other woods. In places the existing trees were left intact and planted trees were squeezed in between them. Among the older oaks and ashes are now languishing or dead Norway spruce, a picture of wasted effort. The plantations were rather more successful on the sites of coppices, of which little remains except stumps of timber trees and a row of hazels on the woodbanks.

A few wood-pasture trees survive. In one field half-a-dozen 'great olde okes' remain from the Prince's Waste. There are two remaining oaks from Middlemarsh Common: one a curious 'elephant's-foot' tree, the other an ancient pollard. The Hilfield Oak is the last relic of a common. The grandest of these trees, however, stands in the middle of a long narrow pasture, a former tongue of common behind Middlemarsh hamlet: a giant spreading pollard oak, the last survivor of several on the 1887 Ordnance Survey.

Woods outside the physical Forest

Foresters in the Locust Years usually went for the bigger woods. Smaller woods away from the central core of Blackmoor Forest escaped. They are usually surrounded by banks and ditches. Great Wootton Wood, though only 22 acres (9 ha), has a perimeter bank which follows nearly every turn of its complicated outline. Hay Wood nearby has banks indicating several phases of subdivision.

There are three types of woodland. The first, like the core woods as they seem to have been, is of ash or hazel in various proportions. (Maple, although recorded for many woods, is more of a hedge than a woodland tree in Dorset.) Some still retain a high density of oaks, left over from Hardy's time. Ground vegetation is usually dominated by bluebell, or ramsons where there is a spring-line. Even smaller woods have a rich flora, with toothwort, herb paris, autumn crocus, archangel, saw-wort and several orchids including helleborine. In places *Carex pendula* is abundant and increasing.

On hilltops, or where greensand or clay-with-flints give acidity to the soil, this woodland gives way to oak–hazel with increasing holly. Bluebells are more strongly dominant, with bracken on the most acid soils. Birch would be expected, but is not yet common. Around springs or in wet hollows of landslips alder becomes dominant, with ramsons, *Carex pendula,* or golden saxifrage where the soil turns to black ooze.

The wood on the cliff below High Stoy, with its centuries of landslipping, coppicing and lime-burning, is mainly ash and hazel with dog's-mercury. In places it would have been what Peterken called the ash–wych-elm Stand Type, but Elm Disease and deer have eliminated most living elm. Patches of ramsons are surprising for a wood on a dry chalk hill. On the hilltop, oakwood with bracken indicates an acid soil, perhaps due to a local accumulation of clay-with-flints.

Ash–hazel-wood, carpeted with ramsons, is repeated in a steep grove called Mount Sylva, immediately below Dogbury; it may contain strip-lynchets from prehistoric cultivation. Although only weakly embanked this is an ancient wood, depicted on the 1615 map, and with huge ancient ash stools. Here, too, is an area of oaks and bracken, where badgers dig up greensand.

Parks

Dorset is one of the most parky of counties; Forest Law notwithstanding, there were several parks in Blackmoor. A mysterious one is represented by a massive bank and internal ditch (p.159f), enclosing the southern part of the Clinger estate, adjoining the boundary of the Buckland Newton perambulation. It has long been recognised and mapped as a park, but no written record is known.

Of the Abbey at Cerne, which owned much of the central woods of Blackmoor, almost nothing survives above ground save the Abbot's deer-park, a little south of the rim. In a chalkland dry valley there are steep coppice-woods and grass-lands, within a huge bank with internal ditch and in places a wall. Some of the ash stools are gigantic, up to 14 feet (4½ metres) in diameter. Presumably this was a compartmental park.

A fragment of another park, also with ditch inside the bank, is Prior's Wood in Stockwood. To the north, Stock-Gaylard Park, probably of later date, is a wonderful setting for an old-fashioned country mansion.

Non-woodland trees

Dorset has long been known for giant and ancient oaks. Hardy thought 'the hollow-trunked trees that shade so many of its pastures' were relics of a greater wooded Forest of White Hart. He was wrong: they seem always to have been hedgerow and field trees, usually pollards. Several yet stand, such as the Cavalier Oak in Stock-Gaylard Park. The Stockbridge Oak, already a famous ancient tree in the 1830s, is another pollard, standing on what was a roadside common. When the common was made into an oak plantation, the Big Oak Strip, in the mid-nineteenth century, a gap was left for this giant tree.

Dorset has a surprisingly unpolluted atmosphere: ancient trees develop their full lichen flora, including large and now uncommon species such as *Lobaria pulmonaria* and *Usnea articulata*.

Another great oak is depicted as my tailpiece to *Ancient Woodland*. It is a pollard, with a massive trunk and small head of branches. I estimate it at about 1,100 years old: older than the Forest, older than the churches, and the oldest living thing in Blackmoor; King Edmund the Magnificent could have seen it.

CONCLUSION

Blackmoor is an 'average' specimen of a wooded, compartmented Forest. Hatfield Forest (Essex) is the best known: others include Cranborne Chase (Dorset and Wiltshire), Grovely (Wiltshire), Wychwood and Bernwood (Oxfordshire), Rockingham (Northamptonshire), Writtle (Essex) and the Forest of Horwood (Gloucester) (see Fig. 184).[31] Blackmoor was smaller than most of these.

As an institution, Blackmoor Forest apparently had a short life, although as Professor Jack Langton points out, Forests passing to the Duchy of Cornwall are poorly recorded and could have endured as institutions much longer than the latest known record. Most of the Forest's fabric lasted into the nineteenth century; its survival is a counter-example to the theory that Forest Law was effective in preserving woodland. It was destroyed, not because its land uses were unsustainable, but because of outside pressures and changes of fashion.

The written record, as far as is yet known, is not especially rich. Blackmoor did not give rise to the disputes between lords that made Hatfield such a supremely well-documented Forest.

The plantations are a depressing epitome of beautiful woodland wrecked for nobody's benefit. They are not high on the list of sites capable of being rehabilitated, although recent advances begin to raise hopes even for places such as this.

Blackmoor is not 'a microcosm of English history' like Hatfield Forest; but it is not lacking in distinction, especially in the relation between geology and function. It has many layers of significance. Iron Age hillforts, Anglo-Saxon perambulations, Forest records, ancient trees, coppice stools, estate maps and the works of Thomas Hardy give structure and meaning to the present landscape.

CHAPTER 21

EXPERIMENTS AND LONG-TERM OBSERVATIONS

New technology and understanding ... can have a devastating effect on long-term projects: there is always a loss of interest in continuing with a project set up using outmoded techniques, recorded on outmoded software (such as paper cards!), and set up to answer problems long since considered irrelevant.
JONATHAN SPENCER, 1995[1]

This chapter is addressed to professional ecologists, teachers devising exercises for students, conservationists in charge of nature reserves and amateur naturalists or historians with a long-term interest in a wood or group of woods.

As all conservationists know, it is easier to start a new project than to sustain an existing one. Funds for new activities are much easier to raise. Volunteers love cutting down trees, but are most reluctant to return, even next year, to record the consequences. There is thus surprisingly little information about the effects of conservation activity. Have woods belonging to conservation organisations fared better or worse than those remaining in private ownership? The answer seemed obvious during the Locust Years. In the 25 years since grubbing and coniferisation ceased to be widespread the question has seldom been asked, but one day it will be, and conservation bodies ought to have an answer.

Investigators may persuade themselves that time sequences can be short-circuited: that comparing plots in 2005 that were felled in 1996, 1999 and 2002 is equivalent to following the same plot through three, six and nine years after felling. In practice this is seldom true: similar, even adjacent, plots have an infuriating habit of going through different trajectories in different years. There is no substitute for real time sequences.[2]

The anthropology of ecological science

Ecology has been forced into a cultural mould determined by other sciences: a world of full-time research, large grants of money to be spent within a limited time, PhDs to be gained within three years, careers to be pursued. Long-term, cheap, interdisciplinary, or exploratory studies are marginalised and tend to take place, if at all, outside the academic establishment.

These constraints limit the range of problems that can be studied, and create a bias towards certain kinds of interpretation. Change tends to be emphasised over stability: students — and referees of learned journals — are excited by change, but discouraged on discovering only stability. Gradualist explanations are favoured over catastrophist. The effect of ordinary rains can be studied with one year spent getting the apparatus together, one year of observation and one year writing up; but what research supervisor will advise a student to study the effect of a deluge that is unlikely to occur within the middle year?

Ecologists, taking 'hard' sciences like physics for their model, have striven towards a reductionist world where everything can be explained in terms of a small number of quantitative laws; in which observations can be repeated and notebooks thrown away when the work has been published. Even a century on, they have not fully come to terms with a real world in which the laws of nature are complex and semi-quantitative and have exceptions; in which observations are time-limited, and the primary data are often of more lasting importance than the theories. The Law of Evolution is not quite a 'law' in the sense of the Law of Gravitation.

Ecologists have become reluctant to investigate the unexpected or inexplicable. Discovery is out of fashion. A scientist recently complained to the British Ecological Society that only 43 per cent of ecological investigations were driven by the desire to confirm or disconfirm a hypothesis. This, for him, was not enough, even though some grant-giving bodies dislike projects that do not test a preconceived hypothesis.[3] The time draws nearer when an investigator has to know (or pretend to know) the approximate answer to a question before applying for a grant to study it. I leave the reader to speculate where new hypotheses will then come from.

Woodland and the teaching of historical ecology

Any ancient wood provides abundant material for demonstrations and student exercises in the long-term functioning of a wood. By maps or transects one can in a few hours investigate the difference between the vegetation on a woodbank and that in the rest of the wood, or the occurrence of different humus types under oak, hornbeam or ash, or the spread of plants of ancient woodland into an extension to the original wood. A more ambitious student project might investigate the correlation between tree species and different types of ground vegetation. But other projects are well worth studying, though one would hesitate to recommend them even as a subject for a PhD, such as how the buried seeds of coppicing plants (p.212) know that the wood has been felled and it is time to germinate.

LONG-TERM OBSERVATIONS

Some of my own studies, written up in *Ancient Woodland* (2003), continue photographic and other records begun by my predecessors B.A. Abeywickrama and D.E. Coombe in the 1940s and 1950s. Here I summarise two others.

Gamlingay Wood over 90 years
In 1911 R.S. Adamson wrote an account of Gamlingay Wood near Cambridge: one of the first ecological descriptions of a natural wood in Britain. His object seems to have been to introduce the American idea of plant-associations to this country. He made detailed maps of trees and shrubs and of the ground vegetation in about one-third of the wood. He drew attention to what I would now call a 'sand-lens': a patch of sandy soil contrasting with the boulder-clay underlying the rest of the wood.[4]

Adamson was unaware that this was (as far as is known at present) the best-documented historic wood in the country. For 650 years before his time the wood, or part of it, had belonged to Merton College, Oxford, which kept excellent archives. Something is known of its ecology in the Middle Ages.

Time rolled on, and Gamlingay Wood passed through various vicissitudes. In 1938 Harry Godwin mentioned 'felling and burning' but alas gave no details. In the 1950s the college sold the wood, and parts of it were replanted in different ways and with varying success. It was bought by the Wildlife Trust for Bedfordshire and Cambridgeshire in 1991, which revived the coppicing and has removed many of the planted trees. Since then Gamlingay Wood has escaped the worst deer damage, but muntjac have become abundant and the wood now looks distinctly deer-bitten.

In 1991 and 2002 I was able to map the vegetation again, and in particular to repeat Adamson's observations (Fig. 209). Table 25 is a summary of the findings.

Hybrid poplars (a fashionable tree crop in the 1950s) were inserted into small gaps in the otherwise intact wood. They had no measurable effect on the native trees or the ground vegetation. The effects of the other planted trees were not always what would be expected. Areas where ash was planted did not necessarily show an increase in ash. The most notable change in trees was birch, which had not been planted. In 1911 birch was confined to the sand-lens, which would traditionally be thought its proper habitat. By 1991 it had declined on the sand-lens, but become abundant everywhere else, especially in some of the planted areas. This is how birch increased generally in the twentieth century, taking advantage of the disturbance created by planting other trees (p.372). Planted trees (other than poplar) were particularly antagonistic to aspen, which although clonal is sensitive to competition.

Among herbaceous plants some differences indicate changes in waterlogging. In coniferised areas the effective winter rainfall would have been reduced, by needles intercepting and evaporating some of the rain; this would work in favour of bluebell and mercury and against oxlip and meadowsweet. Other changes in intact areas may result from runs of wetter or drier seasons. Global warming has not resulted in a decline of bluebell (though it may have of primrose). The decline of oxlip, as in many other woods, may be an effect of browsing. I cannot imagine why meadowsweet declined in both intact and replanted areas. This is peculiar to Gamlingay Wood; in nearby woods meadowsweet remains abundant.

Adamson's record furnishes a rare if not unique opportunity to test how stable plant distributions and communities have been, and to measure the effect of different types of replanting. It confirms that planting damages a wood's individuality, promoting commonplace plant communities, such as a monoculture of dog's-mercury, at the expense of rare ones. However, in forestry terms this was barely a successful replanting. If it had yielded a reasonable crop of planted oak or pine, little of the ground vegetation, let alone the native trees, would have survived.

Lady Park Wood over 60 years

In a corner next to Gloucestershire and Herefordshire, Lady Park Wood climbs the northeast-facing crags of the Wye Gorge just inside Wales. It comprises some 90 acres (36 ha) (projected on to the horizontal) and adjoins other, more extensive, plantations and woods. It has been so called since 1608; who the Lady and the Park were is forgotten. The wood, on hard limestone, clays and scree, is most varied in its soils and vegetation. Ash, beech, lime, hazel and wych-elm predominate; sessile oak occurs on the acidic plateau above the cliffs. There are many other trees and shrubs. Ground vegetation ranges from wood-sage to *Luzula sylvatica* and dog's-mercury.

After centuries as a coppice, the wood was last cut partly in 1902 and partly in 1943. Surrounding woods were coniferised gradually, beginning in the nineteenth century. This difficult terrain escaped, and in 1944 was set aside as a non-intervention nature reserve by the Forestry Commission, British Ecological Society and Oxford University Department of Forestry. It has been maintained, watched over and recorded by E.W. Jones, G.F. Peterken and E.J. Mountford.

By the 1970s there had been quite big changes. Beech increased in dominance; shade increased and understorey trees such as maple were killed; hazel was largely eliminated. 'A perpetual rain of mature trees' fell off cliffs and steep slopes, the limes remaining alive. Then came Elm Disease, which killed most of the elms to the ground. Then came the great drought of 1976, which killed some of the beeches and set back the others, to the benefit of ash and lime.[5]

By 1987 the investigators concluded that 'succession is seen as an unpredictable process without a definite outcome'. Changes were driven by outside events, which varied from one part of the wood to another. Some, such as cessation of coppicing and Elm Disease, applied to many woods. Others, such as storms and trees falling from cliffs, were more or less local. Beech is unusually susceptible to drought, and is a 'catastrophist' tree, coming and going in response to unusual events.

Further changes have occurred in the last 20 years. Fallow deer had been present in modest numbers possibly since the time of the park; they have now proliferated to an all-too-familiar degree – they probably learnt to take refuge here from culling in neighbouring woods. They have eliminated ground vegetation, especially brambles, which survive inside exclosures. Grey squirrel damage is unusually severe, and probably affects the longevity of the trees. Sycamore threatens to invade. Felling of adjacent plantations increases windblow on the edges of the reserve. Pollution, which used to emanate from the mines and factories of South Wales, now takes the form of nitrogen compounds from nearby farms.[6]

Lady Park Wood is probably much more unstable than most 'old-growth' woods that result from non-intervention after coppicing. Of the factors promoting change, one – trees falling off cliffs – is rare, and another – the unstable behaviour of beech – is confined to beechwoods, but the others are widespread. However, it is unusual to find such a conjunction of instabilities in one site. Hayley Wood from 1965 to 2005, or Madingley Wood from 1950 to 1990, have been more stable than the first 40 years of observations were in Lady Park.

Thirty years in a hundred woods: the Kirby– Bunce survey

In 1971 Bob Bunce organised a detailed survey of 1,686 sample plots, each of 200 square metres, in 103 woods, located all over Great Britain, except for East Anglia, Essex, Kent, Cornwall, the Pennines and south Scotland. About two-thirds of the woods are now thought to have been ancient. Within each wood the plots were located at random, some including (for example) woodland grassland, others not. In 2000–3 the surviving 1,648 plots were relocated and re-surveyed by different people, and the results of the two surveys compared.[7]

At the time of writing the comparison was not fully published, and it would be premature to summarise or discuss it in detail. However, I have mentioned some of the findings in other chapters. There was a general change towards greater shade, greater fertility (in woods surrounded by farmland) and increasing deer. In general, plots had fewer species in c.2001 than in 1971, except those 'damaged' by the great storms of 1987 or 1990. The survivors tended to be plants tolerating shade, those of more fertile soils and those tolerant of browsing. Other changes were related to the lengthening growing season.

EXPERIMENTS

Although historical ecology will always be a mainly observational science like astronomy, there are opportunities for experimentation: for example Norman Moore's new wood (p.248), or investigations of how waterlogging affects plant communities. A widely applicable type of experiment is to investigate effects of browsing by fencing various animals out of sample areas, with deer-, rabbit-, or mouse-fences (Fig. 158). One should beware of side effects, for example by the fence intercepting fallen leaves, or zinc dissolved from galvanised wire poisoning plants directly under the fence.

Any wood used for research is littered with remains of experiments that students of yesteryear abandoned to take up careers far away. Amateurs may have more opportunities for continuity. Long-term observations and experiments run the risk of destruction of the site, as happened to Poolthorn Covert (p.248). Management plans for woodland should always take account of the existence of previous investigations, even if they seem not to be still ongoing.

Long-term experiments incur another anthropological difficulty. The question that they were set up to answer, or the hypothesis that they might have confirmed, may turn out to be unimportant or merely unfashionable. Ecology, like many other sciences, is a creature of fashion: in its 150-year history it has been dominated successively by evolution, succession, energy flow, classification, nutrient flow, and recently again by evolution. (Is not a journal called *Trends in Ecology and Evolution*?) Any experiment lasting (by design or accident) for more than 20 years will have been through periods of being deeply un-trendy and unlikely to be continued for its original objective.

My own experiments and observations, set up in Hayley Wood to study the effects of coppicing on herbaceous plants, a few years later became of more interest in relation to the effects of deer. In recent years, with deer excluded from most of the wood, they have gained interest for the recovery of ground vegetation from browsing in relation to whether or not deer had damaged the underwood canopy.

Peterken has related the practical difficulties of maintaining observations over 60 years at Lady Park Wood. Money is less of a problem than lack of continuity of observers and equipment. Even the simplest experiments, using nothing more complex than measuring tapes and permanent markers for plots, are surprisingly difficult to compare with the work of previous observers using different kinds of tape and different methods of locating plots.

Experiments need to be simple and cheap to maintain and their objectives not too narrowly specified; otherwise they can deal only with short-term phenomena. Permanently marked plots that can be recorded or photographed at regular (or irregular) intervals are more robust than apparatus that needs constant maintenance and periodic replacement.

FIXED-POINT PHOTOGRAPHS

Successive photographs from the same point record change and stability as few other methods can do with so little expense or effort. Anyone can repeat a photograph every year or every ten years, beginning (if possible) by relocating a pre-existing photograph or historic painting.

It is important to repeat the exact scene (Figs 160 & 161). By careful observation of sightlines it should be possible in woodland to identify the viewpoint within 8 inches (20 centimetres) or so in three dimensions, even without a marker. For future use it is helpful to take the original picture with one's back to a tree that seems likely to stay in place. A zoom lens is almost essential in order to reproduce the focal length of the original lens. It is not always easy to repeat the pictures at the same equivalent time of year: if anemones are in bloom one year along with their leaves and a bryophyte cover, the next year when the anemones are out the bryophytes may be covered by a layer of fallen leaves that earthworms have not finished eating. One tries to take successive pictures in roughly the same weather and at the same time of day.

An annotated sketch of the scene may be useful for identifying plants in the pictures. The difference between primrose and lesser celandine may not always be apparent in a photograph.

Very often it happens that an original viewpoint is now in the middle of a bramble thicket or otherwise obscured. This, of course, is a useful observation in itself, but it then becomes necessary to take another shot from as near as possible to avoid the obstruction (Figs 162 & 163). I normally think it proper to bend obtruding branches aside.

ECOLOGICAL ARCHIVES

Long-term projects require archives and an institutional memory: without them, the record will remain lost, or its existence will remain unknown. In the case of Lady Park Wood ... the [Nature Conservancy Council] *almost lost the lot when* [X's] *papers were weeded following a promotion, but were saved by a secretary who thought they might be interesting.*
G.F. PETERKEN, 2005

Ecology is time dependent. Stability and change need to be established over periods much longer than the life of a research project, longer than the life of a scientist or the life expectancy of an institution like English Nature. One can still (just) observe what elmwoods are like unaffected by Elm Disease, but to learn what a wood was like before the multiplication of deer depends on the chance of someone having taken and preserved observations.

Present observations will surely be of similar importance to ecologists a century hence. This is not limited to published material. Few ecologists want to publish all their data, even if editors and referees would let them. Some are so perfectionist that they take their knowledge with them to the grave. Notebooks and photographs belonging to deceased ecologists are part of the nation's archives, and need to be properly housed and catalogued. As yet this is not systematically provided for, although some Biological Records Centres have made a valiant beginning.

Electronic storage

There is no remembrance of former things; neither shall there be any remembrance of things that are to come with those that shall come after.

ECCLESIASTES 1: 11

Electronic storage seems attractive, especially with the increasing habit of using Geographical Position Systems. Its limitations are illustrated by a well-known cautionary tale. To commemorate the 900th anniversary of Domesday Book a new project was set up in emulation of the original. A million people took part and promptly forgot about it. Within 15 years, although the disks survived, the equipment needed to read them had passed from 'state of the art' to obsolescence. The data were rescued, just in time, by a difficult recovery project.[8] Had the equipment survived, the disks might not have lasted much longer. Meanwhile, William the Conqueror's original text is still in excellent condition and can immediately be read by anyone who has mastered the abbreviations. The same has happened to other, less famous, electronic databases that were forgotten for 20 years or so.

Curating electronic archives is still in its infancy. Their great advantage in looking up data and saving space is opposed by their great disadvantage in needing frequent, expensive rewriting. Important data should still be preserved with printed copies on acid-free paper as a backup against a future when institutions stop spending money on material that is rarely consulted. Neglect is death to electronic archives in a matter of decades, but does not greatly matter to paper copies, which need only to be kept dry and can be scanned back into electronic form.

CHAPTER 22

THE RECENT PAST AND THE FUTURE

Many owners have found that [public] *access, even to woods supporting a regular shoot, is not a great problem. The relatively few owners who have created Permissive Paths in their wood have found a small extra benefit to themselves: walkers in the wood help to deter wrongdoers – including deer!*

G. ROBERTS, 2005[1]

I am often asked to prognosticate the future. Those who expect me to predict the next 40 years should ask whether in 1966 anyone could have predicted the state of woodland by 2006. Forty years ago there seemed to be no future in natural woodland. Who would have predicted that a goodly number of ancient woods would still be there in the twenty-first century, that plantation forestry would lose the economic base on which it was then justified, that the Woodland Trust would become one of the biggest woodland owners in the country, that the Forestry Commission would be leading the way in recovering replanted woods, and that the idea of new National Forests, presented as imitating natural woodland, would attract huge popular support? It is a fallacy to assume that the future will be no more than a continuation of the trends of the recent past.

The conservation scene is the most rapidly changing aspect of woodland, as old threats and opportunities are replaced by new ones. It has changed even since I wrote the conservation chapter for *Ancient Woodland* four years ago.

ANTHROPOLOGICAL THREATS AND OPPORTUNITIES

Decoupling of woodland

Natural history writers often insist, sententiously, that woods existed because of the part they played in the local economy. That relationship was rather loose. Places with extensive woodland tended to grub it out at times when farming was prosperous, unless there was a fuel-using industry or a city to buy wood. Places without woodland seem not to have suffered much from the lack and did not make much effort to acquire some. France, with ten times as much woodland as England, and Japan, with even more, complained of having too little.

For a thousand years woodland was relatively stable. Woods were assaulted by outside forces, grubbed out into farmland or grazed away into heath. There were gradual changes from within: encoppicement of wood-pastures, lengthening of coppice cycles, shifts in the balance between underwood and timber, or (in the Scottish Highlands) increased grazing and the change from cattle to sheep. All these centuries-long trends, however, were outweighed by the sudden vicissitudes of the twentieth century.

Woods began to lose touch with their local economy about 1800, as woodland owners became more influenced by distant markets for produce. Coal had long been a cheap alternative to wood fuel in cities, but canals and then railways brought it to villages and the countryside. Coal mining itself created well-paid jobs and competed with woodcutting for labour; coppicing retreated from most of Wales and northern England, then prosperous parts of the country. Wood production became less lucrative than timber, but after 1860 timber trees too were less rewarding with the collapse in the markets for oak timber and bark. (Would the story be different if railways had decided, as they did in most European countries, to make sleepers of small oak-trees rather than imported pine?) The plantation ethos began to spread into woodland. Trees were planted for specific purposes which, as often as not, did not wait for the trees to grow.

Specialised coppice crafts lacked organisation, capital and political influence. In the 1920s Fitzrandolph & Hay (p.219) found a multitude of tiny businesses cutting each other's throats and having no control over their supplies or markets. They did not, as ironworks had done, acquire and conserve their own woods. Their problem was disorganisation, not lack of demand or inability to adapt. I understand the position is not much better now. Recently there is the further problem that most coppicing is in East Anglia and southeast England, the most prosperous and expensive parts of the country.

However, coppicing has not been wholly dependent on coppice crafts, and need not be in the future. By far the greatest bulk of underwood has been used for fuel and other non-specialised uses. The future of woodmanship, like its past, depends on marketing produce unsuitable for crafts or surplus to their requirements. A welcome development has been the introduction of miniature forestry machines that handle poles and logs and reduce the greatest labour burden of coppicing, that of getting the produce out of the wood. Biomass fuels mostly involve farmland crops, including willows treated as such, but there are proposals for including woodland.

Decoupling, even if it leads to neglect, is more benign than modern forestry chasing yesterday's industries. However, it carries the risk that some unforeseen new enterprise will treat woods as vacant land, as the present fashion for wind farms is seizing on moors and blanket bogs as vacant land.

Decoupling and modern forestry: In the 1980s confidence collapsed in profit or loss as the factor determining silvicultural practice. Not that profitability is unimportant, but it is unpredictable and even indeterminate. Few plantation owners have cared enough about 'economic viability' to keep the records needed to work it out (p.360). When a plantation is felled who remembers how much was invested in it?

Although forestry 'economics' rarely had a robustly quantitative character, certain lessons can be learnt from the Locust Years. Whether or not a plantation pays its way depends on factors – biological or anthropological – that were not provided against when it was set up, such as workmen demanding higher wages. Technological change can have even more impact on modern forestry than on woodmanship. I know of plantations that were successful in silvicultural terms, but were difficult to harvest because 38-ton lorries (undreamt-of when they were planted) could not get to the site.

Planters concentrated on growing trees, on the basis that once the trees had grown they would sell themselves. But while the trees are growing, fashion rolls on, and selling trees may be more difficult than growing them. Ability, local knowledge and experience are important. Foresters and woodmen both need to know contractors and purchasers who can be relied upon to fell the marked trees and not the unmarked ones, and where to dispose of small quantities of unfashionable trees. People with those skills are rare and valuable: they do not guarantee the profitability of a plantation (that would be too much to ask), but they save their employers many times their salary in cutting losses.

Reduced pressure on land; agricultural collapse?

Edlin wrote *Trees, Woods and Man* during a time of great pressure on land. It seemed essential for every acre of the country to appear to be doing something – even acres that the country managed without in the dark and hungry days of World War II. That time has passed away because of plant breeding. If two blades of grass grow where one grew before, or 2½ tons of wheat instead of 1 ton, what is to happen to the land on which the extra grass or wheat used to grow?

As far as can be foreseen, this is a permanent change. New varieties call for agricultural chemicals at a rate that may not be sustainable, but further plant breeding could probably overcome this restriction. Britain shrinks in area as relative sea level rises and drained salt marshes are reclaimed by the sea. The excessively drained Fens begin to go out of cultivation as the peat soil turns into carbon dioxide. The populations of Britain and Ireland are still rising; fewer people live in each house, so that a village can grow even if its population declines. Human ingenuity finds ways to use up 'spare' land in low-density development: wide-open spaces between buildings, one-storey factories, car parks and acres of unused grass. All these, however, consume only a fraction of the land no longer needed to grow food. Crops for organic fuels, such as rape-oil and willow, could take up some of the slack, though these too consume fertiliser and are economically dubious.

The amount of woodland in Britain is partly determined by the amount of agriculture. Most agriculture is not 'economically viable' but is kept going, precariously, at the whim of politicians. If the subsidies stop, and if Ukraine gets its act together and feeds the rest of Europe, many farmers will go out of business. Farming will survive on a smaller scale and as a part-time or retirement job. Vacant land, sooner or later, will turn into 'scrub' and then into woodland, as it already has done on a vast scale in Scandinavia, the south of France, Italy, Greece and even Japan. In eastern North America an area much greater than the entire British Isles has 'tumbled down to woodland' in the last 150 years.

For conservationists a future like present Connecticut, a landscape that is either urban or forest with the occasional farm surviving as a curiosity, may be superficially attractive. But I foresee the new woods as monotonous tracts of even-aged hawthorn, birch, ash, oak and beech, under which are scanty remains of grassland, threaded through by the outgrown remains of hedges. They will probably swarm with hungry deer and wild pig, feeding on gardens and roadside verges. (They will not, however, be swept by periodic fires, as are the flammable recent woods of southern Europe.) Embedded in them will be patches of ancient woodland, with a greater variety of trees than the recent woodland, but with ground vegetation impoverished by the deer. Any natural non-woodland vegetation will need to be kept alive in nature reserves. The result will not be ideal for woodland plants and animals, and will be bad for everything else.

Public appreciation of woodland

The modern conservation movement grew out of public disgust at the destruction of Hainault Forest (Essex) in the 1850s (Fig. 164) and the need to frustrate the destruction of Epping Forest. The City of London Corporation, having taken over Epping, acquired Burnham Beeches in 1880. Thereafter there was a slow trickle of wood-pastures and woods acquired as public open spaces, such as Hatfield Forest by the National Trust in 1924 and Hadleigh Woods by Southend Borough Corporation in 1936.

In the 1950s woods began to be listed as Sites of Special Scientific Interest, though that did little to save them from being damaged or destroyed. In 1962 Cambridgeshire Wildlife Trust raised no less than £5,000 to buy Hayley Wood to prevent it from being destroyed and to preserve the second-largest population of oxlip in the kingdom. Other nature reserves followed, by purchase or agreement with landowners. A landmark in 1969 was the decision, through a Public Inquiry, to use Tree Preservation Order legislation to frustrate the destruction of the Bradfield Woods (Suffolk).

The trickle turned into a flood as the Locust Years waned. County wildlife trusts had little difficulty in raising six-figure sums to buy wood after wood. The National Trust turned away from modern forestry. The Woodland Trust, founded in Devon in 1972, spread throughout the kingdom to become one of the biggest woodland owners.

In the 1980s the Nature Conservancy published an Inventory of Ancient Woodland. Although this is still not finalised and does not in itself confer legal protection, it institutionalised and gave public support to the idea of ancient woodland. It prepared the way for the reformed Forestry Commission to identify and rehabilitate ancient woods.[2]

Many woods, whether nature reserves or not, are in effect public places. Woods are now appreciated (though not yet understood) as never before. No longer are they something that the public never sees inside and does not care about. Woodland conservation, for the present, is uncontroversial and has become a political force. In the 1990s a proposal merely to bisect Oxleas Wood (Kent) by a major road attracted huge attention and was defeated, even though the road had nowhere else to go. Developers have learnt to recognise ancient woods and work round them: to destroy them is not worth the trouble and risk.

Woodland conservation – or anything presented as such – now attracts public support, possibly at the expense of other, more threatened, habitats. Even in Japan conservation of forests attracts far more support than of wetlands or cultural landscapes, though forests cover two-thirds of the land and are increasing.

Of the big battalions that once were ranged against woodland conservation, the farmers have left the battlefield and the foresters have changed sides. Developers (never so big a battalion) have learnt their lesson: any that have not are promptly denounced by the Woodland Trust.[3] Woods are still so numerous that an attrition rate of zero is unrealistic: there will always be occasional hard cases, mistakes, road-widenings or corruption; but destruction has receded to little more than the level of normal dynamics.

With the countryside shrinking, woods get embedded in built-up areas, which brings problems of rubbish, tidiness, theft of deadwood, and dogs. However, the South Essex woods are a counter-example to any theory that woodland necessarily fares less well in an urban than a rural environment.

Ancient trees

From Shakespeare's time to the 1920s the English, exceptionally among Europeans, appreciated the beauty and mystery of ancient trees. With the rise of the forestry ethos this became unfashionable. Old trees became marginalised, and even the National Trust, at Hatfield Forest and Ickworth Park, tidied many of them away. As Edlin put it, 'all will agree that when old age arrives it is best to fell a tree whilst it is still sound and intact'. Only a few specialists in lichens and invertebrates disagreed, pointing out that decay was an essential part of the value of trees as a habitat.

On 6 March 1991 the City of London Corporation, which had for decades been experimentally re-pollarding in Burnham Beeches, held a public meeting there on pollard and veteran tree management. This attracted an unexpectedly large audience and was the beginning of the Veteran Trees Initiative, taken up by English Nature. Interest in ancient trees, and the wood-pastures in which they occur, has returned to the prominence that it had in Victorian times. England, like Sardinia, Crete and Japan, is especially rich in such trees.

ENVIRONMENTAL AND BIOLOGICAL THREATS

Air pollution

'Acid rain' was a fashionable cause of concern in the 1980s: it was blamed for almost any departure from the supposed normal behaviour of trees (Chapter 17). Air pollution is unlikely to do much damage to trees themselves in Britain today, though it still holds back tree-living lichens and possibly bryophytes.

However, weak levels of pollution, enough to affect the more sensitive lichens, have spread into previously clean regions. Among concentrated local sources, the projected expansion of Stansted Airport, a source of oxides of nitrogen from the airport itself and the associated vehicles, is likely to affect creatures on the ancient trees of Hatfield Forest close by.

Soil pollution

A threat to the British flora is the pervasiveness of fertiliser dust, which blows off farmland and contaminates low-nutrient habitats. I have noticed an increase of plants like goosegrass and ground-ivy round the edges of Hayley Wood. The Kirby – Bunce survey (p.408) identifies this as a main reason for the impoverishment of woodland flora since 1971; another disturbing finding is the loss of very acid woodland soils. The compilers of the *New Atlas of the British and Irish Flora* show that plants of infertile habitats, and low-growing plants generally, are among those that have especially declined during the latter twentieth century.

Increasing shade

Neglect of management makes woods more shady. After some decades the shade in formerly coppiced woodland stabilises or may get a little lighter. Permanent open areas – whose plants, according to historical records, are the most liable to extinction – continue to get overgrown. This has been recognised as a conservation problem for at least 50 years, and is reiterated by another finding of the Kirby – Bunce comparison.[4] For some woods the situation was saved, or the problem postponed, by the great storm of 1987.

Doing nothing does not make a wood revert to wildwood. In general, woods in Britain are now more shady than they have been for a thousand years. On the Vera model of wildwood they are more shady than they have ever been. Even if Vera is to be rejected, open areas in woods are more precarious than they were at any time in the Holocene.

Secondary woodland

New natural woodland may arise rather less readily on farmland than in Tansley's time. A possible reason is that farmland has now accumulated 70 years' worth more nitrate and phosphate from fertilisers, encouraging coarse grasses and thistles. Few tree seeds except acorns can reach the ground through strong-growing cocksfoot grass; grasses are also strong competitors with young trees. Trees get established more easily on the north sides of existing woods, where partial shade keeps the grasses down. They establish more easily still on railway land and abandoned industrial sites, which have escaped being fertilised.

Squirrels

Between 1876 and 1929 landowners made at least 27 attempts to introduce American squirrels to England, two to Wales, three to Scotland and one (but one was enough) to Ireland.[5] They were unanimous that it should be the grey squirrel (*Sciurus carolinensis*) rather than the five other American squirrels.

This bizarre act of folly was irreversible. By 1944 grey squirrels were menacing British forestry and were subtracting the red squirrel. By 2000, red squirrels still prospered only in the conifer plantations of southern Scotland and northern England, in Caledonian pinewoods, and on the Isle of Wight and Brownsea Island (in Poole Harbour), which greys had not reached.

Grey squirrels are often cited as the greatest menace to 'woodland', especially through their habit of pulling the bark off trees, especially beech, hornbeam and sycamore. This chiefly injures the estate branch of modern forestry producing high-quality timber, which is ruined by even slight squirrel damage. For natural woodland a worse consequence is the loss of hazel regeneration. Even in a good hazelnut year like 2004, grey squirrels kill all the nuts by taking them while still green; this makes hazel a threatened species in the long term.

Hitherto this has been a British problem: European countries do not have *Sciurus carolinensis*, who behaves himself in America. However, help may be at hand from animal liberators. They recently stopped the town council of Turin from trying to exterminate the grey squirrels that some fool had introduced. From Italy these will spread into France, chief producer of high-quality beech, and the squirrel problem will attract international research. (The losers, regarding animal welfare, will be grey squirrels, who will probably be massacred by less agreeable methods than Turin city fathers would have used.)

Introduced plants

As regards woodland, our islands have been let off lightly. The most troublesome invader is rhododendron, one of the seven 'villains' (p.267), which has taken over western oakwoods, eliminating all other plants – including oaks in the long term – by its heavy evergreen shade. The Irish have attempted the heroic task of removing it from Killarney with chainsaw, fire and poison, lest it destroy the *Arbutus* and the oakwoods. Lesser threats are from cherry-laurel, sycamore and holm-oak, and a few introduced conifers which can grow from seed.

Whether lookalike trees (p.267ff) will be a problem remains to be seen. They advance the modern, anti-conservation trend to homogenisation, mixing up all the world's plants and animals: they bring closer an age in which there will be no difference between *Quercus robur* in Wales and in Hungary. How much this will matter depends on whether they stay where they are put or displace or hybridise with the natives. So far, imported variants of *Quercus robur* and *Q. petræa* have not filled the gap left by the loss of shade-tolerance by native oaks.

In the rest of the world, matters are worse. Mixing up different continents' fauna and flora is arguably the second-greatest threat to biodiversity, after destruction of habitat. It is tragic to go to California (Fig. 165) or New South Wales and find savanna landscapes in which the trees are native, but the grassland is a hotch-potch of European plants. The wonderful undershrubby *fynbos* of the Cape of Good Hope, confined to an area no bigger than Wales, is being shaded out by a hotch-potch of alien trees.

One reason why it is so surprisingly easy to destroy tropical forests is the introduction of robust giant grasses, which have become universal tropical weeds. Cutting down a forest might not matter too much (forests blow down in hurricanes), but the site is then overrun by an 'elephant-grass' such as *Imperata cylindrica* or *Saccharum spontaneum* which competes with the trees' regrowth and alters the fire regime. Every year or every other year, the grass catches fire, burns hotly, and the flames lick into the edges of the forest and enlarge the clearing.

Invasive native plants include bracken in wood-pastures. Although bracken has long been present and was even a crop, it now displaces all other vegetation except bluebells. This is damaging in itself, and also the dead fronds are a fire hazard, as on Ashtead Common (p.47). Bracken reduction should be at the top of the agenda with wood-pastures containing old trees.

Is beech a problem? It gets into woods outside its native range, especially northern and western oakwoods; it overtops the oaks, and – arguably – threatens to turn all the woods into replicas of Chiltern beechwoods. Some say that this should not be opposed: the absence of beech from north and west Britain and from Ireland is a mere historical accident; if wildwood had not been fragmented beech would by now have become as widespread as a native as it is as an introduction. Against this, the spread of beech is partly a result of human intervention (p.283). My view is that the threat exists, but should not be exaggerated; it should be dealt with wood by wood.

Climate change

Beyond question, the carbon dioxide content of the earth's atmosphere has increased by one-third since 1700, owing to people burning fossil fuels and draining peatlands, and to a lesser extent digging up forests. (It has been argued, less plausibly, that this began in prehistory.) This is a big change in the composition of the atmosphere, and it would be surprising if it had no obvious effect on climate. The change is not yet complete: there are plenty of coal, oil, peat and forests left, and human ingenuity will doubtless find ways of turning them into yet more CO_2.

Whether the effect has yet gone beyond the bounds of normal dynamics is less certain. There have been suspiciously many hot summers and other exceptional events: in Britain the great winter of 1963, the great summers of 1975 and 1976, and so on. Are these outside the normal dynamics of climate? The baseline against which they can be compared is 1800 – 1950, the period since extensive instrumental records began.* This seems to have been an unusually 'quiet' age with only one major fluctuation, the 'year without a summer', 1816, after the giant eruption of the volcano Tambora in Indonesia. In earlier centuries what by modern standards would be violent fluctuations of weather may have been more usual. The well-known Little Ice Age since 1320 is now seen to have had predecessors at intervals all through the Holocene.[6]

Another shortcoming of a simple interpretation of global warming is that it seems not to be enough. If every day next year were to be 1°C warmer than the corresponding day this year, people and most animals and plants would barely notice the difference; yet an average increase of 1 degree is a big change in global-warming terms. What matters more is variability and the incidence of extreme events. Great droughts and great frosts kill plants, rather than long runs of slightly warmer years.

---

* A complication is urban heat islands. The weather station in Cambridge was established, 150 years ago, in the Botanic Garden when that was on the edge of town. It is now well inside the built-up area and is subject to the local warmer microclimate of a city. This has happened to most long-running weather stations and is difficult to allow for.

I would not expect any foreseeable increase of temperature to have a radical effect on trees. No tree species has its southern limit in Britain. Beech has been affected by recent extreme summers, which is surprising for a tree whose natural southern limit is far to the south; but most of the effect is in planted beech, put on chalklands and other soils to which it is not suited.

Effects on herbaceous plants: I note a marked decline in primrose in woods round Cambridge after hot summers (Fig. 210). Primrose is a drought-sensitive plant of Atlantic climate, and the Cambridge area, the most Continental part of Britain, is marginal for it. I have not heard of primrose declining in its strongholds further west. Oxlip, in contrast, is a plant of Continental climate. This too has declined, but here the primary cause appears to be deer, which eat the flowers and leaves. Oxlips are not immortal and are killed by drought, but without deer are replaced from seed.

Bluebell, a plant of strongly Atlantic distribution, has been claimed as potentially the first victim of global warming. In these woods, successive mapping shows it to be not quite static, but with no evidence of general decline.[7]

Phenology: The dates at which plants and animals do things are linked to temperature, and often to daylength as well. In the urban heat island of London trees come into leaf several days earlier and lose their leaves later than in the country. Many trees keep their leaves longer into autumn on a branch near a street light.

From many data sets it appears that the time of leaf opening has generally got earlier in the last 50 years. Part of this may be due to changes in the trees, to the fashion for planting early leafing varieties of native trees, like the 'false native' hawthorn that leafs earlier than native hawthorn.

In my own experience in eastern England, leaf-opening events in trees that happened (on average) in April around 1960 moved into May in the cold springs of the 1970s and are now in early April. The effect varies with different trees. Oaks, which respond to February and March temperatures, came into leaf on average at the beginning of May in the 1950s and 1960s, in mid-May in the 1970s, and early May around 2000. I find the same effect with ash (typically about 11 days later than oak), but beech has been less responsive.

Leaf-fall changes are smaller and more variable. Oak passed through a particular stage of leaf-fall around 11 November c.1960, around 21 November in the 1980s, and around 12 November c.2000; oak leaf-fall is delayed by warmer Octobers. Ash leaf-fall, hastened by hotter Augusts, shows a smaller effect.

These differences could affect woodland. If the tree-leafing season has been extended by about three weeks, this reduces the amount of light available to evergreen and early leafing herbaceous plants. The effect would be comparable to that of substituting an early – for a late – leafing kind of tree. (I find no statistically significant change in the time of peak flowering season of oxlip in Hayley Wood since 1970, although in individual years it is advanced by higher temperatures in March.)

Deer

Deer are a really serious problem. There are now more deer running around Britain than for a thousand years, and more species than there have ever been. In the 1990s it was plausibly argued that there were one-quarter of the number of red deer in Great Britain that there were in wildwood times, and one-half the number of roe deer;[8] there will be more now. Britain no longer had elk, aurochs or wild swine – the last loss has since rectified itself – but it had gained fallow deer, muntjac, Japanese deer and Chinese water deer. In Scottish and South Welsh woods the deer are joined by sheep, and in North Wales and Ireland by feral goats.

The quantity of big game is now a considerable fraction of what it was in the pre-Neolithic, and most of them are concentrated around the much-reduced area of woodland. On the 'forest' and even the 'savanna' model of wildwood there could have been, in prehistoric times, only a small fraction of the deer per square mile of woodland that there are now. The present landscape is super-favourable to deer, with its mixture of farmland and woodland, warm winters, plenty of ryegrass or winter wheat to feed on, tolerant farmers, an unarmed public, and no effective predator save the motorcar. Any number of deer (especially gregarious species like red and fallow) can crowd into a wood. They are not supported by the woodland: when they have eaten everything edible in the wood (Fig. 166), they go out into the fields and eat crops.

Superficially, this might satisfy those who want to get back to wildwood. But exotic species and excessive numbers of deer have disrupted the normal dynamics of woodland. English woods are not wildwood: for a thousand years their ecology has become adapted to regular woodcutting and little browsing – or episodic browsing in compartmental Forests. In a few decades many of them changed to no woodcutting and excessive browsing all the time. Deer affect ground vegetation, small mammals, birds and invertebrates.[9] This is not just a change from one management 'system' to an equally valid one. Nearly all the effects are anti-conservation: they subtract features from woodland without adding features.

Deer now occur in most middle-sized and big woods. They render any management problematic: they are the chief obstacle to restoring coppicing. They eat the foliage of woodland herbs and shrubs and of trees up to a definite browse line. The first thing to do when visiting an unfamiliar wood is to assess deer activity by crouching down and looking horizontally: if deer are active one can suddenly see a long way. The height varies from about 3 feet (0.9 metre) for muntjac (lower for rabbits) to 7 feet (2.1 metres) if one travels to Sweden and encounters elk. Deer have their likes and dislikes: fallow prefer ash and roe birch. Most species are fond of ivy, which is the first plant on which to look for a browse line (Fig. 167).

Deer subtract herbaceous plants. In *Ancient Woodland* I wrote up 35 years' observations and experiments in Hayley Wood, especially on oxlip, the plant for which the wood was made a nature reserve in 1962. Oxlip fared worse in Hayley than in almost any other wood; fallow deer ate out the middles of the plants, which died in the next hot summer and were not replaced. Deer encourage coarse grasses, *Carex pendula*, bracken and ground-ivy, which are unpalatable and flourish in the extra light resulting from damage to trees and shrubs (Chapter 10). Their effect can be to convert a wood into trees plus grass, with no prospect of replacing the trees.

This happens elsewhere. France claims more deer per square mile than in wildwood times. In eastern North America, where in places there is more than ten times the density of white-tailed deer as in aboriginal times, they have subtracted the hemlock tree (*Tsuga canadensis* – also threatened by an introduced insect, p.427) and many of the spring flowers. In western North America the Pacific coast woods swarm with black-tailed deer. In southern North America it is white-tailed deer and pigs – European wild swine and feral tame pigs. Japanese deer cause havoc in Dorset and Japan. One learns to recognise the subtraction of palatable shrubs such as *auki* (*Aucuba japonica*) from Japanese evergreen forests, but the deer congregate on certain mountain tops and destroy the trees – beginning with the rare conifer *Abies homolepis* (Fig. 168) and going on to produce a browse line even on rhododendron.

The world's deer are becoming globalised. Texas ranchers keep fallow and other exotic deer, and lose them into the wild. Red and Himalayan deer eat up New Zealand. Japanese deer are hybridising away the historic red deer populations of northern England and southwest Ireland.

What is to be done about deer? 'Eat Bambi!' He is very tasty and should be the meat of first choice for anyone pernickety about animal welfare. Marketing deer meat is a first objective. But it is difficult to keep deer damage down to an acceptable level merely by killing the animals: the survivors spend more time in the woods and do the same amount of damage. Shooting the last few deer is more easily said than done.

Fencing deer out of woods is not prohibitively difficult. After 30 years of experiment, Cambridgeshire Wildlife Trust, with the support of English Nature, summoned up the courage to fence most of Hayley Wood against fallow deer in 2001–2. The deer were removed by simply closing the fence when they were out feeding in the fields. The results were dramatic. In three to four years oxlip plants have grown to lettuce size and many new ones have arisen; they could even recover to the levels of the 1940s. Recovery of the trees and shrubs may take longer. In previous exclosures young ashes, 'crippled' by many years of deer browsing, shot up into trees (Fig. 85); this time there has not been such a change, perhaps because ash did not set seed in the critical year. Deer have concentrated their activities in the one-eighth of the wood that is still unfenced.

The little, nimble, strong, delicious muntjac are more difficult: they can jump 6 feet (1.8 metres) and force their way through an 8-inch (20-centimetre) hole. It is difficult to devise a gate that will let badgers through, but not muntjac. In Hayley Wood such fencing has lately been tried, lest muntjac increase to fill the vacuum left by fallow. So far they are fewer and do much less damage: although they eat oxlip flowers they do not damage the leaves, and they leave enough flowers to produce adequate seedlings. But Monks Wood, Huntingdon, was reduced to a 'muntjac slum' in which the palatable species were first eaten, such as privet, ivy and bramble, and then the distasteful or poisonous bluebell, dog's-mercury and even arum.[10]

Deer fences are not too difficult for big, compact woods like Hayley, but would be expensive for small or awkwardly shaped woods. Given good materials they probably last 40 years, but need inspection and repair; trees fall on the fence and gates get out of adjustment.

'Bring back the wolf'? This has been talked about for decades. It might just be feasible in the Scottish Highlands. But who knows what reintroduced wolves would live on? Wolves in America eat useful numbers of deer in winter, when deep snow and lack of food make them slow of foot; but why, in warm-wintered Britain, should wolves go after swift and dangerous deer when there are plenty of rabbits, sheep, mice and beetles?

Globalisation of diseases and pests
The last hundred years have seen the subtraction of young oaks from woodland,

probably through American mildew and the subtraction of big elms through two epidemics of Elm Disease; the subtraction of alder by *Phytophthora* will probably affect woodland. Ups and downs of elms go back to the Neolithic and could be part of the normal dynamics, and tree-ring dating specialists tell us that there have been previous periods when oaks have not much regenerated. However, as James Bond would have said, four such events in a century look like enemy action: the enemy being globalisation of plant diseases.

Chapter 17 recounted how foreign diseases and pests have been subtracting tree after tree from the world's forests and savannas. A Japanese fungus removed chestnut from American forests, and an American nematode is removing red pine from Japanese forests. This vendetta continues: *Adelges tsugæ*, an aphid-like insect that lives harmlessly on *tsu-ga* (*Tsuga sieboldii*) in Japan, has reached America, and is eating up eastern hemlock (*T. canadensis*) from Virginia to Massachusetts.

In Ohio in 2005, I found that most big elms (except *Ulmus rubra*) had been subtracted by Elm Disease, chestnut by chestnut blight, some of the oaks by oak wilt, *Cornus florida* by *Discula*; a desperate attempt was being made to contain the emerald ash borer, a bark-beetle-like insect arrived from China, which was about to subtract ash, one of the commonest remaining trees; hemlock *Adelges* was just outside the state border. How much will be left if such events continue for as little as a hundred years?

Globalisation of human, animal and plant diseases is probably as old as shipping, and has brought tragedy after tragedy.[11] Roman traders from India brought rats to Europe, preparing the way for the great plague epidemics. In 1844 *Phytophthora infestans* fell off an American ship, spread into Ireland and Skye, destroyed the potatoes (themselves South American) that were the staple food, and created famine that killed or exiled half the people. America gave European vines powdery mildew in the 1840s, the root-aphid *Phylloxera* in the 1860s, and downy mildew in the 1870s, which destroyed nearly every vine in Europe and came within an inch of killing wine growing. Although technologists just managed to save wine, its production ever since has involved grafting vines and soaking them with chemicals in order to get a crop at all.

Catastrophes are not necessarily abnormal. Perfect health is not the normal state of trees; Elm Decline was matched by a similar, prehistoric decline of hemlock in America. It is the rate of catastrophes – every few years instead of once in a millennium – that matters.

Nursery practice, mass-producing millions of rooted plants in warm damp environments, favours the spread of pathogens that are not immediately mortal.

In New England in 1981 I admired *Cornus florida*, one of the world's most beautiful small trees, the State Flower of Virginia. Now it is mostly gone, subtracted by the canker fungus *Discula destructiva*. *Discula* has turned up several times on *C. florida* imported to Europe; chance alone has kept it from subtracting dogwood and cornelian-cherry from the European flora.

The lesson of what happens when pests and pathogens are separated from the hosts that co-evolved with them has still not been learnt. When tree-planting moved up a gear in 1973, so did globalisation. No longer are introductions merely a matter of eccentric astronomers being careless with moths, or explorers struggling to bring Japanese plants in Wardian cases round Cape Horn. The new industry is geared to the behaviour, not of trees, but of administrators with budgets to spend and voters to woo and time-limits to keep. They would rather plant 10,000 cheap trees than 1,000 expensive ones. If oaks do not produce acorns this year they refuse to wait. Millions of trees, and thousands of tons of soil, are shipped from countries with cheaper labour or where trees fruit every year.

How any parasite gets from continent to continent is seldom known: rarely does a hapless Monsieur Trouvelot earn a place in history by knowingly introducing a new pest. By the time a new disease has been noticed the evidence of how and whence it arrived has usually disappeared. Globalising tree-planting inevitably tends to globalise tree diseases, particularly *Phytophthoras* that can hybridise and generate virulent strains.

But are there not regulations to stop this from happening? Don't Customs persecute travellers who bring back little Christmas trees in their luggage? Shouldn't people be told to scrape the mud off their boots before getting on a plane? What matters, however, is commercial importing of millions of rooted trees. As the *Discula* story shows, it is vain to hope to keep diseases out by inspection: nobody can provide against unknown contingencies. Even Customs are not superhuman; they can hardly search a million containers for a microscopic organism, not knowing what to look for. (According to Dr Podger, a fingernail quantity of infected soil is enough to establish the *Phytophthora* that has devastated southwest Australia.) As John Gibbs points out, the regulations are reactive: they are a gesture against known diseases and not a means of keeping out unknown diseases.

The last time I passed through Heathrow Airport I picked up a leaflet warning the traveller (the *returning* traveller!) about strict controls and dire penalties on importing plants from other continents, but giving the impression that Customs had largely given up trying to control plants brought from Europe. If this is so, any of the world's plant diseases is at liberty to get into Britain provided, like *Discula,* it does so via some other European country.

The problem is not controlling existing diseases – those battles have already been fought and mostly lost – but forestalling the introduction of future diseases. Once a new disease has been detected and the bureaucracy has clanked into action it is too late. It is very exceptional for a tree disease to be controlled once it has got in. Chestnut blight furnishes half an example; but it was not defeated because anyone did anything, but because God raised up a fungal virus to hold down *Endothia* in Europe, but not America.

In 2004 I was at a conference in Ireland. I thought the Irish had had enough experience of *Phytophthora* to last them a thousand years. I put this point to an official speaker, who bleated that nothing could be done because of rules against restriction of trade. The World Trade Organization will not let the stable door be shut until the plant pathologists are quite certain that the horse has been stolen.

Tree-planting practice, as now organised, is probably the greatest long-term threat to existing woodland: greater than pollution or global warming, and at least as great a threat as deer. As yet the only effective countermeasure seems to be restraint of trade, which raises it to a constitutional matter. I hesitate to flatter politicians by telling them they can make even the trees grow, but in this case their inaction can well make the trees not grow.

WOODLAND NATURE RESERVES

In the Locust Years nature conservation was an affair of amateur enthusiasts, who included many ecological scientists, with clear objectives ('Save the Bradfield Woods') and well-defined opponents. It achieved famous successes against heavy odds. Since 1980 conservation has grown into a middle-sized industry, spending eight- and nine-figure sums of mostly public money. It has an ethos of bland triumphalism against no well-defined enemy. Its staff are professional conservationists with degrees in environmental management rather than ecology. This might be a good thing, but professionals seldom remain long in one post: they leave to pursue careers elsewhere, or are promoted or sacked for reasons unrelated to their work, and are replaced by others who have to begin afresh. Sometimes most of the staff go at once, taking their knowledge with them. Moreover conservationists tend to marginalise people with other sorts of expertise, both those with local knowledge and professional ecologists. They spend much of their time on public relations, fund-raising, plans, safety regulations, committees, bureaucracy

– any one of which is worthy, nay essential, but fieldwork and getting to know the sites are low-status activities that go to the bottom of the pile. Such a culture is ill-matched to an activity depending on resolution and continuity of purpose. Conservation becomes reductionist and loses attention to detail.

Conservationists have a record of trying to play God and rectify God's mistakes as well as humanity's. Often they make woods fit a predetermined theory (which theory depends on how long ago they were at college) rather than listening to the woods and discovering what each wood has to contribute to conservation as a whole. The framers of the Epping Forest Act in 1878 knew what was special about the Forest, especially the pollard trees and the bogs. Those who actually managed the Forest never read the Act, and modelled the Forest on an ideal Chiltern beechwood.

In the 1990s it was urged, in effect, that conservationists ought to drop whatever else they were doing and turn all their energies to preserving wildwood; or, since there was no wildwood left in Britain, to restoring wildwood. Coppicing was frowned upon for a time on the plea that it had no place in the theory of wildwood.[12] After Vera published his theory of wildwood in 2002 it was urged that deer and cattle were beneficial to woodland as a substitute for the animals that had grazed in wildwood. At the time of writing, the tide of scientific opinion seems to be turning against Vera: will browsing again go out of fashion?

Whatever the outcome of this particular debate, not enough is known about wildwood to be the basis for woodland conservation in Britain. Wildwood restoration would be an instructive experiment, but is too insecure to be imposed on every woodland nature reserve. Conservation should be based on practical observation rather than unstable theory. Coppicing may be inappropriate for a particular wood because it will be bad for herb paris, or because deer will eat the regrowth; not because scientists lack the imagination to hypothesise what use trees made of the ability to coppice before people invented axes.

I have heard it said that there is enough inertia in conservation practice to protect it from the extremes of these debates. However, any site that has long been in conservationist hands illustrates successive fashions. Not all conservationists play God in the grandly disastrous manner of Yellowstone National Park in America; but the history of any long-standing conservation site, such as Wicken Fen or Hatfield Forest, reveals an alarming series of changes of direction: doing nothing, planting trees, stopping pollarding, removing dead trees, encouraging visitors, doing nothing, ... as well as successive attempts to accommodate the interests of (or attributed to) visitors. Each of these has subtracted something from the special features of the site.[13] (I do not suggest that the National Trust has done worse at Wicken and Hatfield than another conservation body would; it has probably done better than most.)

Conservationists may smile at the vicissitudes of fashion in forestry, but their own profession has them too. Fifteen years ago the rumour got about that bonfires in woodland nature reserves were bad, which arbitrarily deprived 50 species of 'phœnicoid' fungi and bryophytes (those requiring burnt ground[14]) of a habitat. Forestry and conservation fashions have something in common that differentiates them from other kinds of fashion. If I order a fashionable shirt I expect to wear it before it goes out of fashion. But activities that depend on the growth of trees and plants can never catch up with a fashion before it changes.

Characterisation – the genius loci
All ancient woods are different, much as every medieval church is different from every other. What makes a wood special can have many dimensions, such as:
* topography, for example whether a wood is on a cliff or a plateau, and whether it contains ravines;
* tree communities (especially underwood);
* shade-bearing communities of ground vegetation;
* coppicing plants;
* archaeological features;
* structural features, especially ancient coppice stools;
* bryophytes and lichens on trees;
* cultural and spiritual features: it may be a famous bluebell wood, or a battlefield, or the inspiration of Wordsworth, or the haunt of St MacDuagh the hermit;
* existence of past knowledge: this is a place where we know what the tree species were 400 years ago, or the ground vegetation 100 years ago, and whether they have changed or not changed; this is where Tansley made some early observations on plant succession, which one day an interested student may resume.

This is not an exhaustive list of dimensions of variation. One expects birds to be not too different from wood to wood: many birds are notoriously indifferent to tree species, and have no difficulty in getting from one wood to another. Atlantic oakwoods of western Britain lack much variation in their tree composition, but are very variable in their bryophyte communities. Fungi can be very different from wood to wood, but it is impracticable to know them fully for more than a very few woods. Spiders offer scope for another dimension, but are nearly as difficult to study as fungi.

These variables are not to be kept in separate compartments. They interact to create the *meaning* of a wood (or other landscape), which is more than just a list of its features. (Meaning is what differentiates a real ancient wood from a plantation imitating an ancient wood.) The archaeology influences the structure, which interacts with the trees, which interact with the ground vegetation. Any wood that has been a nature reserve for many years comes to be appreciated for reasons different from those for which it was originally selected.[15]

This affects management. Hatfield Forest, as its name implies, has been inhabited by fallow deer for 900 years. They are part of its *genius loci*; deer damage to its woods should be tolerated as it should not be in, say, Garnett's Wood 6 miles (10 kilometres) away, which is not a Forest.

All too often, professional conservationists look for how a wood resembles other woods, rather than what makes it special. The former was made easy by the woodland volume of the *National Vegetation Classification*, published in 1991. Although not intended for this purpose (as reviewers pointed out at the time), it was taken up with surprisingly little dissent as a basis for conservation. Use of it was not confined to those aspects, such as bryophyte communities, where it added to the previously known categories. Its coarse-grained but rigid categorisation, giving no room for further discovery of rare woodland types, was useful to anyone needing to pigeonhole a wood without doing much fieldwork.

Research and understanding include looking for resemblances, but conservation is about protecting differences. It is important to keep an open mind and be prepared for unexpected categories. Staverton Park (see Fig. 21), to the NVC, is a specimen of W10: *Quercus robur – Pteridium aquilinum – Rubus fruticosus* woodland, of which there are thousands of other examples, and a rather poor specimen with few species of herbs. True but trivial: the point of Staverton is that it is one of the biggest collections of ancient trees in Europe: oaks of vast bulk and surrealist shape, giant hollies, giant birches, trees that are part oak, part holly and part birch, and a hundred years' accumulation of dead wood. Besides its unique qualities as a habitat, Staverton is a place of mystery and wonder; it has a peculiar effect on first-time visitors who have no foreknowledge that the world contains such places.

Management plans
In the 1990s there was a vogue for management plans; every nature reserve in the kingdom was supposed to have one. Management plans ought to remedy the problem of discontinuity of personnel, but they were approached as a bureaucratic exercise ('to get English Nature off our backs') rather than a practical tool.

Some wildlife trusts even hired people specifically to write management plans, which suggests that they did not attach much practical importance to them. They were written to a predetermined form, like an income tax return, and rarely published. They were reductionist: they began by saying how a site resembled other sites, rather than what made it special. They missed features that did not have a box to tick. Woods that had been studied for many years were treated the same as new reserves. Plans were supposed to last only five years (on the model of Stalin's Russia?), which defeated continuity. No attempt was made to make them readable, and many of them languish unread. (I make an exception for the National Trust's management plan of Hatfield Forest, which is a model of careful attention to detail.)

When Barsetshire Wildlife Trust appealed for funds to acquire Plumstead Frith it was 'to save a unique ancient wood' – they emphasised the differences from other woods. Now that they have got it, the management plan describes it as an example of the NVC's W10. This saves trouble; it allows someone to write the plan without finding out much about the wood, but does it do justice to the site or the people who subscribed to 'save' it? At best it leads to the site being treated the same as any other W10; at worst the bosses look up the guidelines for what a W10 is supposed to be, and by G** they will make it conform to those guidelines.

Features of a proper management plan
1. It should run for a length of time depending on how long the site has been a nature reserve and how much is known about it. A new site should have its first management plan after two or three years' investigation and experiment. A wood that has been a reserve for 20 years might have a plan covering the next 20 years.
2. It should begin with what makes this wood special and how it differs from other woods.
3. It should specify an annual cycle of operations.
4. It should be a public document, to be given to new members of the management committee and to visiting ecologists, and to anyone wanting to know more about the wood than the visitors' leaflet contains. This is a safeguard against the management plan being forgotten or ignored.
5. There should be maps of archaeological features, tree and plant communities, and dates of coppicing; there will often be a *constraint map,* identifying features (woodbanks, badger setts, localities of rare plants) to be treated with special concern, for example when felling trees. (Many a good management plan is

spoilt by using as a base map the latest edition of the Ordnance Survey. It is well worth getting a photocopy of the earliest-edition OS at 6 or 25 inches to the mile (1:10,560 or 1:2,500). These maps are far more detailed and accurate, and real changes since they were made, 100–150 years ago, are easily allowed for. Moreover they are out of copyright.)

6. There should be an archive of actions and investigations, going back to the beginning of the reserve. If this is in electronic form it is essential to keep a print-out against the time when the disks decay or the software becomes obsolete.

7. There should be a statement of the *core features* of management, principles to be remembered and maintained through future changes of organisation and policy in the parent body. Changes calling for major alteration will be few, and should depend on real changes in knowledge or events on the ground, such as the arrival of deer, the invention of an effective means of controlling deer, or the resumption of regeneration by oaks.

Fragments or islands?

A wood is an island of woodland surrounded by farmland, heath or moorland. Conservationists often assume that woods are fragmented, scraps of what was once a much larger continuum of woodland, and that this is an unfortunate accident. On this theory big woods have more species than small woods, and a wood of 100 acres should have more species than ten woods of 10 acres.

Some woods have indeed been fragmented. In the Blean, northwest of Canterbury, Ellenden Wood and Blean Wood, now nearly a mile (1½ kilometres) apart, were part of one huge wood a century ago. After a proposal to link them by a rubbish dump had been seen off, they are now being rejoined by planting a 'Victory Wood' between. This is wholly commendable, provided one remembers that a new plantation is not the same as an existing wood.

Some conservationists go further: they proclaim their duty to join up woods by new plantations, even if there is no historical evidence that the woods were linked. It is thought self-evident that plants and animals should be able to move freely from wood to wood. Recently it has been claimed that climate is changing and plants and animals need a continuous extent of woodland in order to migrate northwards: the implication is that to be fully effective woods need to be so vast as to have climatic gradients within them. (Is this a practical possibility?)

It is a matter of history that heaths are fragmented: only 200 years ago most heaths were joined up to others. However, churchyards are not fragments of what was once a wider continuum of Churchyard. Are woods like heaths or like churchyards? Have the pinewoods on the Aberdeenshire Dee demonstrably benefited from being joined by plantations?

Species – area relationships:[16] The theory that large woods have more species than small probably originated with ornithologists.[17] It has been verified many times for vascular plants, and at least once for bryophytes. The relationship is not linear: typically, a wood of ten times the size has twice the number of species. For ancient woods it usually takes the form:

$$\log S = a + b \log A$$

where S is the number of species, A is the area of the wood, and a and b are parameters (that is, numbers that are constant for a particular group of woods, but which vary from one group to another). The relation is statistical, not absolute: there are instances where a smaller ancient wood has more species than a bigger. For trees and shrubs the value of b is lower than for herbaceous plants; that is, the size of the wood has more effect on herbs. For ancient-woodland plants the value of b is not different from that of the rest of the flora.

A similar relationship is well known for animal species on islands; it is the basis of the theory of island biogeography.[18] It is explained in terms of a balance between species dying out at random on individual islands and recolonising from neighbouring islands. This is a zoologists' theory, and it will be objected that most woodland plants, being longer-lived than most animals, are less likely to die out at random and less able to recolonise. Nevertheless, I find that the relationship (though not necessarily the theory) holds for flowering plants and ferns on the islands of the south Ægean.

It is known from historical records that plants die out from woods, but from general causes and not at random. Plants of woodland grassland disappear as woods get more shady; if such a plant dies out from one wood, its survival in the next wood becomes precarious and recolonisation unlikely.[19]

Large woods have two other properties. A wood above a certain size may be necessary for an animal to hold a territory or make a living; this may explain why certain birds avoid small woods, but makes less sense for plants. Big woods tend to have a wider range of habitats than small ones – just as a big island is far more likely to have high mountains than a small.

Which plants are confined to big woods? The most definite association is with plants of disturbed ground (e.g. silver-weed, great plantain) and woodland grassland (e.g. devil's-bit). These habitats are less likely to be present in small woods. Some clonal plants, such as aspen and wood-anemone, are less common in small woods: a plant that occurs as one clone every 10 acres (4 ha) can easily be missing from a 5-acre (2 ha) wood. One of the few shade-bearing annuals, the three-veined sandwort (*Mœhringia trinervia*), may be an 'island biogeography' plant, for it is missing from most woods smaller than 5 acres (2 ha).

Metapopulations are groups of local populations of some creature inhabiting patches of suitable habitat, such as woodland, within a region. Individual populations have their ups and downs, and sometimes go extinct if their numbers get too small to be viable. They are renewed by migration from surviving populations not too far off. This is mainly a butterfly phenomenon;[20] I know of no examples of between-wood metapopulation behaviour among plants.

On seven occasions I have been able to compare the species list of a large wood with the aggregate list of ten nearby small woods of similar total area. Each time the ten small woods have more plant species than the one big wood.[21]

Large woods have real disadvantages. They are more likely to have been attacked by modern forestry; their deer problems are more severe.

Is the analogy between woods and islands more than a metaphor? Plant ecologists mostly think of evolution as happening in the remote past. Apart, perhaps, from annuals, plants have been thrust into the cultural landscape much as they are now, and have come to terms with it as best they may. But could evolution have had a significant effect within the span of the history of a wood?

Evolution depends on sexual reproduction, and is more effective with creatures that have short generation times, but even with the human species it is not negligible if the agent is powerful enough. Over a few thousand years humanity has evolved genes that mitigate malaria, and most of us (but not everyone!) have guts that cope with the toxin in wheat (a transgenic plant invented by Neolithic farmers).

A wood has been isolated for, maybe, a thousand years: perhaps 25 generations of oak-trees, 10 of ash and 3 of lime. (Medieval oaks were felled young (p.230), whereas ashes and especially limes form ancient stools.) There might be 40 generations of primrose and 1,000 generations of *Mœhringia*. Clonal plants will have had fewer: possibly four generations of anemone, or one generation of bracken. Annuals have more opportunity for evolution than clonal plants: in the few decades since the invention of weedkillers, some annual weeds have evolved multiple resistance.[22]

What of plants with life cycles linked to coppicing? Maybe the wood was felled every seven years for the first five centuries, then every 14 years. This makes about 100 fellings at any one point, and 100 generations of coppicing plants. Could this be enough for coppicing responses, especially the buried-seed response, to evolve? Is a variant of ragged robin evolution's answer to a thousand years of coppicing in Hayley Wood, but forget-me-not in Hempstead Wood and wood-spurge in Bradfield Woods (p.212f)? Is this why dandelion and cowslip are coppicing plants on Øland (p.23), but are not woodland plants in Britain?

Is the thought of woods as islands more than just a metaphor? Is island biogeography at work, producing different coppicing ecotypes in different woods? Conservationists do not disapprove of real islands: they never recommend 'conserving' endemic plants by translocating those of Crete to Cyprus and vice versa. Why propose the equivalent with the special floras of ancient woods?

Conclusions: Large areas of woodland should be valued where they exist. There are not many places in Britain where a series of woods goes on with little interruption for as much as 10 miles (15 kilometres). The Blean is one such, and modern gaps in it should be repaired when opportunity arises. I am sceptical of attempts to create continuity where it did not exist. It is premature to say 'This wood is too small to be an adequate nature reserve; let us join it to another wood to make up enough area'.

Maybe woods as islands are indeed an unfortunate effect of fragmentation. Maybe, far enough back, perhaps in the Bronze Age, woods were much as they are now except that they went on for hundreds of miles. Or, on Vera's theory of wildwood, woods have always been islands: even in Mesolithic times woods were patches of woodland among grassland, forever shifting under the influence of wild oxen and wild horses. Or, maybe, being an island is inherent in becoming a wood as we know it: the conversion of wildwood to woodland, like the formation of churchyards, never happened on the scale of whole landscapes. Conservationists should not yet behave as though they know the answer.

Grazing
For woods in the Highland Zone and Caledonian pinewoods, the ecologist's instinct is to regard grazing as an abuse: 'the best conservation measure is three strands of barbed wire', as I have said myself. However, research is wanted on how continuous the protection needs to be and what will be its consequences.

As Professor Smout has shown, in many Scottish woods grazing is not a twenti-eth-century innovation, like deer in ordinary English woods, but has a history of at least 400 years: how did the woods get through those four centuries?

Stopping grazing may not of itself bring back missing woodland flowers. In exclosures the sparse moorland-type vegetation may merely turn into denser moorland-type vegetation, or moorland plus woodrush (*Luzula sylvatica*). This may be undesirable if the interest of the wood is in its ground bryophytes.

There are three simple methods to investigate browsing: watching the live-stock and seeing what it is they are eating; setting up exclosure plots; and study-ing cliffs (if there are any that the animals cannot climb). Protection for part of the time will probably be necessary to assure the long-term existence of the wood. But here too I would warn conservationists to be sensitive to the *genius loci* of the wood, to find out what makes it special as it is, and not to force it into a pattern determined by a top-down theory of what a wood ought to be. They should not think they have failed in their duty if a bryophyte-rich wood in Argyll still lacks the rich ground vegetation of an English coppice-wood.

Further deconiferisation

We considered in Chapter 19 the recovery of ancient woods that were replanted in the Locust Years. A step forward came in 2002 with Jonathan Spencer's survey of ancient woodland owned or leased by the Forestry Commission.[23] Ancient wood-land and wood-pasture, or plantations on the site thereof, covers about 1.7 per cent of England. One-quarter of this, 130,000 acres or 530 square kilometres, is still managed by the Commission. Ancient woodland forms a smaller proportion of the Commission's total woodland and plantation than of other owners', but includes some very big woods and notable areas, for example in the Wye Valley.

Spencer's findings are encouraging and surprising. Excluding the peculiar situations of the New Forest and Forest of Dean, only a little more than half of the Commission's plantations on ancient-woodland sites were successful in that less than 20 per cent of the original woodland now remains. One-quarter is still classifiable as native woodland; this is probably somewhat of an overestimate, since it includes some plantations of native trees, but nonetheless in a substantial proportion of woods either replanting was not attempted or the planted trees disappeared. In a further one-tenth the planted trees lived, but native trees are reasserting themselves.

The published survey is subdivided according to the *National Vegetation Classification*, and is thus not very informative as to which types of woodland were more resistant to replanting. However, plantations were notably unsuccessful on woods of the ash – maple – hazel group, and more successful in oakwoods and beechwoods (cf. Table 24).

Protection and restoration of 'ancient and native woodland' and ancient trees are now the official policy of the Forestry Commission, as set out in the document *Keepers of Time*, published in June 2005.

TREE-PLANTING

What are trees for? The twentieth century was the great age of tree-planting. Since 1973 writers have enlarged, often at vague and tedious length, about the values that 'we' associate with trees. But many millions of trees have been planted without proper concern for whether future trees will indeed replicate the values of past trees. There is still a general belief that new woods can routinely be created on randomly chosen sites. That is a power still reserved for God and not given to mankind. (I can sympathise with the Nemoralian Trust's embarrassment on receiving a big legacy specifically to create 100 acres (40 ha) of woodland in southeast Barsetshire!) There are other good reasons for planting trees: to grow timber; as a public or private amenity; to hide old-fashioned modern architecture; to make a stately approach to Cambridge city; as a memorial; even (as Richard Mabey points out) for a public-relations exercise to help the Nemoralian Trust to do better things.

Tree-planting, as we have seen, is risky, especially on a commercial scale. It carries the perils of disseminating invasive species or varieties or tree diseases that may imperil native trees.

Sequestering carbon dioxide
Growing trees on mineral soil – or, better, not destroying forests – takes carbon dioxide out of the earth's atmosphere and hence may stabilise climate. The effect would be cumulative if the trees were to be cut down and put into permanent store, for example by sinking them in the deep ocean. However, Britain is far too small: exhorting people to plant trees to sequester carbon dioxide is like telling them to drink more to hold down rising sea level. To have an appreciable effect it would be necessary first to re-establish the British Empire; and even then it is hardly likely that growing timber, which lasts a few decades, will balance the release of carbon accumulated in fossil fuels over hundreds of millions of years.

Much of the 'vacant' land on which trees could (by heroic technology) be grown is moorland, which is already sequestering carbon very effectively for the rest of this interglacial. If trees are planted on peat, will they absorb as much carbon as is released by damaging the peat in planting them?

Conservation and re-creation

Tree-planting in Britain is popular because of the assumption that it preserves ecology: that present plantations will be a substitute, as a habitat, for woods destroyed in the recent or distant past. Appeal leaflets display photographs of pretty bluebell woods, implying that the plantations will one day look like these. On such assumptions an industry has grown up. But what evidence is there for them? What happens to wildlife in plantations, including when a plantation is harvested (Chapter 19)?

In Britain the need for conservation tree-planting is limited. One tree, black poplar, depends on people's intervention for its survival. There are many rare and a few threatened woodland plants, but I know of none where the threat comes from not having enough trees. If there are conservation objectives in new plantations – for example promoting the goshawk (p.370) – have they not been achieved by those already created? What is to be gained by having more? Only recently and seldom have these questions been asked.[24]

Much that is called conservation is really re-creation; but there is more to creating a wood than planting trees and checking that they are still there five years later. Some features, such as giant coppice stools, depend on a historic sequence of events that would take an impossibly enduring human purpose to repeat. Phrases such as 'How to Plant an Ancient Wood' or 'Planting the Ancient Woods of the Future' or 'Eurotunnel Moves Ancient Wood' imply a serious under-taking, whose success or failure depends on following it up for longer than a human life span or the life expectation of a development agency. What are the criteria for knowing whether a scheme has succeeded?

From observations of past re-creations the omens are not good (Chapter 12). Adding plantations to the landscape tends to favour 'common-or-garden' species, not low-nutrient, weak competitors such as primrose and anemone, let alone rarities. Or, as R.S. Key put it for insects:

Low powers of dispersal of many woodland species means that the neediest species are the ones least likely to benefit ... the creation of new woodland is never mitigation against the loss of [existing old] *woodland.*[25]

Can planting provide followers for existing historic trees that are not replacing themselves? If our successors decide that Hayley Wood needs a new generation of oaks, and invent a method of persuading planted trees to survive where natural seedlings now do not, 'local' stock (from Forestry Commission Zone 402, which extends from Yorkshire to Oxfordshire) will not do. The oaks of Hayley are part of the wildlife of that wood, and need to be replaced from Hayley acorns. In Groton Wood (Suffolk), although the wood is partly medieval, most of the oaks are not wild-type, but derive from a planting in c.1925; their replacement will raise different questions.

This is especially a question for ancient parks. Staverton Park is a simple medieval park, unaffected by planting: here followers for the ancient trees are being raised from Staverton acorns. Moccas Park (Herefordshire) has ancient wild-type oaks together with several cohorts of planted oaks, each with its distinctive features, resulting from successive phases of planting after it became a country-house park (Figs 169 & 170). The Beetle Oak or Stagshorn Oak, a massive, gnarled medieval pollard with a 'mossy' growth of tiny twigs, is the unique home in Britain of the beetle *Hypebæus flavipes*. The Club Oak is a tall columnar tree without epicormic twigs, probably of the seventeenth century. Both trees have changed little since the Woolhope Club photographed them in 1870.[26] Another 250 years will not turn the Club Oak into a second Beetle Oak – and probably would not do so even if the Club Oak had been made into a pollard when young. Anyone wishing to perpetuate the *genius loci* of Moccas Park into a new generation of trees has to provide separate successors to the Beetle and Club Oaks and the other distinctive oak variants. This includes management (especially starting new pollard oaks and perhaps hawthorns) as well as propagation.

Will planted trees reproduce the values of their predecessors?
New planting will not replicate veteran trees and the wildlife that goes with them. Veteran trees are rare, not because of a shortage of young trees, but because middle-aged trees have not been allowed to grow on. The future of veteran trees depends on not felling middle-aged trees when they start to decay.

'We' go to France and marvel at the magnificent timber oaks of the Tronçais, and admire the perseverance of French foresters, upholding their traditions for 350 years through all the vicissitudes of economics, revolutions, invasions, pestilence and falls of kings. Yet a world in which all oaks were like Tronçais oaks would have lost nine-tenths of the value and meaning of oaks. Elizabeth Roberts points out that Sitka spruce in its native coastlands of Washington State and British Columbia is a marvellous conifer, with specialised uses, variation, folklore, magnificent old trees (worthy of photographs by Thomas Pakenham), associated plants and animals, poetry and spiritual values. However, most of these values depend on trees old enough to develop individuality, which has not happened with Sitka spruce transported to Britain: nor is it likely to, for the trees in Britain are meant to be felled young, and they do not sprout. The other values were left behind in Sitka, and what got to Scotland was a general-purpose conifer, what Pakenham calls a 'money tree' (or, rather, a tree that it was hoped would produce money).

Anyone planting trees should consider whether commercial stock, of 'local' origin or otherwise, will be necessary or sufficient for the objectives. If the object is timber, then timber-quality material should be used (remembering that what constitutes timber quality has repeatedly changed before the trees came to be felled). If the object is something else, timber-quality stock may be inappropriate. In generalised 'amenity' planting, foreign material may be acceptable. If the object is to imitate an ancient wood, professional standards require appropriate materials, including trees derived from ancient woodland.

Are planted trees meant as an addition to existing trees, or a replacement or substitute for them? If the former, it matters less whether they are 'local' or imported. However, people who introduce plants or animals have little control over how they behave once introduced, as the grey squirrel illustrates.

Conclusion

In the 1970s trees and plants seemed to be in such a precarious state that only immediate action could save them: tree-planting – any trees – was thought to be needed in a hurry. Rare trees needed to be saved by making them into common trees: there was no thought that the natural distribution of lime or service might have meaning and be worth protecting.[27]

A third of a century on, the threats have diminished or disappeared. Programmes then started have achieved many of their objectives, and there is no longer such a need for haste. People now should stop and think and get the details right. This may involve waiting a year or two, or planting fewer but better-chosen trees; or doing nothing and letting natural succession do the job. The time for playing God is over.

REFERENCES

Author's Foreword and Acknowledgements

1 Behrensmeyer, A.K., *et al.* (1992). *Terrestrial Ecosystems Through Time*. University of Chicago Press.

Chapter 1

1 For more on storms see Rackham (2003) Chapter 27.
2 Roberts, A.J., Russell, C. *et al.* (1992). Regional variation in the origin, extent and composition of Scottish woodland. *Botanical Journal of Scotland* 46: 167–89.
3 Rackham (1998).
4 For example, Fairhead & Leach (1998).
5 Rackham (1986*a*) Chapter 9.
6 Dymond, D. (Ed.) (2004). *The Churchwardens' Book of Bassingbourn, Cambridgeshire*. Cambridgeshire Records Society.
7 Preston, C.D., Pearman, D.A., & Dines, T.D. (2002). *New Atlas of the British and Irish Flora*. Oxford University Press.
8 Wigston, D.L. (1974). The Cytology and Genetics of Oak. *In* Morris & Perring (1974): 27–50.
9 Peter Sell, of Cambridge University Herbarium, will shortly be publishing a taxonomy of British elms.
10 Richens, R.H. (1983). *Elm*. Cambridge University Press.

Chapter 2

1 Moffat, A.J. & Buckley, G.P. (1995). Soils and restoration ecology. *In* Ferris-Kaan (1995): 74–90.
2 Rackham (2003) Chapter 27.
3 Harley, J.L. & Harley, E.L. (1987). A checklist of mycorrhiza in the British flora. *New Phytologist* 105 Supplement: 1–112.
Francis, R. & Read, M. (1994). The contributions of mycorrhizal fungi to the determination of plant community structure. *Plant & Soil* 159: 11–25.
Simon, L., Bousquet, J. *et al.* (1993). Origin and diversification of endomycorrhizal fungi and coincidence with vascular land plants. *Nature, London* 363: 67–9.
Read, D.J., Duckett, J.G. *et al.* (1998). Symbiotic fungal associations in 'lower' land plants. *Philosophical Transactions of the Royal Society* B355: 815–30.
Fitter, A.H. (2005). Darkness visible: reflections on underground ecology. *Journal of Ecology* 93: 231–43.
4 Spooner & Roberts (2005) Chapter 4.
5 Wright, S.F. & Upadhyaya, A. (1996). Extraction of an abundant and unusual protein from soil and comparison with hyphal protein of arbuscular mycorrhizal fungi. *Soil Science* 161: 575–86.
Redeker, D., Kodner, R., & Graham, L.E. (2000). Glomalean fungi from the Ordovician. *Science* 289: 1920–1.
6 Perez-Moreno, J. & Read, D.J. (2001). Exploitation of pollen by mycorrhizal mycelial systems with special reference to nutrient recycling in boreal forests. *Proceedings of the Royal Society of London* B268: 1329–35.
7 Rackham & Moody (1996) Chapter 17.
8 Shigo, A.L. (1983). *Tree Defects: a photo guide*. Washington: United States Department of Agriculture, Forest Service.
Lonsdale, D. (1999). *Principles of Tree Hazard Assessment and Management*. Forestry Commission (HMSO).

9 Schwarze, F.W.M.R. (2001). Development and prognosis of decay in the sapwood of living trees. *Arboricultural Journal* 25: 321–37.

10 Warren & Key (1991).

11 Rackham (2003) p.257.

12 Read, H. (2000). *Veteran Trees: a guide to good management*. English Nature.
    (2001) *Biodiversity: linking the Habitat Action Plan for wood-pasture with the requirements of priority and other species.* English Nature Research Report 432.

13 Rowe, N.P. & Jones, T.P. (2000). Devonian charcoal. *Palaeogeography, Palaeoclimatology, Palaeoecology* 164: 331–8.
    Scott, A.C. (2000). The pre-Quaternary history of fire. *Palaeogeography, Palaeoclimatology, Palaeoecology* 164: 281–329.
    Bond, W.T., Woodward, F.I. & Midgeley, G.F. (2005). The global content of ecosystems in a world without fire. *New Phytologist* 165: 525–38.

14 Ashton, D.H. & Willis, E.J. (1982). Antagonisms in the regeneration of *Eucalyptus regnans* in the mature forest. *In* Newman (1982): 113–28.

15 van Niewstadt, M.G.L. & Sheil, D. (2005). Drought, fire and tree survival in a Borneo rain forest … *Journal of Ecology* 93: 191–201.

16 Rackham (2002a).

17 Mellars, P. (1976). Fire ecology, animal populations and man: a study of some ecological relationships in prehistory. *Proceedings of the Prehistoric Society* 42: 15–45.

18 Walker, D. (1982). The development of resilience in burned vegetation. *In* Newman (1982): 27–44.

19 Thompson, D.A. (1971). Lightning fires in Galloway. *Scottish Forestry* 25: 51–2.

20 Hart (1966) p.63.

Chapter 3

1 Day, P. (1993). Preliminary results of high-resolution palaeoecological analysis at Star Carr, Yorkshire. *Cambridge Archaeological Journal* 3: 129–33.

2 *English Heritage Conservation Bulletin* 48 (2005): 9.

3 For a statistical analysis of perambulations see Rackham (1986a) Chapters 5, 6, 9, 10.

4 Rackham (1986a).

5 Watt, A.S. (1919). On the causes of failure of natural regeneration in British oakwoods. *Journal of Ecology* 7: 147–56.

6 Rackham (2003) p.297.

7 Joel 2:25.

Chapter 4

1 Behrensmeyer, A.K., Damuth, J.D. et al. (Eds) (1992). *Terrestrial Ecosystems Through Time: evolutionary paleoecology of terrestrial plants and animals*. University of Chicago Press.

2 Rossetto, M. & Kooyman, R.M. (2005). The tension between dispersal and persistence regulates the current distribution of rare palaeo-endemic rain forest flora: a case study. *Journal of Ecology* 93: 906–17.

3 Pointed out to me by J.A. Moody.

4 Pitts, M. & Roberts, M. (1997). *Fairweather Eden*. London: Century.

5 Rackham & Moody (1996).

6 Kelleher, C.T., Hodkinson, T.R., & Kelly, D.L. (2004). Species status, hybridisation and geographic distribution of Irish populations of *Quercus petraea* … and *Q. robur* … *Watsonia* 25: 83–97.

7 Evans, J.G. (1993). The influence of human communities on the English chalklands from the Mesolithic to the Iron Age: the molluscan evidence. *In* Chambers, F.M. (Ed.), *Climate Change and Human Impact on the Landscape*, 147–56. London: Chapman & Hall.

8 Godwin (1975) p.114.

9 Miller, S.H. & Skertchly, S.B.J. (1878). *The Fenland Past and Present*. Wisbech.

10 Godwin (1975) pp.273–6.

11 Information from Richard Bradshaw, citing M. O'Connell for the pollen.

12 Rackham (2003) Chapter 8 (summarising data from H.J.B. Birks and others).

13 Hockham Mere 1 and 2: Godwin, H. &
Tallantire, P.A. (1951). Studies in the post-
glacial history of British vegetation. XII.
Hockham Mere, Norfolk. *Journal of Ecology*
39: 285–307.

Old Buckenham Mere: Godwin, H.
(1968). Studies of the post-glacial history
of British vegetation XV. Organic deposits
of Old Buckenham Mere, Norfolk. *New
Phytologist* 67: 95–107.

Hockham Mere 3 and Seamere 1: Sims,
R.E. (1973). The anthropogenic factor
in East Anglian vegetational history:
an approach using A[bsolute] P[ollen]
F[requency] techniques. *In* Birks, H.J.B.
& West, R.G. (Eds) *Quaternary Plant Ecology*,
223–36. Oxford: Blackwell.

Oxborough: Bradshaw, R.H.W. (1981).
Quantitative reconstruction of local
woodland vegetation using pollen analysis
from a small basin in Norfolk ... *Journal of
Ecology* 69: 941–55.

Hockham Mere 4 and Stow Bedon
Mere: Bennett, K.D. (1986). Competitive
interactions among forest tree
populations in Norfolk ... during the last
10 000 years. *New Phytologist* 103: 603–20.

Saham Toney Mere and Seamere 2:
Bennett, K.D. (1988). Holocene pollen
stratigraphy of central East Anglia ... and
comparison of pollen zones across the
British Isles. *New Phytologist* 109: 237–53.

Quidenham Mere: Peglar, S.M. (1993).
Mid- and late-Holocene vegetation
history of Quidenham Mere ... interpreted
using recurrent groups of taxa. *Vegetation
History and Archaeobotany* 2: 15–28.

14 Rackham (2003) pp.379–87.

15 Scaife, R. (1988). Pollen analysis of the Mar
Dyke sediments. *In* Wilkinson, T.J. (Ed.)
Environment and Archaeology in South Essex,
109–14. *East Anglian Archaeology Report* 42.

16 Turner, J. & Hodgson, J. (1979). Studies in
the vegetational history of the northern
Pennines. I. Variations in the composition
of the early Flandrian [i.e. Holocene]

forests. *Journal of Ecology* 67: 629–46.

17 Rackham (1998).

18 Cæsar, *De Bello Gallico* vi.28.

19 Rackham (2002*b*) Chapter 4.

20 Bradshaw, R. & Mitchell, F.J.G. (1999).
The palaeoecological approach to
reconstructing former grazing–vegetation
interactions. *Forest Ecology & Management*
120: 3–12.

21 Grove & Rackham (2001) p.167.

22 Allen, D.L. (1979). *Wolves of Minong: their
vital role in a wild community.* New York:
Houghton Mifflin. [I am grateful to Dr
J.A. Moody for drawing my attention to
this book.]

Nelson, M.F. & Mech, L.D. (1981). Deer
social organization and wolf predation in
northeastern Minnesota. *Journal of Wildlife
Management Suppl.* 77: 1–53.

Ripple, W.J. & Beschta, R.L. (2003).
Wolf reintroduction, predation risk, and
cottonwood recovery in Yellowstone
National Park. *Forest Ecology & Management*
184: 299–313.

23 For further critiques of Vera's thesis see
Rackham (2003) pp.499–503; Hodder *et al.*
(2005).

24 Mitchell, F.J.G. (2005). How open were
European primeval forests? Hypothesis
testing using palaeoecological data.
Journal of Ecology 93: 168–77.

Birks, H.J.B. (2005). Mind the gap: how
open were European primeval forests?
Trends in Ecology and Evolution 20: 154–6.

25 Information from Professor H.J.B. Birks.

26 Simmons, I.G. (1996). *The Environmental
Impact of Later Mesolithic Cultures.*
Edinburgh University Press.

27 Bennett, K.D., Simonson, W.D., & Peglar
S.M. (1990). Fire and man in post-glacial
woodlands of eastern England. *Journal of
Archaeological Science* 17: 635–42.

28 Godwin (1975) pp.119–24.

29 Peglar, S.M. (1993). The development of
the cultural landscape around Diss Mere
... during the past 7000 years. *Review of*

Palaeobotany and Palynology 76: 1–47.

30 Buckland, P. (2005). Palaeoecological evidence for the Vera hypothesis? *In* Hodder *et al.* (2005): 62–114.

31 Rackham, O. Holocene history of Mediterranean island landscapes. *In* Vogiatzakis, I.N., Pungetti, G., & Mannion, A.M., *Holocene History of Mediterranean Island Landscapes*, forthcoming.

Moody, J.A., Nixon, L., Price, S., & Rackham, O. *The Sphakia Survey*. Oxford University Press, forthcoming.

32 Stuart, A.J. (1982). *Pleistocene Vertebrates in the British Isles*. London: Longmans.

Chapter 5

1 Roosevelt, A.C. (1980). *Parmana: prehistoric maize and manioc subsistence along the Amazon and Orinoco*. New York: Academic Press.

Nimuendajú, C. (2004). *In pursuit of a past Amazon: archaeological remains in the Brazilian Guyana and in the Amazon region*. Göteborg: Etnologiska Studier.

2 Peterken (1996) p.282, Fig. 3.4. See also Bradshaw (2005).

3 Information from Professor Martin Canny and Algonquin National Park, Ontario.

4 Donahue, B. (2003). *The Great Meadow*. Yale University Press.

Cronon, W. (1983). *Changes in the Land: Indians, colonists, and the ecology of New England*. New York: Hill & Wang.

5 Bennett, K.D., Simonson, W.D., & Peglar, S.M. (1990). Fire and man in post-glacial woodlands of eastern England. *Journal of Archaeological Science* 17: 635–42.

6 Rackham (2003) Chapter 16.

7 Peglar, S. (1990). The mid-Holocene *Ulmus* decline at Diss Mere ... a year-by-year pollen stratigraphy from annual laminations. *The Holocene* 3:1–13.

Peglar, S. & Birks, H.J.B. (1993). The mid-Holocene *Ulmus* fall at Diss Mere ... disease and human impact? *Vegetation History & Archaeobotany* 2: 61–8.

8 Larsson, L. (2000). Human response to natural resources since the last glaciation. *In* Sandgren, P. (Ed.), *Environmental Changes in Fennoscandia during the late Quaternary*, LUNDQUA Report 37, Lund: 59–68.

9 Cowling, S.A., Sykes, M.T., & Bradshaw, R.H.W. (2001). Palaeovegetation model comparisons, climate change and tree succession in Scandinavia over the past 1500 years. *Journal of Ecology* 89:227–36.

10 Fleming, A. (1988). *The Dartmoor Reaves: investigating prehistoric land divisions*. London: Batsford.

11 Ruddiman, W.F. (2003). The anthropogenic greenhouse era began thousands of years ago. *Climatic Change* 61: 261–93. [I am indebted to A.T.S. Grove for this reference.]

12 Grove & Rackham (2001) p.171–4.

13 Cleere, H. (1976). Some operating parameters for Roman ironworks. *Bulletin of the Institute of Archaeology* 13: 233–46.

Rackham (2003) p.108, using data from Cleere.

Tylecote, R.F., Austin, J.N., & Wraith, A.E. (1971). The mechanism of the bloomery process in shaft furnaces. *Journal of the Iron and Steel Industry* 209: 342–63.

Crew, P. (1991). The experimental production of bar iron. *Journal of the Historical Metallurgy Society* 25: 21–36.

14 Calculation based on Millet, M. (1990). *The Romanization of Britain: an essay in archaeological interpretation*. Cambridge University Press.

Sim, D. & Ridge, I. (2002). *Iron for the Eagles: the iron industry of Roman Britain*. Stroud: Tempus.

15 Peglar (see Chapter 4 n.12).

Day, S.P. (1991). Post-glacial vegetational history of the Oxford region. *New Phytologist* 119:445–70.

Rackham (1990) p.46f.

16 Everitt, A. (1980). *Continuity and colonization: the evolution of Kentish settlement*. Leicester University Press.

17 Hooke, D. (1981). *Anglo-Saxon Landscapes of*

the West Midlands: the charter evidence. British Archaeological Reports, British Series 95. Rackham (1990) p.44f.

18 For a detailed analysis of Domesday Book see Rackham (2003) Chapter 9.

19 Rackham, O. (1980). *Ancient Woodland: its history, vegetation and uses in England*, 1st ed., Chapter 9. London: Edward Arnold.

20 Rackham (2003) pp.144–6.

21 Wager, S.J. [1998]. *Woods, Wolds and Groves: the woodland of medieval Warwickshire*. British Archaeological Reports, British Series 269.

22 Jones, M. [1998] The Coal Measure woodlands of south Yorkshire: past, present and future. *In* Atherden & Butlin [1998]: 79–102.

    Gledhill, T. [1998]. Medieval woodland in north Yorkshire. (*ibid.*): 103–19.

23 Fourquin, G. (1964) *Les Campagnes de la Région Parisienne à la Fin du Moyen Âge: du milieu du XIIIe siècle au début du XVIe siècle*. Paris: Presses Universitaires de France.

24 Rackham, O. (1998). The Abbey woods. *In* Gransden, A. (Ed.), *Bury St Edmunds: medieval art, architecture, archaeology and economy*, 139–60. Leeds: British Archaeological Association.

25 Rackham (2000).

26 Calculations are based on data from:
    Wrigley, E.A. (1988). *Continuity, Chance and Change: the character of the industrial revolution in England*. Cambridge University Press.

    Hatcher, J. (1993). *The History of the British Coal Industry. I. Before 1700: towards the age of coal*. Oxford: Clarendon.

    Collins, E.J.T. (1996). The wood-fuel economy of eighteenth century England. *In* Cavaciocchi (1996): 1097–123.

27 Jones, M. (1998). The rise, decline and extinction of spring wood management in south-west Yorkshire. *In* Watkins (1998): 55–71.

28 Pryce, W. (1778). *Mineralogia Cornubiensis*. London: Phillips.

    Lewis, G.R. (1908). *The Stannaries.*

London: Constable.

    Hatcher, J. (1970). *Rural Economy and Society in the Duchy of Cornwall 1300–1500*. Cambridge University Press.

29 Linnard (2000) p.84.

30 Smout, Macdonald & Watson (2004).

31 Rackham (1986a) pp.113–15.

    McCracken, E. (1971). *The Irish Woods since Tudor Times: their distribution and exploitation*. Newton Abbot: David & Charles.

32 Trinity College, Dublin: MS 1209(9). Published in Aalen, F.A.A., Whelan, K. & Stout, M. (Eds) (1997) *Atlas of the Irish Rural Landscape*, 122. Cork University Press.

33 Wrigley, Hatcher, Collins (n. 26 above).

34 Collins, E.J.T. (1990). Woodlands and woodland industries in Great Britain during and after the charcoal iron era. *In* Métailié, J.P. (Ed.) *Protoindustries et Histoire des Forêts* 109–20. Toulouse: Cahiers de l'ISARD.

35 Rackham (2003) p.495.

Chapter 6

1 Essex Record Office: D/DB LI/9/I.

2 Warren, M.S. & Key, R.S. (1991). Woodlands: past, present and potential for insects. *In* Collins, N.M. & Thomas, J.A. *The Conservation of Insects and their Habitats*, 154–211. London: Academic Press.

3 Grove & Rackham (2001) pp.193–4.

4 *II Samuel* 18: 9.

5 Colebourn, P. (1983). *Hampshire's Countryside Heritage. 2: Ancient Woodland*. Hampshire County Council.

6 Columella, *Res Rustica* ix: 1.

7 Liddiard, R. (2003). The deer parks of Domesday Book. *Landscapes* 4: 4–23.

8 Cantor, L. (1983). *The Medieval Parks of England: a gazetteer*. Loughborough. Rackham (1986a) p.123ff.

9 Taylor (2000).

10 Rackham (1990) p.158f.

11 Taylor, C. (2004). Ravensdale Park, Derbyshire, and medieval deer coursing. *Landscape History* 26: 37–57.

12 Rackham, O. (2004). Pre-existing trees and woods in country-house parks. *Landscapes* 5: 1–16.

13 Harding & Wall (2000).

14 Chafin, W. (1818). *Anecdotes and History of Cranborne Chase*. 2nd ed. London: J. Nichols.

15 Gilbert, J.M. (1979). *Hunting and Hunting Reserves in Medieval Scotland*. Edinburgh: John Donald.

16 Jones, G. (2005). New research on Forests and chases, c.1500 – c.1850. *Society for Landscape Studies Newsletter* spring 2005: 6–9.

17 Szabó (2005).

18 Kaner, J. [1998]. Historic woodland in the Vale of York. *In* Atherden & Butlin [1998]: 120–39.

19 Marañon, T. (1986). Plant species richness and canopy effect in the savanna-like 'dehesa' of S.W. Spain. *Environmental Management* 12: 131–41.

Grove & Rackham (2001) p.199.

20 Austad, I. (1988). Tree pollarding in western Norway. *In* H.H. Birks, H.J.B. Birks *et al.* (Eds) *The Cultural Landscape: past, present and future*, 11–30. Cambridge University Press.

Moreno, D. & Poggi, G. (1996). Storia delle risorse boschive nelle montagne mediterranee. *In* Cavaciocchi (1996): 635–54.

Grove & Rackham (2001) pp.51, 210.

21 Grove & Rackham (2001) p.205ff.

22 Fairhead & Leach (1998).

23 Hodder *et al.* (2005).

24 Mayhew, H. (1851). *London Labour and the London Poor*. London: Griffin.

25 Waterton, C. (1870). *Natural History Essays*. London: Frederick Warne. p.463.

26 Jones, M. (2003) p.21.

27 Harper-Bill, C. (1998). *Dodnash Priory Charters*. Woodbridge: Boydell. §9 *et passim*.

28 Peterken, G.F. & Lloyd, P.S. (1967). Biological Flora of the British Isles: *Ilex aquifolium* L. *Journal of Ecology* 5: 841–55.

29 Stubbs, W. (1874). *Memorials of Saint Dunstan, Archbishop of Canterbury*. London: Longman & Trübner.

30 William of Malmesbury, *Gesta Regum* iii: 275.

31 Thompson, E.P. (1975). *Whigs & Hunters*. London: Allen Lane, Chapter 1 (quoting J. Swift).

Hore, J.P. (1895). *The History of the Royal Buckhounds*. Newmarket.

32 Alfonso XI (c.1350). *Libro de la Monteria* … Ed. Seniff, D.P. (1983). Madison: Hispanic Seminary of Medieval Studies.

33 Birrell, J. (1996). Hunting and the royal Forest. *In* Cavaciocchi (1996): 437–57.

34 Derived from the Deer Collisions Project: *Surveyor* 21 October 2004: 15–6.

35 *Calendar of Close Rolls* 41 Henry III p.131.

Chapter 7

1 Rackham (2002a).

2 Kemble (see below) no.705.

3 At the time of writing there was no up-to-date corpus of charters. The chief sources were:

Kemble, J.M. (1839–48). *Codex diplomaticus*. London, 6 vols.

Birch, W. de G. (1885–93). *Cartularium Saxonicum*. London, 3 vols.

Sawyer, P.H. (1968). *Anglo-Saxon charters: an annotated list*. London: Royal Historical Society.

4 Szabó (2005).

5 The distribution of charters having perambulations is mapped in Rackham (1986a), Fig. 2.1. Analyses of various features are given in later chapters of that book.

6 Essex Record Office: D/DCM Z18/7.

7 Hooke, D. (1981). *Anglo-Saxon Landscapes of the West Midlands: the charter evidence*. British Archaeological Reports, British Series 95.

8 Rackham (1986a) p.79ff.

9 Rackham (1975); Rackham (2000).

10 Three thirteenth-century copies exist.

British Library: Cotton Claudius C.xi;
Gonville & Caius College: MS 485–9;
Cambridge University Library: Ely
Diocesan Registry 6/3/27.

11 Public Record Office: E143/9/2. m. 12, 42.
Aberth, J. (1996). *Criminal Churchmen in
the Age of Edward III: the case of Bishop de
Lisle*. Pennsylvania State University Press.

12 Public Record Office: E318/1271.

13 Harvey, P.D.A. (1986) Boarstall,
Buckinghamshire. *In* Skelton, R.A. &
Harvey, P.D.A. (Eds), *Local Maps and Plans
from Medieval England*. Oxford: Clarendon.

14 Denney, A.H. (1960). *The Sibton Abbey Estates.
Select Documents 1325–1509*. Ipswich: Cowell.
Essex Record Office: D/DHf M19.

15 Dickinson, G.C. (2003). Britain's first road
maps: the strip-maps of John Ogilby's
Britannia, 1675. Landscapes 4: 79–98.

16 Smout, C. (1997). Highland land-use
before 1800: misconceptions, evidence
and realities. *In* Smout, T.C. (Ed.) (1997),
Scottish Woodland History, 5–23. Edinburgh:
Scottish Cultural Press.

17 Smout, MacDonald & Watson (2004)
p.59ff.

18 Kain, R.J.P., Chapman, C. & Oliver, R.
(2004). *The Enclosure Maps of England and
Wales 1595–1918: a cartographic analysis and
electronic catalogue*. Cambridge University
Press.

19 Kain, R.J.P., & Oliver, R. (1995). *Tithe Maps
of England and Wales: a cartographic analysis
and county-by-county catalogue*. Cambridge
University Press.

20 See Grove & Rackham (2001) and many
articles in the journal *Environment &
History*.

21 Rackham (1978).

22 Boulton, H.E. (1965). *The Sherwood Forest
Book*. Nottingham: Thoroton Society.

23 Brought to the author's attention by Dr
David Morfitt.

24 Rackham & Coombe (1996); Rackham
(2003) pp.56ff.

25 Davis, G.R.C. (1958). *Medieval Cartularies of*

Great Britain. London: Longmans.

Chapter 8

1 Egler, F.E. & Niering, W.A. (1976).
*The Natural Areas of the White Memorial
Foundation*. Litchfield (Conn.): Friends of
the Litchfield Nature Center.

2 Broich, J. (2001). The Wasting of Wollin:
environmental factors in the downfall of
a medieval town. *Environment & History* 7:
187–99.

3 Norfolk & Norwich Record Office: Dean &
Chapter Rolls 4750–1.

4 Wheaten, W. & Birmingham, E. (2002).
Archaeology and surviving features. *In*
Holmes & Wheaten (2002): 49–64.

5 Gulliver, R. (1995). Woodland history and
plant indicator species in North-East
Yorkshire ... *In* Butlin, R.A. & Roberts, N.
(Eds) *Ecological Relations in Historic Times:
human impact and adaptation*, 169–89.
Oxford: Blackwell.

6 Jones, M. (1993). South Yorkshire's ancient
woodland: the historical evidence. *In*
Beswick *et al.* (1998): 26–48.

7 Smout *et al.* (2004) p.165ff.

8 Tack *et al.* (1993) pp.207–12.

9 Information from Professor Katsue
Fukamachi and Dr Hirokazu Oku.

10 Stephens, E.P. (1956). The uprooting of
trees: a forest process. *Proceedings of the Soil
Science Society of America* 20: 113–6.

11 Carver, M. (1998). *Sutton Hoo: burial ground
of kings?* London: British Museum Press.
p.94.

12 Calvi, C. (1885). *La Coltura Forestale*. L'Italia
Agricola Milano.

13 Theophrastus, *History of Plants* V.ix.4.

14 Pasmore, A. (1964). Surviving evidence of
the New Forest charcoal burning industry.
Journal of Industrial Archaeology 1: 27–35.

15 Ardron, P.A. & Rotherham, I.D. (1999).
Types of charcoal hearth and the impact
of charcoal and whitecoal production on
woodland vegetation. *Peak District Journal
of Natural History and Archaeology* 1: 35–48.

16 Barker, S. (1998). The history of the Coniston woodlands, Cumbria ... *In* Kirby & Watkins (1998): 167–84.

17 Rackham (1986*a*) p.323.

18 Montanari, C., Prono, P. & Scipioni, S. (2000). The study of charcoal-burning sites in the Apennine mountains of Liguria (NW Italy) as a tool for forest history. *In* Agnoletti & Anderson (2000): 79–91.

19 Crossley, D. (1993). White coal and charcoal in the woodlands of north Derbyshire. *In* Beswick *et al.* (1998): 67.
   Clayton, C. (2000). An archaeological survey of Parkbank Wood, Sheffield. *Peak District Journal of Natural History and Archaeology* 2: 31–41.

20 Rackham (1986*a*) Chapter 16.

21 Sparks, B.W. & West, R.G. (1972). *The Ice Age in Britain*. London: Methuen.

22 Beresford, M. (1957). *History on the Ground*. London: Methuen, p.230ff.

23 Dalling, J.W. & Tanner, E.V.J. (1995). An experimental study of regeneration on landslides in montane rain forest in Jamaica. *Journal of Ecology* 83: 55–64.

24 Holmes & Wheaten (2002) *passim*.

25 Rackham (2003) p.401.

26 Linnard (2000) p.27ff.

27 Essex Record Office: Ph 1/105.

28 Rackham & Coombe (1996).

29 Wheaten, A. (2002). Evidence of human activity. *In* Holmes & Wheaten (2002): 19–48.

30 Rackham (1986*a*) Chapter 8.

31 Oosthuizen, S. (2003). The roots of the common fields: linking prehistoric and medieval field systems in West Cambridgeshire. *Landscapes* 4: 40–64.

32 Upex, S. (2004). A classification of ridge and furrow by an analysis of cross-profiles. *Landscape History* 26: 59–75.

33 Steele & Welch (1973).

34 Woodward (1992).

35 Grove & Rackham (2001) Chapter 6.

36 Cæsar, *De Bello Gallico* V.21.

37 By D.S. McOmish and N.A. Smith of the Royal Commission on Historical Monuments (England).

38 Rackham (1986*b*).

39 *La Grande Encyclopédie*, *c*.1882. Lamirault, Paris, under 'Bois'.

40 Roberts, E. (2004). Forestry at the front. *Tree News Sylva* 2004: 1–2.

Chapter 9

1 Rackham, O. (1978). The flora and vegetation of Thera and Crete before and after the great eruption. *In* Doumas, C. (Ed.), *Thera and the Aegean World I*, 755–64. London: Thera & the Aegean World.
   Rackham, O. (1990). Observations on the historical ecology of Santorini. *In* Hardy, D.A. & Renfrew, A.C. (Eds) *Thera and the Aegean World III*. 2: 384–91. London: Thera Foundation.

2 Andronicos, M. (1984). *Vergina: the royal tombs and the ancient city*. Athens: Ekdotike Athenon.

3 Kren, T. & McKendrick, S. (2003). *Illuminating the Renaissance: the triumph of Flemish manuscript painting in Europe*. Los Angeles: J.P. Getty Museum.

4 Tack *et al.* (1993) p.210ff.

5 Foister, S. (1997). Young Gainsborough and the English taste for Dutch landscape. *Apollo* (Aug. 1997): 3–11.
   Ashton, P., Davies, A. I. & Slive, S. (1982) Jacob van Ruisdael's Trees. *Arnoldia* 42: 1–31

6 Smith, S. (1988). *Horatio McCulloch 1805–1867*. Glasgow Museums & Art Galleries. (I am grateful to James Dickson for drawing my attention to his work.)

7 Staley, A. & Newall, C. (2004). *Pre-Raphaelite Vision: truth to nature*. London: Tate Publishing.

8 Strutt, J.G. (1822). *Sylva Britannica: or, Portraits of Forest Trees, distinguished for their antiquity, magnitude, or beauty*. London: Strutt.

9 I am grateful to Mrs J.M. Davies for correspondence on this point.

10 Grove & Rackham (2001) Chapters 1, 14.

11 Menzies, W. (1864). *The History of Windsor Great Park and Windsor Forest*. London: Longman.

12 Carranco, L. & Labbe, J.T. (1975). *Logging the Redwoods*. Caldwell (Idaho): Caxton.

13 Hill, R. (1924). A lens for whole sky photographs. *Quarterly Journal of the Royal Meteorological Society* 50: 227–35.

14 Evans, G.C. & Coombe, D.E. (1959). Hemispherical and woodland canopy photography and the light climate. *Journal of Ecology* 47: 103–13.

Anderson, M.C. (1964). Studies of the woodland light climate. I. The photographic computation of light conditions. II. Seasonal variation in the light climate. *Journal of Ecology* 52: 27–41, 643–63.

15 For examples see Rackham (2003) Chapter 25.

16 Evans, G.C., Freeman, P. & Rackham, O. (1975). Developments in hemispherical photography. *In* Evans, G.C., Bainbridge, R. & Rackham, O. (Eds) *Light as an Ecological Factor II*, 548–57. Oxford: Blackwell Scientific Publications.

17 Rackham, O. (1992). Woodland ecology in recent and historic aerial photographs. *Photogrammetric Record* 14: 227–39.

18 United States National Archives: RG373: GX10008/GB1044R/102.

19 Robbins, C.R. (1931). An economic aspect of regional survey. *Journal of Ecology* 19: 25–33 [repeated in Tansley (1939) Plate 46].

20 Rackham, O. (1975). Temperatures of plant communities as measured by pyrometric and other methods. In *Light as an Ecological Factor II*, 423–50.

Chapter 10

1 Lutz, H.J. & Chandler, R.F. (1946). *Forest Soils*. New York: John Wiley.

Kubiëna, W. (1953). *The Soils of Europe*, London: Murby.

[Other books on soils are mainly about agricultural and non-woodland soils.]

2 Darwin, C. (1881). *The Formation of Vegetable Mould Through the Action of Earthworms*. London: Murray.

3 Mitchell, R.J. *et al.* (2005). A study of the epiphytic communities of Atlantic oak woods along an atmospheric nitrogen deposition gradient. *Journal of Ecology* 93: 482–92.

4 Grove & Rackham (2001) Chapter 12.

5 Hæggström, C.A. (2000). The age and size of hazel … stools of Nåtö Island, Åland Islands … *In* Agnoletti & Andersen (2000): 47–57.

6 Szabó (2005).

7 Wager (1998).

8 Morfitt, D.R. (2000) *The Historical Ecology of the Woods of Binley, Warwickshire*. Coventry University: Ph.D. thesis.

9 Wigston, D.L. (1975). The distribution of *Quercus robur* … and *Q. petraea* … and their hybrids in south-western England. I. The assessment of the taxonomic status of populations from leaf characters. *Watsonia* 10: 345–69.

10 Dolan, K. Letter to *The Times*, 13 February 2004.

11 Medieval woodland areas were often underestimated: Rackham, O. (1968). Medieval woodland areas. *Nature in Cambridgeshire* 11: 22–5.

12 Rackham (2003) Chapters 7, 25. For individual species see also the *Biological Flora of the British Isles* accounts as published year by year in *Journal of Ecology*.

13 Phillips, J. (1934). The plant or biotic community behaves as, and actually is, an integrated whole. *Journal of Ecology* 22: 554–71.

14 Abeywickrama, B.A. (1949). *A study of the variations in the field layer vegetation of two Cambridgeshire woods*. Ph.D. thesis, Cambridge University.

Martin, M.H. & Pigott, C.D. (1975). Soils. *In* Rackham (1975): 61–71.

15 Rackham (2003) p.77ff.

16 For further details see Rackham (2003) Chapters 7, 26.

17 Decocq, G. *et al.* (2004). Plant diversity in a managed temperate deciduous forest: understorey response to two silvicultural systems. *Journal of Applied Ecology* 41: 1065–79.

18 Rackham (2003) Chapter 25.

19 Peterken, G.F. (1976). Long-term changes in the woodlands of Rockingham Forest and other areas. *Journal of Ecology* 64: 123–46.

    Best, J.A. (1998). Persistent outcomes of coppice grazing in Rockingham Forest. *In* Kirby & Watkins (Eds) (1998): 63–80.

20 Rackham (2003) Fig. 22.3.

21 Rackham (1989) p.198f, Plate 18.

22 Rackham (2003) p.490f.

23 Rackham (2003) p.374f.

Chapter 11

1 Collins, E.J.T. (1989). The coppice and underwood trades. *In* Mingay, G.E. (Ed.), *The Agrarian History of England and Wales.* Cambridge University Press 6: 484–500.

2 Olive, G. (2002). *Farm and Cottage Furniture in the West Country.* Regional Furniture Society.

3 Mellars & Dark (1998).

    Brown, A.G. & Keough, M.K. (1992). *In* Cading, P.A. & Petts, G.E., *Lowland Floodplain Rivers*, 185–202. Wiley, Chichester.

4 Coles, J.M. & Orme, B.J. (1976). The Sweet Track, Railway Site. *Somerset Levels Papers* 2: 34–65.

5 Rackham, O. (1977). Neolithic woodland management in the Somerset Levels: Garvin's, Walton Heath, and Rowland's Tracks. *Somerset Levels Papers* 3: 65–72.

6 I am indebted to Richard Darrah for pointing this out.

7 Mellars & Dark (1998).

8 Totman (1989).

9 Goodburn, D. (1992). Woods and woodland: carpenters and carpentry. *In*

Milne, G. (Ed.) *Timber Building Techniques in London c.900–1400.* London & Middlesex Archaeological Society.

10 Killen, G. (1994). *Egyptian Woodworking and Furniture.* Princes Risborough: Shire.

11 Cummings, A.L. (1979). *The Framed Houses of Massachusetts Bay, 1625–1725.* Harvard University Press.

    Smout *et al.* (2004).

12 *Country Life* 4 November 1992.

13 Hall, R.A. (1982). 10th century woodworking in Coppergate, York. *In* McGrail, S. (Ed.) *Woodworking Techniques before A.D. 1500. British Archaeological Reports International Series* 129: 231–43.

    Rackham, O. (2002). *Treasures of Silver at Corpus Christi College, Cambridge*, Chapter 6. Cambridge University Press.

14 Corpus Christi College, Cambridge: MS 128 f. 401.

15 Canterbury Cathedral, Dean & Chapter: DCC REII4A. Conveyed to me by Alex Wheaten: see also Holmes & Wheaten (2002).

16 Colvin, H.M. (1963). *The History of the King's Works.* London: Her Majesty's Stationery Office.

17 *Statutes of the Realm* 34–5 Henry VIII c.3. Cambridge University Archives (information from Mary Stoutja).

    Letters & Papers Foreign & Domestic, Henry VIII. 3: §3062(1).

18 Milne, G. (1992). *Timber Building Techniques in London c.900–1400.* London & Middlesex Archaeological Society.

    Milne, G. (1995). *Roman London.* London: English Heritage.

19 Rackham (2003) pp.144–7, Chapter 29.

20 Rackham, O., Blair, W.J. & Munby, J.T. (1978). The thirteenth-century roofs and floor of the Blackfriars Monastery at Gloucester. *Medieval Archaeology* 22: 105–22.

21 Kirk, J.C. (2004). Butts Cottage, Kirdford: the conversion of trees to timber in the rural Sussex Weald. *Vernacular Architecture* 35: 12–20.

22 For details see Rackham (2003) p.146; Rackham (1986*b*) p.44.

23 I am grateful to John Bloomfield for drawing my attention to them.

24 Rackham, O. (1993). Woodland management and timber economy as evidenced by the buildings at Cressing Temple. *In* Andrews, D. (Ed.) *Cressing Temple: a Templar and Hospitaller manor in Essex*, 85–92. Chelmsford: Essex County Council.

25 Rackham, O. (2002). The Blean woods and timber-framed buildings. *In* Holmes & Wheaten (2002): 77–82.

26 Rackham (2003) pp.462–5.

27 Essex Record Office: D/DBa M3.

28 Dymond, D. (Ed.) (2004). *The Churchwardens' Book of Bassingbourn, Cambridgeshire*. Cambridgeshire Records Society.

29 Simpson, G. (1998). English cathedrals as sources of forest and woodland history. *In* Watkins (1998): 39–53.

30 Crone, A. & Watson, F. (2003). Sufficiency to scarcity: medieval Scotland 500–1600. *In* Smout (2003): 60–81.

31 Rackham (2003) p.465.

32 Walker, J. (Ed.) (2005). *Report on Vernacular Architecture Group Tour of North America*. Vernacular Architecture Group.

33 Phelps, H. (1982). *The Craft of Log Building*. Ottawa: Lee Valley.

34 *A-zero-no-kioku* [*architectural drawings of temples and pagodas*] (2002). Nara.

   Dendrochronology and the Latest Imaging Equipments: applications to ancient architecture ... (2004). Nara: National Institute for Cultural Properties.

35 Frost, T. (1985). *From Tree to Sea: the building of a wooden steam drifter*. Lavenham: Dalton.

36 Grove & Rackham (2001) p.168.

37 Hutchinson, G. (1994). *Medieval Ships and Shipping*. Leicester University Press.

38 Davis, R. (1962). *The Rise of the English Shipping Industry in the 17th and 18th Centuries*. Newton Abbot: David & Charles.

39 Friel, I. (1995). *The Good Ship: ships, shipbuilding and technology in England 1200–1520*. London: British Museum.

40 Holland, A.J. (1971). *Ships of British Oak: the rise and decline of wooden shipbuilding in Hampshire*. Newton Abbot: David & Charles.

   Guillery, P. & Herman, B. (1999). Deptford Houses: 1650 to 1800. *Vernacular Architecture* 30: 58–84.

41 Miller, S.W. (2000). *Fruitless Trees: Portuguese conservation and Brazil's colonial timber*. Stanford University Press.

42 Ramsbottom, J. (1954). *Mushrooms & Toadstools*. London: Collins New Naturalist.

   Lambert, A. (1991). *The Last Sailing Battlefleet*. Conway.

43 Cook, S.E. (1834). *Sketches in Spain during the Years 1829, 30, 31 and 32*. London: Boone.

   Lane, F.C. (1934). *Venetian Ships and Shipbuilders of the Renaissance*. Baltimore: Johns Hopkins University Press.

44 Stammers, M. & Kearon, J. (1992). *The Jhelum: a Victorian merchant ship*. Stroud: Alan Sutton.

45 Millett, M. & McGrail, S. (1987). The archaeology of the Hasholme Logboat. *Archaeological Journal* 144: 69–155.

   Mowat, R.J.C. (1996). *The Logboats of Scotland*. Oxford: Oxbow Monograph 68.

46 Jane (1970); Hoadley (1990).

Chapter 12

1 Beevor, H.E. (1924). Norfolk woodlands, from the evidence of contemporary chronicles. *Transactions of Norfolk & Norwich Naturalists' Society* 11: 448–508.

2 Woodruffe-Peacock, EA (1918). A fox-covert study. *Journal of Ecology* 6: 110–25.

3 Moore (2002).

4 Peterken, G.F. & Game, M. (1981). Historical factors affecting the distribution of *Mercurialis perennis* in central Lincolnshire. *Journal of Ecology* 69:

781–96.

Peterken, G.F. & Game, M. (1984). Historical factors affecting the number and distribution of vascular plant species in the woodlands of central Lincolnshire. *Journal of Ecology* 72: 155–82.

Peterken (1993).

5 For details see Rackham (2003) Chapter 25.
6 The main source is the county volumes of the *Ancient Woodland Inventory*, produced by the Nature Conservancy Council in the 1980s.
7 For example: Gulliver, R. (1995). Woodland history and plant indicator species in North-east Yorkshire ... *In* Butlin, R.A. & Roberts, N. (Eds) *Ecological Relations in Historical Times: human impact and adaptation*, 170–89. Oxford: Blackwell.
8 Rackham (1986a) Plate XV.
9 Rackham (2003) Fig. 30.4.
10 Hill, M.O., Preston, C.D. & Roy, D.B. (2004). PLANTATT: *attributes of British and Irish plants: status, size, life history, geography and habitats*. Monks Wood: Centre for Ecology & Hydrology.

Ellenberg, H. *et al.* (1991). Zeigerwerte von Pflanzen in Mitteleuropa. *Scripta Geobotanica* 18: 1–248.

11 Holmes, D.S. (2005). Sexual reproduction in British populations of *Adoxa moschatellina* L. *Watsonia* 25: 265–73.
12 Pigott, C.D. & Huntley, J.P. (1978). Factors controlling the distribution of *Tilia cordata* at the northern limit of its geographical range. I. Distribution in north-west England. *New Phytologist* 81: 429–41.
13 Lundström, A.N. (1887). *Pflanzenbiologische Studien. II. Die Anpassungen der Pflanzen an Thiere*, p.79. Upsala: Akademische Buchdruckerei.
14 Sernander, R. (1906). *Entwurf einer Monographie der europäischen Myrmekokhoren. K. Svenska Vetensk. Handl.* 41 [Do not be put off by the author calling this a 'sketch'; it is a serious work of 400 action-packed pages.]

Ulbrich, E. (1909). *Deutsche Myrmekochoren*. Berlin.
[I am indebted to Dr Max Walters for these references.]

15 Coppins, A.M. & Coppins, B.J. (2002). *Indices of Ecological Continuity for woodland epiphytic lichen habitats in the British Isles*. British Lichen Society.
16 Pentecost, A. (1987). The lichen flora of Gwynedd. *Lichenologist* 19: 97–166.
17 Rose, F. & James, P.W. (1974). Regional studies on the British lichen flora I. The corticolous and lignicolous species of the New Forest, Hampshire. *Lichenologist* 6: 1–72.

Gustafsson, L., Fiskesjö, A. *et al.* (1992). Factors of importance to some lichen species of deciduous broad-leaved woods in southern Sweden. *Lichenologist* 24: 255–66.

18 Warren, M.S., Thomas, C.D. & Thomas, J.A. (1984). The status of the heath fritillary butterfly ... in Britain. *Biological Conservation* 29: 287–305.
19 Girling, M.A. (1982). Fossil insect faunas from forest sites. In Bell, M. & Limbrey, S. (Eds) *Archaeological Aspects of Woodland Ecology. British Archaeological Reports International Series* 146: 129–46.

Buckland, P. (2005). Palaeoecological evidence for the Vera hypothesis? *In* Hodder *et al.* (2005): 62–114.

Rackham (1989); Warren & Key (1991).

20 Koerner, W., Dupouey, J.L. *et al.* (1997). Influence of past land use on the vegetation and soils of present-day forest in the Vosges mountains, France. *Journal of Ecology* 85: 351–8.
21 Honnay, O., DeGroote, B. & Hermy, M. (1998). Ancient-forest plant species in western Belgium: a species list and possible ecological mechanisms. *Belgian Journal of Botany* 130: 139–54.

Bossuyt, B., Hermy, M. & Deckers, J. (1999). Migration of herbaceous plant species across ancient–recent forest ecotones in central Belgium. *Journal of Ecology* 87: 628–38.

Verheyen, K. & Hermy, M. (2001). The relative importance of dispersal limitation of vascular plants in secondary forest succession in Muizen Forest, Belgium. *Journal of Ecology* 89: 829–40.

22 Brunet, J. (1993). Environmental and historical factors limiting the distribution of rare forest grasses in south Sweden. *Forest Ecology and Management* 61: 263–75.

Brunet, J. & von Oheimb, G. (1998). Migration of vascular plants to secondary woodlands in southern Sweden. *Journal of Ecology* 86: 429–38.

Brunet, J. & von Oheimb, G. (1998). Colonization of secondary woodlands by Anemone nemorosa. *Nordic Journal of Botany* 18: 369–77.

23 Fali´nski, J.B. & Canullo, R. (1985). La recolonisation des champs abandonnés par l'espèce forestière *Anemone nemorosa* L.: I. Distribution et dynamique. *Giornale Botanico Italiano* 119: 1–26.

24 Dzwonko, Z. & Loster, S. (1992). Species richness and seed dispersal to secondary woods in southern Poland *Journal of Biogeography* 19: 195–204.

Dzwonko, Z. (2001). Assessment of light and soil conditions in ancient and recent woodlands by Ellenberg indicator values. *Journal of Applied Ecology* 38: 942–51.

25 Matlack, G.R. (1994). Plant species migration in a mixed-history forest landscape in eastern North America. *Ecology* 75: 1491–502.

Matlack, G.R. (2005). Slow plants in a fast forest: local dispersal as a predictor of species frequencies in a dynamic landscape. *Journal of Ecology* 93: 50–9.

26 Whitney, G.G. & Foster, D.R. (1988). Overstorey composition and age as determinants of the understorey flora of woods of central New England. *Journal of Ecology* 76: 867–76.

Singleton, R., Gardescu, S. *et al.*

(2001). Forest herb colonization of postagricultural forests in central New York State ... *Journal of Ecology* 89: 325–38.

27 Donohue, K., Foster, D.R. & Motzkin, G. (2000). Effects of the past and the present on species distribution: land-use history and demography of wintergreen. *Journal of Ecology* 88: 303–16.

28 Takahashi, K. & Kamitani, T. (2004). Effect of dispersal capacity on forest plant migration at a landscape scale. *Journal of Ecology* 92: 778–85.

Chapter 13

1 The impact of planting for restoration of remnant bushland on its scientific and educational values: implications for conservation planning. *Pacific Conservation Biology* (1997) 3: 27–38.

2 Gordon, A. (1998). Whence British trees? *Tree News* autumn 1998 p.15.

3 *Forestry Commission Practice Note*, August 1999.

4 Jones, A.T., Hayes, M.J. & Sackville Hamilton, N.R. (2001). The effect of provenance on the performance of *Crataegus monogyna* in hedges. *Journal of Applied Ecology* 38: 952–62

5 Sell, P.D. Introduced 'look-alikes' and other difficult introduced plants in our Cambridgeshire flora. *Nature in Cambridgeshire*, forthcoming.

Sell, P.D. & Murrell, G. *Flora of Great Britain and Ireland*. Cambridge University Press, forthcoming.

Rich, T.C.G., Motley, G.S. & Kay, Q.O.N. (2005). Welsh endemic *Sorbus* species. *Watsonia* 25: 381–8.

6 Akeroyd, J. (1992). A remarkable alien flora on the Gog Magog Hills. *Nature in Cambridgeshire* 34: 35–42.

7 Wilkinson, D.M. (2001). Is local provenance important in habitat creation? *Journal of Applied Ecology* 38: 1371–3; reply by Sackville Hamilton, N.R. (ibid.) 1374–6.

8 Saltonstall, K. (2002). Cryptic invasion

by a non-native genotype of the common reed, *Phragmites australis*, into North America. *Proceedings of the National Academy of Sciences* 99: 2445–9.

9 Rackham (1986a) p.57ff.

Chapter 14

1 Harper, J.L. (1982). After description. *In* Newman, E.I. (Ed.) *The Plant Community as a Working Mechanism. British Ecological Society Special Publications* 1: 11–26.

2 Rackham (2003) Table 31.1.

3 Moss, C.E., Rankin, W.M. & Tansley, A.G. (1910). The woodlands of England. *New Phytologist* 9: 113–49.

4 Rackham (1983) p.383.

5 Rackham (2003) Chapter 31.

6 Wardle, P. (1959). The regeneration of *Fraxinus excelsior* in woods with a field layer of *Mercurialis perennis. Journal of Ecology* 47: 483–97.

7 Moss, C.E. (1907). *Geographical Distribution of Vegetation in Somerset: Bath and Bridgwater District.* London: Royal Geographical Society.

8 Robinson, M. [*c*.2000]. Charred cereals, fruits and nuts. *In* Fairbairn, A.S. (Ed.) *Plants in Neolithic Britain and beyond.* Oxford: Oxbow.

9 Oosthuizen, S. & Taylor, C. (2000). 'John O'Gaunt's House', Bassingbourn, Cambridgeshire: a fifteenth-century landscape. *Landscape History* 22: 61–76.

10 Gurr, A. (1997). Shakespeare's Globe: a history of reconstructions and some reasons for trying. *In* Mulryne, J.R. & Shewring, S. (Eds) *Shakespeare's Globe Rebuilt*, 27–47. Cambridge University Press.
    Rackham (1989) p.136.

11 Schjølberg, E. (1988). Cordage and similar products from Bryggen, in Bergen. *The Bryggen Papers, Supplementary Series* 3. Norwegian University Press.

12 Rackham (2003) Chapter 14; Rackham (1986b).

13 Rackham (2003) Chapter 28.

14 Tansley (1939) Chapters XVIII–XX.

15 Hepple, L.W. & Doggett, A.M. (1992). *The Chilterns.* Chichester: Phillimore.

16 Cowling, S.A., Sykes, M.T. & Bradshaw, R.H.W. (2001). Palaeovegetation-model comparisons, climate change and tree succession in Scandinavia over the past 1500 years. *Journal of Ecology* 89: 227–36.

17 Rackham (2003) p.293.

18 Barrington, D. (1769). A Letter … on the Trees which are supposed to be indigenous in *Great Britain. Philosophical Transactions of the Royal Society* 59: 23–38.
    Ducarel, A.C., Hasted, E. & Thorpe, J. (1772). A Letter … concerning Chesnut Trees. *Philosophical Transactions of the Royal Society* 61: 136–69.
    Rackham (2003) Chapter 21.

19 Rackham (2003) p.250.

20 Roberts (1999); Holmes & Wheaten (2002).

21 Bertolotto, S. & Cevasco, R. (2000). The 'Alnoculture' system in the Ligurian Eastern Apennines: archive evidence.

Chapter 15

1 Dickson, J.H. (1980). A pollen diagram from the Auld Wives' Lifts, Craigmaddie Muir, Strathclyde. *Glasgow Archaeological Journal* 7: 13–8.

2 Stevenson, J.F. (1990). How ancient is the woodland of Mugdock? *Scottish Forestry* 44: 161–72.
    Smout *et al.* (2004) p.175.

3 Tittensor, R.M. (1970). History of the Loch Lomond oakwoods. *Scottish Forestry* 24: 100–18.
    Smout *et al.* (2004) pp.263, 268.

4 Idle, E.T. & Mitchell, J. (1968). The fallow deer of Loch Lomondside. *Deer* 1: 263–5.
    Smout *et al.* (2004) pp.154, 250.

5 I am indebted to Professor C.D. Pigott for introducing me to this wood.

6 Mitchell, F.J.G. (1998). The investigation of long-term successions in temperate woodland using fine spatial resolution

pollen analysis. *In* Kirby & Watkins (1998): 213–23.

7 Smout *et al.* (2004) p.173ff.

8 Smout *et al.* (2004) p.118ff.

9 Sinclair, J. (Ed.) (1814). *General Report of the Agricultural State ... of Scotland*. Edinburgh.

10 Atherden (1992) p.77.

British Lichen Society Bulletin 94 (2004): 19–21, 45–50.

11 The British Vegetation Committee's excursion to the west of Ireland 1908. *New Phytologist* 7 (1908): 253–60.

Tansley (1939) p.474.

Chapter 16

1 Review, *Landscape History* 19: 112.

2 Kinloch, B.M., Westfall, R.D. & Forrest, G.I. (1986). Caledonian Scots pine: origins and genetic structure. *New Phytologist* 104: 703–29.

3 Kamada, M., Nakagoshi, N. & Nehira, K. (1991). Pine forest ecology and landscape management: a comparative study in Japan and Korea. *In* Nakagoshi, N. & Golley, F.B. (Eds) *Coniferous Forest Ecology from an International Perspective*, 43–62. The Hague: SPB Academic Publishing.

4 Bennett, K.D. (1984). The post-glacial history of *Pinus sylvestris* in the British Isles. *Quaternary Science Review* 3: 133–55.

Birks, H.J.B. (1989). Holocene isochrone maps and patterns of tree-spreading in the British Isles. *Journal of Biogeography* 16: 503–40.

5 Atherden (1992).

6 Durno, S.E. (1959). Pollen analysis of peat deposits in the Eastern Grampians. *Scottish Geographical Magazine* 75: 102–11.

Pears, N.V. (1968). Post-glacial tree lines of the Cairngorm Mountains, Scotland. *Transactions of the Botanical Society of Edinburgh* 40: 361–94.

Vasari, Y. & A. (1968). Late- and post-glacial macrophytic vegetation in the lochs of Northern Scotland. *Acta Botanica Fennica* 80: 1–120.

Birks, H.H. (1970). Studies in the vegetational history of Scotland. I. A pollen diagram from Abernethy Forest, Inverness-shire. *Journal of Ecology* 58: 827–46.

Birks, H.H. (1972). Studies in the vegetational history of Scotland. III. A radiocarbon dated pollen diagram from Loch Maree, Ross and Cromarty. *New Phytologist* 71: 731–54.

7 Pliny, *Natural History* IV. xvi.102; Ptolemy, *Geography* II. iii. 12.

8 Rackham, O. (2001). *Trees, Wood, and Timber in Greek History*. Oxford: Leopard's Head Press.

9 Breeze, D.J. (1992). The Great Myth of Caledon. *Scottish Forestry* 46: 331–5.

Dickson, J. (1993). Scottish woodlands: their ancient past and precarious present. *Scottish Forestry* 47: 73–8.

10 McVean, D.N. (1963). Ecology of Scots pine in the Scottish Highlands. *Journal of Ecology* 51: 671–86.

11 Barrow, G.E.S. (1999). The background to medieval Rothiemurchus. *In* Smout & Lambert (1999): 1–6.

12 See for example Smout *et al.* (2004) Chapter 4.

13 Smout *et al.* (2004) p.86f.

14 Stone J.C. (1989). *The Pont Manuscript Maps of Scotland: sixteenth-century origins of a Blaeu atlas*. Tring.

15 Macfarlane, W. (Ed. Mitchell, A.) (1907). *Geographical Collections Relating to Scotland*. Edinburgh: Scottish Historical Society. 2: 241f.

16 Michie J.G. (Ed.) (1901). *The Records of Invercauld*, p.125. Aberdeen: New Spalding Club.

17 Michie (ibid.) pp.126, 151.

18 Michie (ibid.) pp.142, 131, 154.

19 Michie (ibid.) pp.143–4.

20 Michie (ibid.) pp.127, 153, 143, 148, 316.

21 Macfarlane (ibid.).

Smout & Lambert (1999).

Smout *et al.* (2004) *passim*.

22 Smout & Lambert (1999).

23 Steven & Carlisle (1959) pp.96, 99.

24 Smout & Lambert (1999) pp.29, 38.

25 Staines, B.W. & Balhamy, R. (2002).
Red deer and their management in the
Cairngorms. *In* Gimingham, C. (Ed.) *The
Ecology, Land Use, and Conservation of the
Cairngorms*, 130–8. Chichester: Packard.

26 Sinclair, J. (Ed.) (1791–9) *The [Old]
Statistical Account* of Scotland. Edinburgh
14: 463.

27 Pennant, T. (1771). *A Tour in Scotland, 1769.*
Chester.

28 Farquharson of Invercauld, J. (1774). Of
Scotch Pines. *Appendix to Pennant's Tour in
Scotland*. London: White.

29 *Old Statistical Account.*

30 Queen Victoria (Ed. Helps, A.) (1868).
*Leaves from the Journal of Our Life in the
Highlands*. London: Smith, Elder.

31 Pictured in Rackham (1994) p.105.

32 Smout *et al.* (2004) p.74f.

33 Fowler, J. (2002). *Landscapes and Lives: the
Scottish forest through the ages*, Chapter 19.
Edinburgh: Canongate.

Chapter 17

1 *Philosophical Magazine* 62: 252–4.

2 Dugdale, W.D. (1658). *The History of St Paul's
Cathedral* ... London: Warren.

3 Brimblecombe, P. (1987). *The Big Smoke: a
history of air pollution in London since medieval
times*. London: Methuen.

4 Hawksworth, D.L. & Rose, F. (1976). *Lichens
as pollution monitors*. London: Edward
Arnold.

5 Bottacci, A. *et al.* (1988). *Inquinamento
Ambientale e Deperimento del Bosco in Toscana*.
Firenze: Società Botanica Italiana.

6 I am indebted to B. Bache for the
magnesium story.

7 For example: Innes, J.L. & Boswell,
R. (1988). *Forest health surveys 1987. Part
2: Analysis and interpretation*. Forestry
Commission Bulletin 79.

8 Kirby, Bunce *et al.* (2005).

9 Rose, F. & Hawksworth, D.L. (1980).

Lichen recolonization in London's cleaner
air. *Nature* 289: 289–92.

  Hawksworth, D.L. & McMann, P.M.
(1989). Lichen recolonization in London
under conditions of rapidly falling
sulphur dioxide levels, and the concept of
zone skipping. *Journal of the Linnean Society,
Botany* 100: 99–109.

10 Rackham (2003) p.388.

11 For example: Robinson, E.G. (1927).
Mortality among oak. *Quarterly Journal of
Forestry* 21: 25–7.

12 This section is based on my report to the
Conservators. I am most grateful for the
advice of Dr John Gibbs, Dr John Rishbeth
and Dr Donald Pigott, and for the help of
Paul Moxey in the field. The conclusions,
however, are mine.

13 Rackham (1978).

14 Baker, C.A., Moxey, P.A. & Oxford, P.M.
(1978). Woodland continuity and change
in Epping Forest. *Field Studies* 4: 645–69.

15 Lonsdale, D. (1986). *Beech health study
1986*. Forestry Commission Research &
Development Paper 149.

16 Layton, R.L. (1985). Recreation,
management and landscape in Epping
Forest: *c.*1800–1984. *Field Studies* 6:
269–90.

17 Crombie, J.M. (1885). On the lichen-flora
of Epping Forest, and the causes affecting
its recent diminution. *Transactions of Essex
Field Club* 4: 54–75.

  Hawksworth, D.L., Rose, F. & Coppins,
B.J. (1973). Changes in the lichen flora
of England and Wales attributable to
pollution of the air by sulphur dioxide.
In Ferry, B.W., Baddeley, M.S. *et al.* (Eds),
Air pollution and lichens, 330–67. London:
Athlone Press.

18 The Survey was directed by Professor
Nancy Wilkie. I was accompanied in the
field by Dr Jennifer Moody.

19 Worrall, J.J., Lee, T.D., & Harrington,
T.C. (2005). Forest dynamics and agents
that initiate and expand canopy gaps in

Picea–Abies forests of Crawford Notch, New Hampshire, USA. *Journal of Ecology* 93: 178–90.

20 *The Homeowner and the Gypsy Moth: Guidelines and Control* (1979). United States Department of Agriculture Home and Garden Bulletin 227.

    Gypsy Moth Control (1979). [United States] Agriculture Handbook 542.

    The Gypsy Moth in Connecticut (1981). Connecticut Agricultural Experiment Station, New Haven, Bulletin 797.

    See also United States Department of Agriculture (Forest Service) website. I am indebted to Dave Houston for introducing me to the problem.

21 For details of the story see Rackham (1986) Chapter 11 and Rackham (2003) Chapters 16, 28.

22 Anagnostakis, S.L. (1978). The American chestnut: new hope for a fallen giant. *Bulletin of Connecticut Agricultural Station, New Haven* 1978: 777.

23 Podger, F.D. (1972). Phytophthora cinnamomi, a cause of lethal disease in indigenous plant communities in Western Australia. *Phytopathology* 62: 972–81.

    Podger, F.D., James, S.H. & Mulcahy, M.J. (1996). *Review of Dieback in Western Australia*. Perth: Western Australia Dieback Review Panel.

24 Gibbs, J. & Lonsdale, D. (1998). *Phytophthora Disease of Alder*. Forestry Authority Information Note.

25 Brasier, C.M. & Strouts, R.G. (1975). New records of Phytophthora on trees in Britain. I. Phytophthora root rot and Bleeding canker of Horse chestnut ... *European Journal of Forest Pathology* 6: 129–36.

Chapter 18

1 Rackham (2003) p.290f.

2 Rackham (1986a) p.153f.

3 Norfolk & Norwich Record Office: MR208

(241 × 4).

4 *Victoria County History, Bedfordshire* 2: 144f.

5 [*Scottish*] *Acts of Parliament* 2: 51.

6 Harmer, R. & Kerr, G. (2005). Creating woodlands: to plant trees or not? In Ferris-Kaan (2005): 113–28.

7 Standish, A. (1611). *The Commons Complaint* ... London: William Stansby.

    Standish, A. (1615). *New Directions of Experience ... for the increasing of Timber and Firewood* ... [no publisher].

8 Menzies, W. (1864). *The History of Windsor Great Park and Windsor Forest*. London: Longmans.

    Rogers, J. (1941). *The English Woodland*. London: Batsford [citing letter of R. Daye, 1625].

9 Hart (1966) Chapter 8.

10 Taylor (2000).

11 Ketton-Cremer, R.W. (1962). *Felbrigg: the story of a house*. London: Rupert Hart-Davis.

12 Grigor, J. (1841). *Eastern Arboretum*. London. p.316f.

13 Tubbs (1986).

14 For example: James, N.D.G. (1981). *A History of English Forestry*, 168. Oxford: Blackwell.

15 House, S. & Dingwall, C. (2003). A nation of planters: introducing the new trees, 1650–1900. *People and Woods in Scotland: a history. In* Smout (2003): 128–57.

16 Neeson (1991) pp.93ff.

17 Smout *et al.* (2004) p.68.

18 Fowler (2002).

19 Hart (1966) Chapter 10.

20 Norfolk & Norwich Record Office: 30D5 12554.

21 Rackham (1989) p.130.

22 Jones, M. (1998). The rise, decline and extinction of spring wood management in south-west Yorkshire. *In* Watkins (1998): 55–71.

23 Thirgood, J.V. (1987). *Cyprus: a chronicle of its forests, land and people*. Vancouver: University of British Columbia Press.

24 Grove (1983).

25 Ryle (1969).

26 *Forestry Commission Bulletins* 27 (1956) and 33 (1960).

27 Neeson (1991).

28 Neeson (1991).

29 For details see Grove (1983).

30 House of Lords (1980).

31 *Woodland Heritage Journal, passim.*

32 Gilbert, M. *et al.* (2005). Forecasting *Cameraria ohridella* invasion dynamics in recently invaded countries: from validation to prediction. *Journal of Applied Ecology* 42: 805–13.

Chapter 19

1 Coke, R.L. (1980). *In* House of Lords (1980) pp.289ff.

2 St Barbe Baker, R. (1931). *Men of the Trees in the Mahogany Forests of Kenya and Nigeria.* London: Lutterworth. p.240.

   St Barbe Baker, R. (1944). *I Planted Trees.* London: Lutterworth.

3 St Barbe Baker, R. (1954). *Sahara Challenge.* London: Lutterworth.

   St Barbe Baker, R. (1966). *Sahara Conquest.* London: Lutterworth.

4 Essex, S.J. & Williams, A.G. (1993). Ecological effects of a less-intensively managed afforestation scheme on Dartmoor ... *In* Watkins (1993): 110–26.

5 Yalden (1999) pp.183–8.

6 Gibbons, D.W., Reid, J.B. & Chapman, R.A. (1993). *The New Atlas of Breeding Birds in Britain and Ireland: 1988–1991.* London: Poyser.

7 Lavers, C. & Haines-Young, R. (1993) The impact of afforestation on upland birds in Britain. *In* Watkins (1993): 127–52.

8 Ozanne, C. (1997). Creatures of the canopy. *Tree News* (spring 1997).

   Prinzing, A. & Wirtz, H.-P. (1997). The epiphytic lichen, *Evernia prunastri*, as a habitat for arthropods ... *In* Stork, N.E., Adis, J. & Didham, R.K. (Eds) *Canopy Arthropods*, 476–94. London: Chapman

& Hall.

   Ozanne, C.M.P., Hambler, C. *et al.* (1997). The significance of edge effects in the management of forests for insect biodiversity. In Stork *et al.* (ibid.): 534–50.

9 Southgate, G.J. (1969). Helicopter spraying to kill overhead cover in Lavenham Forest, Suffolk. *Journal of the Forestry Commission* 36: 58–9.

10 Pigott, C.D. (1990). The influence of evergreen coniferous nurse-crops on the field layer in two woodland communities. *Journal of Applied Ecology* 27: 48–59.

11 Elwes, H.J. & Henry, A. (1913). *The Trees of Great Britain and Ireland* vol.7. Edinburgh: [Clark].

12 Public Record Office: E315/83 f.36.

13 Perring, F.H., quoted by Grove (1983): 21.

14 Rackham (2003) pp.248ff.

15 Goldberg, E. (2003). Plantations on ancient woodland sites. *Quarterly Journal of Forestry* 97: 132–8.

16 Rackham (2003) pp.524–7.

17 Blaschke, H. (1977). Untersuchungen über das Vorkommen und die Wirkung von biogenen Wachstumsregulatoren in wässrigen Nadelstreuauszügen. *Flora* 166: 537–45.

Chapter 20

1 Horsfall, A. (1993). *An Introduction to Ancient Woodland in Dorset.*

   Horsfall, A. (1997). Domesday woodland in Dorset. *Proceedings of Dorset Natural History and Archaeology Society* 118:1–6.

2 Winchester College Muniment 21378; Dorset Record Office photocopy 369. I am indebted to Mr Seaward for bringing this to my attention.

3 Camden, W. (1586). *Britannia.* London: Newbery.

4 Dorset Record Office: D.148/38/8 *alias* D/FFO 38/8.

5 Watkin, A. (1947, 1952, 1958). *The Great Chartulary of Glastonbury.* Somerset Record Society. [From Longleat MS 1; another MS

with variant readings is Bodleian MS Wood Empt. I, published by Kemble (p.000 note, §768)]

6 Rackham (1986a) p.335.

7 Hutchins, J. (1874 ed. of 1774 original) *The History and Antiquities of the County of Dorset*. London: Nichols. 4: 517, 519.

8 Hutchins, *Dorset* (1874 ed.) 4: 518.

9 Hutchins, *Dorset* (1874 ed.) 4: 517.

10 Watkin (*ibid*.) I: 178ff.

11 *Calendar of Close Rolls*, 1254, p.56.

12 *Victoria County History: Dorset* 2: 229.

13 Birrell, J. (1996). Hunting and the Royal Forest. *In* Cavaciocchi (1996): 437–58.

14 *Dictionary of National Biography*.

15 *Victoria County History: Dorset* 2: 291, 290.

16 Particulars of deer are derived from *Rotuli Litterarum Clausarum, Calendar of Close Rolls*, and *Calendar of Liberate Rolls*.

17 Calthorp, M.M.C., in *Victoria County History: Dorset* 2: 96ff.

    Field, N.H. & Musty, J. (1966). A thirteenth century kiln at Hermitage, Dorset. *Proceedings of Dorset Natural History and Archaeology Society* 88:161–75.

18 Hutchins (note 7) (1874 ed.) 4:518.

19 Traskey, J.P. (1978–9). *Milton Abbey: a Dorset monastery in the Middle Ages*. Tisbury: Compton Press. [Quoting Winchester College archives.]

20 Dorset Record Office: D/WLC/M217.

21 Winchester College 14210, 14211b.

22 British Library Add. MS 52,522.

23 *Hermitage map, 1615*. Dorset Record Office: 362 (copy).

    Minterne-Hartley map, 1616. Winchester College Muniments 21378 (Dorset Record Office photocopy 369).

    Seaward, D.R. & Barker, K. (1993). Maps and Minterne Magna: a diverting story. *Proceedings of Dorset Natural History & Archaeological Society*. 114: 1–7.

    Hermitage-Minterne map, 1723. Dorset Record Office: D148/38/8 alias D/FFO 38/8.

    Isaac Taylor map of Middlemarsh and Hurdley, c.1770. Dorset Record Office:

Photocopy 1/9.

24 Dorset Record Office: Dorset County Museum D1/10.730. (I am grateful to Dennis Seaward for transcribing this.)

25 *Victoria County History: Dorset* 2: 291.

26 Hutchins (note 7) (1874 ed.) 4: 478.

27 Lea, H. [c.1906]. *A Handbook to the Wessex Country of Thomas Hardy's Novels and Poems*. London: Kegan Paul.

28 Dorset Record Office: D/SHA E71.

29 Barker, K. & and Seaward, D.R. (1990). Boundaries and landscape in Blackmoor: the Tudor manors of Holnest, Hilfield and Hermitage. *Proceedings of Dorset Natural History and Archaeology Society* 112: 5–22.

30 Hutchins (note 7) (1874 ed.) 4: 519a.

31 Martin, M.H. (Ed.) [c.2004]. *Lower Woods Nature Reserve: guide and species list*. Gloucestershire Wildlife Trust.

Chapter 21

1 Spencer, J.W. (1995). To what extent can we recreate woodland? *In* Ferris-Kaan (1995): 1–16.

2 Bakker, J.P. *et al.* (1996). Why do we need permanent plots in the study of long-term vegetation dynamics? *Journal of Vegetation Science* 7: 147–56.

3 Crogan, P. (2005). The use of hypotheses in ecology. *Bulletin of the British Ecological Society* 36: 43–5.

4 Adamson, R.S. (1912). An ecological study of a Cambridgeshire woodland. *Journal of the Linnean Society (Botany)* 40: 339–87, Plates 12–7.

5 Peterken, J.F. & Jones, E.W. (1987). Forty years of change in Lady Park Wood: the old-growth stands. *Journal of Ecology* 75: 477–512.

6 Peterken (2005).

7 Kirby, Bunce *et al.* (2005).

8 www.si.umich.edu/CAMILEON/ domesday/ what.html

Chapter 22

1 Roberts, G. (2005). England's Regional Woodlands. *Quarterly Journal of Forestry*

2 Tsouvalis-Geber, J. (1998). Making the invisible visible: ancient woodlands, British forest policy and the social construction of reality. *In* Watkins (1998): 215–29.

3 www.woodsunderthreat.info

4 Kirby, Bunce *et al.* (2005).

5 Yalden (1999).

6 Grove & Rackham (2001) Chapters 8, 9.

7 For further details see Rackham (2003) Chapter 25.

8 Yalden (1999) pp.74, 258f.

9 Jones, M., Robertson, I.D. & McCarthy, A.J. (Eds) (1996). Deer or the New Woodlands? *Journal of Practical Ecology & Conservation, Special Publication* 1.

Tabor, R.C. (1997). The effects of Muntjac deer ... and Fallow deer ... on the Oxlip. *Deer* 11: 14–19.

Articles on deer, *Forestry* 74 (2001): 209–309.

10 Cooke, A.S. & and Farrell, L.T. (2001). Impact of muntjac deer ... at Monks Wood ... *Forestry* 74: 242–50.

11 Elton, C.S. (1958). *The Ecology of Invasions by Animals and Plants.* London: Methuen.

12 Hambler, C. & Speight, M.R. (1995). Biodiversity conservation in Britain: science replacing tradition. *British Wildlife* 6: 137–47.

13 Chase, A. (*c.*1986) *Playing God in Yellowstone: the destruction of America's first National Park.* Boston (Mass.): Atlantic Monthly Press.

Friday, L.E. (1997). *Wicken Fen: the making of a wetland nature reserve.* Great Horkesley: Harley Books.

Rackham (1989) Chapter 6.

14 Spooner & Roberts (2005).

15 Rackham, O. (1991). Landscape and the conservation of meaning. *Journal of the Royal Society of Arts* 139: 903–15.

16 This section summarises Rackham (2003) Chapter 30.

17 Moore, N.W. & Hooper, M.D. (1975). On the number of bird species in British woods. *Biological Conservation* 8: 239–50.

18 MacArthur, R.H. & Wilson, E.O. (1967). *The Theory of Island Biogeography.* Princeton University Press.

19 Rackham (2003) pp.56–9.

20 Freckleton, R.P. & Watkinson, A.R. (2002). Large-scale spatial dynamics of plants: metapopulations, regional ensembles and patchy populations. *Journal of Ecology* 90: 419–34.

21 Rackham (2003) p.477.

22 Vila-Aiub, M.M., Neve, P. *et al.* (2005). Ecological fitness of a multiple herbicide-resistant *Lolium rigidum* population: dynamics of seed germination and seedling emergence of resistant and susceptible pheno-types. *Journal of Applied Ecology* 42: 288–98.

23 Spencer, J. (2002). *Ancient Woodland on the Forestry Commission Estate in England.* Forest Enterprise.

24 Ferris-Kaan (1995).

25 Key, R.S. (1995) Invertebrate conservation and new woodland in Britain. *In* Ferris-Kaan (1995): 149–62.

26 Moccas Park book.

27 Spencer, J.W. (1995). To what extent can we recreate native woodland? *In* Ferris-Kaan (1995): 1–16.

BIBLIOGRAPHY

Agnoletti, M. & Andersen, S. (Eds) (2000). *Methods and Approaches in Forest History.* Wallingford: CABI.

Atherden, M. (1992). *Upland Britain: a natural history.* Manchester University Press.

Atherden, M.A. & Butlin, R.A. (Eds) (1998). *Woodland in the Landscape: past and future perspectives.* Ripon: PLACE Research Centre.

Beswick P., Rotherham I.D. & Parsons, J. (Eds) (1993). *Ancient woodlands: their archaeology and ecology: a coincidence of interest.* Landscape Archaeology and History I.

Bradshaw, R.W. (2005). What is a natural forest? *In* Stanturf, J.A.A. & Madsen, P. (Eds) *Restoration of Boreal and Temperate Forests,* 15–30. Boca Raton: CRC Press.

Cavaciocchi, S. (Ed.) (1996). *L'Uomo e la Foresta.* Prato: Le Monnier.

Edlin, H.L. (1949). *Woodland Crafts of Britain.* London: Batsford.

Edlin, H.L. (1956). *Trees, Woods and Man.* London: Collins New Naturalist.

Fairhead, J. & Leach, M. (1998). *Reframing Deforestation.* London: Routledge.

Ferris-Kaan, R. (Ed.) (1995). *The Ecology of Woodland Creation.* Chichester: Wiley.

Fitzrandolph, H.E. & Hay, M.D. (1926). *The Rural Industries of England & Wales. I. Timber and underwood industries and some village workshops.* Oxford: Clarendon.

Fowler, J. (2002). *Landscapes and Lives: the Scottish forest through the ages.* Edinburgh: Canongate.

Godwin, H. (1975). *The History of the British Flora,* 2nd ed. Cambridge University Press.

Grove, A.T. & Rackham, O. (2001). *The Nature of Mediterranean Europe: an ecological history.* New Haven: Yale University Press.

Grove, R. (1983). *The Future for Forestry.* Cambridge: British Association of Nature Conservationists.

Harding, P.T. & Wall, T. (Eds) (2000). *Moccas: an English deer park.* English Nature.

Harris, E. & J. (1991). *Wildlife Conservation in Managed Woodlands and Forests.* Oxford: Blackwell.

Hart, C.E. (1966). *Royal Forest: a history of Dean's woods as producers of timber.* Oxford: Clarendon.

Hoadley, R.B. (1990). *Identifying Wood: accurate results with simple tools.* Newtown (Conn.): Taunton. [Deals mainly with North American woods, but useful for European species of the same genera.]

Hodder, K.H., Bullock, J.M. *et al.* (2005). *Large herbivores in the wildwood and modern naturalistic grazing systems.* English Nature Research Report **648**.

Holmes, W. & Wheaten, A. (Eds) (2002). *The Blean: the woodlands of a cathedral city.* Whitstable: White Horse Press.

House of Lords (1980). *Select Committee on Science and Technology: Scientific Aspects of Forestry.* London: Her Majesty's Stationery Office.

Jane, F.W. (1970). *The Structure of Wood,* 2nd ed. London: A & C Black.

Jones, M. (1998). The rise, decline and extinction of spring wood management in south-west Yorkshire. *In* Watkins (1998) 55–71.

Jones, M. (2003). *Sheffield's Woodland Heritage,* 3rd ed. Thorpe Hesley: Green Tree.

Kirby, K.J. & Watkins, C. (Eds) (1998).

The Ecological History of European Forests. Wallingford: CAB International.

Kirby, K.J., Bunce, R.G.H. et al. (2005). Long term ecological change in British woodland (1971–2001). English Nature Research Report 653.

Linnard, W. (2000). Welsh Woods and Forests: a history, 3rd ed. Llandysul: Gomer.

McVean, D.N. (1964). Woodland and scrub. In Burnett, J.H. (Ed.) The Vegetation of Scotland. Edinburgh: Oliver & Boyd. 144–67.

Mellars, P. & Dark, P. (1998). Star Carr in context. Cambridge: McDonald Institute.

Moore, N.W. (2002). Oaks, Dragonflies and People: creating a small nature reserve and relating its study to wider conservation issues. Great Horkesley: Harley.

Morris, M.G. & Perring, F.H. (1974). The British Oak. Faringdon: Classey.

Mynors, C. (2002). The Law of Trees, Forests and Hedgerows. London: Sweet & Maxwell.

Neeson, E. (1991). A History of Irish Forestry. Dublin: Lilliput.

Newman, E.I. (Ed.) (1982). The Plant Community as a Working Mechanism. British Ecological Society Special Publications 1.

Peace, T.R. (1962). Pathology of Trees and Shrubs with special reference to Britain. Oxford: Clarendon.

Peterken, G.F. (1993a). Long-term floristic development of woodland on former agricultural land in Lincolnshire ... In Watkins (1993) 31–44.

Peterken, G.F. (1993b). Woodland Conservation and Management, 2nd ed. London: Chapman & Hall.

Peterken, G.F. (1996). Natural Woodland: ecology and conservation in northern temperate regions. Cambridge University Press.

Peterken, G.F. (2005). Natural woodland reserves: 60 years of trying at Lady Park Wood. British Wildlife 17: 7–16.

Rackham, O. (1975). Hayley Wood: its history and ecology. Cambridgeshire & Isle of Ely Naturalists' Trust.

Rackham, O. (1978). Archaeology and land-use history. In Corke, D. (Ed.) Epping Forest – the natural aspect? Essex Naturalist NS 2: 16–57.

Rackham, O. (1986a). The History of the Countryside. London: Dent.

Rackham, O. (1986b). Ancient Woodland of England: the woods of south-east Essex. Rochford District Council.

Rackham, O. (1989). The Last Forest: the ecology of Hatfield Forest. London: Dent.

Rackham, O. (1990, 1st ed. 1976). Trees & Woodland in the British Landscape. London: Dent.

Rackham, O. (1991). Landscape and the conservation of meaning. Journal of the Royal Society of Arts 139: 903–15.

Rackham, O. (1994). The Illustrated History of the Countryside, 1st ed. London: Weidenfeld & Nicholson.

Rackham, O. (1998). Savanna in Europe. In Kirby & Watkins (1998) 1–24.

Rackham, O. (2000). Woodland in the Ely Coucher Book. Nature in Cambridgeshire 42: 37–67.

Rackham, O. (2002a). The Holy Mountain [Athos]. Plant Talk 27: 19–23.

Rackham, O. (2002b). Treasures of Silver at Corpus Christi College, Cambridge. Cambridge University Press.

Rackham. O. (2002c). Observations on the historical ecology of Laconia. In Cavanagh, W., Crouwel, J. et al. (Eds) Continuity and Change in a Greek Rural Landscape: the Laconia survey. London: British School at Athens. vol. I: 73–120.

Rackham, O. (2003). Ancient Woodland: its history, vegetation and uses in England, 2nd ed. Dalbeattie: Castlepoint Press. (1st ed. (1980) London: Edward Arnold.)

Rackham, O. & Coombe, D.E. (1996). Madingley Wood. Nature in Cambridgeshire 38: 27–54.

Rackham, O. & Moody, J.A. (1996). The Making of the Cretan Landscape. Manchester

University Press.

Roberts, G. (1999). *Woodlands of Kent*. Ashford: Geerings.

Ryle, G. (1969). *Forest Service: the first forty-five years of the Forestry Commission of Great Britain*. Newton Abbot: David & Charles.

St Barbe Baker, R. (1948). *Green Glory: the story of the forests of the world*. London: Lutterworth Press.

Smout, T.C. (2003). *People and Woods in Scotland: a history*. Edinburgh University Press.

Smout, T.C. & Lambert, R.A. (Eds) (1999). *Rothiemurchus: nature and people on a Highland estate 1500–2000*. Dalkeith: Scottish Cultural Press.

Smout, T.C., Macdonald, A.R. & Watson, F. (2004). *A History of the Native Woodlands of Scotland, 1500–1920*. Edinburgh University Press.

Spooner, B. & Roberts, P. (2005). *Fungi*. London: Collins New Naturalist.

Squires, A. & Jeeves, M. (1994). *Leicestershire and Rutland Woodlands Past and Present*. Newtown Linford: Kairos.

Steele, R.C. & Welch, R.C. (Eds) (1973). *Monks Wood: a nature reserve record*. Nature Conservancy.

Steven, H.M. & Carlisle, A. (1959). *The Native Pinewoods of Scotland*. Edinburgh: Oliver & Boyd. (Reissue 2001, Dalbeattie: Castlepoint Press.)

Szabó, P. (2005). *Woodland and Forests in Medieval Hungary*. British Archaeological Reports, International Series 1348.

Tack, G., van den Bremt, P. & Hermy, M. (1993). *Bossen van Vlaanderen: een historische ecologie*. Leuven: Davidsfonds.

Tansley, A.G. (1939). *The British Islands and their Vegetation*. Cambridge University Press.

Taylor, C. (2000). Medieval ornamental landscapes. *Landscapes* 1: 18–35.

Totman, C. (1989). *The Green Archipelago: forestry in preindustrial Japan*. Berkeley: University of California Press.

Tubbs, C.R. (1986). *The New Forest: a natural history*. London: Collins New Naturalist.

Vera, F. (2000). *Grazing Ecology and Forest History*. Wallingford: CABI.

Wager, S.J. (1998). *Woods, Wolds and Groves: the woodland of medieval Warwickshire*. British Archaeological Reports, British Series 269.

Warren, M.S. & Key, R.S. (1991). Woodlands: past, present and potential for insects. In Collins, N.M. & Thomas, J.A. (Eds) *The Conservation of Insects and their Habitats*. 155–211. London: Academic Press.

Watkins, C. (Ed.) (1993). *Ecological Effects of Afforestation*. Wallingford: CABI.

Watkins, C. (Ed.) (1998). *European Woods and Forests: studies in cultural history*. Wallingford: CABI.

Woodward, S.F. (1992). *Swithland Wood: a study of its history and vegetation*. Leicestershire Museums.

Yalden, D. (1999). *The History of British Mammals*. London: Poyser Natural History.

TABLES

		Methods of regeneration			
		Seed	Suckers	Coppicing	Pollarding
NATIVE					
Alder	*Alnus glutinosa*	++++	0	++++	++
Ash	*Fraxinus excelsior*	++++	0	++++	++++
Aspen	*Populus tremula*	+	++++	0	0
Beech	*Fagus sylvatica*	+++	0*	+++	++++
Birch	*Betula pubescens and*				
	B. verrucosa	++++	0	+++	+
Blackthorn, sloe	*Prunus spinosa*	++	++++	0	0
Cherry (wild)	*Prunus avium*	++	++++	+	0
Crab-apple	*Malus sylvestris*	+	0	++	+
Elm, wych-	*Ulmus glabra*	+++	0	++++	++++
Elm, East Anglian	*U. minor*	+	++++	+	++++
Elm, English	*U. procera*	0	+++	0	++++
Hawthorn	*Cratægus monogyna*	++++	0	+++	++
Hawthorn					
('woodland')	*C. lævigata*	++	0	+++	0
Hazel	*Corylus avellana*	no longer	0	++++	+
Holly	*Ilex aquifolium*	++++	0	+++	+++
Hornbeam	*Carpinus betulus*	+++	0	+++	+++
Lime, small-leaved	*Tilia cordata*	+	+	++++	++++
Maple	*Acer campestre*	+++	0	++++	++++
Oak, pedunculate	*Quercus robur*	++	0	++	+++
Oak, sessile	*Q. petræa*	++	0	+++	++
Pine, Caledonian	*Pinus sylvestris scotica*	+++	0	0	0
Poplar, black	*Populus nigra*	0	0	+++	++++
Rowan	*Sorbus aucuparia*	+++	0	++	+++
Sallow	*Salix caprea and S. cinerea*	++++	0	++++	++
Service	*Sorbus torminalis*	+	+++	+++	+++
Whitebeam	*S. aria*	+++	0	+++	?
Willow	*Salix alba and S. fragilis*	++++	0	++++	++++
ARCHAEOPHYTE					
Chestnut, sweet-					
(p.370)	*Castanea sativa*	+++	0	++++	++
NEOPHYTES					
Rhododendron	*Rhododendron ponticum*	++++	0	+++	

*Except in Kew Gardens.

Table 1. *Properties of trees.*

'Preference for woodland': + prefers woodland, o indifferent, − avoids woodland. 'Palatability' is a *rough* guide to which trees are preferred by browsing animals. It takes no account of differences between animals: for instance fallow deer hate aspen, but sheep will eat it.

Preference for woodland	Ability to form secondary woodland	Tolerance of poor soils	Gregarious-ness	Palatability	Liability to uprooting in storms	Survival of uprooting
−	+++	++	++++	+	0	++
0	+++	+	0	++++	++	++
+++	+	+++	clonal	+	++	?
++	+	++++	+++	+++	++++	+++
0	+++	++++	+++	+++	++++	+
−	++	+	clonal	++++	0	+++
+++	++++	++	clonal	+++	+++	+
++	?	+	− − − −	+++	++	+++
0	0	0	++	++++		
++	+++	+	clonal	++++	++	+++
−	++	0	clonal	++++	++	?
0	++++	++	0	++++	+	++++
++++	0	+	0	++++	0	?
+	no longer	++	0	+++	+.	+++
+	+	++++	++	++++	+++	++++
+++	+	+++	++++	++	+++	+++
++++	0	+++	++++	++	++++	++++
−	+	+	+	+++	+++	++
0	++++	+++	−	+	+++	+++
++	+	++++	+++	+	+	+++
++++	+++	++++	++++	++	+++	+
− − − −	0	0	0	+++	++++	++++
++	++	++++	+	?	+++	++
0	++++	+++	+	++++	++++	++++
++++	0	++	clonal	+++	?	?
− −	+++	++	++	+++	?	?
− −	+++	+	+++	++++	++++	++++
+++	planted	+++	+++	0	++++	++++
0	+++	+++	++++	0	+++	++++

Table 2. *Differences between woodland and wood-pasture (omitting woodland within compartmental wood-pasture).*

WOODLAND (FOREST)	WOOD-PASTURE (SAVANNA)
Tree canopies touch	Gaps between trees above ground (although roots may meet below ground)
Trees often tall	Trees often low and spreading
Ground vegetation of shade-adapted plants (except for woodland grassland)	Ground vegetation consists of plants adapted to open ground
Browsing animals few or none	Browsing animals abundant
Trees coppiced, not pollarded (except on boundaries)	Trees pollarded, not coppiced
Usually no old trees (except coppice stools)	Ancient trees may be abundant
Can have ancient-woodland plants	Usually lacks flowering plants of ancient woodland, but may have characteristic lichens and invertebrate animals

Table 3. *The two native oaks.*

	PEDUNCULATE	SESSILE
Habit	Spreading	Upright, with long main stem
Leaves	Short stalk with two 'ears' at base of blade	Blade tapers into a long stalk
Acorns	Stalked	Sessile
Geography	Throughout Britain, including far north; uncommon in Ireland	North and west Britain; Ireland
Gregariousness	Scattered at random	Gregarious
Habitat	Standard tree in woods of other species; recent woodland; wood-pasture; hedgerow and non-woodland	Oakwoods with few other trees
Soils	Almost any, except thin chalk and limestone	Acid, infertile
Treatment	Timber tree; pollard; rarely coppiced	Coppiced
Planting	Preferred species from c.1800 (when difference became widely recognised) until 1950s	Preferred in later twentieth century

Table 4. *Characteristics of four sites in eastern England.*

	BRANDON PARK	BRADFIELD WOODS	HAYLEY WOOD	BUFF WOOD
Location	Breckland	SE of Bury St Edmunds	West Cambridgeshire	West Cambridgeshire
Approximate area visited, acres	150	150	120	40
Character	Park of *c.*1805 on former heath or arable, infilled with Forestry Commission plantations	Ancient mixed coppice including plateau alderwood still maintained	Ancient mixed ash–maple–hazel coppice	Ancient mixed ash–maple–hazel coppice + elm and hornbeam, partly shrunken village
Soil	Acidic blown sand	Boulder-clay + loess + sand-lenses, calcareous to very acid	Boulder-clay, calcareous with surface acidification	Boulder-clay, calcareous, unusually fertile
Recording began	1959	1969	1964	1959
Total number of mycorrhizal fungi so far	131	126	113	40
Percentage of total count of fungal species	28	27	22	19

Table 5. *Associations between mycorrhizal agarics and trees.*

The last column contains the associations given by Spooner & Roberts.

Frequency of occurrence: •••• most years ••• fewer than half years
•• few years • rare

Trees: al alder ap aspen as ash be beech bi birch bt blackthorn
cd cedar el elm fr fir hb hornbeam ht hawthorn hz hazel
la larch li lime ma maple ok oak pi pine pp poplar
sl sallow yw yew

Rare and uninformative species are omitted.

	BRANDON PARK	BRADFIELD WOODS	HAYLEY WOOD	BUFF WOOD	SPOONER & ROBERTS
Amanita citrina	•••• be>>ok, pi	•	—	—	
A. excelsa	—	•	•		
A. muscaria	•••• bi=pi	•••• bi	—	—	bi
A. phalloides	•••• be	• hz	•	—	ok
A. rubescens	••• pi>be,bi	•••• bi>hz &c	—	—	
Amanitopsis fulva	—	•••	—	—	
A. junquillea	• pi	—	—	—	
A. vaginata	•	•• as,sl	••• hz	—	
Boletus badius	•••• pi>>be &c	•• bi,hz (+ wood)	—	—	pi
B. chrysenteron	••• be>>fr,cd	• bi	•• ok	—	
B. edulis	•• pi, be	•	—	—	
B. piperatus	• pi	• bi=hz	—	—	
B. subtomentosus	•• pi>be,cd	• bi=hz	•	—	
Cantharellus	•• pi	—	—	— ?*cibarius*	
Clavulina cinerea	• be	•• bi=hz	•••• el &c	••	
C. cristata	• be	••• bi	• ok	—	
C. armillatus	•• pi>bi	—	—	—	
C. cinnamomeus	•• pi>bi	—	—	—	pi
C. decipiens	• pi>be	—	—	•	
C. delibutus	—	•• bi,hz	—	—	
C. evernius	—	—	••	—	
C. flexipes	• be	—	—	—	
C. hemitrichus	• be	—	—	—	bi
C. hinnuleus	•• be,pi	•	•	—	
C. obtusus	•• be	—	• ok	—	
C. paleaceus	—	—	•	•	
C. saniosus	—	•	•	• hz,ok	
C. semisanguineus	•• pi>bi	•	—	—	pi
C. uraceus	• pi	•	••	—	
Entoloma rhodopolium	• be,bi	• sl,hz	•••	••• pp &c	
*Gomphidius roseus**	•• pi	—	—	—	
*G. rutilus**	••• pi	—	—	—	
Gyrodon lividus	—	• al	—	—	al
Hebeloma ?crustuliniforme	••• be	•	••• bi,sl	•• hb &c	ok
H. fastibile	• be	•• al	—	—	

Table 5. cont.

	BRANDON PARK	BRADFIELD WOODS	HAYLEY WOOD	BUFF WOOD	SPOONER & ROBERTS
H. leucosarx	—	• al,sl	—	—	willow
H. longicaudum	• be	• al,hz	•	•	
H. mesophæum	•• be>pi	•	•••	•• hb,hz	pi
H. pumilum	—	• el,li	•	—	
H. sinapizans	•• be>syc,yw	•	••	• hb	
Hygrophorus hypothejus	•• bi,pi	—	—	—	pi
Inocybe asterospora	—	•	•	—	
I. calamistrata	• pi	—	—	—	
I. dulcamara	• be	—	•	•	
I. eutheles	• be	—	—	—	
I. fastigiata	•• be>pi	••	••	• hz &c	
I. geophylla	•• be>>pi	•••	•••• hz,as,el	••• hb &c	
I. griseolilacina	•• be>>yw	—	—	—	
I. lacera	• pi	• al,as	•	—	
I. lanuginosa	• pi	—	•	—	
I. perlata	• be	•	•	•	
Laccaria amethystina	•••• be>>pi	•••	••	• hb	
L. laccata	•••• pi>be,ok	•••• hz &c	•••• hz>ap	••	
L. proxima	• pi	—	—	—	
Lactarius blennius	•••• be>bi,pi	—	—	• hb	
L. camphoratus	—	• bi, ok	••	—	
L. chrysorrhœus	—	• ok	—	—	
L. cimicarius	—	—	••	• hb	
L. controversus	—	•••	—	—	pp
L. deliciosus	•• pi>la	—	—	—	pi
L. fulvissimus	—	—	•	•	
L. glyciosmus	• ok,pi	• bi>ok,hz	•	—	bi
L. hepaticus	•• pi>>la	—	—	—	pi
L. mitissimus	• be	••	•••• bi, hz	—	
L. pyrogalus	—	•• hz &c	••	•• hz &c	hz
L. quietus	• ok	••• ok>>hz &c	•••• ok>hz	•• hz &c	ok
L. rufus	•••• pi	•	—	—	pi
L. subdulcis	••• be>ok,pi	••• bi>hz,ok	•••• hz	• hz>el>ok	
L. tabidus	•• be,ok,pi	•• hz,bi &c	••	—	
L. torminosus	•• be,bi	•• bi>hz &c	•• bi	—	bi
L. turpis	••• bi	••• bi>>hz,li	—	• bi	
L. vellereus	—	•• hz &c	•	—	
Leccinum carpini	—	•	•	• hb	hz,hb
L. scabrum	•• be,bi,pi	••• bi>hz &c	—	—	bi
Naucoria (Alnicola) bohemica	—	• bi,hz	•	—	
N. escharoides	—	• al	—	—	al
Paxillus involutus	•••• pi>>be,bi	•••• bi>hz>al	•	• ok>hz	
Russula æruginea	• pi,bi	• bi	—	—	
R. atropurpurea	••• pi>>be,ok	••• bi,ok	•••	—	
R. betularum	—	•• bi	—	—	bi
R. claroflava	—	• bi	—	—	
R. cyanoxantha	• pi	••• hz, bi	••• hz	• ok>hz	

Table 5. *cont.*

	BRANDON PARK	BRADFIELD WOODS	HAYLEY WOOD	BUFF WOOD	SPOONER & ROBERTS
R. delica	—	• al, bi, hz	•	—	
R. farinipes	—	•	•	—	
R. fellea	• be	—	—	—	
R. fragilis	••• pi>be,bi,ok	••	•••• ok,hz	—	
R. gigasperma	—	• as, ok	—	—	
R. grisea	—	• bi	—	—	
R. lepida	—	•	••	••	
R. luteotacta	• bi	•• bi,hz	• ok,ht	—	
R. mairei	•••• be	•	•• hz	• hz>hb	
R. nigricans	• be,pi	••• bi,hz,ok	• ok	• hb	
R. nitida	•• pi>bi	• bi	—	•	
R. ochroleuca	•••• be>pi>bi,ok	••• bi,hz &c	••• hz	—	
R. olivacea	—	• ok,hz	—	—	
R. pulchella	—	• bi, ma	•	—	
R. rosea	—	• bi,hz	•••	••	
R. sardonia	•• pi>bi	—	—	—	
R. turci	• be,pi	—	—	—	
R. velenovskyi	—	• bi	—	• pp	
R. vesca	•• pi>>be	•• bi,hz	•	—	ok
R. xerampelina	•• pi>be,bi	•	—	•	
Scleroderma citrinum (aurantiacum)	•• be,pi	• hz,bt	—	—	
Suillus æruginascens	••• la>>pi	—	—	—	la
S. bovinus	•••• pi>>bi	—	—	—	pi
S. granulatus	•• pi	—	—	—	pi
S. grevillei	••• la>>pi	—	—	—	la
S. luteus	•• pi>>la	—	—	—	pi
Tricholoma album	—	• bi,hz	••	—	
T. columbetta	• be>la	—	•	—	
T. equestre	• pi	—	—	—	
T. fulvum	• be	•• bi,hz,al	•	•	bi
T. lascivum	• be	•	• ok	—	
T. pessundatum	• be	—	—	—	pi
T. sulphureum	•••• be>>pi	• hz,ok	—	—	
T. terreum	•••• be>pi>>la	•	•	—	
T. ustale	• pi	—	•	—	

*Apparently parasitic on *Suillus bovinus*.

Table 6. *Numbers of mycorrhizal fungi in relation to trees.*

Species are those included in Table 5.   a: only host recorded.   b: main host.   c: minor host.

	BRANDON PARK		BRADFIELD WOODS		HAYLEY WOOD		BUFF WOOD	
	Frequency of tree	Number of mycorrhizal fungi	Frequency of tree	Number of mycorrhizal fungi	Frequency of tree	Number of mycorrhizal fungi	Frequency of tree	Number of mycorrhizal fungi
Pine	+++++	52 (13a 29b 10c)						
Larch	+	7 (2b 5c)						
Cedar	+	1c						
Yew	⊦	2b						
Beech	+++	45 (18a 20b 9c)						
Birch	++	19 (2a 5b 12c)	++++	35 (9a 22b 3c)	+	3 (1a 1b)	(+)	1a
Oak	++	9 (1a 1b 7c)	+++	14 (1c 5b 8c)	++++	8 (5a 3b)	++++	4 (3b 1c)
Hazel			++++	31 (1a 20b 10c)	++++	10 (5a 2b 3c)	++++	9 (7b 2c)
Alder			++++	9 (3a 3b 3c)				
Hornbeam			+	0			++	10 (6a 3b 1c)
Ash			++++	3b	++++	1c	++++	0
Sallow			+++	3b	++	1b	++	0
Maple			++	1b	+++	0	+++	0
Lime			++	2 (1b 1c)				
Aspen			+	0	++	1c	+++	0
Poplar							+	2 (1b 1c)
Elm			+	1b	++	2 (1b 1c)	++++	1c
Hawthorn			+		++	1b	++	0
Blackthorn			+	1b	(+)		++	0
Sycamore	+	1c					+	0
no tree identified		2		25		40		12

Table 7. *Differences between Ancient and Planned Countryside.*

ANCIENT COUNTRYSIDE	PLANNED COUNTRYSIDE
Hamlets and ancient isolated farms	Villages and modern isolated farms
Open-field either absent or of modest extent, abolished before c.1700	Strong tradition of open-field, beginning early and lasting until Enclosure-Act period
Roads many, crooked, often sunken	Roads few, straight, on the surface
Many antiquities of all periods	Antiquities usually prehistoric
Most hedges ancient, mixed, not straight	Most hedges modern, of hawthorn only, straight
Pollard trees, if present, away from habitations	Pollard trees (except riverside willows) absent or only in villages
Woods many, often small	Woods absent or few and large
Woodland area averaged 19% in 1086	Woodland area averaged 8% in 1086
Ancient Woodland area now averages 3.1% of land area	Ancient Woodland area now averages 1.8%
Many place-names ending in *-ley*, *-hurst*, *-thwaite*, *-field*, indicating former woodland	Few place-names indicating former woodland

Table 8. *Commonest trees in the fully developed dry-land wildwood, south Norfolk.*

The figures are the number of cores (out of 12 or 13) in which each species was the commonest tree at each stage.

	EARLY IN ATLANTIC PERIOD	AVERAGE FOR PERIOD	JUST BEFORE ELM DECLINE	JUST AFTER ELM DECLINE
Hazel	7	3	3	11
Elm	0	0	0	0
Oak	0	1	2	0
Lime	3	7	4	0
Ash	2	2	3	1

Table 9. *Comparison of the Tansley and Vera models of wildwood.*

IN FAVOUR OF VERA (SAVANNA-LIKE)

Allows a place for hunter-gatherers to make a living from large herbivores

Allows a place for Neolithic farmers to begin growing crops and keeping domestic livestock

Allows a place for ancient trees and the animals and plants that depend on them

Allows a place for the many butterflies associated with woodland grassland

Allows a place for 'common-or-garden' birds that require both trees and open ground

Wildwood samples contain pollen of herbs that do not flower in shade

AGAINST VERA AND IN FAVOUR OF TANSLEY (FOREST)

Tree-to-non-tree pollen ratio is high in most pre-Neolithic pollen samples (but is this because the significant non-trees produce little pollen?)

Britain and Ireland were not very different from the rest of Europe despite having different animals and trees

Lack of pollen evidence for cyclical succession of different trees

Poor historic correlation between browsing and regeneration of oak

Not enough hawthorn, blackthorn or grass pollen before Neolithic

Too much pre-Neolithic elm, which is very sensitive to browsing

Long time-interval between decline of wild herbivores and earliest records of present woods

Table 10. *'Virgin forests' in west and middle Europe.*

Czechoslovakia	123 sites
Sweden	38
Finland	29
Yugoslavia	25
Norway	21
Austria	9
France	5
Poland	4
Switzerland	4
Bulgaria	3
Germany	3
Greece	3
Hungary	3
Italy	3
Spain	2
Britain, Ireland, Low Countries, Denmark	0
Portugal, Mediterranean islands	0

Table 11. *Woodland in Domesday Book and later, as a percentage of land area, by Ancient and Planned Countryside provinces.*

1895 figures from Agricultural Returns. Ancient Woodland figures are calculated from county surveys by the Nature Conservancy (*alias* English Nature).

	WOODLAND AND WOOD-PASTURE, 1086	WOODLAND AND PLANTATION, 1895	ANCIENT WOODLAND, c.1930	INTACT ANCIENT WOODLAND, c.1990
Ancient Countryside (NW)	16	4.4	2.12	1.16
Ancient Countryside (NW) excluding moorland*	21	6.7	3.19	1.73
Ancient Countryside (SE)	26	8.8	5.55	3.29
Ancient Countryside (total)	19	5.7	3.14	1.79
Planned Countryside	8	3.6	1.76	0.81
All England	15	5.1	2.71	1.48

* Calculated on the basis that moorland now covers one-third of the total area, but one-quarter of the area included in Domesday.

Table 12. *Woodland in the Irish Civil Survey, 1654.*

Thousands of modern acres.

COUNTY	WOODLAND	TOTAL AREA	PERCENTAGE OF WOODLAND
Carlow	8.2	221	3.7
Clare	51.1	788	7.0
Cork (part)	16.7	310	5.7
Donegal	5.3	1,170	0.5
Dublin	0.8	227	0.4
Galway	36.5	1,468	2.5
Kildare (most)	5.5	331	1.7
Limerick	24.4	662	3.6
Londonderry	9.3	509	1.8
Mayo	18.2	1,333	1.4
Meath	2.6	575	0.4
Roscommon	38.3	608	6.3
Tipperary	36.1	1,048	3.4
Tyrone	8.2	774	1.1
Waterford	17.1	453	3.7
Wexford (most)	18.9	540	3.5
TOTAL	297	11,087	2.68

Table 13. *Some guilds of coppicing plants.*

	CALCAREOUS WOODS	WEAKLY ACID WOODS	STRONGLY ACID WOODS
Spring perennials	anemone archangel early purple orchid bluebell oxlip primrose	anemone bluebell pignut primrose	
Summer perennials	meadowsweet sanicle *Viola reichenbachiana* *V. riviniana* *Viola reichenbachiana* *V. riviniana* water-avens	*Brachypodium sylvaticum* *Bromus ramosus* *Holcus mollis* meadowsweet	bracken *Holcus mollis* *Luzula sylvatica*

Buried-seed plants	bugle
	creeping Jenny
	Deschampsia cespitosa
	Galium palustre
	ground-ivy
	Hypericum species
	Juncus species
	Myosotis sylvatica
	Scrophularia species
	wood-spurge (and rare
	  Euphorbia species)
	Veronica species
		brambles
		Chenopodium polyspermum
		Deschampsia cespitosa
		hemp-nettle
		Hypericum humifusum
		  (under lime)
		Hypericum species
		Juncus species
		raspberry
			broom
			Corydalis claviculata
			foxglove
			heather
			Juncus species
			Melampyrum pratense
			raspberry
			Rumex tenuifolius

Mobile plants	burdock enchanter's nightshade *Epilobium* species marsh thistle rosebay willowherb	burdock enchanter's nightshade *Epilobium* species marsh thistle	rosebay willowherb
Unresponsive	lords-and-ladies dog's-mercury herb paris	lords-and-ladies *Dryopteris* species ramsons	

Table 14. *Comparison of certain species of trees and ground vegetation in relation to browsing, Rockingham and Hatfield Forests.*

Rockingham data are after Best. **Bold** indicates significantly greater frequency.

Species	Rockingham grazed	Rockingham ungrazed	Hatfield Forest number of woods out of 12, and notes on abundance	Purlieu (2 woods)	Outside Hatfield: number of woods out of 12, and notes on abundance
TREES AND SHRUBS					
Maple	**markedly favoured**		**12 (2nd or 3rd commonest underwood, after hornbeam and sometimes elm)**	2 (variable)	12 (3rd to 5th commonest underwood, after hazel, hornbeam, ash, elm)
Hawthorn	**markedly favoured**		**11 (abundant in 11)**	2 (occasional in both)	12 (abundant in one)
Blackthorn	**favoured**		12 (abundant in 8)	2 (occasional in both)	12 (abundant in 2)
Crab	**favoured**		4	2	7
Aspen			6 (abundant in 2)	2 (abundant in 1)	11 (abundant in 3)
Oak as underwood			**7 (abundant in 3)**	absent	absent
Elm (all species, before 1980s Elm Disease)			**12 (15 to 40% of area in 10 woods)**	2 (10–20% of area)	11 (exceeds 20% of area in 3 woods)
Ash		favoured	12 (always less abundant than maple)	2 (variable)	**12 (never less abundant than maple)**
HERBS AND UNDERSHRUBS					
Deschampsia cespitosa	**more frequent**		10 (abundant in 7)	2 (not abundant)	9 (abundant in 1)
Barren strawberry *Potentilla sterilis*	**more frequent**		10	1	6
Ground-ivy *Glechoma hederacea*	**more frequent**		**11 (abundant in coppiced areas)**	2	9 (seldom abundant)
Burdock *Arctium* species	**more frequent**		5	2	7
Hound's-tongue *Cynoglossum officinale*			**formerly abundant**	absent	one record
Wood-sorrel *Oxalis acetosella*	**more frequent**		9 (frequent in 2)	2	5
Sanicle *Sanicula europæa*	**more frequent**		4	1	5

Table 14. *cont.*

Species	Rockingham grazed	Rockingham ungrazed	Hatfield Forest number of woods out of 12, and notes on abundance	Purlieu (2 woods)	Outside Hatfield: number of woods out of 12, and notes on abundance
HERBS AND UNDERSHRUBS					
Nettle *Urtica dioica*			**12 (frequent in 5)**	2 (uncommon)	11 (abundant in 1)
Carex pendula			8	2	9 (locally abundant in 2)
Bramble (*Rubus* species)			12 (never widely dominant)	2 (widely dominant in 1)	**12 (widely dominant in 7)**
Primrose *Primula vulgaris* (before 1990s			7 (frequent in 2)	2 (abundant in both)	4 (abundant in 2)
Oxlip *Primula elatior*	outside geographical area		4 (rare in all)	**1 (frequent)**	**7 (abundant in 4)**
Bluebell *Scilla non-scripta*		**more frequent**	2 (rare)	2 (local)	**9 (abundant in 7)**
Dog's-mercury *Mercurialis perennis*		**more frequent**	12 (widely dominant in 9)	2 (widely dominant in both)	12 (widely dominant in 7)
Anemone *Anemone nemorosa*		**more frequent**	absent	1	**5 out of 10* (abundant in 1)**
Herb paris *Paris quadrifolia*		**more frequent**	4 (rare)	0	1 out of 10* (rare)
Pignut *Conopodium majus*		**more frequent**	rare	0	rare
Veronica montana		**more frequent**	rare	0	rare

* These figures include only woods recorded in springtime when the plants are visible.

Table 15. *Density of oak timber. Measured on air-dry samples.*

Fast-grown medieval 'English' oak	0.64, 0.72, 0.75, 0.77 grams per cubic centimetre
Slow-grown medieval Baltic oak	0.43, 0.55
Modern, slow-grown English oak	0.43 (Hayley Wood)

Table 16. *Indicators of ancient woodland in England and Wales.*

Includes all indicators recorded on five or more lists, together with those on four or fewer lists for which there is good evidence that they are at least local indicators.

Coppicing responses: bs buried-seed, sp spring-leafing perennial, su summer-leafing perennial.

Ant dispersal: •••• indicates the strongest connection with ants.

Belgian list: ••••• indicates strongest connection with ancient woodland.

	No. of lists out of 18	Habit	Coppicing response	Ant dispersal	Where plant is indicative (if in a particular region)	Remarks	Belgian list
Melica uniflora	18	clonal grass	su	•••	also Sweden	the 'woodbank grass'	••••
Galium (Asperula) odoratum	17	clonal	su		everywhere except Chilterns; also Sweden		•
Anemone nemorosa	15	clonal	sp	••••	also Sweden and Poland		•••
Luzula pilosa	15		bs	••••	also Poland		•••••
Sorbus torminalis	15	clonal tree	sprouts				
Melampyrum pratense	14	annual parasite	bs	•••	also Poland	wildwood record	•
Milium effusum	14		bs	•	also Sweden and Poland	said to have been planted by gamekeepers, on unknown evidence	•••••
Tilia cordata	14	tree	sprouts			very common in wildwood	
Adoxa moschatellina	12	clonal	none			readily colonises attached recent woodland in Belgium	
Euphorbia amygdaloides	12		bs	•		absent in N	
Paris quadrifolia	12	clonal	negative		also Sweden and Poland	absent in far W	•••
Carex strigosa	11		bs			wildwood record; rare in N, absent in W	•••
Carex pallescens	10		bs	••	not in W		•
Carex pendula	10		su		not in SW	wildwood record	•••
Carex remota	10		bs		not in SW		
Neottia nidus-avis	10	parasite			mainly in Midlands & E		
Oxalis acetosella	10	shade-bearer; weakly clonal			not in W or N; also Sweden	wildwood record	•••••

Table 16. cont.

	No. of lists out of 18	Habit	Coppicing response	Ant dispersal	Where plant is indicative (if in a particular region)	Remarks	Belgian list
Veronica montana	10	clonal	bs	••	not in S; also Sweden		•••••
Allium ursinum	9		negative	••	SW, E, N		•••
Convallaria majalis	9	clonal	su		mainly Midlands & E; also Sweden	beware garden throwouts	•••
Galeobdolon luteum (*Lamiastrum galeobdolon*)	9	clonal	su	•••	not in W or N; also Sweden	beware invasive lookalike	•••
Agropyron (Elymus) caninum	8				not in SW		
Carex lævigata	8					absent from most of Midlands	
Corydalis (*Ceratocapnos*) *claviculata*	8	annual	bs		mainly in E & N		
Malus sylvestris	8	tree	sprouts			crab, not to be confused with cultivated apple; wildwood record	
Orchis mascula	8	orchid	sp				
Carex sylvatica	7		bs	••	also Sweden		••••
Conopodium majus	7		sp			also ancient grassland	
Festuca gigantea	7		casual		mainly in W	woodland grassland	
Lathræa squamaria	7	parasite			mainly in W		
Campanula trachelium	6				mainly in Midlands	woodland grassland	•••
Dryopteris borreri (*pseudomas, affinis*)	6	fern	none		not in most of W or N		
Epipactis helleborine	6		su		not in Scotland		
Lathyrus montanus (*linifolius*)	6	clonal			not in most of W or N		
Luzula sylvatica	6	clonal	su		not in most of W or N	wildwood record?	••
Lysimachia nemorum	6	clonal	bs				•••••
Platanthera chlorantha	6	orchid	su			also grassland	
Viola reichenbachiana	6		su				
Bromus (Zerna, Bromopsis) ramosus	5		su				

Table 16. *cont.*

	No. of lists out of 18	Habit	Coppicing response	Ant dispersal	Where plant is indicative (if in a particular region)	Remarks	Belgian list
Calamagrostis epigejos	5	clonal	mobile			can be aggressive in felled woods	
Epipactis purpurata	5	parasite	negative?			mostly in dense shade	
Geum rivale	5		su		not in Wales or N		
Helleborus viridis	5		none	••••		can be exceedingly stable	
Hordelymus europæus	5		bs				
Hypericum androsæmum	5		bs			reputed not native in most of Midlands	
Poa nemoralis	5		casual				•
Sanicula europæa	5	clonal	su				•••
Scirpus sylvaticus	5	clonal					
Vicia sylvatica	5	clonal			E Midlands & W		
Aquilegia vulgaris	4					woodland grassland; beware garden escapes	
Colchicum autumnale	4				W	woodland grassland; also grassland	
Cratægus lævigata	4	shrub	sprouts			mainly in Midlands & E	
Dryopteris æmula	4	fern			Wales & NW		
Mœhringia trinervia	4	annual	bs	••	Caermarthen, E. England, Lincolnshire	wildwood record	
Myosotis sylvatica	4		bs		Surrey, E. England, Lincolnshire	beware introduced lookalikes with big flowers	
Narcissus pseudonarcissus	4		sp			also grassland; beware cultivars	•
Polygonatum multiflorum	4	clonal			S England		•
Populus tremula	4	clonal tree	sprouts		said to be indicative in W England & Pembrokeshire		
Ranunculus auricomus	4	shade-bearer	bs	•	not in N or Scotland	also churchyards	
Scrophularia nodosa	4		bs		Lincolnshire & N England		
Chrysosplenium ?oppositifolium	3	clonal			Beds, Hertfordshire, Lincolnshire	wildwood record	••••

Table 16. cont.

	No. of lists out of 18	Habit	Coppicing response	Ant dispersal	Where plant is indicative (if in a particular region)	Remarks	Belgian list
Endymion (Scilla, Hyacinthoides) nonscriptus	3		sp		E England & Lincolnshire	wildwood record	•••••
Epipactis leptochila	3	parasite	negative		E England	in dense shade	
Hymenophyllum wilsoni	3	clonal epiphyte			SW Wales & Lancashire		
Melittis melissophyllum	3	clonal	bs		Dorset & SW Wales		
Mercurialis perennis	3	clonal	negative	•••	E England, Lincolnshire, Yorkshire; also Sweden & Poland	wildwood record	••
Primula vulgaris	3		sp	•••	E England & Lincolnshire		
Sedum telephium	3	clonal	none?		Worcestershire & E England		
Tilia platyphyllos	2	tree	sprouts		Hereford, Worcestershire, Warwick	wildwood record	
Calamagrostis canescens	2	clonal	su		Lincolnshire		
Dipsacus pilosus	2				Lincolnshire	woodland grassland	
Hymenophyllum tunbridgense	2	clonal epiphyte			SW Wales		
Hypericum hirsutum	2		bs		E England & Lincolnshire		••
Potentilla sterilis	2	clonal	sp		Lincolnshire & Bedfordshire	wildwood record	•••
Primula elatior	2		sp	••		confined to E England	•••
Quercus petræa	2	tree	sprouts		Midlands, E England, elsewhere		
Ruscus aculeatus	2		none		E & S England	beware garden-escapes	
Salix caprea	2	tree	sprouts		said to be indic. in SW Wales	wildwood record	
Maianthemum bifolium	1	clonal			Lincolnshire; also Sweden and Poland		•••••
Melampyrum cristatum	1	annual parasite	bs			also woodland grassland; largely confined to E England	

Table 17. *Distinction between wild and planted stands of oak.*

	WILD	PLANTED
Species	pedunculate or sessile	usually pedunculate, even where sessile would be expected (p.285)
Age	variable	uniform
Appearance	individualistic	uniform, except for occasional survivors of previous stand
Management	timber trees or coppice stools	always timber, usually close-set
Trunk	variable	straight
Epicormics	variable	typically present but few
Leafage	variable in leaf-shape, density, timing	uniform
Other planted trees	usually absent	conifers often present (now or on early Ordnance Survey maps)

Table 18. *Summary of situations in which oak occurs, and the frequency of species and type of tree.*

	SOIL TYPE	*Quercus Robur*	*Quercus Petræa*	MAIDEN TREE	COPPICE STOOL	POLLARD
1. Natural timber tree among underwood of other species	any except chalk or very infertile	++++		++++		on boundary
2. Timber tree planted into existing underwood	any	++++	+	++++		
3. Underwood stools in woodland	acid, very infertile	+	++++		+++++	on boundary
4. Wood-pasture	any	++++	++	+++	+	++++
5. Natural recent woodland	any	++++	++	++++	+	
6. Oak plantation	any	before c.1970	after c.1970	++++	+	
7. Hedgerow and field	any	++++	+	++++	++	+++

Table 19. *Changes in the lichen flora on trees in the main body of Epping Forest, in relation to the Hawksworth – Rose pollution scale.*

Abridged from the original by Hawksworth and others, except for the last line, which is discussed on p.330.

DATE	POINT ON POLLUTION SCALE	MEAN WINTER SO_2 EQUIVALENT, MICROGRAMS PER CUBIC METRE
1784–96	9–10 (unpolluted)	<30
1865–8	7	40
1881–2	5	60
1909–19	4	70
1969–70	3 (polluted)	125
1989	4–6	70–50

Table 20. *Percentage of rain-days on which rain collected at High Beach was of particular degrees of acidity.*

YEAR	1983 (Oct–Dec)	1984	1985	1986	1987 (July–Dec)	1988	1989
Number of measurements	32	147	145	127	47	77	108
Percentage of rain-days with pH:							
2.6–3.6 (very acid)	–	14	2	13	21	1	–
3.6–4.6	69	54	60	63	53	46	36
4.6–5.6	28	31	31	15	13	23	33
5.6–6.6	3	1	8	8	13	22	25
over 6.6	–	1	–	–	–	8	6
Most acid pH	3.6	2.8	3.0	3.0	2.6	2.9	3.7
pH exceeded by half the measurements	4.4	4.3	4.4	4.2	4.0	4.6	4.9
Most alkaline pH	6.5	6.8	6.3	6.5	6.2	7.3	7.7

Table 21. *Mean width of annual rings in Hayley Wood oaks, 1974 – 81.*

Based on 43 cores from 26 trees, ranging in age from 132 to c.220 years in 1980. Measured (in millimetres) and evaluated by Martin Bridge.

	ALL TREES	OMITTING 2 TREES THAT DECLINED BY LESS THAN 10% AND ONE THAT INCREASED
1974	1.61	1.63
1975 (drought year)	1.71	1.72
1976 (extreme drought year)	0.86	0.87
1977	1.47	1.51
1978	1.68	1.71
1979	1.66	1.70
1980 (caterpillar year)	1.15	1.14
1981	1.21	1.22

Table 22. *Approximate date at which the area of plantations overtook that of ancient woodland.*

Ireland	c.1720
Scotland	c.1800 [1880s, according to Smout]
Wales	c.1820
England	c.1870
Essex, (old) Cambridgeshire	not yet

Table 23. *Habitats of fungi recorded in Brandon Park, 1959–2005.*

Species with more than one habitat are counted in each.

SUBSTRATE	RELATIVE ABUNDANCE OF HABITAT ON SCALE OF 1 TO 6	NUMBER OF SPECIES			
		Exclusive to the habitat	*Mainly in the habitat*	*Partly in the habitat*	*Total species*
Ground under:					
Pine	6	28	13	71	112
Beech	5	81	40	70	191
Birch	4	1	–	25	26
Oak	3	1	–	12	13
Larch	2	3	2	13	18
Cedar	1	2	–	6	10
Other trees	2	2	–	9	12
Grassland	4	53	6	51	110
Heather	2	5	1	13	19
Mosses	2	6	1	12	19
Fire sites	1	4	–	2	6
Wood of:					
Pine	4	32	3	12	47
Birch	2	1	–	5	6
Beech	1	20	1	11	32
Oak	1	4	1	6	11
Other trees	1	7	–	2	9
Parasitic		11	–	–	11
On other fungi		3			3

Table 24. *Resistance and resilience of native and archaeophyte trees.*

	RESISTANCE TO REPLANTING	RESILIENCE (ABILITY TO RETURN)
Oak	0 (easily destroyed)	1 (unlikely to return)
Beech	0	1
Chestnut	2	1
Maple	2	3
Wych-elm	2	3
Sallow	2	5
Hazel	3	0 (owing to grey squirrel)
Ash	4	3
Hornbeam	4	3
Birch	4	6 (easily returns)
Aspen	5 (but later succumbs to competition)	3 (if any part of the clone remains alive)
Elm (suckering)	5	4 (ditto)
Lime	6 (difficult to destroy)	0

Table 25. *Summary of changes in Gamlingay Wood since 1911*
(For the full version see Rackham (2003) pp.362–73.)

	TREATMENT IN THE 1950S				
	INTACT	PLANTED WITH POPLARS	PLANTED WITH OAK, ASH, CONIFERS	PLANTED WITH CONIFERS	SAND-LENS PLANTED WITH OAK AND CONIFERS
TREES:					
oak	decline (felling not balanced by recruitment)	decline (felling not balanced by recruitment)	no change (felling balanced by planting)	decline	severe decline
ash	little change	little change	decline	decline	great increase
hazel	decline (no recruitment)	decline (no recruitment)	decline	decline	severe decline
maple	slight increase	slight increase	decline	decline	rare
aspen	increase	increase	severe decline	severe decline	severe decline
birch	increase	increase	great increase	increase	decline
HERBS:					
oxlip	decline	decline	severe decline	severe decline	rare
meadowsweet	severe decline	severe decline	severe decline	severe decline	—
Deschampsia cespitosa	no change	no change	decline	increase since 1991	decline since 1991
bluebell	increase	slight increase	increase	great increase	increase then decline
dog's-mercury	increase then decline	increase	great increase	increase then decline	rare
bracken	—	—	—	increase	decline

Table 26. *Produce taken or ordered by Henry III from the Forest of Blackmoor.*

DEER, 1222–72

	EATEN BY THE KING	GIVEN AS CARCASES ETC.	GIVEN LIVE STOCK PARKS
Red	0	7	
Fallow, male	0	84	31
female	0	37	102
total	4 unspecified orders	121	133
Roe	10	0	0

TREES, 1222–39

	USED BY THE KING	GIVEN AS GIFTS
Oaks for buildings	170 + 10 unspecified orders	209
Robora	0	40
Busca	3 orders	0

INDEX

Mitchell, F.J.G. 81
mites 199, 319
Mljet (Dalmatia) 84
moats 69, 119, 178
Moccas Park (Herefordshire)
176, 441
Moehringia trinervia 249, 436, 482
Tab. 16
Mogeely (Co. Cork) 109
Molinia cærulea 210, 314, 326
Moneses uniflora 315
Monks' Park (Suffolk) 119, 180
Monks' Wood (Huntingdonshire)
176
Moore, N.W. 248, 408
moorland 24, 53, 80, 101, 127,
158, 258, 302, 313, 314
fire 48, 82
Forests 119, 120
origin 58, 95, 112, 168
plantations on 263, 345, 357,
361, 363, 367
effect on birds 369
recent woods on 25, 294
woods adjoining 107, 291,
295–6, 305
moose 80
mor: leaf-mould type of soil 199,
279, 286, 292, 298
Morfitt, D. 136n, 179, 204, 207–9
moschatel (*Adoxa moschatellina*)
173, 397–8
mott (N. America): a *clone* of
certain savanna trees 79,
131–3, 204, 339
mountain ash see *rowan*
Mountford, E.J. 407
Mousehold Heath (Norfolk) 102,
117, 158
Moxey, P. 329, 330
Mugdock Wood (Glasgow) 292–3
mull: earthworm type of soil 199,
279, 298
mullein (*Verbascum* species) 212
Murray, S. 311
mycorrhiza: fungi that are
symbiotic with a tree or
other plant and perform
some of the functions of
its roots 12, 22, 34–43,
71, 247, 252, 264, 315, 343,
370–2 Tab. 5, 473 Tab. 6
planted trees 264, 342, 369–70,
372, 374
Mynors, C. 148

National Archive 151
National Forests 363, 413
National Nature Reserves 293,
316, 377

National Vegetation Classification
209, 210, 274, 291, 296,
315, 432, 438
National Trust 229, 417, 433
mistakes 133, 359, 375, 418,
430–1
native: kind of plant or animal
that came by natural
means 30
'true' and 'false' 30, 266–71
Native Americans 46, 91, 93, 116
natural woodland: woodland
where the vegetation has
not been planted or sown
naturalised: plant or animal,
originally introduced by
people, that perpetuates
itself without further
human intervention 29–30
Nature Conservancy (Council):
24, 250, 379, 410, 417
nature reserves 429–39
Nelson, Admiral 353
nematodes 319, 339, 343, 342, 427
Neolithic 12, 20, 74, 83, 86, 281, 284
carpentry 97, 241
culture 52–3, 92–4, 95, 116,
164, 174, 220–1, 387, 436
neophyte: post-medieval
introduction 30, 466–7
Tab. 1
Netherlands 80
nettle (*Urtica dioica*) 25, 249, 253,
255, 289, 479 Tab. 14
phosphate plant 158, 178, 181,
200, 210, 216, 260, 282
New England 164, 169, 202, 234,
259, 333, 345, 428
New Forest (Hampshire) 25, 79,
122, 128, 256
history 119, 129, 167, 284, 285
modern forestry 351, 354,
357, 438
New Zealand 66, 92, 425
Niering, W.A. 157
nitrogen 35, 36, 200, 253,
258, 289, 407
oxides of 321, 419
non-compartmented: a *wood-
pasture* in which deer
and other livestock had
access to the whole area all
the time 27
non-woodland trees 21, 27–8
see also *hedgerow trees*
Norden, J. 144, 145, 349
Norsey Wood (Essex) 174
Northwold, Hugo de 140
Norway 69, 125, 204, 235, 306, 337,
475 Tab. 10
nurseries 28, 205, 269, 342, 348,

350–1

oak
acorns 17, 29, 78, 243, 264, 265,
267, 268, 347, 348, 349, 350,
351, 354, 420, 428, 441
ancient trees 119, 176, 177,
206, 256, 400–1, 441 see
also *oak, pollard*; *staghead*;
Staverton
annual rings 42–3, 335
archives 136, 138, 147, 153
Baltic 31, 43, 232, 242–3
bark 57, 112, 205, 225–6, 230,
240, 256, 264, 265, 293, 295,
354, 414
behaviour 17, 25, 203, 404–5,
466–7 Tab. 1
bog 70, 76
browsing and 81–2, 215, 295,
478 Tab. 14
caterpillars 334–5
charcoal 167, 168, 227
coppiced 177, 212, 229, 468
Tab. 3, 478 Tab. 14, 484 Tab.
18 see also *oakwoods*
ancient stools 177, 208, 286
dieback and decline 42, 192,
323–4, 328, 342
diseases 41n, 340, 341
mildew (*Microsphæra
alphitoides*) 59, 335–6, 343
wilt (*Ceratocystis fagacearum*)
338–9, 427
drought 323–4
evolution 29, 64, 65, 436
felling 358–9
fire and 44, 47
fungi 369
galls 189
as habitat 41, 42
longevity 38, 39
mast year 17
mycorrhiza 22, 36, 38, 470–2
Tab. 5, 473 Tab. 6
in oakwoods and other woods
273–4
phenology 423
pictures 187, 188–9, 190, 192
place-names 138
in plantations of other trees
147, 359, 369
planting 247, 264–6, 347, 349,
350, 353–4, 365, 374, 377,
484 Tab. 18
poisoning 359, 376
pollard 38, 42, 116, 123, 125–6,
256, 399, 484 Tab. 18
pollen 68, 69
pollution 321, 323–4, 326,